LOUIS XIV

LOUIS XIV

By JOHN B. WOLF

The Norton Library

W·W·NORTON & COMPANY·INC·

NEW YORK

To THETA, MITZI AND JOHN FRANZ,
AND CAROLYN AND CLARK

CONTENTS

IV

V

MAPS

THE COAT OF ARMS of Louis XIV appears on the title page. It is the coat of arms of France. It was customary in heraldic representations to show the coat of arms in black and white reproduction with lineal patterns to indicate color. The horizontal lines represent blue and the dots represent gold. This coat of arms appears throughout paintings and engravings of the period.

PREFACE

THE AUTHOR OF a one-volume biography of Louis XIV must be prepared to give more attention to some aspects of the king's career than to others; the choice that he makes reflects his appraisal of the king's impact upon our civilization and his place in history. This probably accounts for the remark of a distinguished clinical psychologist who read the manuscript: "But John, you have given more attention to war than to sex!" I could excuse myself by saying that other writers have long since explored some aspects of Louis' life beyond the frontiers of credible evidence, but, in fact, my interpretation emerges from my conviction that his part in the development of the bureaucratic, military, police state and in the rise of the European balance cf power as the governing mechanism for European society was the most important contribution of his reign. Therefore I have, first of all, attempted to present the king as he appeared to his ministers, his soldiers, and his diplomats rather than the picture of him we might get from the gossips, place-seekers, and others who inhabited his court and produced so many of the *mémoires* that have served as sources for the story of his life. I have not ignored the part of his life that scandalized his contemporaries as well as his historians, but I have emphasized the story of the king whose career as king was the most dramatic representation of that role ever played on the European stage. Louis was king in his court, in his council chambers, with his armies; I have tried to follow his career as soldier-statesman, as administrator, and as ceremonial official. It has proved to be a difficult task, for, unhappily, many of the materials that we would like to use have not survived.

Obviously Louis XIV was not alone responsible for the impact of his reign on Europe's history; his collaborators, his friends and allies, his enemies, those indifferent to him, and a host of people whose lives and labors rarely find any recognition in the pages of history have all contributed to the era of Louis XIV. Indeed, in this story I have even suggested that the king *may* have been merely an accomplished actor who played out a role which *may* have been written by others. Nonetheless,

Louis was the king and, consequently, at the center of much of the significant action of his times; his personal part, therefore, is important. The biographer has the formidable task of explaining both the history of the period and the importance of his subject; he must hope that the reader will understand that it is impossible not to insist, perhaps too strongly, on the importance of the subject when the biography deals with Louis XIV.

A host of myths have accumulated around Louis XIV, so many that there is not enough space in a single-volume history to correct them all. These myths often are the result of dependence upon *mémoires* as sources for the history; this evidence is always suspect and it usually results in a relatively sterile anecdotal study. I have read these *mémoires,* and here and there I have used them gingerly, but I have relied principally upon letters, proclamations, preambles to laws, sermons, pamphlets, accounts of fêtes and celebrations, and other similar contemporary materials not written to persuade the historian of this or that interpretation of events. This sort of material allows us to see men at their daily tasks; sometimes it gives us insight into their motives, but it is not altogether satisfactory since the witnesses are very often not addressing themselves to the questions that we would like to ask. Every student reads a great amount of material that proves of little use. The registers of secretaries, of master gardeners, of masters of ceremonies and the like, the invoices of jewels, furniture, clothing, food and drink, and the orders for the daily needs of the royal family provide familiarity with the king's environment, but they are often of limited value for a biography. Nevertheless, visits to châteaus, to battlefields, to galleries of engravings and paintings, along with these records of the court life, all help to solidify impressions even though they produce few footnotes in the text.

In the process of writing this book it became evident that my picture of Louis XIV was somewhat different from the one that usually stalks the pages of history. From Saint-Simon to Lavisse and down to the latest popularizations of the king, Louis stands out as a man suffering more or less from egomania—an arrogant, proud ruler seeking an undefined *gloire,* and subjecting his state and his people to his own inflated ambitions. There can be no doubt that Louis wished to fulfill his *gloire.* His mother and Mazarin had deeply impressed upon him the obligation to play out the role assigned to him by his heredity and his talents, his duty to God, to his state, and to himself. This is what his *"gloire"* meant. Like other seventeenth-century princes, Louis was taught that he must, to the best of his ability, fulfill his destiny and his place in the world or face the punishment of God. He probably was not more anxious to fulfill himself than other princes of his day; he simply worked harder at the task and lived on a larger stage than any of the others.

When we read his letters to his soldiers, his ministers, his diplomats and clergymen, we do not find an arrogant megalomaniac; indeed, I was surprised to find myself seeing Louis as a man who frequently felt psychologically insecure. Time and time again, behind the mask that he wore on ceremonial occasions, we find a man who had trouble trusting his decisions or believing in his actions. He was the king who sought the advice of "experts" whenever he could find them, and, unhappily, seventeenth-century "experts," like those of other times, were often mistaken. There is another facet of the problem that also grew out of these studies; we see Louis in the ceremonial role when he stood before the world *en roi,* and many of the onlookers mistook this for egomania when it actually was a dramatization of the *mystique* that justified the enormous extension of power exercised by his government. Anyone wishing to understand Louis' conception of *gloire* will do well to read Corneille's *Le Cid* or *Polyeucte* rather than the crude nineteenth-century ideas about "national glory."

Another interesting aspect of Louis' life emerging from my studies places important emphasis on his religious beliefs. Fénelon's famous remark, "You do not love God, you only fear the devil," was probably inspired by Madame de Maintenon and undoubtedly contained a bit of truth, for Louis seems never to have understood deep religious emotions; his dislike for Rome and the papal power and the irregularities of his own life have added to the doubts about his religious beliefs. Even so, in reading the king's letters it becomes evident that he was a seventeenth-century man who lived in a theocentric world that God had created and continued to sustain. This cosmology was an important part of his intellectual make-up. As a matter of fact, the cult of the king and the *mystique* developed to justify the exercise of royal power can be understood only in light of the religious preconceptions of the king and of the men around him. He also was his mother's son; that is to say, he had from her a Spanish conception of cult that he never shook off.

On another level my findings call into question some of the traditional interpretations of the king's politics. The remark "I loved war too much" has been taken as evidence to explain Louis' wars, whereas a consideration of the record would suggest that this simplified version of his motivation, given on his deathbed, should be reconsidered in light of the facts in the history. If one looks at the record, it soon becomes evident that Louis' wars were not begun simply for personal reasons and that the length of these wars resulted more from his inability to disengage from war once it began than from any overweening love of conflict. Louis' wars often began with the same unwarranted optimism and shaky moral and political justifications that we find in the actions of other seventeenth-century monarchs; however, although they began with relatively limited objectives, his military potentials were not great enough to ensure success. His correspondence, replete with fruitless efforts to convince his enemies of his desire for peace, sounds strangely familiar to a mid-twentieth-century scholar.

These wars, in their turn, became worth studying for their part in the process that built the European state. The new military institutions cured French society of its endemic revolutions and revolts—the *mêlée,* as Sir George Clark has called them—and thereby assured more domestic tranquillity than had been characteristic of European society in the preceding centuries. These same institutions imposed new strategic as well as tactical ideas upon the king, his soldiers, and his ministers. Once these become understood some of the policies of Louis XIV that have been painted as the work of an egocentric king become the natural consequences of new military processes. What has been portrayed as impudent aggression by a megalomaniacal ruler may not be more acceptable when it becomes aggression as the result of the experience of the Dutch War, but at least it will be a more accurate picture of the problems involved. The part played by the king himself in these wars will probably never be adequately understood, but the *Archives de Guerre* at Vincennes have yielded hundreds of letters that give us a bold outline of his role. These letters also definitely contradict the so-often-told tale of his timidity in face of possible military confrontation; he clearly was not afraid of a battle if there were good chances for a "happy success."

My study, like so many made by my colleagues, owes much to the financial assistance available to scholars today: the Fulbright Commission, the John Simon Guggenheim Memorial Foundation (whose prototype is to be found in Louis' regime), the Social Science Research Council, the Graduate School of the University of Minnesota, two sabbatical leaves from that great University, and the Department of History of the University of Illinois, Chicago Circle, have all contributed to the progress of this book. No student of seventeenth-century France can express enough his gratitude to the *Bibliothèque Nationale* for opening to him its rich collections, nor to its staff for their assistance; we are all grateful to the talented nation that so generously allows foreigners to use its libraries and archives. The *Archives Nationales,* the *Archives de Guerre,* and the *Archives des Affaires Étrangères* also were opened to me, and like so many of my countrymen, I was kindly treated by their staffs. I would like particularly to thank M. Georges Dethan of the *Archives des Affaires Étrangères* for his help and understanding. Other collections also have been very useful: the *Bibliothèque Mazarine,* the Walter Library of the University of Minnesota, the Newberry Library, and the Royal Danish Archives in Copenhagen have all contributed to this study.

I am, of course, indebted to my colleagues, students, and friends. My former students, Professors Lloyd Moote, John O'Connor, Frank Place, Orest Ranum, and George Rothrock, read and criticized part or all of the manuscript; my graduate students in residence at the University of Minnesota during the years 1962–1966 all were burdened with my efforts and generously gave me their attention and critiques; my colleagues Professors Harold C. Deutsch and Marian Miller, as well as my good friend Dr. Starke Hathaway, gave me their advice and encouragement, and Professor Herbert Rowen went through the entire manuscript with a red pen in a way that could only be a labor of friendship for which I am deeply grateful. On another plane Dr. John Harris, an ophthalmologist at the University of Minnesota Medical Schools, made this manuscript possible by the operation through which he restored sight to my right eye; the skill of his knife gave me a chance to complete this work. And finally, my Theta has been most important at every stage of the development of this manuscript: when we might have been enjoying ourselves in Europe, she stood by with aid and advice; her critical comments on my ideas helped me to find solutions for problems, while her understanding of personal psychology saved me from gross errors, just as her feeling for English usage smoothed rough passages in the text; my luckiest moment was when she consented to be my wife— little did she realize the trials that she was undertaking. It is unnecessary to say that none of these people can be blamed for my sins of omission or commission, even though they must be thanked for their aid.

JOHN B. WOLF

Bone Lake, May 26, 1967

PRINCIPAL PERSONAGES

ADÉLAÏDE *Marie-Adélaïde of Savoy, Duchess of Burgundy, 1685–1712.*
Granddaughter of "Monsieur" and Henriette; wife of Louis,
Duke of Burgundy; mother of Louis XV.

ANNE *Anne of Austria, Queen of France, 1601–1666.* Daughter of Philip
III of Spain; wife of Louis XIII; and mother of Louis XIV.

BOSSUET *Jacques-Bénigne Bossuet, 1627–1704.* Bishop and moralist in
the court of Louis XIV; tutor of the Grand Dauphin; noted
funeral orator.

BURGUNDY *Louis, Duke of Burgundy, 1682–1712.* Son of the Grand
Dauphin and Marie-Anne of Bavaria; father of Louis XV.

CATINAT *Nicolas de Catinat, 1637–1712.* Marshal of France; commander in Italy during the last two wars of Louis XIV.

CHARLES II (STUART) *Charles II, King of England, Scotland, and Ireland, 1630–1685.* Grandson of Henry IV and Marie de Médicis;
brother of Henriette, Duchess of Orléans.

CHARLES II (VON HAPSBURG) *Charles II, King of Spain, 1661–1670.*
Brother of Marie-Thérèse; last Hapsburg king of Spain.

COLBERT *Jean-Baptiste Colbert, 1619–1683.* Chief minister of commerce
and internal affairs after Fouquet's disgrace. Father of Seignelay.

CONDÉ *Louis II of Bourbon, Duke of Enghein, Prince of Condé, 1621–
1686.* Son of Henry II of Condé. Became known as "Le Grand
Condé" at his father's death.

CONTI *Armand of Bourbon, 1629–1666.* Prince of Conti; son of Henry
II of Condé; brother of "The Great Condé."

CRÉQUI *François, Chevalier de Créqui, 1625–1687.* A marshal of France.

CROISSY *Charles Colbert, Marquis de Croissy, 1625–1696.* Brother of
Jean-Baptiste Colbert; secretary of state for foreign affairs after
Pomponne.

ELIZABETH-CHARLOTTE *Elizabeth-Charlotte of Bavaria, Duchess of Orléans, 1652–1722.* Second wife of Philippe (1671); chronicler
(through her letters) of this period. Known as "Liselotte," or
"Madame."

FÉNELON *François de Salignac de la Mothe-Fénelon, 1651–1715.* Archbishop of Cambrai; preceptor of the Duke of Burgundy.

FOUQUET *Nicolas Fouquet, 1615–1680.* Superintendent of finance; imprisoned in 1661.

GASTON *Jean-Baptiste Gaston, Duke of Orléans, 1608–1660.* Younger brother of Louis XIII.

LE GRAND DAUPHIN *Louis, Dauphin of France, 1661–1711.* Son of Louis XIV and grandfather of Louis XV.

LA GRANDE MADEMOISELLE *Anne-Marie-Louise of Orléans, Duchess of Montpensier, 1627–1693.* Daughter of Gaston and Marie of Bourbon; cousin of Louis XIV.

HENRIETTE *Henriette-Anne of England, 1644–1670.* First wife of Philippe (becoming the Duchess of Orléans); sister of Charles II.

LAUZUN *Antoine Nompar de Caumont, Duke of Lauzun, 1632–1723.* Courtier and soldier (captain of the king's guards). Probably married "La Grande Mademoiselle."

LE TELLIER *Michel Le Tellier, 1603–1685.* Secretary of state and war; later became chancellor.

LIONNE *Hugues de Lionne, 1611–1671.* Secretary of foreign affairs.

LA VALLIÈRE *Louise de la Baume le Blanc, Duchess de La Vallière, 1644–1710.* Mistress of Louis XIV.

LOUIS XIII *1601–1643, King of France (1610–1643).* Son of Henry IV and Marie de Médicis; father of Louis XIV.

LOUIS XIV *1638–1715, King of France (1643–1715).* The "Sun King."

LOUIS XV *1710–1774, Duke of Anjou, Dauphin; King of France (1715–1774).* Son of Louis, Duke of Burgundy, and Marie-Adélaïde of Savoy.

LOUVOIS *François Michel Le Tellier, Marquis de Louvois, 1641–1691.* Son of Le Tellier and followed him as secretary of state and war.

LUXEMBOURG *François-Henri de Montmorency-Bouteville, Duke of Luxembourg, 1628–1695.* Marshal of France.

MAINE *Louis-Auguste of Bourbon, Duke of Maine, 1670–1736.* Son of Louis XIV and Montespan.

MAINTENON *Françoise d'Aubigné, Marquise de Maintenon, 1635–1719.* Widow of poet Scarron; educated children of Louis XIV and Montespan and later (1684) secretly married Louis XIV.

MANCINI *Marie Mancini, 1640–1715.* Niece of Mazarin; early love of Louis XIV, who later became Princess of Colonna.

MARIE-LOUISE *Marie-Louise of Savoy, 1687–1714.* Sister of the Duchess of Burgundy; wife of Philippe.

MARIE-THÉRÈSE   *Marie-Thérèse of Austria,* 1638–1683. Known as "Infanta." Daughter of Philip IV of Spain; first wife of Louis XIV (1660).

MAZARIN   *Jules Mazarin,* 1602–1661. Cardinal and minister to Anne and Louis XIV after the death of Richelieu.

MONTESPAN   *Françoise-Athénaïs de Rochechouart de Mortemart, Marquise de Montespan,* 1641–1707. Mistress of Louis XIV and mother of seven of his children.

PHILIPPE   *Philippe of Bourbon, Duke of Orléans,* 1640–1701. Younger brother of Louis XIV; known as "Monsieur." Married first Henriette of England and later Elizabeth-Charlotte of Bavaria.

PHILIPPE II   *Philippe, Duke of Chartres,* 1674–1723. Son of Philippe I; Duke of Orléans; regent for Louis XV. Later became Duke of Orléans.

PHILIPPE V   *Philippe, Duke of Anjou,* 1683–1746. *King of Spain* (1700–1746); second son of the Grand Dauphin.

POMPONNE   *Simon Arnaud, Marquis de Pomponne,* 1618–1699. Minister of foreign affairs after Lionne. Disgraced after the Treaty of Nymwegen; returned to power after the death of Louvois.

RICHELIEU   *Cardinal Richelieu, Bishop of Luçon,* 1585–1642. Favorite minister of Louis XIII; introduced Mazarin to the French court.

SEIGNELAY   *Jean-Baptiste Colbert, Marquis de Seignelay,* 1651–1690. Son of Jean-Baptiste Colbert; secretary of state for marine.

TORCY   *Jean-Baptiste Colbert, Marquis de Torcy,* 1665–1746. Son of Croissy; successor as secretary of state for foreign affairs.

TURENNE   *Henri de la Tour D'Auvergne, Viscount de Turenne,* 1611–1675. Marshal of France.

VAUBAN   *Sébastien le Prestre, Seigneur de Vauban,* 1633–1707. Marshal of France; builder of military installations.

VILLARS   *Claude Louis Hector, Duke of Villars,* 1653–1734. Marshal of France.

VILLEROI   *Nicolas de Villeroi,* 1598–1685. Marshal of France; governor of Louis XIV.

VILLEROI   *François de Villeroi,* 1644–1730. Marshal of France; son of Nicholas.

(For an explanation of titles in the court of Louis XIV,
see pages 271–273)

I

I

LOUIS LE DIEUDONNÉ

AT ELEVEN-TWENTY on the morning of Sunday, the fifth of September, 1638, a male child was born at the Château de Saint-Germain; his mother was Anne of Austria, Queen of France, his father was Louis XIII, the king. It is hard to believe that any other child of the century was more anticipated or more welcome; the whole future of France seemed to depend upon the birth of a live male child who could assure the succession to the throne. When the queen became pregnant after more than two decades of childless marriage, Louis dedicated his kingdom to the Virgin,[1] enlisting her powerful support to ensure the birth of a son. With the same intention, Anne had made a solemn vow to construct a handsome church at Val-de-Grâce in honor of the Mother of God and Her Son, if only the Queen of France could also have a male child. When it was announced that the child was a boy, both the king and the queen knew that their prayers had been answered; and the kingdom knew it, too, for the boy was called Louis le Dieudonné, the gift of God.

The women of the royal family and the queen's ladies of honor in attendance in the birth chamber, the bishops, the princes of the blood, and the other great lords who were in the next room, and the king who arrived at Anne's bedside shortly after the birth, all joined the queen in thanking God for the "miracle," and then gave themselves up to more earthy forms of rejoicing. Miracle or not, it was a happy occasion and one that demanded toasts and merrymaking. As the news of the dauphin's birth spread in ever widening circles from the château to the town, from the town to Paris, from Paris to all France, the rattle of muskets, the booming of cannons, the ringing of church bells, the chanting of *Te Deums,* the offering of masses in thanksgiving, the bonfires and fireworks, the singing, drinking, and dancing in the streets with free wine for the people, all testified to the joy and excitement of the kingdom. "Now we have a dauphin," rang out the popular song that told of the joy of France, of the bonfire on the Île de la Cité that almost burned down a building on the other shore of the river, and above all of the promise of a happy future under this prince given to

France by God to be the king. The eternal hope of mankind for a better day never seems brighter than at the birth of a new king whose patterns of life are still to be formed.

While the people danced in the streets and the courtiers congratulated the king, poets and orators all over France memorialized the great event in verse and prose. They vied with each other to sing of the real or imaginary virtues of the king and his infant son. One astrologer, delicately side-stepping the church's denunciation of his art, noted that the young prince was born under the sign of the Virgin when "this constellation had its greatest force." He went on to say that the sun itself had come closer to the earth than usual in order to associate itself with the new dauphin.[2] Richelieu, whose personal satisfaction over the arrival of an heir probably equaled that of the king's, followed these waves of appreciation with delight: "Never has there been," he wrote, "such great rejoicing as for this new favor that Heaven has granted to the kingdom of France." Like his fellow countrymen, Richelieu believed that France had just witnessed a miracle.

Not everyone was as happy as the royal family and the people singing in the streets. The king's brother, Gaston of Orléans, and his cousin, the Prince of Condé, had no reason to rejoice, for the dauphin's life came between them and the throne of France. To Gaston, who had long "known" that he would some day replace his sickly, morose elder brother on the throne, the news of Anne's pregnancy had come as something of a shock. When he arrived at Saint-Germain some fifteen days before the birth of the young prince, he gave no indication of his anxiety, but after a boy was actually born, Gaston abruptly left the court for his own estates where he "complained of his misfortunes with thousands of tears" (Goulas); Louis' birth made it unlikely that he would become Gaston I. The Condé household also received the news of Anne's delivery with reservations. Gaston had been the nearest heir to the throne, but he had only daughters, and a woman could not inherit the crown of France. Next in the line of succession came Prince Henry II of Condé; he was already too old to expect much for himself, but he had two sons, the Duke of Enghien (the future Grand Condé) and the Prince of Conti, and their chances for the succession were dimmed by this birth.

The princes of Europe could share more easily the happiness of the royal family; a child born so late in a marriage to so sickly a king almost inevitably meant that they could look forward to a regency in France, and a regency was, in the nature of things, a weak government. The letters of congratulations that poured into France from the Catholic and Protestant princes alike were not so discourteous as to mention this fact that made their joy in the birth of a dauphin quite sincere; indeed, if one reads the letters that came to the king, it would seem that the whole Christian world unreservedly shared the happiness of the royal couple. Even the King of Spain, at that moment locked in desperate war with France, sent his sister Queen Anne and her husband the king his greetings and congratulations. Pope Urban VIII, along with his apostolic benediction, sent a princely gift of clothing for the new baby; on one garment, as a delicate suggestion, there was beautifully embroidered in gold lace the picture of Saint Louis and Saint Urban in peaceful conversation with each other.

Neither the pope nor the lay princes appreciated the fears of the Swedish minister, the learned Hugo Grotius, who, upon hearing that the child had been born with two fully developed teeth and that one wet nurse after another proved to be unable to sustain the punishment of feeding him, wrote to his master, "The Dauphin is not satisfied to dry up his nurses, he tears them to pieces with his bites. It is for the neighbors of France to fear this precocious voracity."

Everyone agreed that the royal infant was a beautiful child and that he was extraordinarily robust; good health and physical beauty were to be characteristic of this prince until he was well along in middle age, and the fact that he was to live seventy-seven years testified to his physical toughness. Geneticists speak of hybrid vigor that results from the crossing of strains that have long been separated; something like this may have happened in the case of Louis le Dieudonné, for his grandparents carried the genes of the Burgundian Valois, the Hapsburgs, the Médicis, the Béarnais, and the Bourbons at a time when there had been less intermarriage between these families than was later to be the case. His father, uncle, and brother looked more like the Médicis and the Béarnais than either the Bourbons or the Hapsburgs, but Louis XIV seems to have inherited the physical make-up of the Burgundian ancestors of Charles V. The family tree was studded with famous names: Ferdinand and Isabella of Spain, Emperor Maximilian of Austria, Charles the Rash of Burgundy, Lorenzo the Magnificent of Florence, Emperor Charles V and his son Philip II, and of course Henry IV. These men who had left their marks on the history of Europe all contributed to the blood of the young prince; in fact, of the important rulers of the preceding century, only the English Tudors and the French Valois were absent from the list. On the French side of the family the pious figure of a remote ancestor, Saint Louis (and of his mother, Blanche of Castile), assumed great importance as the source of the Bourbon line, and in the even more remote past, Clovis I was honored as the champion of the church and a model for kings by a generation that badly understood history. Many other men, less celebrated by history, also were forebears of the young prince born at Saint-Germain who was more Spanish and German than French, in both inheritance and appearance.

The little boy's own father and mother had not gotten on well together. They had been married while still in their early teens, but the sickly, ill-favored Louis XIII had been terrified at the beauty and animal vigor of his young wife. It was several years before the king consummated the marriage; poor Louis XIII, always somewhat repelled by physical contacts with women, had almost to be dragooned into Anne's bed. There was one pregnancy early in the marriage that resulted in a miscarriage, but no others followed. As time went on, Louis refused to visit the queen's bed in spite of the admonitions of his confessor, of Cardinal Richelieu, and of other advisers and courtiers, all of whom urged the necessity of an heir. There is a story of a rainstorm that caught the king far from his own bed, and forced him to have recourse to the queen both for dinner and for a place to sleep, and that from this brief encounter, Louis XIV was born. Be that as it may, there were many who had called upon the king to perform his marital obligations, and his joy was great when the pregnancy was announced, for if the child were a boy, then the king's irresponsible brother, Gaston, would not be allowed to undo the work that he and Richelieu had begun.

Anne's position in France had been difficult from the very beginning. A large section of the court had not been friendly to the Spanish marriage, and when the young king seemed to reject her, her situation became very uncertain. She was willy-nilly involved in some of the plots against Cardinal Richelieu, whom she regarded as her personal enemy, but more important, she was childless and thus there was always the nagging fear that she would be sent back to Spain as a woman who had failed in the most important obligation of a royal princess. There were stories about peccadillos with the Duke of Buckingham and others, but no one has ever seriously suggested that Anne of Austria forgot that she was the daughter of one king and the wife of another. Her *confidente* and friend, Madame de Motteville, summed up her position as follows: "She was born to make the late King her husband the happiest man in the world and if he had wished it he certainly would have been, but that fatality that almost always separates the hearts of sovereigns, came between the King and the Queen. The love that she could have given to that Prince, she gave to her children and particularly to the King, her son, whom she loved passionately."[3] When Anne discovered that she was pregnant, and later when she gave birth to a son, her status at the court changed radically. She was no longer the foreigner to be suspected of treason because she wrote to her brother, but rather the mother of the dauphin and, after Louis XIII's death, the regent for her son, and completely identified with the Bourbon kingdom of France and its place in the world. It is small wonder that Anne never ceased to regard that chance encounter of a December night and the subsequent birth of her son as a miracle, as God's answer to her prayers. Two years after the birth of Louis le Dieudonné, a second son, Philippe, was born. Anne was thirty-nine years old; the succession in the Bourbon line was secure.

By the time Louis le Dieudonné was born Anne had outgrown much of the frivolous behavior that had characterized her earlier life. Should one criticize her for her former foolishness? What should be expected of a beautiful, passionate woman ignored and despised by her husband? There had been no real scandal, of course, but the queen's love of the theater and of the gaming table where she "gambled as a Queen, without passion and without the urge to win" (de Motteville), her pleasure in dancing with scatterbrained companions, and her self-indulgence at the table had not created an image of a queen who might someday govern the realm. On the other hand, her hostility to her husband's policies and to his minister, as well as her involvement with his enemies, raised serious questions about her loyalty to the kingdom. In her late thirties much of this was put aside as she became the pious queen who spent hours every day praying to God, the loving mother who cared for her son, the Spanish-bred princess whose judgment might someday be of value to the kingdom. She still loved the theater and refused to listen to the clerical prophets of doom who condemned it; she still loved to gamble and to participate in the ballets of the court; she still rose late, drank too much chocolate for the good of her figure, and enjoyed the air of doing nothing; but as the mother of two princes, her position and her loyalties were now no longer in question.

The little Louis benefited from both her maturity and her need for an emotional outlet. Most young princes were left to grow up under the care of governors and governesses, seldom experiencing maternal or paternal love —indeed, hardly acquainted with their parents at all. Anne refused to abdicate her rights as mother; she "seldom leaves him," wrote Mademoiselle Andriéa to a friend when Louis was about eighteen months old; "she takes great pleasure playing with him and wheeling him in his carriage in good weather. He is her principal pleasure, so much so that there is no other in her heart."[4] This was the picture given by all the contemporaries who watched the queen lavish her love upon this "child of the miracle." The relationship between mother and son resulting from this outpouring of love aroused the envy and the ire of the king. One day after the child, upon seeing his father in nightcap, beard, and bedraggled costume, ran terrified to his mother's skirts, Louis wrote to Richelieu wondering whether it might be wise to remove his son from the queen's influence. Fortunately for all concerned, he resisted the impulse. All his life Louis XIV remembered his mother and honored her memory. Her love and devotion were undoubtedly factors of paramount importance in his life, and her ideal of monarchy probably formed Louis' basic assumptions about his own obligations to the world. Anne had two goals for her son: like any pious Christian woman, she wanted him to grow up to be a good man; like a true Spanish princess, a granddaughter of Philip II, she also wanted him to become a great king.

Unlike Marie de Médicis, who had always favored her second son, Gaston of Orléans, over his brother, Louis XIII, Anne never gave her second son, Philippe, anything like the same attention that she showered upon Louis. Philippe could be sick and his mother would not visit him. When he was well he was expected to give in to his elder brother in everything. So fearful was the queen that Philippe might someday play the part of plotter and rebel against Louis XIV, as Gaston had done to Louis XIII, that she treated this younger son like a girl, often clothing him in female dress, bending his will to be submissive, and even calling him "my little girl." His later homosexual tendencies, his love of trinkets, jewels, lace, and ribbons, and his fatal lack of self-confidence could stem as much from Anne's decision that he must never become a threat to her beloved firstborn, as from characteristics possibly inherited from Louis XIII. Many years later Louis XIV wrote in his memoirs for the education of his own son that brothers can be a problem; "My care," he went on to say, "will be to raise them [any brothers that might appear; but at this time there was only one, who died as a child] as well as I raise you, but you ought to raise yourself above them and make the whole world recognize that you merit this rank that seems to be given to you by birth alone." He, like many people, preferred to see himself as a self-made man;[5] he did not tell his son how Anne had treated his brother.

Louis' relationship with his father was less well developed. Louis XIII was ill much of the time; he was loaded with cares of state and war, he loved the chase and the company of his newly found *mignon,* Cinq-Mars; his morose, ill-humored disposition did not help him appreciate a small child who could neither follow the hunt nor understand the coarse jokes of the stable. Louis XIII never really grew up emotionally, and it would have been asking too much to expect him to find himself in this son of his later years. From time to time, however, the little boy does appear in the king's correspondence with Richelieu: "I am dissatisfied with my son . . . when he saw me he cried as if he had seen the devil, and ran to his mother." Clearly the child did not know papa very well at this point in his life. Again: "My son [at eighteen months] has demanded my pardon on his knees" [sic!]. Or again, when things were going better: "My son played with me [in the king's office] for more than an hour; we are the best of friends. . . ." But Louis XIII was never sure of anyone: "I believe that the friendship that my son shows toward me will last, but in case it changes . . ." Let Anne beware if the child fails to honor his father—she will lose custody over him.

Father and son met formally as well as informally. In the *Bibliothèque Nationale* there are several prints illustrating life at the court at this period. In one the child stands on his mother's lap while "papa" hangs the cordon of the Order of the Holy Spirit around his neck. In another the king and queen sit on the palace steps and fondly watch their child, accompanied by a governess and the ubiquitous dogs, as he walks toward them. No very important deductions are possible from any of these "snap-shots" on canvas or paper, for they may have been only the dream of the artist. What we can be sure of is the fact that Louis XIII saw very little of his son during these last years of his life. He traveled about a great deal; he spent time with his hunting dogs and horses; he was deeply concerned by the conspiracy, trial, and execution of Cinq-Mars, as well as over the health of his faithful servant Richelieu. His own death followed so closely upon the cardinal's that it almost seems that he had no will to live without his great minister.

Louis was at Saint-Germain during his father's last illness, and there are stories that indicate his concern over the impending death, but the little four-and-a-half-year-old surely did not understand death, and there is nothing in his later behavior that would suggest that Louis XIII on his death bed, or any other time, had made a great impression upon him. Few would remember the morose, sickly king; Saint-Simon, who believed Louis XIII to be the greatest of kings, probably because he had raised the family of Saint-Simon to the peerage, often complained that no one but himself ever attended the annual mass for his soul. As a man, Louis XIV neither honored his father's memory nor spoke of him with any affection. Indeed, Louis apparently accepted the mythology that surrounded the relationship between his father and Richelieu,[6] for he did not want to hear about either one of them. Colbert, who appreciated Richelieu's statesmanlike papers as well as his place in history, often prefaced an argument with the remark, "Sire, that great statesman Cardinal Richelieu said . . . ," only to draw from the king a wry comment or a shrug of the shoulders. Louis probably adopted his mother's estimate of her late husband; Anne never appreciated the king's place in the government, and Louis XIV, like the numerous historians who wrote before the twentieth century, shared the popular misconception of that unfortunate, sick, emotionally maladjusted man.

After Richelieu's death Louis XIII, knowing that he had not long to live, became fearful for the fate of his kingdom with so small a boy as its king. In December 1642, he registered a document in the Parlement of Paris banning his brother Gaston from any connection with the regency that would govern after his death. Listing his brother's past crimes, he proceeded to deprive Gaston of his soldiers and his position as governor over the province of Auvergne, and ordered that he must never have any part in the administration of the kingdom.[7] The king had not much more faith in his wife than in his brother. She had never been openly in revolt, but she had made friends with almost all those who had opposed Richelieu, and she was associated with the *Dévot* party that regarded the war against the Hapsburgs as sinful; indeed, she was a Hapsburg and had been in correspondence with her brother in Spain. The mother of the king could not actually be excluded from a regency government, but Louis wished to limit Anne's power to undo his work.

The king placed his hope in an Italian diplomat who had been one of Richelieu's creatures. Jules Mazarin, educated in Rome and in Spain, had first served the papal court as a diplomatic "trouble-shooter," and then had been attracted into the French service by Richelieu who sent him from one court to another. When Père Joseph died, Richelieu persuaded the pope to give Mazarin the cardinal's hat that had been intended for the Capuchin, and kept the young Italian in Paris where he learned more fully the problems of governing France. On Richelieu's death Mazarin simply stepped into the vacated place of the great minister. There seems to have been no formal consideration of his position: the king needed help, and Mazarin was there to give it to him.[8] The Italian was clever, he was unobtrusive and modest, and his rank as cardinal made him a "cousin of the King." It is impossible to know when the king decided that Mazarin should have a large place in the regency, but when he asked him to act as godfather in the baptismal ceremonies for his son, it became obvious that Louis XIII expected Mazarin to be important in the government that would follow his death.

Baptism was the little boy's first ceremonial introduction to the court. A sober child of four, clothed in a long robe of silver taffeta, knelt on the *prie-dieu* of the chapel of the Château de Saint-Germain; on either side were his godparents, the Princess of Condé, and Mazarin. The Bishop of Meaux asked his name. "Louis, the gift of God," replied the Princess of Condé, and the bishop poured the water on his brow, placed the salt in his mouth, and asked him if he were willing to give up Satan and all his pomp and works and to accept the doctrines of the church. "*Abrenuncio—Credo*": These were the words of the little boy whom the *Gazette* described as "handsome as an angel, manifesting by all his acts a modesty and a self-control extraordinary for his years." There is a famous story, probably untrue, that the child, returning from the ceremony to his father's bedside where the king asked him his name, replied, "Louis XIV." "Not yet, not yet!" replied the sad king. The memoirists repeat this story so faithfully that it must have had a wide circulation, but it is improbable that either Louis or his father ever referred to themselves with a numeral; perhaps the story is one of those that should have happened even if it did not.

Before he died, Louis XIII relented in his decision to exclude Gaston from the regency, because he decided to use his brother as a check on Anne. His final will provided for a regency council composed of Anne as regent, Gaston as lieutenant general of the realm, and Mazarin as its president. This council would include both princes of the blood and members of the king's government, and its decisions were to be binding on the regent, thereby making it a possible source of much trouble.[9] Any protests that Anne may have had, however, were stilled by Mazarin's assurances that she would not have to worry about her eventual powers in the regency. There was a touching scene at the king's deathbed when Gaston and Anne promised faithfully to live up to the dying king's wishes, and another brilliant presentation in Parlement where Louis sought to give his will the force of law. No one bothered to remind him that in France a dead king could not bind the hands of a living one, nor that the traditions of the kingdom always gave the regency government of a minor king into the hands of the queen mother. So Louis XIII was able to die in peace after preparing himself with the spiritual consolation of the church and the gentle counsels of the good man who was to be known to posterity as Saint Vincent de Paul.

The death watch at Saint-Germain must have been trying for the little boy of almost five. His father's blessings, equivocal talk of God's will, endless discussions in the halls and passageways about the reign to come, the knowledge that something awful was about to happen to his father, something that a child could not understand, and finally, the apparent distress of his mother who kept up the semblance of a woman about to be bereaved of a beloved husband: all these things must have been very upsetting to the child. Philippe at three probably understood little or nothing; but Louis must have had curious misunderstandings. A widely repeated story tells us that a *huissier* asked the boy, "Monseigneur, if God takes your good father, would you wish to be king in his place?" "Non!" cried the weeping child, "I do not wish to be king. If he dies I shall throw myself into the moat of the château!" The exaggerated responses sometimes characteristic of this era may suggest that the child had heard something like this from someone in the court, and childlike, repeated the words.

Louis XIII did die, but not before he had had a prophetic vision of a great victory over the armies of Spain, a vision that surely had the wish as father to the thought, for nothing had been more hoped for than some sign that the armies of France would prevail. Louis XIII died on May 16, 1643; a few days later news came that the Duke of Enghien (the Grand Condé) had won a great victory over the Spanish at Rocroi.[10] What an auspicious opening for the reign of Louis XIV, a reign that was to last until September 1, 1715.

2

THE FORMATION OF
THE REGENCY GOVERNMENT

WHEN LOUIS XIII drew his last breath guards immediately surrounded the new king. Fearful that a clique might kidnap her son and seize the government of the realm, Anne had arranged this precaution weeks before Louis' death. She had little reason to trust anyone, and much cause to be suspicious of several factions in the court. When she left her husband's deathbed she immediately sought out her son, knelt before him, and did homage to "her King." The whole court followed suit. "The King is dead. Long live the King!" There was to be no pretense that the new ruler had to wait for the burial of his predecessor before assuming the status of king; Henry IV was the last king whose royal existence had been prolonged by an effigy representing the sovereign.[1]

Within a short time the royal family and most of the court had packed up their belongings and set out for Paris, leaving the corpse of Louis XIII to physicians, embalmers, monks, and faithful servants of his household. This was the custom of the Bourbons; after a death everyone departed, leaving the dead in the hands of those responsible for preparing the body for burial at Saint-Denis several months later. There were rituals to be perfomed, but these were not for the royal family to see. In the case of Louis XIII there were few real tears shed by those who left the Château de Saint-Germain on that fine spring day; the fresh new green leaves, the wild flowers, and the soft air all promised better things to come.

The cavalcade of horsemen and carriages that made its way to Paris was long remembered. Anne and her two sons, riding in an open carriage, were cheered by peasants, bourgeoisie, and noblemen who turned out to see the new king; at every village the clergy showered blessings upon mother and sons, blessings and expressions of hope and expectation. Louis XIII, sometimes cruel, usually remote, had never been loved, and the exactions required by war had made him even more unpopular. Now there was a new king, and the handsome, robust, sober child who received the applause with solemn eyes, as well as the gracious, still beautiful queen, seemed to indicate that a new era was being born. People have always hoped for a golden age, a time when the evils that beset them would be banished. Louis XIV's subjects wanted to see that promise in the little king that God had given them to be their master. When the procession reached Paris, cheering crowds lined the streets all the way to the Louvre, where great decisions had to be made.

The problem was the regency council provided for in the dead king's testament. It could easily fall into a deadlock, creating confusion and disorder. At forty-two, Anne was a vigorous woman who felt that she had triumphed over the two sickly men whose regime had oppressed her youth; she was ready to live and quite unwilling to accept dictation from the grave. Mazarin assured her that the testament could be put aside; he was too loyal to the royal family, and perhaps too sure of his own ability, to allow any advantages that he might personally reap by this testament to blind him to its dangers. Neither the Duke of Orléans nor the Prince of Condé was in any position to challenge the queen's desires. Anne had carefully courted her brother-in-law, paying him the honor of consulting him freely, and holding up the possibility that one of his daughters might become Queen of France. Condé was a spiritless man, enormously rich, but neither brave nor resourceful. He had had his day; he had allowed himself to be paid as rebel against Marie de Médicis' regency three decades earlier, but when he saw the fate of those who plotted against Louis XIII and Richelieu, he had quickly become "reconciled" to the king's will. In 1643 he pinned all his hopes on his twenty-two-year-old son who had commanded the victorious army at Rocroi. When Anne assured the prince a place in the council and promised to reward the soldier-hero, Condé was ready to agree to anything that she might wish.

The Parlement was only too happy to set aside the late king's will and to register decrees establishing a regency in the name of the queen. As lawyers, the members of the sovereign court were impressed by the tradition that the queen mother had always become regent for a minor king, but they had another, perhaps more pressing, reason for setting aside the will of Louis XIII. The Parlement of Paris, the most important of several Parlements in the kingdom, acted as a court of appeal for suits at law. It registered edicts, orders, and commissions of the king, and exercised a wide variety of administrative duties ranging from control over certain aspects of the royal forests to censorship of books and inquisition of heresy and witchcraft. As a specialized offshoot of the royal council, it represented the king's justice. Tradition had given it a considerable range of powers. By refusing to register a royal decree on the grounds that it was incompatible with the traditions and customs of the realm, Parlement exercised a sort of "judicial review" over royal legislation, but since all the Parlements were only extensions of the royal will, these objections could be overruled by the king in a *lit de justice*, that is, by his attending Parlement in person or in the person of a member of his family, to demand registration of a contested edict. But the members of Parlement owned their offices and could not be removed except by royal repurchase, and they also held the firm belief that their court was a quasi-independent institution. From the king's point of view this often created an intolerable situation, for it was difficult to accomplish political objectives with officials who were not in sympathy with the king's projects and who could not be removed.

Louis XIII and Richelieu had many conflicts with Parlement. When it proved impossible to win its support by persuasion or petty bribes, Louis had gone to their chamber in person and brutally demanded that the Parlement cease interference with "my state" and confine its activities to the giving of justice. Nor was that all; the king's council also acted as an agency of justice, quashed Parlementary writs, and interfered with business that had traditionally been within Parlementary jurisdiction. And finally, Louis and Richelieu had extended the practice of sending out intendants, the council's "circuit riders," as it were, into the provinces to act on urgent matters of police, taxation, and justice. Armed with royal authority, these intendants cut across the traditional patterns of justice and administration, sometimes antagonizing members of Parlement, town governments, and royal governors. With so many offices either hereditary or venal, there was no other way of bringing the wishes of the central authority to the country. Parlement had complained about this practice, but what could be done with such redoubtable men as Richelieu and Louis XIII? The Parlementarians could only grind their teeth and wait.

When Anne came to Paris with her infant son-king, they knew that they had outlived their late enemies. And when Mazarin obligingly assured them that compliance with the wishes of the queen would guarantee future cooperation between Parlement and the king's council, they were only too happy to show that their authority was great enough to put aside the last wishes of their old enemy, the late King of France.

Everything was arranged before the royal family entered the Grand Chamber of Parlement for the *lit de justice*. Mazarin had smoothed the path and made all things possible. The child-king and all the court attended mass at the Sainte-Chapelle next to the house of Parlement, and then marched in state down the great corridor into the gilded hall where the king, carried by a peer of the realm to emphasize the fact that he was a child, was placed on the high throne. "With a grace uncommon to those of his years," said the *Gazette,* he solemnly spoke out the lines that he had learned: "Messieurs, I have come to testify my affection and my good will toward my Parlement. My Chancellor will tell you the rest." The quick glance toward his mother and her reassuring smile of approval, was an interchange quite normal for a four-year-old boy eager to carry off satisfactorily his first official act.

Then the queen spoke up to assure the Parlement that she "would be happy to have their counsel at all occasions"—welcome words to ambitious men so long excluded from politics. She was followed by Orléans and Condé, who protested their loyalty and devotion to, and faith in, the queen, and urged that she be appointed regent. Finally Chancellor Séguier, resplendent in violet robes trimmed with ermine, the blue cordon of the Order of the Holy Spirit about his neck, and heavy with the prestige of his immense wisdom and experience, arose to explain that the king wished the Parlement to name his mother as régent with the power to appoint her council and her ministers, and to govern the kingdom "with full power and freedom" in the name of her son. The Parlement happily agreed to the formula that seemed again to reinstate that august body in an important place in public affairs: "The King, sitting in a *lit de justice* in his Parlement, has declared and declares the Queen his mother Regent of France, confirming the wishes of the late King, his honored lord and father, for the care and education and development of his person, and for the free, absolute, and entire administration of the affairs of the kingdom during his minority." It was not necessary to note that this latter condition set aside the will of the late king. The decree went on to name the Duke of Orléans to the post of lieutenant general of the kingdom, but subject to the authority of the queen. The members of the court with an interest in the outcome of the session already knew what positions in the new government had been promised them, conditional upon their support.[2]

Before the decree was voted, Omer Talon, one of the most distinguished and eloquent members of Parlement, took the floor to address the king. He spoke of the duty of kingship, of the virtues of Louis' ancestors, of the clemency of Henry IV, of the piety and justice of Louis XIII, and exhorted the child to follow their best examples. "Be, sire," he went on to say, "the father of your people that in the extremity of their misery they may find in you comfort, and give to France that which is worth much more than victories. Strive to be the prince of peace." After this, Séguier polled the Parlement—dukes, peers, marshals, and councilors—and the verdict was unanimous in favor of the reconstituted regency. The little boy stood up, bowed gravely to the audience, and then the royal party withdrew. Everyone was impressed with the beauty, the maturity, the dignity, and the earnestness of the new king. He was nearly five years old; we may be allowed to believe that the occasion left some impression on his mind—but what it was no one can know.

Armed with authority as regent, Anne had now to decide what she would do about the government of the kingdom. What course could she follow? The kingdom of France traditionally had been governed by the king and his family with the aid of servants and ministers who carried out their wishes. But who were the members of the "family" of Louis XIV? The heads of the cadet lines of the house of Bourbon were Gaston of Orléans and Henry II of Condé; could they be expected to help govern the kingdom for a minor king? Gaston had already piled up a record of rebellion, weakness, desertion of friends, and incapacity; only the royal blood in his veins had kept his head on his shoulders when those of his accomplices had been struck off. Middle age and the birth of the dauphin had calmed his turbulence but had not given him wisdom. Anne probably had no reason to fear that he might emulate his remote ancestors by a plot to murder his nephew and seize the throne, but she also had no reason to expect much real help with the problems of government from such a man.[3]

Prince Henry II of Condé was even less useful: he had wealth, but lacked both wisdom and courage. Richelieu had taken Condé's measure when he forced him to marry his eldest son, the Duke of Enghien, to the cardinal's misformed niece, in spite of the young man's love for another woman. The young man was then given an army command in the Spanish Netherlands; as a relative of both the cardinal and the king he was deemed to be "safe." But from Prince Henry II one could expect nothing; an ex-rebel whose spirit had long since been broken, he had little to offer anyone. His sons were still too young to claim a position in the regency, although the time would soon come when the hero Duke of Enghien would demand his place.

In addition to these cadet lines of the family, there were the legitimized descendants of Henry IV, the house of Vendôme. One member of this house, the Duke of Beaufort, tried to attract Anne by gallantry. She accepted his sighs and his admiration of her beautiful hands (Anne's principal vanity), and she used him to guard her son in the first days after her husband's death. But Beaufort was only thirty and Anne had no reason to suspect that he had any wisdom or interests beyond his own ambitions. He could not be of any great help. Obviously the regent would have to look beyond the family for assistance in governing the kingdom.

When Richelieu had died the year before, the doors of the prisons began to open and a few exiles trickled back to the court; when Louis XIII followed the redoubtable cardinal to the tomb, the prison doors were flung wide and the exiles returned en masse, all of them filled with expectations. Had not the poor queen suffered from the persecutions of those two wicked men? She had been spied upon, accused, mistreated, misunderstood, excluded from council. Now that she had power, the time for revenge had come. The cardinal's creatures must go, his relatives must be deprived of their offices, pensions, titles, and honors, his policies reversed, and most important of all, his enemies rewarded for their sufferings. Their feelings and aspirations might well have suited Anne before her son was born, but as regent for a boy-king, she needed and wanted other kinds of advice.

Among the returned exiles there were several who had been close friends in her frivolous youth: Madame de Chevreuse, Madame de Hautefort, Madame de Motteville, Monsieur de la Porte (who claimed that his silence had saved her reputation), and others. These people returned to court hoping to see the reversal of their enemies, but Anne seems to have sensed that they were particularly interested in forwarding their own, rather than the crown's, interests. All of them failed utterly to understand that the queen mother, Regent of France, was no longer the poor princess fearful of the tyranny of a misanthropic husband and a hateful cardinal. Anne was the mother of the king, and as a granddaughter of Philip II, a princess brought up to understand the problems of monarchs, she knew well that her task was to preserve the kingdom for her son during his minority.[4] The returned exiles wished for revenge, but Anne knew that revenge would not preserve the kingdom. Several years later she passed by a portrait of her late enemy Cardinal Richelieu, and is said to have remarked softly, "Were you alive, you would be surprised at the honors and power that I would bestow upon you," and the story may even be true. As regent she understood that Richelieu's policies had been directed toward the creation of a powerful kingdom, and she knew that her own should have the same goal.

Cardinal Mazarin became her minister in much the same way that he had assumed power for Louis XIII after Richelieu's death: he knew what had to be done, he was comparatively disinterested,[5] and he had skill. When Jules Mazarin first arrived in France, Cardinal Richelieu introduced him to Anne with a bantering, almost insulting remark: "You will like him, Madame, he has the air of Buckingham about him." He was just about

Anne's age, handsome, brilliant, subtle, and charming. But it is unlikely that Anne noticed him much before her husband's death, for he was away on missions much of the time or deeply engrossed in the king's business. When she had to attend to these things herself, Mazarin was at hand to initiate her into the mysteries of public affairs. It was he who showed her how to avoid the crippling provisions of her husband's will; at the same time he assured her of his own intention of retiring to Italy as soon as she should find someone to replace him. It did not take long for Anne to realize that this Italian was probably the only person in her entourage to give her disinterested advice; at the same time, he also was the only one who understood the problems of state primarily in terms of the greatness of the house of Bourbon.

After being married to Louis XIII for more than a quarter of a century, it was agreeable to talk in Spanish to this elegant cultured man who understood how to pay court to her both as queen and as a woman. Anne was in her early forties, she was becoming a bit too fat, but she still was beautiful and she knew it, and probably was pleased to find that Mazarin found her attractive. Perhaps Mazarin did have something of the air of Buckingham about him; it was a welcome relief after the air of Louis XIII. In any case, she put off accepting his resignation, and began an association that lasted until his death, an association in which Mazarin exercised power more securely than Richelieu ever had.

Mazarin began by seeing the queen every evening to discuss the affairs of state. He soon discovered that Anne did not know much about the day-to-day problems of government and that there were many people who were trying to use her by protestations of past friendship, by playing upon her piety, by making demands upon her gratitude. He urged her not to listen to the monks when they talked politics, even not to spend so much time at Val-de-Grâce. "God," he said, "is everywhere; the Queen can pray to Him in her oratory." At first the court did not realize that Mazarin was achieving an ascendency over her. The court watched unbelievingly: Mazarin was closeted long hours with the queen; she refused to act without consulting him. The relatives of Richelieu retained their offices; the policies of the late king continued unchanged. All through the court there were men who saw their hopes blasted by this Italian who seemed so humble, so anxious to please, so unobtrusive, so deferential. Here was a man who seemed to say that he was sorry that "his rank as Cardinal would not allow him to humble himself even more than he did"—and yet he was all-powerful.

Mazarin himself was surprised and worried at his success. "Your Eminence will learn," he wrote to Cardinal Bichi in Rome late in August of 1643, ". . . of my position in the French Court. I will tell you only that I receive each day the favor of Her Majesty the Queen and the Duke of Orléans, but at the same time jealousy over the place I occupy irritates more and more those who do everything possible for my downfall. If I could please everyone, I would do it willingly, but my crime consists of serving well and having the good graces of the Queen. I am obliged to efface myself as much as I can, not to become more of a criminal . . ."[6] Mazarin worried unnecessarily about his future; he was slowly but surely securing his place in the mind of the queen, the mother of a minor child with a kingdom to preserve, and in the heart of the queen, the woman who had never really known love.

Just as Anne was not a Louis XIII, Mazarin was not a Richelieu. Lacking the late cardinal's brutality and cruelty, he made up for it in subtlety. Where Louis and Richelieu had used the public executioner and the prison, Anne and Mazarin were to govern by indirection, by persuasion, by diplomacy, by combinations. Mazarin has been accused of duplicity, of guile, of double-dealing; it was even said that he would act by indirection whether it was necessary or not. This sort of tactic at first confused men accustomed to Richelieu, but before long they discovered that even though the tactics were changed, the policies were the same. Like Richelieu before him, Mazarin worked against the great nobles who wanted to control the patronage of the regime for their own interests, and maintained the foreign policy that allied France with Lutheran and Calvinist heretics against Catholic Spain.

Those whose hopes for peace and power had been aroused by the deaths of Louis XIII and Richelieu now saw in Mazarin a new roadblock to their programs and ambitions. Plots against the Italian fomented. The Duchess of Longueville, a sister of the hero Duke of Enghien, and as brilliant and beautiful as he was brave and enterprising, the Duchess of Chevreuse, an intriguer whose career dated back at least two decades, and several other women in the court tried to show Anne that her relationship with the handsome Italian was creating a scandal. Anne blushed to the ears, but refused to give up her minister. The masculine counterpart of this intrigue was led by the Duke of Beaufort, later to be known as the "king of *les Halles*" when he aroused Paris against the king during the *Fronde*. After Beaufort discovered that his own suit was getting nowhere with the queen, he planned to assassinate Mazarin as a simple way of being rid of this foreign intruder. As Henry de Campion[7] describes this plot, one sees how primitive were the morals of the high nobility of this period. The plotters missed one opportunity to murder Mazarin because he was in the carriage with the Duke of Orléans, who would not have objected to the murder, but undoubtedly would have resisted an assassination that would have compromised his own honor. Before another opportunity presented itself to this son of a bastard line of the royal family, the plot was discovered and its leaders were quickly clamped into prison. Had they had to deal with Richelieu and Louis XIII, a number of them would have lost their heads, but Anne and Mazarin contented themselves with imprisoning some and exiling others. Even the Duchess of Chevreuse was to discover that her playmate of yesterday could send her into an exile as unhappy as the one that Richelieu had ordered. When the plots were quashed, a raucous song —the "Ballad of the Important Ones"—spread like wildfire over France, telling of the folly and callousness of the cabal that had failed.[8]

After this plot Mazarin doubled the number of muscular young rapier-carrying Italian "valets" in his suite, but this would not solve the real problems that faced the government. The plain fact was that the battle of Rocroi, even though it had dealt Spanish military prestige a staggering blow, had not ended the war. In Germany, in the Spanish Netherlands, on the Spanish frontier, French armies—or armies paid for by France— fought against Spanish and imperial forces. The diplomats had begun to gather at Münster and Osnabrück, but the fighting did not stop. It cost money to subsidize allies and pay for troops—a great deal of money— and Bourbon France never solved the fiscal problem, never had enough money to mobilize the full potential military strength of the kingdom. Often the costs fell unequally and provoked rebellion. The regency government had its share of these rural uprisings against the authority of landlords and tax collectors.[9] In some ways they were almost as dangerous as the plots of disgruntled noblemen, and they did require the disposition of troops that could be better used against foreign enemies. But Mazarin's policies toward these rebellions were less rigorous than Richelieu's had been. One of them at Rouergue, led in part by local nobility, was quickly suppressed, and the government decided upon clemency. The *arrêt* was one of the first of its kind signed by the minor king: "The rapidity with which the said provinces have been brought into submission has led me by the advice of the Queen Regent to forget their errors." Such clemency did not solve the fiscal problem, nor end rural dissatisfaction, but it did indicate the temper of a new regime that tried to govern by softer measures.

Rebellions against tax collections were symptomatic of the wartime problems of the regency. Even with stepped-up collections, there was not enough money—more taxes and extraordinary fiscal measures were absolutely necessary. Mazarin never understood fiscal problems; he knew only that he needed more money to accomplish the European objectives of the monarchy, and so money should be forthcoming. Parlement, however, took a less sanguine attitude, and resisted the imposition of new taxes. By 1645 the government decided that the king must again go to Parlement to register his will. Louis was now seven years old, and everyone was impressed by his "perfect beauty," his maturity, his "confidence beyond his years," his "dignified carriage" (*Gazette*). This time he was not carried to Parlement; he walked into the chamber holding his mother's hand. "Messieurs," he said from the throne, "the needs of the state have led me to come before my Parlement to speak of my affairs. My Chancellor will explain to you my wishes." The *Gazette* reports that "his natural grace surprised all the assembly, which acknowledged it by prolonged applause." But applause did not conceal the fact that Parlement was becoming hostile to the government of the regency. The more it changed, the more it became the same old government that had been so unsatisfactory in the eyes of Parlement, and these new fiscal measures did not make the war any more popular. Before Parlement bowed to the royal will in a *lit de justice,* the boy-king had to listen to tales of the misery of the kingdom, the poverty and ruin of the peasants, and the distress of the whole land. These stories had been recounted many times before when rulers had asked for money, but the speeches of this session portended troubles to come. The abortive revolt of the "Important Ones" had been a warning that the high nobility was dissatisfied. Parlement now indicated its displeasure. Even a little boy could get the idea that things were not going well.

3

THE BOY-KING

EVERYONE who has left us a verbal picture of Louis as a child was impressed by his robust constitution, his solemn dignity, his grace and noble appearance. The child very early showed the reserved self-possession that was to be characteristic of the man; he seems to have looked out on the world without revealing his own feelings. There is a posed picture at Versailles by an unknown artist showing Anne and her two children: Louis seems serious and reserved yet eager in his searching regard. Anne's beautiful hands and Philippe's girlish face suggest that the artist accepted the conventions of the memoirists. And yet we must not conclude that the child-king did not behave as a child. Loménie de Brienne tells us that Louis loved to hammer his drums, trying to imitate the beat of the Swiss guards, that he had a passion for playing soldier with Madame de Salle, one of the queen's women, calling out the commands for the little troupe of children in his company. This latter is not surprising to anyone brought up during a war; the talk of adults must have been almost solely about armies, and the pageantry always featured soldiers. Children of the Thirty Years' War were like children of any other war; and in a king's court, where the colorful guards added additional military flavor, it would be even more certain that war and soldiers would be the center of their interests.

According to his confessor, Father Paulin,[1] the children had daily exercises that helped to make them strong; Louis excelled in these—"He easily fatigues all his courtiers, being almost indefatigable himself." At seven he learned to shoot at a target, and soon became a crack shot, a skill that he retained most of his life. He also had some emotional difficulties. Like any small boy he jealously resented the time that Mazarin spent with his mother over affairs of state, and there is an amusing story of rivalry with his brother that resulted in each wetting the other in bed. Thus even though courtiers tended to note his more sober moments, we can assume that this king, who was "handsome as an angel," "precocious," "bright," and "dignified," was also a child and sometimes acted like one.

When he became seven years old, Louis was taken from the custody of women and placed under that of men. Anne appointed Mazarin as the supervisor of his education. In the royal commission[2] she explained that Mazarin was the choice of the Duke of Orléans, the Prince of Condé, and, indeed, the late king himself, who in making Mazarin godfather of his son, had pointed to him for the supervision of the boy's education. The Marquis de Villeroi, a wise and honored soldier, became Louis' governor, while Dubois and La Porte were named his valets. Hardouin de Péréfixe, a scholarly clergyman who had served both Richelieu and Mazarin, became preceptor, and a battery of instructors in mathematics, writing, Spanish, Italian, drawing, fencing, horseback riding, and dancing were employed to teach the boy the skills that he would need in the world. Not all of these appointees were loyal to Mazarin. La Porte, for example, a victim of Richelieu's wrath when he had shielded Anne years before, did everything he could to undermine the cardinal. His chance came when Louis asked for fairy tales like the ones the ladies used to tell him before he went to sleep; La Porte read to him sections from Mézeray's *Histoire de France,* which had begun to appear in 1643, particularly emphasizing those sections dealing with *fainéant* kings. It was easy to arouse the wrath of the child-king over the behavior of these early do-nothing rulers; La Porte persuaded him that he should never become Louis *le Fainéant,* and seems even to have developed in him a temporary dislike for Mazarin who could be identified with the mayors of the palace in Mézeray's book. Someone also taught Louis a few of the anti-Mazarin songs that were current at this period, but most of the child's instruction was directed by men anxious to please the powerful minister in every way possible.

A host of critics, headed by Saint-Simon and Louis XIV himself, have voiced disapproval of the education that these men gave the king. Their collective judgments, however, may be somewhat unfair, for despite the civil disorders of the *Fronde* that broke out when Louis was only ten and disrupted the regularity of his instruction, Louis at twelve had learned to speak and write elegant French, he could handle Italian easily, and he had enough Spanish to get along in that language. His handwriting left much to be desired, but he could write, and he knew as much mathematics as a king needed. He had become an excellent horseman, a skillful fencer, and an accomplished dancer; his natural grace and physical coordination may have accounted for these athletic accomplishments, but the teachers should be given some credit. He also had acquired a little Latin—enough to translate Caesar's *Gallic Wars*[3] as a surprise for his teacher, but not enough to allow him any real access to the ideas or literature of classical antiquity. Perhaps the most important accomplishment of this early period was the fact that Louis learned to speak French properly; when one considers the violence that Anne and Mazarin did to the French tongue, it is surprising that the boy learned it without a thick accent.

While several priests contributed their part to the religious education of the king, the queen mother may well have been the most decisive figure in the formation of Louis' religious ideas. Anne had grown up in the court of her father, Philip III, who was more suited to be a monk than a king, and while the celestial voices that spoke to him in pure Castilian Spanish never seem to have visited his daughter, Anne nonetheless absorbed the religious symbolism, the elaborate externals of Catholic worship, and the pious atmosphere of her father's court. Her first books were on the Christian mysteries or books of devotion; her love for the theater began with the strange religious dramas written by Lope de Vega; she early learned of the spiritual consolations of the *prie-dieu* and of visits to the convents where nuns talked knowingly of God. Before her marriage, Anne's life had been wrapped up in a texture of religious observances, cults, mysteries. When she first came to France her "Spanish Catholicism" was not as apparent as it was to become later, for her playful enthusiasm in these younger years produced frivolous behavior sometimes bordering on folly. However, one has only to read the *Mémoires* of her faithful friend Madame de Motteville to see that, after forty, Anne reverted to the pious patterns of her youth. She spent hours on her *prie-dieu,* visited convents and chapels, and listened attentively to the words of holy men.

Louis XIII had also had something of this pattern of religiosity, though perhaps a little less flamboyantly than his wife. His dedication of the kingdom to the Virgin to secure her aid in making his unborn child a boy, his habit of ordering *Te Deums,* public prayers, masses of thanksgiving and other religious services on every occasion, was the usual pattern for a Catholic prince of his time. The fact that a man like Saint Vincent de Paul was a frequent and welcome visitor to the palace both before and after the death of Louis XIII gives us an indication of the family religious attitudes. Saint Vincent was no theologian; he was a pious man, a doer of good deeds, a preacher of pious acts, a gentle soul sometimes naïve but always reverent before God.

These were the religious values that the child breathed in as he breathed air. Father Paulin, who prepared Louis for his first communion, wrote to the general of his order (the Jesuits): "There is no lamb more sweet, more tractable than our King . . . he has in him the piety which the most Christian Queen has inculcated in him from early childhood."[4]

The reader of the *Gazette* knows that Anne took her son with her on an endless round of visits to churches, convents, and monasteries. Val-de-Grâce, where she built the magnificent baroque chapel decorated with the symbols of motherhood, and the Theatine chapel given by Mazarin and dedicated by Louis himself to Saint Anne, were most often favored by the royal presence. However, Anne and her son visited all the churches in the Paris area and made pilgrimages to the wonderful Cathedral of the Virgin at Chartres, where she and the young king attended the services held in the crypt in honor of the Queen of Heaven. These visits to churches and shrines contributed to Louis' total education, as well as to his religious instruction, for ambitious or inspired priests could not resist the opportunity offered by this captive audience to lecture the king. Most of the pompous, often tedious, speeches and sermons are happily lost forever, but enough of them have been preserved in pamphlets for us to know their general tenor. Louis and the queen were always urged to love God and the church; to emulate Saint Louis and his mother, Blanche of Castile, as pious rulers, and Clovis, of a more distant age, as extirpator of heresy. Henry IV, the first Bourbon king, usually also came in for a share of praise. Later in the era of the *Fronde,* some of these orations took on a more contemporary political tone.

Anne always had the twin aspirations for her son that he should become a great king and a good man; by "good man" she meant a man who lived the Christian life as she understood it. Her teaching was by precept, example, and even punishment. For slight infractions Louis was sent to his room. Once, for example, when the child tried out language that he had heard in the stable, he was imprisoned for two days. The purity of his later language may have stemmed from his mother's insistence that he must not take the name of God in vain, just as his later devotion to the forms of religious cult and the externals of Catholic worship—the pomp and circumstance of ritual—probably have their deepest origin in Anne's teachings.

What other things intruded into the consciousness of the little Louis XIV? Like other men, he undoubtedly learned much that was not explicitly taught him by parents and preceptors; in the process of living one learns much of what is expected of one and what one means to others. Who knows what are the effects of being a king from the age of four? Of having grown men and women obviously in awe of a child? Of being constantly reminded that one is of the race of the gods? And yet that is what happened to this boy whose good will could mean fortune and position to those about him.

The royal family moved from the Louvre to the palace that Cardinal Richelieu had built and willed to Louis XIII, henceforth called the Palais-Royal. It was more comfortable than the Louvre and its excellent enclosed garden provided a fine play yard for the boy. When Louis was ten or eleven a miniature fort was constructed in the garden, conforming to the best military engineering of the day and large enough for the children to ride their horses in the enclosure. Children of that day loved to play at war, and a child who was also a king played war royally. The Palais-Royal also had a little theater where Richelieu had put on his own and others' dramas; it now became the stage for both the French troupe and the Italian pantomime players whom Mazarin imported for Anne's pleasure. To this day the *Comédie Française* still plays at the Salle Richelieu next to the Palais-Royal. In the palace theater Louis first saw *Le Cid,* with its conception of personal *gloire* so like that which he later professed for himself; *Polyeucte,* with its portrayal of Christian heroism; and others of the plays of the day loaded with Christian and feudal idealism. Corneille's French and the control of his poetic meter must have contributed to Louis' general culture.

With the royal family installed in the Palais-Royal, Mazarin bought three mansions on the other side of the garden and joined them into a town house appropriate for a minister (now the *Bibliothèque Nationale*), which he decorated with pictures and statuary imported from Italy. He also brought his sister Madame Martinozzi with her son and daughters from Italy to share his good fortune. Madame de Senecay, who had been a governess of the small king, undertook the education of these girls, and the queen practically adopted them as their foster mother. With the little group of boys—sons of noblemen and royal officials—who were in attendance on the king, Mazarin's family completed the picture of the royal entourage. There are stories of the children attending parties at the Palais-Royal, at Saint-Germain, or out at Fontainebleau when Louis was eight, nine, and ten years old. There were bathing parties in swimsuits that must have discouraged swimming. The boys played at war, listened to huntsmen tell stories of Louis XIII's exploits at the chase (six wolves in one day!), learned to shoot, and to ride after the dogs with a naked sword or a spear in hand. If we are to believe contemporaries, Louis excelled in everything. The portraits and medals of him at this period show him to be a handsome, winning child whom everyone could love. Yet it is not improbable that the constant adulation and deference with which he was surrounded also gave him some of the airs of a little prig.

The child learned other things as well. How could he have missed the fact that his mother distrusted his uncle Gaston and his cousins the Condés? And what of those relatives by the left hand, the legitimized Vendôme family? How much did he understand of Beaufort's plot to murder Mazarin? Could he have been pleased to hear the hero Duke of Enghien criticize his mother's court for its feminine character? Louis was far too bright not to have learned very early in life that the crown had enemies, and that some of them were uncomfortably close—within the family. His *Mémoires,* written to instruct his own son, strongly suggest that he learned this early. It was also at this time that his Aunt Henriette, Queen of England, returned to Paris demanding asylum in her father's kingdom. Madame de Motteville unfolds the story of the English civil wars and the tragic execution of Charles I as it was told in the royal circle in Paris. These were stories not lost on the impressionable mind of an eight- to eleven-year-old boy; the tears of his aunt, his cousins the Prince of Wales and the Duke of York, and the gawky English princess (who would one day look more beautiful to him) undoubtedly left impressions not easily erased from memory. When he remembered his cousins' poverty and distress in exile, the erection of the barricades in Paris and the civil war of the *Fronde* must have been terrifying to him. He probably was too young to understand why men rebelled against the authority of kings, but he could not miss the fact that they did.

In the spring and summer of 1647, when Louis was still eight, he learned firsthand something of the uncertainty of high politics and war. The negotiations at the Westphalian towns of Münster and Osnabrück were dragging on slowly while the armies in Germany, the Low Countries, and on the Franco-Spanish frontier were still arguing the case with guns; it seemed that the war would never end. In the preceding year Mazarin had indicated that France would like to annex the Spanish Netherlands either in exchange for Catalonia or perhaps as a dowry of a Spanish princess who would become Queen of France. This project aroused objections from France's ally the United Netherlands. The provinces of the northern Netherlands had welcomed French aid for their independence, but after the battle of Rocroi, their leaders eyed French actions with increasing suspicions. Spain may have been their enemy, but a weak Spain seemed preferable to a vigorous France as a neighbor. When Mazarin suggested French annexation of the Spanish Netherlands, the Dutch assured the Spanish that they would not attack them, thus freeing an army of some twenty thousand infantry and eight thousand horsemen under an Austrian archduke for an invasion of France. This army laid siege to Armentières. The garrison was weak, and the French field army in miserable condition. Mazarin boldly decided to send the boy-king to the frontier to bolster the morale of the soldiers and to force some of the gentlemen of the court to join the army.

Louis made the trip from Saint-Germain to Compiègne and thence on to Amiens by carriage with the cardinal and his mother, and undoubtedly he heard enough talk to understand that things were going badly. He was disappointed that he was not allowed to travel on horseback, but he did what was expected of him: at each stop he listened to the oratory of local dignitaries eager to show off their forensic talents, and replied "with firmness of voice and assurance well beyond his years."[5] He was unable to save Armentières, nor could he prevent the capture of Landrécies, but the French army revenged itself by attacking and capturing two small Spanish fortifications, Dismude and La Bassée. Mazarin developed a grandiose plan worthy of a great captain: he would bring Turenne's army from Germany as one point of a pincer on the Spanish, with Marshals Rantzau and Gassion, who commanded the forces in the southern Netherlands, as the other prong. It was a fine plan, but Turenne's army, the Weimarians, mutinied and refused to leave Germany—a marvelous example of the unreliability of a mercenary army. The whole campaign came to nothing: a bitter lesson for a boy who had hoped to begin his career as a soldier.

And there was more bad news to come. The young Prince of Condé (Enghien had become Condé on his father's death) was in Catalonia besieging Lerida. The governor of the city, Don Antonio Britte, sent him *limonade* every morning, but the Spanish sorties were as destructive as the drink was refreshing. The French army became discouraged and began to melt away in desertions—and Condé had to raise the siege. Immediately there was a song in Paris declaring that the Spanish had fought so well because they failed to recognize the victor of Rocroi under his new name—they thought that they were dealing with his father. There were many in the court not secretive in their satisfaction over the frustration of the hero-prince. Thus the boy-king learned that his subjects could make merry over the defeat of his armies. Several of the poets were put in jail, but songs continued to be written; within two years they would be pointedly directed against Mazarin and the queen.

The summer did not pass without some satisfactions. The court visited Dieppe after a trip across Normandy during which the king and the queen mother were showered with cheers and benedictions "in a way agreeable to their Majesties." These trips had long been the monarchy's way of advertising itself; the people were eager to see and honor the king, and their cheers in turn strengthened the king's government against other powers in the state. At Dieppe Louis saw the sea for the first time. Neither the Bourbons nor their Valois predecessors had ever appreciated the meaning of the ocean; their attention was land-directed, their policy continental-minded, a fact that came to plague Louis severely after 1692. The boy boarded a splendidly appointed ship, a gift from the Queen of Sweden, and took part in a sham naval battle in which, as one might expect, the king's side won.

In August the court returned to Saint-Germain. The war was not forgotten, but there was a round of hunting parties, balls, ballets, and theater presentations. Madame de Motteville noted that the king seemed more serious than ever; perhaps his experiences of the summer had been sobering for a nine-year-old boy. Other memoirists, less perceptive, noted that Louis danced marvelously. Then, early in November, the whole court became serious: the king came down with the dreaded smallpox.

Here was the first great crisis of the regency. There was no immunity from the ravages of smallpox; it impartially killed men in the hovel and in the palace, and every victim's life hung by a thread until the disease passed its crisis. Several of Gaston of Orléans' intimates had the bad taste to toast "Gaston I," for they assumed that Philippe would follow Louis to an early grave; but they failed to count on Louis' robust constitution, which withstood both the onslaught of the smallpox and the lancets of the physicians. Louis was badly pocked by the disease, but who did not carry its marks in this era? Perhaps this brush with death also brought more maturity.

The crisis had momentarily allowed Parlement to reconsider the regency. Many of its members were no longer satisfied with their handiwork following the death of the late king. If there was to be another regency for Philippe, the Duke of Orléans and the Prince of Condé should have a larger place in the government, and foreigners (Mazarin, of course) should be excluded. Louis did not die, and no new regency had to be established, but the court heard rumbles of Parlement's discussions. When Condé returned from Lerida, somewhat chastened by his frustrating failures, he offered Anne his full support and Mazarin gave him command of the army in Flanders. At the same time, Mazarin urged his agents to make haste in the negotiations at Münster.

Public rejoicings and *Te Deums* celebrated the recovery of the king, but there was also agitation in the Paris streets, initiated by an economic crisis partly caused by war and taxation, but mostly by bad harvests. The queen's carriage was surrounded by wretched women begging for assistance. What was worse, the government needed more money to guarantee victory, and there was no way to avoid another direct appeal to Parlement.

In January 1648, Louis made his third visit to "his Parlement," and this time the atmosphere was much less cordial than it had been on earlier occasions. The first president was moderate enough, but then Omer Talon made a speech that created a sensation. He spoke of the economic distress in the kingdom, of the misery of the peasants, and the burdens of taxation. Omer Talon was never one to deny that the king ruled by the grace of God, but he insisted that Frenchmen must not be governed "like Scythians or other barbarians," for France is a land where "men are born free." In former reigns, he said, kings came to Parlement ceremonially to announce the beginning and ending of wars, to participate in ceremonies, and the like; he deplored the practice of kings visiting Parlement to force registration of unpopular acts, particularly taxes. He took cognizance of the problems of the war—it is "easier to fight than to make peace"—but "victories and conquests do not diminish the misery of the people." He turned to Anne, respectfully to be sure: "It is for you, Madame, to think of these things and of the misery of the people. When you are in your cabinet and at your oratory, recall that many women must suffer in the provinces to carry on the war. . . ."[6] When the queen returned to her apartments, she wept from chagrin. "My son will punish them!" she muttered. "My son will punish them!" Anne's love of God did not create in her compassion for the people. In this she resembled most European royalty of her time.

This session was the first gauntlet thrown down in the conflict between the regency government and Parlement. Before it was over there would be barricades in Paris, sieges of the city, and a civil war in France. Louis probably understood what was happening and grasped the reason his mother was "showing" him to the people at every opportunity—as Madame de Motteville so naïvely put it, "to attract by their presence the hearts and the love of his subjects."[7] Anne and Mazarin were politicians perfectly willing to use this seventeenth-century form of "baby kissing" to try to win support for their program. The people of Paris remained loyal to the king, but still were willing to rebel against his government. It was quite a *leçon des choses*—instruction in the political facts of life—for a boy not yet ten.

4

THE "FRONDE" I:
PARLEMENTARY, 1648-49

MANY YEARS after the *Fronde* had been crushed, Louis still recalled the awful misgivings that he felt during the revolt. He became "of age" in 1652, at fourteen. But as he wrote in his *Mémoires*, it is "the age that the laws of France have established to avoid greater evils," but ". . . not that at which private individuals begin to handle their own affairs." He must have keenly felt his own inadequacy for dealing with the situation. The kingdom "suffered terrible agitations . . . : a foreign war in which domestic difficulties cost France a thousand advantages; a prince of my blood, and a very great name, at the head of the armies of our foes; many cabals in the state; the Parlement in possession of, and with a taste for, usurped authority; in my court little fidelity without personal interest. . . ." His mother was forced to dismiss the minister she trusted, a man of whom Louis wrote, he was "very clever, very adroit; . . . [he] loved me and I loved him . . . [he] rendered me great service." And yet he had to go. Paris closed its gates on the king's army while it sheltered the *tercios* of Spain. It was cold comfort to Louis to hear troops defending a town against the royal army cry out "*Vive le roi!*" while they continued to resist the king's forces. Like everyone of the time who knew anything about world affairs, Louis must have connected these stormy days with the events in England that had cost his uncle Charles I both crown and head, and made England into a republic. Neither at fourteen nor at any other time in his life did Louis understand the *Fronde* as anything but the brutal attempt of willful men to usurp royal authority and to curb royal power. All his life he labored to prevent its ever happening again.

The disorders that began in the summer of 1648 were inspired by men who neither understood nor sympathized with Mazarin's war policy. They did not even know what he was trying to achieve for the kingdom and the Bourbon dynasty by the negotiations at the Westphalian peace conference. Seventeenth-century monarchs did not maintain "ministries of propaganda" or "offices of information" to explain their policies to their subjects. There were no regularly established channels of communication between the king's government and the public; a king did not want his people to presume to tell him how to manage his affairs. Louis XIII had been explicit in forbidding discussion of the business of "his state," and Anne and Mazarin were not less anxious to maintain control over their policy.

This meant that while there was little or no public discussion of politics, there also was no "public" to support the policy that was undertaken. Indeed, quite the opposite was true. Whatever "public" there was, was made up of persons frustrated by their exclusion from public affairs, and therefore often selfishly interested only in their own fortunes. This certainly was the case with many of the great nobles whose forebears had sat in the councils of kings. They were now avid place hunters, and when these favors were refused them, they blamed the "foreigners" (Mazarin) who excluded them from the king's council. Moreover, when these men became malcontents, they were capable of causing trouble, for in the first half of the seventeenth century no king in Europe had military forces strong enough to awe into obedience great noblemen nursing grievances worthy of rebellion.

We have already seen that the Parlement of Paris had become a center of opposition to the regency by the opening of 1648. In an effort to force the regency to listen to their grievances, its leaders were resolved to use to the very hilt their right to refuse to register the edicts of the king. They wanted control over taxation; they wanted to force the royal council to recognize their prior rights in all matters of justice; and they hoped to end the practice of sending intendants of justice and taxation (the "circuit riders" of Richelieu's time) to the provinces as representatives of the council. When a new tax proposed to find revenue by measures that fell heavily upon the members of Parlement and of the other sovereign courts, their cup ran over. During the spring and summer of 1648 the crisis in the relationship between the regency council and the Parlement mounted month by month.

It should have been obvious that fuel for serious trouble was piling up at a great rate. The Parlement and many of the great noblemen not only disliked Mazarin's policy, they also disliked Mazarin personally. Xenophobia has long been characteristic of the French, especially if the foreigner in question happened to achieve power over them. More than a quarter-century earlier, Concini and his wife, favorites of Marie de Médicis, had been brutally murdered in a frenzy of anti-foreignism. Mazarin, another Italian favorite of another foreign queen, now not only governed France, but like Concini, also was becoming exceedingly rich in the process. As soon as rebellion removed the fear of punishment, there was no lack of inflammatory sheets urging Mazarin's murder. Curiously enough, this dislike of the foreigner has followed Mazarin on into the twentieth century; even now many French historians have trouble admitting that the Italian minister was almost the only person in the France of 1648–52 to understand the historic structure of the kingdom.

It is one thing to object to a minister, or even to urge his murder, and yet quite another to erect barricades and risk death to overthrow him. The nobles or the Parlement might engineer a murder, try a *coup d'état,* but they needed the support of the mob for a riot in the streets. This was not hard to get in 1648: the annals of the seventeenth century are replete with accounts of rebellions against all authorities.[1] The common people had small stake in the civilization of the land; they always lived close to the edge of starvation, and they were predisposed to violence by public hangings and other brutalities. In 1648 there was no problem in rousing a Parisian mob, for famine stalked the land when bad harvests drove up the cost of bread beyond the reach of the city poor.

The regency's fiscal policies must also share the blame for the storm. Mazarin was no financier and not interested in fiscal reforms; his finance minister, d'Emery, was always only one jump ahead of disaster, always forced to rely upon "extraordinary" measures. In 1648 sale of new offices, forced loans, and new excise taxes were evoking increasing protests from the Parlement; only the presence of the king had assured registration of these measures.

When Louis was taken to the Parlement to assure compliance, he had to listen to some blunt language intended for the queen and Mazarin. Omer Talon remarked, "God may govern Heaven without counsel, but even though kings are of the race of gods, they are nonetheless men, and all men need counsel!" On June 26, 1648, the first president softly remarked, "Sovereigns ought to secure obedience by love and kindness rather than by constraint and violence. They should not deprive magistrates of their rightful power [to nullify edicts contrary to the constitution]." A month later he said, "Sire . . . the laws are fundamental to the happiness of states, they are not the work of men; God is their author. . . ." Kings had the obligation to see that these laws were obeyed for the good of the people. At every session the Parlementarians harped upon the distress and misery of the poor people who were overburdened by taxes. The tax that they themselves wished to avoid became hidden behind the "burdens of the people."[2] The Parlementary orators never denied the time-honored formulas of divine right, nor did they suggest that Frenchmen need not submit to the "king given to them by God," and yet they also insisted that "it is not kings who make the kingdom, but rather the multitude . . . who maintain and submit to the Crown." As Louis listened to these discussions, he must have pondered the copy-formula that his instructors had given him to write: "Kings may do anything that pleases them."

The nine-year-old king probably did not hear everything that was said. A pamphlet broadside either written or inspired by a member of Parlement explained that the worst thing that can happen to a prince is to believe that he can do as he pleases—this is the advice of flatterers, of evil counselors. This pamphlet went on to explain that the Parlement held the same position in France that the senate had had in Rome: all good Roman emperors consulted the senate, but bad ones did not; it followed that good kings would consult the Parlement, and the people would willingly obey laws approved by Parlement.[3] The argument was spurious, for the Parlementarians were not, by any stretch of the imagination, Roman senators. Nonetheless, confusion of the name "Parlement" with the English "Parliament" during these years of the English Revolution added to the confusion with the Roman senate, to give Parlement popular prestige and support. It is highly improbable that anyone ever explained all this reasoning to the young king.

As the summer wore on it was increasingly evident that the government had to do something dramatic to check the onward course of the opposition. The Parlement and the other three sovereign courts in Paris had taken the bit in their teeth, and were meeting jointly to consider a program for the reformation of the monarchy; these meetings in the *Chambre Saint-Louis* were undoubtedly illegal and revolutionary, yet the government could do nothing about them without endangering its own existence. At this point Mazarin appealed to Condé, then commanding the army in the Spanish Netherlands, to see if a military victory could not be engineered; Mazarin scraped together all the troops and money that he could find, and Condé agreed to try his luck in a field battle. Several weeks later he attacked the Spanish at Lens[4] and won a clear-cut victory. When the news was announced at the court, Louis piped up, "The Messieurs in Parlement will be quite unhappy about this!" The remark indicates that the boy-king was already well aware of the fact that "his Parlement" was staffed by men who might be "unhappy" over the successes of "their king."

The victory at Lens precipitated the first *Fronde*. The regency government felt strong enough to stand up to its critics, and ordered the arrest of three of the most objectionable (and at the same time most distinguished) members of the Parlement. Included among these was Broussel, an old man who had been particularly outspoken in his demands for a reduction of taxes, in his attacks on the luxury of the court and the evils of the tax collectors, and who had acquired a following in Paris as protector of the poor. The arrests turned out to be a blunder that brought down a hornets' nest. The crowds, accepting the Parlementarians as "fathers of the people," almost succeeded in preventing the arrest of Broussel, and then raised barricades all over the city. Chancellor Séguier and his brother, a bishop, narrowly escaped with their lives into the house of a friend. The Swiss and the French guards were able to defend the Palais-Royal, but the city was in the hands of the crowds.

A deputation from Parlement, headed by the first president, appeared at the palace to request the restoration of the arrested members and to insist that the regent had badly treated Parlement.

The queen: "I have made my decision; I shall do nothing about it."

The first president: "I wonder if you are not deceived, Madame, when you are not told about the state of your kingdom and the situation here in the city of Paris . . . the evil is so great that it is almost beyond remedy. I fear, Madame, that Your Majesty will be obliged to grant to violence and the mutiny of the people what you have refused to grant at the humble supplication of Parlement."

The queen: "You should not speak to me that way; the King my son will demand account for this some day."

The first president: "We do not fear his wrath; we are the ones who render his justice."[5]

When the deputation left without a promise of the release of the prisoners, the mob handled the Parlementarians roughly.

While this was going on, Louis was playing in the courtyard of the Palais-Royal with the troupe of young courtiers who grew up with him. But this does not mean that he did not know of these events. The story that he heard was undoubtedly the one that Mazarin and his mother told him. Here is Mazarin's account of what happened, written a few weeks later:

> The affront given to the King by the Parlement and the people of Paris could not be greater in form or substance . . . there is not only no corner of France, but not even of all Europe that does not know about it, and now awaits to see what one will do. . . . Authority must be reestablished at any price, and placed higher than before, or it will perish and be ridiculed and despised. . . . The Parlement has assumed the functions of the King, and the people defer entirely to it; it has made Broussel an associate of the King; it has taken up arms to compel the King to give in . . . it has barricaded the front of the Palais Royal and spoken impudently to the Queen and to me; it has made unheard of demands, insolent proposals—to seize the person of the King; to force my dis-

missal; to put the Queen in a convent. Several persons in Parlement have suggested the creation of a Regency for Monsieur [the Duke of Orléans], and have tempted the Abbé de la Rivière [Gaston's closest adviser] with my post. They sell defamatory pamphlets against me; they wanted to kill the Chancellor and the First President [when he failed to secure the release of Broussel]; there has been open and public sedition and the Parlement has approved it by its conduct . . . its officers have also fomented the other Parlements of France to revolt, urged the people not to pay taxes and the officials of the realm to request the purchase price of their offices . . . commerce has ceased . . . and it is impossible to find a cent for the expenses of the war. . . . With twenty thousand *écus* it would be possible to harvest the fruit of our great victory [of Lens] and attack Tarragona [in Spain] . . . the lack of money threatens to undermine the effort in Cremona [Italy] and in Germany: without money . . . the army commanded by M. de Turenne will mutiny . . . we have therefore the reason to punish, indeed the obligation to do so . . . the King would have cause to demand an accounting from me one day—particularly from me—for allowing his authority to be destroyed.[6]

Anne's first response to the rioting was an angry urge to pick up the gauntlet and fight back, but Mazarin understood that there was too much at stake to risk such a conflict. In Westphalia the draft treaties ending the war in Germany were almost ready to sign, and these treaties were very favorable to the Bourbon interests in Europe since they separated the Austrian and the Spanish Hapsburgs and gave the French king an entry into Germany. If the riots in Paris developed into a civil war, the enemies of France could take heart and perhaps refuse to sign. Mazarin was as ready to deal harshly with the rebellion as was Anne, but he advised caution; one must temporize, dissimulate, pretend. The wily Italian rarely attempted to storm a position by frontal assault; he preferred to outflank an opponent, concealing his objectives until the last moment. On his advice, the captive "Fathers of the Country" were released from prison; even the illegal meetings of the *Chambre Saint-Louis* were allowed to continue. Indeed, on October 22 the government accepted a "charter" that the Parlementarians had drawn up for the reform of the state, which greatly limited arbitrary royal power in matters of taxation, administration, and justice; it even ended the use of the *lettres de cachet,* by which the king could arbitrarily enforce his will. Mazarin seemed to agree to all this, but he really had no intention of living up to his concessions. On October 24, 1648, the treaties of Westphalia that concerned France were signed; it was then only a matter of the time for ratifications to give the French government a freer hand in internal affairs.[7]

Unfortunately for Anne and Mazarin, underneath the stormy waters of the Parlementary *Fronde,* other *"Frondes"* were gathering. The noble families of Vendôme-Beaufort and Longueville, both issues from bastard children of former kings and both related by marriage to legitimate cadet lines of the royal family, were becoming the center for a cabal involving their own hangers-on, as well as other important noble families and frustrated place-hunters like Châteauneuf (one of Richelieu's former creatures), Gondi (soon to be Cardinal de Retz, the Coadjutor Archbishop of Paris), La Rivière (the principal adviser of Gaston of Orléans), as well as other malcontents. Some of these men had political skill approximately equal to that of Mazarin; some of the women had easy virtue, and were willing to use their sex to involve young blades in the adventure. Madame de Longueville, for example, finally succeeded in catching none other than Turenne, the first soldier of the kingdom, who turned his sword against the king when this lady turned his head. These people were willing enough to be loyal to the regency if Anne would also be willing to bow to their interests. Like their ancestors who had forced Henry IV and later Marie de Médicis to bribe them for their loyalty, all they wanted were military governorships and royal offices, a reversal of the policies of Louis XIII and his formidable minister, gifts of money, and the dismissal of Mazarin and the other officials who were defending the boy-king's inheritance. These requests may have seemed reasonable to Madame de Chevreuse, who had a score to settle with both Richelieu and Mazarin, but the granddaughter of Philip II found them exorbitant. Fortunately for her and for the king, not all important people joined the *Fronde* at once.

How much did Louis understand? De Mesmes, who waited on Anne with his fellow magistrates, tells us that he saw Louis playing in the garden—"While the Prince played," he remarked, "he was losing his crown." Other observers tell us that a usually sober young man was even more sober when he entered his eleventh year. However, he kept his own counsel and said so little that his cousin Condé came to suspect that he might not be too bright. Did Louis miss the fact that he and his mother were practically prisoners in the Palais-Royal; that Anne's tears of anger and frustration boded ill for the future; that everyone about him was concerned for the fate of his uncle in England as well as for the near future in France; that these days seemed to be creating massive evidence of the feebleness of kings, perhaps of the near end of the monarchical principle? Louis' later career and his dislike of Paris crowds, the Parlement, and the idea of representative government, all seem to emphasize that he did come to understand how dangerous his situation had been. How could it have been more dramatically brought home to him than by flight from Paris in the early hours of January 6, 1649, when Mazarin spirited him and his mother out of the city to Saint-Germain with no warning, no preparation? There had not even been beds at Saint-Germain, and the king had had to spend the rest of the night on straw.

It was Mazarin's decision to desert Paris and then besiege the city and force its surrender; Condé had wanted to bring in professional soldiers and fight it out with the rabble in the streets, but Mazarin had been fearful of the barricades that would prevent the use of cavalry, and of the roof tiles that so easily became lethal missiles. He also wished to avoid the destruction of property and life that could result from street fighting. Bloodshed, he believed, was less easy to forget than a siege that forced submission by hunger. This reasoning was in line with Mazarin's teaching that a king was strong in the countryside surrounded by his soldiers, but weak in the towns where the crowds presented a constant threat to his safety.

The authorities in Paris were dismayed by the flight of the king, which amounted to a declaration of war against the city. Could the Parlement, its city friends, and the assortment of malcontent noblemen hold the city against the royal army long enough for the disturbed feelings in the provinces and the war in the Netherlands to compel the regent to admit failure? A torrent of pamphlets spewed from the Paris presses, attacking Mazarin and the queen, and demanding, requesting, finally begging the king to return to Paris where "he belonged!" Many of them urged violence. *Le second parti de l'aveuglement de la France,* for example, fairly shouted, "Long live the King, the Duke of Anjou, his Royal Highness [Orléans], long live the princes of the blood, but murder him who knows neither joy, nor law, nor religion. Murder, murder, murder Mazarin!" This theme pervaded the polemic flood aroused by the *Fronde*. These pamphlets, some written by clever men who knew how to turn a phrase, others by crude men who knew only how to vilify; still others by learned men who drew upon history and law for argument, seeped out from Paris into the provinces where they often found a receptive audience.[8]

The king probably knew little of their contents. He would have been shocked to see how they treated his mother: Why had she not been virtuous, wise, and pious like Blanche of Castile? Why had she allowed the relatives of Richelieu to keep offices and positions? Why had she allowed the dispatch of the robber intendants of justice and taxation to be sent to the provinces? Why had she kept Mazarin, a foreigner, in high office? Why did she attend the theater while an insolent foreign "Mayor of the Palace" controlled the destiny of the king? Again and again these pamphlets came back to Mazarin: He should be killed—"*Vive le roi, Mazarin, non!*" Again the pamphleteers queried: Why had the king departed from Paris? The country is the place for sport, not a place to live; kings are the image of God, but God shows himself in the universe—kings should not remain hidden. "We want no other sovereign: the nobility recognizes you as chief, the people as father, the church as son; our sole desire is to die in your service, but you must return to the city . . . We want the King, but no companion [Mazarin]."

Where the pamphleteers left off, the song writers took up the chase, endlessly repeating each other in their vilification of queen, cardinal, and government. One of the most famous started with the verse:

> Do you know the difference
> Between his Eminence
> And the late Cardinal Richelieu?
> The answer is not moot:
> The one led his animal
> The other mounts his brute.

There were a dozen verses, most of them more pointedly attacking the queen in unprintable language, and always with the raucous refrain. The singers of the seventeenth century stood somewhere between the editorial writer and the street entertainer; their songs often provided release from the frustrations men felt about their world.

Neither songs nor pamphlets could break the grip of Condé's army; his soldiers not only checked the flow of grain into Paris, but they also gave France its first real taste of the disorders that could be created by mercenary troops trained in the Thirty Years' War. "Pillagers!"—that was the name given indiscriminately to the armies of friend and foe alike. While the army held the ring around Paris, Mazarin continued to negotiate with his enemies in the city.

These negotiations attempted to separate the Parlementary and other leaders of Paris from the handful of noblemen who had thrown in their lots with the first *Fronde*. This latter group included not only the Prince of Conti and the Duke of Longueville (brother and brother-in-law of Condé) and the Duke of Beaufort as its most distinguished members, but also the Marshal de la Mothe, the Prince of Marsillac, the Duke of Elbeuf, and others with ancient or at least famous names. Frenchmen who remembered the religious wars and the rebellions against Marie de Médicis must have noted that many of these men were the grandchildren of former rebels against royal authority. Like their forebears, they did not hesitate to follow rebellion with treason by inviting the archduke in Brussels to come to Paris to discuss possible Spanish aid. Had not the Catholic League, led by one of Marsillac's ancestors, brought Spanish troops into that city? And well they might try to get Spanish aid, for the trainbands and the riffraff that they assembled were no match for Condé's seasoned troops. This treason, however, made the court at Saint-Germain even more unwilling to listen to Father (Saint) Vincent de Paul when he naïvely tried to bring the queen and her enemies together on the latters' terms. There was no hope for a negotiated peace: Condé's forces were strong enough to starve the city to surrender.

Actually the defeat of the Parlementary *Fronde* was a foregone conclusion. When the court heard of the tragic execution of Charles I in England, Mazarin carefully pointed out that weakness had cost the English king his head. The moral was clear: there could be no weakness in face of the threat from Paris. And the possibility that the *Frondeurs* would obtain help from abroad melted away when a friend of Mazarin's, the banker Hervart, poured money into the pockets of the German mercenary officers in Turenne's army; as Madame de Longueville had hoped, Turenne joined the *Fronde,* but contrary to her expectations his army remained in Germany. Nor could the archduke do much better; the Spanish had not really recovered from the mauling Condé had given them the preceding summer. Paris was ready to negotiate; and so was the government, for it feared an invasion from the Spanish Netherlands.

In the negotiations that followed, both parties had to give in. While Parlement did not have to humiliate itself as the crown wished, it also was unable to dictate Mazarin's ouster. The treaty signed at Reuil was a compromise that met the government's needs of the hour; it would be several years before the crown became strong enough to reverse the whole program of the *Fronde.*[9]

The noble *Frondeurs* desperately tried to salvage what they could from the fiasco. Their "demands" ran from requests for seats in the council and elevation to the peerage, to the right of *tabouret* for a wife (the right to sit down in the presence of the king). Some wanted restitution of offices; others asked for new places—admiral of the fleet, commander of the galleys, governorship of a province, assurance that a son could succeed to his father's position as commander of troops, governor, etc. And of course there were requests for pensions.

The court at Saint-Germain did not take these requests seriously once the Parlement and the city had folded up. When a negotiator for the noble *Frondeurs* arrived at the court with demands for his fellows and the suggestion that Mazarin should now be dismissed, he was received by the court "as a man who has come to play a farce after the serious drama was finished." The city had already surrendered its fortifications and arms; it was prepared to welcome the king, the queen-mother, and Mazarin, if they would return. There was no need to placate the noble *Frondeurs* beyond the grant of amnesty that had been given by the Treaty of Reuil.

The Parlementary *Fronde* left a mark on the king that was never to be erased. Perhaps this is not surprising when we recall that the barricades, the talk of rebellion, the demands of the *Frondeurs* to "see" that the king had not been spirited away, the flight from Paris—all came while he was still a young boy, at a time when he could not defend himself or even understand the forces that seemed to be governing his life. Louis never really trusted Paris again; he never really trusted the Parlement; and he never forgot that the greatest misfortune that can come to a king is the loss of his power to govern his kingdom. In his *Mémoires,* in his letters, and in his conversations for the rest of his life, traces of the fears and terrors caused by the barricades and rebellion always remained. His experience in these years with men—both those who joined the rebellions and those who remained at his side but secretly corresponded with the rebels—made him suspicious of everyone, and this was to remain a firmly established trait of his character until the day he died. The *Fronde* taught lessons in statecraft so vividly that they could not be forgotten.

5

THE "FRONDE" II:
THE PRINCES

LOUIS II OF BOURBON, Prince of Condé, was only twenty-eight years old when he commanded the royal army that besiged Paris in 1649, yet by his victories at Rocroi, Lens, and in a dozen lesser actions, he had already earned the sobriquet Le Grand Condé. With his high nose, his protruding teeth, his piercing eyes with their deep-set wide lids, his lithe body and proud carriage, the great Condé looked every inch a soldier—perhaps even more, he resembled a bird of prey. Cadet lines of the French royal family had often acted out the roles of hawks or vultures in the political life of the realm; few of them looked the part as much as did this young man.

The house of Condé had sprung from the sixteenth-century constable Charles of Bourbon, who had turned traitor to Francis I. The first to carry the name of Condé some years later escaped execution for treason only because of the death of Francis II; his later career as leader of the Huguenot rebellions provided an aura of glamour that did not, however, conceal the fact that he was a rebel. The father of the great Condé, Prince Henry II, was born somewhat under a cloud: his mother was suspected of poisoning her husband to prevent him from learning that she was pregnant. King Henry IV several times contemptuously hinted that Prince Henry II of Condé might not be legitimate, but he never actually attempted to deprive him of the rank of prince of the blood. The mother of the great Condé was the beautiful daughter of the Constable of Montmorency, and her loveliness attracted none other than that old satyr Henry IV, who married her to his cousin Prince Henry II in the belief that a spiritless fellow would tolerate royal attentions showered upon his bride. The young couple fled to Brussels and did not return until after Henry's death.

The subsequent history of Henry II of Condé shows him to have been a sorry dissolute fellow, lacking in courage and intelligence; his attempts to put pressure on Marie de Médicis' government failed conspicuously. Perhaps his wife summed up his career best when she said that he made her happy twice in his life: when he married her and when he died. As long as Louis XIII and Richelieu governed France with brutal hands, he kept himself aloof from politics, perhaps fearing that the execution of his brother-in-law for rebellion could mean that his own head might not be safe if he became involved in treason. He fawned upon the cardinal; as we have seen, he even married his eldest son, the Duke of Enghien, to the cardinal's misshapen niece, Mademoiselle de Brézé. This was a personal and a family tragedy for young Louis: he was in love with another woman whom he never quite forgot, and Mademoiselle de Brézé was a dwarf and a hunchback whose genes were to mark the Condé children for several generations to come. But Louis II could not defy his father, the cardinal, and the king, so he married the girl and hated her the rest of his life.

Upon his father's death this young man easily assumed his place as first prince of the blood. "*Monsieur le Prince*," they called him. His possible future was intriguing. Between him and the throne there were three lives: Louis XIV, his brother Philippe, and the aging Gaston of Orléans. In an age when death stalked so freely, this was no multitude; the two boys could easily die before either could sire a son, and Gaston, whose children were all girls, probably would have no further issue. But even if the elder branch of the Bourbon line should manage to retain the throne, the dashing soldier-prince who could command armies would be able to demand a place in the royal government. The Parlementary *Fronde* showed clearly how important he was to the regency. He had been asked to join his sister and brother as a *Frondeur,* but when he recalled "that my name is Louis de Bourbon," the royal victory was practically assured. In an age when everyone expected to be paid for political favors, Condé had every reason to expect great things from the future.

Everyone about him recognized this fact as well as he did. The Orléans family watched the ascent of Condé's star with considerable distaste: Gaston's eldest daughter, *la Grande Mademoiselle,* frankly admitted that she regretted every victory he won, and Gaston himself quietly advised the queen to be cautious in her gifts to the hero. Neither Anne nor Mazarin needed to be warned that Condé could be dangerous, and yet, if they were to win the war against Spain and control the disorderly elements within the kingdom, they needed his bravery, his dash, his willingness to order a charge that risked life and fortune. But these talents could be hazardous: seventeenth-century soldiers like Wallenstein, Mansfield, Saxe-Weimar, and others had confidently moved into the ranks of imperial princes. Would Condé be satisfied with less? And yet where was there a throne for him that would not split the inheritance of the rightful king?

When the court again controlled Paris, Condé fully expected to reap his reward. He asked for the position of Admiral of France vacated by the death of his brother-in-law; he asked for new military governorships in the south of France; he requested favors and positions for his friends. Mazarin and Anne managed to evade so many of these requests that their gratitude seemed niggardly and mean, but they were fearful of the prince's ambitions and his obvious intention to create a "party." They even interfered with a marriage project of the Condé family. All this made Condé more difficult and intransigent, and the gap that had always existed between him and Mazarin widened. It soon became evident that the contest of power was between the prince and the cardinal. In the first round Mazarin had many of the best cards, for the Parlement did not forget that Condé had starved out Paris, the Orléanists were fearful of his influence, and the noble and clerical *Frondeurs* recalled that he had not joined them. Furthermore, Condé's people did not always help: one of his officers, Jarzé, made improper advances to the queen; and Condé felt he should avenge one of his lackeys who got himself killed in a street riot. Even Coadjutor Archbishop de Retz was antagonized and began to cooperate with Mazarin. On January 18, 1650, Mazarin felt strong enough to strike: he had Condé, his brother Conti, and his brother-in-law de Longueville arrested and put in prison.

The arrest came after Condé had been in what seemed to be friendly conversation with the queen and her minister. When he left the room with his brother and brother-in-law, the captain of the guards announced that all three of them were under arrest. At first the prince was sure that it was a joke, then demanded to see the queen, but finally the whole company was marched away to prison. Everyone seemed happy at the *coup*. "A lion, a fox, and an ape—all caught in the same net," said Gaston. The drama must have been relished at the royal palace, too, for within a decade the king twice plagiarized the scene: first with the arrest of de Retz and later with that of Fouquet. As for Condé, this arrest embittered him much: "You do not understand my imprisonment?" he asked Cominges. "Eh, Monsieur, do you recall why Tiberius could not put up with Germanicus?" Later he remarked that he entered prison an innocent man and left it a guilty one.

The arrest of the princes solved nothing. Condé had friends willing to take up arms in his defense, the noble *Frondeurs* were soon ready to help, and the Parlement relished the embarrassment of the government. The queen and her son must have been appalled to watch the political maneuvers in the court and field. When Condé was arrested, Mazarin was at the center of the political picture; before the year was out he had been isolated by a series of agreements that gave a cardinal's hat to de Retz, a place in the government to Condé's friend Châteauneuf, promises of marriage between Gaston's daughter and Condé's son, and between Conti and a daughter of Madame de Chevreuse, an alliance between the Parlementary *Frondeurs* and Condé's people (the so-called treaty of the two *Frondes*), and even an alliance between Condé and the King of Spain. Condé may have been in prison, but his influence was so great that much of the south of France was in arms on his behalf, while the court was riddled by the intrigues of his party. Mazarin finally decided that it would be best for him to withdraw from politics temporarily. In the first week of February 1651, he went to Le Havre where Condé was in prison, released the three princes, and left France for an exile in the Rhineland.

Condé seems not to have realized that Mazarin's exile at Brühl did not mean that Mazarin was no longer important in France. In sharp contrast to Condé's agreements with Spain, Mazarin refused to accept employment from the Spanish crown on the grounds that his loyalty belonged to the Bourbon monarchy; indeed, not only his loyalty but also his advice continued to support the queen and her son. This is not the time to raise the question about the possibility that Anne actually married Mazarin, yet we should note that his letters to the queen in this period are not those of a fallen minister, exiled and forgotten, but rather of a man who expected to be obeyed. He may have written to some of his creatures in France lamenting his neglect, but when he wrote to the queen, his letters had the tone of a masterful *pater familias* giving commands. These letters and the handful of Anne's letters that have survived suggest that there was a secret marriage between these two people.[1] Mazarin was not a priest, so no vows stood in the way—and Anne was far too pious to tolerate the irregularities that her letters would imply if a less formal relationship were assumed. Moreover, the letters between the minister and the queen, Mazarin's obvious love for the young king, and the total relationship between the three all give the impression of a close-knit family, tied together by real affection.

When Condé returned to Paris, he was in no mood to be contradicted. In short order he established his hold upon the south of France so completely that Mazarin sarcastically wrote that there was nothing left for Monsieur le Prince to do but go to Reims to be consecrated. His arrogance and his demands soon began to produce a harvest of hostility, and the queen, following Mazarin's advice, started to reform the coalition that had allowed her to arrest the princes in 1650. By the fall of 1651 she could announce that the king must be recognized as of age. This would end the regency and with it Louis' dependence upon his mother and the princes;

a major king could call anyone he might wish to his government and expect to be obeyed. Condé, recognizing that he was being outmaneuvered at court, withdrew to his estates at Saint-Maur, and began a series of negotiations that seemed to indicate that he now forgot that he had called himself "Louis de Bourbon," or that he had disdained to join the *Fronde* in 1649 as a battle of "chamber-pots and paving stones." Rather than risk another imprisonment, the "hawk" was willing to raise the flag of rebellion.

On September 7, 1651, as a formal gambit against Condé, Louis XIV declared his majority in the Parlement of Paris. The king and court arrived at the Sainte-Chapelle for mass, and then the whole procession—peers, members of the order of the Holy Spirit, marshals, and members of the household and government—marched from the chapel to the chamber of Parlement. "Gentlemen," the king announced, "I have come to my Parlement to tell you that in accordance with the law of my state, I am going to take upon myself the management of my government, and I hope that the goodness of God will grant that this will be with piety and justice . . . My chancellor will give you my intentions."[2] The chancellor announced three edicts: the first against blasphemers, the second against dueling, and the third offering clemency to Condé who was absent and clearly in rebellion. The next day, the feast of nativity of the Virgin, Louis publicly attended mass at Notre-Dame. Father Paulin wrote to his vicar describing the events:

> Yesterday the King . . . made his entry in the courtyard of Parlement on horseback in the midst of a magnificent cavalcade . . . and declared himself to be of age . . . he has promised to rule . . . with piety for his guide and justice for his companion. How great was the applause of the witnesses, the cries of joy, the striking sounds of drums and trumpets. . . . Alas, the Prince of Condé did not see the public joy. . . .[3]

Indeed, the Prince of Condé had withdrawn toward the south where he remarked, "You have forced me to draw my sword . . . you will see that I will be the last to return it to the scabbard." On September 13, the king and the royal army followed Condé southward, and shortly thereafter Mazarin, summoned by the king, prepared to invade France from the east with an army raised in Germany.

With the proclamation of the young king's majority, Gaston had announced that he would retire to his estates "without becoming further involved in anything," but when the Parlement of Paris placed a reward upon Mazarin's head and asked Gaston to join in repulsing the Italian, the prince decided to throw his lot in with the new *Fronde,* and ordered his troops to counter those of the cardinal. Thus began the second *Fronde,* the *Fronde* of the princes, which was to teach the young Louis how dangerous it is for a king to have relatives with any military power at their disposal.[4]

Gaston's career could not have given much comfort to his allies. During his brother's reign he had stood aside while his friends were executed for their part in plots that he had fomented, or at least joined; indeed, the only time that he had ever balked his brother's will was his refusal to put aside Margaret of Lorraine, whom he had married in exile without his brother's consent, so that he might marry one of the Cardinal Richelieu's nieces. In a charming book[5] Gaston's latest biographer presents him as a prince—charming, if somewhat soft—as a patron of the arts, a dilettante in philosophy and learning, a sensitive, frustrated man whose hopes had been crushed by the birth of the Dieudonné. He was not a man to play a decisive role either as friend or as foe of the king. In the first *Fronde* he had played a mediocre role; he had agreed to the arrest of Condé; indeed, he made a solemn treaty with the queen by which they undertook not to free the princes without mutual consent. On the other hand, he suspected Mazarin; he did not like to hear the minister compare the *Frondeurs,* many of whom were his friends, with the English revolutionaries and Cromwell. His advisers persuaded him that the situation in France required the assembly of an Estates General. And after Mazarin's exile, Anne had been too weak to refuse to consider the proposal, even though she remembered that previous Estates General had not been reassuring for the monarchy—in fact, they had been downright dangerous. After the declaration of Louis' majority, Gaston probably realized that there would be no Estates General; this may have influenced his decision to throw in his lot with the *Fronde.*

At this point another member of the family of Orléans emerged as an important figure. Gaston's second wife and their children were political ciphers, but not so Anne-Marie-Louise, Duchess of Montpensier, the only child of his first marriage, who was known to her own time as to ours as La Grande Mademoiselle. Left motherless almost at birth, and neglected by her father who was in exile during much of her childhood, this little girl was brought up by governesses and servants who feared to oppose her will; Queen Anne, whom she called "little mama," was as close to a mother-figure as she ever had. La Grande Mademoiselle possessed two characteristics that made her very important throughout most of her life: first of all, she was her mother's sole heir, and therefore the richest woman in all of France—perhaps in all of Europe—and secondly, she was the granddaughter of a king. In her own way she was clever, but her utter insensitiveness, her complete lack of a sense of humor, her proud, uncritical, and arrogant estimate of herself, her single-minded ambition for a throne, and finally, her naïve sense of loyalty to her *gloire*—one is almost tempted to say her baroque conception of herself—all combined to rob her of the sympathy that her career might have evoked. When Louis was born in 1638, Anne, half in fun and half to please her father, told her that one day she should marry the dauphin. Scandalized, Richelieu ordered the twelve-year-old girl to stop referring to the baby dauphin as her "little husband." At twenty-three she had not yet given up the idea that she might one day marry the young king, even though he was almost twelve years her junior. Nearly all of her interests centered around marriage—for the throne that she might thereby acquire. The only trouble was that she rejected princes who wanted her, like the young Prince of Wales, whom she regarded as a fortune-hunter, anxious to use her money in a vain attempt to recover a throne. And on the other hand, princes whom she might have married, the Austrian archduke for example, did not want her. All this did not bother the Duchess of Montpensier; she had not given up hope that she might one day become Queen of France.

In the early days of the princely *Fronde,* she played a gallant role. There was a contest for control of the Loire valley where the king's army cruelly devastated the estates of the Duke of Orléans at Blois. Up the river, the town of Orléans closed its gates to both armies in the hope of remaining neutral in this contest between the great ones of the land. Gaston sent his daughter with a mixed army of his own troops and Spanish regulars to take the city and check the progress of the royal army. When La Grande Mademoiselle found the gates closed to her, she crossed the river without escort, and managed to enter a back gate; then by judicious use of her rank and sex, she "captured" the city and took over its government in the name of the princes. It was hardly a brilliant action, but out of it she managed to identify herself with the Maid of Orléans, and as might be expected, obtained the delighted congratulations of both her father and Condé.

Several months later she again took the spotlight. The fortunes of war turned against Monsieur le Prince, and Turenne, again a loyal servant of his king—for men changed sides easily—was pressing the rebel army against the gates of Paris. Upon hearing of Condé's plight, Gaston of Orléans muttered something about the happiness of people who do not become involved in affairs, and refused to act. Mademoiselle, appalled at her father's indecision, marched to the Bastille, ordered the guns turned from the city toward the fields, and then fired them at the king's army to cover

Condé's forces as they passed through the gate St. Antoine. Mazarin and the boy-king watched the engagement from the high hill that today is the cemetery Père-Lachaise. The cardinal's cynical remark—"Mademoiselle has just shot her husband!"—was more truth than jest; she saved Condé, but that day earned her an exile from the court that ended her hopes of becoming Queen of France.

If the pamphlets sold freely in the streets of the city are any indication of the feelings of Parisians, their loyalty was on the side of the princes. They carefully attempted to separate the young king from his ministers and even his mother: they were loyal to the king, but not to those evil advisers who surrounded him. Mazarin was again the principal target. *La Sybille Françoise* urged the princes to raise a large army capable of repulsing him; *La voix du peuple au roi pour la paix générale* urged Mazarin's murder, and even suggested in a veiled manner that Anne might share the same fate. *La décadence visible de la royauté* pointed out that those who sustained the king's power (Mazarin and his friends) lacked authority, that the people no longer respected royal decrees, that the royal council resorted only to trickery, that the king's honor in the land was weak. The king must free himself of his evil counselor and discover by his own travels the true state of his kingdom. These are only samples of the hundreds of anti-Mazarin pamphlets that flooded Paris and France, giving the princes assurance that the kingdom was on their side in this contest for power.

However, when Condé's army entered the city of Paris on the day Mademoiselle's heroic artillery barrage decided the "battle of Porte St. Antoine," time began to run out for the princely *Frondeurs*. Condé's army was largely made up of foreign troops: Spaniards, Lorrainers, and "Germans" (many of whom were Poles, Czechs, and other central European peoples), and the presence of Spanish and Lorraine officers betrayed the fact that the prince was really allied with the foreigners. A pro-royalist party in the city opposed his stay. Several days after he entered, a tragic event further underlined the tenuous nature of his power: a riot broke out in which the troops became involved; the Hôtel de Ville was burned, several important people were killed, and many of the people of the city were further estranged from Condé, who had to shoulder the blame. After the riot, the *Frondeurs* seized the government of the city, making Beaufort governor and Broussel the *prévot des marchands,* but their days were strictly numbered. Condé had to move most of his army outside the city walls, and even the most sanguine *Frondeur* understood that he soon would have to withdraw from Paris.

The court, in the name of the king, ordered the Parlement of Paris to leave the city, since it was no longer under the king's jurisdiction, and to reassemble at Pontoise. The more timid and perhaps the more responsible members of the Parlement obeyed the order; those men were never to regret their decision for Louis XIV provided each of them with a life-long pension. Then Mazarin played his *coup de théâtre*: the princes and the pamphleteers insisted that his presence made peace impossible, so voluntarily leaving the court, he again went into exile in Germany. This placed Condé in a predicament; he now had to make public his conditions for peace, and they conclusively proved that it was not Mazarin alone who stood in the way of a settlement. Condé wanted the return of all the offices and honors that he had held, marshal's batons and other new offices for his friends and supporters, pensions for his followers, the right to keep his army and remain in alliance with the King of Spain, and finally, full control over the negotiations for peace between France and Spain. He did not ask for a crown, but that was about the only thing not on his list; had these demands been granted, he would have exercized the authority of a sovereign within the kingdom. The terms were patently impossible. They cost the prince support of the city of Paris as well as that of the entourage of Gaston of Orléans. The bourgeois circles were now insisting upon a quick settlement. By October 1652, Condé's position in Paris had become impossible; just three months after he had entered the city, he had to withdraw, and his puppet government collapsed. Paris and the surrounding countryside were not unhappy to see the army of pillagers depart.

Men loyal to the king took over the government of the city and sent assurances of their loyalty to the court. They humbly begged the king to return to "his good city of Paris," to recall the sovereign courts to their usual chambers, to give the population amnesty for its follies. "These are our wishes, sire," their spokesman said, ". . . not conditions that we would impose upon you; for we reserve for ourselves only the glory of obeying you. . . . I would be repudiated by my fellow citizens if I spoke otherwise." Louis thanked the heads of the city militia, and the representatives of the restored city government for their loyalty, but he must have recalled bitterly how different had been the behavior of the city only a few weeks before. On October 21, 1652, he made a solemn reentry into Paris. The royal train passed between lines of soldiers, but even the troops were unable to hold back the enthusiastic crowds who shouted greetings and tried to kiss their king's boots.

That same evening Gaston of Orléans left Paris for his estates on the Loire under the threat that force would be used if he did not. His elder daughter, an unrepentant *Frondeur,* watched the royal procession from her window; shortly afterward she received an order to retire to her estates and to stay there until permitted to leave. It was an exile that she found dull and boring.

On August 29, 1652, Louis had sent a letter to his uncle in his own hand-writing: "I would like to believe," he wrote, "that being as close to me as you are, you who have given evidence of affection in every meeting as you have done, and that having the interest that you have in the conservation of my state and my authority, you would not have adhered to those who have undertaken action against me if you had not been led into it against your own inclinations. . . ." He expressed astonishment that Gaston had blamed Mazarin for troubles that had been going on when Mazarin was in exile. Then in a sterner tone: "I am not more astonished that you were persuaded that I would not be offended when you raised troops against me, when you commanded my revenues, that you might employ them in war against me, or that you would exercise authority against my will, or that you would try to make the cities of my kingdom recognize a power without right, or that the officers of justice have given you [authority] . . . which they undoubtedly would have refused [without duress]. . . . Do you realize what a scandal it is when my subjects see you refuse to obey my letters to you? . . ." Louis went on to urge his uncle to return to his duty, and offered to forget the past so that Frenchmen could fight against the common enemy.[6] Who knows how much of this letter was actually written by the king? Possibly very little of it, and yet it is clearly in character; it sounds like the king, and undoubtedly represents Louis' point of view during the days when the rebellion was collapsing.

As for Gaston, there was no reason to fear him. The songsters were soon chanting of his disgrace. One of the verses announced that "of all the princes of the earth, poor Gaston is the most unfortunate; his arms are only glass, his blows have no force. He is valiant as he is faithful; he is in no way a good model."[7] The song went on and on, telling of the man whose rebellions always fizzled out.

In Paris, Louis dealt with the Parlement by convocation and a *lit de justice*. The members who had been with him at Pontoise, he graciously invited to the Louvre, where he explained his intentions; the rest, with the exception of some ten of the most hardened *Frondeurs* who were ordered into exile, were simply commanded to appear at the royal session by *lettres de cachet*. This was the first session in which Louis met with Parlement as a major king. He was a big, handsome, dignified boy of fourteen; his solemn, serious mien betrayed his feelings about himself and his place in the world. His government had triumphed over a rebellion; this session was a public affirmation of his authority. The decrees registered by that *lit de justice* left no room for doubt about the future of the kingdom. There was a general amnesty, but only if the guilty unqualifiedly submitted to royal authority in proper haste. All acts of the Parlement, including the decrees against Mazarin, were annulled. The Dukes of Beaufort and Rohan and a number of other gentlemen involved in the usurpation of power, as well as the president of the *Chambre des Comptes* and ten members of Parlement, including Broussel and de Thou, were exiled to the provinces. Members of the sovereign courts were henceforth forbidden to have any commerce with members of these princely or ducal families, to accept any pensions from them, or in any way to "attend to their affairs." Even more important, the members of Parlement were expressly and pointedly forbidden henceforth to interest themselves in the affairs of the kingdom, in finances, or in the activities of men charged with the administration of the kingdom. No language could be more specific: Parlement was forbidden to meddle with the business of the king.

Condé and his family scorned the amnesty offered them and withdrew with the Spanish army into the Low Countries. On November 13, Louis again went to Parlement, to register a declaration against Condé, Conti, and Longueville, declaring them guilty of *lèse-majesté* and thus as criminals before the law. Their goods were confiscated. Any friends that the prince still had in Parlement remained silent. The *Fronde* obviously was dead.

Gaston proved more than willing to accept the king's forgiveness. He not only signed a letter of submission dictated by the court, but also supplied information that incriminated Châteauneuf and Cardinal de Retz. Gaston had not changed much in thirty years; his friends and supporters could depend upon him to leave them in the lurch to save himself. Châteauneuf was ordered to go to his estates, but de Retz presented a slightly more difficult problem: as Coadjutor Archbishop of Paris, he could easily find sanctuary. Louis allowed him to feel safe and then took him unawares. The little comedy of his arrest unfolded another side of Louis' emerging personality. Cardinal de Retz appeared at the Louvre to pay his respects; the king received him graciously even though Anne spoke to him sarcastically. Father Paulin wrote to Mazarin to tell him of the event:

> I was there when the King gave the command in the very presence of the Cardinal . . . his Majesty conducted himself with great sagacity . . . no one could have carried out a more refined policy. I was beside the Cardinal, I made him admire the bounty and grandeur of the King . . . The King came up to us and spoke of a comedy that he had in his head; first speaking aloud to M. de Villequières, then, as if laughing, he whispered in his ear (this was the moment

of command) . . . he left shortly . . . as if he were an actor on the stage . . .
saying that the King was going to mass . . . In the middle of mass, **M.**
Villequières came to whisper to him . . . the King turned to me and said: "I
have just arrested Cardinal de Retz!" I replied, "Your Majesty has only been
attending mass; the Cardinal is waiting below!" "That's not the way it is," replied the King.

The Jesuit, obviously impressed by Louis' indirection, assured Mazarin that
the queen was pleased with her son's firmness. Why should she not be:
Louis was paying her and Mazarin the compliment of imitation, and
punishing one of her enemies.

After punishing the guilty, royal justice required that the "innocent"
should be returned to position and honors. This meant the recall of
Mazarin, an act close to the hearts of both the king and his mother. Mazarin,
however, did not return immediately. He first undertook to close the frontier to the Condé-Spanish forces. This proved to be easier than might have
been expected, for with the defeat of the *Fronde* in Paris, Condé's French
troops melted away, and the Lorraine-Spanish forces were not strong
enough to stand up to Turenne's army that joined Mazarin on the German
frontier. By the first of the year, loyal troops were firmly established in the
frontier fortifications, and Mazarin arrived in Paris. The king received him
with great honor, and the crowds on the street that so shortly before had
cried for his blood, cheered his cortege as it passed. Within a very short
time Conti begged for pardon, and as pledge of good faith, asked for the
hand of one of Mazarin's nieces. It is small wonder that the songsters
chanted:

> In spite of everyone,
> In spite of the princes and the *Fronde,*
> In spite of our complaints and cries,
> After terrible tempests,
> Jules returns to Paris
> And remounts his beast.[8]

And still Condé refused to submit; he had promised that he would be
the last to return his sword to the scabbard; he preferred to command the
troops of Spain rather than bow and ask for forgiveness. Louis wrote to his
uncle Gaston:

> . . . you know how I have given the Prince of Condé all that he could
> desire from me to return to his duty . . . and you yourself have worked for this
> end without success . . . instead of accepting my bounty, he has scorned it and
> has associated himself more and more with the enemies of this Crown. He is
> not content to put himself at their head, but even urges them to attack my
> fortifications, and having taken them, appropriates them to himself, doing things

unworthy of his birth and quality . . . these things cannot be further tolerated without becoming an indulgence prejudicial to my state and my person. . . .[9]

Louis asked his uncle to associate himself with a declaration against Condé. The *Fronde* might be over, but the problems of the kingdom were still far from solved.

The first *Fronde* taught Louis much about rebellions in his cities as well as the difficulties that could arise between the crown and venal royal officials who could not be removed. The second *Fronde* was even more important, for it reaffirmed the military lessons of the civil wars of the preceding century. Richelieu may have started the building of a royal army under the control of a minister and a bureaucratic apparatus, but the *Fronde* of the princes imperiously demanded that such an army must come into being. Mazarin, Louis, and the men around them all got this message; in the following years the ordinances of Le Tellier that became the foundation for the new army began to delimit the military organization of the kingdom. Never again did a French king find himself less powerfully armed than his relatives or the great lords of his realm.[10] Louis undoubtedly learned many other things from the *Fronde,* but this was the most important for the future of the kingdom.

6

THE EDUCATION OF
THE KING: I

ANNE ONCE REMARKED THAT kings do not need to read history since they "live it," and anyone who reads the *Mémoires* that Louis dictated for the education of the dauphin, or who follows closely his policy as king, cannot miss the fact that the history that Louis "lived" between 1648 and 1652 left an indelible mark upon his personality and on his relations with people and institutions. Why not? The years between ten and fourteen are impressionable ones, especially when the experiences are as vivid and as perilous as were those of the *Fronde*. But Louis also learned other things, more formally, that contributed to his character and his conceptions of himself, his place in the world, and the world itself. Even during the *Fronde,* when the lessons were sometimes broken off for weeks on end, Louis was still a "school boy," more or less subject to the discipline of his tutors and preceptors.

One critic after another has called attention to the feebleness of his instruction. One does not have to look far to discover what these critics mean: Louis did not receive a "humanistic" education, and his lack of interest in books and reading prevented him from ever repairing the omission or even really discovering what he had missed. He might translate Caesar's *Gallic Wars,* but this did not mean the acquisition of enough Latin to enable him to read and to understand the great Latin essayists, poets, historians, orators, and statesmen with profit and pleasure. The king did return to the study of the language several times after he became a grown man, but his objective was to be able to read letters from the papal court, rather than Ovid or Cicero.[1]

Louis did not learn to be king from the great writers of antiquity, the men of the renaissance, or even the bookish people of his own day. It almost seems that he was allergic to books; as a boy he read as little as possible; as an adult he spent many long hours reading dispatches, memoranda, and letters dealing with current problems of government and politics, but there is little evidence that he spent much time with the printed pages of men either living or dead. It may be that his experience with the books written for him by his preceptors was the root of his disinterest in literature.

Of all the men who attempted to shape his mind, two were the most important: La Mothe le Vayer and Péréfixe, the Abbé of Beaumont. We have the books that they prepared especially for the king. La Mothe's essays on geography, rhetoric, and morals were written in 1651; on economics, in 1653; on politics, in 1654; on logic, in 1655; and on physics, in 1658. In addition, he wrote an undated *History of France* addressed to Louis' brother, but since the two boys shared lessons, it can be assumed that the king also had to read it. Even a cursory glance through these essays gives the impression that they were designed to discourage the reader from concerning himself with such things; they are dry, dull, and factual without ever suggesting the significance of the "facts" to be learned. The style lacks either distinction or elegance. It has usually been assumed that the good La Mothe filled in the outlines by discussion with the boys, thereby showing how wise the preceptor was; perhaps this only confirmed the king in the idea that writers keep the important things out of their books, so why bother to read them? In any case, the *Gazette* did not know whereof it spoke when it assured its readers that "the King has no less inclination for sacred writings and *belles lettres* than for other forms of exercise worthy of a great monarch . . . which promises us in his time a golden age."

Péréfixe's most important literary contribution to the boys' education is a little more readable than those of La Mothe, but hardly a literary monument. He wanted the young king to understand the life and works of his grandfather, the first Bourbon ruler of France, both as an object lesson in the art of government and as a pious excursion in family history. Like most historians with a conscience, Péréfixe was concerned about the accuracy of his account: "History," he wrote in the preface, "is attended by so many circumstances that it is almost impossible not to make some mistakes." He assured the king that he had "not advanced anything for which I cannot provide proof" and adds that if contrary things are to be found in other histories, we must remember that "our historians differ so among themselves that if you follow one, you necessarily contradict another." Péréfixe was not the only seventeenth-century man to regret this melancholy state of affairs; many men pointed out that there were "histories of France, but no history," and some therefore concluded that all history was false—"a set of lies more or less agreed upon." Péréfixe's *History of Henry IV* is a straightforward account, largely chronological, with events following one another without analysis or interpretation; judgments are made simply *ex cathedra,* without explanation. He condemns the Saint Bartholomew's Day massacre, the murders of Guise, Lorraine, Henry III, and, of course, of Henry IV. He usually finds Henry IV both gallant and brave.[2] Péréfixe's method of instruction seems to have merit for a prince who must make decisions: he discussed Henry's decisions, asked his young pupil to consider possible alternatives as well as the reasons for the action that finally was taken. Undoubtedly these discussions with the wise clergyman were more exciting than the reading of his book.

Seventeenth-century boys were expected to learn their duty toward God and man—as well as wisdom about the world—by copying maxims, sets of moral precepts, catechisms; a king was no exception to this procedure. There were a number of royal catechisms, preaching the duties of kings, prepared for Louis. At least one of them was banned by Mazarin because it was too outspoken about foreigners and ministers, and such forbidden topics. We know of one set of maxims, still preserved in the *Bibliothèque Nationale,* that under Péréfixe's direction, was copied by the king both in French and in Latin in 1651. It is impossible to guess what they meant to a thirteen-year-old boy, but the intentions of the teachers are clear from the content and tone. The collection begins, "I know that the first duty of a Christian Prince is to serve God, and that piety is fundamental to all royal virtues." Later: "I wish to put my entire hope in God and support myself by His goodness, for I know that a prince who confides himself to God frustrates without arms the legions armed against him." Farther on: "It often happens that people are not ashamed to despise the orders of a prince when the prince is not ashamed to despise the orders of God." And then: "I wish to render honor to priests for they are the interpreters of religion and the masters of piety. . . . The Pope being first among them, reason demands that I honor him particularly." In another tone: "The greatest difficulty for me is to control my passions and to chain them like ferocious beasts [for] they are furies that, having become masters of the soul, impose their law on reason and make men slaves. . . . Has not that king lost his liberty who obeys his passions and does not dare to do things that they forbid, nor to refuse what they demand?" The reader must wonder how this sounded to a young teen-ager—and what he understood by "passions" at that moment of his life. The Boy-Scout-like admonition— "I ought always to remember that I am King so that I do nothing unworthy of my name"—surely had more substance at thirteen than the attack on passion. The lines "When pride carries me to a glorification of power, I ought to remember that I am under God," and "If I bring myself to treat

my subjects as slaves, I should consider that the hatred of men is particularly inflamed by outrages" may have recalled the orations in the Parlement, or they may have been copied mechanically. The preceptors did not
forget that Louis was the grandson of Henry IV: "Whenever the pleasure
of the body counsels me to renounce chastity, I will resist courageously
. . . but of all the passions, I wish most to control wrath, because with it
one can do nothing that requires reflection." Were we to try to assess the
effect of these maxims, this one might be given high place, for Louis did
control his temper, but so did his mother control hers, and her example was
undoubtedly worth more than precepts. As for virtue: "The four virtues that
I must have are prudence, justice, courage, and temperance, if I wish to
succeed in private or in public life." This sample is enough to taste the
temper and spirit of the exercises.[3]

We have already seen that as a child, Louis was obliged to listen to
the words of wisdom—or otherwise—of the clergymen in the churches and
the monasteries that he visited with his mother. Even as in our own day when
priests, rabbis, and clergymen of all denominations seize upon the opportunity to pronounce a public prayer at the inauguration of a president
or a governor, to tell God and the audience how rulers should conduct
themselves and how the world should be governed, so the clergy of the
seventeenth century delighted in the visits of royalty that provided a captive audience for their lectures. These men hammered away at a few
simple themes. Like the preacher at Auxerre in 1650, they emphasized
the injunction "Give unto Caesar . . . as well as to God." Or the importance of the church as the unifying force in society: "your arms are
not as strong as religion, and should not be used against rebels except in
the last extremity . . . religion will gain and hold the hearts of men. . . ."
The altar supports the throne: "Henry IV could not have held the throne
without the church." Others repeated the refrain that the society was in
trouble when the church was in trouble, and that heresy (Huguenots) was
an evil for both. "Heresy caused the death of Charles I of England. . . ."
asserted an orator, and another said, "God has blessed France because
Louis XIII and Richelieu disarmed heresy in France."[4]

Louis was undoubtedly instructed by these clergymen, but they taught
him more than they wished. "I have never failed to call your attention,"
he wrote for his son, "to the respect we should have for religion and the
deference for clergymen in the things that particularly regard their mission
—the celebration of sacred mysteries and the teaching of the evangelic
doctrine—but . . . clergymen are apt to be a little too proud of themselves
because of their profession. . . ." He willingly listened to their sermons

about God, but excluded them from the conduct of affairs. Mazarin taught him to be suspicious of the clergy, and hostile to the extension of clerical foundations that absorbed wealth and manpower to the detriment of the state. But the clergymen who lectured to Louis may inadvertently have given him an even deeper insight into their ambitions and aspirations.

There were a number of "handbooks on government" published while Louis was still a schoolboy, some of them obviously in the hope that the king would read them; but we have no evidence that any of them was actually placed in his hands. One of these books, however, was important, since many of the orators in Parlement, some of the clergymen, and probably some of the king's entourage when Mazarin was in exile seem to have been influenced by it. The book, written by Claude Joly, was entitled *A Collection of Maxims for the Education of the King.* Mazarin had the book burned in 1653, but it enjoyed several subsequent printings. It opens with the assertion that the king should always be a minor in the sense that he should never act without counsel, and should never himself assume responsibility for his acts. It also insists that a king's power is definitely limited: "Power is not absolute, not without limits . . . the King must understand this fact." After making these two basic assumptions, Joly proceeds to analyze the institutions of the French monarchy: king, councils, Parlement, the Estates General, the church, the law. It was a textbook on French government as Joly, a *Frondeur,* understood it. Louis did not need Joly to tell him about the limitations on royal power during these years of the *Fronde,* but there is no evidence that he ever accepted Joly's conception of those limitations as a constitutional rather than a political fact.

The religious and moral education so carefully begun by his mother when he was only a child, was continued by his confessor, his teachers, and the general spirit of the court under Anne and Mazarin. The solemn little boy of six who said his prayers and attended mass grew up to be the adolescent who feared God and respected His sacraments. At fourteen we see him at mass praying for the soul of a companion, Mazarin's nephew, who was killed in the battle of the Porte Antoine. At eighteen he wonders how "anyone could go to bed at night safely with a mortal sin on his soul," and a little later upbraids his brother for eating meat on a fast day. The literary portrait of the king drawn by La Grande Mademoiselle late in the 1650's emphasizes this attention to the details of religious observance. After praising his features and carriage, she continues, "He has great piety and devotion, not too austere nor too severe. He has been well raised, since his mother the Queen is a Princess of the most solid piety . . . one sees the effects and the graces given by God in the personality of the King."

In the years following the *Fronde,* when Anne was in her fifties, many of the characteristics that had been observable in her earlier years became more pronounced, and the fact that she had no difficulty in retaining her son's love and affection perhaps helped to reinforce in him some of these attributes. In this period, Madame de Motteville tells us, Anne's disposition became more calm: ". . . she is rarely in wrath, her passion never dominates her." Indeed, she seemed never moved by anger except when the interests of the crown were involved. Her manners were civil, she refused to listen to gossip—"If the young people of this century follow her maxims, there will be more good and polite people than now." Anne never confused herself with the saints, for she well knew her petty weaknesses (the ones people are always willing to admit),[5] and yet her modest virtue was exemplary in an age when many women flaunted their sex or their bad manners. As we have already seen, Anne's Spanish Catholicism was a thing of cults and observances, of reliquaries and hours on the *prie-dieu.* ". . . she has a great respect for the laws of God and her desire is to see them installed in the hearts of Frenchmen . . . she is indefatigable in the practice of devotions; voyages, sickness, troubles, and pleasures are never allowed to interfere with her retreats and prayers. She has an extraordinary confidence in God . . . she is exact in observance of fast days, and I have often heard her say that kings ought to obey the commandments of God and the church more precisely than other Christians, for they are obliged to serve as examples to their people. . . ."[6]

The queen's observance of cult and ceremony was not unique with her. This mid-seventeenth century was a period in which a *Te Deum* sung at the cathedral, a high mass for thanksgiving or to beg intercession, public prayers and novenas, were at once religious ceremonies and dramatic methods of influencing public opinion or communicating news, either good or bad, to the people. Even Condé was not above this. During the *Fronde* he had walked bareheaded through the streets of Paris with the relics of Sainte Geneviève in a procession organized to "banish Mazarin and bring peace." For him it may have been a cynical act; but as propaganda for the people, it was most effective. Thus we must be careful to distinguish between pious public proclamations and private religious devotion: Louis did not need his mother to teach him to order the chanting of *Te Deums,* the exposition of the Blessed Sacrament, processions of relics (on one occasion, to bring down the price of bread), and masses for thanksgiving or to request favors. He did these things because he was a seventeenth-century ruler in a Catholic land; if he did them more effectively than other kings, it was because he was a better showman and realized how important they were to bolster the regime. On the other hand, Louis' sense of personal piety, his almost superstitious insistence upon the observance of both the sacraments and the sacramental cults, which testifies to his fear of God and the devil, may well have come directly from Anne. All his life Louis punctiliously followed the observance of the Catholic worship and attempted to live up at least to most of the external requirements of the church's law.

Both Anne and Mazarin were concerned that the *Confident* (their code name for the king) should not fall into evil ways because of bad companions. The cardinal's informers told him both of plots against his government and of gossip about the court. As a result of this sort of information, several boys, a little older than the king, were quietly removed from the troupe of royal companions.[7] Mazarin often seems to have been a man who feared neither God nor the devil, but he was anxious to see that his charge should grow up to achieve the *gloire* that his capacities entitled him to earn; thus we find him almost as solicitous as the queen for Louis' moral well-being. Mazarin clearly expressed his feelings when he once wrote to the king, "I have nothing to add to the sentiments that you express, and I hope that God will bless them and affirm them so that you will never have others than those needed to be the most glorious among kings and the most accomplished and best of all men."[8]

One might object at this point that Louis in his twenties and thirties committed adultery, scandalously paraded his sexual irregularities before the world, and clearly lived outside the teachings of his church. A closer look at his life in these days, however, will show that his conscience never allowed him to enjoy the pleasures of the flesh without some reservations. Tears over his mother's reproaches, and pious resolutions (often enough soon forgotten) when churchmen rebuked his sins, were not enough to overcome the demands of the flesh while he was young and vigorous, but they did trouble his mind. The last thirty-five years of his life, spent largely with the pious and somewhat prudish Madame de Maintenon, whose resemblance to Anne cannot be missed, plainly reflect the experiences of his youth.

Like his mother, Louis was no theologian—indeed, he had no interest in theology. Anne's instructions to his first confessor, Father Paulin, who prepared the king for first communion, did not emphasize the intellectual side of religious instruction. "She has given into my hands," the pious Jesuit wrote, "a child most dear to her, and she urged me in the most pressing manner to keep in mind the salvation of his soul . . . she hopes that I will join his Majesty each day in his devotions when he prays to

God in the morning, when he studies his letters, when he attends mass. . . ."
Father Paulin prepared Louis for both first communion and confirmation,
using Godeau's *Royal Catechism*[9] for instruction in Catholic dogma. This
book is simply an affirmation of the Catholic doctrine of divine right of
kings, asserting the idea that monarchs are called to a sacerdotal office, but
failing to give any considerable understanding of the formal thinking of
the great theologians of the church. Nineteenth-century critics who complain that Godeau not only failed to condemn war but actually presented
war as God's way of punishing an evil world, failed to understand that
moralists of the seventeenth century shared their century's belief in
providential history; war was unfortunate for many people, but for a king
to regard it as sinful, would have been considered bizarre.

The king was confirmed by his first chaplain, the Bishop of Meaux,
on November 3, 1649; he received his first communion on Christmas of
the same year, rather than on the traditional Easter, in "symbolic recognition of Clovis' conversion." Perhaps even more important than Clovis was
the fact that these were the days when the Parlementary *Fronde* was building up toward its climax. Royal visits to the churches were redoubled, calling attention to the piety of the royal family, and the public was well
alerted to the gala ceremony that was to come. Louis may have realized
that Mazarin was using this display of royal piety to improve his position
over the *Frondeurs,* but at the same time it was a personal experience for
the young king. Louis confessed to Father Paulin at 10 P.M., December
24. (He had been practicing confession for several days so that all would
go smoothly.) At eleven he mounted the royal carriage with Mazarin, his
younger brother, and his governor, to drive to the church of Saint-Eustache.
Guards stood at intervals all along the half-mile of the route between the
Palais-Royal and the church. The royal carriage "preceded by guards of
the Grand Provost and the Hundred Swiss . . . and followed by the Body
Guard and numerous valets . . . [passed] in the midst of a multitude of
people who appeared to have been disgorged from all the churches on this
principal festival of the year." There were cries of "Long live the king!"
and at the church door the king was received by numerous clergy with
cross and holy water. The church was richly decorated with flags and
tapestry. Louis heard mass and in proper time approached "the holy table
with humility and zeal that testified to the example of the Queen." Mazarin
presented the Gospel for him to kiss, and the officiating bishop gave him
the Host. Later in the day the royal family made a solemn visit to Anne's
favorite chapel at Val-de-Grâce, to the accompaniment of public cheers
from the streets. It was only a few days later that the royal family fled

Paris in the middle of the night and then besieged the city; Louis could not have missed the connection between these events.[10]

During the *Fronde* this lesson of the usefulness of public ceremonies as a method for capturing the imagination of men was many times reenforced. At Chartres, for example, on Assumption Day, 1650, the king and the queen mother solemnly reaffirmed the vow of Louis XIII, dedicating the kingdom of France to the Queen of Heaven. "The city cannons were fired," explained the *Gazette,* "but it was clear that neither the noise of all these city cannons . . . nor the affairs of peace and war . . . could trouble the devotion of their Majesties." Two years later Father Annat, a provincial of the Jesuit order, was "delighted with the piety of the King." Louis performed these religious ceremonials very much as would any adolescent boy with a pious Catholic education; his outward piety perhaps concealed the fact that he may have wondered why he was not more moved inwardly.

The most important politico-religious ceremony for any French king was his consecration at Reims cathedral with the holy oil that had come "directly from Heaven for the consecration of Clovis." This anointment emphasized the sacerdotal character of kingship and endowed the ruler with religious as well as secular prestige and stature. Louis' consecration came when a sizable part of his kingdom, headed by a prince of the blood, was under arms against him; could there be any more striking affirmation of his authority than this consecration with the holy oils that came directly from God? However, just like his first communion, this consecration had political overtones, and it was obviously in defiance of the Prince of Condé and his followers. But the imagination of an adolescent boy must nevertheless have been fired by the pageantry, the chanting, the tolling of bells and firing of cannons, the incense, the cross, the monstrant with the Host. Although there had been a grand procession when Louis announced in Parlement that he was now a major king, this celebration that included religious as well as civil authorities was even more imposing.

The court arrived at Reims several days before the ceremony. On the day before the consecration, Louis was received at the abbey of Saint-Rémy, where the holy oil was kept, "by the Grand Prior who presented him with holy water, a splinter of the true Cross to kiss, and then lectured him on the duties of kings." After mass at Saint-Rémy he went to Sainte-Niçaise where the monks received him with ceremony before reading a low mass. That evening he attended vespers in the great cathedral, and then, in preparation for the next day, he went to confession, and retired to his *prie-dieu.* His preparation for the consecration was much the same as that made by a bishop for his consecration.

On the morning of June 7, 1654, at 4:40 A.M.,[11] the high clergy robed themselves and began the ceremonies at the cathedral; by 6 A.M. the court and a great press of people were in the church and on the grounds between it and the archepiscopal palace. Then came a procession headed by the Bishops of Beauvais and Châlons marching to the palace and pounding on the door. The Duke of Joyeuse, playing the part of Grand Chamberlain, called out, "What do you wish?" Beauvais: "The King. We ask for Louis XIV, son of that great King Louis XIII, whom God has given us for King." This formula was repeated three times before the doors were thrown open and the great crowd pressed into the king's bedroom, where Louis, clad in rich clothing, awaited them. With holy water, incense, oboes, flutes, drums, chants, and prayers, they led him to the cathedral for the age-old ceremony of the anointment and consecration.

The great church was magnificently decorated. The rich Reims tapestries[12] illustrating Bible stories curtained off the area of the high altar like the inner sanctum of an Egyptian temple, leaving only the traditional small door through which "the unimportant masses" might see what was happening. Scaffolding ran entirely around the choir of the church, creating a balcony some ten to twelve feet from the floor for the invited spectators: the box for the Queens of France and England (Henriette was still in France) was directly between the high altar and the beautiful rose window of the church; just below them, in front of the altar, was the throne, luxuriously hung with fleurs-de-lis and exquisite Turkish carpets. The clergy, peers of the realm, marshals of France, high officials of the crown, and the secretaries of state—each had assigned places on the benches at either side of the throne. A series of engravings preserved in the *Bibliothèque Nationale* illustrates the steps in the ceremony as well as the elegance of the setting.[13]

Important noblemen, including the king's own brother, acted out the parts that formerly were taken by the now nonexistent original peers of the realm. At one step in the ceremony, reminiscent of the consecration of a bishop or the ordination of a priest, Louis, clad entirely in white, prostrated himself before the altar flanked by the high officers of his household, while in the rear of the scene, three marshals of France held the crown, the sword, and the scepter of the kingdom. Roll of drums, fanfare of trumpets, and melancholy wail of oboes preceded the solemn chant of the kyrie, the litany of the saints, and finally the *Agnus Dei*. Then came the moment of tension: "Monsieur," said the Grand Prior of Saint-Rémy, "I place in your hands this precious treasure sent from Heaven to the great Saint-Rémy for the consecration of Clovis and the kings who succeed him. I beg you to return it to me according to the ancient custom after the consecration of our great King Louis XIV." Wherewith he gave the Bishop of Soissons the holy ampule. Thus began the ceremony of consecration. Louis was invested with the robes and the symbols of office and placed on the high throne where he was revered in the way Byzantine emperors of the past had been "adored." He received the "kiss of peace" from Cardinal Grimaldi, wine in a rich vessel from de Souvre, "bread of gold" from d'Orual, "bread of silver" from de Sourdis, and the purse with thirteen pieces of fine gold from the Duke of Saint-Simon. During the subsequent reading of the high mass, a large number of birds were released in the church and royal servants scattered money for the crowds. After the services, Louis "cured" over two hundred people by the "king's touch."

Neither Gaston of Orléans nor the Prince of Condé was present at Reims: the one sulked in semi-exile on his estates, the other was under arms, allied with the Spanish against his own king. But their absence did not seriously mar the ceremony; at least, it did not prevent the king from proclaiming to the world that he was the ruler of France, blessed by God, and anointed by the church, and that rebellion against him was a crime. How better could a young king learn the importance of ceremony and pageantry? How better learn the value of harnessing the prestige and power of the clergy to the chariot of monarchy? How better learn that great noblemen and wealthy churchmen could be given harmless occupations reeking with prestige to divert them from the exercise of real power?

7

THE EDUCATION OF
THE KING: II

TRADITION AND HISTORY assigned to the King of France three important roles: soldier, statesman, and judge. He was first of all a soldier. Indeed the very title "king" is a military one; the king was the leader of a warlike race of noblemen who made up his entourage. When a young prince came to the throne, the question was not Will he fight? but rather, Whom will he fight? A king who remained at home and at peace would soon hear sharp words from the young noblemen who surrounded him, for to them war was the way to wealth, power, and fame. Thus every young prince was brought up to be a soldier, for a king's *gloire* depended upon success in the field.

A king was also a statesman and a politician. He had to deal with the turbulent and clashing forces in the pluralistic society that made up these seventeenth-century kingdoms: noblemen great and small, town corporations, hereditary office-holders, often with little or no dependence upon the Crown, religious institutions of many different kinds, often antedating the monarchy, and a host of economic bodies with links to church, towns, feudal fiefs, privileged companies, and the like. These were realities with which a king must cope if he were to be successful in his career. In addition to the tangle of internal politics, a seventeenth-century monarch was confronted with the difficult fact that his kingdom was becoming part of the larger community of Europe whose manifold complexities also required the skills of a statesman and a diplomat.

Finally, the King of France was a judge; like the role of a soldier, this function came to him from the distant past when the king went from place to place settling disputes and giving justice. The seventeenth-century king had lower courts of several kinds, his Parlements, his chancellor, and his council of state to assist him in this duty, but Louis was destined to spend much time as judge and arbiter dealing with the affairs of private individuals.

Few princes achieved great success in all of these facets of their functions; even fewer were given realistic and systematic educations to prepare them for the many duties for which they were born. Although Louis lacked the bookish education of the humanist scholar, he had professional education far in advance of that given to most princes of his day. Mazarin played the important and decisive role as educator of the king. Superintendent of his education, godfather, first minister, confidant and intimate of both the boy and his mother, Mazarin had an unequaled opportunity to influence Louis' development. Turenne, as soldier and administrator, and the secretaries and officers who assisted in the management of the government and the army, all played a part secondary to that of the cardinal. Mazarin was a politician, a diplomat, perhaps even a statesman; Turenne was a soldier and an administrator; neither was a financier nor a judge. Neither regarded the inner organization of the kingdom as much more than a platform upon which to conduct the business of war and high politics. How could it have been otherwise? Throughout almost the entire period of Mazarin's administration, war was the most important business of state. Thus, by the time that Colbert arrived in the king's council in 1661 to instruct the young king in finance, internal economy, colonies, and naval affairs, Louis had already absorbed so many of the assumptions, attitudes, and interests of his earlier instructors that he was unable to appreciate fully Colbert's teachings.

Mazarin's place as surrogate father of the king was well established in the royal family. Anne wrote to him in code in 1653: "15 [Anne] cannot have other designs than those that please 16 [Mazarin] and, to show him that there is nothing in the world equal to the attachment [*amitié*] that 22 [also Anne] has for 16, 15 does not wish to displease him even in her thoughts. . . ." Louis probably never quite shared this complete submission to Mazarin, but he grew up hearing his beloved mother sing the praises of the cardinal, and he became a man in an environment in which it was an article of faith that Mazarin had saved the Bourbon throne, and where there were, as Mazarin wrote, "no secrets among us [Anne, Mazarin, and Louis]." Both the course of events before and after Mazarin's death, and Louis' own words, fully discredit the memoirists whose hatred of Mazarin led them to assume that the king must also share their attitudes. In fact, so complete was the unity between the two men that Mazarin could once write to the queen that there was no need for a letter from both him and Louis, since she probably could not tell which one was writing.[1]

Mazarin's position was also solidly grounded in his own love for Louis. The accusations of his enemies have tended to blind some historians to Mazarin's motives. To be sure, he loved money and the things that money could buy—jewels, palaces, books, art objects, dowries for his nieces, and the like—but most men who served seventeenth-century monarchs also loved these things, and it should not hide from us the actual work of the man who educated the *Confident* and prepared him and his kingdom for an era of greatness. Péréfixe, who lived in easy familiarity with the royal family as preceptor of the young king, well understood what Mazarin was up to. He wrote in a dedication that is of course laudatory, but need not have taken the form that it did: ". . . how many times have you [Mazarin] told me that nothing was as important as to impress upon the mind of the King that he should apply himself well to the things that he does, and that he should apply himself to serious things? . . . I believe that I am not mistaken [in thinking] that those who write the story of your life will scarcely find anything more worthy of their praise than this [education of the king]."[2]

Mazarin believed in Louis, and probably knew him better than anyone in his entourage. He often expressed the opinion that Louis "had the stuff for several great kings and one good man." To Villeroi he once wrote, "I believe that we can expect that this will be a prince as accomplished as any that we have seen in several centuries." His letters to the queen beam with fatherly pride in the accomplishments of the *Confident,* even when Louis was resisting Mazarin's insistence at sieges that he should be careful not to expose himself unduly. Mazarin's letters to friends and associates testify to his affection for "the best friend I have in the world." Indeed, it is hard to read his letters in the decade before his death without gaining the impression that he saw himself and his *gloire* as the statesman who saved the Bourbon inheritance from the rigors of foreign and domestic wars and prepared the young king to achieve the positions of power and prestige that his talents warranted.

Mazarin's system for instruction would satisfy the "progressive educators" of the twentieth century: Louis learned by listening, reading, and doing. From the time that Louis was fourteen or fifteen Mazarin had the custom of receiving him each day in his chambers for a discussion of current problems of state. Any chart of the movements of the two men will show that they were together most of the time during these years, so these conferences were practically daily affairs. What did they talk about? We know that they discussed the dispatches of the day, that Mazarin urged Louis to read the documents, and to write about them for practice in formulating his ideas. How better to learn the complexities of European affairs than at the side of an old master who had had personal experience in most of the countries of Europe, who understood the inner workings of high politics from years of study and practice? It is small wonder that Louis later astonished a Polish ambassador with his knowledge; he had studied with a man whom Richelieu had picked because of his diplomatic skill and his understanding of Europe.

Mazarin also introduced his charge into the meetings of the council where decisions of state were made. In the first years of his apprenticeship Louis apparently attended only those meetings at which relatively simple problems, susceptible to an easy solution, were discussed. But as time went on he was gradually introduced to the more thorny ones, some of which had no easy solution, perhaps no solution at all. Ten years later Louis was to explain for his son that politics consisted in the application of reason to the conjuncture of events, but that sometimes there is insufficient evidence for a solution based upon reason. "Wisdom," he says in one passage in which we can almost hear Mazarin's voice, "teaches that one leaves much to chance in certain things; therefore, reason itself counsels the following of blind movements or instincts above reason; these seem to come from Heaven . . . and are worthy of great consideration by those whom it [Heaven] has put in first place." Every seventeenth-century statesman knew that reason could not always direct policy, that there were foggy areas where information was missing and intuition as well as reason had to play a decisive part.

Louis' presence at council meetings became more and more frequent as he grew older. During the last years of Mazarin's life, the king presided at most of the meetings when important decisions were made, but he deferred to the cardinal's judgment on the policy to be adopted.

Louis seems to have cooperated well with Mazarin's system of instruction. He explained to his son that he developed the practice of testing his judgment by reasoning about problems under consideration "in secret and without a confidant, reasoning alone and by myself. . . . I was greatly pleased when I discovered that my first thoughts were the same as those reached by able and experienced men." How better to test one's judgment? How better to gain the impression that "God has not placed me on the throne without . . . giving me the means to fulfill my duty." All his life Louis submitted his problems to the council, but unlike his cousin Leopold I of the Danubian monarchy, who always accepted the majority opinion, Louis believed that he could depend upon his own judgment after he had listened and considered the opinions of others. He firmly believed that God had endowed princes with the judgment they needed to govern on this earth; it was only necessary for them to know the facts and the fan of opinion. Perhaps Mazarin taught him this as well.

It is one thing to educate a prince to play out his role; it is quite another to persuade him that the business of state deserves his complete attention. Princes of this world lived in courts where pleasure often beckoned more ardently than the business of state, where many men sought their own interests by turning the king's attention to frivolous things, and only a few princes really gave their lives to "the great *métier* of the king." Somehow Louis was persuaded of his responsibilities and literally gave his life to his *métier*. In this, too, we must see the hand of the cardinal, probably ably assisted by the queen mother. As we have noted elsewhere, there were good reasons why the young king should accept the attitudes and the standards of value presented by Mazarin and Anne, but in addition to these forces inherent in Louis' environment, Mazarin consciously labored to give his charge the ambition and the desire to rule. As early as 1653 we find the cardinal writing to Anne: ". . . if anything should prevent his applying himself to the things that he should [be doing], and lead him into laziness from which there would be difficulty in arousing him, . . . all would be lost." As Péréfixe said, Mazarin wanted Louis to apply himself to the things that he did and to do serious things; should he fall into the traps set for princes, the work of the queen and cardinal would be lost. Mazarin never allowed him to lose sight of the fact that the fulfillment of his *gloire,* that is, the full use of the talents with which God had endowed him in behalf of his kingdom, was a duty that could not be shirked. How many times in the cardinal's letters do we find the expressions: "You can become the greatest king. . . ."; "God has given you talents. . . ."; "You owe your God and your *gloire.* . . ."? In one of his most eloquent exhortations during the Mancini crisis:

> God has given you all the qualities for greatness; you must put them to use, and that you can easily do . . . acquiring by the application that you give to affairs the necessary knowledge and experience. . . . When you are at the helm of state, you will do more in one day than one more clever than I could do in six months; for it is of a different weight and a different *éclat* and impression when a king acts . . . than when a minister acts, no matter how authorized he may be . . . I will die happy when I see you prepared to govern by yourself, using your ministers only to present you with advice, profiting from it in the manner that pleases you, and giving them . . . the orders on which they are to act. . . . If you begin to take pleasure in this [affairs of state], I say to you without flattery or exaggeration that you will make more progress and that you will profit more in a month than another will in six. . . .

This was the argument: you can do it; you have the talents; you owe it to your *gloire* and your God. With such words Mazarin urged Louis to fulfill his destiny. They also became the dominating ideas of Louis the king. His

Mémoires fairly bristle with this message; and the long hours at his desk, in the council chamber, and in the field, where he acted out "the *métier* of the king" (one of Mazarin's expressions), testify to the impact of the cardinal's teachings. Marshal de Gramont tells us that Mazarin "trained his master in the art of governing"; he might also have said that he gave the king the ideal by which he governed. Some historians have seen this dedication to *gloire* and his consequent pride in the role of king as evidence of Louis' megalomania; it more properly is a response to ideals and goals that, as a child and a youth, he was taught to respect and to follow.

Louis understood that the place in the world to which he was born required of him humility as well as pride. As he wrote, "If there is a legitimate pride in our rank, there is a modesty and a humility that are no less praiseworthy. Do not think that these virtues are not for us. To the contrary, they belong to us more properly than to the rest of men. For after all, those who have no eminence by fortune, by birth, or by merit, no matter what small opinion they may have of themselves, can never be humble or modest. . . . If I can explain my thought, *it seems to me that we should be at the same time humble for ourselves and proud for the place that we occupy* [author's italics]." This is a conception of pride in the achievement of one's *gloire* that Mazarin would understand and teach; he was the man who "removed" flatterers from the entourage of the young king, for flatterers only try to bolster the ego, they do not strengthen pride in rank and obligation. This conception of pride of rank, rather than pride of self, lies at the very foundation of the value-system of a hierarchically organized society; it must be understood if one wants to know Louis XIV.

If Louis' memory of his earliest reactions to the do-nothing Merovingian kings is correct, Mazarin need not have advised him to govern without a first minister, and yet he did tell the young king many times that he should be his own first minister. The question has been raised: why should the man who himself governed as first minister advise the king to avoid choosing a successor to his position? Some believe that Mazarin wanted no successor because he wished to be the only man ever to reach so exalted a position; others suggest that the cardinal knew better than anyone the personality and the abilities of the king, and realized that he could govern by himself. Choice between these positions depends upon one's opinion of the cardinal's character. If we see Mazarin as the man of devious routes (and he surely was that at times), his letters and actions can be interpreted as ruses behind which we find the selfish motives of the minister. On the other hand, if we take Mazarin at his word, we find that he believed in the king's abilities and that he wanted him to achieve the full measure of prestige and power that his talents merited. Mazarin was a seventeenth-century man who could find his own *gloire,* in part at least, in the achievements of his *Confident.* If we are forced to make a choice, the simpler solution, namely that Mazarin really meant what he wrote, seems to be the better one.

What exactly did Mazarin teach the king? Fénelon rather smugly wrote, "Sire, you were born with a good heart, but those who brought you up, gave you as the art of governing, only defiance, jealousy and dislike of virtue, fear of all notable merit, a taste for devious and servile men, pride and attention for your interests alone. . . ." One after another of the anti-Mazarin pamphleteers insist that he taught the king only Machiavellianism. These views are on a par with much of the propaganda against the cardinal. They neglect the fact that Machiavelli did not invent the idea that states' interests know no morality; he discovered it from the study of politics. Nor was the so-called Machiavellianism, like Mazarin, simply a product of Italy; Henry IV and Richelieu could have taught Machiavelli things that he only imperfectly understood. It is probably true that Mazarin's teachings did not rise above the milieu of his century; he taught the king the art of politics as it was practiced by contemporary men. To do this he used the march of current events as object lessons and added to that the wisdom that he had gained from a life dedicated to the art. Fénelon's pious, lofty, and somewhat impractical idealism was offended by the policies of the middle-aged Louis; that is no excuse for condemning everything that he was taught, and by implication, all those who served in his government.

Later critics have objected that Louis' policies did not conform to their particular notion of political morality, thereby overlooking the fact that a man's basic assumptions as well as the direct conclusions that he draws from experience, both condition his behavior. Mazarin and Louis did not live in an era that shared the liberal, democratic, or socialist ideals of our times; since their world had not yet coined the word "humanitarianism," it is hard to censure them for not understanding its implications. The society of the mid-seventeenth century lived by assumptions rooted in theological rather than in secular patterns. Seventeenth-century rulers started with the belief that while God had delegated power to kings as His lieutenants on earth, He retained the authority (right) in his own hands, but He did not become the author of evils that the kings might commit. This distinction between the *power* to govern and the *right* (authority) to rule is a nice one; it did not prevent kings from seeing rebellion as a crime. As Louis wrote, ". . . bad as a prince may be, revolt on the part of his subjects is always infinitely criminal. He who has given kings to men has wished that they be respected as His lieutenants, and *reserves to Himself the right to examine their conduct* [author's italics]." Thus *Frondeurs* who "appealed to Heaven"—that is, to arms—were impious men; they should have had recourse to prayers and tears. But as Louis said, the assumption that God has given kings power to rule does not mean that they may act as they please. This is the error of those who would contrast the "despotism" of the so-called "Age of Absolutism" with the more felicitous period in which they live. Perhaps we should note that no seventeenth-century French king could exercise power as complete as that given to twentieth-century rulers.

Louis well understood that he was to govern a pluralistic society in which custom and law, tradition and friction of time, space, and inadequate personnel, all limited the power of the king. Even though he might develop overwhelming military strength, the king's power to command and to exact obedience was in fact strictly limited in this society in which there were many stubborn wills to be reconciled and many traditions to be recognized. This does not mean that the king's government was not often brutal and arbitrary, only that its acts were constrained by the structure and traditions of the society, as well as by the monarch's interpretations of God's will. Nor should this restriction be taken as mere formality in the sense given it by the secular societies of the twentieth century. Mazarin fairly shouted at Louis that "God did not establish kings so that they could satisfy their own passions," and every moralist and preacher of the era insisted that God would hold kings responsible for their actions. Anne believed that God would be more exacting in his examination of kings because He had given so much into their hands. Louis was most eloquent in his own belief:

> You must know, my son, that you cannot show too much respect for Him who has made us respected. . . . The first lesson in politics is that which teaches us to serve Him well. . . . Submission to Him is the best lesson we can give of that which is due to us; we sin against prudence as well as justice when we lack the veneration that we owe as His lieutenants. . . .
>
> He is infinitely jealous of his *gloire*. . . . He has perhaps only made us great so that our respect will honor Him more. And if we fail . . . perhaps He will let us fall into the dust from which He raised us.[3]

Moral compulsion threatened a bad king both with reversal of his rule on earth ("disturbances and revolutions," wrote Mazarin) and eternal damnation for his soul.

A further assumption inherent in all that Mazarin did or taught was the belief that each generation of kings had the obligation to pass on to its successors the complex of rights, privileges, prerogatives, and powers that had come to it from its ancestors. Just as Louis XIII believed that his primary duty was to preserve the French throne as it was left to him by his father, so Mazarin and Anne attempted to maintain the crown for Louis XIV just as Louis XIII had left it. In his own day Louis XIV wrote to his son: ". . . when it concerns . . . the rights of your crown, of the king . . . hold onto them stubbornly, with the elevation of heart and mind of which you are capable, do not betray the *gloire* of your predecessors nor the interests of your successors to come, for which you are only the depository." It is this that Louis means when he speaks of his duty to "defend the rights of his Crown," or of his gratitude to Mazarin and his mother for their defense of his crown at a time when he was unable to act for himself. To defend the rights and dignity of the crown was an obligation descending with the throne from former kings; it must be maintained intact for successors.

This confusion of state and dynasty sometimes makes seventeenth-century politics difficult to understand in an era that no longer regards the acts of God (e.g., inheritance) as the basis for sovereignty. Yet we must see that seventeenth-century men saw both the power of the crown and the territory of the prince as entities to be inherited and cared for—to use Burke's expression—as an "entailed trust." Although these seventeenth-century princes might take territory by the sword or change institutions by arbitrary power, they tried to justify their acts as based upon tradition or dynastic right; even in his most flagrant land grabs, when a legitimate prince was involved, Louis piously insisted upon his right based upon treaties or inheritance.[4]

The *Fronde* and the Spanish war formed the young king's political laboratory. Where better to learn the problems of parties and factions than in the "combinations" that Mazarin had to make in order to emerge victorious in the *Fronde?* Indeed, where better to learn the danger of factions to the crown? Louis did not draw from this the lesson of "divide and rule" that Catherine de Médicis had used. "I have never believed," he writes, ". . . that the art of government was to create division and disorder. . . . Feeble and poorly established princes who cannot sustain themselves by their own force, hope to find help in the animosity of individuals." Louis learned that factions must not be allowed to come into being; all must accept the will of the king.

The war was an excellent arena for the student of politics. Mazarin had to deal with the unstable situation in Germany following the Thirty Years' War; with the problems of Italy rising out of both the Franco-Spanish conflict and the variant interests of the papacy and other Italian states; and above all with the Low Countries and England. Under Mazarin Catholic, monarchical France made an alliance with Cromwell, the regicide responsible for the death of Louis' own uncle. In dealing with Republican

Dutchmen and regicide Englishmen, Louis learned the lesson that one could sup with the devil so long as one had a long spoon. This was a lesson that he did not forget when the Turks became his only friends in Europe. So well did Louis absorb Mazarin's conception of politics that long after the cardinal's death, Madame de Lafayette could observe, "It seemed that the King sought to govern his politics by the ideas that he [Mazarin] had inspired."

Louis' *Mémoires* prepared during the first decade of his personal reign are an excellent source for understanding the teachings of the cardinal. These pages written or dictated by the king so often express ideas that we find in Mazarin's letters that it probably is not far from the mark to assume that the "reflective" passages in them are Louis' condensations of Mazarin's wisdom. Many of them are surely more mature and more sophisticated than we would expect from a Louis under thirty. These passages cover many of the basic problems of kings, and taken together, they probably constitute the most pointed and practical counsel ever prepared for the education of a prince. Here and there the tone is lofty and moral, as Louis exhorts his son to give "his heart to God" or expatiates on "virtue." But for the most part the advice is practical and pragmatic, the words of an experienced politician: How shall a king live with his neighbors? How shall he pick his ministers? How shall he reward those who serve him? The importance of keeping one's pledged word. Why one must always support a minister and refuse to listen to a subordinate. Care in not believing the words of flatterers (here we almost hear Mazarin's exact words). Do not presume too much; it is better to wait until success is sure before announcing victory. Do not hope for luck; indeed, be suspicious of such hopes. On faithful and faithless servants. On the clergy. On the lower classes (they must be protected from the soldiers). These are typical of the many topics discussed for the dauphin; we can almost be sure that they were also the topics discussed by the cardinal.

Mazarin's counsel covered little as well as big things. Louis, for example, scrupulously followed the cardinal's practice of thanking profusely those who served him: this sort of letter looms large in the correspondence of both men. Both managed people by indirection rather than by force; both were extremely polite at all times. As Louis explained to his son: a king can do himself great damage by being rude, for it may cost him a loyal servant, while politeness costs nothing. Mazarin was a reader of dispatches and taught that only thus could a man govern; Louis spent his whole professional life studying the letters, memoranda, and reports of diplomats and officials. It may even be that the practice of keeping the *feuillets,* from which he dictated the *Mémoires,* was copied from Mazarin's use of the little *carnets.*[5]

In the last year of Mazarin's life, perhaps feeling that death was almost upon him, the cardinal gave even more attention to the training of his charge. The Venetian ambassador told his government that the daily interviews between the two men sometimes lasted hours on end: ". . . the Cardinal informs him of everything, instructs him and educates him in such a manner that if his Majesty observes the precise advice and the strong maxims and all that which the genius of so great a man reveals to him . . . one cannot doubt that, if he does not fall under the influence of another minister, he will become a very great prince."

In Mazarin's last hours there were many touching scenes, but the most important of these for the training of his master was his deathbed list of rules that Louis must follow to become a great king. The awesomeness of approaching death gave dramatic force to Mazarin's words. As Louis wrote, "The Cardinal, sensing that he approached his end and desiring to divest himself of the business of this world . . . gave the last moments of his life on earth to the love that he has always had for the good of my state and my *gloire.*" Is it small wonder that Louis never doubted Mazarin's sincerity? Facing the unknown of death, he still held to his task of preparing the king. What did he advise? He spoke of the necessity of picking worthy men to fill clerical offices, and the importance of supervising their morality. He urged the king to preserve the nobility as the "right arm of the monarchy." He went on to speak of the necessity of holding the magistrates within bounds, of honoring and rewarding the faithful in the company, and of the importance of caring for and preserving the common people who pay taxes to the state. This advice concerning the "orders of society" was not greatly different from that to be found in Richelieu's *Political Testament* intended for Louis XIII; admittedly, only the solemnity of the occasion prevented it from being almost trite. The rest of the topics deal with the employment of men according to their talents, the rewards for good service, the need to govern as a king, the importance of suppressing libertinage and scandal at court, and finally a warning against Mazarin's old enemies, the Jansenists. There may have been other topics, but Louis did not go further in his recording. These were things that Mazarin had already discussed many times, and as an old man with the declining comprehension of his deathbed, he repeated them in almost fossilized language.

Turenne was Louis' most distinguished teacher in the art of war; but a king learns to be a soldier from many sources. As a child Louis drilled with his companions in imitation of the Hundred Swiss; as a boy he learned the manual of arms for the pike and the musket, the use of the lance and the saber from horseback, of the rapier as a weapon for the duel, and of the art of fortification warfare in the play-fortress of the garden of the Palais-Royal. As a youth he joined the royal army and soon learned that the presence of the king gives courage and enthusiasm to soldiers. There were heady thrills that made war attractive, especially to princes brought up in the shadow of the Thirty Years' War. He presented a dashing figure of a man; clad in rich clothing with a gleaming steel breastplate, a velvet cape, and riding a spirited horse, he always could evoke a "Hurrah!" from the troops. Furthermore, since Louis proved to be a hardy campaigner, accepting the discomforts and fatigues of the march without complaint, the soldiers responded by idolizing him. All this well suited the young king. There may be nothing to the idea that his Bourbon blood made him a soldier, but there surely is something to his Bourbon traditions that made him want to be one.

La Grande Mademoiselle was undoubtedly wrong when she wrote that Louis at twenty understood the *métier* of the soldier from the place of the simple infantryman to that of the general commanding in the field, but she knew whereof she spoke when she wrote, "He shows the greatest passion for war, and is in despair when he is prevented from going [to the front] as often as he wishes . . . he has as much courage as anyone could ever have . . . if he had to reconquer his kingdom as Henry IV did, he could do it."[6] He particularly loved the details of campaigning; Mazarin wrote to the queen, "The *Confident* is indefatigable; he goes the entire day with the army, and on arriving here [at camp] he makes a tour of the advance guards' posts . . . he has just returned . . . not worn out by fifteen hours on horseback . . . those about him cannot sustain such fatigue." This was long to be the story—Louis' unconcern for fatigue, inclement weather, and all external circumstances was not always shared enthusiastically by those about him.

The troops taught him how important it was for the king to be a soldier; his presence might not guarantee victory, but it did ensure high morale. As Mazarin wrote once when Anne wanted her son in Paris with her, "I had planned to have the *Confident* visit you . . . but I have changed my mind; that voyage would have a bad effect on the troops, and give courage to the enemy. . . ." In a letter to Lionne he wrote, "One cannot tell with what joy and applause the troops received his Majesty. . . ." In this era before the ideas of nationalism and fatherland provided rallying cries, the person of the king could often produce a similar effect. Men were royalist; they loved the king blindly, especially when he was a handsome, energetic, daring boy of fifteen to twenty. For the young king, war was exciting and fun, as well as a political necessity; it is small wonder that Louis found the first years of his personal reign a little dull; Europe was calm, and there was no need to put himself at the head of his soldiers. War to the young Louis was the sport of kings; only the old Louis, beset by illness and age, would realize that war could also mean disorder, disaster, defeat.

Naturally the business of war in the seventeenth century was something more than loud hurrahs from the soldiers and a camping trip in the country air. It entailed the administration of the army, the organization of maneuvers, the planning of a campaign, and the command in battle; these were an important part of the *métier* of the king. He had Turenne for his preceptor. Turenne was one the last of the old-style marshals: a member of a great family of counts and peers, sovereign lords in their own names. Turenne was a Huguenot, and began his career with the king as a hostage for the good behavior of his brother, the Duke of Bouillon. Like great noblemen of earlier times, he rallied to the support of the king on his own terms. He had not hesitated to be on the other side during the early days of the *Fronde,* but once returned to the royal armies, he soon assumed the role played by the constables in the past. Louis was not the only one of Turenne's "cadets"; the many young men who learned war at his side commanded the soldiers of French and enemy armies during the later wars of Louis XIV. Turenne was famous as the master of maneuvers by which the army always assumed defensive stands, forcing the opponent to withdraw or attack a fortified position or camp. Marlborough must have been on hand when Turenne explained that "in the end, the army must fight," for "handsome Jack" became the "terrible Marlbruk," the master of the field battle in which a province, a kingdom, indeed an entire war could be won—or lost—in an afternoon. Louis, on the other hand, seems to have been on hand when Turenne explained the necessity for caution. One must wonder what would have been Louis' career if Condé rather than Turenne had been his teacher. Condé was the dashing leader who taught that you must "fear the enemy when he is at a distance, but despise him when he is in front of you." He knew how to seize the moment for attack, how to take in a battlefield at a glance, how to give the order for an impetuous charge. Could Condé have overcome Louis' natural caution? We shall never know.

Louis had an avid interest in the administrative details of command. Seventeenth-century armies moved slowly—from two to five miles a day unless there was urgent need for hurry, and then eight to ten miles was a very long march for a day. The reasons for this slowness are easy to find. The roads were poor in quality, inadequate in number, and, often enough, part of the army had to march over·fields where no road existed. Another important reason was the fact that the army had first to take down and pack its camping equipment and then reassemble it at the new location; this was a slow process, for some of the wealthier officers had elaborate tents and baggage. And lastly, the army could not camp just anywhere; every campsite had to be a fortified position. This meant that a ridge long enough to accommodate the army and near enough to water for men and horses had to be found for each change. Anyone following the marches of one of these armies in Belgium today is immediately struck by the fact that armies camped on the same sites time after time, in war after war.

To move from one camp to the next required an enormous amount of paper work. Depending upon its size, the army would march in one to five columns, each with its baggage, its scouts, its predefined route. Each regiment had specific tasks at the old and again at the new campsite. Here was a problem of administration and control that very early became a passion of the king. Louis liked to make up the orders of the day, replete with secret passwords and trumpet fanfares; he liked to superintend the details of the march, as well as of the fortification of the new site. In warfare largely made up of maneuvers and sieges, these details became important elements of command. In the mid-seventeenth century, two field armies could maneuver within forty miles of each other all summer without contact except for clashes of scouting parties.

Another of Louis' avid interests was strict discipline. Whether it was the counsel of Turenne, of Mazarin, of Le Tellier, or simply the facts of warfare in the years following the *Fronde* that taught Louis the necessity of greater control over his soldiers, we cannot say. There were two important facets to this idea: the first, that the king must have a disciplined army, strong enough to prevent future *Frondes*; the second, that this army must not be a danger to the king's peaceful subjects. The undisciplined forces that had learned the art of war and pillage in Germany proved that an army was dangerous to the people who lived in its line of march. When Louis took over the government of his kingdom himself, no small part of his correspondence was concerned with the problems of the discipline of troops. In his advice to his son, Louis becomes eloquent over the need for discipline, training, and especially for royal supervision over the details of military organization and personnel. Writing in 1666, before his personal government had embarked upon a serious military enterprise, Louis explained to his son the importance of exercising, drilling, and reviewing the troops, of reforms in the army organization, and of the application that a king must himself give to the administration of the army. It was probably Turenne, the soldier, and Le Tellier, the war secretary, who taught the young king this lesson of military administration that was so congenial to his personality.

It would be a mistake to believe that Louis learned nothing about his profession as king after the death of Mazarin. As we shall see, Colbert, Le Tellier, Lionne, Vauban, and perhaps others continued to assist him and to explain the art of governing the kingdom. On the other hand, Louis at twenty-three, like other men of that age, had formed a relatively stable personality, with predictable attitudes.

8

THE YOUNG KING:
FAMILY AND COURT

WE KNOW that a man's character is made by things other than the formal schooling that he receives, but how are we ever to unravel the totality of significant experiences that somehow become important in the development of a personality? We may surely believe that Louis learned much more than he was explicitly taught, but what were the "meaningful experiences"? We have a description of "the King's day" written by Dubois, a gentleman servant attached to the royal household, about the time that Louis was approaching thirteen. Are these important events?

The King takes pleasure in walks that he makes to the house outside of Paris, in his little hunting parties, in the fortress in the garden of the Palais-Royal where he conducts the company of princes and seigneurs in sieges, defenses, sorties, and military exercises.

· · ·

May 2, 1651: The King danced a ballet before a great crowd. He amuses himself by dancing and watching others dance. . . .

He usually takes his meals with his mother . . . or Marshal Villeroi. . . .

· · ·

He studies in the morning after saying his prayers . . . then he takes dancing lessons, does exercises of arms [he learned the manual of the pike as well as of the musket and sword], breaks a lance [from horseback], then takes his lunch usually with his ten violins playing very prettily so that there are often several people who come to see him eat. He then goes back to his studies until the Queen awakens [he visited her several times each day].

· · ·

His studies [include] the *Commentaries* of Caesar in Latin, which he translates into French. . . . He writes, reads the history of France, studies Italian, maps, and mathematics. . . .

· · ·

June 19, 1651: Madame de Lansac read the letters of Catherine de Médicis written for the education of her son, Henry III. . . . Louis listened attentively. [There was considerable reading aloud in the court—both of letters and of memoirs, etc., that could bear on contemporary problems.]

· · ·

He showed Chancellor Séguier his translation of Caesar; the Chancellor urged him to continue, pointing out that it was an advantage for a king to combine letters with arms. . . .[1]

In these activities we see a growing boy with a normal and healthy interest in a wide variety of activities, but we do not see any indication of the Sun King that was to be in the future.

We get a little more understanding of the young king's progress if we follow the royal family in its travels. Here Louis saw the magic effects of the king's person. The court passed through Normandy in 1649; Father Paulin wrote to Father Piccolomini in Rome:

> All passed well here . . . it is a grace to see the King . . . in France that is the most important and the most sought-after grace . . . such is the majesty of our Prince, in spite of his dozen years, such is his bounty and the ease of his humor, joined to the gracefulness of his body and the sweetness of his appearance that I know no philtre more powerful for the enchantment of men's hearts. All Normandy could not see enough of him . . . everyone says that if the Queen should wish to conquer all the kingdoms of the world, she has only to make a tour with the King, saving just enough time to show him [to the people].

It was almost the same everywhere the young king traveled in the provinces, and he could not have missed the fact that this gave his mother's government advantages over the malcontent *Frondeurs* who opposed her. When the *Fronde* was over, there were periods when the court stayed in Paris, but the royal family never really trusted the city again. From the time of the barricades of 1648 until the storming of the Bastille in 1789, the Bourbon rulers preferred to live elsewhere. While they were in Paris, the king and queen mother usually lived at the Palais-Royal, with Philippe staying at the Tuileries, which was empty since La Grande Mademoiselle was in exile; the Luxembourg Palace, now empty because Gaston usually stayed at Blois, was occasionally occupied by the Queen of England or the Queen of Sweden, both of whom often followed the court. The Louvre seems to have been used only for receptions, theatricals, and parties that could be held in the stately rooms built by Henry IV and Marie de Médicis a half century earlier.

When not in Paris, the court retained its traditional peripatetic customs, visiting Saint-Germain, Vincennes, Fontainebleau, Saint-Cloud, Compiègne, or Versailles. The royal châteaus in the Loire basin were largely unused. During these years most of the available money went into the war, and so except for Vincennes, none of these royal palaces received any considerable attention in the form of new construction or decoration. Mazarin wanted to build a royal residence at Vincennes inside the great walls of the old fortifications; it was close enough to Paris to keep the city under surveillance, and yet strong enough to hold off any attack by the Parisian mobs or militia. The two handsome pavilions that still grace the fortification were completed in these years, but this example seems to have had no effect upon Louis, for when he came to build his great château, he relied upon his army for protection and built out at Versailles—with no great walls around it—proving both his wealth and his military power. In later life Louis used the château at Vincennes only as a base for hunting parties in the magnificent forest beyond the fortifications.

Perhaps we can find the development of the king in the complexities of his court in the first decade of his majority. It was a motley crowd of soldiers, administrators, ladies, and gentlemen attached to the households of the king, his mother, and his brother, and the usual crowds of servants, scribes, clerks, aids, huntsmen, guards, and others whose presence in the council chambers, in the palace, the gardens, and the stables made life at court both simple and complicated. With the Prince of Condé in rebellion, the Duke of Orléans in self-imposed exile, and La Grande Mademoiselle ordered to stay at Saint-Fargeau, there were none of the king's immediate family at court except the Prince of Conti, who had made his peace with Mazarin when he married one of the cardinal's nieces; Conti, however, almost immediately became a "dévot," giving up everything for his religious devotions so that his young wife complained that she had to live like a "woman of fifty." The inner circle of the court was made up of the queen mother, Philippe, the cardinal and his little family of nieces, and the Queens of England and Sweden (when they were in France). Of this group, the real inner circle was composed of Anne, Louis, and Mazarin.

As we have seen, the relationships among the queen mother, the cardinal, and the young king were undoubtedly of great importance in the development of Louis' character, but these things were difficult to ferret out and even more difficult to assess. Mazarin's part in this triad was certainly grounded in the first instance in his relationship with Anne. When Mazarin was away from her, Anne's letters were filled with the despondency created by his absence, with expressions of affection, protests that his affection was less than hers, even assertions that she could not stand his being away from her. She ended these letters by scrawling the code symbol for her love of Mazarin all over the bottom of the page as a teen-age girl might mark x's on a love letter to her boyfriend. Anne's writing and spelling were so bad that one wonders how Mazarin ever made out what she had to tell him.[2] These letters are important to the historian, for even if we had none of Mazarin's letters, it would be hard to read Anne's without concluding that she was Mazarin's wife.

Mazarin, for his part, was both more articulate and more literary than the queen. Some of his letters were gallant, some a bit drippy in sentiment, some very clever. "I will close by assuring you," he wrote, "that the sea [code for Mazarin] is not calm nor the sky [also code for Mazarin] serene, and that the Sarafin [code for Anne] is the cause, but 26 [Mazarin] will always be faithful, zealous, and passionate in his service of [code sign for Mazarin's love of Anne]." Another time: "I tell you . . . that I have no other joy in the world than to be received by the *Confident* [Louis] and the *Confidente* [Anne] [triple sign of his love]." Again: "I am unable to stop without saying something to you in favor of the sea [Mazarin] whom I recommend to you with all my heart. . . . [sign for Mazarin's love] is more than ever before" and it "gives me complete belief in [sign for Anne's love]." On another occasion when he was badly crippled with gout he wrote, "I hide as well as I can from my gout the knowledge that you are coming . . . for if it knew this, it would stubbornly refuse to leave me because then it could pride itself that no other gout ever had such happiness." This is not an ungraceful gesture for a sick man two years before his death. Skeptics have dismissed these letters as the mere flattery of a courtier, but the sentiments expressed in them could well have been the strong motive in Mazarin's devotion to the house of Bourbon. Surely anyone who sees Anne joining the sick cardinal on the Paris balcony to watch the triumphal procession when Louis brought his bride into the city for the first time must recognize that strong ties existed between these two, and these ties surely affected Louis.[3]

Anne's daughter-in-law, the gossipy Elizabeth-Charlotte who became Philippe's second wife, many years later wrote that the "Queen Mother, widow of Louis XIII, did much worse than love Mazarin; she married him. He was not a priest and there were no orders to prevent the marriage." Proponents of the marriage theory set the date as sometime in 1647. There is much circumstantial evidence to support the marriage (but not necessarily the date) thesis—not least that it is inconceivable that Anne would have lived in disorder, and that Louis XIV many years later made a secret morganatic marriage with Madame de Maintenon. On the other hand, some scholars have doubted that a daughter of the Spanish Hapsburgs could have married beneath her, and point out triumphantly that not a single shred of contemporary evidence either in France or in Rome conclusively supports the idea of marriage.[4]

One thing that we can be sure of is that Louis was privy to the relationship between his mother and Mazarin. During the last decade of the cardinal's life, Louis and Mazarin lived on terms of easy familiarity. They traveled together while following the course of the war or simply visiting the provinces. Whenever they were separated from Anne, a steady stream of letters in both directions kept the three united. Louis and Mazarin shared most of the queen's letters, and Anne was willing to accept a letter from one of them as "her letter" for the day; on some days, however, she would receive as many as four. There is much charm in the picture that emerges from Mazarin's letters: "The *Confident* never fails to embrace me every evening." Or again: "The *Confident* was never better. He is continuously in my chambers, and I leave you to know that I have good company." Anne often worried about her son's health. Mazarin would write, "The King is well . . . his health is excellent . . . he is as safe as if he were in the Louvre." In another: ". . . he had seen with great pleasure the letters that you were pleased to send me, and I have not failed to point out to him . . . your solid and tender love [for him]. . . . I must tell you that his appreciation [of your love] . . . is as great as anyone could hope for. . . ." On one occasion Louis said to his mother, "I have seen the letter you wrote and I am delighted with the tenderness you have for me. I beg you to believe that I will have it for you until death." Sometimes Anne protested that she was neglected, and Mazarin would have to assure her that he was very busy, and simply did not have more time to write.[5]

His letters show great pride in the accomplishments of the *Confident*. He tells Anne about Louis' being received by the troops, about his gallant behavior at the front, about his physical vigor, which was as phenomenal during this period as it was later in his life. If Mazarin showed fatherly pride, he also had fatherly concern. Anyone who has raised a son knows that the boy must try to find himself—find his ego, separate from the adults who frame his life. This leads to conflicts. "He won't listen to me . . . ," Mazarin complains. "Nothing that I say has any effect on him. . . ." Sometimes Anne's help was needed in handling her son. But by and large, Louis did "listen" to the cardinal, and the remarkable series of letters that Mazarin sent him during the Mancini crisis (see next chapter) is most compelling evidence of the frank, often brutally frank, exchange that could exist between these two men.

Mazarin was the only man in the court with the courage and authority to speak up candidly to the young king. His power and position, firmly grounded in the affection of both the queen mother and the king, could not be jeopardized by crossing the monarch's will. We have seen that he supervised the young companions of the king, even dismissing some. Mazarin watched his reading, reprimanded him for unseemly behavior, praised him when he merited it. Mazarin was never more the "father" than when he would say to Louis, "You can be a great king if. . . ." The "if" was attention to details, careful reading of dispatches, writing of reports (in which Mazarin says that Louis excelled, but none of these early papers seems to have survived), recognition of obligations to God and self, that is, to one's *gloire*. Mazarin's letters show that he believed in this talented boy who would make a "great king and a good man."[6]

Louis' love for his mother was even greater than his love for Mazarin. Unlike some young men who turn against their mothers and resent them for the rest of their lives, Louis always spoke of Anne with affection and honored her memory.

> I cannot tell you [he wrote for his son], of my distress [at her death] . . . or explain to you the merits of this Queen . . . it is enough to tell you that, knowing better than anyone the vigor with which this Princess sustained my Crown at a time when I could not act for myself . . . [this] to me is a mark of her affection and virtue. The respect that I had for her was not a simple duty . . . the custom that I had of keeping only one household and only one table with her . . . [of seeing] her several times a day in spite of the pressure of my affairs, was not a law . . . but a mark of the pleasure that I had in her company. . . .

This seems to sum up his attitude. Anne and Mazarin had saved his kingdom, and he knew that they had; they also loved him and gave him every reason to love them. This made the queen mother's personal influence very important. Like Mazarin, she had a vision of Louis' *gloire* as the fulfillment of his potentialities as a man, of his obligations to God and to himself. We do not know how she transmitted these values, but her attitudes, her point of view, her "words for good and evil" correlate so well with those of her son that we have the right to infer the close relationship between them. Anne had the exaggerated sense of majesty, insistence upon formal dignity, upon etiquette more Spanish-Hapsburg than Bourbon. She also had the belief that her grandfather Philip II was right—and so like Mazarin —in his insistence that a king must labor to fulfill his profession, his duty to God and man. She also had that urge for revenge on those who caused her to be afraid; her religious values bordered upon superstition, with hell's fire threatening kings more than other men because God had entrusted more to them. For all her little vices and personal softness, Anne of Austria was a strong woman who had stood up to the redoubtable Richelieu, to her husband Louis XIII, to her critics, and to the *Frondeurs,* both bourgeois and noble; she knew how to hate with intensity, and she also knew how to forgive when it was expedient to do so.

What is it that makes a personality; how is the so-called superego formed in a man? All accounts of the king tell us of his self-assurance, of his "adequacy" to situations, of his poise and emotional stability. Where did he get the vision of himself, the ego-identity that both allowed and forced him to play out the role of king as a grand *métier,* as an actor on the stage of history? Personality theorists are more or less agreed that the relationship between a growing personality and the adults that he loves, respects, and admires is a primary factor in the formation of values, attitudes, and character traits. If this be true, then Louis' life with his mother and Cardinal Mazarin must have been of great importance in the development of the man and the king. One thing is certain: Louis grew to manhood in an atmosphere in which he could be sure of the affection of those closest to him; an atmosphere that allowed a young man to mature free from some of the worst stresses that beset an adolescent. He had nightmares during these years, but war and politics rather than rejection probably were responsible. This assurance about the positive feelings of others has its advantages. Many historians have commented upon the poise and serenity of the king when, as an old man, he was stricken by tragedy in his family, defeat in war, and illness in his person. It may well be that his strength of character, as well as his vision of himself that allowed him to play so well the part of Job, were firmly grounded in his relationships with his mother and the cardinal.

His other near relatives seem to have had little or no influence upon his development during these years. The Prince of Condé's treason perhaps left a scar that never completely disappeared, but there was one amusing incident that must have given Louis considerable satisfaction. At one point in the war the Spanish army captured a number of French banners carrying the device of the fleur-de-lis. Condé, perhaps feeling guilty when he saw his own coat of arms on the captured flags, sent the standards back to Louis with his compliments. The young king immediately returned them with a note that Spanish soldiers capture so few French flags that it would be unjust to deprive them of those they actually did win. The prince was not discussed much; in the secret code used by the family his name changed from Valiant to Uncertain, to Credulous, and finally to Embarrassed. In his *Mémoires,* however, Louis leaves no doubt about the fears that Condé aroused; at one time he believed that there was danger that the kingdom would be divided between Condé and himself.

His uncle the Duke of Orléans seems to have aroused no comparable antagonism. When Paris opened its gates to the king in 1652, we have seen that the duke retired to his estates at Blois after signing a "reconciliation" with his nephew. In the years that followed, Louis wrote to him a number of times on the occasions of political or military victories. In several of these letters he thanked his uncle for "signs of appreciation and pleasure" over royal victories (Gaston must have written first, but his letters are lost); in other letters Louis announced royal "triumphs" that "undoubtedly will interest" Uncle Gaston, since he is concerned "for the prosperity of my state." Others requested that the duke order the churches of his apanage to give thanksgiving to God for royal victories. The manuscript copies of these letters do not tell us whether they were actually written in the king's own hand or by a secretary. Louis never took Gaston very seriously. The family code names for the Duke of Orléans were War, Farce, and Rome.[7]

In one of his letters to Louis, Mazarin exclaims, "It is up to you to become the most glorious king that has ever been. God has given you all the necessary talents, and nothing remains but to put them to use; this you can easily do . . . acquiring by the application which you give to public affairs . . . the necessary experience, and still it is not necessary that this will prevent you from enjoying yourself . . . for by employing a little time to resolve those things that must be done . . . you will still be free for those things that please you." This would seem to indicate that Mazarin accepted the proverb about "all work and no play. . . ." There was no reason to fear that the court would not provide amusement. Mid-seventeenth-century men loved their horses, their dogs; they practiced all sorts of martial games, from fencing to riding with a lance at a ring; they enjoyed the gaming tables, dances, theaters, and spectacles. Indeed, there was so much of this sort of activity at the court that one gets the impression that these people were driven in a frantic search for pleasure to escape the essential boredom of their lives. Most of the people around the court had no significant work to do; the cardinal and his trusted friends and secretaries ran the king's government without consulting the hangers-on; the army was becoming increasingly a professional force that would welcome recruits, but had no use for fair-weather warriors. The people who held assignments in one or another of the royal households did not actually have much work to do, and they, along with the seekers for place and favor, the visitors, the curious, wanted to be entertained. Some critics have blamed Mazarin for not seeing that Louis read the classics. Such talk ignores the structure of the court, which must have had a tremendous appeal to a teen-aged boy.

Dubois has given us another example of "the King's day" when Louis was about seventeen; his activities have changed somewhat since he was twelve:

> As soon as he awakes, he recites the office of the Holy Spirit and his rosary; that being done, his preceptor enters for a study period . . . reading from Holy Scripture or the history of France. After that he gets out of bed and we [four members of the household] enter . . . he then sits on the "cut-out chair" in the alcove of the chamber . . . he then enters the grand chamber where usually there are princes and great lords who attend his *lever*. He is clothed in a dressing gown and goes before them speaking familiarly first to one then to another . . . which enchants them. After he has eaten his first breakfast, he washes his hands, mouth, and face . . . takes off the cap that had been tied about his head because of his hair . . . he then prays to God in the passageway behind his bed, accompanied by his chaplains while everyone is on their knees, and if anyone dares to talk or make any noise a *huissier* removes him. The prayer of the King finished, he brushes his hair, puts on his suit, stockings of serge . . . and goes out to the large chamber behind his anti-chamber where he does his exercises: he jumps to and fro with remarkable agility; then he rides his horse at full caper . . . and drills with the pike. After this he returns to the chamber where he dances (under the direction of Maître Beauchamp). . . . He next goes back to his grand chamber where he changes clothes. . . . Leaving the chamber each morning, he makes the sign of the Cross, and then goes up to the Cardinal's rooms . . . where a secretary of state makes his reports on the most secret affairs of the Kíng—requiring a half hour to an hour and a half. After that the King goes to greet the Queen [probably between eleven and twelve, for Anne was a late riser] . . . and then goes to hear mass. After mass he returns to his rooms, changes clothes, either to go on a hunt or to remain in the palace. If it is to be a hunt, he wears an ordinary hunting costume; if he stays, it is a modest one . . . his body is so well-built that one cannot say more about it. After dressing he goes to dine, often with the Queen; sometimes after dinner there is an audience with ambassadors to whom he listens attentively. . . . In truth, he has a charm that makes it an honor to be near him and that merits that a Queen of Sheba should come to see and hear what God has seen fit to put in this vessel of election.

Dubois goes on to tell us that after dinner there were often innocent pleasures with the queen mother and other intimates: reading, conversation, gambling, and the like. Late at night supper was served, and after that everyone went to bed. The other memoirists of the period largely confirm this picture of a day in which the king divided his time between study, exercise, hunting, and pleasure of one kind or another—and between the cardinal, his mother, and his religious duties. There is no evidence that Louis indulged voluntarily in reading or even in the "literary games" that amused his cousin La Grande Mademoiselle during her exile, or that the court ever fell into the traps and follies of the fashionable salons ridiculed by Molière. There was no place for a *précieuse* in Anne's company; she probably spoke Italian or Spanish to her son as often as she spoke in French, and with better accent. In addition to these pictures there are others of a sort of "family life" in which the cardinal's nieces, the Queens of France, England, and Sweden, Louis, his brother, the young English princes and princesses, and a few favored noblemen make up an inner circle.

Let us look at the month of January 1655, when Louis was going on seventeen. Here we see a troupe of young people finding their pleasure in group activity that would amuse any high-school senior. On the sixth there was a supper at Cardinal Mazarin's palace, after which Louis danced a ballet. On the seventh Philippe had a party at the Tuileries: a ball, a comedy, and a buffet late in the evening. On the eleventh everyone went on a big hunt out at the forest of Vincennes, and on the fourteenth there was a performance of the Italian comedy troupe at the Louvre; on the sixteenth a hunt for upland game birds (with fowling pieces) on the plain of Grenelle, and the next day another ball at the Tuilleries at which Louis danced with the Duchess de Mercoeur, one of Mazarin's nieces who had earlier attracted his attention. On the twenty-sixth some young men with Louis at their head dressed in masquerade and marched off to the lodge of the Palais-Royal to serenade the Princess of England, and then invaded the house of Chancellor Séguier (presumably for food), who several days later presented the whole group with a theatrical party and a magnificent buffet. At the end of the month there was a party at the hotel of the Duke of Créqui with a dance and a ballet in which Louis played the part of a shepherd.

January in Paris was a busy social month; war was on winter vacation and the social calendar could occupy the energy of the court. But throughout the year there were events to relieve the tedium of life. When evenings were not spent with dance or theatricals, there was always the gaming table: *reversi, lansquenet, trente et quarante,* and *grande et petite prime* were the current favorites.[8] Anne was an inveterate gambler; Mazarin even more so. He is supposed to have introduced the Italian game *hoca,* an ancestor of roulette, that was later to make many men who played with Marie-Thérèse very rich, for she could not resist taking the ultimate chance. At the gaming tables rank dropped aside for the moment, and those who could not otherwise sit in the presence of the king had that right when they were risking their money. There is one pointed story about Louis' gambling: One evening he won a large sum from the Chevalier de Rohan, who tried to pay the debt in Spanish pistols. When Louis refused to accept the coin of his enemy, de Rohan threw the pistols out of the window as "useless."

Louis complained to Mazarin about de Rohan's behavior, but the cardinal rebuked him: "Sire, the Chevalier de Rohan acted like the king, and you, like the Chevalier de Rohan!"

At the parties given for the royal family, Louis learned more than how to dance and play. There is a story about a ball given in 1655 when the king wanted to dance only with girls his own age, and particularly with one of Mazarin's nieces. Little Henriette, his English cousin, was only eleven years old, and somewhat skinny for her age (Louis called her "the bones of the holy innocents"); she was a wallflower without anyone to dance with her. Anne suggested several times to Louis that he should dance with his cousin, and finally got up, brusquely separated him from the Duchess de Mercoeur, and ordered him to dance with Henriette. After the party there was a scene between the mother and son; Louis insisted, like a normal seventeen-year-old, that he "didn't like little girls," but his mother demanded that a king be polite and considerate to everyone. This was only one of Anne's many lessons that perhaps were to make Louis' behavior the model of politeness and gallantry.

Anne's Spanish upbringing in a court where Lope de Vega had provided exciting entertainment gave her a lifelong interest in the stage. Before the *Fronde,* both the French theater and the Italian pantomime theater that Mazarin imported to please her, gave frequent productions for the court. Corneille's *Le Cid,* in particular, was played time and again, presenting a conception of *gloire* and a pattern of honor that could have been influential in the life of the boy-king. When the *Fronde* was over, the theater again assumed a prominent place in the festive activities of the court. Many of the plays of this era were short pieces that could be finished in an hour, and therefore easily combined in an evening with a dance and a late supper. It was in these years that Molière emerged as a royal favorite. His pointed social criticism and his humor satisfied the taste of the day. Molière has left us eloquent testimony of his admiration and love for the king who applauded his performances and loaded him with favors and wealth—at a time when some critics were heavily attacking the tart playwright. During the last decades of Molière's life, as is testified by the *Impromptu de Versailles* and other pieces, his company, with himself as the lead actor, played before the court with great success. The drama was an easy way for a king to absorb literary culture.

We do not need the *Gazette* or Mazarin's letters to assure us that Louis enjoyed "perfect health" during these years; all his pictures show him to be a fine-looking young man, bursting with energy. His Italian riding instructor Arnolfini must have been pleased to see him handle a spirited horse, ride at the ring with a lance, or course wildly through the woods after a stag or a wolf. He could shoot from the saddle and put a horse through paces resembling a figure dance. This latter type of "horse show" was a popular form of entertainment; in its most elaborate form the riders dressed as Turks, Iroquois, Russians, Romans, or some exotic tribe, and showed off their mounts in complex maneuvers, each ending with a tableau. To do it properly required both practice and good horsemanship. Louis may not have been as good as the flatterers around him said, but he must have done very well.

This was the period when fencing and dancing required the same skills. The classical ballet emerged in the seventeenth century as a form of indoor activity in which amateurs as well as professionals could participate. The basic stance for the ballet and for the fencer was the same, so the two forms of activity could be studied together. Louis from age ten to thirty enjoyed participating in the ballet very much. With great gusto he took the part of the "shepherd of his people," of "Apollo, the Sun God," of "Spring," or of some other mythological character. He and the young men around him worked off their energy, much as young men of other periods of history, by doing the things that were "smart," or popular, or just fun; one should expect a healthy young king to assume that his status might entitle him to a stellar role in the group play of his day.

Of all the sports, Louis loved the chase best. In this he was a true Bourbon; it was fun to ride after the stag, the wolf, the wild boar, with spear or sword in hand and a pack of dogs leading the way. These were colorful, exciting events: the horns of the huntsmen, the baying of the hounds, the rush of the horses, and the final melee when the quarry was brought to bay or pulled down. These were scenes that the artists loved to paint or to weave into tapestries, that the story-tellers loved to recount. In the forests of Vincennes, Boulogne, Versailles, Saint-Germain, Fontaine-bleau, and Compiègne, game was plentiful and the scenery beautiful; Louis probably would have preferred them to Paris even had there been no *Fronde*.[9]

The other form of hunting that was popular in the mid-seventeenth century was the shooting of upland game birds and rabbits with a fowling piece. The plains and hills around Paris abounded in game during this period when the people did not have the weapons or the right to hunt; stories of the funeral processions from Saint-Germain to Saint-Denis tell of the soldiers popping off at birds and rabbits all along the route. The royal hunting party had the proper weapons for killing birds on the wing and rabbits on the run, and never had to lack for something to shoot. Louis learned to handle a gun by the time he was ten, and much of his life he easily passed as a crack shot. This was not as much fun as following the deer or the wolf, but it did provide an amusing change.

In these same years he had his first sensual contacts with women. A vigorous boy (with the blood of a Charles V and a Henry IV in his veins), he could be expected to find the opposite sex interesting. As Voltaire remarked, Louis liked women, and it was reciprocal. By the time he was fourteen, his attractiveness was already evident to the doggerel poets of the court:

> Who does not admire the youth
> Of a King more handsome than the day?
> When he sings and dances
> The women sigh at the sight of him
> And each blushingly admits
> That it is well that he is not mature.

Perhaps he was more "mature" than the poet knew. Indeed, the first account of his "gallantry" came when he was going on twelve. "The King gave a ballet . . . his promenades outside the city are no longer so frequent," writes an anonymous informant to Mazarin, "and rumor has it that he gives himself to gallantry . . . a thing not to be desired . . . yet all begin to notice that he is at great effort to please a young beauty . . . recently come to Court . . . the sister of Madame de Novailles. . . ."[10] Nothing much could come of the "affair" of an eleven-year-old, and in the years that immediately followed, horses and dogs seem to have been more interesting to Louis than the coquettish Martinozzi, Mancini, and other girls who were everyday companions in the innocent activities of the court.

But when he was sixteen he appears to have been abruptly introduced to sex. There are several more or less untrustworthy accounts of the circumstances, but there seems little doubt that Madame de Beauvais—one of Anne's women, whom she called the "one-eyed one"—waylaid the boy-king, fell into his arms while scantily dressed, and forthwith gave him his first experience with female flesh. The lady was in her late twenties and something less than a ravishing beauty, but Louis apparently was grateful, for all her life she lived at court on a pension and was treated by the king as "a privileged person with much consideration."

La Beauvais was only the first of the conquests of our "Don Juan." However, it would not have been easy for a handsome young king to remain chaste in any court of Europe in the seventeenth century: women had a way of seeing relations with the king as a route to fortune. There was a little gardener whose child married an obscure nobleman, and there may have been several other girls before a daughter of an *avocat* of the Parlement refused to meet the king alone. One of these girls gave the king a case of gonorrhea that caused his doctors to worry about loss of fertility.

Affairs with women of high rank were not so easy to manage: Anne and Mazarin combined to break up an affair with Mademoiselle de la Motte-Argencourt, whose mother apparently threw her at Louis; the girl herself was not too bright, for she also gave her favors easily to other young swains. In the end Louis did not object when she was "rewarded" by imprisonment in a convent. One of Mazarin's nieces, Olympe, inspired such intense "puppy love" that the Queen of Sweden thought that they should marry, but Mazarin saw to it that Olympe became a duchess instead. The cardinal is said to have rebuked Louis by telling him that his niece wanted a man, not a boy who trembled when he touched her. None of these girls seems to have become a grand passion; it was to be reserved for Marie Mancini to inspire him with his first real love.

9

THE MANCINI CRISIS

IN THE SEVENTEENTH CENTURY, disease visited the palace, the convent, and the peasant's hut with equal severity, and often brought the careers of men to a sudden end. In the summer of 1658 Louis, who had been the very picture of health, came up to death's door in a serious illness; his career as soldier, statesman, father of his country, and playboy almost came to an end before it was properly launched.

After the fall of Dunkirk, the king and cardinal were with the army at an encampment near Mardyck. The weather was particularly hot and the air heavy with the odor of half-buried men and horses. Who knows what caused his illness or why Louis, of the whole company around him, was the one to be susceptible? On the last day of June the young king complained of a headache and went to bed; the next day he had a high fever; by the third of July it was evident that he was in great peril; from the fifth to the tenth of July, death seemed about to win the battle; on the eleventh the fever began to break, and by the thirteenth the king was out of danger. It was probably typhoid fever. We can follow the course of the disease in Mazarin's troubled letters.[1] To Turenne: "The King was bled last night . . . the doctor [Valot] assures me that there is not the shadow of danger." To Lockhart: "I would hope that God does not wish to punish this kingdom by taking from us the one who brings joy . . . the father of the country." To another: "It is not only the King my master who is dangerously ill, but . . . the best friend that I have in the world." On the sixth Louis took communion and preparations were made for extreme unction. Mazarin wrote to Colbert that the king's piety and devotion edified everyone, and that Louis, realizing his danger, said to him, "You are a man of resolution and the best friend that I have; therefore, alert me when I am near to death, for the Queen would not dare to do it for fear of augmenting the illness." By the thirteenth Mazarin knew that the king would live. He wrote to Turenne: "I rejoice anew with you over the grace that God has given us in conserving the King." Toward the end of July, when Louis could travel,

Anne took him to Compiègne for rest and recuperation; everyone knew that the air at Compiègne was better than anywhere else.

Six doctors had attended the young king. They knew that he had a high fever; they also finally admitted that he was in dire danger. Their remedies? They bled him, they gave him enemas, they fed him physic, a "tisane tea" that "sent him to the pot fourteen to fifteen times in a day," and emetics to clear out his stomach. Valot wrote, "This evacuation continued for nine days with the same force, and was so advantageous that it achieved a cure of his Majesty without any accident and without relapse . . . one could say with truth that God directed the cure by methods so extraordinary, and by assistance and grace so particular . . . that it ought to be credited as a miracle rather than to the industry and experience of the physicians." In this *Journal of the Health of the King*[2] it was always the same story: God worked through the skillful physicians to battle for the King's life; in the end, with the aid of God, the physicians always won and stood by to collect their reward. But when we read of their remedies, we wonder if Mazarin did not make a mistake in urging them to cure the king with the same methods that they would use for any other person; he was afraid that the physicians might shrink from using their violent, but "sure," cures on his majesty. It should be noted that not all the medical advice of the period agreed with Valot's methods: Dr. Patin, professor of medicine at Paris, took a dim view of the royal physicians who held their office in near-hereditary trust. "The King," he wrote, "was saved by his innocence, his age, his strong and robust constitution, *nine good bleedings,* and the prayers of good people like us . . . [author's italics]." Patin, an ex-*Frondeur,* was not welcome at court; his judgment may have been correct—that Louis got well in spite of the medical attention of his physicians.

Louis and his subjects alike believed, as did both Valot and Patin, that God's grace had much to do with the cure. While the king struggled for his life, there were public prayers in churches all over France, and religious processions in Paris and other cathedral cities. When the crisis passed, *Te Deums* of thanksgiving replaced the prayers of supplication. This was the pattern of the French monarchy under Louis XIV: it assailed Heaven with pleas for God's favor; and it never forgot the *Te Deums* when thanksgiving was in order.

During the critical days, many courtiers naturally turned their eyes to Philippe, the younger brother and heir. This foppish young man had been brought up to accept Louis' leadership, for Anne did not want her second son to be another Gaston of Orléans rebelling against his brother. His mother encouraged feminine ways, pleasures, behaviors to curb his will to power. When Louis fell ill, Anne refused to allow him to visit his brother's bedside for fear that he might also catch the infection. Madame de Motteville tells us that this brought a flow of tears from Philippe (he was eighteen), for apparently he did love his brother. It is hard to say whether these courtiers who looked expectantly to Philippe would have succeeded in using him for their own ambitions; had he become king, his reign unquestionably would have been different from that of his brother, but it is not clear that he necessarily would have dismissed Mazarin and established the cardinal's enemies in power, for he was subject to his mother's influence perhaps even more than Louis was. Nonetheless, both Anne and Mazarin were greatly disturbed to learn that at the moment their *Confident* was threatened with death, there were men plotting to gain ascendancy over the mind of his successor.

If Louis' bout with fever pointed to anything, it was the fact that he should sire an heir. Philippe may have been a nice boy, but he had not been brought up to be king—quite the contrary. There was only one solution: Louis must marry. For some time he had been old enough to marry; many French princes married at fourteen, and Louis was twenty. But there was a little problem about his marriage. Anne had always assumed that he would marry the Spanish Infanta Marie-Thérèse, who was about his age, and now was the most eligible young woman in Christendom. But her father's kingdom was at war with France. It was awkward to discuss marriage and not peace, and the King of Spain would not agree to peace on French terms. Nonetheless, Philip IV and the girl herself had also always assumed that she would become Queen of France, for Louis also was the most eligible prince in Christendom. It was simply a problem of finding a way.

When Mazarin was negotiating with Cromwell for an English alliance, he had sent Lionne to Madrid on a secret peace mission to see if it were possible to find an alternative to an alliance with a regicide. Lionne tactfully brought up the question of marriage: upon seeing a picture of the Infanta he suggested that peace would be easy if France could have the "original," but when the Spanish, loyal to Condé, insisted upon including that prince in any settlement, nothing came of the negotiations. The growl of cannons, the tramp of cavalry, the thrust of pikemen were still necessary before cupid could strike the royal couple.

By the summer of 1658 the English Alliance, victories on the Channel coast (Battle of the Dunes), and the growing power of Turenne's army had considerably softened the Spanish will to resist. In fact, by the end of the summer Turenne stood ready to drive deep into the Spanish Netherlands, and he was sure that in the campaign of 1659 victory would be complete. Unfortunately it was not so clear to Mazarin. He understood only too well from the Dutch action in making a separate peace with Spain ten years earlier, that they were glad to be friends of the French, but fearful of becoming their immediate neighbors. If Turenne should sweep the Spanish from the Netherlands, he knew that the Dutch might create a new situation to prevent peace. Was there another way to bring the Spanish to a conference table? If Philip IV understood that Louis might marry some princess other than Marie Thérèse, perhaps the Spanish would not wait for Turenne to force the issue. There were other princesses: Louis' cousin, Princess Marguerite of Savoy, who, like Louis and Marie-Thérèse, was a grandchild of Marie de Médicis and Henry IV; another cousin, a younger daughter of Gaston of Orléans (the idea of this match touched off considerable jealousy in the heart of La Grande Mademoiselle, her half-sister); and the Princess of Portugal, whose mother offered Mazarin "great treasures" if he would bring off a marriage. Of the three, Marguerite of Savoy was the most probable choice, even though the Elector of Bavaria had passed her by for her younger sister.

Mazarin ostentatiously opened negotiations with Savoy for a marriage alliance, and made a date to meet the Savoyard court at Lyons in the late fall of 1658 to see if the young people would like each other. There could be no doubt about Madrid's hearing all about it. At first Anne refused to consider going to this meeting, so great was her distaste for the possibility that the marriage might actually occur, and perhaps her conscience was pricked at the hypocrisy. Then upon Louis' urgings she decided to go with the intent, Madame de Motteville assures us, "to work to break the project." Mazarin took most of the court, including his nieces, to the meeting at Lyons; perhaps he, too, felt the need of some other personalities to help control the king.

It was at this point that Louis fell passionately in love, a love that perhaps was the only romantic one he was ever to know, and one that threatened to upset all the plans for peace and power. Louis had been interested in other girls—but he had also been interested in sports, in parties, in war, in God, in politics, in life. Like many a young man of nineteen or twenty, he had liked girls, but they had not dominated his life. But now, just when there was a powder train laid to bring the King of Spain "to his senses," Louis fell in love and threatened to upset the well-made plans for his kingdom, his dynasty, and his *gloire*. The object of this love was Marie Mancini, one of Mazarin's nieces who had for some time been living in easy companionship with the young people who made up the entourage of the king.

According to her own story, Marie had grown up in the shadow of her two more attractive elder sisters and the baneful supervision of super-stitious parents who were convinced that she would bring them ill luck.[3] To prevent this, at seven she had been put in a convent to become a nun, but her parents had to take her back home two years later because of ill health. When Mazarin called the family to France her mother wanted to leave Marie in a convent in Italy, but the little girl somehow persuaded her that if God wished her to be a nun, there were convents in France. The trip to France on a sumptuous Genoese galley and the meeting with her famous uncle did little to sweeten the life of this unloved girl who stood in the shade of her sisters' beauty and her mother's dislike. For a year and a half the three Mancini girls were housed in the Visitation Convent in the Faubourg Saint-Jacques to "be fattened up a little," to learn to speak French, and to "acquire all that culture . . . judged necessary for young women of our rank and age." Sister Marie-Elizabeth, whose brother was first president of the Parlement of Paris, had charge of their education. If the memoirists of the period are correct, Marie did need to be "fattened up a little"; they all speak of her plainness, her lack of color, her skinny figure, and several called her homely. Obviously she was a gawky girl of twelve or thirteen, so unsupported by love or any self-assurance that years later she could not write about her mother or sisters without bitterness. When the girls went to court, the younger son of Marshal Meilleraye proceeded to fall headlong in love with Hortense, the king paid courtly attention to Olympe, and poor Marie, undeveloped physically and very much under her mother's thumb, practically played the part of Cinderella, the girl who had to stay home while others had a good time.

Marie's chance came when her mother fell ill. Madame Mancini had been warned by a seer that she would die in her forty-second year, and to fulfill the prophecy, she fell ill in the later months of 1657, and managed to die just before she reached the age of forty-three. Her mother's death released Marie from surveillance, but more important, her mother's illness brought her into closer contact with the king. For Louis, dutifully at first, and later because he wanted to do so, made daily visits to the bedside of the dying lady. As Marie told the story years later, it was not clear whether the young girl waylaid the king, or vice versa, nor did it matter much.

> . . . his Majesty [she wrote] paid her [Marie's mother] the honor of visiting her every evening, and as he noticed in me much fire, vivacity, and playfulness, he always said something to me in passing; that was a small solace for the evils that my mother made me suffer. . . .

Actually her mother would not allow Marie to be in the bedroom when she had visitors, but Louis somehow managed to talk to the girl after visiting the sick woman. At one point in her illness "mama" almost recovered; then a relapse sent her to the tomb she knew was awaiting her.

Her mother's death changed Marie's life. Hortense, Marianne (her younger sister), and herself were placed under the tolerant guidance of Madame Venelle; Olympe married the Count of Soissons; and her brother Alphonse went to Clermont to school where some time later he was killed in an accident. Marie was very pleased with her new arrangement; the Mancini family began to live in easy familiarity with the rest of the court, and that gave her opportunity to talk more freely with Louis, as well as to show off what she had learned when enforced solitude had driven her to books for comfort. In the evenings she read aloud to the little circle in the queen's chambers—from Corneille, from Italian poets, from the romantic popular literature of the day. She also discovered that "the King was not displeased with me" and somehow let Louis know that she liked him. These things sometimes move very fast; sometimes they take time to mature. Louis was well aware of the fact that he was attractive to the young ladies around him. Why not? He was young, strong, handsome, charming—and the king. He also had enough judgment to know that his being king may have been as important as his personal charm, and his natural caution made him move slowly. By spring, however, Marie could know that she had his attention; then the affair was broken off by the king's leaving to join the army, and in the summer, by his grave illness. When he began to recover, he learned that while some of his court had looked to the reign of his brother, Marie Mancini had shown real distress over his illness; she wept real tears and prayed to God when the king was in danger. Louis was delighted.

What sort of a girl had this young lady become? The young woman who won the heart of the king was no longer the gawky girl that she had been when she arrived in France. There are several canvases painted about this time, including a fine one by Mignard, that confirm the suspicion that she had changed considerably between thirteen and eighteen; the pictures show us a blooming young woman with flashing dark eyes, elegant dark hair, well-formed attractive lips, beautiful neck, shoulders, and breasts, and a well-proportioned body. Moreover, in the years when she played Cinderella she had stocked her head with ideas about art, literature, and even politics; here was a girl who could talk wittily and intelligently about a great many things. A contemporary pen picture in the *Dictionnaire des Précieuses* described her under the name of Maximiliane:[4] ". . . she is one of the wittiest people in the world . . . she has read all the good books . . . she writes with a facility that one would not expect . . . even though she is not from Greece [France] she knows the language as well as the wittiest of the Athenians [French] . . . even as well as those in the Assembly of the Forty Barons [French Academy]. . . ." Before Louis' affair with her was over, he found himself reading poetry, playing the guitar, and talking about literature—she almost cured him of his distaste for books. Whether she talked in his mother's salon, or rode horseback with him wildly through the forest of Fontainebleau, or danced in the great hall of the château; whether she was dressed in the tight-fitting blue velvet riding habit trimmed with gray fur, or in the elegant low-cut dress that exposed her firm shoulders and bosom while swirls of silk and lace gave charm to her figure, Marie was a girl who could attract many a young man, no matter what might be his status in life. Louis found her friendly, sympathetic, witty, intelligent, and concerned for his welfare; he also knew that she found him much to her liking. Such is the stuff from which romance is made.

Mazarin and Anne could not have been completely unaware of what was going on, but they may have thought that a little innocent love affair might hasten the recovery of the king's health and give him a little excitement before settling down to marriage. They did not interfere; perhaps before the trip to Lyons there was no real need to do so, for it was the return trip that seems to have set the spark for the more intense part of the affair. Before the trip to Lyons, the French court made all the necessary arrangements to meet the Savoyards, and with loud enough talk and excitement to be sure that Philip IV would not miss what was at stake. The Savoyard family only imperfectly understood that Marguerite might be exposed to another humiliation like the one that had ended the Duke of Bavaria's courting. Perhaps it was that the dowager duchess, a daughter of Henry IV and Marie de Médicis, was quite willing to take the chance that her daughter might not win the French throne for the chance that she might. Marguerite herself tried to find an excuse for not going to Lyons; perhaps she had a premonition of the fiasco to come.

The little comedy had to be played out. The French court with all its tinsel and finery slowly journeyed toward Lyons, while the Savoyards, not to be outdone in show or elegance, outrageously taxed the duke's resources to present a brave front to their French relatives and moved north to try their luck.

The weather was crisp and bright, making the trip a grand opportunity for the young people, who loved horses and the pleasure of travel.

Local noblemen joined the cavalcade as it passed through their districts and peasants turned out to cheer the king. Louis acted out the ceremonial role of his office like a veteran, delighting his mother, the cardinal, and his subjects alike. From the descriptions of the journey, the young people seem to have galloped and romped pell-mell as long as the cavalcade was in the woods or the open fields, but when they came to a settlement, Louis regained his hat and his dignity so that no one missed which one of the young people was the king. All the memoirists agree that he was in high spirits; their cause is not so clear. In contrast to his mother and Mazarin, Louis seems to have made the trip to meet Marguerite in good faith and without reservations; perhaps his high spirits were simply those of a young man going to meet his possible bride. On the other hand, all the memoirists also speak of the increasing intimacy between him and Marie; for months he had given her more or less of his time, but on this excursion he saw Marie flushed with the thrill of the gallop from the wild horseback races, and then quietly talked to her as the horses walked side by side through the autumnal sunshine in the beautiful Burgundian hills.

But Louis had not yet fallen in love with Marie when the court reached its rendezvous at Lyon with the Savoyards, for he was interested enough in Marguerite to be the first of the French party to greet the visitors. He returned immediately to tell his mother about it. Anne: "Well, son?" Louis: "She is shorter than the Marquise de Villeroi . . . she has a charming body, her complexion is olive . . . it suits her well. She has beautiful eyes . . . she pleases me . . . I find her to my taste." Anne was appalled; Marie, who seems to have known her own feelings better than Louis knew his at this moment, was shocked and terrified. Years later she wrote in her memoirs that she had never believed that Louis would marry Marguerite. For Louis, however, Marguerite was a new girl, and he seems to have been momentarily interested in her.

He invited Marguerite to ride in the same carriage with him and La Grande Mademoiselle, whose presence was apparently no brake upon Louis' effort to become better acquainted with his Savoyard cousin. "The King started to talk to Princess Marguerite," she wrote, ". . . as if he had known her all his life and she him; this surprised me, for the King is normally cold and ill at ease in making up to people . . . the King talked to her about his musketeers, his heavy and his light horses, the regiment of guards, the number of his troops, those who commanded them, and how they marched. I judged that he took pleasure in entertaining her. These are for him the most interesting subjects [of conversation]; he is much taken by [his soldiers and his guards]. He asked her about the guards of the Duke of

Savoy. . . . I did not dare to continue to listen for fear of being noticed . . . The King spoke to her of the pleasures of Paris, and she of those of Turin." Louis, at twenty, made up to a girl with the same show of insight into feminine interests characteristic of young men of other periods. He was a soldier just returned from the war, a war that was a game for kings; he knew that Marguerite was eager to know all about it. And she, just as have many girls before and since, seems to have played the good-listener. This scene does raise a question: When did Louis actually "fall in love" with Marie? It is clear that he did not yet know that he wanted to marry her, and as such, it is an interesting "bench mark" for understanding the coming love affair.

While the meeting between Louis and Marguerite went off famously, the one between Anne and her sister-in-law the dowager duchess was somewhat less cordial. In spite of the fact that the young people were first cousins, Anne regarded a Savoyard marriage as a misalliance for her son. Faced with the possibility that it might become a fact, she became cold and hostile. That evening there was a scene between her and Louis in which she argued against the marriage, while he spoke hotly in favor of it—even going so far as to say that "he was the master." Madame de Motteville tells us that Mazarin refused to intervene in the discussion. Shortly afterward, there was another encounter: when Marie met her prince charming, whose flagrant fickleness might have caused her to accuse him bitterly, she met him with an utterly feminine attack—"Aren't you ashamed that they wish to marry you to such a homely woman?" What else she said, Mademoiselle does not report, but this was an effective barb striking directly at masculine vanity. The decisive word, however, came from Spain; it was a word that smoothed Anne's fears and lulled Marie into false security.

When the news reached Spain that the French court would go to Lyons to make a marriage alliance, Philip IV announced, "That cannot happen, and it will not!" He had always assumed that his daughter would be Queen of France. A courier immediately left Madrid to follow the French court to Lyons with a suggestion of peace and a marriage alliance; it was just what Mazarin had hoped would happen. The evening after the scene between mother and son, Mazarin came into the queen's rooms with the announcement that he had news that she "did not expect and that would surprise her to the utmost." Anne: "Does the King, my brother, offer me the Infanta?" Her relief must have been extreme; she had played for high stakes and won.

It was a bad blow for the dowager duchess; when Anne regained her composure, the duchess lost hers. Marguerite, who had noticed that Louis had cooled off even before the news from Spain, accepted the situation with good grace; perhaps she had never really believed that the marriage would take place. Mazarin assured the Savoyards that in case the Spanish marriage should fail, Louis would marry Marguerite; but, he pointed out, it was a duty to Christendom to attempt to bring peace between France and Spain. Before the two courts parted, there was a brilliant ball at which tensions were more evident than pleasure, and then both parties turned toward their own capitals. Marguerite's brother, the young Duke of Savoy, was rather too enthusiastic in shaking the dust of France from his feet; after all, he had failed to find a formula by which he could marry the beautiful Hortense Mancini, who had much taken his interest; Mazarin had no sovereign territory to give him as the dowry that he would have to have if he married a girl without royal blood in her veins.

What happened when the court returned to Paris? Years later Marie wrote vividly of the events:

> On our return our sole care was to enjoy ourselves. There was not a day, or to tell the truth, a moment not given to pleasure, and I can say that no one ever had a better time than we had. His Majesty, wishing to assure the continuation of our entertainment, ordered our troupe to meet every day. There followed a series of festivals, balls, and all those things that one can do in the country . . . there was never anything more magnificent . . . these entertainments were for the people of the first quality . . . love was the mode . . . there was not a cavalier who had not made his choice. The Grand Master [Meilleraye] made every effort to please my sister Hortense; the Marquis de Richelieu . . . Mademoiselle de la Motte-Argencourt; the Marquis d'Alluy . . . Mademoiselle Faulloux . . . His Majesty and I had an extreme confidence, and there were several others who had similar engagements of whom it would take too long to talk about here. . . .
>
> The gallant adventures that accompanied our meals, our promenades . . . would require an entire volume, and so I shall pass them over in silence . . . only reporting one occasion . . . his Majesty wishing to give me his hand, and mine having struck against the pummel of his sword, hurting it slightly, he drew it bruskly from the sheath and threw it away. . . . I will not try to tell with what air he did this; there are no words to explain it.[5]

Louis and Marie were living in a fool's paradise. They somehow were able to rationalize their situation by believing that the Spanish would never consent to a treaty, and therefore that no Infanta would ever arrive in France. They also made themselves believe that Anne and Mazarin would consent to their marriage as a token of the great debt that the house of Bourbon owed to that of the cardinal. Love blinded Louis to more than the reality of his love object; he had also lost sight of his destiny and role as king. When Anne and Mazarin came to realize that this was more than a weekend romance, they quickly ran down the curtain on the show. Marie was exiled to Brouage near La Rochelle, and Louis was sent to Chantilly to recover from his infatuation.

The separation of the two lovers has since become famous, celebrated by poets and memoirists alike. Madame de Motteville's account is probably as close to the true story as any other; she, at least, was there:

> The King must be praised in that he understands that the misfortune the Queen is bringing upon him . . . is similar to that done by surgeons when they cure a wound by incisions and caustics . . . [She actually did not know what the King thought; she saw only his actions]. On the evening before Mademoiselle Mancini departed the King came to the Queen broken with sorrow. She drew him apart and talked to him for a long time; but as the feelings of a heart that loves demands solitude, the Queen took the candle herself . . . and going from her chamber to the bathing room, asked the King to follow her. After they were there together for about an hour, the King and the Queen came out also deeply touched . . . she did me the honor to say: "I am so sorry for the King; he is both tender and reasonable. . . . I have just assured him that one day he will thank me for the evil that I am now doing him." . . .

Many parents have been sure that their children would "thank them in the future"; but both Madame de Motteville and the queen were more sanguine about Louis' willingness to accept the situation at the moment than was warranted. He did allow Marie to be exiled, but his subsequent behavior indicates something less than full consent. The parting of the lovers was a touching scene; tears, earnest conversation, and Marie's much-quoted remark, "You weep, but I part, and yet you are the master!" There are several variants of Marie's farewell; this one is probably as correct as any of them. Many years later she wrote in her *Mémoires:*

> I cannot remain silent about the sadness that this separation caused me; I have known nothing like it in my life. All that one could possibly suffer seems as nothing by comparison with this absence; there was not a moment when I did not wish for death as the supreme remedy for my troubles. . . .[6]

Her situation was actually worse than she knew, for her younger sister, who went along with her, acted as a spy to tell Madame Venelle, her "jailor," all that Hortense and Marie planned and did to evade the cardinal's decision.

It is unfortunate that of all the letters that passed between Marie and Louis, between Louis and Mazarin and the queen, only those of Cardinal Mazarin remain to help us reconstruct the course of the crisis. The cardinal's letters[7] make inferences possible about what was contained in those of the king and others. We can only regret that we do not also have the love letters that passed between the young couple.

Louis was obviously smitten very hard. Mademoiselle tells us that he begged on his knees that Anne should change her mind; he also returned again and again to the theme that the Bourbons really "owed" so much to Mazarin that it was only proper to reward him by marrying one of his family. When Marie was taken away from him, he must have confided his problems to his friends, for the queen and cardinal had to "remove" Vivonne, who was counseling Louis to escape from under the thumb of the cardinal and marry the girl.

Against Mazarin's better judgment, Anne allowed Louis to correspond with Marie; he undoubtedly would have done so anyway, for the young couple established a clandestine correspondence as well as a legal one; there were plenty of people who believed that Marie would be Queen of France in spite of Mazarin and Anne, and wanted to be in her good graces. Finally, to Mazarin's near despair, Anne even allowed the two young people to have a last meeting that, as the cardinal had foreseen, only poured oil on the fire. Perhaps the best way to follow the crisis is through quotations from Mazarin's letters. These not only illuminate the Mancini crisis; they also speak volumes about the relationships between Mazarin, Louis, and the queen mother.

On June 22, Marie and her two sisters left for Brouage, and Louis for Chantilly. There were a number of letters between Louis and Mazarin in which Mazarin believed that Louis was resigned to his duties. On June 28, Mazarin wrote to the king:

> You will recall . . . that when you have asked me to point out for you the road that one must take to become a great king . . . [I have said that you] must begin by making the greatest effort not to be dominated by your passions, for when this misfortune occurs, no matter how much good will one has, one cannot do what must be done. I speak to you with liberty . . . you have no other servant who is more interested than I am in your *gloire,* and to see you the greatest king on earth . . . as a result of the talents that . . . you possess.

The next day another letter added:

> . . . I received your letter with joy for it is well written and commits you to apply yourself to the business of state . . . do not overlook anything that is needed to make you a great king . . . God having given you all the qualities [necessary] . . . it only remains for you to put them to use. . . .

And on July 2, in the same tone (Louis obviously was still able to deceive the cardinal):

> . . . I continue to be very satisfied with the content of your letters, and with the firmness that you show . . . in applying yourself to the business [of state]. . . .

God has given you so liberally all that is needed to become the greatest prince in the world that you cannot complain with justice if you fail to do so . . . [he urges Louis to play tennis, ride horseback, and read dispatches]. . . . I say again that great things will happen to you if you wish them; I rejoice in advance for the reputation and glory that you will acquire. . . .

Few wise fathers would have failed to use this same line of argument to control the behavior of a son under like circumstances; but Mazarin was wrong in believing that he would succeed in quieting Louis' passion with a promise of future greatness.

Louis spent all his time writing to Marie, reading Marie's letters, thinking about Marie; the flow of letters from Brouage did not help to resolve his problem, for Marie, even more than Louis, was quite unwilling to accept her uncle's decision. Mazarin, now engaged in the process of tying up the Spanish negotiations for peace and the royal marriage, became horrified when he learned that Louis had promised Marie that he would marry no one if he could not marry her. And perhaps even worse, that the noise of the king's passion was being bruited about by newsletters that must eventually find their way into the hands of the Spanish. What if Spain broke off relations? The war would start up again more stubbornly than ever, and all of the work toward peace would be irreparably lost. On July 16, Mazarin was at Cadillac suffering both physical (gout) and mental anguish. His letter to Louis is one of the most remarkable that ever passed between a minister and his king:

> I have seen the letter from the *Confidente* [Anne] touching your distress . . . but as I know . . . that your natural goodness, more than your sense of duty, would cause your discontent if you displeased her and would immediately bring you to show her your tenderness . . . I tell you that I am extremely surprised [by what I hear] . . . at a time that you have promised me that you were resolved to apply yourself completely to affairs . . . to become the greatest king on earth.
>
> Letters from Paris . . . say that you are not the same since my departure . . . because of something belonging to me [Marie] . . . that the engagements that you are making will prevent your giving peace to Christendom and making your people happy. . . .
>
> . . . It is said that I am in accord with you and have a secret understanding with you . . . to satisfy my ambition and prevent peace. . . .
>
> . . . It is said that you are in difficulties with the Queen, and . . . that you avoid seeing her. . . .

Mazarin went on to tell him that he knew of the voluminous correspondence, of Louis' brooding over these letters, and that this was creating a scandal. Louis should know what this meant to his subjects; as a result of it,

Mazarin himself was loaded with grief and unable to sleep. This was willful behavior unworthy of a king. He then turned on Louis:

> . . . God established kings to guarantee the good, the security, and the peace of their subjects, and not to sacrifice these goods and that peace for their own individual passions. And when it happens . . . that because of their conduct, Divine Providence abandons them, history has become full of revolutions and disorders that they have drawn upon their persons and their states.
>
> That is why I tell you boldly that this is no time to hesitate . . . even though you are the master in a certain sense, to do what you think is right . . . You owe accounting to God for your actions, for your own salvation, and to the world for the maintenance of your *gloire* and your reputation. . . .
>
> You assured me that you would do everything necessary for this *gloire* and honor . . . let me say that in writing otherwise to La Rochelle [Marie] I cannot see your true intention. . . . It is not a question of your desires . . . your subjects' welfare and your kingdom are at stake . . . Let me assure you that the Prince of Condé and others are alert to see what will happen . . . hoping to profit by any plausible excuse that you may give them. . . .

He went on to ask what the Spanish would think about his attitude toward marriage with the Infanta, and to suggest the danger of a break in the negotiations for peace. Mazarin then resorted to threats:

> I conclude this letter by telling you that if I see by your reply . . . that there is no hope that you will put yourself on the road that will lead to your good, your honor, and the preservation of your kingdom, I have no other gambit to play to give you a final proof of my fidelity and my zeal for your honor and kingdom than to sacrifice myself, and, after having placed in your hands all the gifts that it has pleased the late King, you, and the Queen to pile upon me, to put myself and my family aboard a ship and go to some corner of Italy to pass the rest of my days and to pray God that His action will . . . produce the cure that I hope for.

Many writers hostile to the cardinal have assumed, upon reading these lines, that Mazarin had no intention of doing this, that it was an act of hypocrisy. Others have suggested that he was so startled at his own temerity that he became fearful that he might have to resign. The subsequent correspondence, however, tends to show that these judgments are of the same cloth of so many of the anti-Mazarin attitudes of Frenchmen. That same day Mazarin wrote to Anne, telling her of his worries, that he could hardly eat or sleep, that her letters were a comfort to him. But he added that if Louis did not mend his ways, he was "resolved to do what I threatened [to resign]. I will be happy enough [if it cures him] and at least I would have this advantage that the world would see what I had done, even to the sacrifice of myself to serve my master. . . ." Seven days later, in another letter to Anne: "I will tell you confidentially that nothing will stop the execution of that which I am resolved to do if he does not change. . . ."

On July 25 Mazarin, somewhat recovered from the gout, moved farther south toward his rendezvous with Don Luis de Haro, the Spanish statesman heading Philip IV's peace commission. From Bidache he wrote to the king that he hoped:

> . . . to confer with Don Luis and to be sure to deceive him in that I will tell him of your intentions and your desire to complete the marriage. . . . And nevertheless, I know that in your present state, and one from which it seems to me you have no desire to emerge, if the person whom you should marry were an angel, she would not satisfy you. That is all that I have to say to you, praying God to help you . . . make the decisions that both human and divine reasons require of you.

At this point Louis conceived the idea that he should visit Marie for one last time. Mazarin was horrified to hear that the queen permitted him to do so; Anne was obviously much moved by Louis' sorrow, and less able than the cardinal to say no to him. Mazarin wrote to both of them on July 29, arguing against the meeting. To Louis he reproached the queen's "half-measures," insisting that he must break cleanly with Marie to become master of his own conduct. He went on to say:

> I love my niece . . . but without exaggeration I love you better, and I am interested in your *gloire* and the conservation of your state more than anything else in the world. . . .
>
> The Queen loves you [and hates to see you suffer] . . . for my part I believe that I have for you the same tenderness that the *Confidente* has, but [it] . . . makes me harder and more firm in my opposition to that which is contrary to your service. . . . If I did otherwise, I would be asking you to destroy yourself. . . .

In the rest of the letter he argued that meeting Marie would do Louis no good, that it would result in scandal that might get to the Spanish negotiators and endanger the treaty of peace. In his letter to Anne he argued against the meeting, but part of the letter was just for her:

> I have been extremely sorry not to be able to write to you, for this is one of the greatest consolations that I have . . . in the agitation of my spirit as it now is. I read your four letters several times and I cannot thank you enough for your natural goodness, without which I would pass a most unfortunate life, being away from you and the *Confident*. . . .

He then went on to discuss the problem of Louis' visit, hoping that "the *Confident* will have the goodness to grant me the favor of not going . . . for . . . it would be badly received and would cause a public scandal."

Louis did make the rendezvous with his loved one, and as a method of calming his passion, the interview, of course, proved to be a complete failure. The letters between the two apparently became more frequent and more ardent; it is a shame that there is no account of what really happened at the interview. Anne, however, believed that it had resulted in a cure, for we find Mazarin writing to her on July 26:

> I am delighted with the news you write to me of the *Confident*'s application to business; for *I hope for nothing with greater passion than to see him capable of governing this great kingdom* [author's italics]. But I also hope with almost equal passion to see him happy in his marriage. . . .

He went on to say that Louis must forget Marie.

Louis, however, was not yet cured of his desire for the black-eyed Italian. He wrote to Mazarin, again explaining all the good reasons why he should be allowed to marry her. Mazarin's answer to this letter should be placed beside the one of July 16; again he answers all the arguments, and urges that the king give up his folly:

> I am not surprised at your manner of talk since it is passion that prevents you from knowing . . . what is right. . . . Without this passion you would be in agreement with me. . . .

He then took up some of Louis' arguments, and at the time wrote very frankly about Marie's faults. He then indicated that the king seemed to leave him not much choice but

> . . . to execute the design that I wrote to you about from Cadillac, for there is no power that can take from me the free disposition of my family that is given to me by God and the law, and you will be one of the first to give me praise for the service that I will have rendered you . . . by my resolution I will have given you the peace and put you in the state of being the happiest and the most accomplished prince in the world. . . . [He then returned to Louis' folly.] You have begun since this last visit . . . to write not only letters, but entire volumes. It is incomprehensible. . . . You practice the expedients to heat up your passion on the very eve of your marriage. Thus you are working to make yourself the most unhappy of all men for there is nothing quite like marrying against one's heart. I ask you . . . what does that person [Marie] think she will do after you are married? Has she forgotten her duty to the point that she would believe that I would be such a dishonest person, or more, such an infamous one, as to allow her to practice a trade that would dishonor her? [There is no evidence that Marie planned to be the king's mistress; she wanted to be his wife!]

He went on to say that his duty forced him to speak very frankly to the king about Marie as well as about the French kingdom. The arguments were the same: the king's *gloire,* the peace of the kingdom, the welfare of his subjects, his duty to God—all were endangered by this folly. He even threatened Louis with God's wrath:

> How could I conceal from you . . . that you will expose yourself to . . . the wrath of God if you marry, hating the Princess that you make your wife . . . having the intention of living dishonestly with her . . . ? Do you believe that God will bless such a marriage and that . . . you will not thus run the risk of His indignation. . . . ?

After further involved argument, he added:

> . . . I tell you that nothing will stop me from dying of chagrin if a person belonging so closely to me causes you the supreme misfortune . . . at the moment that I have . . . procured advantages and glory for your person and your state. . . .

In the end, it was Marie who brought the affair to a conclusion. During the first week in September she decided that the negotiations with Spain had reached the point at which there was no longer any question about the marriage, and no shred of evidence has appeared that she ever had had the intention of becoming Louis' mistress. Thus there was nothing to do but to break off the correspondence with the king. Mazarin was overjoyed. In his letter to Madame de Venelle, obviously intended for Marie's eyes, too, he wrote:

> Let me tell you again that I have no greater joy in the world than to have such a niece, seeing that she herself has taken the generous resolution conforming to her honor and my satisfaction. . . . I beg you to tell her for my part that I love her . . . that I am going to care for . . . her marriage and her happiness. [He indicated that he realized that Marie must be in considerable distress from her decision. His advice:] . . . Tell her from me that she ought to read books . . . particularly Seneca, in which she will find consolation and confirm her satisfaction in the decision that she has made. . . .

Mazarin's enemies have pointed to his failure to suggest either the *Bible* or *The Imitation of Christ* or any other religious book as evidence that he was a heathen. There is much in his life to suggest that he feared neither God nor the devil; this does not seem important to his relationship with the king.

Louis' reaction to the catastrophe that overtook his first love affair presents the historian with problems. We have no direct evidence from his pen; the indirect evidence in Mazarin's letters suggests that at first he was deeply hurt, and perhaps not completely convinced, for Mazarin finds it worth his while to attempt to turn Louis against Marie *after* the affair was presumably finished. When she would write no more, however, Louis too stopped the flow of letters, and it appears that the pain was soothed by time and attention to the multitudinous details of the negotiations for peace and plans for his forthcoming marriage.

The Mancini crisis was of great importance to the later life of the king. No one reading Mazarin's letters will miss the goals that were held up to Louis: he must renounce personal satisfactions, personal happiness, personal desires, to achieve his *gloire,* to make himself worthy before God and the world for the title of Most Glorious King, and to satisfy the needs of his state. These were unquestionably the goals that Mazarin and Anne had held up to him for more than a decade. It was for them that he gave up the only romantic love that he was ever to know, the love for a woman whose beauty, wit, and brains satisfied his needs as a man. In her place they put a queen who turned out to be a woman of very limited intelligence and even less wit; it was a hard bargain that he had agreed to when he set out to become a great king. This renunciation of his first love, added to the misfortune of marriage to a dull woman, probably accounts for some of the disorder that came to his personal life during the next twenty-odd years.

THE LAST ACT UNDER MAZARIN

ONCE HE WAS RECONCILED to the fact that he could not marry Marie Mancini, that he must do his duty toward his dynasty and his kingdom, in short, that he must follow his *gloire,* Louis could settle down to the business of making peace with Spain and his coming marriage to the Infanta. There was much preparation to make before the French court could meet its Spanish relatives. Elaborate protocol, new clothes for everybody, new carriages for the royal family, new uniforms for the guards: all these were necessary to match the expected Spanish display. Many a French nobleman nearly bankrupted himself to keep up with the royal family's expenditures. Fortunately there was time; the negotiations for the treaty of peace were drawn out, for the Spanish court, which would not travel in the wintertime, could not arrive at the meeting place until spring.

This gave the royal family a chance to visit the tourist attractions of southern France; Avignon, Nîmes, Marseilles, Montpellier, Bayonne, and other less well known cities all had a chance to play host to the royal family. La Grande Mademoiselle tells us of her visit to the Pont-du-Gard and describes in detail Louis' entry into Marseilles through a breach in the wall, a symbolic recognition of the city's punishment for a recent rebellion. It was the young king's first trip to the south, his first sight of the Mediterranean, the famous galley fleet, and the commercial cities that traded with the Levant. Everywhere he was received with cheers: all France was happy with the prospects for peace, with the marriage that would guarantee the peace, with the sight of the king whose handsome figure seemed to promise good things to come. France of the mid-seventeenth century was profoundly royalist, and the attention paid to the young king was very near to adoration.

Louis cut a handsome figure on the eve of his marriage. One lady, who probably was in love with him, wrote a pen portrait for a volume presented to La Grande Mademoiselle:

His body is tall, free, ample, robust; his chest and shoulders broad; his arms and legs big, well-proportioned and perfectly turned. A countenance that is at once proud and sweet . . . even should he˙disguise himself, one would recognize immediately that he is the master, for he has the air . . . by which we recognize those whom we speak of as having the blood of the gods. . . .

His eyes are brilliant and piercing . . . the eyelids that cover them make them seem like the light of the sun that dissipates the mist. . . . Smallpox has left some slight marks on his face, but his vivacity and his good color shine through . . . his chin has the first sign of a beard.

. . . He must be seen dancing the ballet . . . he is Heaven's masterpiece, the gift of God to France. . . .

. . . He treats no one badly; a prince who never wounds by raillery. . . . His age and station and physical advantages make him naturally attractive to women; he is sensitive to their charms . . . [but] so submissive to reason and conscience that he will permit only innocent acts . . . [sic!].

. . . It is enough to say that there has never been one person with so much courage without vanity, justice without ferocity, prudence without artifice, reserve without austerity. . . . In him one recognizes that magnanimity includes elevation of grandeur and moderation of power. . . .[1]

Mademoiselle, who probably knew Louis better and who had already suffered exile at his hands for her folly in the *Fronde,* was hardly less bubbly in her picture of the king. She starts by insisting that only the three persons of the Trinity could really write properly about God, and likewise only Louis could really draw his own portrait; and yet, just as it is permissible for man to write about divinity, so she should be allowed to write about her king. With this attitude or worship so nearly universal in the entourage of the royal family, it is surprising that Louis ever got any objective view of himself. Perhaps without Mazarin it would never have been possible. Mademoiselle went on to write of Louis:

. . . He has an elevated, distinguished, proud, intrepid, agreeable air . . . a face that is at the same time sweet and majestic. His hair is the most beautiful in the world . . . his legs are handsome and well made, and to take him as a whole, he is the most handsome and the best-built man in the kingdom. He dances divinely, he loves ballet. . . .

. . . His manner is cold; he speaks little except to people with whom he is familiar . . . [and then] he speaks well and effectively, and only says what is apropos. He jokes agreeably, and always in good taste . . . he has natural goodness, is charitable, liberal, and properly acts out the role of king. . . .[2]

Mademoiselle and her friend were unquestionably a bit *précieuse,* but their pictures of the king correspond with those drawn by others at this period. "The King is good," said his mother, and all who knew him supported her contention and added that he also was handsome. Such was the prince destined to wed the Infanta of Spain: handsome, athletic, kind, reserved, sober, a little diffident. The time had not come when the responsibility of office and the pressures of politics and war would bring out the flaws inherent in his character. La Grande Mademoiselle herself might well have revised her picture had she known that Louis would forbid his new wife to kiss anyone but himself and his mother, for thus he could establish the gap that he wished to exist between the king and his immediate family.

While the royal family occupied itself with clothes and etiquette and preparations for the marriage, Mazarin was completely involved in the duel with Don Luis de Haro on the island in the middle of the Bidassoa River. The conference building on the Isle of the Pheasants, erected exactly on the line of the frontier, had been Don Luis' first triumph. By insisting that the King of Spain could never leave his kingdom even for a marriage or a peace treaty, he had established a sort of symbolic equality between the two kingdoms, an equality that did not exist in fact. The treaty was negotiated and signed with both rulers remaining always inside the frontier of their own kingdoms. Before the treaty was finally written Mazarin had many good reasons to respect the steel of his opponent.

Actually the Spanish were at a considerable disadvantage in the negotiations. The French armies occupied more Spanish territory than the French king actually demanded, and they were in a position to quickly extend their control over much more of the Spanish Netherlands should the negotiations fail. The war had gone badly for Spain, her treasury was empty, and she was obviously unable to exert further efforts. Furthermore, the Spanish had asked for peace, and offered the Infanta as a gauge of their good faith. Philip IV had one other disadvantage: he had given his word to the Prince of Condé and considered himself morally obligated to include the prince in the treaty. Several years earlier, negotiations had broken down precisely on this point. In Louis' eyes Condé was a rebel, a man convicted of treason and condemned to death by the Parlement of Paris for having taken up arms against his king; the French were in no mood to forgive him without extracting great advantages for themselves. On the other hand, Don Luis knew that Mazarin counted heavily upon making a treaty that would crown his career and firmly establish his reputation as a statesman. France was also in financial difficulties, and the French people wanted peace. Moreover, both Mazarin and Anne were deeply committed to providing the king with a wife and the possibility of a suitable heir to the throne. Don Luis knew all this, and he also knew how to use it to his advantage.

Condé's return to France with all his former honors and wealth was the source of much discussion. Mazarin wrote several letters to Louis about it; on one occasion he had to calm the young king's fears that Condé might force him to permit the refortification of places that the royal army had recently razed. We do not have Louis' letter to which Mazarin was replying, but obviously the young king was looking into the future and wished to be sure that Condé would never again have places of *sécurité* to which he could retire should he raise the standards of revolt. Mazarin assured the king that he would tolerate no such privileges for the ex-rebel; that the Spanish would pay dearly for espousing his cause; and that Condé would not come back except under conditions that made him promise to be a loyal subject of the king.[3] In the preliminaries of the treaty, France expected to obtain Roussillon and most of Artois; in the final treaty, Condé was forgiven, but the Spanish gave, in addition to Artois and Roussillon, Gravelines, Bourbourg, Bergues, and Saint-Venant in Flanders, a large slice of Hainaut with the fortifications of Landrécies, Quesnoy, Avènes, Philippeville, and Marienbourg, and finally Thionville and Damvillers. Condé's pardon cost the King of Spain dearly.

The marriage contract also presented some problems. Marie-Thérèse was the elder daughter of Philip IV; her younger sister was destined to become the bride of Leopold I, emperor and ruler of the Hapsburg Danubian lands. Philip did not want his crowns to pass from the Hapsburg family, and yet Marie-Thérèse's marriage would make that possibility real, for his sons were sickly and hardly expected to live. Therefore a formula had to be found to deprive Marie-Thérèse of her birthright, and thus to assure for her sister's children the right of succession should the Spanish Hapsburg line fail. The contract made when Anne became the bride of Louis XIII provided the model for the renunciation, but Marie-Thérèse, as the elder daughter, was giving up much; so to compensate, she had to be richly dowered. Spanish pride would not have it otherwise, nor would the French. The sum finally set was 500,000 *écus* of gold, by Lionne and one of the Spanish negotiators, secured the formula: "In consideration of payment of this sum, the most serene princess Marie-Thérèse renounces her claims"[4] to her father's crowns. Don Pedro Coloma tried to resist this formula, but Lionne blandly asked him whether the Spanish did not intend to live up to the treaty. The dowry was much too big for the Spanish treasury, and it was never paid. Thus the "in consideration" clause was destined to be much discussed by diplomats and publicists for the next half-century.

The text of the Treaty of the Pyrenees, including the terms of the marriage contract and the political settlement between the two crowns, fills 79 folio pages with its 74 articles. Condé's pardon was issued in January 1660 in letters patent sealed with the great seal of France with pink and green silk threads, signed by the King of Aix.[5] The pardon also covered those who had served the prince. During the months following the treaty, Mazarin and the secretaries of state were busy with letters, proclamations, pardons, and orders necessary for the implementation of the treaty.[6] It would seem that Louis had little or nothing to do with these routine affairs; in any case there is no evidence in the documents of his participation.

In 1659–60 the most important fact about the treaty must have been the peace between the two kingdoms, but in the years that were to follow, the importance of the marriage pact grew and grew, for the male line of the Spanish Hapsburgs ended with Charles II, the sickly, dull-witted son of Philip IV, and long before his death, the question of the Spanish inheritance willy-nilly became an important axis for much of the politics of Europe. Too much, however, has been made of the renunciation clause, and of the expression *"moyennant de"*—"in consideration of." Even if the dowry had been paid, there would have been a Bourbon claim. As early as 1646, when the diplomats at Münster were considering the marriage and peace between France and Spain, Mazarin wrote, ". . . The Infanta, being married to his majesty, we can hope for the succession to the thrones of Spain no matter what renunciations she has to make . . . this expectation is not at all remote since the life of only one prince, her father, excludes her. . . ."[7] In this Mazarin was saying what every statesman knew about paper barriers to the succession to a throne. It was a nice question whether or not a princess could actually give up her birthright, and it was even more of a question whether she could bind her as-yet-unborn children to give up their rights. These rights came from God, not from a king or a paper treaty. If Madame de Motteville's account is correct, Philip IV also understood that the renunciation probably was not valid, just as Louis himself was to understand in 1714 that Anglo-Dutch diplomacy probably could not really exclude his grandson from the throne of France. A treaty could be written, and if it were never challenged it would be regarded as valid, but if the prince in question should actually become claimant of the throne, it would be difficult to exclude him by a paper treaty. Thus it was not Mazarin's "Machiavellian diplomacy" that involved France in future wars over the Spanish inheritance; the issue of war and peace that came later was inherent in the fact of the marriage itself—a marriage desired by both Anne and Philip as a family affair.

In reading French historians the impression often emerges that their judgment of Mazarin is colored by the military decisions of the War of the Spanish Succession, which a half-century after his death cost France heavily in blood and treasure, and brought nothing in return. The statement that a Richelieu would have known better how to end the war in 1659 since he was a born Frenchman, or the castigations of Mazarin's "duplicity," fail to point out that Mazarin was dealing with the real situation of his day; it involved both a queen (Anne) who was determined to have her son marry the Infanta if it were at all possible, and a problem created by the fact that Louis, several years older than his Hapsburg cousin, Leopold I, married the elder of the two Spanish princesses. It was a world with assumptions different from those held by nineteenth- and twentieth-century nationalists who are concerned with "national frontiers" and national interests; Mazarin, Anne, and Louis were making a dynastic alliance between the Hapsburg and Bourbon families, and family politics were as important to them as the "interests" of France—or even more important.

Louis was obviously satisfied with the treaty. In one of the last letters to his uncle before Gaston died, he wrote, ". . . I cannot doubt that the joy that you expressed is sincere, for in addition to the fact that your birth attaches you to the good of my state, I am also assured by the affection that you have for my person, and nothing is more natural than for you to take pleasure in that which you believe to be to my advantage and my *gloire*. . . . I think that we have as much of the one as of the other in the treaty that I have just made with the King of Spain . . . nothing is lacking for our satisfaction."[8] This letter illustrates many of Louis' basic assumptions about himself, his kingdom, and his relations with the King of Spain: if one misses the fact that the Treaty of the Pyrenees was first of all a family agreement between Hapsburgs and Bourbons who were already related, rather than merely a Franco-Spanish settlement of outstanding problems, the treaty becomes almost unintelligible. Not only the marriage of the king, but also the reinstatement of Louis II of Bourbon, Prince of Condé, in favor at the court, underscores the dynastic and family nature of the treaty. Even the territorial clauses were subordinated to these family considerations.

The marriage ceremonies provided the great excitement for the spring of 1660. Who was this young lady destined to become Queen of France and mother to the next dauphin? Marie-Thérèse's family background was very much the same as Louis' and she looked so like the young king that she might have passed for his sister.[9] This was not surprising, for the two young people had identical grandparents. Her French mother had gone to Spain when Anne came to France. From the time Marie-Thérèse was a little girl, her French-born mother had told her of the delights of Paris and the French court, and had led her to assume that one day she would become the bride of her cousin in France. Thus Marie-Thérèse from childhood had been emotionally conditioned to love the prince charming in Paris, even though her father's kingdom was at war with his.

We have many pictures of her; perhaps the most famous is the one, now hanging in the Louvre, painted by Velasquez. There she stands in her "Spanish" clothes and wig, as stiff as a manikin, her eyes revealing the vacant childish stare of a mind intellectually unfavored, uneducated, uninformed. Velasquez did his best to present her beauty as the gift of her youth, but he was too honest to fail to comment upon her dull and uninteresting personality. Her years in France were to bear out this estimate; poor Marie-Thérèse was a severely limited woman.

Madame de Motteville has left us the classic description of the young queen's physical appearance:

The Infanta queen is small but well-built; we admire the striking whiteness of her skin . . . her blue eyes seemed to us beautiful; they charmed us by their softness and their brilliance. We recognized the beauty of her mouth; her lips, perhaps a bit too large, but still beautiful, also received our praise. To tell the truth if her body were a little bigger and her teeth more beautiful, she would merit a place among the most beautiful women of Europe . . . but her costume was horrible, neither the cut nor the style pleased the eye. . . .

The Infanta's dress and wig drew universal criticism from the French women whose standards of elegance were somewhat above those of the Spanish dressmakers. All who saw her in these first days commented upon her white skin, obviously long protected from the Spanish sun, and none of them asked what she was to do as the wife of Louis XIV, who loved the outdoors, the elements, and insisted that his entourage ignore the hazards of weather as he did himself. Nor was there anyone to comment on her intelligence, beyond the fact that she could not properly speak French. Madame de Motteville, whose Spanish background gave her ready access to the conversations in Spanish that went on around her, has given us, quite unwittingly, some insight into the new queen's mental processes; there can be little doubt about it—Marie-Thérèse's responses to situations were very elementary.

Louis did not yet know that the bargain he had made when he exchanged duty to his dynasty, his kingdom, and his *gloire* for Marie Mancini, would tie him to a naive, simple-minded woman. Surely in the long run Marie-Thérèse could not hope to make him forget that a vivacious, intelligent girl could be good and exciting company. His first letters to his bride, however, were models of propriety, if hardly model love letters:

It is not without constraint that I have yielded to the reasons that have up to now prevented me from telling Your Majesty of the feelings of my heart. Now that things have reached the stage that gives me the right . . . I am delighted to assure [Your Majesty] . . . that this happiness could not come to anyone who hoped for it more passionately, nor who esteemed himself more fortunate to have it than I. . . .

Marie replied in Spanish:

> I have received Your Majesty's letter . . . accompanied by the demonstrations of attachment and joy. . . . I have received this evidence with the deference that should be given to Your Majesty's gallantry and that the good fortune of having it requires. I shall always try to merit it by conforming to the obligations that Your Majesty imposes upon me, and by desiring for Your Majesty that God guard Your Majesty with all the happiness that I desire for [your Majesty].

The stilted tone might be accounted for by the fact that the writers knew each other only from hearsay and pictures. Louis sent substantial evidence of his willingness to have her for his bride in the form of a coffer encrusted with gold and filled with jewelry. The necklace that Mademoiselle describes leaves no doubt as to their priceless character; Marie-Thérèse wore the jewels of the king when she was married in the French ceremony.

The first marriage was celebrated at Fontarabie on June 2, 1660; Don Luis de Haro wedded the Infanta by procuration in the name of the King of France. Custom had it that a Spanish princess could not leave the kingdom until she was married, while the French king had to be married on French soil. The French court was not invited to this first ceremony, and those who attended incognito were given no special consideration. To their surprise, the Spanish seemed to play it down: those who attended were dressed in black rather than in the gay clothes usual for a marriage, so that it almost seemed that this were an occasion for mourning, as if this marriage of the Infanta were simply a tragedy resultant upon the loss of the war. The Spanish carried this attitude further in the exchange of gifts between the two families; the French were lavish in their presents, but Philip sent his sister several pairs of Spanish gloves of questionable quality. Even Anne, who usually wanted to hear no criticism of her Spanish relatives, was disappointed.

The meetings between the two families were also somewhat unsatisfactory. According to the protocol the two kings were supposed to meet only once, when they signed the treaty and swore to keep the peace between the two kingdoms. It worked out otherwise, because the French were less formal than the Spanish. Anne and her ladies, accompanied by most of the French court, visited the Spanish king at Fontarabie on the fourth of June. The queen tried to kiss her brother, but he managed to hold her off. Marie-Thérèse went to her knees before her aunt who raised her up and kissed her tenderly. The French court paid its compliments to Philip IV, who was particularly friendly to Mazarin and complimented Turenne by saying that he had caused him some "bad moments." Then Anne and her brother sat down for a conversation in Spanish. They had not seen each other for a half-century, and most of the correspondence between the two had been in the nature of announcements of births, deaths, marriages, and the like, usually written by secretaries; there was little to talk about. Anne excused herself for having been so good a Frenchwoman during the late war: "I owe it to the King, my son, and to France," she said. Philip replied, "I respect you for it. The Queen, my wife, would have done the same, for although she was French, in her heart she had only the interests of my kingdoms and the desire to please me." Anne, who had counted much upon seeing her brother, was sorely frustrated by the whole scene.

At this moment Mazarin announced that an "Unknown" wanted the door opened so that he could look into the chamber and see the new queen. This was the first view that the young couple had of each other. Philip admitted that he was to have a handsome son-in-law, but he forbade the Infanta to express her opinion of Louis until she had "passed the door." Marie-Thérèse did say that the "door" seemed handsome to her. When Louis left the scene he told Conti and Turenne that the "homely headdress and costume" of the Infanta surprised him, but after the first shock, he realized that she had "considerable beauty" and that "it would be easy to love her." A few minutes later he galloped his horse on a gallant cavalcade so that the royal party across the river could see his excellent horsemanship. Marie-Thérèse: "What? Do I find him to my taste? He certainly is handsome, and he performed that cavalcade like a very gallant gentleman."

On Sunday, June 6, the Treaty of the Pyrenees was solemnly signed in a room of the temporary structure on the Isle of Pheasants.[10] The room was decorated with rich rugs, tapestries, and flags; half was in the Spanish style, and half in the French. As usual, Madame de Motteville had a comment on the taste: she found the blue and gold of the French more pleasing than the red and yellow of the Spanish. A press of courtiers and officials from both kingdoms crowded into the room to witness the ceremony; their bright costumes provided additional color for the scene. The household troops of the two kings were drawn up in battle array on either side of the river. We have a contemporary engraving and several literary descriptions depicting the event; the soldiers with their gaudy colors and streaming banners, the officers riding back and forth, contrast strikingly with the disorderly tents, wine kegs, butchering activities, outdoor commissary restaurants, dogs, and other figures that also were there. Inside, a secretary of state from each kingdom read the text of the treaty in French and in Spanish, and then the two kings took the simple oath on the Bible to maintain the treaty and keep the peace between their lands. Amid pageantry that probably can be called baroque, this simple oath established peace in Catholic Christendom, and then the treaty was signed. We wonder what went through Louis' mind while he affixed his signature.

On June 7, Marie-Thérèse left Spain. The parting was painful, replete with tears and embraces. Anne, Louis, and Philippe were also present. King Philip IV described the scene: "I feel half dead. The sight of my daughter's tears and those of my sister [were expected] but to have those two boys hanging on my neck and crying like children. . . . I am sentimental like that myself, and I can't take any more of it." The tears and farewells over, Marie-Thérèse mounted the elegant French carriage, resplendent with gold and silver embroidery, and was driven to the temporary residence of the French court at Saint-Jean-de-Luz, followed and preceded by a crowd of horsemen and carriages that churned the dust and made merry the voyage. France had a queen, and in due time there might be a dauphin.

The next day was a busy one. The young queen received the oaths of the officers of her household, submitted to the demands of the French dressmakers who were preparing her wedding gown, and struggled to accustom herself to the ways of the French court, where the royal family lived a life in the public gaze with very little privacy for anything. It is hard to know whether she was aware of the many conflicts that raged around her: the king had ordered that she kiss no one but his mother; the Princess Palatine wished to wear a "train"; there were dozens of questions of precedence. La Grande Mademoiselle was chagrined over not receiving a gift of perfume from Philip IV; and her sisters were miffed at not receiving a kiss from Marie-Thérèse; Mazarin ruled against Princess Palatine's pretensions, whereupon that young lady threatened to boycott the ceremony. Of all this and more, the Infanta probably knew nothing.

On June 9, the second marriage ceremony made Marie-Thérèse the Queen of France. Dressed in a gown covered with gold fleurs-de-lis, the new queen seemed beautiful to all observers, while Louis in severe black made a brave figure as the groom. The ceremony was long: a solemn high mass, gifts of gold and silver pieces, the kiss of peace for the bride (given by Mazarin), and finally the marriage vows. As was usual in French ceremonies, where more people always tried to enter the room than could easily be accommodated, the scene was a little rowdy with talking, pushing, jostling, and complaints. But it was always thus; even at a funeral ceremony the French court was disorderly.

That evening the queen mother, followed by her ladies, led the young queen to the house where the king was staying. The two queens, Louis, and his brother, ate supper together in public, and immediately afterward Louis announced that he wanted to go to bed. Marie-Thérèse with tears in her eyes exclaimed, "Oh, there is much time yet!" But she submitted to her ladies, who led her off. While she was undressing, someone said that the king was ready. "Quickly! Quickly!" she cried. "The King awaits me." Tradition has it that she made only one request of Louis on her wedding night—that he never abandon her. This may even be true; the young princess seems to have been deeply moved by leaving her father's court for a strange land, and she probably realized that it would take more than the love that Anne, as aunt and mother-in-law, so freely offered for her to find happiness in the court of France. Louis was often to be unfaithful to her, but he never abandoned her, and even when he was most involved with mistresses who made the queen seem dull and dowdy, he did not neglect his duties as husband.

The trip from the Spanish frontier to Paris consumed a leisurely two and a half months. Louis had never seen much of this part of France, nor had these people ever seen their king. Now they had many chances to cheer Louis and his Spanish bride, to harangue the court, and to watch the ceremony of royalty. At one point on the journey the party was shaken up by a slight earthquake, but for the most part it was a simple, triumphant procession. They spent several days at Chambord, passed on to Fontainebleau, and then, stopping at Fouquet's château Vaux-le-Vicomte, to Vincennes where preparations were completed for the triumphant entry into Paris. This pageantry was typical of the seventeenth century. A procession or parade was a means of advertising or flaunting power and place, of crystallizing public opinion. When a new diplomat arrived at a foreign capital, he held a formal "entry" with guards, pack horses, mules, and carriages; when a king married or triumphed at arms, he held a formal entry, sometimes through a breach in the walls, sometimes through a triumphal gate, sometimes simply through streets decorated for the occasion. Thus when Louis brought home a Spanish bride, as token of the fact that a successful war had been concluded, it was fitting that there should be a magnificent entry into Paris, followed by three days of celebration.

The parade has been preserved for us by a pictorial representation made at the time, as well as by pamphlets that "explained" to the people who watched it what they were seeing. Paris took three days off to welcome the king and his bride; its inhabitants had to have "programs" to help them enjoy the spectacle. The parade was led by representatives of the religious houses of Paris (Carmelites, Augustins, Jacobins, Cordeliers), then thirty priests of Paris, followed by the faculty of the Sorbonne; then three hundred archers and the guards; the government of the city, representatives of the merchant corps, and other bourgeois notables; and next the archers of the Châtelet and the notaries, lawyers, and judges of the sovereign courts, the Parlementarians resplendent in their magnificent robes. Then came the royal party. Mazarin's personal contribution was the largest, even larger than that of the king: 72 mules in 24 rows covered with rich harness, the cardinal's carriage with its blinds drawn to indicate that he was not there, and then the gentlemen and guards of his household. Next the queen mother's household and pack animals, then the king's 60 mules and 24 horses followed by the members of his government; Fouquet, the four secretaries of state, a company of master of requests, and the chancellor on horseback with his umbrella and the six young men who marched at his side. Then more soldiers, gentlemen of the court, governors and lieutenants of the king's provinces, the Hundred Swiss, and with a fanfare of trumpets, the marshals of France, the high officers of the king's household, and finally the king himself mounted on a splendid horse and followed by his brother, Philippe, the Princes of Condé and Conti, and the Duke of Enghien and their officers. Then came the triumphal chariot bearing the new queen. It was drawn by six Danish gray horses and entirely covered with embroidery of gold and silver. The queen was clothed in a golden robe and decorated with pearls and other jewels that set off her splendor. She was gracious with her smiles as she replied to the cheers that welcomed her to the capital. Following her were the carriages with the ladies of rank: princesses of the blood, foreign princesses, and the wives of dukes and peers of the realm. Then came more soldiers, the bodyguard of the king, and at the end, the officers and gentlemen of the king's falconry. It took hours for the parade to pass a given point: Paris had not seen such a sight in a generation—perhaps never before. Some writers would give this procession the title "baroque" on the assumption that such display was typically baroque and also typical of this epoch; a more perceptive understanding of the display would relate it to the pageantry that men have always loved to act out, whether it be a ticker-tape parade on Wall Street to welcome a Lindbergh, a G.A.R. parade on the Fourth of July in Plainsville, U.S.A., or a victory march down the Champs-Elysées. Such displays provided entertainment for men in the drabber days of yesteryear before television and the mobility of the automobile made them seem old-fashioned, or even bizarre.

Mazarin did not ride in the parade to take the cheers that were rightfully his for having ended the war. During the course of the negotiations of the Ile des Faisans and the marriage ceremonies of June, his health showed signs of deterioration. Old and sick, he probably sensed that he soon must die, and did not want to, or could not, put the added strain of the parade upon his health. Instead he reviewed the procession from a balcony in Paris. The queen mother joined him there; perhaps it was in defiance of all those who had written such horrid things about her, perhaps simply to associate herself with Mazarin in the double triumph of the peace and the marriage. These two people who had held together the kingdom and its constitution as they understood it were there to wave to the king and his bride as they passed in review. Neither of them needed the "programs" that were being sold on the streets to tell them what was passing before their eyes![11]

During the celebrations and receptions that followed the parade, Mazarin must often have meditated upon the fickleness of men. The very people who had exiled him and placed a price on his head now praised him as the greatest statesman of the age. It probably gave him some satisfaction, but he was too sick to look forward to long enjoyment of his triumph. He suffered from gout, kidney stones, hydrothorax, and probably other maladies not identified by his physicians; he often was wracked with pain and yellow with jaundice; obviously he had not much longer to live.

During the months that were left to him, he concerned himself with the innumerable details of the peace settlement, the problem of the restoration of the Stuarts in England, and the negotiation of the peace of Oliva that ended the war in the Baltic and Poland. He also seems to have redoubled his efforts to prepare Louis for the task of governing the kingdom that must soon be his. All those who watched him during these last months of his life testify that Mazarin realized that his death was near, and prepared himself, his family affairs, and the kingdom for that fact. Mazarin met death as he had met life: resolute and serene in the face of conditions that he could not control. Madame de Motteville, who had little use for him as a person, admitted that he died like a philosopher as well as like a Christian, even though she obviously had some reservations about the ultimate destination of his soul.

Before we leave Mazarin, a most important influence on Louis' early life, we must consider the most telling criticism leveled against the cardinal: his avarice. All favorites and ministers of seventeenth-century rulers became rich, fabulously so. Sully, Luynes, Richelieu, Colbert, Le Tellier, Louvois, and others close to the throne were all loaded with worldly goods; so was Mazarin, and after his return to France in 1652, he seemed even more avid than most for money and lands. Charles Péguy may have explained his situation in a moving essay on *Misère,* in which he points out that anyone who has ever been faced with want attempts to pile up insurance against its ever happening again. In exile Mazarin found himself without resources, probably forced to rely upon the charity of others; when he returned to France he did pile up funds and wealth both inside and outside of the kingdom. Had he not been a foreigner, the French might not have condemned him so strongly, but he *was* a foreigner who ruled France, and he did become rich—the combination was sinful. One of the stories most quoted to prove Mazarin's greed tells of a visit to his art gallery, when he realized that it was probably the last time that he would ever see his beautiful statues and paintings: he shook his head and sadly remarked that it was a shame to "leave all these things." Curiously enough, what seems to have been an appreciation of beauty in face of the tragedy of approaching death has been interpreted as evidence of avarice. There is no need to whitewash Mazarin. He did use the knowledge that he had as chief of state to engage in profitable speculations; he did lend money to the king's government at usurious terms; and undoubtedly he did urge the king to reward him handsomely for his labors. But all this was well within the usual framework for a seventeenth-century minister of state. Moreover, Mazarin used his wealth for the king's service when it was needed, and even his worst enemies cannot accuse him of taking money needed by the vital activities of the state. Moreover, it must also be pointed out that no small part of the great fortune that he had at his death was given to him after the signing of the Treaty of the Pyrenees, and the preamble of the gift document states clearly that the royal family considered his services to be beyond the possibility of adequate reward.[12] Louis and his mother both believed that Mazarin had saved the Bourbon throne in the years 1649–54, and by defeating Spain, had given the Bourbon family the preeminent position in Europe. What kind of money or what gifts of lands could repay a minister for such service? Before he died, Mazarin, at Colbert's suggestion, gave all his wealth to the king. Louis waited a decent time and then returned it to his minister, thus confirming once and for all that the royal family considered the great wealth of this remarkable man to have been legitimately acquired.

Most of Mazarin's wealth went to his family. Like Richelieu, Mazarin arranged brilliant marriages for his nieces—the Mazarinettes, as they have been called. These girls became the wives of men from the royal and princely families of Bourbon, Savoy, Modena, and Colonna (the latter was the husband of Marie Mancini, whom Mazarin believed to be better married to a Colonna in Rome than to someone in France). One of these nieces (Hortense) married a relative of Cardinal Richelieu who took the title Duc de Mazarin. But Mazarin also founded the College of the Four

Nations, in which he hoped to teach the king's non-French subjects to love the throne; he gave money to religious foundations and for the building of chapels; he collected books and manuscripts that have become the core of two great French libraries, and art works that have enriched the kingdom; and his personal archives began one of the world's great archival collections, the Archives of the French Ministry of Foreign Affairs.

How should we judge this man who from relatively humble origins came to rule a great kingdom more absolutely than any minister before or after his time? The political education of the king was unquestionably his most important legacy, but not everyone is convinced that he should be praised for these labors. The *Catéchisme des Courtisans,* published in Cologne in 1668, dealt with his influence thus:

Q. What is the doctrine of Mazarin? A. It is the same that the French tyrants have taught, and that their followers embrace with all their hearts.

Q. What is the faith of Mazarin? A. To believe that all belongs to the King; that he may take all without returning anything.

Q. What is the Credo? A. I believe in the King for my own interest, he is all powerful and can do all things; and in his only favorite, Mazarin, conceived in the mercenary spirit, born of Richelieu, suffered under Gaston and the *Fronde,* died for his ministry, and descended into hell where he sits at the right hand of Lucifer to persecute the living. I believe in his spirit and in the church of the devil, or rather the congregation of partisans, in the government of the Estates, in the maintenance of the finances, the resurrection of tariffs, and the eternal extortion of the people.

This is the judgment of an enemy of both the cardinal and his royal pupil, but one assumption is correct, namely that Mazarin's work and his position in history must in large part be judged by the fruits of the regime of Louis XIV. Mazarin the politician and the statesman, the patron of arts, letters, and sciences, was the prototype for the regime of his successor. Louis did not have Mazarin's intelligence, but he did have enough to appreciate his work and to build upon his system. He respected, perhaps even loved, Mazarin enough to wish to continue his regime long after the cardinal was dead.

Mazarin's last days lend further evidence to support the belief that he and the queen were more to each other than just minister and sovereign. Anne moved into the room next to that of the dying man to be better able to care for him; her vigil was that of a woman still in love, or at least still under the spell of deep affection. Louis, too, stayed at Vincennes after it became obvious that the Cardinal must soon die. There were many touching scenes at the bedside when these three, who had gone through so much together, prepared to say good-bye. Before he died Mazarin made magnificent presents of jewelry to the two queens, to Louis and his brother, Philippe, to Condé and Turenne. Anne's was a superb, large diamond ring; Louis' was a cluster of beautiful diamonds, valued at almost two million livres, that is to say, about two-fifths of the value of all the crown jewels.[13] Toward the end Mazarin insisted that the royal family discontinue its visits and that Anne should move to a room where she could not hear his difficult breathing, and where she could get some rest. He did not want them to remember him as he must become in the last stage of life, and he wanted the opportunity to make his peace with God and his own conscience.

Mazarin accepted death calmly; he called in his servants and asked their pardon; he sent his greetings to the Parlement and to the assembly of the clergy; he finally asked pardon for saying sharply to his physicians that they had killed him. He died after receiving the last sacraments of the church and the consolations of a pious priest who stayed with him to the end.

Early in the morning of March 9, 1661, Louis was awakened with the sad news. His first act was to seek out his ministers and his mother, and before the morning was well advanced, the whole court was on the road to Paris. That same day Anne went to Val-de-Grâce for prayer and devotions. As we have seen, the Bourbons never stayed long in a house with a corpse. The King of France faced death only once—when it was his own. After the family left, the body was cared for by monks, embalmers, the dead man's household servants, and prelates who directed the devotions, prayers, and vigils. Louis ordered full mourning for his dead minister, an homage never before and never afterward given by his line to anyone outside the royal family. It was Anne who finally called a halt to further talk about the dead man, for as she wisely understood, nothing useful could be accomplished by going over and over again the loss that they had suffered.

Mazarin had ruled France from the day of his return from exile in 1652 until his death in 1661 virtually as a monarch; Louis had deferred to him in all things. Now that the minister was dead, the young king faced the task that he "had both feared and hoped for." There is every reason to believe that he regretted the death of the cardinal. He wrote that he had hoped that Mazarin would live on a few years more to give him a longer time to learn his "trade" before he must himself take full responsibility for realizing his *gloire*. One has only to read the sheaf of letters that Louis wrote to family and friends to announce Mazarin's death to see that the king was deeply affected by his loss. "God has visited upon me the greatest affliction that I could experience," he wrote on March 9 to Philip IV. "The only consolation is that . . . he died in consonance with his religion so that

I can hope for the divine bounty. . . ." On March 13, in another letter to Philip IV, he speaks of the "great loss that I have just experienced of which I have already written your majesty. . . ." On March 17, in the formal letter of announcement to the King of Spain—a letter that may have been written by a secretary at the king's dictation: ". . . the sole consolation that I have now is to tell your Majesty that he died experiencing feelings of religion, piety, and repentance of his errors, so that I can hope of the divine goodness that it has already given him rewards for his labors. . . . " "Human condolences," he wrote to the Duke of Modena, "are feeble in face of this rude blow . . . the memory of so worthy a minister will always have on me the same effect as his presence. . . ." To the Duchess of Modena, one of Mazarin's nieces: ". . . in waiting until it pleases God to send me the consolation that I need, nothing will comfort me more than to send you . . . evidences of my friendship. . . ."[14] Even if one separates the letters that had to be sent as formal announcements of the cardinal's death to the governments of Europe, there still remains enough evidence of Louis' feelings for his minister to discount the oft-repeated suggestion that Mazarin might have been disgraced if he had not had the fortune to die at the right moment.

II

THE NEW GOVERNMENT:
THERE SHALL BE NO
MINISTER-FAVORITE*

EVEN AS Mazarin sank into his grave, the new government began to take
form; while the cardinal made his peace with God and no longer concerned
himself with the minutiae of politics, Louis started to meet with the
secretaries and ministers of state to discuss the affairs of the day. On the
morning of March 9, after Mazarin's nurse announced that the cardinal was
dead, the young king's first act was to summon the secretaries of state, the
superintendent of finance, the chancellor, and Lionne, to order them to
meet in Paris the next morning. Louis was already acting *en roi;* it remained
to be seen what he would find that role to be.

His speech on that March 10, 1661, has become famous. Addressing
the chancellor, he said:

> Monsieur, I have called you, together with my secretaries and ministers
> of state, to tell you that up to this moment I have been pleased to entrust the
> government of my affairs to the late Cardinal. It is now time that I govern
> them myself. You will assist me with your counsels when I ask for them. Out-
> side of the regular business of justice, which I do not intend to change, Mon-
> sieur the Chancellor, I request and order you to seal no orders except by my
> command, or after having discussed them with me, or at least not unless a
> secretary brings them to you on my part. And you, Messieurs, my secretaries
> of state, I order you not to sign anything, not even a passport . . . without my
> command; to render account to me personally each day and to favor no one. . . .
> And you, Monsieur the Superintendent [of finances] I have explained to you
> my wishes; I request you to use M. Colbert whom the late Cardinal has recom-
> mended to me. As for Lionne, he is assured of my affection. I am satisfied with
> his services. . . .

Shortly thereafter the president of the Assembly of the Clergy asked
to whom he should henceforth address himself for the settlement of
business. "To me, Monsieur the Archbishop, to me," replied the king. Louis

later wrote to his son that he was sometimes timid and frightened during those first days when he had to talk in public *en roi.* If it was to this session of March 10 that he referred, no one but the king himself knew of his fright.

This was the day Mazarin had referred to when he wrote that he would die happily when he knew that Louis could govern the kingdom by himself, using his ministers when and as he wished. It was a significant reversal of the political practice of a half-century. Since the death of Henry IV, the actual government of the kingdom had been entrusted to a minister-favorite, who, while he derived his power from the king, formulated and administered policy and governed in the name of the crown. The king or regent retained the right to review policy and the minister's tenure was entirely dependent upon royal satisfaction with his work. But in fact this was a doubtful power for the monarch, since the king or regent was usually completely dependent upon the minister for the conduct of the government; thus the right of review frequently merely meant the right to approve.

There were serious disadvantages to this form of government. Neither Louis XIII nor the two queens who had headed regency governments in the half-century before 1661 had been strong enough or wise enough to govern the kingdom, but there was no reason to assume that weak rulers would have the wisdom to pick and support strong ministers. Indeed, Marie de Médicis' regency and Louis XIII, in the first years of his reign, both failed to do so. With no political machinery to regularize government outside the royal will, the politics of the kingdom were unhappily dependent upon the chance that the king would find and use a minister capable of governing.

The system created by Richelieu and Mazarin had had a profound impact upon the political life of the kingdom. These two ministers had begun the process of centralization that was eventually to undermine the traditional pluralistic structure of French political society. Traditionally the governors of provinces, the judges of the so-called "sovereign courts," the councils and magistrates of towns and cities had shared the government of the kingdom with the king's council; but under the two cardinals, the council and its officials gradually encroached upon these traditional corporations and officials by reversing their decrees, taking jurisdiction out of their hands, and putting them under the supervision or even control of royal officials, intendants of justice, police, and taxation. Complaints about the activity of the king's council were at the very top of the lists of grievances presented by the Parlementary *Frondeurs* in 1648 and by the princely *Frondeurs* two years later. The ancient federal structure of the kingdom, in which noblemen and royal officials with tenure independent of the king were in a position to control large segments of power, was at stake. The two "revolutionary" cardinals had begun the centralization of this power and had aroused considerable antagonism. The *Frondeurs* who urged the young Louis to "govern without a companion" (i.e., without Mazarin) were simply asking him to reverse this process that the ministers had introduced.

With Mazarin gone, the big question was: How will the king govern without a first minister? The two cardinals had governed using the traditional royal officers: secretaries of state, chancellor, superintendent of finance, etc. But in the course of the years it became apparent that they had created new institutions out of these older ones, and even more important, that they had developed new machinery for the organization of power. The basic fact was that each of the cardinals had developed a "team" made up of relatives and friends who were completely dependent upon him, and who worked with him to manage the government of the kingdom as well as the king or regent. The cardinals tried to surround the king with their own creatures.[1] Sometimes they had been able to disgrace officials who would not cooperate; sometimes they merely isolated and bypassed them. Thus the posts in the government, the church, the army, and the royal households were staffed whenever possible by the friends of the favorite. Much has been written about the "spy services" of Richelieu and Mazarin—it was no formal organization like those developed by modern states; the minister simply placed his friends where they could hear about all sorts of things and report them to their "patron." Mazarin's correspondence, preserved in the Ministry of Foreign Affairs Archives, is filled with letters from men and women who were in his debt, or hoped to be. Everyone understood this system. When Richelieu and Louis XIII were dead, their enemies tried to secure the disgrace of Richelieu's "creatures and relatives"; during the *Frondes* the cry was against the "creatures of the cardinal."

What would happen to this system if there were no first minister? Could the king create a "team"? He would not have a host of relatives to place in key positions, and even if he did have, he would not give them places of power, for in France a king's relatives were always dangerous to his government. He could not marry his nieces to officers of the army and household; they were needed for dynastic politics. He would not have a party of friends and "creatures," for a king was supposed to give equal justice to all his subjects. Thus the question on that March 10 was: What would now be the apparatus of power? Louis obviously assumed that he could step into the dead Mazarin's shoes without causing a ripple, for he planned to take over the cardinal's "creatures" as his own. Mazarin's last advice seems to have concerned the men whom he was leaving for the king's service. Le Tellier, Lionne, Fouquet, and Colbert were designated for the top echelon, but a host of lesser people like Rose, Mazarin's secretary, who was to be Louis' personal secretary for nearly three decades, were also now to become "creatures" of the king. Even the governor of the Bastille was on this list; "Console yourself," Louis said to him in Mazarin's antechamber on the morning of the cardinal's death, ". . . serve me well . . . you have found a good master."

But could these men risk becoming the king's creatures? Louis knew that he would govern the kingdom, but there were many in the court who did not believe it. How could anyone expect a young man of twenty-two to assume such a burden? If he did not, who would? Would there be a new first minister? Opportunists wanted to be on the team of the winner.

Louis may have believed that he could become his own first minister without altering the mechanism of government, but it could not be that way. When Le Tellier, Lionne, and Fouquet emerged as his chief ministers of state, as the members of the highest council of the king, a wholly new situation arose. They were the ministers of the king, not the "creatures" of the king's minister; each of them was henceforth dependent upon the favor of the king for his own future and that of his family and friends. Each realized that he was in competition with the others for that favor, and even more important, each of them realized that there was the possibility that the young king might tire of his task and that one of them would step into the role of the late cardinal. Even the queen mother was not at all sure that her son would persist in his new role. Louis himself had not yet written that it was his decision to "abolish the very word 'First Minister' " in the kingdom; and only Louis, of all the people in the court, knew that he was enjoying the *métier* of the king, that he was thrilled to "find in myself skills that I did not know I had." It was an exhilarating experience. Louis knew that there would never be another first minister. But in their ignorance, the men in the court began to speculate on the question of Mazarin's successor and to prepare to greet his rising star in time to share his fortune and favor.

Who were the possible successors of the cardinal? Those who looked to Villeroi—who had been Louis' governor—somehow failed to recognize his incompetence; Louis allowed him ready access to his person and obviously was fond of him, but he did not even use him in the government. Others remembered that the Cardinal de Retz had hoped to be next in the line of cardinal-ministers; he had the skills, the daring, the cunning. But Louis detested him, and he was in Rome as a refugee from the king's justice. The king's preceptor, Péréfixe, was a scholar, but not the man to dominate the king, and he had no ambition to do so. This left the three men whom Louis had called to be his ministers of state: Lionne, Le Tellier, and Fouquet. Of the three, Lionne could quickly be dismissed as a candidate. He was an experienced diplomat, he had done Mazarin's business in Spain, Germany, and Italy; he knew the languages of Europe and the courts of the great, but he was not ambitious to govern. Le Tellier might have thought of himself as a possible successor to Mazarin. He had great experience with the government of the kingdom and he was an excellent, efficient administrator. But Le Tellier probably also knew the young king better than either of the other ministers, and probably understood that Louis would not tire of the job. Le Tellier was not a man to push himself. For all the power he exercised and all the skills he must have known to be his, Le Tellier always appeared as a modest, retiring, self-effacing man. Thus, of the three, Fouquet alone was a possible candidate for Mazarin's place.

The superintendent of finances was a man of parts. He was intelligent, highly skilled, and his vision of himself placed few limits upon his possible advancement. His motto *que non ascendam* asked to what heights might he not aspire. In his own mind, Fouquet set few limits to his career. He knew that he had the talents needed to govern; he probably was the only man in the entourage of the late cardinal with a vision of grandeur large enough to qualify him as Mazarin's successor. Fouquet also well understood the system of government by first minister, and even before Mazarin's death, from the relatively independent position allowed him as superintendent of finances, he had begun the creation of an apparatus of "creatures" to help him take over the affairs of the king. The superintendent had money to give, he had offices to fill, and he had influence with Mazarin, for the cardinal had needed his skills: these were the ingredients with which to create a political machine.

The young king understood this very well and also saw that Fouquet was ambitious to dominate him and the kingdom. In his *Mémoires,* Louis tells us that he was anxious to right the wrongs that Fouquet had committed, anxious to give relief to his subjects who cried out against the finance minister. "But," he went on, "that which made him most guilty in my eyes was that far from profiting from the generosity that I had shown him by retaining him in my councils, he found new reasons for believing that he could fool me; far from becoming more wise, he simply became more clever. But whatever artifice he might attempt, I was not long in recognizing his bad faith. For he could not stop his excessive expenses, his fortifications of his château, his decoration of his palaces, the formation of cabals, and *placing his friends in important places which he secured for them at my expense in the hope of thus making himself sovereign arbiter of the state* [author's italics]."[2] The young king might well have been able to forgive this man had he simply clustered about himself playwrights, artists, musicians, architects, and landscape gardeners, but he could not forgive him the cabals, the "creatures," the fortification of Belle-Isle, the obvious plan to make himself indispensable and therefore all-powerful.

Fouquet was, indeed, more clever than wise. He lent his money freely, he gave little pensions and gifts, he even tried to give money to Mademoiselle de la Vallière when she became a "friend" of the young king. He pensioned Lionne, who always seemed to be short of funds.[3] It is probably true that Fouquet needed a tribe of assistants to help him manage the king's finances, but, unless his ambitions soared beyond the office of superintendent, he did not need the courtiers and others around the king who took his money in return for information and perhaps more. Fouquet was also unwise in his conquests among the ladies of the court; he may have fancied himself a lady-killer, but attentions to women could be the result of political ambitions as well as personal ones. After the superintendent's arrest there were a host of people in the court who feared the revelations in his letters and books; they had taken of his bounty and often enough asked for more.

Fouquet obviously took the two previous minister-favorites as his models. He built up a coterie of people dependent upon him for favor, patronized men of letters who might become his publicity men, artists who could help him build and decorate his beautiful château at Vaux, and entertainers who could provide the "delights" that were so prized by his day; these things had been done before by Richelieu and Mazarin. Had he been a little more perceptive, Fouquet might have realized that these outward manifestations of power might impress the courtiers with his rising star, but they would also alert Louis XIV to his ambitions. Had he remembered that the young king had come of age during the *Fronde* when noblemen and courtiers had military forces that could and did challenge those of the king, he would have avoided the impression that he was fortifying his château at Belle-Isle so that it could be used against the king as well as against the English.

There were signals that a more alert man would have recognized. Louis plainly announced that he did not intend to have a first minister. The fact that the king seemed to accept Fouquet should not have lulled the superintendent; he needed only to recall that de Retz before him had hoped to dominate the king, only to find himself under arrest. Fouquet should have known that Louis could dissemble his intentions and act before his victim knew what was happening, that Louis had learned the lesson when Mazarin and Anne arrested Condé and would not need further instruction. The most important danger signal that he missed was the appointment of Colbert to the finance department. Somehow Fouquet saw in Colbert only Mazarin's manager of personal affairs who now needed a job and surely could not be dangerous to the superintendent. He failed to see Colbert as a rival whose position as an executor of Mazarin's will gave him entrée to the king. His spies should have told him that Colbert was a cold, calculating, crafty schemer whom the dying cardinal had strongly recommended, and who was willing to go to great lengths to secure his own future. Colbert tells us that the king was scrupulous in his insistence that Mazarin's will be carried out to the letter; he does not tell us anything of the conversations that he had with Louis while discussing it, but it takes little imagination to see that this was Colbert's chance to undermine the superintendent. He had been placed in the office to watch Fouquet, to see whether or not he was honest; as might be expected, the evidence of Fouquet's "wickedness" piled up fast under Colbert's careful examination.

Why was Fouquet so blind? At twenty-two Louis was a reticent young man who well understood how to conceal things that went on in his mind, but it was common talk in the court that he was determined never to be dominated by anyone. Fouquet should have known, but through his ambition to rule he seemed oblivious to the danger he ran. Perhaps he was doomed anyway: Louis was clearly afraid of him[4] and Colbert stood in the shadows anxious to bring him down.

Fouquet not only failed to read the signs; he also committed the supreme blunder of giving the king an opportunity to be ruthless against him. At his château, Vaux-le-Vicomte, Fouquet entertained the young king perhaps more royally than Louis himself could have entertained. Why not? Mazarin had often given expensive parties with exotic foods, excellent entertainment, and prizes for everyone. It is not true, as the story is so often told, that this was the first time Louis saw this beautiful château;[5] he had stopped at Vaux with his bride on the way to Paris the year before. But it is true that the party advertised the luxury of Fouquet's way of life, and it was easy for Colbert to suggest that Fouquet could not pay for such an affair if he were strictly honest with the king's money.

It was a party to talk about: Molière's troupe of comedians, Lully's musicians, decoration by the very men who were to create Versailles, food under the maître d'hôtel who was destined to make Condé's household famous. It was obviously entertainment for a king, and Louis decided that it must have been paid for out of money that should have been in the king's treasury. But if Louis' own words are significant, and if his acts are to be considered, it was not Vaux-le-Vicomte that worried him as much as Belle-Isle, which the superintendent had purchased at Mazarin's suggestion. At Belle-Isle Fouquet had a château fortified with cannon that was, as far as Louis knew, capable of standing off a royal army. This is why the superintendent was arrested at Nantes rather than at Paris or Fontainebleau; Louis wanted to have an army at hand to occupy Belle-Isle before a new *Fronde* could be organized around the superintendent and his party.[6] Fouquet's supreme blunder was not that he excited the envy of the king, but that he aroused Louis' fear of a new *Fronde* as the alternative to domination by Fouquet as a first minister.

Colbert must have been gleeful to see Fouquet slip his head into the noose, but Louis worried that the trap might fail. How could Fouquet be brought to "justice"? The timing must be right. When he had become the superintendent of finance, he had not given up his appointment in the Parlement of Paris, and so if he were accused of crime, the Parlement would have jurisdiction over his case. There were several reasons to believe that they would not convict him; but even more important, there were men in Parlement who would have had a field day in such a process— with Mazarin on trial rather than Fouquet. This would not do; if Fouquet were to be tried, it had to be before a special commission drawn up to convict him. Therefore Fouquet's arrest was postponed until after the king persuaded him to sell his post in Parlement. Somehow Fouquet did not see the implications of the request that he sell his office.

And there were other difficulties that gave reason for delaying the arrest. The king's treasury was empty and Fouquet was at the time negotiating new contracts with the financiers who farmed the taxes; he alone knew all the details, and he alone could deal with these men. Also, Louis did not want to arrest Fouquet until he had military forces ready to take over Belle-Isle. Historians who now know that no new *Fronde* would break out have trouble understanding how much Louis feared the possibility of such a rebellion. In 1661 the memory of those years was still very green, and the men who had been responsible were still around, and some of them in positions of power.[7] Louis well understood how dangerous the *Fronde* had been; he knew that although Mazarin had stilled the rebellion, he had not yet built the military establishment that could easily prevent a new challenge to the central authority. The fear of another *Fronde* remained constant throughout Louis' life, even after his armies made rebellion no longer possible.

Fouquet's arrest came in the middle of September 1661. It was the second time Louis had used the technique that he had seen his mother and Mazarin employ against Condé ten years earlier. But let us have the young king tell the story himself, as he explained it to his mother in a letter dated at Nantes, September 15, 1661:

> Madame, my Mother, I wrote to you this morning of the execution of my order for the arrest of the Superintendent; but I am now pleased to send you the details. You know that for some time I have had it in my heart, but it was impossible to do it earlier because I wanted him to pay the 30,000 *écus* for the navy, and moreover it was necessary to adjust several other things that could not be done in a day. You should have seen the difficulties I had in speaking to d'Artagnan [Captain of the Musketeers], for I was burdened with a crowd of people, all of them alert, and they would have guessed my intention at the slightest inclination. . . . Nonetheless, two days ago I ordered him to be ready. . . . Finally this morning the Superintendant came to work with me as usual; I received him in one way or another, pretending to look for papers until I saw d'Artagnan through the window in the court . . . then I dismissed the Superintendant, who, after whispering a little with La Feuillade, disappeared . . . poor d'Artagnan thought that he had missed him, and sent Maupertuis to me to say that he suspected that someone had warned him to flee. But he caught up with him in the square before the church and arrested him on my order at about noon. He demanded the papers that he carried, in which I am told that I will find the true state of Belle-Isle, but I have so many things to do that I have not had time to look at them. Nonetheless, I commanded Boucherat to seal the Superintendant's house, and Pellot to seal Pellisson's [one of Fouquet's men who later helped Louis to write his *Mémoires*], whom I have also arrested. . . . I have also ordered the companies of the guard . . . to maneuver . . . so that they would be ready to march on Belle-Isle . . . if by chance the Superintendent should make resistance there. . . . I have talked about the incident with the gentlemen around me. . . . I told them frankly that I had formed the project four months ago. . . . I told them that I would not have another superintendant . . . that I would work on the finances myself with the aid of faithful people who would act under my direction, that this was the only true method of creating abundance [the seventeenth century's word for "prosperity"] and comfort for my people. You will have no trouble believing that these people are sheepish, but I am satisfied that they see that I am not so much of a dupe as they thought, and that it would be wise to attach themselves to me. . . .[8]

This letter, so evidently from the king's own hand, is a most interesting and revealing document. Louis is euphoric in his tone and proud to be able to tell his mother how well he carried it all off, but who can miss that he also felt that he was surrounded by people whom he could not really trust, men who were indebted to Fouquet, men who had considered the king to be a "dupe"? Would he trust them more if they really did "attach themselves to me"? No one will miss the point that Belle-Isle and not Vaux was on the king's mind. Fouquet was not the last man to be "disgraced" by Louis XIV, but he was the only one whose disgrace required so much preparation and whose fall caused the king to worry about rebellion. In arresting Fouquet, Louis obviously believed that he was removing not merely a man whose peculations deprived the king of revenue, but also a man whose position and party might give him power over the kingdom and the king himself.

The subsequent trial only underlined this fact. A special commission was appointed to convict Fouquet, and it was a badly kept secret that the king would not object to a death sentence. The evidence, however, was not conclusive, and not even Colbert's relatives and friends on the commission could convince all the judges that Fouquet should die. The trial was a sensation, for the bundle of papers that fell into the king's hands contained names of men and women who had accepted Fouquet's generosity, as well as ladies who had known his gallantry. It was indiscreet of the superintendent not to have burned some of those letters, but he may have hoped to use them as levers to hold the loyalty of those who owed him much.

What did the papers prove? That Fouquet had been a successful seducer, that he had been generous to people in high places, perhaps even that he was building up a party or a network of "creatures" to help him run the state. But he was being tried for treason and dishonesty, and the papers did not really substantiate these charges. Fouquet probably did misappropriate the king's money; during the preceding decade there had been times when his own and the king's fortunes were both exhausted by Mazarin's needs for soldiers and cash, and it may have been difficult for him to distinguish between his own and the king's money. One thing came to light: Fouquet may have lived lavishly, but he was not a rich man on the scale of a Mazarin, or a Sully, or even of a Colbert a few years later. Perhaps had he become first minister he also might have become immensely rich, but the evidence did not support the charge of greater dishonesty than was usual in and around the king's treasury.

Even in prison Fouquet proved himself to be a formidable opponent, and when he was brought into court he was devastating. Chancellor Séguier urged the charge of treason, only to be asked by Fouquet what he, Séguier, had done during the *Fronde* when Fouquet had stood loyally beside Mazarin and the king. Séguier had been on the other side. Fouquet was just as forceful in defense of his honesty, and it proved hard to show that the man who had provided money for the late war had stolen the king's money. As stories about the trial leaked out, the Colberts began to appear in the role of tyrants and Fouquet as a victim of persecution. The pro-Fouquet–anti-Colbert party continued to grow as Colbert used this same court to force the financiers who had dealt with Fouquet to disgorge their "ill-gotten gains." Even Turenne added his bit; he understood that Fouquet's trial was a contest for power rather than the trial of a swindler when he remarked, "I believe that M. Colbert had a greater desire that he [Fouquet] be hanged, and M. Le Tellier a greater fear that he would not be." As for Louis, how could he tell the court that he wanted Fouquet convicted because he had made the king afraid?

Indeed, it was impossible to find a man guilty of treason simply because the king feared his intentions. In spite of the fact that the court was packed with Colbert's friends and relatives, it would go no further than to find Fouquet guilty of dishonest practices and to order his exile. Louis decided that Fouquet was too dangerous a man to allow him to leave the kingdom where he might conspire to return. He therefore changed the superintendent's sentence from banishment to perpetual imprisonment. Poor Fouquet was sent to the fortress of Pignerol in Italy, far from the possibility of a dramatic break or rescue. He was placed in close confinement, and if Louis read any of the pitiful letters that he composed, protesting his innocence, he gave no sign of it. For almost two decades Louis received regular information about Fouquet's activities and tried to have the jailer "discover" Fouquet's "secrets." Only toward the last of his life did the unfortunate man have the company of other political prisoners (Lauzun) and finally visits from his family. Such treatment at the direct command of the king shows the depths of Louis' feelings: no one, not even Marlborough or Eugène, ever caused Louis so much fear. *This* was Fouquet's crime.[9]

Fouquet was not the man to raise a new *Fronde*. He was a clever man, perhaps even a gracious one; he sought men's affections with his money and his wit, and at the trial he showed himself to be a capable, intelligent, at times too witty opponent. Beside Colbert's chilly manners, or his Uncle Pussort's "hunting-dog bayings" for blood, or Sainte-Hélaine's brutal demands on the court, Fouquet appeared as a gentleman unjustly accused. There was a song of some thirty verses that was sometimes heard in the theater of the fair, or in drawing rooms around the court that mocked the men who had "tried, but failed, to cut off Fouquet's head."[10] The song was in the spirit, and even set to the music, of the *Mazarinades* of the era of the *Fronde,* but there was no one to draw a sword for the fallen superintendent of finance.

Colbert's day had arrived. He understood it even though Le Tellier at first missed the signs. When Louis announced that Colbert would assist him in looking after the finances, Le Tellier remembered that Colbert had been in his bureau before he became Mazarin's trusted man, and so he came forward with the suggestion that Colbert could work under his direction. This would never have suited Colbert, nor was it the intention of the king; neither of them wanted to put Le Tellier in a position to inherit Mazarin's place. But Le Tellier was a cautious man, not a person to fight for the position of minister-favorite. He quickly realized that Colbert and his family and friends would be rivals not subordinates of the Le Telliers; both would loyally serve the king.

The Fouquet incident rang up the curtain on the reign of Louis XIV. Up until the disgrace of the superintendent of finance, it was not clear that Louis would not give over most of his affairs to a minister-favorite while he followed the usual pattern of a young king: hunting, partying, philandering, posing. With Fouquet out of the way in so dramatic a fashion, the court and Europe suddenly realized that Louis really meant that he would be king, and his image as the king who worked at his *métier* began to harden. Madame de Motteville, reflecting this new image, remarks that Louis took great interest in the progress of his cousin Charles II, whose career "augmented [his own] desire to become the greatest and most glorious king that had ever carried the crown up to the present." The good lady's dislike for Mazarin prevented her from seeing that this ambition had long since been planted in the king's mind by Mazarin and the queen mother, but she was right in pointing out that the court at last realized that Louis really intended to govern the kingdom himself.

12

THE COLLABORATORS
OF THE KING*

WITH THE FALL OF Fouquet the characteristic forms of Louis' government began to assume firm contours. There was no first minister; the king discussed secret affairs with the trusted three: Le Tellier, Colbert, and Lionne; he met with the secretaries, the chancellor, and many other people who might have business to transact; he poked his nose into the work of the bureaus and the affairs of his government. Everything centered upon his person. "I wished," he explains, "to divide the execution of my orders among several people, the better to bring them under my authority. It was with this in mind that I chose men of diverse talents and professions, fitting the diversity of the materials that ordinarily fall under the administration of state, and I distributed my time and my confidence according to the understanding that I had of their virtues and the importance of the affairs that I gave over to them." This was the crux of the problem, and he recognized that his most important action was the discovery of the proper talent, the choice of the proper men to help him rule the state.

Saint-Simon tells us that Louis placed his trust in the "vile bourgeoisie," in men without blood or family traditions, rather than in the men who should have been his advisers in government. This judgment has been widely repeated, but like so many things that Saint-Simon said, it is only half true. Louis did pass over the claims of the high nobility, even of his mother and brother, and other princes of the blood, and in his choice of men for high position in the state, he also avoided clergymen whenever possible. This does not mean, however, that he staffed his government with grubby sellers of wine and cloth. On the contrary, the men in his service were nearly all people with family traditions for state service. In seventeenth-century France a son very often followed in his father's footsteps, but there was a progression from one generation to another. The son of a merchant might buy an office; his son in turn would either take up the father's position or buy another office higher in the government hierarchy. The offices of the so-called sovereign courts as well as many other offices in the kingdom were thus the property of official families; indeed, the office of secretary of state belonged to the occupant, and if the king would not grant the secretary's son the right to follow his father, the next secretary had to buy the office from his predecessor. It was from this group of professional royal servants that Louis picked the men to serve his state. Most of them were the sons and grandsons of men who had served as officials in the sovereign courts, or as *maîtres des requêtes,* or as civil servants of the king's father and grandfather. An able man like Colbert could move from the office of clerk in the war ministry to minister of the king in one lifetime, but most of the officials were the sons of men who had already proved themselves in the courts, in the king's councils, in the diplomatic service, or in the *hôtel de ville.* In a word, Louis selected his servants from the cadres of civil and judicial officials; these men and their sons were professional servants of the state—a long cry from Saint-Simon's "vile bourgeoisie."[1]

Louis tells us that he chose these people to man his councils, to advise him on secret affairs, and to serve his state, because he "believed it necessary for people to know by the rank of the men who served [him] that [he] had no intention of sharing authority with them." If the great ones of the land were the king's advisers, they would seem to share the royal authority; professional administrators would not. Some have interpreted this statement to mean that Louis wanted the world to know who governed the kingdom; others, that Louis' experiences with the *Fronde* had convinced him that "men of quality" were too dangerous to be allowed power. It is probably better to recognize that Louis was only doing what Richelieu and Mazarin had done before him. They had replaced men of quality by their creatures wherever possible, so that they could have men about them whom they could trust. Their creatures were nearly always men who were professionally oriented, so that they would implement the policies that the minister developed. Louis did the same thing. He wanted his trusted advisers to be men dependent upon him for their place in the world and men who could carry out the policies determined by his council. The result was as unexpected as it was unwanted by the great lords of the land: a new hereditary administrative class emerged to control the state. The men of the pen with political and administrative experience elbowed aside the men of the sword in the places of power.

In passing up the men of quality, Louis did not seek mere rubber stamps or "yes men" for his advisers. He well knew that there were too many men who would hide their opinions to · achieve preference: ". . . while we are in power," he wrote, "we will never lack men who study to follow our thoughts and to agree with . . . our ideas . . . what we have to fear is the lack of men who know how to contradict us . . . when our inclinations become so obvious that only the bravest dare to oppose . . . it is good that there are some that take this liberty. False compliance that one has for us . . . can hurt us more than stubborn contradiction."[2] The men around the king in these early years of the reign were not "yes men," even though they were happy to see themselves as his creatures.

In his *Mémoires* Louis explains that he carefully picked his trusted ministers for their merit and probable usefulness. His critics chide him for claiming credit for his choices on the ground that all the men were in his entourage when Mazarin died. We have already noted that this quite misses the point. Even though Mazarin might have indicated the men who could best serve the state, Louis had to make the decision to employ them. There were many men in his entourage who would have been willing, indeed eager, to become his advisers and his tools; a man of lesser capacity would have thought twice before taking strong men as confidants. Louis' great merit was exactly in this: he chose men senior to himself in experience as well as age, men with an expert knowledge of the problems of the kingdom rather than "yes men" who might have flattered him by their submission. This young man who informed the world that he intended to govern his kingdom was no vain "know-it-all" who wished to be surrounded by flatterers and sycophants.

In many ways Le Tellier was the most interesting of the group; he was also destined for the high honor of chancellor. He came from a family allied both to the magistrates of the Parlement and to the officers of the city government of Paris. His own career included service as *procureur du roi* at the Châtelet, *maître des requêtes,* and intendant of the army in the days of Richelieu; under Mazarin he became a trusted adviser and secretary of state in charge of military affairs. Anne and Mazarin regarded him as their most trusted servant; his code name in their confidential correspondence was "the faithful one." Le Tellier was an excellent administrator as well as an imaginative statesman; he understood well the military and political problems that confronted the kingdom. Even more important, he understood the procedures that were necessary to combat the evils inherent in the system. In contrast to his son Louvois, who became famous for his harsh exterior, Le Tellier was a "soft" man. Like Mazarin,

who as we have seen always tried to dissemble his intentions behind
apparent compliance, Le Tellier had learned that this was the only way an
official of a regency government could operate. He had to deal with princes
of the blood like Condé, with great lords like Vendôme, with soldiers like
Turenne, de Bellefonds, or d'Albret—men who had never brooked civilian
control and who regarded a "mere pusher of a pen" as beneath their dignity.
And yet it was the "pusher of the pen" who reorganized the army and gave
it the form it was to keep with only slight modifications until the Revolution of 1789.

Historians, fascinated with the brilliance and brutality of Louvois, have
tended to give him credit for the work that, in fact, his father actually did.[3]
We can see now that in this first decade of Louis' personal government
when the new army made its bow to the world, the war ministry was
actually headed and controlled by Le Tellier. His son Louvois did have the
right to succeed his father, and he did operate under his father's supervision
as his assistant and mouthpiece; but only gradually did the young man
come to prominence, and even then, he seems long to have deferred to his
father's judgment. Perhaps the best example of the relationship between the
two can be seen in the episode of the Dutch War when Turenne and Condé
seemed to be united in their opposition to the presumptuous civilian Louvois,
and were almost ready to bring him down. At the critical moment Le Tellier
divided the soldiers, enlisted Condé on his side, and saved his son's position. By the end of the Dutch War, Louvois' skill as an organizer of supplies
and men gave him prestige and preference in the eyes of the king, but even
long after Le Tellier had become chancellor and Louvois was fully in command of the war ministry, Louis really had two war ministers, for Le
Tellier continued until his death in the highest councils of the state.

The "new army" had in fact been started under Richelieu, and its first
administrator had been Le Tellier's predecessor, Sublet de Noyers. It had
grown after the *Fronde* under the prodding of Mazarin and the direction
of Le Tellier, but it did not come into flower until the personal reign of
Louis XIV. The political assumptions behind the new army cannot better
be summed up than they were in the commission that Louis XIV presented
to Turenne immediately after the Peace of the Pyrenees:

We find ourselves obliged, for the conservation of our state as much as for its
glory and our reputation, to maintain . . . in peace as well as in war, a great
number of troops, both infantry and cavalry, which will always be ready and in
good condition to act to keep our people in the obedience and the respect that
they owe us, to insure the peace and the tranquillity that we have won . . . and
to aid our allies.[4]

Le Tellier could have written those words; they could also have come directly from the pen of the young king. The *Fronde* and the Hapsburg war had exposed the inadequacy of the old armies; what was needed was an army dependent upon the king, submissive to his commands, and always ready to carry out his orders. The old-style soldiers who were responsive to their *condottiere* captain if to anyone, and who were dismissed when the war ended, so that they became a danger to the countryside and the public tranquillity, no longer satisfied the needs of public power. Le Tellier crowned the creation of the royal army that wore the king's coat, was commanded by the king's officers, and was responsive to the orders of the king's war minister. It was still a mercenary army, but the king now occupied the place that had formerly been the domain of the *condottiere* captain.[5]

Louis never lost interest in military problems. His was of a generation of princes who were born under the shadow and expectation of war and nurtured in an atmosphere of civil rebellions that could be tamed only by soldiers; they recognized the military as a prime factor in their government. Louis explained to his son that a prince should know the exact state of his soldiers, should concern himself with their discipline and their training, and should identify himself with their interests. Thus it is not surprising to find the king closely following his armies, demanding that they maintain discipline and support the good name of the kingdom both by their valor and by their behavior, and insisting that they be properly trained. Richelieu had explained that the creation of a well-trained army under responsible officers should be the aim of royal policy; Le Tellier and Louis XIV brought the first of such armies into existence.[6]

It was a tremendous job. The government of the king could not hope to end the venal system that made the company the property of the captain, and the regiment the property of the colonel, who usually was also captain of the first company; but they could introduce new ratings into the official hierarchy (the major, for example), and bring the general officers under stricter control. In the old armies the great nobility and princes of the blood assumed the right of command as a function of their feudal loyalty to the crown. Thus we find a Condé commanding an army in his early twenties, a Turenne assuming command to be a function of his birth. It happened that these two officers turned out to be capable soldiers, but there was no assurance that the system would always produce great commanders, and there was much evidence that it would produce general officers who assumed the right to decide on their own interests whether or not they would obey their king. Louis and his war ministers strove to break this system by gaining more control over the appointment of general officers, and by regulating the flow of soldiers and supplies so that a general would soon know that the strength of his army was dependent upon his compliance with the orders from the king and his minister. A disobedient soldier, no matter what his talents might be, found that he had neither men nor supplies to accomplish his plans because these were at the disposal of the king. Critics of Louis XIV have insisted that this meant that the marshals of France who followed Turenne in positions of command were "court generals," "sycophants," and "time servers," who earned their batons by flattering the minister, the king, or a mistress. It would be hard, however, to prove that the average talents of the men who commanded Louis' armies were inferior to those who had commanded the old armies. On the other hand, it is difficult to guess how the king's interests would have been served had he given command of the new army to men who would themselves assume the right to decide how they would act and whether they would support the king's projects or those of his enemies.

An even more important consideration that both Louis and his war ministers had to keep in mind was the fact that the new army was really a standing army, rather than merely a palace guard that could be enlarged in times of war or rebellion. Under Louis XIV the French army increased from a few thousand men to an army of nearly 100,000 in time of peace, and 400,000 in time of war. Thus the war ministry had to assume responsibilities over a force that had not even been considered in the earlier era. It had to be sure that the companies actually contained the number of men that were paid for: dishonest captains and *passe-volant* soliders continued to fill the ranks for a "review," so that in actual fact the king might be paying for soldiers that did not exist. The training of soldiers, left to the conscience of their captains, was often problematical, and the discipline worse. General Martinet, Louis' first inspector-general of the army, provided the first real attempt to bring training and discipline under a common pattern. From his day on the word "martinet" has had a special meaning for all soldiers; his was the only way to bring some kind of order out of the anarchy inherited from the old army.

Thus we see Le Tellier issuing regulations to control the recruitment, discipline, training, and command of the army; regulations to organize the billeting, supply, and medical attention of the troops; regulations of all sorts necessary for the creation of a military force responsive to the royal command.[7] Like the good administrator that he was, Le Tellier would follow up a regulation with a study of its effects and actual functioning, and then several years later, reissue the orders corrected by experience that had been gained. It is worth the attention of students of military affairs to follow these ordinances. Between 1655 and 1675 Le Tellier's regulations laid down the basic pattern of the pre-revolutionary Bourbon army; after 1675 new ordinances were never much more than minor revisions of the basic regulations made necessary by changes in weapons or by abuses in organization. These first decades of Louis XIV's reign set a military pattern both for France and Europe that was to last for generations to come. The actual work and most of the ideas came from Le Tellier and his son Louvois, but to the king must go the credit for supporting these ministers against the protests of soldiers, the agitation of the court, and the arguments from Colbert about the costs.

Le Tellier did a great many other things in addition to his primary role as war minister. Seventeenth-century government did not recognize the lines that later came to separate the several functions of government. He played an active part in the king's council *en haut* where high politics were usually the subject for consideration. He also corresponded with his share of the provinces; each secretary of state dealt with the royal and clerical officials of about one-fourth of the kingdom concerning all sorts of questions from justice to fortifications. His reputation both as an administrator and as a man of law made Le Tellier the natural candidate for the high office of chancellor when it fell vacant.

Jean Baptist Colbert was the other "most important" collaborator of the king during these first and formative years of the regime. While Le Tellier may have reflected Louis' politeness, his subtlety, his diplomatic grace, Colbert reflected his firmness, his austerity, his secretiveness, perhaps even his brutality. There can be no question about his being an alter ego of the king. For more than two decades of the reign this "cold, humorless, hardworking, honest, narrow, devoted" man[8] was both a workhorse and a driving wheel in the government of Louis XIV. Where Louis could put off a request with his famous "We shall see," Colbert had no difficulty in refusing or ignoring requests or proposals that were inopportune or unwanted; where Louis was the "politician" anxious to keep his fences mended, his minister could be the "hatchet man" driving ruthlessly toward a desired goal.

When Mazarin died, Colbert was the cardinal's intendant for his personal affairs, secretary of the orders of the queen, and counselor in the king's councils; he had acquired the fief of Seignelay that gave him the rank of a baron. This closeness to Mazarin and the trusts that were given to him were the surest signs of his coming greatness. Within a decade after Louis assumed personal power, Colbert had become intendant of finances (1661), superintendent of the department of buildings (1665), superintendent general of commerce (1665), secretary of state in charge of the navy, the galleys, commerce, horse raising, forests and waters, and a share of internal administration including fortification of the coastal towns. By 1671 he also had charge of the royal household, the general affairs of the clergy, and a dozen lesser things. His correspondence gives evidence that his interests and influence roamed the entire business of the king, both at home and abroad.[9] It is an incredible career that we follow; Colbert seems always to have already exercised the power before he was given the commission; he took on one new area of activity after another without ever giving up the things that he had been doing. We cannot but ask: how could one man do so many things? How could he cheerfully, even gleefully, add more to the already impossible load that he carried? Nor was this man an administrator who could easily push work onto another; while Louis tells his son that he would have liked to do all the work himself, Colbert, in fact, seems actually to have done it all himself. Here was a man after the king's own image, a man willing to work long hours to achieve his own *gloire,* to regulate the affairs of his master's kingdom.

At the height of his power Colbert probably handled more of the king's business than Mazarin had ever had under his control, but he never forgot that he was the agent of the king rather than master of the affairs in his own right. There is a much-quoted letter from Louis to Colbert that so well reflects the relationship between king and minister that we find it to be almost a Leitmotiv of much of Colbert's correspondence. The letter is dated April 23, 1671; Colbert had already achieved great power in the king's service. At the council *en haut* he had protested a decision that Louis had made; the king's letter speaks volumes about the personality of Louis XIV and about his relationship to his ministers.

I was master enough of myself day before yesterday to conceal from you the sorrow I felt in hearing a man whom I had overwhelmed with benefits . . . talk to me in the fashion that you used. I have been very friendly toward you. . . . I still have such a feeling, and I believe that I am giving you real proof of it by telling you that I restrained myself for a single moment for your sake. . . . I did not wish to tell you what I am writing to you, so as not to give you further opportunity to displease me. . . . It is in the memory of the services that you have done for me, and my friendship, which has caused me to do so. Profit thereby and do not risk vexing me again, because after I have heard your arguments and those of your colleagues, and have given my opinion on all of your claims, I never wish to hear more about it. . . . I am telling you my thoughts so that you may work on an assured basis and so that you will not make false steps.

We do not know what Colbert wrote in reply, but Louis sent him another letter a few days later:

Do not think that my friendship for you has decreased. While your services continue that is not possible. But you must render them to me as I wish, and believe that I do everything for the best.

The preference that you believe that I am giving to others should not trouble you. I wish only not to do injustice and to work for the good of my service. [How often does Louis say this!] That is what I shall do when you are all with me.

Colbert must have complained that the king seemed to prefer the Le Telliers before himself; Louis knew how much his favor caused jealousy: "It is necessary," he wrote, "to divide [favor and grace] equitably . . . men are jealous of the things that come from the sovereign. . . ." But Colbert understood that he was not to oppose his king *after* a decision was taken, and we find no further evidence that he did.

This cannot be construed to mean that Colbert was simply a tool of his king. Louis was actually only marginally interested in the details of internal government that occupied most of Colbert's time, and there can be no doubt about the origin of the policies that we associate with Colbert's name. Colbert proposed and directed the reforms that brought some order out of the fiscal system, codified some of the laws of the kingdom, gave a modicum of rational direction to an anarchistic and chaotic economy, and organized the artistic, literary, and scientific talents of the era as a frame for the reign of his king. In all this Louis supported his minister, shared his enthusiasms, and recognized his talents, but Louis was more interested in the increased revenue at his disposal than in the measures that produced it, and he would never allow his finance minister to curb the king's projects by petty talk about lack of money. Thus Colbert, while he was undoubtedly one of the architects of the era of Louis XIV, was not the man who organized the great projects dear to the king's heart that were to be both the monuments of the age and the tragedy of the king's life.

Colbert did find the money that gave Louis the opportunity to build his armies and navies, to bribe foreign and domestic potentates, to repair the old châteaus and build new ones—in short, that enabled Louis to shine in the world as the great king of the age. In doing this, however, Colbert also raised for his master a sackful of enemies who hated both the king and his minister during their lifetimes, and who would attempt to blacken their memories and undo their works. The first of these was the result of the work of the court that Louis brought together to try Fouquet. Not only Fouquet, but also the entire financial world of Paris and the other great commercial cities came under its scrutiny and lash. This court looked into the financial misdemeanors of a whole generation of financiers who had supplied the king with the money to fight his enemies, and who had also feathered their own nests, perhaps outrageously, in the process. When their accounts were looked into and they were called upon to disgorge their gains, their cries of distress and pain could be heard throughout the kingdom, and indeed even down to our times. Small wonder! They were forced to return millions of livres to the king's treasury and a number of them suffered the further indignity of imprisonment. Nor did Colbert's hunting of the unearned wealth of the bourgeoisie stop there. He also carefully scrutinized the funds in the *hôtel de ville* and drastically reduced the payments of the *rentes*. Since he was also responsible for alterations of the coinage, his enemies insist that he started his career by declaring the king bankrupt and ended it as a counterfeiter. This is not the place to analyze the justice of these allegations; like all such claims there is enough truth to give them verisimilitude and enough falsehood to make them absurd.

Colbert's reputation as a statesman varies with the political assumptions of the men who discuss his career. To those committed to *laissez faire,* Colbert is the arch example of regulation that failed; those who look with sympathy upon attempts to control the disorder of the marketplace or who see him fighting an economic crisis with the only weapons available, regard him as an enlightened adviser of his king. He was confronted with enormous problems. The king's treasury was empty, the future revenues were mortgaged, the machinery for the collection of taxes was bled by financiers accustomed to finding their own wealth at the expense of the king. Even if the taxes could be collected, the tax structure was cumbersome, unequal, and inefficient. Nor was that the end of his troubles. The economy of the western world was in the doldrums throughout the latter seventeenth century; the economy of France was troubled by the periodic crisis in agriculture, by antiquated tolls and tariffs, by dishonest, inefficient, and unskillful workers and entrepreneurs who put shoddy goods on the market, by the effective competition of the Dutch. If this economy were to yield more revenue for its king, severe reforms and drastic measures were necessary.

It has often been pointed out that Colbert was not a statesman with the vision necessary to bring order out of the chaos of royal fiscal administration. While this is undoubtedly true, perhaps it is also meaningless, for only a revolution that could overthrow social and political forms could really reform this system. Like Sully before him and the reformers of the eighteenth century who were to follow, Colbert had to work within a socio-economic frame of reference that defied reorganization. Furthermore, like every finance minister who served the Bourbons, he served a king who was quite uninterested in the details of financial reform. Louis may have pretended to "work as his own superintendent of finance," but at bottom he was interested only in having the revenue needed for his projects —not in bringing order out of the system. How could it have been otherwise? Louis had been educated by Mazarin who taught him that the great political goals were the proper aims of politics and that government must never limit its objectives simply because the grubby men of the marketplace might not want to supply the money. Whether it was for the creation of a monumental palace, or the prosecution of a great war, or the sponsorship of culture, Louis was not one to check his course merely because the finance minister found it hard to raise money. This fact made it impossible for Colbert or any of his successors to reform the system, even if they had the will to do so. There were few years during the reign of Louis XIV in which the demands for money did not require the development of "extraordinary" fiscal measures as well as the exploitation of all "ordinary" ones. Under such conditions, the finance minister who succeeded in forcing the collectors and farmers to make reasonably complete returns and who could think up "expedients" to raise additional money was a great financier. This is the basis for Colbert's reputation as a fiscal administrator.

Colbert may not have been a great statesman, but at least he did have appreciation for the ideas of men who were striving to break through the mass of past practices and create states' policy. Louis XIV often chided him in council with the remark, "And now Colbert will tell us that the late Cardinal Richelieu proposed. . . ." Whether it was Richelieu or one of the others who was trying to find the relationship between states' policy and economic well-being (abundance) makes little difference; Colbert was seeking advice from men who did conceive of states' interest, and he was striving to reform the economy of the kingdom to bring abundance for all— including the king. His "New Deal" legislation has been praised as well as condemned; both of these attitudes miss the point, for they fail to take into account the fact that Colbert, supported by the king, was trying to find the elusive formula that would bring some sort of order (and thus assure prosperity) to the economy. Like his fiscal policies, his reform measures had to depend upon the political forces of the reign, and unhappily these included wars that lasted longer than was expected and produced results that were equally unexpected. In addition to the disorder of wars, his policies were also always confronted by inertia, inefficiency, ineffective agents, and deliberate sabotage. The King of France did not have a political machine that could readily translate either his will, or that of his minister, into action. Colbert found this just as did Le Tellier and Louvois. There was always friction in the machinery of state in the seventeenth century.

In the early days of the new regime, Colbert's troubles were further aggravated by the fact that while he was a minister of the king, he was not secretary of state, and thus much of his official correspondence dealing with trade, commerce, and other affairs under his supervision had to be channeled through the secretary who owned the charge responsible for writing the letters. This led to no end of confusion and disorder, until Colbert succeeded in buying the charge of secretary of state; perhaps all creative governments are disorderly and operate in a cloud of confusion, because in order to succeed creative governments have to break down established patterns of action.

The third member of the high council was Hughes de Lionne, who had also been a confidant of the late cardinal. Lionne was fifty years old when Mazarin died and already had had a long career as a diplomat. He was subtle, intelligent, and skilled as a negotiator. He was a specialist, an expert in foreign affairs. He had been with Mazarin at the Isle of Pheasants; he had been important in the negotiations for the League of the Rhine and the defense of "German Liberties"; he had taken part in the negotiations that produced peace in the Baltic just before Mazarin's death; and he was *au courant* with affairs in England, the United Netherlands, and Italy. Lionne had one further qualification: his parents had been petty nobility without either position or wealth, so that he, like the others around the king, had to count upon the royal bounty for his advancement, which was exactly what Louis wanted. At the same time he was not an ambitious man; Lionne was an "expert" in foreign affairs, and he had no desire to become the first minister.

Lionne was more sensitive to the young king's needs and ambitions than most men of the court; he was one of the first to realize that Louis actually intended to govern his own kingdom. "Those who believe that our master will soon give up the direction of affairs deceive themselves," he wrote as early as August 1661. "The more we go along, the more pleasure he [the king] takes in applying himself and giving himself entirely to the affairs of the kingdom." Several years later he wrote to Queen Christine of Sweden of his surprise that so many of the court underestimated the king. He emphasized the "qualities of his Majesty's mind: firm, flexible, vigorous, constantly attending to business and above all sensitive to things that touch his honor. . . ." Here was a servant who appreciated his master, and if we can credit the hundreds of volumes in the Archives of the Foreign Ministry that show Lionne writing the policy of the kingdom, he was a servant who carefully considered his king's interests and ambitions. Even so, Lionne was not unwilling to keep things from Louis if he thought it well to do so. For example, he seems to have prevented a crisis at the time of the Anglo-French controversy over the naval salute to the flag, simply by failing to bring all the problems to the young king's attention.

Like Colbert, Lionne was not a secretary of state at the time Louis called him to his high council. The office of secretary of state for foreign affairs belonged to Lomenie de Brienne and his son, who held the right to follow his father. Neither of these men was admitted to the inner circle, probably because the Briennes were identified with the pro-Spanish party in the court, but Louis explained to his son that he considered the elder Brienne too old and too unwise, and the son too young to be trusted with the conduct of affairs. However, Louis XIV was not the man to deprive a faithful servant of his position and property without considerable provocation; therefore, some way had to be found to circumvent them until a time when they would be willing to sell their charge. Thus one of Louis' first orders placed Brienne under the direction of Lionne who was the minister for foreign affairs, and then the king ordered that all his agents, ministers, and ambassadors to the courts of Europe should direct their correspondence to the king himself. They could write to the secretary of state about minor affairs, but anything of importance had to be sent to the king. This created a paradoxical situation: Louis and Lionne read the dispatches and then composed the letters for the secretary of state to send to the ambassadors. Lionne dealt with the foreign agents in France; the secretary of state in charge of foreign affairs was often ignorant of the course of events. It is almost unbelievable that this expedient actually worked, but it was not until 1668 that the Briennes were so humiliated that they were willing to sell their charge to Lionne and regularize the situation. Even this did not cure all the disorder, for this charge was also entrusted with the correspondence on marine affairs, which had become the prerogative of Colbert. By 1670 the lines of authority and power were finally more or less straightened out.

Lionne's actual influence upon the king is a difficult thing to assess.[10]

Both Louis and Lionne had "studied foreign policy" under Mazarin, and both were deeply influenced by the cardinal's maxims. But Lionne was a skeptic, an anti-clerical, sharing Mazarin's dislike and distrust of papal policy, and he was perhaps responsible for the king's uncompromising attitude toward Rome. The memoirists of the period have left us a less vivid picture of Lionne than of the other ministers, perhaps because he was less colorful and less controversial than Colbert or the Le Telliers. They do tell us that Lionne's personal life was morally irregular to a point of scandal, and since Louis' own life was also irregular, several observers have suggested that the older man should have had a better influence on the king than was actually the case. Who can believe that "the ladies" would not have attracted the king even if Lionne had not been at his side?

While Lionne was Louis' most important adviser on foreign affairs, he was by no means the only one. In these early years of the regime, all of the ministers discussed affairs with foreign ambassadors, wrote to French ambassadors abroad, and presumed the right to discuss these affairs with the king. It was to be a very long time before the business of government was compartmentalized to the point where the minister of foreign affairs had a monopoly on his area.

There was one thing that Louis demanded of all his advisers: absolute secrecy. The king's business was not the business of the court, and the king's ministers were expected to keep the affairs of their master confidential. There was no agenda for the council *en haut,* and the ministers were forbidden to keep notes about its meetings. Thus only the decisions, embedded in letters or orders, have survived. This accounts for the frustration of many men in Louis' court who wanted to know what was happening; it also has made the task of the historian of Louis XIV somewhat difficult.

The song of 1670 insisted that the "carriage of the Sun" was drawn by four horses that "were neither good nor beautiful—Le Tellier, Louvois, Colbert and Lionne."[11] Of these, Louvois was the newcomer to the king's council. He was three years younger than the king and had known that he would be the king's war minister from the time he became aware of his place in the world. At twenty he had the right to succeed his father and already had become an "apprentice" in the war ministry. Historians used to assume that he entered his career at the very onset of Louis' reign, but more recent studies show us that only in 1671 did he gradually assume duties as a prime mover, and that even after he had entered Louis' council *en haut* he carried out his father's orders as much as he originated orders himself.

Louvois was a very different person from his father. He seems to have had very little of Le Tellier's compliancy and self-effacement, except when he dealt with the king himself. It is perhaps true that Louvois was another facet of Louis' own personality: he was harsh, ruthless, aggressive. He brooked no opposition to his orders. With his creatures and others whom he knew to be friendly, he could show a generous, playful side, but this was not his usual face to the world. Still, no one worked harder than Louvois, not even Colbert. He had a prodigious ability to go through masses of detail, to sort out projects that needed to be done, to give directions for the organization of men and materials necessary for military or other operations. When one sees him at work, it is almost incredible that he found time in his private life to build a château, to play with mistresses, to indulge in debaucheries. Louvois' ambitions were no less developed than his abilities. He wanted the favor of the king; he also wanted the *gloire* of the formation of policy. When Lionne died, Louvois briefly occupied the office of foreign minister and the rest of his career finds him meddling in foreign affairs as well as in those of the army.

During the third decade of Louis' reign, after Colbert died, Louvois came as near as anyone ever was to come to the role of first minister, perhaps even minister-favorite. In these first two decades of the reign, however, Louvois' career was primarily concerned with the establishment of ministerial control over the army and its generals. This was a prodigious task, for the increasing number of soldiers and the growing complexity of the art of war greatly expanded the work of superintending the army. At the same time, both Louvois and his king were determined that the general officers commanding the royal army would recognize the rights of the king's government to supervise and direct their activities. As we shall see, this led to "revolts" on the part of marshals of France, to cabals uniting Turenne and Condé, to sabotage by officers of lesser rank who refused to accept the organizational tables that were necessary to establish control. Thus Louvois had to be a politician and statesman as well as an administrator. In these first years of his service, his father's skill was often necessary to keep him afloat.

The other man who came to the king's council *en haut* during the first two decades of Louis' personal reign was Arnauld de Pomponne,[12] who became minister of foreign affairs after Lionne's death in 1671. Like the others, Pomponne was a professional royal servant, an "expert" in the field of foreign affairs. He came from a family famous as theologians (Jansenists) and royal servants. By 1671 he had already established a distinguished career as an administrator and a diplomat. Pomponne, born in 1618, was twenty years older than Louis. Like Colbert, he began his career under Le Tellier in the 1640's, shared the fortunes of Mazarin's creatures during the *Fronde,* and emerged in the later 1650's as a diplomatic agent of the cardinal. His career was almost blighted by his family's relationship with the Jansenists, but Pomponne managed to allay any fears of his connections with "that sect" by refusing to be identified with it in any way. Under Lionne's direction he had been ambassador both to the United Netherlands and to Sweden, and in both situations had distinguished himself as a man of insight and skill. Pomponne was soft-spoken, gentle, yielding, and yet always conscious of the interests of his king. He came to office when the Le Telliers and Colberts agreed with Louis that he was the best man among the "experts" to direct policy. He fell from grace when the Le Telliers and Colberts allied against him. But the king must have had an affection for this well-mannered man, for even though Louis wrote harshly about him in a famous and much-quoted statement about the duties of a king, as soon as Louvois died, Pomponne was returned to favor and a place on the council *en haut.*

It is difficult to characterize these creatures of the king. From the compliant, subtle Le Tellier and the pliable Pomponne, to the hard and cold Colbert and the brutal Louvois, these men all seem to have reflected aspects of Louis' own personality. Also they all were men of prodigious labor. La Bruyère drew their picture thus: they "alone are charged with the details of state . . . who could draw them showing the haste, the worry, the curiosity, the activity? Who would know how to paint their movement? One never sees them seated, never fixed, never at rest. Who has ever seen them walk? One sees them running, talking while running, questioning without waiting for a response. They come from no place, they go nowhere, they pass and repass. Do not stop their precipitous course; you will wreck their machine. Do not ask them questions. . . . They are not the satellites of Jupiter, that is, the crowd that surrounds the Prince, but they announce him and precede him, they hurl themselves impetuously into the crowd of courtiers—all in their way are there at their own peril. . . ." This picture was intended to portray Louvois and Colbert, but it could have been any of Louis' ministers whose careers made the expression "working for the King of France" synonymous with hard and unending toil.

Though they worked hard—and most of them died early—these men also shared in the honors and wealth as well as in the power of the Sun King. Louis' creatures all became men of substance. High noblemen sought their daughters for wives, their estates and châteaus were among the most beautiful of the era, and the great and small stood in awe of their power. As living extensions of the king's own person, they treated the men around and under them with brusque, sometimes unfeeling, contempt that knew no respect for rank. The king could not himself be so ruthless, but he could and did back up his ministers when they acted that way. These were the men who educated and influenced the king as well as carried out his projects. Of all the people in the royal entourage, they were the most important.

13

THE "MÉTIER" OF THE KING*

THE YOUNG MAN who took over the direction of "his"[1] state in 1661 deeply understood that to be king in fact, as well as in name, required effort and imposed responsibilities. "All people," he wrote, "are bound together by reciprocal obligations. The obedience and respect that we receive from our subjects is not a gratuitous gift, but rather an exchange for the justice and protection that we give them . . . and the debts that we owe are greater than those owed to us, for if a subject fails in his ability, or his will, to do as we command, there are others to take his place, but only the sovereign can act for the sovereign. . . ." Or again: ". . . the care for my people is my strongest passion, and I will receive with pleasure any suggestions that you might make to help me [fulfill my desire]." In another place: "In addition to peace and security and good order I wish to contribute by my efforts to the return of wealth and abundance and happiness of my people."[2] These were the words of a young man recalling the admonitions of a pious mother, of a wise mentor, of a cautious confessor—all of whom had taught him that "when God raised kings to their thrones, He intended that they should do their duty." They were also the words of a young man deeply conscious of an obligation to fulfill his *gloire* as an obligation both to himself and to his God.

But it is one thing to speak piously about the role of "father of the people," and quite another to grapple with the daily tasks of government. Any observer of the great in the world quickly realizes that men's *mystiques* nearly always wish the good, nearly always express the highest aspirations of the society, while the *politiques* that men follow, the actual measures that they take to expedite the daily course of affairs, often fall somewhat short of these high goals. No one reading the letters or the dictated *Mémoires* of this young man who took the helm from the dead cardinal will miss the idealism, the aspirations for good, that inspired his actions; he was determined to fulfill his *gloire* as king, to carry the heavy burdens that God had placed upon him to the best of his ability. But what must one do to accomplish this? Indeed, what was the *métier du roi?*

Kings of the past had been soldiers, judges, politicians. Some of them had spent a lifetime in the saddle, others a lifetime with pen and ink; many of them had given more time to the chase, to the gaming table, to balls, parties, and spectacles, or to the pleasures of women, than to the business of state. But Louis XIV had learned "the trade of king" from Mazarin; he understood that the *métier du roi* required a king to decide policy and to superintend the people who administered the state. Almost naïvely Louis explained to his son that he would prefer to do all the work of government himself, but since that was manifestly impossible, he had to be content with projecting and directing the work of his ministers, and above all, with keeping in his own hands the responsibility for the decisions that if he really were to fulfill his *gloire* and his responsibility to God, the king alone could make.

As we have seen, he had to assemble a "team" such as the cardinals had created for their government, and organize it into a government that operated under his direction. This is what he was doing when he realized that Fouquet had visions of personal grandeur. After Fouquet's disgrace, no one again attempted to take the *métier du roi* from Louis' hands, but this meant that he had to subject his pleasures, his leisure, his inclinations to the demands of the state, and Louis himself insists that to do otherwise would be "ingratitude and boldness toward God, injustice and tyranny toward men. . . ."[3] All his life Louis recognized that this was his lot, a lot that "sometimes seemed rude and thorny . . . ," but that also had its "sweetness and pleasure," for to a king "nothing could be more burdensome than inactivity. . . ."

Throughout the *Mémoires* Louis emphasized the fact that a king must decide. This is his greatest function. And the most important of the decisions that he must make are those concerning the personnel that he picks to assist him with his tasks. As he wrote to his son, "To govern alone, not to listen to anyone, are two different things . . . the most able private individuals take advice of able people . . . and what should kings do who have in their hands public interests?" Throughout his life, Louis insisted upon the necessity of obtaining the advice of wise men who were experts in their fields of action, of men whose experience with and information about the problems of the hour would be greater than his own. As we have seen, on Mazarin's death he invited the ablest men in his entourage to become his ministers and join his highest council. He wanted to be sure that he had men about him with the information and the administrative skills needed to operate his government, but their roles were to advise and assist him, not to dominate him or to take over control of the state. Of the four men that he picked, only Fouquet misunderstood the king's intentions; the others recognized the functions that the king had assigned to them. During his long reign Louis often failed to obtain, or perhaps to listen to, the wisest advice for the formation of policy, but he always sought it within his lights. This was the practice of the man who wrote that a king must "fix his mind on the project, and when he thinks that he has discovered the best course, he must take it."

By reducing the number of people who could have knowledge of and influence over the direction of affairs, Louis only continued the pattern of government that had begun to emerge under the cardinals. The traditions of the kingdom demanded that policy decisions should be made only after discussion in council, that the chancellor and keeper of the seals should not seal any document that was not first discussed in council, but there was no fixed pattern that dictated the membership of the king's high council. Under the Valois rulers it was often very large, including all adult members of the royal family and many of the great lords. Under the first Bourbons the size of council began to diminish, and men of the pen elbowed the soldiers and noblemen aside. Even so, Louis XIII had included his mother, and Anne had included the Duke of Orléans and the Prince of Condé in their high councils. Louis XIV made his council *en haut* almost an informal affair; he called to it whomever he wished, and no one had a "right" to join him in his political deliberations.

This little council *en haut* had no fixed membership, no formal organization; it usually consisted of three or four members besides the king. The secretive character of Louis' government angered and offended many people in his court. "The King believes," wrote an anonymous contemporary, "that three is a perfect number and he uses his three ministers just as God uses secondary forces for his own purposes . . . it pleases him to be secretive about his affairs. They [the ministers] alone have any knowledge of them . . . the rest of the Court is left free to meditate on whatever happens. . . ."[4] This is not quite an accurate picture, for occasionally the council would be enlarged to include others—Turenne, for example —but as a rule, before 1700 none of the royal family, not even the queen mother, none of the dukes and peers, not even the marshals of France received invitations. In the first years (1661–70) it was Lionne, Le Tellier, and Colbert, with an occasional session including Turenne; later Louvois was added, and after Lionne's death, Pomponne, who was in turn succeeded by Colbert de Croissy. None of these men had a brevet of membership; they were simply called upon to advise the king and thereby became *ministres d'état.*

These were the sessions that Louis enjoyed most. He was intelligent enough to understand the problems and their ramifications; he liked calm, deliberate discussion in elegant language that lighted up the corners of policy. He enjoyed the conflicts of interest that were never far from the surface in the discussions of his ministers; he understood their rivalry for power and place. Nor did he expect them to agree with each other or with him in the discussions, for he well understood that he was best served by frankness and direct speech. As we have seen, however, in the case of Colbert, once a decision was taken, he exacted complete obedience and agreement from all. In this council *en haut* Louis superbly played his role *en roi;* it was there that he was the king in action, the king as the formulator and director of the destiny of the kingdom.

In making final decisions, Louis did not always decide with the majority vote of the council. As he explained to his son, ". . . in important issues, when we have before us the reasons for and against them, it is for us to decide . . . what should be done. And this choice . . . if we do not lack the intelligence and courage, another could never make as well as we do. Decision needs the spirit of a master, and it is incomparably more easy to make it when one is master than to imitate it when one is not. . . . You will notice almost always the difference between the letter that we take the trouble to write ourselves and those which even able secretaries write for us . . . in the latter there is something less than natural, a nervousness of pen that fears always that it writes too much or too little . . . the difference is even greater between decisions that we [kings] make ourselves and those that we leave to our ministers to make without us."[5] In another place Louis tells his son that God gives the wisdom necessary for the decision, that God gives the king the moral and intellectual strength needed to rule. Fortified by such a belief, prepared for decisions by teachings of Péréfixe and Mazarin, and advised by men whose skill and knowledge he respected, Louis had few doubts about the wisdom of his acts in these early years of his reign. Later, when disaster dogged his heels in war and in politics, he wondered if he had decided rightly, and sometimes concluded that God had withdrawn His protection from the kingdom, perhaps because of the sins of the king.

When not in council, the king spent long hours closeted with the very same men who sat in this council *en haut.* We have only short glimpses of these sessions that show us how Louis tried to keep himself *au courant* even of the minute affairs of state. He believed that "the most important affairs are nearly always conditioned by the smallest ones, and so what would seem lowly in a prince if he were solely concerned about money [the discussion was about finances] becomes elevation and grandeur when it has as its object the well-being of his people, the execution of grand designs . . . for which care of detail is the surest foundation. . . ." Indeed, Louis asserted that a prince could not act effectively unless he had extensive knowledge "of all that happens around him," because a badly informed man "cannot fail to reason faultily." Thus, not "to know" could be a king's greatest fault and greatest danger. Indeed, "in the centuries past, the faults . . . that have been committed by sovereigns nearly always [result] . . . from something that they did not know." This insistence upon having the necessary information was not simple cant parading as advice for the young. Louis' letters to the men who served him in all capacities fairly bulge with demands for information; he wanted to know everything that could be known about his kingdom and about the affairs of neighboring states. Visconti tells us, "He, Louis, wishes to know the affairs of state through his ministers, those of Parlement through his judges, and even the least things, even the gallantries of women of the court . . . there are few things that happen on any day of which he is not informed, and few people whose names and habits he does not know."[6] Visconti should know, for he was one of the people who supplied Louis with information.

Rarely are we allowed to be present at intimate conversations between the king and his ministers or other informers, but every memoirist of the period tells of the countless interviews, of the hours when Louis was closeted with his ministers and secretaries and others. The official correspondence of the reign is replete with remarks such as: "I have discussed this question with his Majesty"; "his Majesty wants to know . . ."; "his Majesty has questioned me closely . . ."; "his Majesty requests that you inform him. . . ." Louis' own letters so often contain the phrases: "You will report exactly what you hear . . ."; "I desire exact and complete information . . ."; "I expect you to give me information of the place where you are. . . ." An undated letter to General Pradel during the Dutch War typified this characteristic of Louis' correspondence: "I reply to you," he wrote, "that from curiosity and, I must add, inquietude, I must know everything that happens in the country where you are now. You must not fail to give me news as often as you possibly can."[7] Did he discuss the replies with his ministers? Probably.

Louis tells us that he took great satisfaction in having "eyes open all over the earth to learn the news of provinces and nations, the secrets of all the courts, the humors and failings of princes and their ministers, to be informed of the infinite number of things that one thinks we do not know, to see around us that which people strive to hide . . . to discover the true views of courtiers, their hidden interests . . . I know of no pleasure that I would not give up before surrendering this one."[8] The statement clearly reveals that he had placed himself squarely in the position Richelieu and Mazarin had occupied before him. To run the government of the kingdom he had to know about the reports of ambassadors and secret agents, of intendants and judges, and at the same time pick up all the gossip about the court and the kingdom.

The cardinal ministers had solved the problem by placing their creatures or their relatives in key positions, and by being generous to those who volunteered information. Louis surely had not been unaware of the numerous letters that found their way onto Mazarin's desk. When he became his own "first minister," he too developed a circle of informers and correspondents who supplied information. Visconti is one of the few who have left us an account of the way Louis recruited him to be an informer. He also tells us about the secrecy and anonymity that Louis assured to the people who provided information. The king knew that the sources would dry up if informants thought they might be betrayed. He also knew that informers liked to be paid; writing to an anonymous correspondent, he said, "Since you have something advantageous to tell me, I find it good that you should come to see me, and if what you propose should be fruitful, I will recompense you in a way that will satisfy you. . . ."[9] There are enough of such letters extant to suggest that they were not uncommon. We do not know how far he was able to separate the relatively true from the relatively false; he must, of course, have obtained a great deal of malicious gossip.

The post also provided a source of information. Mail service in the seventeenth century was somewhat less well organized than it is today, and letters entrusted to the post somewhat less secure from violation. In 1668, when Louvois became superintendent general of the posts in France, there was a reform that assured more privacy for the ordinary letter, but Louvois also organized a "black chamber" primarily to spy on the correspondence of foreigners and others under suspicion.[10] Naturally Louvois supplied the king with information thus acquired. The police officers, especially those in the city of Paris after Louis' police reform, also supplied much information. Most of it dealt with problems of public tranquillity, but the registers of the secretaries of state contain many hints that these reports included information not directly related to public order.

If Louis demanded information, he also always strove to formulate plans of action. The arrest of Fouquet was typical; it may have had fear rather than knowledge as the ultimate mainspring, but it was carefully planned and as carefully executed. Louis never liked surprises. "It is said," he wrote, "that kings have long arms, but it is important that they also have foresight, and that they become aware of things long before they happen, for whether things happen by our orders or happen in spite of us, it is equally advantageous to have foreseen them early . . . one can pardon the failures of a mediocre person if he fails to think of the future . . . but an intelligence more sharp, more elevated . . . ought to use time continuously searching into the future, for thus he will have the leisure to see how he should act to meet events, and will not be reduced to the unhappy necessity of acting precipitously . . . for haste and precipitation either give us bad counsel or deprive us of the necessary means of executing good counsel."[11] One can almost hear Mazarin in these words: the secret of success as a ruler is work, attention to detail, probing into the unknown future so that it will have few surprises.

"I imposed upon myself the rule of working regularly twice a day two to three hours each time with divers persons of government, not counting the hours that I spent myself or the time required for extraordinary affairs." What sorts of things did he have to do? One has to poke about in the masses of papers in the Archives of the Ministries of Foreign Affairs and War, in the National Archives, in the *Bibliothèque Nationale,* and elsewhere to understand the fantastic number of problems that came up to the king as long as he insisted that the chancellor seal nothing and the secretaries dispatch nothing without his knowledge. In the ordinary course of royal business there was a constant flow of decrees, commissions, grants, memoranda, letters, invoices, and other such papers that either required the king's signature or had to be called to his attention.[12] Of course we know that the vast majority of those tall shaky signatures LOUIS were probably written by scribes or secretaries who could sign his name as well as he could himself, but we also know that an astonishing amount of this material actually came to his attention. He may have had only a perfunctory knowledge of much of the paper, but there was much that he insisted upon seeing: *gratifications,* pensions, appointments to office, commissions of all kinds, clerical appointments—in short, all those things that were connected with the staffing either of the church, of his government, his household, or his armed forces, and all gifts that were classed together under the general term *les bienfaits du roi* were of keen interest to him. It may not be true that he never forgot anything that he had given to one of his subjects, but it was almost true. He saw to it that these *bienfaits* were all carefully listed in well-bound manuscript volumes (now in the *Bibliothèque Nationale*) arranged both under the names of the men who had received the bounty of the king and under the rubrics of the several types of gifts or commissions or offices that they had received. This "personnel" work was a significant part of the *métier du roi;* he was "acting in the place of God" by distributing the goods and offices of the world. In his *Mémoires,* Louis assures his son that only the king could act effectively in these matters, for he alone could distribute the gifts without thinking of private interests.

If we wish to find Louis at work, his correspondence deserves a closer scrutiny, for in the letters that were dispatched in his name we find mirrored an important part of the *métier du roi.* No less than his great grandfather Philip II, Louis XIV was a man of parchment and ink, a king who tried to follow the complexities of the business of state through the masses of paper that were required to keep it functioning. During these first years when Louis was young, he may have known about most of the letters that were sent in his name. But as he grew older, particularly after 1686, the flow of paper increased; and poor health or at least reduced vitality curbed his own labors, so that more and more of the details were left to others. Yet even at the end of his life we find him trying to keep abreast of the work of the state.

Some of the king's correspondence was formal, letters copied from a letter book by the secretaries. For example, there were hundreds of letters sent to the princes of Europe and other dignitaries, both foreign and domestic, that were simply in announcement of births, baptisms, marriages, illnesses and recoveries, and deaths in the royal family. Some of these letters are in the same style or form, whether they were written in 1661 or 1715, or for that matter, after Louis' death; for Louis XIV, they were the counterparts of the cards that twentieth-century men buy in the drugstore to greet a friend or to announce some news, to sympathize or to rejoice with an acquaintance over the events of the day. These letters autographed by the king went to fellow monarchs, to Italian cardinals, loyal bishops, faithful soldiers, or any other person whom the king might wish to honor. The fact that Louis found it necessary to send out hundreds of these greetings each year, much as an American senator might shower Christmas cards on his constituents, tells us something about the king of France as a politician who needed to mend his fences and keep his friends.

However, as we go through these "autographed letters" it soon becomes clear that not all of them were taken from a copy book by a secretary, for here and there the king's personality intrudes itself in a message to his father-in-law, Philip IV, to the Prince of Colonna who married Marie Mancini, to the Prince of Condé (again returned to favor through the efforts of Le Tellier), and to many other people whom, for one reason or another, the king wished particularly to honor. These little letters signalizing triumph in a battle, the baptism of the dauphin, or a gracious response to a letter that had congratulated the king are often in his own hand and composed in elegant French. Did Louis actually write them, or were they, too, the work of his secretaries who could duplicate his handwriting as well as his signature? This is a question we often cannot answer.

Letters of another category were so individualized that they could not have been written without the express will of the king, for Louis wrote or caused to be written an enormous number of letters in which he thanked men for their particular services to "my state" or later to "the state." The formula was simple enough: ". . . to thank you for the acts that were for the good of my state . . ."; ". . . to thank you for the acts that were for the good of my service. . . ." We know how distrustful Louis really was of the motives of men, yet in this correspondence it seems that he is surrounded by men who were above all anxious to serve him well. ". . . knowing how interested you are in the success of my projects . . ."; or "realizing how much you have always wished success to my state . . ."; or ". . . thanking you for the good wishes that you have always had for the success of my plans. . . ." These oft-repeated phrases show the king to be both politician and psychologist. Anyone who faithfully fulfilled a task might expect to get a little like the one sent to de Payne: ". . . I have seen by your letter your punctuality in carrying out my orders, and I am satisfied with it. . . ." Or perhaps like the one Turenne received in 1673: ". . . I would have trouble telling you the satisfaction that your last victory gave me." Again, a letter to de Guiche: "I see that I was not mistaken in believing that you would fulfill the task that I gave you. I am not only well-satisfied . . ."; or ". . . the gratification for which you thank me could not be better employed. It is not just that one should ruin himself in serving me as you have done." Or to the Marshal de Plessis-Praslin at the time of the death of his son during the Dutch War: ". . . I pray to God that He will give you the same fortitude to sustain this latest test of your virtue that He has already given you in the past on more than one similar occasion. . . ."[13] No one will doubt that these documents were precious possessions of the men who received them. The minister who received a letter saying, "I have confidence in you and in the fact that you know better than anyone what would be best. . . . I order you to do what is most advantageous to me . . . ," would not fail to appreciate a good master. Such gracious expressions may sound somewhat formal to us, but in an age when loyalty was personal rather than to the state and when men were still forming the rudiments of a service for the state, such letters helped to hold together the labors of the soldiers, diplomats, judges, and others whose work was so important to the kingdom. They gave their loyalty to the king and Louis used his personal touch to keep them loyal servants who would do their duty. As he explained to his son, it would be very embarrassing if one had to secure obedience by force.[14]

When men conjure up visions of the work of a king, it is easy to imagine that he largely makes plans for "grand designs," organizes new political constellations, and penetrates deep into plots against his regime. Such visions neglect the fact that the king had much routine business to do: paper work concerning the adjustment of problems that troubled his subjects, appointments to numerous offices and positions, charters and grants relating to both the agricultural society in which he had to operate as well as the bourgeois business community that was pressing upon him. Many of these documents have survived, some of them on embossed parchment with Gothic script suitable for royal words, properly signed by the king and his officials and sealed by the chancellor. Even though Louis did tell his officials to sign and seal nothing without his consent, it would be a great mistake to believe that he saw or signed all of these papers, and yet it would be equally false to assume that only a few of them went through his hands. As he wrote for his son, in a kingdom like that of France, there were many people who held offices and indeed exercised large concessions of power by hereditary right or near-hereditary right, and this fact led to both corruption and tyranny in which the "public is the victim," for the result is that instead of a "single king that the people ought to have, they actually have a thousand petty tyrants. . . . The orders of a legitimate prince are gentle and moderate, while those of these false sovereigns, being inspired by their irregular passions, are often unjust and violent." This goes back to the king's conception of his office as a gift from God for which he was responsible, and while we have no direct statement to the point, such a view undoubtedly played an important part in Louis' deep concern over grants, commissions, offices, and other acts that relinquished power into the hands of his subjects.

The registers of the secretaries of state who consulted the king every day also provide revealing evidence of the work of the king. In these papers we see him establishing a chamber of commerce and granting a son the right to succeed to his father's commission in the army, in the royal household, even to a professorship in the university, or to some other office in the kingdom. Many of these appointments cost him nothing, for the office was endowed in one way or another, but they did represent areas of power.

Other acts of the king fixed the value of an office, that is, the minimum sum for which it could be sold, thus creating collateral for a loan or a "just price" in case of a sale. Other letters ordered the registry of claims in the chambers of accounts, required tax farmers to check upon the activity of one of their subordinates, or might forbid a stone quarrier at Saint-Cloud to sell stone in Paris. Another might establish the formula for the election of an official of a town, or at the other end of the scale, allow the receiver of the letter to enter freely into the king's châteaus, or to wear certain clothes reserved for the elite of the court, or to regulate the dress that could be worn on certain occasions. One order might give the right to cut wood in the king's forest, while another enjoined a nobleman to desist from killing dogs chasing a stag through his woodland. Indeed, in these papers we find the secretaries of state concerned with the most minute problems in the kingdom, and they often brought them to the king, for their letters abound with the expressions: "I brought this matter to the attention of the King . . ."; "it is the King's personal wish that you . . ."; "the King is much interested in this case. . . ."

A glance at the budgets of the king's household or his government reveals an important fact: while there were some people who held multiple appointments and thereby were able to parlay their incomes to quite handsome sums, the great majority of the men who enjoyed royal "bounty" were scantily paid. Furthermore, their salaries did not go up with years of service—unless they could be fortunate enough to secure a change of office. This is why there was so much excitement when death removed someone from a post—no matter what post—for there were people everywhere who needed more money than their offices provided. A faithful servant could be repaid for his devotion either by being given a better post, or—and this was the more usual—by being granted a royal *gratification*. As we noted above, the word *gratification* covered many things, from the bribing of a minister serving a foreign prince to a huge gift for one of the royal family; but the vast majority of the *gratifications* were really "bonuses" given by the king just as General Motors might reward a faithful employee with a special gift at Christmas. Many of these *gratifications* were in the form of pensions or gifts drawn on the royal treasury, but the king was always on the lookout for gifts that would cost him nothing: a foreigner domiciled in France, or a bastard who had not been legitimized, might die—their property was forfeit to the crown. The registers of the secretaries of state show us the king throwing these confiscated estates, usually very small affairs, to one of his soldiers, a courtier, or an official, as reward for good services. Again, we will find him granting papers of legitimization or naturalization to foreigners or bastards to allow them to pass their property on to their children.[15]

The problems of the church and the clergy intruded into the king's closet. A Jesuit father was exiled for being uncivil to a bishop; and of course there were endless appointments to church benefices. A church might be ordered to display its relics to check the spread of a plague, or even to mitigate a famine (sic!); victory of the king's arms, the birth of a royal child, recovery from illness, and a host of other things would lead to orders for *Te Deums* of gratitude, for it would not be proper to assail heaven with requests for favor without also sending up prayers, songs, and incense of gratitude for divine aid.[16]

By every tradition of the French monarchy, the king was the fountainhead of justice and the officer responsible for public order and peace. Most writers concerned with the reign of Louis XIV discuss the "Grand Days of Auvergne," when the king set up a special court to restore public order in that province. This was most dramatic, for the men who lived on the Massif Central of France had long been unaccustomed to royal justice and the "king's peace." What is often not mentioned is the fact that most of the evil-doers drifted out of the province before the court could get its hands upon them. But Louis' interest in justice and order was a constant throughout his reign. His kingdom suffered from every sort of disorder; murder, robbery, and kidnapping were so common that people accepted them just as they did thunder and lightning. True, many of the murders were duels; many of the kidnappings were cooperative ventures between snatcher and snatched, for only thus could some girls get the husband they wanted; but it simply was not safe to go about in a city after dark, or through a deep woods at any time of day without armed escort. Violence and disorder dogged every man's footsteps. In the years immediately before Louis' personal reign, the erection of "hospitals," which were really poorhouses and places of detention, had begun to attack the problem created by the marginal populations that bred the beggars, cut-purses, and the like, but there was much to be done after 1661. Perhaps the most important single creation of the reign was the police system in Paris with the vigorous **La** Reynie at its head; yet all over France, Louis' reign tightened the police function,[17] and at least attacked some of the problems of public order. One observer tells us that "justice is quick all over the kingdom . . . they capture a criminal today and one hangs him tomorrow . . . that is why we see so much human flesh on the great highways. . . ." These words were written by an Italian and by comparison with Italy, crime was punished readily in France; a twentieth-century man would not have been so enthusiastic. How much of the criminal behavior of his subjects came to the king's desk? A surprising amount, but of course only a small fraction of all the crimes of the kingdom. Louis had regular reports from La Reynie; he took interest in crimes committed in the neighborhood of the court, and he often had crimes called to his attention by people seeking redress that only the king could give. There were few days when some problem of crime and police action did not intrude on the king's attention.

There is a popular engraving preserved in the *Cabinet des Estampes* at the *Bibliothèque Nationale* in Paris that celebrates the king's concern for justice. The artist's conception is a little naïve, but it reflects both popular impressions and perhaps the king's own notion of his role. Louis is pictured receiving complaints of the poor people who pass before him; a secretary of state stands on one side, a captain of the guards on the other. The caption explains, "Here is Louis XIV. He gives audience even to the poorest of his subjects to expedite quickly their differences and their problems."[18] In almost the same spirit Louis explains to his son:

I reformed . . . the manner in which I became accustomed to give justice on my own account to those who demanded it of me. . . . I had not found the form in which heretofore their requests were received satisfactory either to them or to me. And indeed, since most of the people who had requests or complaints . . . were in no condition to secure private entree to my person, they had trouble finding the proper hour to speak to me, and remained several days in my suite separated from their families and their work. For this reason I fixed upon one day each week when all who wished could speak to me or give me memoranda, would have the freedom to come to my cabinet, and would find me ready to listen to them.[19]

Louis' concern for his role as judge may have had its origin in the many speeches that he had listened to as a youth in which the orator praised Saint Louis. Colbert tried to interest him in generalizing his image of himself as judge by assuming the role of Justinian, and did succeed in undertaking an attempt to reform the laws themselves. However, the special commission for the codification of the laws ran into great problems that could not be solved without more help from the king than it received. But it did succeed in laying down the underpinnings of the reform in both the laws and the court procedures that were later used by the men after 1793 to prepare the reforms known as the Napoleonic Codes.

If he failed as Justinian, he was a little more successful as Saint Louis, but in this role much of the royal intervention often seems arbitrary, even tyrannical. Scattered through the registers of the secretaries of state we find orders to courtiers, noblemen, prelates, or simple subjects to present themselves to the Bastille or some other fortress for detention, orders to the guards to see that the prisoners were presented to the governor of the fortress or to a hospital for detention. These people are the unfortunate ones who in one way or another offended the king, their parents or superiors, or perhaps even committed some crime. Some of them had had a trial of a sort; others were sent to jail by royal order alone. The king, acting as father of his people, could punish without any trial those who offended their own natural father or their king. Some of these men were well treated. For example, a man sent to the Bastille for writing a book that offended a foreign prince might find his detention comfortable or distasteful, depending on the attitude of the king toward the offensive book, while someone who had really committed a serious offense might be kept under harsh conditions by order of the king. Thus we find Louvois telling the governor of Pignerol to treat a prisoner "harshly" for he was a *fripon* (rascal) and the king "believes that he merits it."[20]

These people might be kept in prison for years or for only a few days; occasionally a secretary of state would order a review of prisoners, because "it is not just to keep people in prison indefinitely without good cause." Most of the political or personal prisoners probably had means of keeping their cases under some review. We have no definitive studies to show the number of persons, the seriousness of their offenses, or the "justice" of the king's intervention, but we do know that the total number of arbitrary arrests was not large until after the revocation of the Edict of Nantes. These detentions in hospitals and prisons probably did not exceed a hundred or so a year, and most of them seem to have lasted for relatively short periods of time.[21]

Louis was particularly insistent that the edicts issued by his own government should be obeyed. As he wrote to the first president of the Parlement of Toulouse, "I am still firm in the resolution that my edicts shall be observed without exception since I am committed to them by all sorts of divine and human considerations. . . ."[22] The expression is interesting, for Louis undoubtedly believed that God did impose upon him the obligation to see that the law was obeyed. In practice this meant that a great quantity of paper had to cross his desk informing him of the police and justice of the kingdom. Whether it was due to his efforts or not, during his reign there was a significant decrease in murder and violence, and particularly in dueling. Like Richelieu, Louis was insistent that the duel cease to cause death for men whose lives could better be spent in defense of the king's interests, and we see him often intervening in person or through the action of high officers of the army in quarrels that might lead to swordplay.

As we examine the papers requiring the "signature of the king," ranging from heavy parchment to simple chits, from personal letters to administrative orders, we cannot escape the impression that Louis simply could not have examined in detail all this material himself. Charters, grants, orders on the treasury or receivers of revenue, and even many simple letters must have been only briefly called to his attention before they were signed by others who could write his name.[23] Nonetheless, there is enough evidence scattered throughout the papers of the regime to convince any reader that Louis, like Richelieu and Mazarin before him, understood that seventeenth-century government functioned effectively in direct proportion to the personal contacts between the king or minister and the men who helped them operate the machinery of state.

His insistence upon having an important share in the process of government is best illustrated by the remark of one of his ministers: "The King will pass twenty suggestions without question, and then refuse the twenty-first." Louis wanted to have the aid and advice of "those who were most enlightened, most wise, most reasonable among . . . [his] subjects," but important decisions were the responsibility placed by God on the king.

In the seventeenth century it was always a problem to secure obedience; it took great skill on the part of a ruler to find and hold the services of men who would carry out his orders. No one knew this more than Louis and the ministers who aided him; Colbert, Le Tellier, or later on, Louvois, and the others who succeeded them, always had a problem finding ways to have their orders obeyed, and they obviously carried their problems to the king, for his personal intervention was often necessary to secure the modicum of obedience that did occur. His letters to judges in the Parlements are interesting examples. Louis never fully trusted the Parlements, but he had to get along with the men who sat on the benches of these important courts. Contrary to the myths that show the king imposing his will, we find that he used all sorts of gentler methods to secure their cooperation. Louis unquestionably was set upon depriving Parlement of its "usurped powers," but he could hardly hold a *lit de justice* every time a problem arose. Furthermore, not all the questions arose from usurped powers. After Le Tellier became chancellor, the king's government took an active interest in reforming the processes of justice and the organization of the court.[24] We find this sort of sentence in his letters dealing with legal problems: "I am unshaken in my resolution that my edicts be obeyed without question . . . and you may be assured that in serving me well . . . you will have nothing to fear and that my protection will not fail you. . . ." Or another time to the first president of the Parlement at Bordeaux: ". . . this letter is simply to tell you the same thing that I have just written [in an official letter signed by the king and a secretary] . . . which is that once and for all I want you to make your company understand that I wish to be obeyed." When the Parlementarians did comply, they often enough received a gracious letter from the king and on occasion a generous *gratification*; the king could use a carrot as well as a stick.[25]

Sometimes Louis had to intervene personally to obtain results. In several provinces (*pays d'état*) the provincial Estates fixed the amount of the revenue that could be raised for the king's projects; this meant that political manipulation was sometimes necessary for success. Thus we find Louis writing to noblemen, clergymen, and officials to enlist their support in the forthcoming meeting of the Estates of their province. To the Bishop of Montpellier: ". . . not doubting the continuation of your zeal for the good of my service, I would be pleased to learn that in the forthcoming meetings of the Estates in my province of Languedoc, you would . . ."; or to the Duke de Meilleraye: "I know by experience how much you have been able to contrive to the success of my affairs at the Estates of my province of Brittany . . ."; or to the Marquis de Saint-Sulpice: "I am so pleased with the conduct of the gentleman that you sent to the meeting of the Estates of Languedoc last year . . . you would do me a great favor to send him again . . . and remind him to continue to serve me with affection. . . ." These are the letters of a politician who understands that there are many ways to achieve compliance.

Mazarin undoubtedly taught the king his own maxims about the use of persuasion as a means of accomplishing objectives; men are more easily governed by such means than by force. Thus we find Louis writing to his son, ". . . a prince should first employ the means of gentleness and persuasion, for it is more advantageous to persuade than to force." But Louis went on to say, "It is, however, certain that once it concerns either obstacles or rebellion, it is in the interests of [a prince's] *gloire,* and even that of his people, that he make himself obeyed. . . ." Thus Louis could be stern; but he preferred to use soft words and *gratifications.*

Critics, led by Saint-Simon, have charged Louis with being cold, ungrateful, and unfeeling toward those who served him well. To prove their point, they cite the king's apparent unfeeling behavior whenever one of his ministers died. This criticism neglects a cardinal principle of the king, namely, that no person, no event, could disturb the progress of the state. When Louis was in public as the personification of his kingdom, he could not show distress at the death of a Colbert, a Le Tellier, at the German invasion of Alsace, or even at the defeat of his arms at Blenheim, Ramillies, Oudenarde, or Turin. He was a man with a "grand style"; even his own death could not ruffle the "public image of the king." "Why do you weep?" he asked. "You do not expect me to live forever, do you?" But when this same man acted at his desk *en roi,* or when in the privacy of his own chamber, he was simply a man—it was another matter: he could weep over a death, worry that God had withdrawn protection from his kingdom, or concern himself for the welfare of a servant. If a king should die, the cry was "Long live the king!" If a minister should die, "Hail to his successor!" If a marshal should be killed, "We have others!" Yet while they were alive, Louis was not unmindful of their welfare. Colbert was indisposed. The king wrote that he must "care for himself"; he must not "endanger health" that "is necessary to me." He wrote to Madame Colbert urging her to look out for her husband. When Le Tellier fell ill, Louis wrote to Louvois about his father: "I am doubly upset . . . having affection for both you and your father. . . . I fear the result of this illness." He went on to say that although he needed Louvois because of the press of war (1673), perhaps Le Tellier needed his son at his bedside even more, so it was for Louvois to decide whether his father's condition required that he go to him. To this must be added the fact that Louis richly endowed his servants with lands and fiefs and money; he dowered their daughters and arranged wealthy and titled marriages for them; his ministers were the new aristocracy of France and they owed their wealth and power and social prestige to the king's bounty. Both the favors and the goods that he showered upon those who served him and the personal attention that he gave them stand as evidence of Louis' idea of their part in the *métier du roi.*

Up to this point we have watched the king operate as a politician, perhaps even as a statesman, as a judge, as the "father of his people"; the King of France was also a soldier, and Louis was the last French king actually to act as a soldier, leading his people to war. He liked this role best of all—which is not surprising in a prince brought up during the Thirty Years' War and arriving at manhood in the last years of the duel between Hapsburg and Valois-Bourbon. Not surprising in a king surrounded by noblemen who also regarded war as an opportunity and an adventure; it would be astonishing if he had not relished the role of soldier.[26]

However, just as he was a king immersed in pen and ink and conferences, so he was a soldier who preferred administration to command, written orders to cavalry charges. This tended to confuse his thinking about war, but it did not lessen his attention to the art, even though it meant that soldiers like Condé, Turenne, and Luxembourg could not get his ear as readily as a bureaucrat like Louvois. Louis liked the details of military administration. "I have taken great pains," he wrote, "to distribute even the lesser commissions myself for both the infantry and the cavalry. . . . I have assigned quarters for my troops, I have regulated the differences between individual officers . . . you may be assured that such attention given to matters concerning the public good, as well as the service of your army, is the sole means of putting [your affairs] in the state that you desire to see them. . . . I do not understand how princes who neglect their business can believe that those upon whom they depend will care for it any more than they do themselves."

Louis' formula for the army was the same as for other things: personal attention to details, in the belief that thus he could control the development of affairs. When he joined the army as its commander, with competent senior officers to give him advice and counsel, he always personally concerned himself with the paper work of the campaign. The orders of the day that controlled the movement of the army from one campsite to another, perhaps three or four miles away, usually bore marks of the king's personal attention. He liked to organize and direct the several columns of march, to pick the password of the day, to order his brother or some other high officer to assume the responsibility for the king's tent. In an era when maneuver was much more important than pitched battles, these were necessary concerns of a commander, and they fitted into Louis' conception of war.

Efforts to regulate Mars by paper and ink brought cries of distress from commanders in the field who had grown up under the conditions of warfare before 1660. Soldiers like Turenne or Condé, who had always been able to decide what course to take without reference to a civilian minister or a far-away king, hated to be given orders from anyone sitting at a desk two days away. Turenne complained that he got orders that ought never to be given any officer "in whom the King had any confidence." He and other marshals of the old school often managed to circumvent control from the war ministry; some of them actually defied the king. The process that was creating a new army, however, was inexorable. Le Tellier and Louvois used the king's name to enforce their orders, and Louis backed them up to the hilt. A royal army, subordinate to the king's will, was the only force that could curb the violence and disorder that had plagued the preceding century, and such an army would be impossible if the commanders in the field were left free to act as they might wish. Sometimes this administrative supervision might have been responsible for some lack of dash, perhaps even for inaction on the part of commanders, but it also was at the very core of the process that created the new army.

As we shall see later, Louis' own military experience in the field was largely confined to titular command over an army besieging fortifications; he never commanded a field battle. This was partly because of his firm conviction that a king should rely upon the advice of men better informed or more experienced than himself, and partly because many of his high officers did not want to be responsible for the safety of the king as well as for the vagaries of a field battle. A siege was a relatively safe operation as long as the king used some sense about his behavior. The wars were to teach Louis a great deal, but we shall describe his career in this area of his life in the chapters that follow. Writers who try to lump his attitude toward war and battles from the Watteau-like picnic campaigns of the War of the Devolution, when the ladies went along to share in the conquest, to the awful years of the War of the Spanish Succession, simply miss the point and grossly distort the picture.

We should note here that his administrative attitude toward war did not prevent Louis from accepting the hardships of a campaign. Indeed, as long as his health would permit, he joined his soldiers and shared the mud, the cold, the rain, and the other discomforts to which they were exposed. It was probably a deliberate policy: during the *Fronde* Louis learned that troops were heartened and inspired by the presence of the king. He might not stay with the army throughout a campaign, but he did let the soldiers see him in their midst. Later, when he was unable to go with the army because of ill health, he sent his son and his grandsons to take their part in the game of war—always, of course, with a competent commander at their sides. On several occasions he explained that the presence of members of the royal family gave encouragement to the troops and caused fear in the hearts of the foe. But there were other reasons for having the king with the army. We shall see that, in the first part of his reign, his presence was often necessary to be sure that orders would be obeyed, or that men like Vauban would be allowed to direct operations. But this is part of a later chapter.

The King of France lived in a "goldfish bowl" from the moment of his *lever* in the morning to the *coucher* at night; it was a routine that shocked more than one foreign princess who came to France to marry into the royal family. The king and his family dressed in public, ate in public, prayed and lived in public—even went to bed in public. Only a master actor could carry it off with great skill. As Louis became older, his settings became more and more elaborate, perhaps more Byzantine; this was the part of his career that properly can be called baroque. A procession of the knights of the Holy Spirit, a horse show like the carrousel of 1667, the baptism of a member of the family, a marriage, a party given to the court, a hunting party in the forest of Fontainebleau or Chambord or Versailles—indeed, every occasion except a royal funeral was an entrée for the king. When the court was on the march from château to château, or on a tour of inspection to a fortress, a town, or a harbor, or on a pilgrimage to a holy place like Chartres, the king always had to act out his role. He was the *grandeur* of his kingdom; his *gloire* and that of France were confused in the minds of the people, and Louis, who had experienced the *Fronde,* understood this and wished to keep it so.

He seems to have enjoyed these ceremonials. If the registers of the grand master of ceremonies are even nearly correct, he especially relished playing the part of king.[27] It was a function of his *métier* and he knew that he did it well. The magnificent portrait painted by Rigaud showing Louis clothed in ceremonial dress and surrounded by the symbols of his office is still an experience with royalty that few viewers will forget. Here was a man who knew that he had been born to do the *métier du roi,* and on his own confession, enjoyed playing the part very, very much.

14

HIGH POLICY*

IN 1661 DE LA VAUX explained that "France has . . . all of the qualities needed to make her inhabitants powerful, peaceful, and well provided with everything necessary to live graciously . . . she is naturally fortified against foreign attack, being almost surrounded by seas, by high mountains, or by very deep rivers. She produces in abundance the things needed for man . . . she is cultivated and populated and very open to travel for commerce or communication. She has an unusual perfection as a state . . . and her inhabitants are almost infinite in number, robust and generous, born for war, frank, and disciplined. . . ."[1] He found that there were only two evils in the kingdom: religious disunity and vice among the young.

As Louis XIV looked out on the same scene, he too recognized the general picture of tranquillity, but he noted that "it was undoubtedly a little unfortunate to enjoy such tranquillity . . . at a time when my age and the pleasure of being at the head of my armies made me wish for a little more activity abroad." This was the paradox of 1661. Mazarin's policies had won peace with Spain, peace with Germany, peace in Italy, and even peace in the Baltic, and he had willed that peace to a young man who as king was supposed to be a soldier, who had been brought up to be a soldier—a leader of a warlike race. A great war had nurtured a generation of princes and noblemen in the mythology of war and the promise of fame, wealth, and women—to be won by battle. La Grande Mademoiselle reflects her generation when she tells us that she "adored" war and soldiers; for her race and her generation there were few other avenues to success in the great world. Visconti confirms her judgment by saying that women did not want to give their favors to men who were not soldiers, and thereby persuaded young men to give up a career in the king's bureaucracy to join the army.

Who in 1661 saw it otherwise? Who was really happy with the peace? A few merchants and their elected town officials, the men who paid taxes, the members of the sovereign courts who posed as the defenders of the taxpayers' interests, peasants and artisans who feared the incursions of soldiers, and perhaps a few clergymen who dreamed of turning the warlike energy either against Islam or heresy: these "unheroic" people (undoubtedly a majority of the nation) would become important in a later day, but in 1661 they were not. Their voices were not heard in the councils of princes, nor were they wanted there. The prince who came to the throne at a time when there were no wars to be fought, no battles to be won, was the most unfortunate of his rank. To say this neither condones nor condemns; it is only that too often the Sun King and his wars have been misunderstood because writers have failed to grasp the basic assumptions of Louis' century.

Of course foreign affairs, the activity of diplomats and soldiers, the gossip of the courts of Europe were things that deeply concerned a mid-seventeenth-century prince. How could the heir to the Valois and the Hapsburgs fail to see that dynastic politics had reached an apogee, that the chess board of high politics in Europe was set up for the benefit of the successful player, and indeed, that a skillful diplomat and soldier could win great stakes at the game? The staggering luck of Charles V could be repeated by his descendant, perhaps even surpassed. This was also the era when the newer trends of secular politics raised other questions that interested princes and their ministers. Changes in the art of war, new and great opportunities for wealth, and a gradual realization that the humdrum routine of everyday affairs was at the roots of power—all were combining to make states' interests counters in the politics of the world. Louis might tell his son that he was interested in reforming the laws, in building canals and roads, in improving the systems of administration and justice, and in many other everyday affairs that possibly could result in "abundance" for the kingdom, but he had not been educated to handle these problems, nor was he really interested in them. These were things for Colbert, and Louis appreciated his minister, listened to him, and left him to attend to his affairs. But if one wanted the king's eyes to light up and his attention to concentrate, the discussion had to turn to high politics and war. These were the subjects that he had studied under Mazarin and Turenne; these were the proper activities of a prince.

Colbert understood this well. He knew that Louis would and did listen to his plans for making him a "Justinian" by reforming the laws, or an "Augustus" who could assure the peace, or a "patriarch" who would provide "abundance"; but he also knew that Louis' competence and interests were elsewhere. It is a little ruefully that he tells us of the king's meeting with a Polish agent who came to discuss plans for making Condé's son king of that land: "The abbé," he writes, "could not believe that this prince who had taken over the direction of his affairs only four months before would have acquired so much knowledge, short of a miracle." Or again, when Louis discussed Italian affairs with the Spanish ambassador: "This ambassador, who in forty years of service . . . had never heard a prince converse other than in monosyllables . . . found himself surprised with a long and difficult discussion for which he had to assure his Majesty that he was not competent . . . and that he must write to Madrid for instructions."[2] This is in character with the testimony of every memoirist: the young king had an astonishing knowledge of Europe and its problems. He writes for his son, ". . . keep your eyes open to all the earth, know the news from all the provinces and nations, the secrets of all the courts, the humors and weaknesses of all the princes and their ministers. . . ." It was not idle curiosity that inspired him always to insist that his agents abroad must report in great detail all the events of "the land in which you find yourself." As we have seen, he also wanted to know about court gossip as much as about military activity, about ministers, mistresses, soldiers, and plotters. Mazarin had taught him to read the dispatches from ambassadors, and the immense correspondence in the Archives of the Ministry of Foreign Affairs testifies eloquently to the fact that he had learned his lesson.

What were the problems of 1661? Both Colbert and Louis have provided us with panorama discussions of the world that Mazarin left for his protégé. The wars were over, the Hapsburgs had been humiliated and despoiled, the empire lived under a French guarantee that united its most powerful princes in a league to assure the peace. A French-born queen in Poland was working for the election of a French prince to that throne, and in Portugal a French protégeé would undoubtedly win the rebellion against the Spanish king. In Italy, outside of the Spanish provinces, only Mazarin's old enemy Pope Alexander VII resisted French influence. To the north the United Netherlands had been nicely punished for their separate peace with Spain when Mazarin stood aside and allowed Cromwell's England to defeat and humiliate them. In 1661 the restoration in England brought Louis' cousin to the Stuart throne under conditions that suggested that no further trouble could be expected from that part of the world. Both Louis and Colbert emphasize the fact that Mazarin had left a world at peace and one in which the French state was unquestionably the most important factor in the political order of Europe. The young king rather regretted so profound a peace, for it seemed to offer little opportunity for his talents.

A young king in 1661 had to be sure that he would be taken seriously by his contemporaries. His fame, his prestige, his reputation were all deeply involved with the status of his kingdom; his own reputation and fame were what to a nineteenth-century statesman was "national honor," and he had to be sure that they were respected. "A king," Louis wrote, "need never be ashamed of seeking fame, for it is a good that must be ceaselessly and avidly desired, and which alone is better able to secure success of our aims than any other thing. Reputation is often more effective than the most powerful armies. All conquerors have gained more by reputation than by the sword. . . ." This sounds something like the doctrine of "atomic deterrent" mingled with ideas of "national honor" that one hears in the twentieth century.

On the other hand, Louis was not prepared to back down before a similar show of resolution or force on the part of others. When Charles II and his advisers attempted to frighten the French into acceptance of the English version of the right of their ships at sea, Louis wrote to his ambassador in London, "The King, my brother, and those who pretend to advise him do not know me very well . . . there is no power under heaven that can force me to move one step [on a road of dishonor]. . . . I thought that one had a better impression of me than this, but I console myself that only at London does one make such false judgments. . . . I will see that they do not long remain in an error of this kind."[3] Lionne saw to it that the affair did not result in conflict, but the expression of Louis' attitudes must be accepted as representing a point of view common among princes of the period. When he wrote, "In the case of princes like myself who regard honor and *gloire* as being above all other considerations . . . ," Louis was verbalizing the mythology of his period, just as statesmen at all times have talked about the "sacred interests" for which they are responsible. Louis did not confuse himself with his state, but he understood that his reputation and that of his state were inextricably bound together; as a seventeenth-century man, he had seventeenth-century notions of the things that were important both for himself and for the state.

Louis was not alone in holding such notions about reputation, honor, and *gloire;* they were the common property of men of his generation. Thus when an ambassador arrived at a foreign capital, his formal *entrée* was a demonstration of his importance and the prestige of his king. These *entrées* were grand affairs with mule trains, carriages, and marching servitors; other ambassadors and men from the government to which the new ambassador was accredited also joined to make the *entrée* an event in an otherwise dull routine of everyday life. Long before Louis came to power, these *entrées* had given rise to endless contests of precedence and place. Just as the members of the sovereign courts and the men from the Hôtel de Ville in Paris argued endlessly and even jostled each other about the right of place in a parade, a procession, or bench-positions at a funeral, so the several envoys in every capital disputed with one another about rank in these *entrées.*

On October 10, 1661, the French and Spanish ambassadors in London got into such a dispute; the Spaniard had had the vision and wisdom to import as "servants" several thousand Spanish soldiers from the Low Countries, while the Frenchman had only about five hundred. The contest was uneven and a number of French dead were left on the city streets. It was embarrassing to the English king, but he did not have forces at his disposal equal to those of the ambassadors.

The news came to Louis when he was at dinner. He turned white, grasped the arms of his chair, and ran the gauntlet of the expressions of outraged emotions. He could have been play-acting, but it is more than probable that his reactions were sincere; statesmen for the next three centuries were to take a similar attitude toward their "national honor." Noblemen of the preceding centuries had struck similar poses about their "personal honor." Louis stood between these two eras; his reactions fitted both of them. The affront to the French ambassador was an affront to the King and kingdom of France; Louis broke off relations with his father-in-law's kingdom, canceled all Spanish passports, and prepared for war.

Poor Philip IV: he was old and sick, he wanted to hear that his daughter, the Queen of France, had been delivered of his grandchild; his last recollections of Louis had been of a big boy hanging on his neck weeping farewells. Now he had either to fight this young fire-eater or accept humiliation. The Spanish tried to temporize, but Louis would hear nothing of it; he was sure that the insult had been planned and approved as a Spanish response to the marriage between Charles II and the Princess of Portugal, which had been more or less underwritten by French policy. Furthermore, as he explained to his son, the name "French" had acquired dignity, and he did "not consider it proper to leave [his] successor less than [he] had received." The Spanish had to submit utterly. On May 4, 1662, Count de Fuensaldagna appeared at the Louvre before the assembled court and the foreign ambassadors to make a complete repudiation of the pretentions of the Spanish ambassador at London. Louis then asked the foreign envoys to his court to report the scene to their governments "so that they would know that the Catholic King had given orders to his ambassadors to give precedence to mine on all sorts of occasions." Only in Vienna did the Spaniard have the first place; as a result Louis always sent a minister rather than an ambassador to the court of his Hapsburg cousin.

The second test for French prestige came in Rome when papal troops clashed with those of the French ambassador. Pope Alexander VII, who did not like the French very well anyway, was reluctant to humble himself at the demand of the young French king. Louis' reaction was prompt and violent. Every prince in Catholic Europe received a personal letter from the king "written in his own hand," explaining the enormity of the outrage and suggesting that Catholic princes must unite to assure themselves that such events did not reoccur. In Rome, where they had dealt with princes long before Louis XIV was born, it was assumed that delay and procrastination would wear down the edge of French protest. They were, however, dealing with the skeptic Lionne and the Mazarin-trained Louis XIV who had an old score to settle with the pope. When there was no satisfaction, Louis ordered an army to march to Rome, and called loudly on Catholic Europe to support him. Just as Philip IV had been forced to capitulate, so Alexander VII also had to accept Louis' demands; a pyramid was erected in Rome as a monument, and the nephew of the pope went to Paris to apologize. The mere fact that Louis went out of his way to honor the papal ambassador actually advertised—rather than hid—the fact that his presence in Paris was a humiliation for the pope.[4]

These two "flights of the eagle" served notice to Europe that the King of France was not a man to be treated lightly. They are typical of Louis' determination to be sure that he and his kingdom were respected in the world. The conflict with the English over the salute to the flag at sea was on the same general plane, even though it was "solved" by having the two fleets avoid each other rather than by a head-on confrontation. The young king's proud attitude and "brinksmanship" policy were not different in kind from that of other princes of his era; he earned a reputation from it because he had the power to make his prestige respected.

There was one area in the world where the *Pax Mazarina* did not guarantee tranquillity: Christendom's relationship with Islam was to remain a torpid "cold war" down to the opening of the nineteenth century. In the 1660's the onward march of the Ottoman Empire in the Danube basin, the long-smoldering conflict between Venice and the Turks on Crete, as well as the endemic conflict with the North African pirate states, kept the conflict alive. If the King of France should fail to join against the Moslems, he could be sure that many of his nobly born subjects would run off to another army as volunteers anxious for fame, excitement, and perhaps fortune; by allying with the emperor or with Venice, this military ardor could be channelized and perhaps made to reflect glory upon the king.

As a matter of fact, Louis was much interested in sending an "expedition" against the Ottomans (1664), which he pretended would not involve him as the King of France, but rather as the "Margrave of Alsace," aiding the emperor in his struggle at the Danube. The expeditionary force was composed of the flower of the French nobility, and a surprisingly large number of them lost their lives. This was the first serious military effort of his personal regime; he followed the reports of the troops, urged his commanders to be sure that his soldiers maintained discipline and the good name of their king, and took great pride in the critical and decisive part that the French expedition played in the battle of St. Gottart. Indeed, without the French force, that battle might well have been lost. Unfortunately, however, the expedition did not produce the desired results. The French could not resist the temptation to use the expedition to intimidate the Ten Imperial Towns of Alsace whose governments claimed that they remained directly under the emperor's authority in spite of the terms of the Treaty of Westphalia. This pressure on the Germans in Alsace came at the same time that another French army went to the assistance of a German bishop whose subjects were in revolt against his authority. It was all very well to say that the French were only acting under their treaty rights and that these French soldiers behaved properly, nonetheless no one in Germany missed the fact that French soldiers were solving German problems. Perhaps this is the real reason that the imperials, after cordially and generously praising Louis' soldiers for their part at St. Gottart, turned cold and unfriendly and made it difficult to supply the French force with food. The expedition returned to France, a handsome "memorial" volume in the royal library commemorated their glorious effort and recognized the noblemen who took part in the enterprise,[5] and that was about all. There was little satisfaction for France in the knowledge that her soldiers had made it possible for Leopold to secure a twenty-year truce with the Ottoman Empire.

The expedition against the pirates in North Africa turned out even less well. A naval expedition under the Duke de Beaufort, who as a cadet of the Vendôme family could boast of Bourbon blood, and as an erstwhile *Frondeur* had won only mediocre reputation for himself, proved unable to establish a French foothold in Algeria. Louis wrote regularly both to Beaufort and to his friend Vivonne (the brother of Madame de Montespan) to encourage them to cooperate and to accomplish their mission. It was no use. Obviously Beaufort was an incompetent, and his death shortly afterward may have saved him from a well-deserved disgrace; but he was a member of the family, and Louis did not find it easy to act against him.

No one can say what Louis actually learned from these adventures, but they clearly did not satisfy his desire for fame for his kingdom and prestige for his arms, nor did they forward the policies of his state. These early clashes of arms had little to do with the development of the foreign policy that is associated with his reign.

There were, of course, other problems for him to consider. Richelieu had repeatedly emphasized the fact that there were "gates" on the frontiers that could swing open for the foreigner to invade or that might be openings for French military excursions beyond the frontiers. Mid-seventeenth-century statesmen did not think in terms of lineal frontiers; they saw the borders of their states occupied by provinces and dependencies, cities and fiefs with ambiguous relationships. They had no idea of "natural" or "national" frontiers, but they did think of "defensible" ones. In the 1630's and again in the 1650's foreign armies threatened to swarm on to Paris as they had done in the sixteenth century; Richelieu, and after him Mazarin, wished to gain control of the "gates" that these foreigners might use. By the Treaties of Westphalia and of the Pyrenees, Mazarin had secured some control over most of the "gates" in Alsace (except Strasbourg), Flanders, and Artois, as well as on the Pyrenees frontier, but Lorraine and Dunkirk still remained in the hands of foreigners, and from the flatlands of the Spanish Netherlands to the hilly frontiers of Luxembourg, there were roads and cities that might assist an assault on the French kingdom. It would be absurd to assume that preoccupation with the "gates" of his kingdom was the sole axis of Louis' policy, but it is equally false to fail to recognize his concern.

The young king had hardly taken over his government when the opportunity arose to acquire one of these "gates." He understood that Mazarin had been forced to give Dunkirk to England in return for aid against Spain, but as he explained, he also understood that the English "were ancient and irreconcilable enemies of France . . . from whom she was formerly saved only by a miracle. . . ." All Normandy remembered the English of the fourteenth and fifteenth centuries; the Rouen militia had an "English alert" until the end of the seventeenth century. Under English control, Dunkirk was a dangerous point for attacking France. Under French control it was to become a nest for privateers against English commerce. When Charles II, in need of money, indicated his willingness to sell Dunkirk, Louis quickly grasped the opportunity to buy it. He wrote to his cousin Conti that he had originally consented "to turn Dunkirk over to the English, only to advance the peace," and so therefore as soon as he understood that it could be reacquired because his royal cousin in England needed money, he (Louis) "could think of no better way to employ money. . . . For that reason, without even stopping to think of the present state of my finances, I did not hesitate to make a treaty securing this place. . . ."[6] It was with great satisfaction that he revisited the city to receive the cheers of the Dunkirkers who were pleased to be free from a non-French-speaking, foreign, and heretical rule. Louis' government was also "foreign" to the Dunkirkers, but less so than England's. The visit, however, did not give the king any greater love nor appreciation for the sea, which was to remain an alien element that he never understood.

The French acquisition of Dunkirk may have caused some problems for Charles II, whose subjects were unhappy to see the port released from English control, but the King of France had only satisfaction from the transaction. The next "gate" that Louis tried to close, however, created some difficulties both within and without the kingdom. As Louis explained it, Lorraine had been a "gate open to foreigners invading our estates" and under French control it could provide "passage for my troops into Germany. . . ." This German frontier had long been a troublesome one. By the Treaty of Westphalia, the French king became *landgraf* or *landvogt* or Margrave of Alsace, which gave him suzerain rights over a largely undefined complex of cities, fiefs, and ecclesiastical estates. The city of Strasbourg was not included, but the so-called Ten Towns probably were. Lorraine to the north was still under its duke, whose status also had many ambiguities. For generations, historians have wrangled over the legal problems involved; but Louis was not as interested in the legal problems as he was in acquiring the "gates" and establishing his "rights" under the treaties; he understood that the questions were as much political as juridical, but that the important question was a military one.[7]

The impecunious Duke of Lorraine needed money as much as Charles II did, and he was willing to trade off his ducal throne for gold and promises that would guarantee his future and that of his illegitimate son. Thus he listened attentively when Louis offered him money and the assurance that his family would have an important place in the French peerage in return for ceding Lorraine to the Bourbon crown. Duke Charles was a difficult, irrational, indecisive, evasive man; it took a long time to get him to sign a treaty that left him as governor of Lorraine, his family as peers of France immediately behind the Bourbon-Condé lines in the succession to the throne, and his pockets full of French gold, in return for the annexation of Lorraine to the kingdom of France.[8] Louis was jubilant. "I have just made a *coup* of great luck and importance," he crowed to Condé. "It will create a sensation in the world!"

Sure enough, it did. Then French peers were disgruntled to have another family pushed ahead of their claims to the throne, but more important, the German princes in the League of the Rhine were unhappy to hear of a treaty that detached a part of the empire. Rather than showing pleasure at the luck of their ally and friend, they asked each other whether this new King of France might not be a threat to that sacred cow of the princes beyond the Rhine, "German liberties." Unhappily, too, Duke Charles was willing to sign, but not willing to deliver, and so the French threat had to be underlined by a military excursion to Lorraine to secure Louis' rights.[9] Then there was the nephew and heir of the Lorraine duke. The queen mother had intended to marry him off to her niece La Grande Mademoiselle, but the annexation ended these plans and sent that young man off to the imperial service, in which he was destined to earn a great military reputation. Finally, even though the preoccupation with the Turks prevented the men at Vienna from protesting very effectively, the emperor never really accepted the French annexation of Lorraine which he considered to be part of the empire, and in fact, the treaty was reversed at Ryswick some thirty years later.

About the same time that Louis was "closing the gate at Lorraine," he also attempted to assert his suzerain rights over the so-called Ten Towns of Alsace. The Treaty of Westphalia had been deliberately vague about the rights that the French king had acquired in Alsace, so vague that the townsmen could argue that they remained under the empire even though the King of France had become margrave of their province. Lionne and the French ambassador at the Diet realized that French prestige in Germany, and the usefulness of the so-called League of the Rhine to France, rested upon the idea that France was the defender of "German liberties" and that this idea would evaporate if France threatened to impose her will upon Germany. Thus they urged caution in the relations between the king in Paris and the Ten Towns of Alsace. But Louis could not resist the temptation to use the expeditionary force that went to support the emperor against the Turks as a threat to intimidate the townsmen. The result was a series of complaints at Ratisbon and a flutter of diplomatic activity in the Rhineland that boded ill for the future of the French alliance. Louis, more aggressive than the cardinal had been, did not hesitate to frighten the German princes, but in so doing he loosened and finally destroyed the League of the Rhine that Mazarin had brought into being to keep Emperor Leopold I from using Germany against France. The policy seems to have been the king's own making, for Lionne eloquently argued against frightening the German princes.

There were other areas in Europe where successful policy might win great stakes, but caution required that the King must go slowly. In the lands beyond the Rhine there were elective thrones that might be won by policy or bribery. Louis had been a candidate for the crown of the empire at the time that Leopold I had been elected; the fears of German princes made it imperative that he move with caution, yet Louis did not easily give up the hope that he or a member of his family might follow Leopold on that throne. Farther to the east was the kingdom of Poland, where a French-born princess conspired with Louis to place Condé's son on the throne. Louis spent freely of his money and advice in an effort to convince the Polish Diet of the wisdom of such an election, and for a short time it seemed that he might be successful.

At the other end of Europe the revolution in Portugal offered opportunity to weaken the power of Spain and to develop a French satellite power. The Treaty of the Pyrenees explicitly prohibited French interference between Philip IV and his rebellious subjects, but as Louis wrote to d'Estrades, "My ancestor Henry the Great . . . did not hesitate to aid the United Netherlands with men and money even though it was forbidden by the treaty of Vervins . . . and I propose to model my behavior on that great prince. . . ."[10] Louis carefully kept himself in the background, but he authorized Turenne to make all the arrangements needed to sustain the rebellion. Schomburg, commanding an army paid for by Turenne, managed the affair quite successfully, for the Spanish had no soldiers able to fight him. Turenne also arranged the marriage policies that Louis planned for Portugal. He was unable to convince La Grande Mademoiselle that she should marry Don Carlos, the pretender to Portugal's throne, for that lady preferred to be La Grande Mademoiselle in France, to visit her watering places, and to entertain her friends, rather than to marry a prince who murdered for the fun of it and whose personal habits were quite repulsive. Louis was careful not to insist, but the fact that Turenne did try to put pressure on her made Louis seem unscrupulous in the lady's eyes.

Louis also had his hand in the English marriages. Charles II would have been happy to marry La Grande Mademoiselle when he was an exile, for her great wealth could have been used to regain the throne, but once on that throne, there were other considerations. In fact, he married a Portuguese princess who brought a dowry of land and money (presumably paid by Louis) in return for English aid for Portugal. This policy had a double edge: it alienated the Spanish and English thrones at the same time that it aided the Portuguese rebels. The other English marriage united Henriette, Charles' sister, to her cousin Philippe, Louis' brother. It was a match that brought little joy to either, for Philippe had no great interest in women. Henriette returned to France, however, somewhat more attractive than she had been as a teen-age girl, when Louis had referred to her as "the bones of the holy innocents." We will see how the young king was to pay for that remark.

Unhappily for historians, if Louis had a grand design or long-range program for his policy, he failed to leave us its blueprint. Over a century ago Mignet published a great collection of documents dealing with the succession to the throne of Spain, and for two generations historians proclaimed that this was the axis for the foreign policy of Louis XIV.[11] Then historians came to realize that Louis, like any other statesman, had to contend with the day-to-day course of events, and that inevitably his policy was modified and shaped by these events. As a result, it became fashionable to portray Louis and his ministers as men conditioned by the latest dispatches; they lived from hand to mouth, rather than by an established plan. There can be no doubt that statesmen of the caliber of the king and his advisers do take advantage of events as they develop and do not hold to an "axis" as though they were following the pole star. And yet it is also probable that these men did not overlook the obvious possibility for great political success that was inherent in the political structure of their time. When Louis wrote to Turenne that "projects roll about in my mind," he undoubtedly meant that there were possibilities for his dynasty and his state in the political organization of Europe at the time.

Mignet was unquestionably right, however, in pointing out that of all the possibilities, the most glittering was the throne of Spain. In this seventeenth-century world, dynastic inheritance was the key to sovereignty, and therefore the stakes of politics were often confused by the accidents of birth and death, which were conceived to be the work of God. Both Anne and Mazarin had understood that the Spanish marriage of 1659 could result in a Bourbon succession to the thrones of the Spanish Hapsburgs. The dowry clause that made the renunciation dependent upon payment of a huge sum of money had been put in the treaty by design, but even if the dowry were paid, it was always questionable whether an act of man could nullify an act of God. As long as Philip IV had sons to succeed him, the question would not be raised, but were the Spanish Hapsburg male line to end, then it would become a disputable point: could Marie-Thérèse actually renounce the rights that belonged to her unborn children? Many years later Louis himself was confronted with the same problem. The Treaty of Utrecht excluded Philippe V of Spain and his heirs from the throne of France, but as the old Louis said, it was not at all sure that the Parlement of Paris would recognize any king who did not come to the throne with the sanction of the Salic law. The King of France might not understand much theology, but he did understand that God disposed the fate of kingdoms on this earth. This does not mean, of course, that Louis was unwilling to bargain and to compromise; for while he understood "his rights" and the will of God, he also was a politician who had to confront the events of the day by policy that recognized the political structure of Europe.

If the acquisition of the Spanish inheritance could be considered as one aspect of a grand design for Bourbon France in 1661, the other side of that program was an effort to control the Holy Roman Empire. Indeed, a book published in Paris during these early years of Louis' personal regime indicated that the Bourbon line was in fact heir to Charlemagne's empire of the west,[12] that the Hapsburgs in Vienna were at best late comers, at worst usurpers, and must be replaced by the Bourbons. The book created a scandal. In Germany there were men who had already become fearful of France and the intentions of the French king; this pretension to universal empire presented by an official of the French Parlement seemed to accentuate their premonitions for the future. Louis sent the author to the Bastille for a short stay as a sop to the foreign critics, but no one missed the fact that this book had merely proclaimed openly what many men were privately considering as a future possibility. The emergence of France as a great military force in Europe was creating a situation that offered many opportunities to an ambitious prince, and no one doubted that Louis was aware of this.

However, as Europe looked from Paris in 1661–65, the biggest problem was not the crown of the empire, nor even succession to the Spanish inheritance. What concerned men like Turenne and Lionne and Louis was the same thing that had bothered the late cardinals, namely the Spanish Netherlands. Within the memory of living men, foreign armies had several times either threatened to invade or actually had invaded France from the north; these provinces were in effect "gates" to the kingdom of France. Thus we have seen that Mazarin tried in 1646 to secure them as a "dowry" for Marie-Thérèse, and again, in 1658, Turenne was anxious to sweep the Spanish out of these provinces and thus to end the war by conquest. The Treaty of the Pyrenees temporarily halted the effort to gain control over these provinces, but men in high places in France knew that for many good reasons the acquisition of the Spanish Netherlands must have a high priority in French policy. Were France to gain control over Antwerp, Colbert argued, the city could again become one of the first commercial ports of Europe, and the rich industrial hinterland would come to life economically as it had in the era before the Dutch closed the Scheldt river to seagoing traffic. Thus the dynastic interests of the Bourbon family were joined with the military and economic considerations of soldiers and bureaucrats to intensify the need for annexation of these provinces on the northern and eastern frontiers of the kingdom.

But as we have seen, the problem was complicated by a complex of interests centered around these provinces. Neither the Dutch nor the English wished to see Antwerp regain its commercial preeminence, and especially they did not wish to see a French Antwerp become a trading center rivaling London, Rotterdam, and Amsterdam. Nor did the Dutch relish the idea of French military forces on the Scheldt; the French were good as allies, but bad as neighbors. In the German Rhineland, too, there were fears that French occupation of the Spanish Netherlands would endanger German "liberties." Louis and his advisers were very much aware of all of these conflicting forces and of their implications for French policy. In light of their past experience with Dutch diplomacy, it is hard to understand how they could believe that the United Netherlands would ever allow them to annex these provinces.

The chance to discuss the problem with the Dutch came almost immediately after the death of the cardinal, for a delegation of Dutch politicians arrived at the French court with a request for the renewal of the Franco-Dutch alliance. At the time of the Congress of Westphalia, the Dutch had deserted French interests precisely over the question of the Spanish Netherlands. This act cost them dearly, for Mazarin had stood aside and allowed Cromwell's England to punish them severely in a naval war that injured Dutch commerce and cost considerable blood. In 1661, when Charles II returned to the throne in England, the Dutch patrician regime anticipated that the new English king would intervene in Dutch domestic politics to favor the Orange party, headed by his nephew, the young William of Orange. The merchant families wished if possible to exclude the Orange factions from power. There was also the chance that Charles II would embark upon Cromwell's anti-Dutch commercial policy to endear himself to the trading interests in England. Considering all this, Louis and his advisers convinced themselves that the Dutch would relent in their opposition to French annexations of the Spanish Netherlands. Louis appointed a committee composed of Lionne, Villeroi, Colbert, and the two Briennes to negotiate an agreement. Even though the Dutch shied away from recognition of the French right to annex the Spanish Netherlands, an alliance was finally signed, for Louis seemed to believe that they would eventually agree on this delicate point.

While Louis made a treaty of alliance with the Dutch, he did not hesitate to develop policies that would seriously antagonize them. The complex of politico-economic ideas that we commonly call "Colbertism" had been current in France long before Louis came to power, but no government had been strong enough to put them into effect. The strong support that permitted the other reform movements of the new government allowed Colbert to draft new commercial legislation to unify the economic order in the kingdom. Louis was interested in this program and strongly backed up his minister. As Colbert saw the economic world, the total amount of commerce possible was strictly limited; his conception of the economy posited a rigid machine in which a fixed amount of goods, requiring a fixed number of ships, circulated in the markets of Europe. The only way to increase the trade of one country was to decrease that of another. Thus trade was, in effect, commercial warfare by which the merchants of one land brought distress to those of another. Colbert expounded this doctrine in memorandum after memorandum for the benefit of the king, until Louis shared it completely. Colbert tried to teach him that economic warfare could be as exciting as the more conventional military operations.

In the 1660's the problem was simple enough: the Dutch had a lion's share of the trade of the European world. Goods of all Europe went to the Netherlands where they were graded, perhaps adulterated or finished, and reexported in return for other goods. The United Netherlands, as wholesale jobbers, sold English tin, Spanish wool, Swedish iron, French wine, Asian, African, and American wares, and became rich both on the carrying trade and the profits of the exchange of goods. Cromwell's England had fought this Dutch monopoly with Navigation Acts and battleships; the monopoly also aroused the envy and cupidity of the French. The only way to cut into the trade was to prevent Dutch traders from exporting their goods to France. Therefore a tariff became the weapon in this commercial war.

Nothing could be done in 1661 and the years immediately following, because the French fiscal system and customs structure were too disorderly and archaic to be used as economic weapons. Thus when the alliance was made, there were no problems of economic friction: the Dutch bought French brandies and wines and sold the goods of the world in French markets without hindrance. In 1664, however, Colbert achieved his first tariff reform. If one looks at this tariff from the twentieth century, it becomes painfully clear that it was only a partial reform of an almost hopelessly complex and disarrayed system, but from the viewpoint of a seventeenth-century politician, it was a reform that gave the king much more power for the control of commerce, as well as a bigger bite of the available revenues. Foreign merchants were not particularly disturbed by this tariff;

it raised their eyebrows rather than their wrath, for its most important effect was to unify the tariff rates of the entire kingdom. In 1667, however, Colbert was ready to strike; he prepared a new tariff that would make serious inroads on the commerce of both English and Dutch merchants who traded with France. By this time France, as an ally of the Dutch, was already at war with England, but Colbert was striking his allies as well as his enemies.

The French were not the only ones envious of the Dutch. Charles II knew that he could be sure of support from England's commercial classes for a policy similar to the one that Cromwell had adopted a decade earlier. In 1664 his brother commanded a naval expedition that occupied New Amsterdam, while another English squadron attacked several Dutch installations in Africa; at the same time he reimposed the navigation laws. Obviously England wanted war.

The Dutch fluttered to Paris demanding Louis' aid as an ally. The discussions about the fate of the Spanish Netherlands that had preceded the alliance treaty of 1662, as well as Colbert's realization of the economic hostility of the Netherlands, made the French court somewhat less than anxious to rush to the aid of their "ally." It was embarrassing, as Louis saw it: ". . . if I execute the letter of the treaty of 1662, I will prejudice my principal interests for people from whom I shall never obtain any assistance, indeed, whom I would find against me in the only case in which I might . . . need their aid, and thus the aid that I would give them would be turned against me." Lionne explained to the Dutch ambassador, "It is bad business; we will assist you and break . . . an engagement that we have with England, and tomorrow you will break with us. And all this trouble because of that miserable policy requiring a barrier [in the Spanish Netherlands] between the United Provinces and France." The French did not want to break off their relations with England, and especially they did not wish to force England into an agreement with Spain, and yet they had made the alliance with the Dutch in hopes that some agreement could be reached over the Spanish Netherlands.

The best solution seemed to be to attempt to mediate between the Dutch and the English. Louis sent his uncle (of a bastard line), the Duke de Verneuil, at the head of a mission to London to try to find a way to peace. The discussions came to nothing. In June the English won a naval victory that convinced them that they could win without negotiations, and the Dutch, believing that Louis was playing false to his alliance, became more and more insistent that the French join the war, especially since they were threatened with an invasion from Germany by a *condottiere* bishop in the English service. The French temporized, but on September 17, 1665,

Philip IV of Spain died, leaving a sickly baby boy as his sole male heir. Should this child die, the Spanish succession would be an immediate problem. On January 26, 1666, Louis declared war on England. As he explained his action to his son, he had the choice of declaring war on Spain to protect the interests of his wife and infant son who had "rights" to the Spanish succession, or of declaring war on England and thereby honoring his alliance with the Dutch. Louis tells his son that he decided upon the latter policy to which he had pledged his word.

French policy however, was not as simple as that. Louis did declare war on England, and in spite of the innuendoes to the contrary, he did try to give the Dutch help, both on land and on sea, but he did not enter the war simply to support his allies. The war became a screen behind which he could prepare for the conquest of the Spanish Netherlands. The French were convinced that their intervention in the Anglo-Dutch war would force the Netherlands to support their claims to these provinces. It had taken months to reach the conclusion, for Louis' advisers were anxious not to create a situation that might throw England and Spain into an alliance. "A prince," Louis wrote, "gains *gloire* by conquering difficulties . . . but if he puts himself in the danger of being accused of imprudence; if he throws himself too easily into situations that a little caution would avoid [he can be in trouble] . . . the more one loves *la gloire,* the more one ought to be sure to achieve it with safety." By declaring war on England, the French would have an excuse to build up the forces necessary for the conquest of the Spanish Netherlands, and at the same time, perhaps, the opportunity to bind the Dutch to a policy that would allow France to keep these provinces— or that is what Louis and his advisers hoped would happen.

15

THE WAR OF DEVOLUTION*

ON SEPTEMBER 17, 1665, Philip IV died in Madrid leaving his thrones to a five-year-old son, Charles II, whose general physical condition was so bad that no one expected him to live. In light of Marie-Thérèse's renunciation of the Spanish thrones, Philip IV had named his second daughter, Marguerite-Thérèse, then the intended bride of Leopold I, as next in line of succession after his son, thereby excluding the Bourbons from the Spanish throne. Did he have the right to do this? The Treaty of the Pyrenees had in fact provided for Marie-Thérèse's renunciation, but it was conditional upon the payment of a dowry that had not been paid. No one in the court of France doubted that Marie-Thérèse and her son had legitimate claims to the thrones of Spain, or that Louis, as husband and as father, had the obligation to see that his wife and son were not deprived of their rights. For the moment the question was not really serious, for young Charles II was still alive; but with the death of Philip IV, the Spanish empire stood revealed as a hollow giant governed by a weak regency. It was a situation that invited bold projects.

There was no lack of ideas in France for such projects. Both politicians and soldiers had long believed that the French kingdom should somehow annex the Spanish Netherlands. As we have seen, this idea was an old one; it also was tangled in the high politics of the United Netherlands, England, and Germany, as well as of France. Louis' council well understood what was at stake, and Louis did not lack advisers who could find good reasons for taking action.[1]

Since the Spanish child-king "refused to die" and leave the inheritance to the decision of politics and war, the French decided to press a claim that would allow them to partition the Spanish inheritance even though the little Charles II still lived. The claim was based upon the law of inheritance common to several of the provinces of the Spanish Netherlands, which provided that a daughter of the first bed could insist upon her share of her father's goods, even though there was a son by a second bed who had been declared universal heir. This was a law tailored for Louis' situation, and his advisers easily provided him with an elaborate and skillfully argued brief proving that Marie-Thérèse and her son had a right to assume control over a large part of the Spanish Netherlands. Since Turenne's secretary prepared the argument, Louis must also have been assured of the military practicality of the move.

The *Traité des droits de la reine très chrétienne*[2] that presented the case was translated into several languages and widely circulated throughout Europe. The regency government in Spain quickly rejected it, and a shower of pamphlets pro and con rained from the presses of Europe. While Louis assumed the stance of a husband and father defending the rights of his family, his opponents painted his demands as stark aggression. The French argument was shaky and yet it should not be summarily rejected. International law in 1667 was not a firmly established code and especially not for questions that were essentially dynastic. This was not a question of law between states as much as it was a contest within the family, and yet it was a problem that could easily involve the resources of the states concerned. As the French presented their case, their armies did not march into the Spanish Netherlands as a hostile force bent on conquest, but rather as the army of their queen occupying territory that was rightfully hers. The whole argument revolved around a concept of law that matched the dynastic assumptions of the seventeenth century; it had nothing to do with the ideas of international law that were developing out of conceptions of "states' interest" and the emerging new political structure of Europe that conceived of a community of states living together under vaguely defined rules of international law based upon custom, a state's interests, and power. This French "aggression" threatened the states' interest of France's neighbors, so that the attempt to impose a rule of "dynastic" law became a question of high politics and power that could be challenged as a violation of the emerging international law.

It would be folly to believe that the French were ignorant of the implications of their action; but the men around the king believed that the political situation created by French intervention in the Anglo-Dutch naval war would prevent any interference with their plans. If one keeps the public morality of the seventeenth century in mind, their course of action seems more unwise than unjust.

Louis could not foresee how unwise his demands were. As he explains it, everything seemed to favor the enterprise: "Flanders was short of troops and money; Spain governed by a foreign princess [Mariana von Hapsburg]; the emperor irresolute; the House of Hapsburg reduced to two heads, its forces weakened by diverse wars and its partisans cool to its interests."[3] With England and the United Netherlands engaged in war with each other, there seemed to be little to do but occupy what rightfully belonged to the queen.

The preparations for this "occupation" had started the year before, when Le Tellier and his son Louvois began the assembly of the army and the concentration of supplies under the mask of war against England. An army of over 70,000 men, the finest that France—or for that matter, Europe—had seen since Roman times, was brought into being, drilled, and prepared for the great adventure. Louis' part had been to attend frequent reviews of these troops, a gay and exciting activity well suited to his moods and self-image. He took the court with him to see the soldiers, making the review into a grand fête, as well as a military parade. The country people had a chance to see his queen, his mistress, the ladies, and the great press of courtiers who followed everywhere. Saint Maurice describes their forces: "The King left . . . with the most handsome and pretentious suites that anyone could ever see. There were eight in his carriage; the King, the Queen, Monsieur [Louis' brother], Mme. the Duchesse of Orléans, Mlle. de Montpensier [La Grande Mademoiselle], the Duchesse de la Vallière, the Countess de Bethune, and the Marquise de Montespan." La Vallière had just been made a duchess and her daughter by Louis declared legitimate; and she was pregnant again. But her star was on the wane, for Louis' roving eye had made contact with the fairest flower of them all—de Montespan. Saint-Simon was not a witness to the scene, but he is probably right when he writes that the "people came from all parts to see the three queens . . . and asked themselves with simplicity if they had seen them." The king's court with its magnificence was as much a part of the preparations as the army of Swiss, German, French, and Italian soldiers that were so ostentatiously reviewed.

When Louis campaigned with his army, his personal equipment was sumptuous to a high degree. When he took the ladies of the court with him to see the soldiers, Darius the Persian never was better housed in the field. His tent, made entirely of Chinese silk, had three rooms in addition to a sleeping chamber and two offices. It was populated by "cavaliers" who would attract the enemy rather than cause them to flee, for the troop included Mademoiselle de la Vallière, Madame de Montespan, Princess d'Harcourt, Madame de Roure, and a dozen other beauties who stayed in the tent during the heat of the day, but occasionally rode with the king to see the assembly of more serious warriors. De Noyes, writing to the queen of Poland, was probably a bit sarcastic when he remarked that it was doubtful if the king would find Flanders "as agreeable as it seems to be here," or that Flanders would provide as much pleasure. Louis was anxious to take the war seriously, but in 1666–67 that did not yet mean that he must deprive himself of companionship and comfort. When the campaign began in earnest, Louis sent the ladies to Compiègne and then joined Turenne to direct the occupation of the queen's "rightful inheritance."

The plans for the campaign were unquestionably the work of Turenne, but, as kings often do, Louis took credit for them. "Since I knew that the Spanish lacked . . . soldiers," he wrote, "I decided to terrorize them from all sides at once to oblige them to divide the few troops that they did have into a great number of garrisons . . . thus making them equally weak everywhere." The French forces were overwhelming, and Spanish resistance was very weak; yet there were difficulties for the Bourbon armies. Fortresses do not surrender unless the governor is sure that re- sistance would be futile, nor do armies retreat unless the enemy is obviously overwhelming in power. Louis was faced with the omnipresent facts of seventeenth-century warfare: the soldiers needed food, the horses needed fodder, and a siege required munitions and guns. This was an era when an army moved under horsepower over roads that seemed to have no bot- toms, and through country that could provide little beyond forage—and sometimes not enough of that. The carts and carriages and gun caissons cut the already poor roads to pieces, and men, horses, carts, and guns were either mired down in mud or bedeviled by dust and chuckholes. Since the townsmen did not like to risk their houses to the vicissitudes of cannon fire, the Spanish garrisons usually surrendered as soon as the French siege lines were drawn and ready to begin the siege, for it would be folly to fight when there could be only one result. But guns and munitions did not move themselves, and soldiers would not surrender until the besieger was actually in place. Thus the campaign depended as much upon transportation as it did upon the heroism of the troops. Even this French army, excellent by contemporary standards, was not free from the vexing trials of seven- teenth-century warfare, which included—in addition to logistics—deser- tion, cowardice, and inefficiency. Turenne had had experience with all of these problems and advised Louis to move cautiously. There might not be much fighting, but the occupation of the land presented formidable prob- lems.

Louis learned this lesson very quickly. "It is not enough," he ex- plained, "to make grand plans without thinking of the means for executing them; projects . . . that at first seem marvelous have little solidity if they are not sustained by foresight that understands how to arrange the many things that must go along with them. . . . This is the great difference between a good and a bad captain. The clever general never undertakes an affair that requires time without having examined all the things necessary to sustain his men . . . it is inhuman to put brave men in danger of losing their lives under conditions in which valor will not guarantee success . . . in which they cannot even console themselves in death by the hope of fame. . . ." Indeed, he writes, "other disasters can nearly always be blamed upon cowardice or just bad luck, but in a case where supplies are lacking, the failure of foresight of the general is alone responsible." This was a lesson that Louis was never to forget; his correspondence for the next forty-five years is filled with advice about forage, food, munitions, carts, and problems of logistics. When he found that Louvois was a man who could manage supplies, Louvois' position in his government was established, no matter what else that difficult individual might do.

The plan of the campaign called for an invasion of the Spanish Netherlands by three armies. The middle one "commanded by Turenne under the King's orders" was the important thrust, while detachments under Marshal d'Aumont and Lieutenant General Créqui operated on its wings, one facing the sea and one facing Germany. When Louis joined the army about the middle of May, he announced that as one of Turenne's cadets, he proposed to learn the art of war under Europe's most famous general. This does not mean that the king was useless baggage. He did not direct the activities of the soldiers, but his presence gave strength to the morale of the troops. In striking contrast to the picnic-like parts of the campaign, when the serious invasion was under way, Louis shared the hardships of war with his soldiers. "Even in this terrible weather," writes a fellow-soldier, "the king rode horseback at the head of the army . . . the same as a simple officer . . . nor does he seek shelter in houses, no matter where we are, while his troops camp out. . . ."[4]

Turenne's cautious invasion marched with clocklike precision. With a superb army, plentiful supplies, and a weak enemy, the campaign was largely a problem of moving so many men and horses over the roads. It was hardly necessary to fire the guns to force a city to surrender. All France was soon ringing with *Te Deums* ordered by the king to thank God for His bounty. While Louis fully realized the importance of the work done by the Le Telliers and by Turenne, he also believed that the ease with which this campaign progressed was indication of Divine approval of his projects and claims. As he wrote to the Archbishop of Paris after the surrender of Douai, "It is from the hand of God that I receive these happy successes . . . and I wish to give thanks for His divine bounty. . . ."[5] When the Parlement sent a delegation to congratulate him on his glorious campaign, and as courtiers, to beg him not to expose his precious person to further danger, Louis brusquely rejected the idea that he had done anything to warrant praise. The war was grave enough, but it was not a difficult operation as long as Turenne's caution and the supplies provided by the war ministry dominated the situation, and God continued to bless the campaign.

When the weather improved in July, Louis decided that the time had come to bring the queen and the court to Flanders so that her subjects could see their rightful ruler. The fact that his affair with de Montespan had progressed to a stage that might be called "ardent" may have been an added inducement. Louis returned to Compiègne, picked up his court, and then started a grand tour of conquest to show the queen's new subjects the wonders from Saint-Germain and Fontainebleau, the plumes and silks, the sumptuous gowns, the magnificence of the carriages and the harness of the horses, the superb tents and equipment of the court. It was not just the simple Flemish peasant who gaped at the splendor of the king of France: as Coligny wrote to a friend, "All that you have seen of the magnificence of Solomon and the grandeur of the King of Persia does not equal the pomp displayed on this trip . . . plumes, gold embroidery, chariots, mules superbly harnessed, parade horses with equipment embossed in gold . . . all the courtiers, the officers, the volunteers [every army of the period was accompanied by 'volunteer' noblemen who did not belong to any of the regular companies]—all are sumptuously equipped . . . one counts 30,000 horses for this equipment alone." This figure may have been a little high, but all evidence points to the fact that the court must have consumed mountains of forage that might better have been used by the cavalry if the war had been a serious affair. But Louis was doing several important things by this invasion of his court: it served notice to Europe that the King of France was the first soldier of the day, and that his kingdom was the most powerful force in the world, and it was a display to attract the attention and the loyalty of the new subjects of the house of Bourbon. These seventeenth-century parades and pomps were calculated to amuse and to control the minds and the hearts of men, and no one ever understood this better than Louis XIV, the man of *Te Deums,* of carrousels, of parades, of Versailles.

When the king rejoined the court, there were personal satisfactions for some, and terrible problems for others. Mademoiselle de la Vallière, pregnant and partially in disgrace because of a bold attempt to hold her lover, knew the tortures of jealousy; the poor stupid queen wondered why her husband had to spend so much of his nights with the business of war, and Madame de Montespan blossomed forth as the radiant beauty of the day.

The English ambassador, watching all this, cynically remarked that these things might be unfortunate, but since "kings were no more constant than other men," they probably have to happen. Louis has left no indication of his own feelings at this moment when La Montespan's charms won their place in his heart, but there, for all to see, Venus had joined Mars in occupying the king's attention.

Even in a war where the cards are all stacked in favor of the invaders, there is the possibility of a snag, and this is just what happened. Turenne decided to invest Dendermonde, an important city on the Scheldt that would assure the conquest of the rest of Flanders, but Duras moved too slowly and the Spanish were able to throw reinforcements into the town and then open the sluices to flood the countryside. With his usual good sense, Turenne decided to abandon the operation, in spite of the caustic comments of the younger hot-bloods in the king's entourage who were sure that nothing could stop them. Louis was embarrassed. He knew that Turenne was right, and yet it was humiliating to hear the comments of his friends, and even more so, to receive "condolences" from his cousin the emperor in Vienna, where men pretended that the French had suffered a severe setback. Nonetheless Louis wisely decided to back up his general: "The same people who blamed me the most," he commented, "would be the very ones to condemn me . . . if I attacked without success, or, if in taking the place, I ruined my army. . . ." To show Europe that the "promenade" was a serious venture and the army a force to be considered, the French invested the great fortress of Lille. This siege was the first important assignment for Vauban, a young engineer whom Louvois had "found" in Condé's entourage, who was destined to be the first engineer officer ever to become a marshal of France.

There was relatively little serious fighting in the campaign of 1667, and still it was enough to cause Louis to worry about the cost in blood. Although much of his reign was taken up by war, he never easily accepted the "butcher's bill." Letters like the one sent to d'Humières, about to besiege the château of Tournai late in June 1667, are fairly typical: ". . . since it is not of importance to take it one day rather than another a little later, I desire that you be as careful as possible of the troops who attack it. . . ." Later in the summer when Turenne captured Alost, but at the cost of about 600 casualties, Louis sent him a letter of congratulations and appreciation, but added, "I am upset that there were so many men wounded in an attack on a place like that one. . . ."[6] He was willing to take a loss if it was important, but he hated to see brave men, especially officers, killed.

While Louis was satisfied with the progress of his arms and sure that it was evidence of the blessings of God for the righteousness of his cause, other men in Europe were not quite so well pleased. Naturally in Madrid and Brussels this assault was regarded as an act of piratical aggression, but also in the United Netherlands, England, and Germany there were many who could not share Louis' conviction about God's intervention in the course of history. Many well-informed Dutchmen became convinced that the French would not stop until the whole of the Spanish Netherlands was conquered, while Germans were equally fearful for the fate of the Rhineland. The English and the Dutch were trying to negotiate a peace for the Anglo-Dutch war when the invasion began. While there were many complex factors that led to the Treaty of Breda, unquestionably one of them was the desire of both countries to free their political and military forces for a consideration of the emerging problems in the Spanish Netherlands. The Dutch attack on the English fleet in the Thames River undoubtedly hastened the treaty, but there were many men in both countries who foresaw that Anglo-Dutch cooperation against France might be necessary. Nor was this reaction altogether unexpected in France. Louis' *Mémoires* are filled with suggestions that he understood the Dutch neurosis about France as a neighbor, but he did not expect the two trade rivals to cooperate so quickly.

Louis sought to disarm Dutch hostility to his expansion by a generous offer: he would be satisfied with Luxembourg, Cambrai, Aire, Saint-Omer, Bergues, and Douai, providing that the General Estates would support his claims at Madrid, and as good allies, threaten the Spanish with military action in case of refusal. When he got no response, he suggested that there would perhaps be other places that would satisfy him: Franche-Comté, Charleroi, Tournai, or indeed simply the places that he had conquered in Flanders during the past summer. The DeWitts and their colleagues in the United Provinces, quite unhappy about the French action, wanted to find some procedure that would tie Louis' hands and keep France away from their frontiers. They were pleased to have Louis willing to grant three months of truce to allow the Spanish to make up their minds to surrender some of the Netherlands to France, but they also wanted to have him promise not to extend his conquests.

It is not surprising that the last four months of 1667 and the first ones of 1668 were filled with feverish diplomatic activity. The pope, who offered his mediation, the princes of the moribund League of the Rhine, the courts in Berlin and Munich, the Spanish governments at Madrid and at Brussels, the emperor's court at Vienna, and of course the governments at London and The Hague were all concerned. Lionne showed himself to be a masterful negotiator by persuading the Electors of both Brandenburg and Bavaria to adopt a policy favorable to France, and then securing from the Austrians a treaty providing for the partition of the Spanish empire upon the death of the sickly Charles II.[7] This latter treaty was a triumph for French diplomacy almost equal to the victories won on the field of battle. As Louis explains it, this treaty was "a marvelous confirmation of the rights of the queen, and a strong avowal of the nullity of the renunciations; an act made even more important, since it was made by the very party that had an interest in sustaining them."[8] From Louis' point of view, it was hard to see how anyone in the future could reasonably contest his wife's legitimate rights to a part of the Spanish inheritance.

But at the very time that the emperor was becoming accommodating, an Anglo-Dutch agreement presented another face to the problem. In England, Charles II was forced to dismiss a pro-French minister and to agree to cooperation with his recent enemy against Louis, at the very time when Louis was secretly informing him of French plans for continuance of the war. This Anglo-Dutch treaty, which became the famous Triple Alliance by the addition of Sweden, was made with so much secrecy that the French were unaware of it until it was a *fait accompli*. DeWitt and Sir William Temple, its architects, believed that to abandon Spain would be tantamount to giving the Spanish Netherlands to Louis, so it became imperative to find some formula by which they could persuade the Spanish to make a sacrifice rather than lose everything, and at the same time, provide them with a means of limiting French acquisitions. Since Louis himself was willing to limit his demands to a part of the Spanish Netherlands, they could offer him this territory as a basis for negotiations without seeming to be tweaking the king's nose. Thus the Triple Alliance offered its mediation for the reestablishment of peace on the basis of the proposals made by Louis himself. They did not mention the secret article by which the parties of the alliance agreed to make war on France and return her to the frontiers of 1659 in case their good offices were rejected.

While these diplomatic negotiations were occupying Europe's attention, Louis "took his own measures" to assure the rights of his queen. With the advice of Le Tellier, who probably wanted some counterweight to the prestige of Turenne, he recalled his cousin Condé to command a French army, his first commission since the *Fronde*. Under cover of his activities as Governor of Burgundy, Condé, supported by the war ministry, prepared for a winter invasion of Franche-Comté. The attack began in February, when Louis joined the army. It was simply a reproduction of the preceding summer's campaign in the Low Countries. The cities of Franche-Comté were in no way prepared for siege, and so they surrendered almost without contest as soon as the French appeared in force. A wave of emotion ran through Switzerland similar to the one that had upset the United Provinces the preceding summer: like the Dutch, the Swiss also preferred not to have France as a neighbor. But Louis, now in possession of almost all the property under contest, was in a position to negotiate. The situation in Europe made it necessary that he do so.

He understood that the Anglo-Dutch league, even though it appeared to treat Spain and France in the same manner, was "nonetheless made solely against me" and that peace depended upon his willingness to accept limited gains. What should he do? He did have the military forces ready for another round in the Netherlands that undoubtedly would result in complete conquest of the Spanish provinces, but his advisers disagreed with each other about policy. Condé, Turenne, and Louvois, in the field, realized how great was the military power of France, and how complete was the weakness of her enemies. They wanted to continue the war in spite of the Anglo-Dutch league. Lionne, Le Tellier, and Colbert, who were responsible for the government in France, the conduct of foreign relations, and obtaining money and the materials of war, wanted to accept the mediation on the condition that Spain would give to the French all the territories Louis had demanded in the preceding fall.

With his principal advisers divided upon policy, the decision was up to the king. Louis understood that the men "who had conducted the war were attached to reasons for continuing it," while the others "who had not been able to follow the armies . . . were in accord in their advice . . . for peace." "The one side," he tells us, "pointed out to me the number and the vigor of the troops that I had determined to use, the weakness of the Spanish, and the indifference that seemed to encompass Germany . . . all the measures were already taken for the next campaign, the recruits enlisted . . . the magazines filled, and a good part of the expenses paid for . . . [and] that the Dutch . . . had more bad will than power, that the English . . . had neither troops nor finances ready for any important effort, that the Swedes . . . wavered back and forth between their alliance with France and with her enemies . . . finally that all these powers joined together would have only a half of my power, without counting, as one pointed out, my own presence, my vigor and my application . . . in short, they promised infallibly the conquest of the Netherlands."

The other side also had arguments, arguments that Louis finally decided were more solid. ". . . they did not deny that I was stronger than the Spanish; but they pointed out that it does require more power to attack than to defend, that the greater my progress, the more my armies would be used up by garrisons . . . left with the newly captured peoples, while my enemies would augment their number . . . by the jealousy that one would have of [my acquisitions] . . . that at the end I would have either to return a good part of my conquest or to resolve to retain it by eternal war against my enemies; that, having publicly declared in the first days of the war that I would demand only what was justly mine, it would not be possible to refuse to be satisfied with what I had myself asked for without arousing against me all those states that had accepted my words . . . that the Emperor, who still appeared indifferent, would not lose an opportunity to check the weakening of his house, and would enlist to his aid . . . the states and princes of Germany." The attitudes of the Swiss, the pope, the Turkish conquest of Crete, all added to their argument, and finally that "my peoples, frustrated by the expenses of this great war [from enjoying the] comfort they expect of me, would suspect me of preferring the interests of my personal fame to those of their advantage and tranquillity." Louis tells us that in addition to these reasons, there were "others depending upon secret views . . . for I expected not only to profit by the present situation, but also to put myself in position to take advantage of those that might develop." The "secret" views seem to have considered the danger of a coalition or league that might arise "and remain permanently opposed to my most legitimate pretensions. . . ." In other words, by being agreeable at this point, it might be possible to achieve the same things later without arousing a hornet's nest against him. Mazarin's council to avoid rousing coalitions, may have been the final factor in Louis' decision.[9]

Since the facts of the military situation, as well as the pressure of the Anglo-Dutch diplomats, made the Spanish willing to be accommodating, peace became possible. But the conventions signed at Saint-Germain and later incorporated into the peace of Aix-la-Chapelle obviously were no more than a temporary compromise. Louis was clearly fearful of the extension of the league that Anglo-Dutch diplomacy had brought into being. As he wrote, if the kingdom persisted in the war, "the League that was forming . . . would remain a barrier to my most just claims [obviously not yet satisfied]." It was therefore important to dissolve it and convince his smaller neighbors of his "probity and moderation," and thereby "soften in them the currents of fear that each naturally felt in face of so great a power." Moreover, as he fully understood, the Anglo-Dutch proposals were in fact no more than he himself had already made, and they may actually have been more favorable, for "by ceding part of the Spanish Netherlands

Scale of Miles
0 20 40 60

ENGLAND

Strait of Dover

Calais

Dunkirk-1662

FLANDERS

Bruges

Antwerp

NETHERLANDS

Cassel

Courtrai

Scheldt R.

Brussels

St.Omer

Aire

Oudenarde

Liège

Aix-la-Chapelle

Lille

Ath

Tournai

Charleroi

Bouchain

Condé

Valenciennes

Meuse R.

Somme R.

Amiens

Rocroi

Rouen

FRANCE

Aisne R.

Seine R.

Meuse R.

France after the Treaty of Aix-La-Chapelle

▬▬▬▬ Border of France and the
        Spanish Netherlands-1668

Courtrai Cities underlined〰〰
        acquired by treaty-1668

▨▨▨ Gains by treaty-1668

to France . . . through a free treaty . . . [they] carried with it the abandon-
ment of the renunciations by which the Spanish pretended to exclude the
queen from all successions of her family." Louis could happily make peace
if he could dissipate the "League at its birth" and lay the foundations for
future action along the frontier. Therefore he decided upon peace.

The treaty that was made drew the frontier between France and the
Spanish Netherlands on the basis of the conquests of 1667, rather than on
any rational plan. This line was surely not a "military frontier," for the
war in the Netherlands stopped before any military conclusion had been
reached; indeed, from a military point of view this frontier was folly, since
it left French and Spanish fortifications mixed pell-mell, with no plan along
the entire frontier. Nor, for the same reasons, was it a "political" or
"economic" frontier. The enclaves of French territory surrounded by
Spanish, and Spanish territory surrounded by French, cried aloud for a
more rational solution. Louis was not responsible for this disorder. He
would have preferred to annex Franche-Comté and leave the Netherlands
for a later adventure, but the Spanish, anxious to give the Dutch more
reasons for fearing France and defending the remainder of the Spanish
Netherlands in the future, preferred to have it this way. The men who
wrote the treaty must have known that it was not the final settlement of
the problem of the Spanish Netherlands.

Louis gained much from appearing reasonable. But his greatest gain
was time—time to strengthen his military forces and mend his diplomatic
fences. It was indisputable that the United Netherlands had again stood
squarely in the way of "the just pretensions" of the house of Bourbon to
the Spanish Netherlands; from the middle 1640's onward, the Dutch had
resolutely refused to accept the proposition that the kingdom of France
should absorb these provinces. In 1668 the French recognized this situation and agreed to peace, but they only bided their time. A young engineer
who had recently joined Louvois' entourage summed up in few words the
thinking of many of the men around the king: "There is no judge more
equitable than cannons. They go directly to the goal and they are not
corruptible. See to it that the king takes them as arbiters if he wishes to
have good and quick justice for his rightful claims."[10] Louis may not have
seen that letter, but the idea was well understood in the ruling circles around
the king. Peace, therefore, was only a breathing spell that would allow the
diplomats to break up the coalition; it was not a solution for the frontier
of the kingdom.

There were many in France, however, who rejoiced over the end of
the war without realizing that the peace was only a truce. Boileau dedicated

a poem to the king that said, "You can be a hero without ravaging the land. . . . There is more than one route to *gloire;* it is the error among kings to give first place to conquerors. Among all heroes they are the most common. Every century has its rash heroes. But a king truly a king, who understands his prospects, who knows how to maintain his subjects in a happy tranquillity, realizes that public happiness guarantees his *gloire.* . . ."[11] Louis did not pay much heed to the ideas of the poet; indeed, he may never have read the poem.

THE DUTCH WAR: ASSAULT*

WHEN "to no avail I requested that Spain should recognize the just pretensions of the Queen [to the Southern Netherlands] . . . I took up arms to validate the rights of that princess. . . . In my successful campaign neither the English nor the Emperor opposed my cause. . . . I found in my way only my good, faithful, and longtime friends, the Dutch, who rather than being interested in my fortune . . . wished to impose their law upon me and oblige me to make peace, even dared to threaten me in case I should refuse to accept their mediation. . . ." Thus did Louis describe the intrusion of the United Netherlands in his affairs. Had he not already known of the Dutch resistance to French ambitions for control of the Spanish Netherlands, this dramatic move by the Dutch-inspired Triple Alliance should have been enough to let him understand that his "just pretentions" would be frustrated as long as the Dutch had the power to intervene. In Louis' mind this was a monstrous act of ingratitude. Had not his father and grandfather protected these people against the Spanish? Had not he himself just prevented the invasion of the Netherlands by the Bishop of Münster, and joined his naval forces to theirs against the English? These people were ingrates; they "had not only never aided [the enterprises of the Kings of France] . . . with money or troops, they had not even departed from simple and lukewarm neutrality . . . [and] they had actually tried to undermine either overtly or underhandedly our progress and our advantages."

There would be no advantage for us to discover or discredit the truth of the king's beliefs; it is enough to know that Louis regarded the war that he planned to bring down upon these Dutchmen as entirely the result of "[their] ingratitude, [their] bad faith, and [their] insupportable vanity."

In light of the conflict inherent in the situation and political morals and customs of seventeenth-century men, this war was probably inevitable. Interests of the French state as well as the "just pretentions" of the Bourbon family both demanded that the Spanish Netherlands should be united to the kingdom of France; on the other hand, Dutch fear of the military, political, and economic consequences of such an event made resistance a matter of life and death for them. Men went to war for less important things than the "just claims" of a queen and the political and economic needs of a kingdom. This was an era that saw the great German war and the treaties of Westphalia, the Anglo-Dutch trade wars, and the Hapsburg-Bourbon war—none of these rooted in problems more important to the contestants than those involved in the French pretensions to the Spanish Netherlands.

It is impossible to justify the often-given interpretation that this war was simply the result of the wounded pride or the insupportable arrogance of the young French king. The thesis that interprets the reign of Louis XIV in terms of his search for *gloire* or his overweening vanity is open to serious revision. Louis' advisers were friends and followers of Cardinal Mazarin; like him they believed that the acquisition of the Southern Netherlands was very important for the political, military, and economic well-being of the kingdom. Colbert, no less than Turenne, Le Tellier, and Louvois, advocated policies that would bring these provinces under the rule of the king. The war ministers and soldiers argued the need for defensible frontiers, for control of the "gates" to the north of the kingdom. Colbert dreamed of the day when France would control Antwerp, open the Scheldt, and reestablish, to the advantage of the kingdom of France, the ancient prosperity of the whole region drained by that river. The Dutch who stood in the way of this project were Colbert's enemies in the commercial world as well. He "knew" that there was only a limited amount of trade in the world, and he also knew that the Dutch monopolized most of it. They had over 16,000 ships, while France had only a few hundred; this balance would be rectified by war.

For a very long time many historians have painted Colbert as the man of peace opposed to Louvois the man of war; this is simply a myth that has suited the anti-militarist assumptions of bourgeois historians. Colbert was as anxious as Louvois to crush the Dutch. He may have disagreed with Le Tellier and his son on the method of attacking the United Netherlands, but he did not disagree with the project itself. Colbert's commercial policies, his tariffs and other harassment of Dutch trade, were all of a piece with his predatory attitude toward the men who owned the lion's share of the merchant shipping of the world. He was as vindictive against them as Louvois, and his suggestions for the proposed peace in 1672 not only included the nearly complete destruction of of Dutch commercial power, but also vetoed any suggestion that the Dutch provinces might be annexed to France, for fear that these same Dutchmen would regain their place in the world's commerce under the flag of the Bourbons. Colbert, like the others, voted for their annihilation.[1]

The men who managed Louis' military forces were as anxious for war as Colbert.[2] Turenne's projects for the conquest of the Spanish Netherlands had been foiled twice by the Dutch; and now Condé joined him in anticipation of the advantages that soldiers could gain from a new war. Both of these great soldiers had added to their reputations by the easily won victories of the past war; they assumed that another war would be the same. The Le Telliers, father and son, while nourishing serious reservations about the two great warriors, were equally anxious to show their king what devoted administration could do. They understood Louis' military ambitions, and they knew that their own favor and place would grow along with the rise of an army and the conduct of a war. Moreover, as devoted servants of the king, they, like Turenne and Colbert, saw the advantages that would accrue from the acquisition of the Netherlands and the destruction of Dutch power.

Lastly, Lionne added his voice to the chorus advocating war, for ever since the Treaty of the Pyrenees, the acquisition of the Spanish Netherlands had been a task reserved for him. He, better than any of the others, understood that it could be accomplished only by war against the Dutch.

Nor were these reasons of state all that urged the young French king to consider war on the Dutch. In 1670 religious flags were no longer popular cloaks for political action, and yet religious issues still rancored men's souls. Louis had trouble understanding why he, the most Christian king, should grant toleration to the "so-called reformed church" in his kingdom, while the Dutch Calvinists refused to allow Catholics in the Netherlands to practice their religion publicly. Louis persuaded himself that religious hostility had united "heretical potentates" in the Triple Alliance against him. A religious issue probably could not have been enough to justify war, but added to other issues, it gave moral justification for such action. The same was true of political differences. In Louis' writings there is ample evidence of his contempt and hatred for "republican" principles, and especially for these revolutionaries who had founded their regime by a revolt against an hereditary ruler. When he added up his griefs against the ingrates, he did not forget that his "ancestors once ruled these people," nor that their rebellion had been against his own great-grandfather. The mere fact that another great-grandfather had aided that rebellion only made their attitude toward his "just pretentions" more reprehensible. Furthermore, in the French court there was a general attitude of contempt for the "herring merchants," as Lionne called them: they could have no notion of honor or faith or nobility. How could such men balk the just plans of a king who represented the hereditary order that God had intended for the world? To call this attitude "arrogance" misses the point: it was an attitude ingrained in the society of kings and noblemen of seventeenth-century Europe. Thus the awkward, sometimes brutal, insolent, and uncouth, and always pretentious[3] behavior of the Dutch ambassador, van Beuningen, deeply offended the French and confirmed their king in his prejudices. With reasons of state, reasons of dynasty, and personal feelings all urging war against the Dutch Republic, is it any wonder that Louis decided to undertake that war? As we have already said, in the seventeenth century the question for a young prince was not "Will you make war?" but "Against whom will you make war?" The Dutch were an obvious target.[4]

The preparation for the Dutch War was characteristic of Louis XIV. How many times did he tell his son that a king must plan for the future with great care, that he must iron out the possible obstacles long before they are actually encountered? "One can pardon the feebleness of mediocre minds who are concerned only for the present . . . ," he writes, "but those with greater and more elevated gifts ought to . . . look ahead . . . so that they will never be reduced to making precipitous judgments." In war or politics the wise king makes his plans far ahead. While he signed the Treaty of Aix-la-Chapelle, Louis decided upon war with the Dutch, but he also decided that the plans for that war must be carefully prepared both inside and outside the kingdom of France. He needed money, soldiers, and allies; he also needed to isolate his victims so that they could have no hope for assistance from Europe. He allotted three years for this task; it actually required four. The Dutch War, then, was no haphazard, spur-of-the-moment affair; it was a venture carefully planned by men who believed that they were acting rationally.

The burden of the preparations, however, fell to others than the king. Louis was only thirty years old; the life of the court was fascinating and filled with pleasure. His new mistress provided an excitement that La Vallière had never been able to create, and the full-blooded vigorous young man worked off some of his energy in the hunt, the parties, the gambling, and the pleasures of the court. This does not mean that he was not informed of the work that went on in his name, nor that he did not take a keen interest in the raising of armies, the building of fortifications, the extension of commerce, and the negotiations with foreign princes. It was only that the king's role was to preside over the making of policy and to follow the proceedings, while the actual work was left to the experts who made up the governing team he had assembled. Colbert worked on the navy and the finances; Louvois, under his father's tutelage, prepared the army and pushed the work of fortification on the new frontiers; and Lionne spun the webs of diplomacy and bribery to prepare Europe to accept destruction of the Dutch power.

Louis followed the progress of the preparations for war with keen interest, and soon discovered that in the son of Le Tellier he had a man with energy, ruthless persistence, and administrative genius who could be depended upon to complete the projects of the king and to disprove the German proverb that said that Frenchmen "start many things but never finish any of them." Louvois brought together a magnificent army. Regiments of foreign troops were recruited in Italy, Germany, England, Scotland, Ireland, and Switzerland; the French regiments were filled and disciplined. Training, fortifications, magazines filled with supplies, weapons, carts, and river boats—all these were the grist for Louvois' mill. The fortifications on the frontiers and in the new provinces recently acquired were inspected, redesigned, and rebuilt. It was an immense labor that fell heavily upon the shoulders of this young man who was determined to win the favor of the king for himself and his family. Louvois brought many men into the king's service to help him. The names of at least two have military significance for all the western world: Martinet was his inspector-general for the infantry whose strict discipline left an indelible mark upon the army, and Vauban was a young engineer who emerged as the most effective designer of fortifications. When Louis found that Vauban's drawings were always the best ones submitted, Vauban's future was assured, for the king was vitally interested in building fortifications that would guarantee the integrity of his territory against invasion. Louvois did not make the new French army during these years; the ordinances regulating the army were his father's work in the preceding decade. But Louvois did assemble and organize the army so that the King of France could march down the Rhine and into the very heart of the Dutch Netherlands with little more trouble than he would have making a trip of similar length in his own kingdom.

While Louvois and his father prepared the war machine, Lionne and his diplomats undermined and destroyed the Triple Alliance, and attempted to erect a political structure to allow the king to strangle the Dutch without interference from Europe. Superficially Lionne succeeded as well as the soldiers, but in actuality he did not, for there were too many factors in the political climate of Europe that could not be controlled. In Germany, by a nice mixture of persuasion and bribery, he committed the princes to either neutrality or actual assistance. Even the emperor's court seemed willing to stand by and see the Dutch punished. Only the Elector of Brandenburg escaped Lionne's spell. In the Iberian Peninsula, the Portuguese provided the distraction to keep the court at Madrid occupied, and in the north, French money persuaded the Swedish regency government that it had no further interest in the Triple Alliance. In the middle Rhine the Duke of Lorraine, whose political gyrations had long provided an *obligato* to French policy, gave Louis an excuse for occupying his territory and thereby assuring the French army access to the lower Rhine. But of all the diplomatic preparations, the treaty with England was the most important, for it provided for the shift of English power from a Dutch to a French alliance, and at the same time promised to return England to the Catholic fold.

Charles II of England had had no taste for the Triple Alliance, but his dependence upon Parliament gave him little choice. When Louis proposed to give him a large French subsidy in return for an alliance against the Dutch, Charles seized the opportunity to free himself from the financial dependence upon Parliament. He even believed that another war against the Dutch would be popular in England. And yet Charles was a clever politician; he wanted to be sure that he would not commit a foolish move that might deprive him of his throne. Thus the discussion went slowly— at times bogged down entirely. Louis followed these negotiations with avid interest. He loved secret parleys and greatly enjoyed the idea that this was personal diplomacy. The Treaty of Dover that consummated the agreement between the two kings was finally effected by Henriette, Louis' sister-in-law, who went to meet her brother at Dover, while the French court waited on the other side of the Channel—in ignorance of her mission. Even Philippe was not aware of his wife's errand. Henriette carried off her assignment with great skill, and it surely was not her fault that her brother was later forced by his English subjects to go back on his word. As for Henriette, shortly after her return to France she died of convulsions, convinced that someone had poisoned her; we are reasonably sure today that "natural" causes, perhaps a ruptured appendix, were to blame for her death. With the Treaty of Dover (1670), the most important link in the diplomatic chain was forged, but the actual attack had to wait until the spring of 1672 so that final plans could be completed. The French wanted no surprises.

Louis described the activities of his ministers with an egocentrism typical of his rank. "After having taken precautions of all sorts," he writes, "as much by alliances as by raising troops, magazines, warships, and great sums of money. . . . I made treaties with England, the Elector of Cologne, and the Bishop of Münster . . . also with Sweden, and to hold Germany in check, with the Dukes of Hanover and of Neuburg and with the Emperor so that he would not take any part in any interference that might arise against me. . . ." When Louis wrote these words he had not yet realized that his enterprise was to be far from a success. Almost naïvely he exclaims, "I made my enemies tremble, astounded my neighbors, and brought despair to my foes. . . ." As an afterthought he added, "All my subjects supported my intentions . . . in the army with their valor, in the kingdom with their zeal, in foreign lands with their industry and skill; France has demonstrated the difference between herself and the other nations!" He might have added that this demonstration of force caused enough consternation in Europe to arouse a great coalition against him.

Louis and almost all of the men around him were land-oriented—men who saw the sea as a hostile, foreign element, unsuited for French genius. Colbert may have understood that this was not true and he did try to give France a "blue-water orientation," but his was a lone voice that did not find a responsive chord in the heart of his king. The army, more specifically the cavalry, was the service most favored, and continental politics concerned with frontiers, fortifications, and inland travel fitted Louis' predilections. Thus, although war against the Dutch had also to be fought at sea, Louis was really interested only in the operations by land. His ships and those of his cousin Charles II might operate in the Channel and the North Sea, but it was the war in the Rhineland, the war that carried French standards to Utrecht and the outskirts of Amsterdam, that was important to the young king.

When all was ready in the spring of 1672, Louvois presented him with a magnificent army. The king was its supreme commander; his brother Philippe, his cousin the Prince of Condé, the great Turenne, and a stellar galaxy of marshals and lieutenant generals assisted him. With this invincible force the Dutch seemed doomed to quick defeat. The plans had been so well laid that French soldiers were already in control of key points on both sides of the middle Rhine, and huge quantities of supplies were already assembled deep in Germany before the invasion began. This was the work of Lionne and Louvois, who made lands of the bishops of the Rhineland practically into French provinces. It seemed that there was nothing to do but march in and subdue the miserable merchant republic that stood in the king's way.[5]

This was the first time that Louis "officially" left French soil.[6] Like his grandfather, Henri IV, who also planned to campaign in the Rhineland, Louis went to Parlement to register an edict granting his queen the power of command in France while the king went "in person to make the Dutch feel the results of their ingratitude to the kings of France. . . ."[7]

Then, proclaiming a manifesto of war, he established the hierarchy of command that placed the members of the royal family at the top, but subordinated all the marshals of France to Turenne. Then Louis joined the army and invaded Germany.

The first thing that marred a brilliant scenario that could repeat the promenades of the last war was the rebellion of three marshals who refused to accept orders from Turenne on the grounds that marshals of France obey only the king and princes of the blood. Louis quickly removed them from their commands for "it would be . . . too much of a limitation on the authority of a prince; he can divide his power as it pleases him, and . . . according to the needs of the state . . . not according to the pretentions of his officers. . . ."[8] It is amusing to see Louvois' role in this little comedy of command. He had been the first to demand that the troops of the king should obey royal authority, but this revolt was against Turenne, who was also his rival, perhaps his enemy. Louvois insisted upon discipline, but the rebellious marshals were not treated as harshly as might have been expected under other conditions.[9]

At first the campaign seemed to be a repetition of the last war. Fortresses surrendered almost without a fight and the army swept onward as an irresistible force, but let us allow Louis to describe it himself. He wrote to Colbert, the last of May 1672:

It seemed to me so important for the reputation of my arms to begin this campaign with an affair of great *éclat* that I thought that only an attack of Maestricht would suffice; however, it would require so many men to take that place in a reasonable time that it would interfere with my other intentions. I judged it more advantageous for my projects and fame to attack four fortifications on the Rhine at the same time and actually to command in person the four sieges. I chose for this Rheinberg, Wesel, Burick, and Orsoy. I took particular charge of the siege of Rheinberg as the best fortified and from which I could visit each day the works of the other sieges. My brother had charge of the details of the siege of Orsoy; M. le Prince that of Wesel; and M. de Turenne that of Burick. I hope that no one will complain that I have failed public expectation. . . .[10]

When he wrote these words, Louis was obviously enjoying the crest of the wave. The Dutch garrisons occupying these fortifications either surrendered before the first shot was fired, or immediately thereafter. The cathedrals of France had trouble keeping up with the king's orders for *Te Deums*.

Louis' role in this early part of the campaign was obviously limited by the fact that the Prince of Condé and the Viscount de Turenne were always near at hand. How could he really command when men with their prestige were with the army? He did have a large part in framing the orders of march, in choosing the password for the day, in enforcing discipline in the ranks. For his brother Philippe he reserved even lesser roles. Louis' orders for June 16 contained the following:

My brother will choose my quarters where he judges it best, and will order the troops to make camp in the usual order, that is, the brigades of the guards nearest to my lodging. . . .[11]

This gave Philippe little to do, for Louis' orders for the establishment of camps were usually very precise. Each section of the army had its place marked out by precedent and prestige, and the *maréchal de camp* was expected to see that each was in its place.

But he also had a part in commanding military operations. The Dutch hoped to stop the French at the point where the Rhine breaks into the several streams that make up its estuary. By the second week in June the hour of truth had arrived, and the defendants took up their positions behind the Rhine, the Yessel, and the Waal. The Waal was so swift and so deep that passage was almost impossible, so the Dutch particularly prepared to defend themselves behind the other two arms of the river. Louis tells us that he looked over the situation and decided to cross the Rhine. "I confided my plan to my brother, the Prince of Condé, and the Viscount de Turenne . . . ," he writes. We shall probably never know who did decide that the Rhine was the river to cross, but the maneuver was well taken, for the Dutch had only slight strength at Tolhuis, the point chosen. In his *Mémoires* Louis gives Condé credit for picking the place where the French crossed the river; he does not tell us there of his anger at the impetuosity of Condé and several of the French volunteers who participated in the crossing.

What happened was that a group of the French soldiers managed to cross the river only to be confronted by a small body of Dutch infantrymen who probably would have either fled or surrendered as soon as the battery that Louis himself was posting on the other bank could open fire on them. At this moment a group of French volunteers led by the young Duke de Longueville, who had managed to cross in a boat, charged the Dutch at full gallop, shouting "Kill! Kill!" Condé's son was in the party and instead of checking their impetuosity, Condé himself joined them. Naturally the Dutch infantry did all they could to avoid being massacred. Louis wrote to Marie-Thérèse that evening, telling her about the crossing, about the death of the young de Longueville, Guitri, and others, about the wound that Condé had received in the action, but he added, "With a little patience we would not have lost one of these men. The Comte de Guiche could have enveloped [the Dutch] from one side, and from the other we could have pushed them with the other squadrons and with infantry . . . in place of this wild-eyed action that cost us so dearly."[12] Louis had told Condé not to go across the river with the first troops. He must have been astonished to see Condé rashly exposing himself along with the stupidly impetuous volunteers. It made a deep impression upon him. He had never favored the impetuous school strategy; henceforth he was even more suspicious of it, and it is not surprising to find him in later years sternly forbidding his officers to act as "volunteers" in any attack—even to the point of severely reprimanding a great captain like Marshal Luxembourg for allowing them to do so.

Later when Versailles was built, the crossing of the Rhine became a theme for decorators and artists, just as it had been for publicists and historians. Jean Racine in his nearly-mythological history of the war explained that ". . . the foe did not dare stand up to [the French]; they fled at full speed, turning somersaults over each other as they ran to carry the news to Holland that the King had crossed [the Rhine]." All this fanfare about the crossing of the Rhine, so dear to men who have read Caesar's *Gallic Wars,* has tended to cover up for later generations the fact that it really was a military measure of considerable merit, and that Louis really did have a larger role in the affair than one would expect. Condé, not Louis, made a fool of himself by forgetting that a general officer does not behave like a subaltern, and Louis placed the battery of guns that got control of the crossing. He did not need to throw his horse in the river to play the important role in the drama. Louis does not make too much of his part in the crossing. "I was present," he writes, "at the crossing, which was bold, vigorous, and full of *éclat,* and glorious for the nation. I hurried the crossing of the troops to strengthen the soldiers of the Prince of Condé; I worked diligently on the bridge of boats over the Rhine; and I remained with my brother, the Viscount de Turenne . . . , and the rest of the army . . . to oppose the Prince of Orange . . . but it worked out that my precautions, however necessary, were useless, for the Prince of Orange . . . took a different gambit." Indeed, there was very little for Orange to do; he did not have power enough to stand against the overwhelming force of his enemies. Thus the crossing of the Rhine opened the very heart of the United Netherlands to the French army. Louis had joined the army at Charleroi the first week in May; by the middle of June complete victory seemed assured.

The French army crossed the Rhine on June 12; ten days later the Dutch cut the dikes and allowed the sea to flow over the part of Holland

between the Zuider Zee and the rivers, making Amsterdam an island im-
mune from attack, while at The Hague preparations for resistance were the
order of the day. Some of the burghers of Amsterdam were ready to treat
with the French as soon as they heard that Louis had crossed the Rhine;
bolder spirits persuaded them to wait and managed to cut the dikes to give
the city immunity until frost would harden the flooded polders and provide
a bridge for the enemy horses. What happened? There has been a large
literature on the subject, and few of the leaders of the French army have
failed to find someone to blame them for the disaster. Clearly there was a
lack of intelligence about the location of the sluices. Rochefort was in
possession of the key town of Muiden east of Amsterdam on the Zuider
Zee before the sluices were opened, but he did not know about them or their
importance. Surely Turenne or Condé should have known about the possibility of inundation, since they had both fought in the Spanish Netherlands enough to be familiar with such tactics; perhaps Louvois, too, should
have known; but Louis cannot be expected to have taken this as his problem. No matter, it happened, and this was the turning point in the war. It
did not matter that over ninety fortified places had surrendered to the invading armies; if the Dutch would not come to terms, the war could not end.

Appalled by the disaster that had overtaken them, the General Estates
were anxious for peace. They offered the cession of Maestricht, the fortifications that the French had taken on the Rhine, and the parts of Brabant
and Flanders that were under Dutch control—that is, all that the United
Netherlands ruled beyond the frontiers of the Seven Provinces that made
up the Republic. In addition, they offered an indemnity of ten million
livres. From our point of view in time, and especially with the hindsight
that we have of the events that were to come after 1672, this offer seems
extraordinarily favorable to France. The Dutch would in effect give up
their possibility of opposing eventual absorption of the Spanish Netherlands in return for their right to live, for without the advanced positions
that they occupied in the Rhineland, on the Maas, and in Brabant and
Flanders, they could not hope to oppose French action in the Spanish
provinces.

But the French had other ideas. Colbert had refused to consider annexing all the provinces for fear of their competition with French merchants if they should become subjects of the King of France, but he and
the other advisers of the king did covet some of the territory of the Seven
Provinces, and they all wanted to impose conditions upon them that would
effectively ruin the future military and financial power of these "herring
merchants." They demanded the cession of Nymwegen, the island of

Bommel, Grave, the Comte of Moeurs, and several lesser places, a 24-million-livre war indemnity, the suppression of all measures taken against French commerce since 1662 (the retaliations for Colbert's tariffs), the free exercise of the Catholic religion in the United Netherlands, and finally, as an ultimate humiliation for their past acts of pride, that the Dutch should send a mission each year to France to present a gold medal to the king thanking him humbly for having given them peace. Had the military situation been such that resistance was impossible, such terms might have seemed justifiable, but they turned out to be folly when it became evident that the inundations had actually stopped the French advance long enough for the Dutch to organize resistance and to find support in a Europe now frightened by the military power of France.

Why did Louis commit such a blunder? In the four years that they were preparing for war, the men around him, with the possible exception of Pomponne, became intoxicated with their own strength and blinded to the realities. The Dutch were their enemy; they would destroy them as a political, military, and economic force in Europe. It was not enough to humble them, to force them to accept eventual French absorption of the Spanish Netherlands: they would break their power once and for all. Such an idea might have been possible had the military situation really warranted it, for the lightning assault on the Netherlands took Europe by surprise and Europe was unable to respond quickly to a changed situation, but when the *Blitz* did not actually cut the jugular vein of the Dutch Republic, the political and economic destruction of the United Netherlands became a chimera that could only lead to disaster unless it were revised.

Louis was thirty-four years old when this problem arose; he was surrounded by soldiers and politicians many years his senior. In his *Mémoires* the king takes responsibility for insisting upon a treaty that would destroy his enemies, but he also takes credit or responsibility for many other decisions, both political and military, that were obviously made by the council. Many historians have seized upon his proud words ". . . ambition and *la gloire* are always pardonable in a prince, and particularly in a young prince as handsomely favored by fortune as I was . . ." to prove that it was simply egomania that prevented Louis from making a peace comfortable to the military situation of 1672. This puts too much weight upon the king's words, and too little upon the counsels of Colbert who would wreck the Dutch commerce, of Louvois, Turenne, and Condé who would destroy Dutch military potential, and of the other advisers who failed to understand that one cannot accomplish politically more than can be accomplished militarily.[13]

The French armies were in the very heart of the Netherlands; the great cities of Arnheim, Doesburg, Utrecht, Woerdern, and Naarden were in their hands, and "Amsterdam trembled, this city superb in its prosperity . . . considered surrender."[14] When the dykes were cut, the soldiers should have understood that the campaign would bog down in the "swamps from which . . . [the French] had formerly saved" the Dutch, but Louis could hardly have been expected to realize this. He was told that the freeze of winter would again open the land to his cavalry, and he, along with his advisers, believed that the Dutch, as reasonable men, would also recognize that their situation was impossible. The *Gazette* of August 4, 1672, printed a letter supposedly from a Dutchman that reflected the same opinion: ". . . peace," he wrote, "under any conditions would be more useful to us than war in which we shall surely lose all. But," he added, "there are those who can profit from our troubles and oppose obstacles [to peace] wherever they can . . . sacrificing willingly to their interests all of the others. . . ." With such advice about the situation in the unconquered part of the Netherlands, why should the king think of taking less than he expected to get?

The Dutch, however, did not make peace. Louis stayed with the army on into July, expecting that his foes would come to reason. As Racine later explained in words reflecting Louis' own ideas about the war, "The King had conquered almost all of Holland. He could impose his vengeance on their cities, but the submission of the vanquished disarmed his wrath. He reestablished Catholic worship, and after having appointed governors and garrisons everywhere, he returned to France . . . where triumphal *entrées* [on the route] were prepared that he did not accept; he contented himself with the acclamations of the people and the universal joy that his return excited in the kingdom."[15] This may have been the way Louis wanted posterity to remember it, but there were a few discrepancies in the account. When he left the Netherlands—as he was soon to learn—he had not broken the will of the Dutch, and further military action had become impossible. When he came to France, he did expect and did receive acclamations in the form of victory parades, fêtes, and *Te Deums* celebrating triumphs that he had not really achieved.[16] At the same time the presses of France unburdened themselves of a literature filled with praise for the royal accomplishment. In Le Clerc's *Paraphrase du XX psaume de David,* it became evident that God himself had intervened "to invest our great monarch with glory."[17]

But in spite of the *Te Deums* thanking God for victory, the Dutch persisted in their refusal to accept the King's terms. There was a revolution in Amsterdam; the DeWitt brothers were murdered and their party discredited. The *Gazette* in France recounted these events, blaming William of Orange for the murders and the violence, but the same issue of the *Gazette* (August 22) told of preparations for war in Turkey, of the canonization of a saint, and of affairs of France and Europe quite unconnected with the revolution in Amsterdam or the war. There was no indication that the campaign had broken down, or that the Prince of Orange might be able to recruit Europe to aid his cause. And yet that was what he was in the act of doing. In Racine's "fairy tale" the "wicked" Elector of Brandenburg is the first one to step up and protest the "rightful" conquests of the French king. He was dissatisfied with French occupation of his Westphalian territories, and threatened to attack the French from the rear. Nor was that all: the emperor, too, made menacing moves in spite of the *Gazette*'s announcement that the pope himself had urged him not "to employ his forces in favor of the Dutch [who were heretics]," and after the elector and the emperor, the governor of the Spanish Netherlands, without authorization from Spain, had lent troops to William of Orange alleging that such aid had been promised by an earlier treaty. To these forces were added the twenty thousand or more soldiers that Louis and his generals had rather contemptuously released from their prison camps at a minimum ransom payment—to avoid caring for them. Turenne could counter the moves of the elector and force him to agree to remain neutral, but the Dutch army of William of Orange was still in the field, and even able to mount a feeble offensive against Charleroi. By winter of 1672–73, when the ice did not freeze around Amsterdam, the French army found itself increasingly embarrassed because of the distances between itself and France and the hostility it was encountering from the population. Louis had not yet begun to have nightmares and cry out in the night, but this, too, was not far away, for even in France it was becoming evident that the war was not over, and indeed, far from won.

The king's reaction to this dramatically changed situation gives us much insight into his character. Louis was no fool; he understood that it had been the flooding of the land that had actually changed his "victory" into an ambiguous situation, and yet when he wrote about it he said:

The resolution to put the entire country under the water was a bit violent; but what will one not do to prevent the domination of a foreigner? I cannot help admiring and praising the zeal and fortitude of those who broke off the negotiations . . . even though their advice, so salutary for their fatherland, brought great prejudice to my service.

Had the situation been reversed, one wonders whether William of Orange would have had as much understanding of the position of an enemy.

But all this did not disguise the fact that the war had failed to achieve its objective. Louis' own share in the military operations had been slight; how could a cadet at war expect to have great influence in the councils when a Turenne and a Condé were in the field? Obviously the responsibility for the failure did not rest with the king, nor with his poor brother, whose role was little more than perfunctory. Turenne and Condé had commanded the armies, and responsibility for the failure should rest upon their shoulders. Condé's "Fear your enemies when they are at a distance; despise them when they are before you" had not won the campaign, but it had won a severe wound for Condé at the crossing of the Rhine. Turenne's maxim "eventually you must fight" also had not won the campaign, because the occasion to fight had never really presented itself. Had these two men not had so inflated a reputation (both in the eyes of their contemporaries and of posterity), Louis would have been justified in dismissing them. But he could not, and probably would not. Turenne did check the Elector of Brandenburg, and was to continue to command the royal armies until a cannon ball ended his career several years later; Condé also continued to command until, shortly after Turenne's death, he retired to his estates, leaving Louis and his administrative bureaucracy in command of the war machine. Not until these two old soldiers of the era of the German war and the *Fronde* passed from the scene did Louis find a solution for the war that he had so confidently undertaken in order to destroy the United Netherlands. Much has been written to prove that the grandeur of Louis XIV owed a great deal to the two generals who accompanied him on the assault against the Netherlands, but the facts of the war hardly support such contentions.

THE DUTCH WAR:
THREAT OF DEFEAT 1673-75

ALTHOUGH the French army occupied much of the Netherlands, the Prince of Orange, brushing aside those who would make peace at any price, called upon Europe for aid and girded the small army under his command to resist. There was a little assistance from the Governor of the Spanish Netherlands, a promise from the Elector of Brandenburg, and some real help from the prisoners of war that the French command so unthinkingly released,[1] but his ill-fated attempt to besiege Charleroi showed how difficult it would be to fight the French without allies. And yet the war was not lost. The invaders had not reached Amsterdam and the Anglo-French navies had not destroyed the Dutch sea power; if Europe could be aroused, the French would soon be in trouble—especially since they were so far from their frontiers. This Dutch resistance was quite incomprehensible to the young king and his advisers who assumed that reasonable men would admit defeat. However, since the water from the sea deprived them of a battlefield, and since Europe began to act threateningly, the French had to consider seriously their next move.

Mazarin had always cautioned avoidance of any situation that would provoke a coalition against the kingdom, and the exposed and distant position of the army in the Netherlands doubly underlined this danger. In the seventeenth century the trip from the French frontier to Utrecht required much more time than it does to move a twentieth-century army from Dallas, Texas, to western Germany: Utrecht was remote from France. When Frederick William of Brandenburg became threatening, Turenne moved into the lower Rhineland to face him; when the emperor began to move, Louis sent honeyed words about his "intentions to observe religiously the treaties of Aix-la-Chapelle and Westphalia" along with not-too-veiled threats of reprisals in case Leopold should act "contrary to the interests of my service."[2] These moves quieted Germany for the moment, but the Spanish governor in the Netherlands and the little group of determined Francophobes in England gave notice that the conquest would be contested. Spain would probably join the Dutch, and England's king might well be forced to switch sides; if this happened, could anyone believe that the German princes would stand by their commitments to France? On his return to court, Louis did not outwardly show any anxiety over this situation. He was gallant to the ladies; he accepted the victory celebrations, the fireworks, the *Te Deums,* the speeches, the sermons, with an outward air of assurance. But it was during this period that his physicians began to report that he "cried out in the night," had bad dreams and sleeplessness. We do not know that we should link this behavior either to concern for his soul, threatened by his double adultery, or for his kingdom, threatened by Europe; but it is evidence that he was not as calm as he appeared to be in public.[3]

Louis was worried for the safety of his army. Throughout his life he was to be seriously concerned when a French army got very far from the frontiers of the kingdom, and characteristically, in the later months of 1672 and the winter of 1673, his letters to Louvois are sprinkled with uneasiness about the army in a hostile land. The council of war with Louvois, Condé, and Turenne did not remove the doubts: it would require 35,000 troops to watch the Germans; this left only about 65,000 to face the Spanish and to undertake any enterprise that might bring the war to a close. And surely something had to be done to end this war.[4]

One of the policies adopted proved to be a disaster to the Dutch, and in the long run, to the French as well. The army took up winter quarters in the Netherlands and required the Dutch to pay for its upkeep through contributions levied on the towns and villages. But that was not all. The French also adopted a policy of systematic destruction of places not occupied. The *Gazette* for January 13, 1673, carried the first story of these "atrocities" to be published in France. The French army had burned the towns of Zwammerdam and Bodengrave so that "there hardly remains a single house standing." More than 2,000 houses in the "most beautiful part of Holland" were gone, and the French army retired, "leaving us [the Dutch] in a state of astonishment from this harsh deed from which we will have difficulty recovering." In the following months Dutch correspondents of the *Gazette* continued to write of the destruction of their country.[5] Almost a century later, Voltaire found that the memory of these French atrocities was still green in the Netherlands.

Who was responsible for this policy? Condé can be exonerated, for he strongly protested having to continue the work that Luxembourg had begun. Undoubtedly Louvois had much to do with the decision; the callousness involved conforms with his disregard for the feelings of others. It is not at all clear whether or not Louis was also responsible. This belief that through "frightfulness" one can create a demand for peace was to come up many times during his reign, both before and after the death of Louvois, and there seems to be no evidence that Louis ever opposed it. On the contrary, when soldiers or sailors resisted the policy of shelling towns with red-hot cannon balls, of destroying whole provinces by fire and explosion, the king's authority was always on the side of destruction.[6] The policy of "frightfulness" has had many imitators in modern times; Sherman, as well as the authors of the systematic bombings of the war of 1939–45, and the advocates of atomic bombing of cities, all agree that by terror, populations can be coerced to make peace. Louis' part in the decisions during his reign must be inferred, since no papers give direct evidence, but there is strong reason to believe that he favored the policy, even though he may not have originated it.

The "frightfulness" of this era, however, presented some difficulties. One of Louis' most cherished programs was his attempt to keep his soldiers under discipline and to prevent his armies from creating much disorder. His letters throughout his life are filled with demands that discipline must be maintained. But what happens when troops are ordered to burn but forbidden to pillage? The *Gazette* tells us that the king first ordered that five men guilty of pillaging a church should be burned alive before their fellows, and then sent the Cardinal de Boullion to the church to "give, in the name of the pious King, chalices, ornaments, and a considerable sum of money as reparation."[7] The same issue of the *Gazette* tells how Louis ordered that Dutch peasants, who had killed several French soldiers contrary to public faith, "be summarily hanged," while the troops confiscated the animals of the whole village as a means of "holding the rest of the peasants to their duty." Could it be that Louis' letter to Turenne a few days later, in which he says, "I am writing to you in my own hand to tell you that it is of the utmost importance for the good of my service that you continue to hold the troops of the army that you command in the most exact discipline," is evidence of schizoid behavior in the army? Probably not; the troops were accustomed to savage discipline, and they were always ready to execute harsh orders.[8]

When plans for the campaign of 1673 finally matured, neither Condé nor Turenne had any considerable part to play. It may be that since his "great" generals had failed to secure peace in 1672, other advisers now had Louis' ear; or it may simply be that the prospect of commanding an army without the tutelage of these "great" generals determined his decision. But there is a third possibility: by 1673 another personality and a new idea were beginning to make an impression on the military thought of the king. A Condé or a Turenne still thought in terms of an army in motion, maneuvers, detachments, and perhaps a decisive victory. This was the conception of war that had grown out of the great German war of 1618–48; it posited a commanding general who was largely autonomous in his actions, and independent in his command. The new idea of war developed out of the war office that Le Tellier and his son Louvois had done so much to create, an idea that would subordinate such officers to a centralized direction and concentrate their actions on the defense—or the attack—of a line of fortifications.

One of the architects of this new conception was the young engineer who had emerged as a vital and vigorous adviser of the war minister and the king—Sébastien le Prestre de Vauban. As we have seen, Vauban first attracted royal attention at the siege of Lille in 1668; in the five following years his progress was rapid. He visited the "new frontier" made by the Treaty of Aix-la-Chapelle, where the French and Spanish fortresses were mixed up in a most chaotic fashion, indicating the lack of thought about frontiers at that conference. Vauban urged a "rationalization" of this situation. His projects and drawings for new fortifications and lines were even more effective. Louis was delighted with him. Louvois piled more and more responsibility on his shoulders, and more and more the idea of lineal frontiers defended by great works at key points came to dominate the thinking of the war ministry. This suited Louis XIV. No one reading his letters can miss the fact that all his life he had an almost pathological fear of an invasion of "my kingdom." He dreaded the thought of raids by detachments of the enemy for contributions and pillage; the very idea of an invasion filled him with terror. It is small wonder that Vauban, the man who made the defenses of the kingdom, waxed strong in the patronage of the king.

The project for 1673 was an attack on the fortification of Maestricht. This great fortification would give the French control over the line of the Meuse (Maas) and assure communications with the Rhine as well as the defense of France from that quarter. The city belonged to the Elector of Cologne, but the Dutch had strongly fortified and garrisoned it to control the river. The elector was upset to learn that the French were willing to rid him of the Dutch only on the condition of taking their place. In 1672 the invading French army had bypassed the fortification, for it was so strong that its capture might have required a whole campaign; in 1673

Louis decided to attack it. The capture of Maestricht should bring much prestige to French arms, it would give Louis control of a section of the Meuse, and it might even encourage his enemies to make peace.

The plan left Turenne in Germany to watch the Brandenburgers and the empire, Condé in Holland to watch the Prince of Orange, while Louis, with an army of about 32,000 men, marched into the Spanish Netherlands as a deceptive maneuver to throw the Spanish off guard. In his *Mémoires* the king explains that he took an active part in the preparations; it "was sweet," he wrote, "to mingle my glory with that of a state so powerful and prosperous as this kingdom." He also took credit for the deceptive march toward Brussels. This was "the grand design" that was needed, since he "was involved with the Dutch and the Germans [and the Spanish were his foes] . . . I pretended to march on Brussels . . . wishing to make them [the Spanish] responsible for beginning the war. . . ." The plan was highly successful. No one realized that Maestricht was the target until the whole of the Spanish forces in the Netherlands were tied down in their own fortifications. They fell into Louis' trap without realizing what had happened to them. The king adds a significant and interesting note to the effect that the maneuver was possible because of the new portable bake-ovens developed by the war ministry; they could be set up in six hours. Louis remarks that if the army had had these ovens the preceding year "I would have done things . . . in Holland that the lack of bread . . . prevented. . . ."

This siege of Maestricht was one of the first in history to be directed almost entirely by an engineer. The normal pattern for sieges was to have the commanding general tell the engineers what was to be done, a procedure that usually, or at least very often, was costly in terms of blood, for even a Condé who prided himself on his knowledge of fortifications, was not really an expert in that field. Louis, however, had long accustomed himself to the consultation of specialists; his *métier* was that of the king; it did not require him to *be* the expert, but it required that he know how to use advice. Both Louis and Louvois were impressed by Vauban's military engineering and they were ready and able to give him a free hand in the direction of the siege. Even so, the king had much to do. He tells us that he kept himself "alert to the actions of the Spanish and the Dutch [armies] . . . sent out parties in all directions to assure control over the roads . . . and an abundance of everything in the camp. Always concerned to see that what . . . [was] ordered was actually done . . . and always in places where . . . [my] presence was needed."

Years later, at the opening of the War of the Two Crowns, Louis wrote out a long memorandum in his own hand on the problem of besieging Maestricht; this document is evidence that he understood the requirements of the siege. But the actual directions of the siege operations in 1673 were in the hands of Vauban.[9] The king's relationship with his engineer is well explained in a letter that Louis wrote to his grandson years later when the latter was about to undertake the siege of Brisack with the assistance of Vauban: ". . . he [Vauban] put himself into the trenches, attacked the fortifications; he gave me his thoughts and explained what he believed should be done, and when I approved it, he gave me an outline of the measures to take and asked me in writing for whatever was required. . . . I furnished it, and he protested only when he did not get what he needed— which never happened."[10] Could there be a more concise description of the partnership that was established?

Jean Racine, writing a mythological history of the war for Louis' edification, gave a somewhat different interpretation of the siege: "Never," he exclaims, "did a city put up so great a resistance, never was fire more cruel and terrible . . . but what could their force and industry do against an army of Frenchmen dominated by the presence of their King?"

Either at the king's command or by his assent, the *Gazette* kept its readers informed about their king's actions. On June 11 he was reported present when the dragoons clashed with the enemy and captured a prisoner. Louis gave each dragoon three gold pistoles (value, about three livres each), and released the prisoner telling him to report that his masters must surrender within one week if they wished quarter. On the night of June 17–18, when the large cannons were in place, the king "began to salute the besieged in a handsome manner." He visited the works on horseback, "appearing at places where lesser officers would hesitate to go . . . so that one attributes the vigor and safety of his sacred person to the particular care of divine providence." In an even more lyrical passage, the *Gazette* exclaims, ". . . come, follow the footsteps of the greatest King on earth, see the prudence with which he gives orders, how he is everywhere where his presence is needed, with what indefatigability he works, and with what boldness he faces danger. . . ." How could even a storybook king do any better? As a matter of fact, Louis, in spite of the cautions we have already noted, was occasionally foolhardy; perhaps this is why years later he was to caution Marshal Boufflers to prevent the Duke of Burgundy from unnecessarily exposing himself to the enemy.

The siege was actually a masterpiece of military art that astonished the besieging army no less than the besieged. The trenches were so effectively placed that the fire from the fortification did practically no damage to the assault forces as they moved closer and closer to the walls. This was to be a rare siege; the besieged lost more men than the attackers, even though an act of folly produced extraordinary casualties in the king's own regiment, including the famous Captain d'Artagnan. The final attack was a two-pronged affair; the false one was led by Philippe, the true one by the king. Louis writes, ". . . at the same time that we carried the half moon, the false attack succeeded better than anyone had hoped for . . . my brother gave his commands well." Of the soldiers under his own command, Louis exclaims, ". . . the guards and the musketeers were marvelous . . . the Swiss did their duty very well . . . the logement was the most beautiful in the world . . . a marvel." Vauban does not appear in this final description of the siege, but without his preparations it could not have been effected. Louis later gave him full credit, saying that a fortification attacked by Vauban was as good as taken, and a fortification defended by him, impregnable.

The fall of Maestricht twenty-two days after the French army camped outside its walls impressed Europe, but did not create any great desire for peace. The Spanish, angered by the French march through their part of the Netherlands and frightened by the obvious power of the French army, prepared to enter the war, and in Vienna and the lesser capitals of the empire, plans matured rapidly for a coalition against France. There was a conference at Cologne to discuss peace, but it was abundantly clear that this conference was not going to achieve it. The problem was simple enough. Both Louis and Charles II were willing to accept much less than they had demanded the preceding year, but Dutch victories at sea, the embarrassment of the French army in the Netherlands, and the rise of an anti-French coalition made the Dutch less and less willing to make peace at any price other than complete withdrawal from their territories. These were not conditions that Louis would accept. His armies were in the Netherlands, he had conquered Maestricht, and France was clearly the only great military power on the continent. Louis was willing to consider substitutes for his conquests. There could be an exchange of territory leaving Franche-Comté and Luxembourg to France, providing that Maestricht also remained in French hands. Louis was proud of his recent conquest; he seemed as disposed to cede Versailles or Paris as Maestricht. If he had accepted the Dutch offer of the preceding year, he could have had Maestricht and a good deal more, but in the summer of 1673 the Congress of Cologne indicated that he could extricate himself from the war only by terms that would practically restore the *status quo ante*. Louis would rather fight than give up so much; he was in possession of the Netherlands, the Rhineland, the Meuse, and the Moselle—let them put him out who could.

With the conference bogging down and Germany girding for war, the province of Alsace became a serious problem. Ever since the Treaties of Westphalia, the status of Alsace had been ambiguous. Strasbourg was a free city of the empire, the league of the Ten Towns pretended to an independence from the margrave (Louis), and indeed French authority over all the land was quite insecure. Louis placed the administration of Alsace under Louvois' office, and left Maestricht about the middle of July accompanied with something more than a token force to visit the province. Readers of the *Gazette* must have thought that the king went to Alsace and Lorraine to attend services in the cathedrals, to listen to sermons, speeches of welcome, to watch fireworks and artillery salutes. But Louis wrote to Colbert that he went there to "free myself from the difficulties that these caterpillars [Germans] can make for me." He stayed in the province for the rest of the summer. The Tén Towns were brought under control, several of them had their fortifications destroyed, others were occupied, and Vauban began his massive labor of developing the defenses of the Rhine. They were none too soon; within a year the Germans would storm over the river and invade the land.

By the summer of 1673 the two antagonists who were to spend most of the rest of their lives in opposition to Louis XIV were ready to take their places as allies and coordinators of the coalition against France. The one, Prince William III of Orange, emerged as the central figure of the United Netherlands after the downfall of DeWitt; the other, Emperor Leopold I, was the hereditary prince of the German Hapsburg holdings and elected ruler of both the empire and Hungary. William had connections with the English royal family through his mother, and important status as Stadtholder of the five most important provinces of the Netherlands and heir to the traditions of the house of Orange. He was an uncompromising foe of France, a stalwart protagonist of the reformed religion, and a stubborn fighter for the rights and interests of his country. He regarded himself as the natural antagonist of Louis XIV and all that Louis stood for. Leopold, himself a staunch Catholic, could not object to the French king's religious policies, but he did react strongly against the expansionist program of the Bourbon house. His German and Central European advisers warned him of the dangers to the empire; his dynastic interests alerted him to the threat of Bourbon claims to the Spanish inheritance. At the time of the War of the Devolution, Leopold had been willing to consider partition of his brother-in-law's hands, but by 1673 he was ready to follow the advice of counselors like Lisola who were sure that Louis intended to create a universal empire at the expense of the "liberties of Europe." Leopold was not as able nor as flashy as his French cousin, but in his stubborn way he was an effective ruler. On August 30, 1673, he signed a treaty with the United Netherlands, the kingdom of Spain, and the Duke of Lorraine. If we discount the Triple Alliance of 1668, this was the first important military coalition against Louis XIV, and in a way, the first important effort to build a continental balance of power as the government of Europe.

The Swedish ambassador may have had dreams of making a treaty of peace, but this Grand Alliance was the death sentence for the congress at Cologne. Louis announced that he was not willing to accept peace at the terms that would "dishonor" the conquests of his soldiers and humiliate their king; rather than give up everything that he had won, he would defend these conquests "one by one." That ended the conference of Cologne. The Dutch War was over, a European War was about to begin.

The last months of 1673 brought serious reversals to French arms: the garrison at Naarden surrendered under humiliating conditions, and the imperial army captured Bonn. Neither Turenne nor Condé could check the progress of the foe. Not only did the prestige gained at Maestricht begin to fade, but even more important was the question of the safety of the French army in the Netherlands. The perplexing problems in the field soon generated other difficulties. Orders from the war ministry to the generals became more and more exact, so that it almost seemed that Louis and his ministers had lost faith in their commanders. The reaction was quick. Turenne resisted orders from a distance; he fairly shouted that no soldier worthy of a command should ever be given such precise orders. What might seem reasonable to men at Saint-Germain had no meaning in the Rhineland. These orders must have been largely the work of Louvois, for later in the reign when Louis acted as his own war minister and chief of staff, he generally gave the commanders in the field in whom he had confidence wide discretion in many matters of military strategy; only now and then did he issue orders that actually tied a soldier's hands. Louvois, however, was quite capable of drafting imperious orders, and especially when he saw the military situation disintegrating. He had labored hard to build the machine that had overrun the Netherlands and overawed Europe, and he was losing faith in the men who had failed to use it effectively. Furthermore, modern war was becoming much too complex an operation to leave all decisions in the hands of a commander in the field; the war office, the intendants, the king's council—all had a need to share in the direction of military policy. A Turenne, or a Condé, whose memory ran back to the German war, the *Fronde,* and the Franco-Spanish War, had an image of the role of a commander quite different from that of the minister at Saint-Germain.

It was a delicate situation that almost led to Louvois' disgrace. The generals joined hands to destroy him. Louis could not have been unaware of the storm that was brewing; this time the rebellious soldiers were not a mere Marshal Bellefonds, but the Prince of Condé and the Viscount de Turenne. They wanted to blame the arrogant young upstart in the war ministry for all the failures of the war and thus discredit him in the eyes of the king. Happily for Louvois, his father was well-versed in court intrigue and politics. For Le Tellier had been the one to reinstate Condé in favor in 1668 as a counterbalance to the influence of Turenne, and he knew well that Condé and Turenne had not only fought each other in the *Fronde* and after, but also that they were still rivals for the king's favor. Turenne was particularly jealous of Condé, for the hero of Rocroi was not only a soldier but also a Bourbon. This was the wedge that allowed Le Tellier to get to Condé's ear and to offer him in return for neutrality, the assurance that Louvois would provide him with a fine army for a campaign in 1674. By himself Turenne could not disgrace the war minister, especially since Louis had come to regard Louvois' administrative talent as indispensable. On the king's request, the old marshal and the young war minister patched up their differences without solving them; on the surface the king's official family was again at peace. Another of the important crises on the road that was to subordinate the soldiers to the king's command had been successfully passed.

By the end of 1673 the French army in the Netherlands was in a precarious position, and indeed with the war becoming a European conflict, France itself was in trouble. "Most of the princes of Europe were leagued against me," writes the king. "My allies were becoming my enemies and all of them wished to frustrate my enterprises. . . . So many powerful foes forced me to take guard . . . to sustain the reputation of my army, the advantage of the state, and my personal *gloire*. . . . My reactions had to be secret and prompt."[11] It was a painful decision, but there was no alternative: the French army had to evacuate the Netherlands and concentrate its efforts nearer the frontiers of France. The Dutch guessed this long before it was announced; they even placed bets on the date of the French retreat. The plan that emerged concentrated all the surplus war materials in the fortress of Grave and then withdrew the French army to a line on the Meuse with Maestricht as an anchor. Alsace and Lorraine were to be defended by a line from Maestricht to Trier (captured in the fall of 1673), and then along the Moselle to the Rhine at Philippsburg. The strategy was not yet worked out in detail, nor were the field fortifications built, but in this scheme we probably see the origins of the famous "lines" that were to make the wars of the next three and a half decades very similar in spirit to the terrible war of 1914–18.

The retreat from the Netherlands was almost frustrated by another rebellion by one of the marshals of France. Marshal Bellefonds, in the pattern of the soldiers of his day, assumed the right to veto the king's order to retreat. It would be shameful, cowardly, and contrary to the interests of the kingdom, he said, so he made his own solution to the problem without even consulting the war minister. At first the presumption on the friendship of the king was met with firm orders to carry out the king's commands, but finally Louis and Louvois had to act more decisively. There were two letters under the king's signature: the first expressed surprise and regret at Bellefond's refusal to obey orders "with exactitude and submission that you owe me!"; the second was directly to the point—"My cousin, being dissatisfied with your conduct, I send you this letter to tell you that it is my intention that you turn over to the Comte de Lorges . . . the command that I gave you over my troops. . . ." Fortunately for the old marshal, the intendant attached to the army was a man of judgment and diplomacy, so Bellefonds was spared the disgrace of immediate dismissal, but he never again had a chance to rebel against royal commands. It was the third time in this war that marshals of France had protested the king's orders without success. The new army would be one in which soldiers and even marshals of France obeyed the government of the king.[12]

The plan for action was well designed. The army withdrew from the lower Rhine leaving the fortifications in the hands of the Electors of Cologne and Brandenburg (who had made peace with Louis for the moment); at the same time, another army prepared to invade Franche-Comté. The Spanish had done nothing to strengthen the defenses of that province, since they believed that the emperor and the Swiss were so frightened by Louis' occupation of 1669 that they would prevent its ever happening again.

As usual Louis' project was carefully planned: French money bought off the Swiss, and Turenne's army screened off the imperials, while the army, under the personal command of the king, quickly subdued the province.[13] It was an easy campaign and Louis generously recognized the assistance of his armies and friends. Condé's son, the Duke of Enghien, was with him at the capture of Besançon, and Louis wrote to the father of the excellent behavior of the son. To the town councilors of Toulouse who had congratulated him, he wrote asking them to "pray to the Divine Providence to continue to protect us so that we can become masters of this country. . . ."[14] When the province was conquered Louis replied to a letter from the wife of the Marshal de la Motte, governess of the king's children, in which she had given him great praise for the victory: "You have too good an opinion of me in giving me all the glory for the taking of Besançon. . . . My troops had a great part in it, and, moreover, I must recognize that it is principally the work of God. . . ."[15] All seventeenth-century rulers had courtiers who would praise their every act; all were obsessed by their *gloire;* it was always a problem for them to keep some perspective on their actions. Louis' belief in Divine Providence often came to the fore in such circumstances. It could have been a polite show of false humility, but as Sir George Clark so rightly remarked, we must take seriously the words of these seventeenth-century people when they speak of God and of His will.

The campaign in Franche-Comté was the only one in 1674 to be directed by the king himself. Condé commanded in Flanders against William of Orange, and Turenne in Alsace and on the Rhine against the Germans. Louis undertook to watch the campaign from his capital, and to shift the troops from one army to another as the situation demanded. This was his first real experience with "chief-of-staff" operations, one that must have been both enlightening and exhilarating. Up to this point he had always been under the shadow of his two famous commanders; now, with the vigorous will and intellect of Louvois to guide him, he began to see war as something more than a campaign in the field.

Thus continued the process that was to change warfare in western Europe; the famous captains of the past had been given, or had themselves organized, armies, and they had conducted their campaigns with little or no interference from the king's government. Tilly, Wallenstein, Bernard of Saxe-Weimar, Spinola, like Condé or Turenne, had been quasi-independent forces. By 1674, however, the armies were so large, and the problems of supply so complex that some sort of control had to be exercised over the will of the commander. This growing control from the war ministry aroused antagonism on all sides. Condé and Turenne spoke of disliking directions from a man "who merited the title valet rather than captain," and as the war progressed, Turenne bitterly complained that "some day generals will be constrained to take orders [from the central government] even though they are a hundred leagues away."[16] Lesser officers ground their teeth and obeyed, because they understood that the war minister could make or break their careers. Louvois was not making himself into a constable; he was the loyal servant of a king who was resolved to make the army responsive to the royal will, and who backed up his minister's orders at every point.

Thus we now find much of Louis' correspondence dealing with the problems of movements of troops. When intelligence reports indicated a need, detachments were sent from one army to the other, or commanders were ordered to assume a defensive position on a line to hold off an expected attack. It was not always easy, however, to get the commander to do as he was ordered. We find time and again that the king had to write in his own hand saying, "[It is] my intention that you send these troops at once . . . without holding them under any pretext whatsoever. . . ."[17] When the Prince of Brandenburg went back on his agreement with France and reentered the war, Louis had almost as hard a time getting Condé to return the troops to Turenne. This was to be the pattern for the next two decades' reign; we shall see that it was often difficult to force a commander to give up a detachment for the service of his rival.

His problems with Turenne in July 1674 are illustrative of the difficulties Louis encountered. Early in June the king expressed "entire confidence in your [Turenne's] zeal for my service. . . . I put it in your judgment to do what you believe apropos, not doubting that you will take every possible advantage of the enemy. . . ."[18] By July 1, Louis had information of an enemy project on the Meuse, and asked Turenne to leave the Palatinate to meet the new threat, for ". . . your long sojourn in the Palatinate has no advantage to my service . . . it would be more advantageous for you to take it to the Meuse below Sedan. . . ."[19] In this letter he also explained to Turenne his plans for "lines" between Philippsburg and the Meuse. Twenty-two days later he writes telling Turenne of the pain he felt "in not being informed about what you wish to do in the Palatinate . . . which can end only by exciting the princes of Germany to send aid to the Elector . . . and oblige you to cross the Rhine." He went on, "I believe that it is to my service and to the reputation of my arms in Germany to make it evident that your return should not be attributed to the march of an enemy army. . . ." He explained that the war in Flanders also required that Turenne should take up a post in Alsace for the defense of the kingdom. The bad state of the defenses "makes me see with great chagrin that you are far distant." He ended by urging the old marshal to obey the orders sent earlier in the month.[20] Without asking too closely whether Louis or Turenne had the better reason, it must be clear that the king thought that he knew what was happening and had trouble persuading the marshal to carry out his orders.

Condé also caused some problems. In fulfilling his father's promise that Condé should command an important army in 1674, Louvois gave the hero of Rocroi the very best part of the forces available for the campaign. But Condé was now in his fifties; he suffered from gout and had lost his will. Louis left to him the decision to attack the enemy, asking only that he be informed where the blow would fall. Poor Condé could not decide; he rejected one target after another. The king then suggested that if the great fortresses were too strong, he should, at least, attack a lesser one. Condé returned with a request that the king should nominate the target, but Louis did not want to be responsible for plans of an attack. He wrote on June 21, "I say to you that I have great confidence in your affection to my service and in your capacity, and I know that one cannot decide on such things without being careful." But Louis urged Condé to decide. When he would not, Louis finally detached part of Condé's army in Flanders to assist Turenne who was hard-pressed in Alsace. Condé did finally fight a battle with the Prince of Orange, but he seemed to have lost his touch. This battle of Seneffe would have been a highly successful encounter with the rear guard of the enemy army had Condé been willing to call a halt to the action after he had achieved an initial success, but the battle that followed his failure to break contact was a sanguinary affair in which a great number of brave men on both sides were killed without either gaining a significant advantage. It was Condé's last battle and the only important one that he commanded during the personal reign of Louis XIV. It is hard to see why historians have made his presence so important a factor in the reign.[21]

Turenne, on the other hand, showed a vigor and a willingness to fight—quite out of character for him—and beyond the resources at his disposal. The Germans burst in on Alsace and forced him back at every point. Turenne had been known as the man of maneuver, but he also was the man who once said, "but there comes a time when you must fight!" This was the time; and it perhaps gave inspiration to a young cadet in Turenne's army, John Churchill,[22] who later—as the Duke of Marlborough —was to be the scourge of the French. Turenne fought a series of pitched battles—at Sinzheim, Ensheim, Muhlhouse, and Turkheim—that may not have destroyed the enemy armies, but they did force the Germans to leave Alsace.

Louis' letters of congratulation were always prompt and gracious, yet he rarely failed to mention his displeasure and sadness over the losses. After Sinzheim, for example, although he sent his congratulations to "all the officers of my army that you command," he added, "I am indeed disturbed by the bad state of the wounds of Saint-Abre and Beauvige. . . . I await with impatience the account of the battle . . . and the memoire on the officers and my troops who have perished . . . and those who were wounded."[23] This concern for the casualties was characteristic of Louis throughout his life.

The campaign of 1674 did not go well. The initial success of the occupation of Franche-Comté was about the only real advantage gained during the year. The imperial army ravaged Alsace before it was driven out; the French garrison at Grave, with a huge amount of war supplies, was forced to capitulate; the enemy captured Huy and Dinant in the Netherlands, and the Spanish captured Bellegarde in the south. Admiral Tromp sailed along the coast of France menacing commerce and awaiting the uprising of the Huguenots that the coalition hoped to inspire. And yet the foes could not win a decision any more than Louis did, for as Louis explained it, "United action is difficult for these people who have separated interests . . . the divided authority is never as strong . . . as when it is united in one person alone. This is the advantage that I have had against my enemies during all this war, and it has contributed to the successes that have come to me."[24]

In the spring of 1675 Louis decided to command the main army himself; the project was a grand sweep through the Spanish Netherlands to assure the French hold upon Maestricht, and perhaps by a demonstration of power, to encourage the enemies to make peace. As usual, when the campaign started, Louis was optimistic about its possible results; this optimism at the opening of a campaign was to be a usual pattern throughout his life. The grass was long enough by May to support the cavalry, and the army began to assemble in north France in the area of Ham. Louis joined the troops on May 13 as commander-in-chief; Condé, Philippe, Marshals Feuillade and Créqui, and an able staff of lieutenant generals stood ready to assist. The progress was slow; on May 15 they were at Cateau-Cambrésis, on May 21 they camped south of Mons, and by May 30 they had crossed into the Netherlands and were camped halfway between Namur and Tirlemont. While the main body marched through the Spanish Netherlands, a detachment under Créqui maneuvered between the Sambre and the Meuse to the south. "The enemies," writes the official account, "not knowing what to think about Marshal Créqui's maneuvers . . . expected an attack on their important fortifications on the Scheldt and the Meuse. . . ." But Créqui actually invested Dinant and soon de Rochefort was detached to invest Huy from the north (June 1). Both of these places quickly fell, and the main army continued its majestic leisurely march toward Maestricht. The Prince of Orange did nothing to interfere with the sieges of Dinant and Huy, but when Créqui went on to invest Limbourg, the Dutch army made threatening moves, for the French capture of this place would assure a better grip on French communications between the line of the Meuse and the Moselle. The Dutch could not prevent the fall of Limbourg, which the French immediately refortified and garrisoned. After this, Créqui turned south to pass by Luxembourg on his road to the Moselle where the Germans were threatening again to invade Alsace, while the main army under the king proceeded to Maestricht where it camped on the high ground to the south of the town. The army stayed at Maestricht until the first of July, when it moved on Tongres and Saint-Trond, destroying both of these fortifications. During these maneuvers, detachments under Condé, Luxembourg, and la Feuillade made forays to collect contributions from the countryside and assemble forage for the army.[25]

From Louis' point of view this sweep through the southern Netherlands was a highly successful operation. Although none of the places captured amounted to very much, the taking of Limbourg and the destruction of several other forts tightened the grip on Maestricht. Perhaps more important, it was a demonstration of the power of the French army, which had marched through its enemy's lands, collected contributions, and lived off the countryside, while the Spanish-Dutch army had been unable to interfere. This should have discouraged the enemies of France. Louis greatly enjoyed the excursion: organizing lines of march, fortifying new positions, and choosing the password for the day. The royal tents were splendidly emblazoned with the insignia of power and garnished with secretaries, guards, and officers; they were the fit habitation for a great king.[26]

By the second week in July Louis was ready to return to Versailles, where problems of a very different sort awaited him. Before giving command of the army to Condé, a very large detachment was sent to join Créqui on the Moselle, and then the king with his guards, the musketeers, his light and heavy cavalry returned to France. This meant that Condé would be in no position to attempt very much against the enemy; he had enough troops to stand off the Prince of Orange, but he could not risk another Seneffe. It is unlikely that he would have done so anyway, since he was feeling his age and had lost much of his *élan*.

The king's personal problems at this point probably disturbed him almost as much as the military ones did. Before he had set out for this sweep through the Netherlands, the scandal of his double adultery with Madame de Montespan had reached proportions that led him to decide to put her aside.[27] But as he was later to remark to Madame de Maintenon, he knew "very well the man who wished to do the right and yet so often did the opposite." He had not taken the precaution to exile the lady from the court; this would have been too harsh a punishment for a crime that he also shared. So when he returned—there she was. The good Bishop Bossuet's fears were more than confirmed when the guilty couple decided that they could not give each other up.

While Louis was marching through the Spanish Netherlands, French forces elsewhere also gave a good account of themselves. In the Caribbean area and in the Mediterranean the French navy proved its mettle. Late in June the battle of Palermo gave the French a foothold in Sicily where the Spanish rule was quite unpopular.[28] At the same time the Swedish intervention against Brandenburg and the uprising of the Hungarian malcontents who had been supplied with French money prevented the Germans from repeating the invasion of the preceding year, and indeed, Turenne was in the act of pressing the imperial army on the German side of the Rhine. The fact that Frederick Wilhelm had defeated the Swedes at Fehrbellin in Pomerania had not yet altered the balance of military power in Germany. But on July 27 a chance cannon ball fired at a reconnoitering party struck and killed Turenne. The effect on the French army was immediate and unfortunate; the soldiers' morale was shaken and the high officers fell into a fight over the right to command. Jean Racine tells us that "the enemies expected to exterminate the whole army, but the Count de Lorges and the Marquis de Vaubrun . . . reassured the troubled soldiers, animated them with a desire for revenge, and then returned to the Rhine. . . ." Racine does not tell the whole story of the shameful conflicts for power and the disastrous retreat, nor of the lost battle that cost Vaubrun his life. The campaign of 1675 that had been so successful up to that moment was now in great jeopardy.[29]

The news was like a bolt of lightning to Louis. He spoke of the loss of the "father of the country," the hero-marshal who deserved so much from both the dynasty and the kingdom. "I have just heard with a sorrow that you can well imagine," he wrote to Condé, "of the news of the unexpected death of our cousin the Viscount de Turenne who has been killed by a cannon shot while he was placing the army that I had put under his charge in order of battle . . . by his loss, my army in Germany is without a chief. . . ." He then ordered Condé to turn his command over to Lieutenant General Luxembourg and to go at once with a detachment of troops to replace the fallen marshal in Alsace. At the same time he announced that Turenne would be buried in Saint-Denis,[30] the basilica in which the kings of France were entombed; no higher honor could be paid a soldier. Louis apparently gave no attention to the pious people who suggested that Turenne's death was God's way of punishing the king for his adultery.

"We have lost a father," he exclaimed, but Louis already had the mien of a king and understood that a king's public reaction to events was a political fact of great importance. "We have lost a great soldier, but we have others." This was his response to Europe, his assurance to his own subjects. On the morrow of Turenne's death the king nominated eight new marshals from the roster of the lieutenant generals. A wag called these men the change (*monnaie*) from Turenne, but since two of the eight were Luxembourg and Schomberg, a third, Rochefort, and a four and fifth, Turenne's nephews Duras and de Lorges, it seems quite unfair to play down the promotions. An honest appraisal will have to admit that half of them were as good as the average commanders in the armies of the time, while the first three were quite superior, and it can be argued that Luxembourg was the peer of any soldier of the entire period.

The promotions were followed by the famous *ordre de tableau,* which henceforth regulated the right to command: when there was more than one marshal of France present on the field, the command fell to the one who had first been promoted to the rank of lieutenant-general. This order would prevent a reoccurrence of the events that followed the death of Turenne; it was an absolute necessity for the development of the army that Louis and his war ministry were creating. The contests for power and the rebellions among the high officers of the army did the king's service no good; the problem would be further complicated as soon as men of relatively lower social rank were promoted to high command. Of the eight marshals only five were dukes, and in the future, men whose forefathers had sold cloth or wine would reach that rank. Unless the rule was established, the rights of blood and social status could easily do great damage to the king's service. Much of the gall and vitriol that filled the pen of Saint-Simon was distilled from this famous order of rank; nor was Saint-Simon the only one who protested, but the king insisted upon the right of the war ministry to structure his army.[31]

The military results of the death of Turenne were very unhappy. Most of the army did get back over the Rhine, but the imperials also crossed the river into Alsace, recreating the serious situation that had existed the preceding year. If the imperial commander Montecuccoli had not been, like Condé, burdened with age and infirmities, the predicament of the French army might well have been most precarious. In the north, on the Moselle, a German army fell upon Créqui's position at Könz-Saarbrück, and completely defeated the army under his command. Créqui managed to get to Trier before the Germans arrived to besiege it, but his bad luck continued, for a mutiny forced him to surrender the fortress long before the military situation warranted it. The only relief from these disasters was the fact that the Germans were not united enough in purpose to follow up their advantage.

Louis took these defeats with outward calm. Madame de Sévigné's letter of August 19 tells us that when Créqui was routed at Könzbrück, the king remarked, ". . . he is a brave man . . . it is disagreeable to be beaten by people who have never played anything but bassetta." When asked why he had been beaten, Louis replied with a story from the battle of Nordlingen where Bernard was defeated "because he thought he would win. . . ." But Louis' calm did not prevent his taking reprisals on the soldiers who had "failed their duty" at Trier. The Marshal de Rochefort was ordered to divide the dragoons and cavalry into groups of twenty and to hang one man, chosen by lot, from each group. The officers were hailed before a court, both the ones guilty of mutiny and those who had done nothing to check it. The court could not act against the latter group for lack of an established law, but one officer was decapitated before the troops and two others demoted in rank and Louis sent the two who had done nothing to check the mutiny to Metz for close confinement. Louvois has been "blamed" for the harsh discipline, but anyone reading Louis' letters cannot miss the fact that he wanted his soldiers "to do their duty," and that he was willing to resort to strict and brutal punishment to achieve this aim.

The campaign of 1675 that had started so auspiciously with the sweep through the Spanish Netherlands, Turenne's invasion of the Black Forest region, and the victories both in Sicily and on the Spanish frontier, ended with Créqui a prisoner, Turenne dead, the imperials again in Alsace, and the Elector of Brandenburg very much in control of the situation on the Baltic coast. Only in Sicily and in the Caribbean Islands could the French find reason for satisfaction. Happily the coalition was not ready for concerted action, since it had no unified plan or will. It was also lucky that Montecuccoli was as infirm and lacking in decisiveness as Condé, so that he was unable to take advantage of his position in the Rhineland. Both he and Condé retired from active command at the end of the year. One day Europe would learn to organize itself for a coalition war and find generals willing to follow up their advantages; then the French position would become difficult indeed.

18

THE DUTCH WAR: LAST PHASE

THE DEATH OF Turenne, the retirement of Condé, the shock of the defeats, and the anxieties of the latter part of 1675 all combined to urge the desirability of peace—if it could be had. The situation inside the kingdom seemed to cry for peace with the same urgency. Prolonged war enlarged the burdens of taxation, while disorders perpetrated by the soldiers and the deserters added to the social discontent. By winter of 1675 the little chorus of protests against the war threatened to grow into a big clamor, and Colbert complained of the problems of finding money for the war. The increased taxation produced a series of revolts; no one forgot that the tradition of rebellion in France was strong, or that the first *Fronde* had been rooted in protests against wartime fiscal measures. Vauban, a chronic worrier, spoke of the threat to the monarchy; Courtin, who knew the country even better, talked about the danger from the drain of money and the dissatisfaction of the people when the king's authority was involved in foreign ventures. In 1675 men in high places understood clearly that the king's government flew on crippled wings and was in danger of being grounded completely. Surely Louis, too, realized that the war must somehow come to an end.

To find a way to peace was not easy. Even though it had been largely fought on foreign soil the war had gone badly. The French had been obliged to retreat from the Dutch Netherlands and the Rhineland, and had seen their German allies one by one join the ranks of their enemies. Early in 1674 the English Parliament forced Charles II to make peace with the Dutch, and there were men in England clamoring to join the war against France. Louis had taken these desertions with surprising grace, even though with Spain, the Netherlands, and the empire joined against him, it became increasingly difficult to see how the war could end. His Swedish ally also had not proven to be of much use, for the Brandenburgers had practically annihilated the Swedish army and had captured Pomerania. Small wonder

LOUIS XIV

that Sir William Temple found the French anxious to make peace, and more than willing to send a mission to Nymwegen to negotiate it. But the congress of Nymwegen was called without an armistice to stop the fighting; therefore, like the previous conferences in Westphalia, its negotiations were to be tied to the action in the field. The congress met first in 1676, but a whole year went by before it got much beyond problems of protocol. In the meantime, the war had to go on.

Without Turenne and Condé in the field to vie for priority, the war ministry could prepare a plan of action based upon a single concept of military strategy. This had not been possible in the preceding three years. In 1676 Vauban had the ear of the king and he was evolving a strategic doctrine based upon lines of defense. As long as the frontiers of the kingdom were made by treaties that ceded a city or province "and its dependencies," the frontier was a thing of shreds and patches, of enclaves that studded the land pell-mell with fortifications of both rulers who shared the frontier, so that no one could say exactly where it did go, or what were its "gates." As Vauban's military thinking developed, the idea of a "line" (for example, the "line of the Rhine," the "line of the Moselle," etc.), then the fortresses scattered helter-skelter and without order became an anachronism. The king needed to straighten out the frontier in Flanders to assure himself a "dueling field" with clearly marked lines.[1] The strategy for 1676 and 1677 was based upon this idea. The reforms of the Le Telliers had recreated the Roman legions; perhaps it was inevitable that with Vauban they would now prepare the way for a reinterpretation of the Roman "lines."

The plans were simple enough: Louis' armies would besiege the fortifications of Condé and Bouchain on the Scheldt and thereby isolate Valenciennes and Cambrai to make them easy prey for the following year. It was no simple thing to prepare for sieges of this magnitude, and every effort was made to prevent the Spanish-Dutch intelligence from learning what was being planned. It fits Louis' own character that they tried to deceive the Duke of Villahermosa and the Prince of Orange by pretending to prepare attacks on Namur, Charelemont, and Ghent. The ruse was so successful that part of the garrison at Condé was actually detached to meet these French threats just before de Lorges arrived before that fortress on April 17. Four days later Louis joined the army, and on April 23 the bombardment of Condé began with Louis ordering that anything that Vauban wished or asked for "to advance the conquest" should immediately be supplied.[2]

The army that invaded the Spanish Netherlands in 1676 was under the command of the king, supported by his brother, by the Duke of Enghien, four marshals of France, and a fine cast of lieutenant generals. The actual sieges were directed by Vauban, even though he was outranked by a dozen officers in the king's entourage. The siege of Condé presented a nice problem because of the swamps that nearly surrounded the fortification, but Vauban quickly subdued it. D'Ostich, its governor, surrendered without even trying a sortie, three days after the cannonade began; the terms allowed him to march his troops to Tournai, while Vauban directed the rebuilding of the fortifications to receive a French garrison. After the fall of Condé, it was Philippe's turn to capture a city. Créqui, under Philippe's orders, moved a large detachment about eighteen miles south to besiege Bouchain, while Louis, with the rest of the army, acted as a screening force to prevent the Dutch from interfering with the siege. This turned out to be the only opportunity that Louis ever had to win a military reputation, but the chance slipped from his grasp.

After the fall of Condé, the Dutch army under the Prince of Orange moved to Perwez with the obvious intention of interfering with the siege of Bouchain or attacking one of the French fortresses, and Louis placed his army between the Prince of Orange and his brother. A beautifully bound official "history" prepared for Louis tells us "that the King with incredible vigilance and surprising activity observed the enemies' movements and countered their efforts." The French army crossed the river below Valenciennes and came face to face with the Spanish-Dutch army. According to this history, it was "the day that [the Prince of Orange] had with great passion hoped to see, and of which he had bragged for so long to the people of the Netherlands, [but it] ended without his daring to do anything."[3] The two armies were face to face in battle formation for a whole day, and nothing happened beyond a little skirmishing and the "three cannon shots" that the French fired to let their enemies "know of the desire" that Louis had "of fighting them." Obviously this was not all: the battle of Hurtebise near Valenciennes did not take place.[4]

There *was* much more to it than that. This was one of the occasions that led Saint-Simon and other enemies of the king to insinuate that he was a coward, afraid of a battle. Perhaps the story can unfold itself a little if we turn to the account that Louvois sent to his father with the clear intention of publishing all or part of it in the *Gazette*. This is an "official" account, and yet it contains an element of the story that should not be missed. Louvois wrote his father about the king's movements from April 27, after the fall of Condé, when his Majesty gave orders to Philippe to besiege Bouchain. The Prince of Orange with the Dutch army came within three leagues of the French camp. On May 6, Louis himself, with a cavalry escort, reconnoitered the enemy position; by May 9, he had placed Villeroi with some 3,500 men and four cannon to control the bridge over the Scheldt, and he himself prepared to follow his enemies to Oudenarde to prevent their besieging that place. He then visited the siege works at Bouchain to tell his brother that he had crossed the Scheldt. Philippe asked him to issue the orders for the siege, "but the King, jealous for his brother's *gloire,* left it all to him." The next morning, after the king had had only two hours' rest following twenty-four hours in the saddle, Schomberg alerted him that the enemy was approaching Valenciennes. Here is Louvois' account of the great event, written several days later:

The King was easily aroused from his sleep . . . he immediately mounted his horse and set out for Hurtevise [Heurtebise] which was only a cannon-shot from Valenciennes, followed by only eight squadrons of the guards, four of his gendarmes, and his light horse. His Majesty, on seeing thirteen squadrons in battle formation under the counter-escarpment of Valenciennes, thought at first that it was the garrison cavalry. He saw a moment later that the foes formed an extended cavalry wing. Wishing to take advantage of the moment, and not to give them time to be reinforced by a larger corps, the King proposed to charge them, but, knowing by the respectful silence, and then, by the opinion of the most experienced officers who had the honor to be with him, when his Majesty ordered them to express their opinion, that the difference in the number—which increased every moment—as well as the decisive advantage of their [the foes']`position, would mean that such an order would not be followed by happy success. He decided then also to await the arrival of the troops, while remaining with the small number that accompanied him in the presence of his enemies, whose batallions extended to the woods and whose squadrons formed a second line. The word reached the army that . . . the King with several squadrons was within cannon shot of Valenciennes and the foe in line of battle. Excited by the ardor and the diligence natural to Frenchmen who know that their master is in some peril, all the officers burned with impatience to have the honor of fighting in the presence of the King . . . the King with an unbelievable coolness placed his army in battle formation as it arrived, extending his right near to Valenciennes and his left up to the woods of Saint Armand. Nothing escaped his Majesty's skill and foresight. He sent Marshal de Lorge with thirty squadrons and a thousand musketeers to the heights behind the woods of Saint Armand. He established his artillery in an advantageous post. He had the dragoons and the infantry occupy the huts and the houses which were in his first line. . . . The general officers took their places after all his orders had been given, and executed in short without confusion. The King wished to command the right wing and his first line; he gave the command of the left wing to the Duke d'Enghien in the absence of Monsieur, who having been alerted of what was happening as his Maejsty had promised him, arrived a little later with the Duke de Créqui and followed by twenty squadrons. Monsieur then took the place destined for him and M. de Schomburg was under his orders. The Marshal Créqui had the honor of commanding under the orders of his Majesty; the Marshal de Feuillade commanded the infantry; the Duke de Lude, the artillery. In this position the King ordered the firing of three cannon shots to tell the enemy of the desire and the intention that he had to give battle, and to assure them that he waited and sought the opportunity.

. . . Those who are impressed by the true grandeur of the King's action, those whom he had loaded with his favors or who hoped to merit them by their faithful services, and those who have respectful love for his Majesty could not on this occasion decide what they should desire. They were first of all moved by the hope of winning a battle that would augment in some manner his Majesty's *gloire,* but his intentions to expose himself to the first and greatest of dangers made their desires uncertain.

. . . The enemies, however, freed of such worries for their generals, set about working to entrench themselves on their heights, their left under the fire of Valenciennes and their right in the woods of the Abbey de Vicogne. Taking extraordinary precautions for an army of 50,000 men that had an important fortification to shelter them in case of necessity, and that had been invited to risk a glorious chance of battle with the King in person, seconded by his brother and a Prince of the blood; even defeat would have been honorable.

. . . The day passed with several slight skirmishes. The Marshal d'Humières returned to join the army with his detachment; Marshal de Créqui returned in the evening to his camp before Bouchain; Monsieur went there also the next day . . . and began the assault in full daylight. . . . The fortification surrendered, and the foe was informed by three discharges of cannon fire. . . .[5]

Louvois' account, however, falls somewhat short of being a full story. Indeed, four days before he dispatched it, he wrote his father that all was quiet even though the enemy was only a cannon-shot away, and added that "the King rode today to the high point above the Scheldt from which one can see the enemy army as if inside its camp . . . anyone seeing their camp knows that they are a third less powerful than his Majesty's army."[6] But he makes no explanation of the reason for not falling on them when the opportunity presented itself several days before, and winning a decisive victory. De la Fare, who was there, but hardly as an unbiased witness, accuses both the king and Louvois of cowardice, but admits that Louvois might have been embarrassed by Louis' presence on the field. From his account and others, we can reconstruct the story of the critical decision.

As soon as the royal army was in position, Louis called his marshals and several of the lieutenant generals to him, but it was to take counsel rather than to order an attack. Louvois argued that the army was in place to cover the siege of Bouchain, and that they should not give battle; if the Prince of Orange wanted to disrupt the siege, it was up to him to attack the French positions. Von Schomberg supported the war minister, perhaps (as it was suggested by several memoirists) on the prodding of Louvois, and then the other marshals and lieutenant generals, with the exception of de Lorges, agreed. Saint-Simon tells us that his father-in-law, de Lorges, sensitive to the king's honor,[7] vigorously urged a battle, but we have no corroborating evidence of this fact. Louis, it seems, accepted the voice of the majority and remarked, "Since you have more experience than I, I will accede, but with regret." These may have been his very words, for he actually seems to have regretted the decision the rest of his life. Dangeau tells us that some twenty-three years later Louis spoke of this day as the one on which he "had made the most errors; that he never thinks of it without sorrow, that he recalls it in the night and always awakens in anger." According to Dangeau, the king blamed Louvois for the decision.

A closer look at the affair reveals some of its contours. Pellisson,[8] who was obviously present at the council, also believed that Louis could have won an easy victory, but he did not question the wisdom or the honor of the men who recommended that the army stand on the defensive. Louis, his brother, and the Duke of Enghien were all on the field. This meant that had the king been killed, the dauphin would come to the throne, and Condé, a cantankerous old man, might well have become the principal personality in the government. The entire efforts of the preceding two decades could have been wiped out. No soldier could ignore this possibility. As Marshal de Luxembourg wrote several days later, battles are not "the *métier* of kings";[9] indeed, in a battle the king's person is an embarrassment, for he must be protected no matter what are the necessities of the fight. We shall see that two decades later Luxembourg was obviously the most important person at another council of war that decided that Louis must not fight a battle. The fate of the kingdom could not be risked in this manner. With testimony from Vauban, Luxembourg, and other responsible soldiers, it is clear that they believed that Louvois was right in preventing a battle at Hurtevise (Heurtebise).

It is interesting, however, to speculate on the king's motives and action. De la Fare says that he was afraid.[10] Rousset insists that he was not afraid to fight, but afraid to be *defeated*. His *pride* rather than his *courage* thus becomes his downfall, for his pride caused him to take counsel with his marshals *so that* they could be blamed in case of failure.[11] This theory had found wide acceptance by historians, because Louis' pride has often been given as the key to his character. There is, however, another characteristic of the king that may well have been a more important factor in the decision. Throughout this period of his life, and in his words of advice to his son, we see Louis as the man who takes counsel from specialists. He recognized that others knew more than he did about many aspects of government and war, and he sought the most expert opinion that could be found. We hear him telling his son that any wise man takes counsel of the best-informed people he can find. At the siege of Maestricht we see him turning over the virtual command of the army to Vauban, who was not even a lieutenant general. His discussions of the problems of finding ministers and advisers, his relations with Colbert, Le Tellier, Louvois, and many others in his entourage indicate that Louis believed that the proper work of the king was to find good advice and to follow it. At this time of his life he recognized the limits of his talents as a soldier. He knew that he "commanded the army" to give heightened morale to the troops, to assure control over the behavior of these divergent personalities who were his marshals, and to impress the foe. It did not occur to him to "command" without a competent general officer "under his orders." This is his pattern of war for himself, and later for his son and his grandson. The King of France is a "soldier," his sons are "soldiers"; but in the complex art of war, the king needed the specialist who made war his business to give expert direction to the campaign. This is why Louis, when he was with the army, limited his own activity to the things that the king could do. When there was a question of an assault, a siege, or a battle, men whose business was war were needed to make decisions. We do not know why Louis did not order an attack at Heurtevise. We could call him a coward or a vain man. But if we are charitable we may see him as a man dependent upon counsel, a man who had advisers quite unwilling to risk the king's person and the destiny of the kingdom to the chance of an unlucky musket or cannon ball. If Turenne could be killed, so could anyone else.

After the fall of Bouchain, the royal army moved off the field near Valenciennes to a position from which it could defend both Condé and Bouchain, while the engineers rebuilt the fortifications. The Prince of Orange, well satisfied to have come off so easily, also withdrew to a new camp to the north. When the forts could defend themselves, the royal army worked its way to a position about three leagues from Brussels where it "fattened on the land" and on contributions from the enemy territory. A letter from the king to Colbert at this time speaks of the necessity of his staying with the army, because his enemies hoped that he would return to France. This has been used as further evidence of Louis' arrogant self-esteem. It may have been a simple statement of fact, for as soon as he actually left the army, squabbles broke out among the commanders, indicating that the "table of rank" created the year before needed time to be accepted. It was not easy to establish the "pecking order" in the army; some demanded position and power because of their "name or the name of their uncle" and refused to accept the "commission of the King" as evidence of authority. De la Fare, who wrote so venomously of Louvois and the king, was one of the men who had to be relieved of commission because of his insubordination later that summer.

In July Louis returned to Versailles, leaving Louvois in the field to direct operations in his place. The letters between the two men in the weeks that followed are a mine of information about the relations between them, and about the problems of the war. When the king left the army, a large detachment under Marshal Créqui was sent to the Moselle, where the unexpected death of Marshal de Rochefort had left a serious vacancy. Schomberg was left in command in Flanders to watch the Spanish and Dutch, but neither army had any orders for an "adventure"; after the capture of Condé and Bouchain the French went on the defensive, awaiting moves from the foe. Indeed, it is abundantly clear that the French had no aggressive plans once the two siege operations were completed.

The Prince of Orange, however, had a very ambitious plan; he attacked the fortification of Maestricht. This was a serious operation, for Maestricht, one of the greatest forts of Europe, was strongly garrisoned, and even though its governor, Marshal d'Etrades, was at Nymwegen discussing peace, the garrison was commanded by a redoubtable soldier, the Count de Calvox. Maestricht could be counted on to hold out for a long time. What should be the king's reply? He could try to relieve the city, or following Vauban's doctrine, he could let the Dutch capture it while the French captured another city in exchange that would better serve the French defensive system than the distant and exposed Maestricht. There were several fortifications that would answer this purpose; finally Aire was decided upon as a suitable "exchange" for Maestricht. Marshal d'Humières was given the command to invest the fort while Schomberg observed the enemy.

At this point Louis became concerned about the "exchange." He expressed confidence in and satisfaction with his war minister's conduct of the siege, but it seemed to be to "the good of [his] service" to take another fortification after Aire capitulated. Louvois, however, suggested that the troops would need a rest and should not be expected to try another "enterprise." Louis insisted: ". . . according to all appearances Maestricht will hold out a long time. . . . I believe that it would be to the good of my service to try one more important affair after the conquest of Aire . . . to make up for the loss of Maestricht. Think of all possible projects and send me your advice." Again: "If the troops that make the siege need a rest, then others perhaps can act. . . . I won't make a positive order, but I desire that we do something with prudence." Louvois finally returned his answer: "Your Majesty should note that the sieges of Condé, Bouchain, and this one [Aire] will have consumed 500 milliers of powder and 30,000 balls . . . and that I do not know about more than 200 milliers of powder that can be used for an attack . . . without dimishing considerably the magazines necessary for the security of your Majesty's fortifications." He suggested that two little forts, Linck and Back, might be attempted; the next day he added Saint-Guillain to the list. Louis' reply is characteristic: the man who refused to accept Colbert's statement that there was no more money could not allow Louvois to say that there was not enough powder. ". . . I saw what you wrote about munitions. If there is a great effort to attempt, we should not fail to try it, for there is no fear that the enemy is in a position to do anything."[12]

Louis' correspondence abounds in admonitions of "prudence"; he warns his soldiers to be "careful" of his army, to seek "advantages" over the enemy, not to attack without "prospects of success," and the like. All this has led to the accusation that he was unwilling to assume risks, that he feared any action. During the siege of Aire, Louis watched the forces of the Duke of Villahermosa from a distance; he "hoped" that Schomberg would "find a chance to fight" the Spanish; Schomberg's maneuvers ". . . can produce important things. He should fight if it is possible to have a good advantage." Later: "There are two possible ways to meet Villahermosa: to go out to fight him or to wait for him to attack . . . if Schomberg attacks, it is best; but if . . . he must await the enemy, find the best way that you can to explain to him my wishes." His letters show that the king knew that the Spanish army was weak and poorly supplied; it probably could be defeated without much risk.[13]

There is another revealing passage in this correspondence. Louis explains to Louvois how satisfied he is with the war minister's operations and how pleased he is to have him on the scene. Then he went on to say, ". . . there are so many important enterprises on all sides that I follow with attention and much worry . . . even though I appear calm."[14] Louis understood how necessary it was for a king to dissimulate his feelings as well as his plans.

After the capitulation of Aire, Louvois suddenly got the idea that it might be possible to save Maestricht. In a forced march of twenty days, Schomberg descended upon the besieging Dutch army like an avenging angel. The king avidly followed the news of his march. The Prince of Orange was appalled; Maestricht would not fall and with the French army coming, his predicament was dangerous indeed. He tried one last assault, using a high proportion of officers to carry it off, but to no avail.

At the end of a two-month siege he had to withdraw as Schomberg's army moved into the high ground to the south of the city. Louis poured favor and wealth on the two men who had saved Maestricht: de Calvo for his defense; Schomberg for his brilliant forced march.[15]

However, the campaign of 1676 did not end on this high note. The imperial army, under Duke Karl of Lorraine, besieged and took the great fortress of Philippsburg (Philisbourg in French documents) on the middle Rhine. This fortification had been the anchor of both the line of the Rhine and the line that stretched to the Meuse. Its loss was a blow to French power and prestige that somehow made up for the Prince of Orange's failure at Maestricht. There is a little story connected with the fall of "Philisbourg" that illustrates both Louis' basic optimism as well as his tolerance of the opinions of faithful servitors. "We shall lose Philisbourg," he remarked. "That is too bad, but I shall still be King of France." The Duke de Montausier, the outspoken governor of the dauphin, replied, "True, Sire, you would still be King of France without Metz, Toul, Verdun, and Franche-Comté, which your predecessors got along without." Louis looked at him and remarked, "I understand, Monsieur de Montausier; you think that my affairs are going badly. . . . I take no objection to your words for I know that your heart is entirely for me."[16] Most of the so-called conversations of the king are open to much question, but this one seems in character with his letters and it may be a true account. Louis was a confirmed optimist about his prospects for success; he never started a campaign without believing that all would go well; and he always seemed a little astonished when it did not.

Two other items of this period also reveal to us a picture of the king somewhat less flamboyant than the usual egocentric portrait of those who follow Saint-Simon. In a letter to Bishop Bossuet, who had written to the king in praise of his campaign, Louis answered, "I am not embarrassed by the praise that you gave me in your last letter, for you have made me understand very well to Whom it is due. . . . I refer to the principles that you have taught me. [God deserves the credit.]" On another occasion, when the French fleet won a victory at Palermo, a courtier handsomely praised the king for the victory, but Louis replied, "You praise me as a devoted servant, and because of that, all that you say does not fail to be agreeable, but I must consider the distance [from Versailles to Palermo] . . . and only use your needle to urge me to [merit] fame."[17] His mail was apparently crammed with letters from men anxious for favor or place or royal attention; all were lavish in their praise of his real or supposed actions. But as Louis tells his son, a king must "be sure that he deserves praise before he accepts it." Too often we see only the hymns of praise that arose from the courtiers around the king without realizing that he knew what he had actually done and how courtiers behave. As the embodiment of the kingdom he could take credit for the successes of the crown, but as a man he was often enough willing to give God or one of his faithful servitors credit for successful actions. Unfortunately we do not have as many of his private thoughts preserved as we would need for a solid judgment, but no one can read long in the literature of the day—in which those near to the king strove to bolster his ego by crediting him with real or imaginary achievements—without feeling that for all the arrogance of his outward façade as King of France, Louis must have been very insecure and self-conscious about his behavior. Just as the world did not see his doubts when he took over the reins of power at Mazarin's death, so later he was able to hide his *inquiétude* and worries about himself and his own actions behind the splendid façade of the monarchy.[18]

After the campaign of 1676 a blind man could know that in 1677 the French efforts would be directed against Valenciennes, Cambrai, and Saint-Omer, so that it was difficult to throw a "smoke screen" around the plans. Only the timing could be hidden, and Louis did this very well by a series of splendid court fêtes that seemed to assure Europe that the king of France had no intention of starting operations early in the season. While the court danced, Louvois went on ahead, and the armies converged upon Valenciennes. Bad weather forced the postponement of the planned simultaneous attack on Saint-Omer; indeed, the weather was so bad that when Louis arrived before Valenciennes all his equipment and most of his party were bogged in the mud miles away.

The capture of Valenciennes is one of the drollest stories of the war. Vauban's trenches drew nearer and nearer the walls; a heavy cannonade battered a breach, and then in full daylight but without warning, some 4,000 soldiers stormed into the fortifications, overwhelming the unprepared defenders. It was incredible. Once on the walls the French had no trouble forcing the city. The first thing that Louis knew, he saw his own soldiers manning the enemy guns that they now turned on the city. The city fathers got to the king asking for a chance to surrender just in time to prevent pillage. When they begged for the safety of their wives and children, Louis scolded them for being so slow to surrender—he must have had his tongue in cheek when he did so.[19] When the Archbishop of Paris tried to compliment him for the conquest, Louis replied, "God Who sees my good intentions has wished to bless them in their execution . . . never doubting that the continuous prayers for the prosperity of my arms that have come from your orders have had a principal part [in the success]." To the Bishop of Strasbourg he wrote, "I pray that God will inspire my enemies with the same desire for peace that he has strengthened in my heart by his constant blessing of my just arms."[20] The conquest of Valenciennes probably should be credited to Vauban's surprise rather than to God's intervention, but at the time it may have been hard to distinguish between the two.

After the fall of Valenciennes, the royal army moved on to besiege Cambrai, while Louis' brother Philippe marched on Saint-Omer. If the game were not so deadly in earnest, it would almost seem that the two brothers were "playing at war," for Louis with the intelligence at his disposal did not believe that the Prince of Orange would interfere with his plans. In a long memorandum he explained to his brother that he did not expect William to try anything, but if "contrary to all appearances" he should, Philippe was to take a defensive position. In any case, the siege of Saint-Omer could be postponed until one should see whether, "contrary to all indications, the enemies would approach." Two days later Louis informed Philippe that the Prince of Orange had very few troops, and probably would attempt nothing; thus Philippe could take any gambit that might seem reasonable to him. Louvois obviously shared Louis' optimism, for he even doubted that the Dutch would have any cavalry or that the Dutch infantry would have "shoes when it arrives in your vicinity."[21] Louvois, like the king, was wrong. The Prince of Orange found some cavalry and his infantry did have shoes. Louvois, seeing them advance, wrote to Philippe's adviser, Marshal d'Humières, "If the Spanish and Dutch armies advance to relieve Saint-Omer, Monsieur will have no alternative but to retire unless he is promptly reenforced by troops from the king. . . . His Majesty wants me to tell you that he does not want Monsieur to commit a bad mistake." It would be almost as bad for Monsieur to lose a battle as for the king to do so.

However, Louis and his minister, not wanting Monsieur to be caught in this tight situation of inferiority, began to collect troops from all sides to reinforce his army: cavalry from all the border fortifications on the Flanders front, detachments from the army before Cambrai, and other small isolated groups that could be picked up and sent on to Monsieur, soon joined the army near Saint-Omer. On April 9, Louis sent his brother another memorandum telling him of the potential threat from the enemy army assembling at Ghent: "The king approves strongly that Monsieur should leave his position only to take a stronger one . . . in which to await the Prince of Orange." Obviously Louis expected Philippe to stand on the defensive, but he added, ". . . the king gives no order to Monsieur, he simply offers advice leaving to Monsieur the liberty to conform if he finds it practicable, and if he judges it apropos for the good of his Majesty's service."[22] Two days later, when it was clear that the Prince of Orange was actually marching against Monsieur's army, Louvois first urged Philippe to throw out a cavalry screen, and then a few hours later he added, "I want you to know that his Majesty waits with great inquietude for news from you. Your Royal Highness will give him great pleasure by a little letter. . . ."[23] The next day Philippe fought a battle at Cassel in which he captured 2,500 prisoners, 40 flags, 14 standards, as well as cannons, munitions, and the personal equipment of his enemy. The French losses were 1,558 killed or wounded. The little man of ribbons, rouge, jewelry, and mincing ways had reached his greatest hour and proven himself to be a Bourbon, the grandson of Henry IV, the son of Louis XIII, and the cousin of the great Condé.[24]

Of course Philippe did not win this battle by himself. Louis had had the wisdom to add Marshal Luxembourg, one of his best—if not *the* best —soldiers on his "team," to join Marshal d'Humières and the others who "commanded under Monsieur's orders." In addition to Luxembourg, he also sent very strong reenforcements. Thus in a very real sense the official history is right in saying that Monsieur "knew that the success of the battle was principally due to the care of the king . . . equally prudent and equally generous care that had sent the aid without which he would not have been able to win."[25] And yet the sycophantic courtiers who tried to give Louis, rather than his brother, the entire credit for the battle by claiming that Louis' wisdom was always fatal to the projects of the Prince of Orange, that he "always penetrated his designs and observed his intentions from a distance . . . [and always] frustrated him," also tells us something. Would Louis have tolerated such talk if he had not been insecure about himself and his actions? The comparison between what happened at Cassel and what did not happen at Heurtevise the year before must have been painful, and undoubtedly Louis knew it was the subject for much discussion.[26]

Yet the affair at Cassel was just the kind of fight that Louis dreaded the most. He had been at the crossing of the Rhine when impulsive action caused unnecessary casualties, and could have jeopardized the whole operation; he surely knew of the bloody inconclusive results of the battle of Seneffe, which could have been a modest victory if Condé had been willing to break off, rather than impulsively insisting on action that could not succeed. All his life Louis was to be afraid of the impulsive soldier who waved his sword and cried, "Kill! Kill!" As we shall see, when he came to direct the course of war by himself he was not adverse to a battle if it could gain an advantage, but he always insisted that his commanders should seek to "gain an advantage" by their position, to fight when there were "good chances for success," and never to risk an "unfortunate affair" that could be "disagreeable to my army."[27]

Philippe never again had a command that could be used to fight a pitched battle, but it may be that Louis' caution rather than the usually attributed "jealousy" was responsible for his placing Philippe in command of the coastal forces rather than of a field army. If he was jealous of his brother (and he may well have been), it does not show in the letter that he wrote to Condé in reply to the old prince's congratulations: "You are right to congratulate me. . . . If I had won it in person, I could not be more pleased either with the grandeur of the action, the importance of the events, or above all for the honor of my brother. . . . I am not surprised that you express joy on this occasion; it is only natural that you should experience what you have allowed others to experience by similar successes."[28] At the public level, on orders of the king, *Te Deums* throughout France, fireworks at the Palais-Royal, and sermons and speeches celebrated Philippe's victory.

The defeat of the Dutch army at Cassel sealed the fate of both Saint-Omer and Cambrai. Jean Racine tells us that thus Louis captured fortifications (Valenciennes, Saint-Omer, and Cambrai) that had "been the terror of his frontiers." A glance at the map will show that Louis was straightening out his northern frontier to give it a defensible line—to make it the dueling field that Vauban had urged. By 1677 the expansionist dreams of 1672 had faded into the mists of Dutch resistance, the military realities of Europe, and the growing realization that in England as well as in the Netherlands there were many men who could not tolerate French control of the outlet of the Scheldt and the city of Antwerp. Charles II had been forced in 1674 to make a separate peace, and now the French ambassador to England wrote to the king saying there was a "hatred of France" in influential parts of England, that although the English king was friendly, he believed that France had taken about all of the Spanish Netherlands the French kingdom needed to round out its frontiers. Thus military strategy as well as political reality joined hands to make Louis satisfied with any peace giving him limited successes in the Spanish Netherlands.

The situation in the kingdom continued to make even more urgent the need for peace. Primi Visconti is only one of many eloquent witnesses to the fact that there was ominous economic distress in France. It was not a crisis on the scale of the 1690's, but the rising death rate, the difficulty in the collection of taxes, the cries of the people—all indicated bad harvests and the danger of famine that stalked so many years of this epoch.[29] Even the "fire-eaters" who surrounded the king and who could hope for great personal gain from war, understood that the kingdom must find peace. Louis ordered his armies to stand on the defensive, and tried to find a way of driving a wedge between the Dutch and their allies, and in the United Netherlands, between the "patrician" politicians and the Prince of Orange. When Prince William managed the great coup of marrying the niece of Charles II, these maneuvers became more and more necessary, for Princess Mary, as the eldest daughter of James, Duke of York, was in line for the throne of England after her father and uncle, neither of whom was expected to produce a male heir. She was a Protestant and acceptable to the Francophobes in England. Now, if ever, was the time secretly to assure the Dutch politicians that France had no intentions of annexing Dutch territory or of threatening the Dutch frontiers; a "rectification" of the frontier made at Aix-la-Chapelle and the annexation of Franche-Comté would satisfy the French king who also would be willing to withdraw Colbert's anti-Dutch tariff laws. Prince William might insist that the United Netherlands was "honor-bound" to stand with its German allies, but the Dutch merchants regarded "honor" as a nobleman's virtue, quite unsuited to the political and commercial arena of Europe. The negotiations at Nymwegen, and behind closed doors at Versailles, went on.

France needed peace; to get it was the problem. "The efforts of my enemies leagued against me," writes Louis, "obliged me to take great precautions. I resolved after finishing the campaign of 1677 to employ my forces only in places where they would be absolutely necessary."[30] Thus the troops that had established themselves in Sicily were withdrawn. They probably could not stay there anyway, for it would be difficult and perhaps unprofitable to hold the island with the English Francophobes concerned about French naval power in the Mediterranean. This was another "retreat" like the one of 1674 when the ideas of Vauban and Chamlay reversed the grandiose schemes of 1672. Mazarin and Richelieu had wished to control the "gates" to the kingdom; the "lines" that were in the process of making the frontiers were a later seventeenth-century counterpart of those "gates." Both sought a defensible military frontier.

Unfortunately for Louis, he could not stop the war simply by saying that he wanted only defensible frontiers, and by assuring Dutch politicians of his good intentions toward them. The Germans wanted to be sure that their interests would be taken care of, and William of Orange had almost convinced the Francophobes in England that they must join the coalition.

If this should come about, there was no way to foresee peace. However, Prince William only imperfectly represented the United Netherlands; many of the magistrates and merchants, as well as the little people who paid heavy taxes, were anxious to end the conflict. Louis tells us that he decided upon a bold plan to tip the balance in the United Netherlands toward peace: he would seek a dramatic victory on the very frontier of the United Netherlands to frighten them into a willingness to discuss terms realistically. The decision undoubtedly was made in council.

There were three possible targets: Luxembourg, Namur, or Ghent. Of these Ghent was nearest the Dutch frontier, and the king "fancied" capturing this "fortification that the greatest captains of our century had not dared to attempt, or before which they had come to misfortune." This description of the city, of course, was the result of naïve pride supported by hindsight and small historical knowledge, but it was true that the capture of Ghent would be a considerable victory. The city could most easily be taken if it were surprised; this the French were determined to do.

As Louis tells the story, he did it all by himself, and if Louvois' orders are to be taken seriously, Louis did have a large part in the plans, for the minister's letters are replete with expressions like—"It is his Majesty's intention . . ."; "the King has ordered me to tell you . . . ," etc. The French pretended that their intention was to attack from Alsace—either Luxembourg or an invasion of Germany. Louvois pretended to be ill; Louis with his guards and other household troops, accompanied by the court, and "the ladies," departed for Metz to take command. Secretly munitions and cannon were on the move, and Marshal d'Humières, alerted to his role, quickly marched into Flanders with 10,000 cavalrymen. The blow fell on Ghent on March 1; two days later there were 60,000 men before the city, and a few days later Louis arrived from Metz after a series of forced marches to take over command. The "ladies," including Madame de Montespan, who was pregnant, were left behind to put up with inconveniences as best they could. The trenches before Ghent were opened on March 5; on March 8 the city government surrendered; on March 10 the Spanish governor gave up the citadel and took his garrison to Antwerp. Louis tells us that he "forgot nothing that could advance the siege," but the ease of the conquest seems to indicate that, next to Vauban, surprise was the most important factor in the operation. Louis and "the ladies" had their part in making that surprise possible.[31]

The fall of Ghent ended the war, even though an English expeditionary force landed at Ostende without a declaration of hostilities. Louis published his terms for peace, which were entirely favorable to the Dutch.

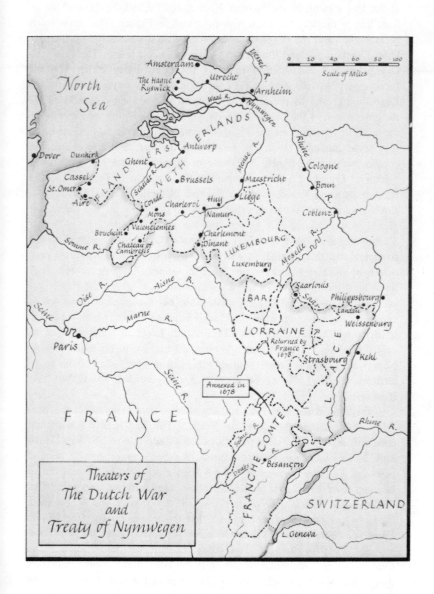

Theaters of
The Dutch War
and
Treaty of Nymwegen

There were a few diplomatic exchanges, and then a Dutch mission arrived at the king's camp in the Spanish Netherlands "to ask for peace," or at least that is the way the scene was presented in France. The terms were "reasonable" and the negotiations at Nymwegen for a treaty between the United Netherlands and France went sailing to a conclusion. The Prince of Orange made one last effort to block the treaty by attacking Marshal Luxembourg by surprise, but Prince William was never a match for Luxembourg, and so the attack was beaten off, and then repudiated by the government of the United Netherlands. Once the Dutch withdrew from the war, the emperor and the King of Spain found themselves isolated, for they could not hope to engage England in the war, nor to continue the conflict without the Dutch. The King of Spain paid the bill for French "victory." Franche-Comté was joined to the kingdom of France, and the frontier between France and the Spanish Netherlands was rationalized. Louis gave up several enclaves that had fallen to him by the last peace, but gained substanially so that he achieved the *pré carré* (dueling field) that Vauban had demanded. It was not what either Mazarin or Louis had wished to secure, but this frontier at least came close to being a defensible one, drawn by military realities rather than by religion, language, commercial lines, or dynastic rights. In the Rhineland the new settlement largely re-affirmed the ambiguous Treaty of Münster, but the emperor remained in control of Philippsburg, while the French acquired Fribourg with a passage to Brisach. The settlement for Lorraine left Louis in occupation of its capital, and since Duke Charles V refused to return to his lands without Nancy and Longwy, French soldiers remained in occupation of the entire territory, thereby assuring France a reasonably suitable frontier on that front also.

Fredrick William of Brandenburg tried to refuse to accept the pro-vision that returned Pomerania to Sweden. This had been his important conquest, and he believed it to be a necessary addition to his lands. How-ever, he was unable to resist the threat of French power, and in the end bowed to Louis' will. Sweden had not been much help to France, but as his only loyal ally, Louis would not allow Sweden to be dispossessed of this territory. There were other clauses in this treaty: one of the most interesting of them was the demand that the emperor must free Bishop Egon von Fürstenburg, a French agent who had been "illegally" im-prisoned early in the war, and whose later career at Strasbourg and Cologne we shall encounter farther on in this book. But the most important thing about the Treaty of Nymwegen was the fact that it straightened the French frontiers with the Spanish Netherlands and confirmed the shadowy provisions of the treaties of 1648, thereby providing Louis with the legal basis for a broad series of annexations that would rationalize his frontiers opposite Germany.

With this treaty, Louis XIV ended a significant chapter in his career. He tells us, "I was resolved to make peace . . . but I wished to conclude it gloriously for me and advantageously for my kingdom. I wished to reimburse myself by the rights of conquest . . . and to console myself thus for the end of a war that I had fought with both pleasure and success."[32] The king understood, of course, that his war aims of 1672 had not been accomplished, but he also understood that his armies had been able to stand off a powerful coalition, until his diplomacy could break the solid wall that his enemies presented to him. The treaties of peace were obviously a victory, and yet they were only a modest victory, perhaps even an equivocal one. Nonetheless, his subjects now hailed him as Louis the Great, and erected statues and monuments to his grandeur; and foreign princes, impressed with the strength of his arms, began to pay him the compliment of imitating the military organization that had proven to be so formidable. After Nymwegen, Louis was on the verge of entering that period of his career that was resplendent with the glamor of the Sun King.

19

THE COURT OF APOLLO*

IN 1638 THE MINT STRUCK A COIN with the zodiacal sign of September 5, 1638, and the inscription *Ortus Solis Gallici* (Thus Rises the Sun of France); it was to commemorate the birth of Louis *le dieudonné*. Throughout his life he was to be associated with the sun. His age knew and used classical antiquity, especially as myth and symbol, and was conscious of the tradition that associated Caesar with the sun, Pharoah with *Re;* why should it not associate its own king with Apollo? Thus the title Sun King was thrust upon Louis XIV even before he understood its meaning, and the society that nourished its literary tastes with stories of pagan deities expected him to pun and play on the theme, and to identify himself with the sun god.[1] Thus the fêtes, the balls, the ballets, the decorations, the *feux d'artifice* that gladdened his days from youth to old age repeated endlessly the symbol of the flaming sun. The father of his people, the one who brought joy, the hero king: the King of France was also the Sun King. He has marched ever since through the pages of history accompanied by the sign of the sun flamboyant.

This does not mean that the King of France stood apart from other men as a ceremonial icon, a figure to be admired—perhaps even worshiped —from a distance, a ruler with only formal contacts with other men. He *was* this ceremonial figure, but he was also a man living with other men within a system of etiquette that defined the limits of familiarity. By the mid-seventeenth century the kings of France had established several levels of power and social importance, and Louis' decision to exclude the great nobles and members of his family from the direction of the government sharpened cleavages of social rank. The king had all power, both its *mystique* and its reality. He shared the latter with his ministers, his secretaries of state, and perhaps with his ambassadors, marshals, high clergymen, and the people who helped him manage the government and the army. For the most part these people were of relatively humble origin and almost completely dependent upon him for their fortunes and places. Thus he could trust them with the realities of power. Louis shared the *mystique* of power with the "people of quality" whose birth and wealth gave social preeminence. These were the princes of the blood, cardinals and bishops of the church, noble families with connections with sovereign princes abroad, dukes, and peers of the realm. Below them were a host of counts and marquis who aspired to rise to the eminence of the peers and dukes. All of these people and their wives had social prestige but little real power. The king's own brother found himself courting the war minister Louvois to secure favor; the Prince of Condé was not above courting Louis' personal secretary Rose to secure a request. But in the social order these "people of quality" had the right to live more or less as companions of the king. They held the honorific offices of the royal households, their sons were enlisted in the guards, and some of them reached high office in the king's army.[2]

In the first few years after Mazarin's death the etiquette was less rigorous than it was to become by the end of the decade. After all, Louis was only twenty-three years old and surrounded by young people who had grown up with him—all of them filled with high spirits, intrigued by pleasures, excited by passions, and eager to live. Mazarin's death released the court from the sober influence of an old and sick man; Louis probably regretted his passing, but most of the young court happily bade him farewell and very likely hoped that Anne would soon follow him. These young people around the king were not allowed to forget who was king, but they lived with him in easy familiarity. In this first decade one did not see the great mob that was later to come to Versailles, for it was not yet customary for men "to live at court" unless they had some reason for being there. Thus the young court was made up of the officials of the king's government and the officers of his army and of the royal households.

French kings had always lived their lives in full view, and under Louis XIV this came to mean that the king's life became a court ceremony. Only when he was closeted with his ministers, or visiting his mother or his wife or a mistress, were his courtiers denied the opportunity of seeing the king. From the moment he opened his eyes in the morning until the candle was blown out at night, Louis lived surrounded by his servants, his household, officers of his army, prelates of the church, and noblemen—all hoping for favor. Thus the dramatic events of the day became almost theatrical: the king's *lever* and *coucher,* his *dîner* and *souper* were all elaborately staged. The masters of ceremony ransacked the past of the kingdom, the practices of foreign courts, and the ceremonials of antiquity to give these occasions solemnity.[3] It became important who "gave the King his shirt," who "held his candle at night," the service of his table; even the bringing of the "pierced chair" took on solemn overtones. There was a crowd in his chamber when his chaplain led him through his prayers, sometimes a noisy mob that had to be warned to silence. There was a crowd when he ate; a crowd followed his strolls through the garden, his expeditions of the hunt, his attendance at the theater. Since it was the king who could give offices in the church, in the army, in the households, in the civil bureaucracy, pensions, and *gratifications* from the treasury—all of these people were on the alert to be noticed and anxious to please. But there were so many of them that their progress often created considerable disorder. Primi Visconti, who was familiar with the practices at Rome and in the courts of Spain, describes the press that followed the King of France:

I was stupefied to see the Cardinals de Retz and de Bonzi, and other ecclesiastics who occupy so high a rank in Rome, reduced to an equality with the mere priests and often jostled by the crowds. And it was the same for all except the princes of the blood . . . the explanation is given that there are too many people of quality to pay any attention to any single one of them.

Primi went on to say that the French despise anyone from whom they can expect nothing; therefore, since the king alone had favors to give, he alone was important.

Louis encouraged this disorder that resulted in bringing the great ones to a plane of equality. His policy toward the "people of quality"—indeed, toward the entire nobility—unquestionably tended to undermine their status. As long as they had to contend with one another for the favor of his glance, it would be easy to curb a "cabal of the Important Ones" or even a *Fronde*. If the great ones of the land must serve the king at his table, carry his candle, and compete for his smiles, they become his slaves. On the other hand, Louis was overly sensitive to their social importance, to the rank that they had a right to maintain vis-à-vis each other, even to their great superiority over the men who actually exercised power in his name. Louis and the kings who had preceded him had created these dukes and peers; therefore, in honoring them, he honored the tradition and the history of the kingdom. All this cannot conceal the fact that by separating the reality and the *mystique* of power and position, Louis began the process that in the next century almost made the nobility into a parasitical class without meaning to the real life of the nation.

The royal family was set off from all the other nobility as "children of France." Their place in the scale of prestige was indicated by their titles. All "children of France" were "Monsieur" or "Mademoiselle" or "Madame," but there were little distinctions that indicated place within this rank: the eldest son of the king was Monseigneur le Dauphin; the brother of the king, Philippe, and his wife, Henriette, were Monsieur and Madame (it was not necessary to add Duke of Orléans). The head of the house of Condé-Bourbon—in the first place the Great Condé, and later his son—as first prince of the blood was Monsieur le Prince;[4] his wife, Madame la Princesse. Their eldest son was Monsieur le Duc. Other sons of the Condé-Bourbon house added the name of their apanage—"Le Prince de Conti," for example. The eldest daughter of Monsieur and Madame became Mademoiselle; the eldest daughter of Louis' late Uncle Gaston was La Grande Mademoiselle. When three sons of the dauphin appeared, they became dukes, but the name of their apanage (Burgundy, Anjou, Berry) was added to the name. Naturally all other noblemen indicated the name of their family as well as of their estate (*terre*) to their titles. Thus, for example, the husband of Louis' second mistress was named Louis-Henry de Pardeilhan de Gondrin, Marquis de Montespan et d'Antin. Their son, in due course, became the Duke d'Antin. One has only to read Saint-Simon to discover how important these things were. The royal family, which alone had access to both the *mystique* and the reality of power, could simplify its titles and thereby indicate its exalted place in the hierarchy.

The lines of precedence in the court were clearly drawn; some of the practices actually went back to the Valois, some to Henry IV, some were obviously dredged up from Byzantine records or copied from the court of Spain. The order of rank had been fixed soon after Henry IV, as the first Bourbon king, mounted the throne. Highest were the princes of the blood in the order of their nearness to the throne; after them came the nobles whose families were sovereign princes outside of the kingdom: the house of Lorraine (Guise, Armagnac, etc.), the house of Savoy (Nemours, Soissons, etc.), the house of Gonzagua and Mantua (Nevers), and the house of Longueville. Louis XIV was to place the Bourbon bastard lines legitimized by him and by Henry IV between the princes of the blood and the "foreign" nobles. Next in line came the peers and dukes and their families. These ranks formerly had been of utmost importance, but Louis XIII and Louis XIV greatly diluted their significance by creating a great number of them. Even so, these families, along with the ones above them and the cardinals, who ranked as princes of the blood, and archbishops and bishops who took their rank from their sees, and the marshals of France, all of whom hoped to become dukes and peers—these were the "people of quality" in the kingdom. There were perhaps 100,000 to 120,000 men, women, and children who, as counts or marquis, counted as "noblemen," but there were not more than 250 men and women in this elite rank of "people of quality" who had the right to live in more or less easy intercourse with the king.

The lesser nobility who wished to enjoy the king's favor joined the army, the clergy, or entered the civil bureaucracy to become officers, counselors, ambassadors, or even, with luck, secretaries of state. In any of these roles they might hope to merit the king's attention and perhaps mount to the rank of bishop, or duke and peer. These lesser people sometimes look like the vultures of a decadent feudal society because of their crude efforts to find place and position; they lived at the court when they could afford it or when they could get an appointment, but they were not in the elite group mentioned above that had privileges of living near the king.

Even among such people of quality there were differences. One test of status was the right to sit down in the presence of the royal family. The dauphin, and later the dauphine and their children, and the princesses of the blood had the right to a tabouret (a sort of footstool) when in the presence of the king; everyone else had to stand. In the presence of the queen, only the princesses of the blood and cardinals (as princes of the church) had the right to a tabouret; the princes of the blood, along with everyone else, had to stand. In the presence of the dauphin and dauphine, princes and princesses of the blood, along with the cardinals, had the tabouret; in the presence of legitimate grandchildren of the king, the royal family and cardinals had the right to a chair with a back, while women of quality had the tabouret, and their men stood. In the presence of princes and princesses of the blood, cardinals and foreign dukes and duchesses could have an arm chair, while men and women of quality were simply seated. The king could, and sometimes did, give the tabouret to this or that person in recognition of great services or favor, and needless to say, these were much sought-after honors. Only at the gaming tables were these rules suspended, for anyone willing to risk his money had the right to sit, even though the king himself was at the table.

There were other marks of distinction. Following Byzantine practices, on January 16, 1665, Louis granted to a favored few the right to wear a special blue coat embroidered with gold, but only those with a registered letter of permission could wear this costume.[5] Later in the reign when the court was en route to, or at, Marly, a special few were allowed to have their doors chalked with the words "for M. de ————" and this "for" became a favor especially sought after. There were other marks of distinction; for example, whenever it became known that a lady enjoying the favors of the king might become his mistress, the other ladies always stood in her presence.

The king's meals were another test of quality. Ordinarily he ate alone, served by the officers of his household and under the eyes of the court. Occasionally he invited his brother to eat with him; sometimes a select group of the ladies who also often shared his carriage. Other princes of the blood might also have this honor. When he was on campaign, he frequently ate with the superior officers and gentlemen of quality who happened to be in attendance, for in the field some of the etiquette was relaxed. This stiffness had its purposes: the seventeenth-century ruler associated his rule with God, and the *mystique* of his court allowed the courtiers to know how the angels felt in the presence of the deity. In the later years of the reign it became part of the "cult of the King."[6]

How did one "live at court"? In these first decades before Versailles became the axis of the king's life, the court moved about from Saint-Germain to Versailles, to Fontainebleau, to Vincennes, even down to Chambord on the other side of the Loire. These trips were colorful affairs, perhaps also painful to the ladies who spent most of their time in springless carriages and without "rest rooms" en route. But the guards, the mounted courtiers, the picnic meals, the decorated carriages and wagons all made a brave show to the peasants and townspeople who turned out to see the progress of their king. In these first years the trips through the countryside were accompanied with wild galloping through the woods; later they were more staid affairs. When the court arrived at its destination, then the business of being king and courtiers took over the order of the day. We can follow these affairs in part through the pages of the *Gazette* and of Loret's *La Muze historique*. The latter was a rhymed news sheet carrying gossipy stories about the personalities of the court, usually speaking in extravagant terms of the bravery and gallantry of the men, of the beauty and charm of the women, of the wonders of court events. Molière would have needed to go no further to find the dialogues for his satires of the *précieuses* of the day. The *Gazette* was only slightly less exuberant in its stories of the court; the *Misanthrope* is probably wrong when he says that his valet's name appeared in this sheet, but it is true that anyone who *was* anyone could read his name there. Did the king read these papers? We do not know, but the kingdom could read them and follow therewith his public life.[7]

In the first two decades of the personal reign, life at court was indeed delightful. Hunting parties during the days; at night boating trips on the moats and ponds, or strolls through the gardens or forest paths followed by violins. It was a life spiced with gallantry, with young men and young women eager for each other's favors. In these early days, several of the young men even dared to contest with the king for the attention of this or that beauty.[8] For entertainment the young people could depend upon their own talents, supplemented by the professional musicians and entertainers attached to the court. They held ballets, balls, horse shows, pageants, and contests of skill of all sorts. The king and his brother, as well as Villeroi or the Duke of Guise, or Guiche, thought it proper to take a role in the ballet, a part in the pageant, or even a try at amateur dramatics. Figure dancing was great fun; dogs and horses were good companions in field and forest; entertainers provided music and comedies, and in the background there was plenty of food and drink to spice the hours of pleasure. Des Noyers, writing to the Queen of Poland, gave her this little picture of the court in 1667:

The French court is not like yours. Its occupations are different, for its study is to find new amusements. The King is at Versailles fêting with his troop of ladies; you know these are Madame de Montespan, Mlle. de la Vallière, Madame de Roure, Madame de Heudicourt, Mlle. de Fiennes . . . and two or three more whom I do not recall. *Voilà* the royal troop!

As Voltaire said, "Louis liked the ladies, and it was reciprocal." In these early years and in his later ones, he always surrounded himself with beauties; they traveled in his carriage, they danced in his ballets, they joined in his games and his gambling. It must be noted, however, that Louis also worked six to ten hours a day with his ministers on the affairs of state; the ladies were not allowed to interfere with the proper *métier* of the king. It would seem that these were the years when Louis worked hard both at his trade and at the pleasures of the world.

Everyone loved the ballet. In the wintertime the court would put on from one to three ballets a week, and everyone took part. Like a modern bourgeois family that secures dancing or music lessons for its children, the king provided the Academy of the Dance to brighten up the court performances. Loret, in 1663, offered a poem commemorating the event:

> The King does not cease to cherish
> The *beaux arts* that he made to flourish
> In his kingdom of France;
> He recognized especially the dance
> Which gives grace and *politesse*
> To both people and *noblesse*.
>
> It is a hundred times more charming
> Than tournaments and combatting,

Which even as symbols so grand
Only upset the peace of the land.
In their place, balls and ballets.
Either serious or diverting,
Make the fruits of peace alluring;
To achieve all this his Majesty,
By virtue of his supreme authority,
Has created the Academy of the Dance.[9]

Often Louis, with "incredible agility and grace," took a part in the ballets. His favorite impersonation was Apollo, but he also appeared as Alexander the Great, as a shepherd, and in many other roles. All the young people in the court enjoyed taking part in these ballets. The *Gazette* and *La Muze historique* were often hard put, it seems, to find new ways of describing the "unbelievable beauty," the "touching grace," the "charm passing all credence" of the women; the gallantry, the "perfect skill," and the "handsome figures" of the men. Loret sang of the charms of each actor, even of the queen when she could not take a part: "the beautiful Thérèse who now goes only in a chair so that she may save the second fruit now formed in her womb." Or of Madame, "who appears in her place with so much charm and grace," and of La Vallière, the "young shepherdess whom the heavens have endowed with that which is given only to the best of its friends: beauty of heart, wisdom, tenderness . . . an object in which glory and modesty are perfectly united." Of Madame de Montespan who has "all the touching graces that make a lady charming." And of course the king, "who merits the title of the most judicious King ever placed under the skies, the King who is the flower of his age, as charming as he is wise." With such a press to applaud its performances, the actors had little need to worry about possible critics.

Nonetheless, Louis danced his last ballet in 1669; and for the rest of his life he remained a spectator of the dance. There has been much speculation about his reasons for giving up a pleasure that he had obviously enjoyed very much, long before age deprived him of the grace and vigor to do it well. It has been suggested that the line in Racine's *Britannicus* intimating that the Romans disdained their emperor for playing in the theater may have given him pause, or that he may have read the passage in Tacitus (*Annals* XIV, 308) from which Racine drew his story.[10] Whatever the reason, Louis gave up the role of actor when he was only thirty-one years old.

These ballets with their formalized *entrées,* their stylized stories, and their fixed patterns were only one form of the royal entertainment. The young court held parties, fêtes, pageants, and balls on every possible occasion. Most of them were in the royal residences, but they did visit other châteaus as well. *La Muze historique* tells us of a party given by Philippe at Saint-Cloud in May 1662. The "pompous and charming palace where one sees hundreds of fountains jetting water and a thousand other wonderful things" was the scene of a magnificent *régale* at which one did not lack violins, or the ball, or theatrical spectacle, for Monsieur "produced such things wonderfully." The whole court was there, they danced all night, they had a marvelous feast. A few years later a similar party given by Condé at Chantilly entertained the whole court with feasting, hunting, dancing, theaters, and the like at a cost of not less than 150,000 livres (an enormous sum of money)! This was the occasion on which Monsieur Vatel—Condé's *maître d'hôtel,* who had filled a similar function for Fouquet earlier—committed suicide, presumably because some fish that he had ordered did not arrive at the proper time. Fortunately, not all the *maîtres d'hôtel* of the era took their tasks so seriously.[11]

Some of these affairs were much more important than others. The Place de Carrousel still marks the place where Louis XIV held a famous "horse show" and tournament in 1662. A carrousel was at once a pageant, a display of skillful horsemanship, military maneuvers, and tests of skill in riding with the lance at a ring. In the preceding century the tourneys included tilting, but the death of Henry II as the result of a split lance piercing the eyepiece of his helmet tended to discourage such violent sport. In the Grand Carrousel of 1662 the men were divided into five troops, including the courtiers and soldiers, so that the whole court was involved. The first company was the "Romans" led by Rex Romanae Imperator, Louis himself! There were three to four hundred horsemen in this troop; the other four had about a hundred and fifty each. The "Persians" were led by Dux Aurelaenensis Persicae, none other than Philippe, Duke of Orléans. They were followed by the "Turks" led by Condeus Turcarum Turmae, the victor of Rocroi—Condé himself! Then came the "Indians" led by his son, Dux Anguiennaeus Indorum, the Duke of Enghien, and last, the "American Indians" led by Dux Guisius Americanae, the Duke of Guise, who as the senior member of the house of Lorraine, was the first nobleman of the kingdom, after the princes of the blood. The whole show was a masquerade as well as a display of skill. The stallions were richly caparisoned with ostrich plumes, ribbons, colorful blankets, and silvered harnesses. Soldiers with kettle drums and trumpets hailed the emperor who stood stiffly at attention, holding the truncheon of office. The Persians with their crooked scimitars, the Turks with their great turbans, the grotesquely clad Americans carrying war clubs, wearing stuffed birds on their headgear and with "snakes" entwined in their horses' tails remind us of the colorful shows that every generation that has known horses—from the tournaments of the medieval era to the rodeos of the American West—has loved to put on. There were "horse quadrilles" to demonstrate the abilities of the companies, races to test the speed of horses, and riding at the ring to show off the skills of the "knights." Marie-Thérèse was the Queen of the Carrousel and gave out the prizes to the victors. It was so much fun that the whole show was repeated later in the summer by a cast of Romans, Muscovites, Moors, Persians, and Turks.[12]

The most famous party of the decade, perhaps of the whole reign, perhaps even in the whole history of France, was the three-day festival at Versailles in May 1664: the Fête of the Enchanted Island. As Louis first planned the party, it was to be a little affair, a lottery similar to the ones that the cardinal used to give; he wrote to Colbert on May 2:

Since I last saw you I have had an idea that will cost me dearly, but it will give much pleasure to the people here, particularly to the Queens. I do not wish it to cost more than 3,000 pistoles, which, well employed, should buy enough jewelry. . . . Take care of it when you get this letter . . . try to find in Paris those things that will be pleasant and agreeable . . . no one knows better than you why I want them . . . [Madame Colbert was caring for Louis' child by Mademoiselle de la Vallière who was still much in the king's favor].

Louis went on to suggest brooches, rings, bracelets, and the like for some thirty-five ladies, including Mademoiselle de la Vallière and Madame de Montespan. When the party actually came off a little later, it had grown to a big affair held at the hunting lodge of Louis XIII at Versailles. The lottery in which "all tickets were good" was only a part of the festivities. Versailles with its forest, its gardens, reflecting ponds, and charming little châteaus provided a bucolic setting. Ostensibly the affair was "for the two Queens," but everyone knew that Mademoiselle de la Vallière was the real queen of the fête.[13]

Versailles became the "island" enchanted by the great magician Alcine, who by a magic spell held the entire court captive for three days. There were pageants, tourneys, races, ballets, dances, dramatics, music, and mountains of food for a troop of fauns, satyrs, gods and goddesses, knights and ladies. On the first day the "knights" displayed their valor. Their leader was Roger (Louis), while Rolland (Philippe), Olger the Dane (de Noailles), Giudon the Wild (Saint-Aignan), Griffon the White (d'Armagnac), and others, also disguised, maneuvered their horses, tilted the ring, and displayed their skills as horsemen. Then there were tableaus marking the four seasons with papier-mâché animals: an elephant, a camel, a horse, and a strange creature resembling a bear. Later in the evening the people of quality ate with the king at a huge semicircular table, while dancers entertained the company. As night fell, torches gave off weird lights suitable for the "spell."

The following days were filled with gay entertainment. A comedy, a ballet, a musical tragedy that might be called an opera, a première by Molière. At night an eight-sided table, loaded with food and decorated by a center piece—a "baroque" architectural structure with columns, statues, floral chains, torches, and papier-mâché figures. Armed men held back the crowds of courtiers until it was time to eat. These guards, presumably the king's bodyguards, were always present at Louis' parties. The final show was held around the grand canal, which was much less pretentious than it is today; all around the edge there were lights of torches and lanterns, while small boats with lights made the water into a fairyland. Skyrockets and other fireworks provided sporadic illumination, and the king's violins made music. The final act came when the spell was broken by the firing of the magic castle at the end of the canal; the gods and goddesses, fauns and satyrs again became courtiers of the Sun King, a humdrum occupation compared with the "delights" provided by the spell of Alcine.[14]

If one reads carefully the accounts of the parties and horse shows, an interesting theme runs through all of them. These "games" are a "substitute" for war, an outlet for the martial spirits of the courtiers, or they are practice so that the courtiers will not forget their military skills. Monsieur de Bizincourt writes, "Your Majesty has established a peace so profound that those of your subjects whose birth and status make them eager to serve in your armies would soon forget the exercises of Mars if they had only ordinary pleasures . . . ," but these tourneys gave them practice for, or an alternative to, martial action.[15]

We should also note that Louis sometimes used these "parties" to mask his intentions in high politics. A big affair at court "covered" the invasion of Franche-Comté in 1668; another, as we have seen, "covered" the attack on the Spanish Netherlands in 1675 and another in 1678. Europe might think that the King of France was concerned only for his own pleasures, and Louis was willing to let Europe believe such things. The king did enjoy the fêtes, but memoirs and letters attest to the fact that he often was absent while the court enjoyed itself. Both his ministers and his mistresses distracted royal attention. Unhappily Louis himself tells us almost nothing of his personal attitude toward the entertainments of the court.

Anyone who follows the court in the pages of the *Gazette* knows that there was a religious procession of some kind in Paris almost every week, and that very often the court either participated or held one of its own. He also will know that the king and his family spent much of their time in religious observances; the King of France was the most Christian king and the church was a real part of his government in the society. The two queens made a great show of their piety; especially Anne, who spent as much time as she could in churches and convents, for her illness warned her that she soon would follow the cardinal to the grave. The court's religious calendar followed the feasts of the church. Lent and preparation for Easter naturally took up much time and attention; on Holy Thursdays the queen "washed the feet of thirteen poor women . . . ," while the king did the same "for thirteen poor men and then served them food carried by princes of the blood." Every year the pattern follows in about the same track. On Holy Saturday, and again after mass on Easter Sunday, Louis "touched" the sick, sometimes hundreds of them. On All Souls' Day Louis, "wearing the collar of the Holy Spirit and accompanied by many courtiers heard low mass at the church of the Feuillants where Cardinal Antoine gave him communion." Then he heard high mass and afterward touched the sick. "The Queen did similar devotions at the Carmelites . . . after dinner their Majesties went to the parish church at Saint-Germain-en-Laye to hear an eloquent sermon by Father Cosme du Boc . . . then to Vespers chanted in the chapel. . . ." On the fête of Saint Hubert (patron of the deer and of hunting), Louis often gave a hunt in honor of some member of the family. At Christmas there was a great round of celebrations as the religious festivities reached the climax of the coming of the Christ Child. The feast of the purification, of the blessing of the candles, of the coming of the wise men, and especially of the Assumption, brought the court, the king, and his family into the churches and religious processions.

When it was a matter of *Te Deums* in thanksgiving for the birth of a child, recovery from illness, or victory over the foe, the cathedral chapters and all local dignitaries were ordered to attend. (There are literally hundreds of pamphlets in the *Bibliothèque Nationale* describing these *Te Deums*.) On the fête of the Assumption nearly all France was required to celebrate. The preamble of a letter signed by the king, ordering the Parlement of Paris to march in the procession, gives the story:

Wishing that the procession which was ordained in the year 1638 by the late King, our honored Lord and Father after he put the kingdom under the protection of the Virgin, should be made the fifteenth of August each year in the Cathedral Church of Paris with pomp suitable to an action filled with piety, we order you to take part in the ceremonies.[16]

A similar letter went to the other sovereign courts and the Châtelet to assure the presence of colorful robes in the procession. Thus could the people understand that the kingdom of France properly celebrated the dedication that had given it Louis XIV. We know, however, that the bishops often failed to hold this special celebration.[17]

Seventeenth-century men made much of military orders of knighthood and decorations, but in France these things were also closely related to religious ceremonials. Henry III had founded the Order of the Holy Spirit to attach the great lords more closely to his court. It was a sort of "lodge" or "secret society" with initiation "mysteries" to which only those who merited membership by their deeds and family trees were invited to join. Like the Hapsburg Order of the Golden Fleece or the English Order of the Garter, the Order of the Holy Spirit conferred great honor on its wearer. In 1662 there were only three members alive from the promotion of 1630, and sixteen from that of 1633. Louis and his brother had received the blue cordon and the cross shortly after their births; there had been no promotions since, except when Louis conferred the Order of Chevalier on Philippe at the time that he himself assumed the duties of Grand Master of the order (June 8, 1654). It obviously was time for another "promotion." On January 1, 1662, eight prelates and sixty-four noblemen were initiated into the order. The list started with the Prince of Condé, his son the Duke of Enghien, and his brother the Prince of Conti, followed by princes of Henry IV's bastard legitimized families, and the dukes and peers, marshals and others who merited the high honor. The eight prelates included the Archbishops of Lyon, Arles, Metz, and Paris, and the Bishops of Lisieux, Albi, and Mans. Next it was the turn of foreigners: in 1663 the Duke of "Mekelbourg" became a member; two years later the Dukes of Bracciano and Sforze and the Prince of Sonnino (Calomna), King John Sobieski and his nephew the Marquis de Bethune were given the cross. The next promotion came in 1682 when the dauphin received the cordon, and then in 1686 when other princes of the family, the Dukes of Chartres, of Bourbon, of Maine, and the Prince of Conti were taken in. Another mass promotion came in 1688.[18]

The members of the order not only wore the *cordon bleu* and the cross, but also, on feast days, the great cape with the insignia of the order on the shoulders. There were frequent solemn processions, eagerly watched by the ladies, when the members of the order marched through the gardens to the chapel, as solemn affirmation that the high nobility of the kingdom, the sword and the church, stood together in the service of God and the king.[19]

In 1665 Louis reestablished the Order of Saint Michel. This order was strictly limited to one hundred members; all must be Catholics, and all must serve the king. High nobility, however, was not a prerequisite, for Louis wished to reward all subjects for their services. The insignia was the same as that for the Order of the Holy Spirit, but half as large and with a small steel statue of Saint Michel on its face. Men who served in the king's household, in his army, in the Parlement could be promoted to membership. This order, like the more prestigious one, also had strong religious overtones.

There were many other ceremonial occasions at the court. Whenever a member of the house of Bourbon-Condé married, the whole family— legitimate as well as illegitimate lines—met to sign the marriage contract and to celebrate the wedding. One of the more elaborate of these came with the wedding of the Great Condé's son and Anne of Bavaria. Anne was the niece of the Queen of Poland, who provided some of the dowry and most of the jewels mentioned in the contract; it was assumed that the young couple would follow John Casimir on the throne of Poland. The ceremony of the *fiançailles* was held in the king's chamber at the Louvre with Cardinal Antoine presiding and the whole family present. The next day they were married, and everybody signed the register. The queen mother gave a dinner that evening, and after the young couple had retired, there was a ball, and finally a supper at which Philippe served the king.[20]

Baptisms were also occasions for fêtes. Those of the children of the royal family naturally created a stir, but the king was quite willing himself to become the godfather to children of friends and favorites. Molière, the Venetian ambassador, and many others had the king as godfather for their children. The lucky child received a gift as well as a name from the king. At the other end of the life-continuum there were also ceremonials, but as we have already noted, the King of France never attended a funeral, or even remained in the same building with a corpse.

Receptions of state when the king met the ambassadors, prelates, or other dignitaries who appeared in his court[21] were grand occasions for ceremony. Seventeenth-century ambassadors always made elaborate *entrées* to the capital city of the kingdom to which they were accredited. When the ambassador finally arrived at the royal palace, his reception depended upon the rank of his sovereign; Louis was highly conscious of the status and protocol that required even a minor ambassador to be led by the "introducer of ambassadors" through lines of guards and the Hundred Swiss presenting arms, and finally to the king, who might be flanked by his brother and other princes of the blood, as well as by the dignitaries of the court. After this, the ambassador would be taken to the apartment of the queen to pay his homage, and finally to a buffet where he would be entertained as a state guest. There were many other similar occasions. The faculty of the University, the Parlement, the other courts, and the Châtelet would send delegations to congratulate the king on victory, recovery from illness, the birth of a child, or to sympathize with him on the event of a death. The protocol was carefully regulated by the masters of ceremonies who were responsible for the event.[22]

One ceremony that Louis relished was the creation of a new prince of the church. Whenever a prelate resident in France was elevated to the rank of cardinal, the pope sent the new hat to the king. The usual protocol called for a mass at which the new cardinal was clothed in red garments, and then led to the king, who put the hat on his head with the words, "I give you this cardinal's hat that I have requested for you from the Pope." The formula was slightly changed when the new cardinal did not owe his elevation to the king's request. After the ceremony the new cardinal was taken to the apartment of the queen to thank her, then to that of the dauphin (even though he might still be a child), and finally to Monsieur, though this might mean a trip to Saint-Cloud.[23]

Not all of the king's life was controlled by such elaborate ceremony. This may be one of the reasons that Louis loved the relaxed etiquette of the hunt beyond almost everything else. He grew up hearing stories of his father's exploits hunting the wolf, the stag, the wild boar, and he himself added a long chapter to the annals of Bourbon hunting expeditions. Louis was a crack shot with the fowling piece; he also rode gallantly with sword or spear in hand, following the baying dogs after a frightened deer. The great forests of Vincennes, Versailles, Saint-Germain, Compiègne, and Chambord rang with the shouts of men and the barking of dogs. Sometimes the ladies would go along; some of them, like the second Duchess of Orléans, Liselotte, rode almost as well as the men. If the etchings that we have of this sport convey the true spirit of the chase, it must have been thrilling to follow the game through the virgin forest with its open floor strewn with fallen trees and branches for the horses to hurdle in their mad chase. Usually the hunters wore regular hunting costume, but at times even the hunt was turned into a masquerade. The *Gazette* tells of one hunt near Chambord in which "the women in the suite of the Queen, and that Princess herself, were clothed as Amazons so gallantly that one could add nothing" to their costumes. After such a hunt there was often a ball, a huge feast, and perhaps a comedy to entertain the company.

But the activity that obsessed everyone was gambling. Games of chance have always been popular with people who have leisure, money, and dread of boredom, and even though the life we have been describing may seem exciting, there were many dull stretches in it that called for flirtation or games of chance. This had long been true of Europe's courts; before Louis was born, men ruined themselves at the gaming tables of kings. Anne and Mazarin both loved to gamble, and Louis encouraged gambling at court, even allowing games there that he forbade his subjects to play elsewhere. Almost every day there were games of chance. Madame de Sévigné's description of the gaming tables is worthy of repetition:

At three o'clock the King, the Queen, Monsieur, Madame, Mademoiselle, the princes and princesses of the blood, Madame de Montespan and her suite, all the courtiers, all the ladies—in a word, all who could be called the court of France assemble in the fine apartment of the King . . . all is furnished divinely, all is magnificent . . . a game of *reversi* gives form to the assembly and makes everyone sit down. The King is with Madame de Montespan who holds the cards, Monsieur, the Queen, and Madame Soubise, Dangeau and company, Langlée and company are at different tables. A thousand louis are thrown on the tables; they use no other counters. I saw Dangeau play and could not help observing how awkward the others appeared in comparison with him. He thinks of nothing but the game, wins where others lose; never throws a chance away; profits by every mistake; nothing escapes him . . . [the ladies and the Queen] talk incessantly: "How many hearts have you?" "I have two," "I have one," "I have three." . . . Dangeau is delighted by their chatter. . . . I observe with pleasure his great skill and dexterity.[24]

Langlée and Dangeau were only two of the most famous of the courtiers who "lived" by gambling. The queen was not always sure what game she was playing, others of the ladies and some of the courtiers were not always sure of the rules, and a great many of them had little or no sense about their play. Nonetheless, they did play. Liselotte, with the indignation of a well-brought-up Protestant German princess, exclaimed, "Here in France as soon as people get together they do nothing but play lansquenet; the young people no longer care about dancing . . . they play for frightful sums, and the players seem bereft of their senses. . . . One shouts at the top of his voice, another strikes the table with his fist, a third blasphemes . . . it is horrible to watch them."[25]

Louis, however, was not "horrified"; the gaming tables kept his court active and out of mischief. Occasionally when Marie-Thérèse or Madame de Montespan lost outrageously he complained; sometimes he paid off the debts of a favorite or a faithful servant like the Marshals de Bellefonds and von Schomberg, who foolishly ventured beyond their means, but for the most part he did not interfere. Practically every memoirist of the era tells us the same story: the gaming table was the most popular of amusements in Louis' court.

Gossip and petty talk took up much of the spare time of people with little to do. La Grande Mademoiselle tells us that at "the Court the least circumstances make for much talk; all there [at court] is futile and of little use. I will be the subject of conversation there all this evening. . . ." How could it be otherwise? The court was crowded with people who had only ceremonial functions; the reality of power was closely guarded by the king and his ministers, leaving the crowd of men and women who had social pretensions only hollow activities to perform. It was not very much to serve the king his meat, to watch him go to bed, to have the honorific function of caring for his clothes while others of meaner rank actually did the task. Gambling, gossip, intrigue for favor inevitably rose to high place in the activities of the court. The king, in whom power and pageantry were united, could enjoy the empty amusement for he also dealt with real and vital problems of state.

Primi Visconti has given us a wonderful description of Louis leaving the château:

It is a beautiful sight to see him leave the château with his bodyguards, his horses, his carriages, the courtiers, valets, and a multitude of people all in confusion, running about with much noise. It struck me that this was the Queen of the bees when she leaves the hive with her escort.[26]

Only the king gave meaning to the court, and in these first two decades of his personal reign he learned to use that court to curb the nobility and to reduce his fears of a renewed *Fronde* that might create havoc for his reign.

20

THE YOUNG KING: HIS WIFE, MOTHER, MISTRESSES*

WITH MAZARIN DEAD and the queen mother excluded from the council chamber, Louis came of age politically. The government of the kingdom was in his hands alone; no one in the family had any right to interfere. His mother could scold and act hurt, his brother and cousins could complain, but as King of France and head of the house of Bourbon, he had no peer. His marriage and the responsibility for the kingdom also moved him to further emotional and personal maturity. Even though he did not really shake off his mother's influence, she could no longer treat him as a child. When the rounds of gaiety began during that summer of 1661, he must otfen have reflected upon his renunciation of Marie Mancini and his subsequent marriage with the Infanta. How differently his life might have turned out if Mazarin had died a little earlier.

The Infanta was the problem. No matter that she was wife and cousin, she had trouble adjusting to the life of the French king and court. In April 1661, Philippe married Henriette of England—the girl that Louis a few years earlier had called "the bones of the Holy Innocents," who now appeared as a charming, vivacious young woman. Monsieur and Madame, with the king and the queen, should have been a gay quartet. They had much in common: all four of them were grandchildren of Marie de Médicis and Henry IV; three of them were grandchildren of Philip III of Spain; Henriette, Philippe, and Louis had been brought up together in France while civil war and revolutionary government troubled England. The "delights of France" were theirs to enjoy. But Marie-Thérèse did not enjoy them. She did not like the out-of-doors, she could not understand the jokes even when she understood the French, and then, as Louis wrote to his father-in-law about the middle of April, "there [was] no room to doubt that the Queen [was] pregnant," and when Marie-Thérèse was pregnant, she was unwell. Louis soon realized that he had given up more than Marie

Mancini when he exchanged his first love for the *gloire* of his crown and the peace of Europe; he had married a dull wife.

Who was this princess? She was just Louis' age, but as Abbé Flechier[1] said, "While Louis received knowledge of the great principles that make up the art of government, Thérèse was given knowledge of Christian virtues that she practiced with great edification." The only trouble is that, when one is twenty-three or so, the "Christian virtues" are not as important in a wife as wit, charm, and a lively personality. She obviously had been born with a simple heart, educated to desire to please God and to do her duty gladly. Her "duty" was to marry the King of France and bear his children, and Marie-Thérèse seems never to have questioned her fate. But it was a frightened girl who had come to France only partly equipped with the language and knowledge of the customs of her new home. She had little to cling to except her handsome new husband, the ladies and servants who came with her from Spain, her "Tia" (the queen mother, who was both aunt and mother-in-law), and above all, her church. Anne died, Louis was unfaithful; small wonder that the church loomed large as a moral support in her life. Abbé Pieche[2] tells us that her apartment was scarcely different from a cloister and that "she passes . . . much of her time in prayer before the feet of Jesus Christ." In the first year of her marriage she received the habit of the Third Order of Saint Francis "with profound humility and extraordinary piety"; she remained superior of that order as long as she lived, and at death was buried in her habit. Marie-Thérèse often signed herself "Soeur Thérèse"; in this way she could indicate her devotion to her religion, and as she understood Him, to her God.

Like Louis' religion, Marie-Thérèse's was a thing of prayers, pious observances, services of cult, reliquaries, candles, novenas, and the like; she understood only the simplest theology. She opposed any innovation that she had not known as a child, and she "had an extreme aversion for all those who wished to introduce any change in cult." Like Anne, she spent regular hours at her *prie-dieu,* and she was disturbed when the court's travels interrupted her devotions. Her confessor assures us that she had great respect for priests, that she cared for the sick and the poor, for the welfare of religious communities, for her family, and for God. The good Abbé de Storia's account of her life underlines her naïveté; God and the king seem to have been the limits of her vision. Occasionally she would have a book read to her: the works of Saint Theresa, of Saint Peter of Alcantara, or of Saint Francis de Sales—no mention is ever made of a secular book or idea. The abbé tells us that her real interests were in the celebration of religious fêtes, particularly those honoring the Virgin, or traditional Spanish fêtes like the "hour of the delivery of the infant" at Christmastime. Were we to listen only to the bishops, priests, and monks who gave funeral orations after her death, we might even be willing to believe in their repeated suggestions that she should be canonized.[3]

Her relations with the king provided much amusement for the court. She was always the last to learn of his infidelities; she loved to babble about his attentions in the bed and his favors during the day. Her sorrow over his behavior aroused scant sympathy. Her confessor tells us that "she looked to him [Louis], after God, as the object of her respect and compliance . . . her principal care being to do exactly what she believed would be pleasing to him and to avoid the least thing that would annoy him." But it was no easy thing to be the wife of Louis XIV. In these early years the court traveled much from château to château; it even had to follow the king to the wars. Since Louis had no objection to any kind of weather, he could see no reason for anyone else's objections to rain, cold, or heat. De Storia tries to tell us what we already know, namely that Louis was not considerate of other people, and especially not of Marie-Thérèse, whose skin was milk-white and sensitive to the sun; nonetheless, he writes "she followed him with joy to all the places this great monarch saw fit to lead her." The "joy" probably was somewhat less than de Storia would have us believe. On these trips Louis took his mistresses along, the roads were often terrible, the carriages were without springs, and there was no provision for creature comforts. There often were bad beds and poor food. La Grande Mademoiselle has recounted several "horrid" experiences. How much did the queen complain to the king about all this? We do not know.

The memoirists leave us a picture of a lady who cried, prayed, had sudden outbursts, but who complained little. Her health was a frequent concern. In 1664, after the stillbirth of a child, she seemed near to death. A priest came to administer extreme unction; the king and the whole court were attentive. Poor Marie-Thérèse decided that, even with Mademoiselle de la Vallière and all the rest of her crosses, life was still important: "I do not want to die," she cried; "I am too young to die; I want to receive communion, but not to die!" Madame de Sévigné who tells this story goes on, "It was the most magnificent and the saddest thing in the world to see the King and all the court with candles . . . conduct the Holy Sacrament, and to see the Queen receive it with a devotion that brought tears to everyone." This touching scene might be matched by another in which Marie-Thérèse tried to find out why her husband came to bed so late; she was the only one in the room who did not realize that Louis' excuses about "work" and "dispatches" were lies, and that his absence had quite a different cause.

On her wedding night Marie-Thérèse asked Louis never to abandon her; in spite of his infidelities, the king kept his promise. Primi tells us that it was common knowledge among the ladies that Louis had "commerce" with the queen at least twice a month, and that the next morning she would communicate to thank God and to ask for children. She had five—two boys and three girls, one of whom was apparently a "blue baby" and perhaps deformed. Only one of them lived to maturity. Seventeenth-century men were always under the shadow of death whether they were the sons of a king or a cotter, and Marie-Thérèse's children were no exception to this rule. When her children died, the queen went "immediately to her oratory or to the church to prostrate herself before God . . . and offer her innocent victims as the most precious gauge of her love."[4] Perhaps her attitude toward life as a queen in a foreign land can be summed up by a remark she made at the time of the death of one of the girls—it is "better that she died in infancy to enjoy eternal happiness rather than to live in the uncertainty of salvation and become the Queen of Spain." The son who lived, the Grand Dauphin, took after his mother in looks, disposition, and intelligence.

Even so, Marie-Thérèse did enjoy some of the "delights" of the court of France. Entertainers, as well as important visitors who came to court, had to go to her apartments; she may not always have understood their words or their actions, but it was pleasant to be the focus of attention. She also loved the gaming table. Some whole days were spent at gambling; she was there usually between eight and ten every evening. Her favorite game was *hombre,* but she tried all of them, and her losses were the principal means of support for a sizable company at the court; Madame de Sévigné suggests that the Princess d'Elboeuf supported herself entirely by her winnings from the queen. At times her losses were beyond the resources of her own treasury[5] and Louis had to settle the debts; on one such occasion, in November 1675, she lost 20,000 *écus* before noon and missed mass in a fruitless effort to recoup. Louis was irritated, "Consider, Madame, how much this is a year!" The next day the blunt outspoken ex-Huguenot de Montausier met her with the remark, "Eh, Madame, will you lose a mass again today for *hoca*?" She became very angry with him.

One of the most sensitive of the observers at Louis' court sums up the queen's life during these years:

> The King treats her with all the honors of her rank; eats with her, sleeps with her, fulfills his family duties, and makes conversation with her as if he had no mistress. As for the Queen, half of her time is passed in devotions. Her

entertainment consists of half a dozen dwarf-fools . . . the Spanish court always
had such creatures around . . . she calls one "my heart," another "poor boy,"
still another "my son" . . . and with a number of little dogs; but the dogs are
better treated than the fools. They are petted and the valets take them for
walks, and they share the table scraps. I do not know who it was that told me
that these little beasts cost 4000 *écus* a year. As to the fools, they have trouble
getting a pistol. It is not as in Spain where the dwarf Nicholas made his
brother president of Milan.[6]

Obviously Primi was not describing a woman who could hold Louis XIV;
it was probably inevitable that his marriage to her be followed by infidelities, for he had to find more satisfying female companionship somewhere.

The women in men's lives are always selected in part as the result of
proximity; men must see and know their women before they can be attracted to them. Louis was in full flight from a stupid queen even before
Mazarin died; the first woman to come into his line of vision was his
new sister-in-law, Henriette of England. Henriette, no longer awkward and
gawky, had a natural wit and vivaciousness that provided a charming contrast to her Spanish cousin. Since Philippe was much more interested in
several of the handsome young men at court than in his bride, Madame
soon found herself at loose ends. It must have been very welcome when
Louis began to pay attention to her. Marie-Thérèse was pregnant and
neither could nor would mount a horse, nor do any of the things that were
fun. This meant that Henriette soon found herself as the companion of the
king. Back in the château waiting for the young people to return from a
hunt or a wild ride, Marie-Thérèse would ask her Tia if the fact that she
was to give birth to a dauphin meant that she had to be left alone. Soon
there were gossipy stories that reached the ears of both mothers. The queen
mother spoke sharply to her son; the dowager Queen of England admon-
ished her daughter. They could not allow their children to live in any disorder. Neither Louis nor Henriette had yet really freed themselves from
their mothers' domination, so when the queens protested, the young
people decided to use a ruse rather than rebellion to avoid parental control.
Louis would pretend to be interested in one of the young women in Henriette's household; under this cover they could continue seeing one another.

Louis' attachment for Henriette started like the opening scene of a grand
passion; so it was a surprise, perhaps even to Louis and Henriette, when
the pale Mademoiselle Louise de la Vallière became the secret mistress of
the king. Louise had been their third choice as "decoy"; the first was
spirited away by her parents, the second "knew how to take care of herself"; Louise was too innocent, perhaps too overwhelmed by the fact that

the king paid attention to her, to escape, and her parents had no objection. But the would-be seducer was himself seduced—Louis fell in love with his "victim," and soon they were meeting clandestinely in one of the little rooms away from the crowd. The contemporary account of the seduction told by Bussy de Rabutin long circulated in many manuscript copies before it was printed; it probably contains more than an element of truth, as well as considerable fiction, but it is too salacious to be repeated unless the author seeks to shock his reader.[7]

Several artists painted Louise de la Vallière, and the memoirists have left us many descriptions. At seventeen she was a delicate, simple, very feminine creature, "very sweet, very pretty, very naïve." Her hair was golden blonde, her eyes a lovely blue, her complexion clear white; she had several pox marks on her face, she was slightly lame, and there is no reason to believe that she had more than a bare average intelligence. Like many a girl at court, she had long "adored" the king from a distance, but it must have been a shock to her to realize that she had become the object of his attention. It is also a question for us. Why he ever fell in love with this girl is a mystery. The romantically inclined insist that he was happy to be loved for himself rather than as king, but this hardly holds up, for Louise apparently never knew or thought of him as any other than the king. Some say that he loved her because she demanded nothing but love in return, but on closer scrutiny this also breaks down; she asked for many other things. There may be a better explanation. Louis seems to have been a little awkward with women, a little unsure of himself, especially in his earlier years. Maybe this sweet, simple little girl, who did not have spunk enough to demand that she be recognized in spite of his mother's objections, was about all that he could manage at this time. Her body and gentleness suited his taste, and once he knew her carnally, he became involved with her too deeply to give her up until her fading beauty and obvious spiritual weaknesses began to pall on him. What Louis needed as long as his mother was alive, was a mistress who could be a "secret," a mistress with whom he could enjoy a tender love affair veiled from the view of the court. Louise was just the woman for this role. As Madame de La Fayette so shrewdly put it, Louise's "limitations prevented this mistress of the King from taking advantage or the credit that so great a passion would have given another. . . ." Louise lacked the style, the brazen insolence, the self-assurance to become uncrowned queen in the French court, and this suited Louis well, for at this moment he did not have the courage to face his mother with a "third queen."

Naturally the women of the court would not allow so simple a girl to carry off the prize without a fight. In every court of Europe there were brazen women who freely flaunted their beauty and their sex, and well understood that with the king, women could gain honors, wealth, and fame at a little risk to their souls. Even this peril was open to question, for there were women who argued that there could be no sin in bestowing oneself upon a king. These women were not going to yield all that could be gained to La Vallière without a struggle. Louise was vulnerable on several fronts: would Henriette keep a "fallen woman" among her ladies of honor, especially considering the circumstances under which La Vallière had happened to attract the king's attention? What would the two queens say when they learned the news? And of course anyone by a direct assault might successfully seduce the king and take him away from this pale flower. All of these routes were explored. Henriette would have dropped Louise if Louis had not insisted otherwise. Anne learned of the danger after it was too late. She could scold, but she could not get Louis to give up his mistress. Many times he emerged from the queen mother's chamber with red eyes, but victorious. And the young women who pushed their charms got nowhere, for Louis was completely involved with Louise. The queen was the last to know. A clique of troublemakers tried to inform her by a "poison pen" letter purporting to come from Spain, but Louis got it first. He failed to find the culprits because he chose one of them as his trusted agent to find the guilty parties. Finally, the Countess of Soissons, formerly Olympe Mancini (mother of Eugene of Savoy) told the young queen the whole story; it was no use, Marie-Thérèse was as helpless as her Tia had been, for Louis would not budge from his course. Naturally the veiled protests of the Spanish ambassador were brushed aside.

At first the affair with La Vallière proceeded like an idyll; Louis could not see enough of his mistress. When the dauphin was born, he went to Chartres to thank the Virgin, but hurried back to be with Louise. Then she became pregnant and had to dress to hide her condition; when the child was born, it was spirited away to Madame Colbert, as were the later children born before the king could recognize La Vallière officially as his mistress. But like all great passions, this one sometimes encountered stormy weather. We do not know all that happened, but Louise ran away to a convent at least once, after carefully telling where she was going. Did she think that Louis would let her go? Probably not. This was one of the ways this sweet, simple, gentle young woman used to dominate her lover; she could not stage a scene, but running away was just as effective. She was the "clinging vine" type and her methods worked well when their love was still young.

Although Louis wept easily himself, he hated women's tears—but he later learned better to cope with them.

Poor Louise! Around her there has grown a mythology that conceals her inadequacies. She is remembered as the "saintly mistress" in contrast to Madame de Montespan, the "wicked one." Her last years in the convent almost led to a move to canonize her. In this myth La Vallière is remembered as the girl who did not ask for anything but love, who even failed to tell the king that she had a brother until he stumbled on the fact by himself. Of course it is a distortion; Louise had a long list of favors to ask from the "man who takes care of my affairs." And this nearly worthless brother, who stupidly offended the king by trying to act like a brother-in-law, was high on the list of those who benefited by her station. There was a host of people who asked her to intercede for them, often enough for petty affairs, and she did not know how to say no. She asked for the property of a deceased bastard, the right to salt fish, the right to control commerce in this or that port, the right to inspect merchandise, for little pensions and gratuities. These things were often enough petty in themselves, but Louis must finally have been tired of her requests and surprised that she used her influence so foolishly. Neither Madame de Montespan nor Madame de Maintenon ever made such mistakes.

In this court where the influence of the queen mother was still important, Mademoiselle de la Vallière needed friends who would help her maintain herself, and she had very few. As a matter of fact, she was surrounded by people who wished her ill. The clergymen were scandalized and blamed her rather than the king. One of them, a young man named Bossuet whom Anne had "found" and whose moral standards matched his eloquence, boldly reminded the king himself of his duties. At the feast of the Assumption he fairly thundered, "I would tear from this heart all the pleasures that enchant it, all the creatures that capture it . . . O creatures, shameful idols, leave this heart . . . which wishes to love Jesus Christ. . . . There is one true love that wishes to enter your heart; false love, deceiving love, do you wish to rival Him?" Bishop Bossuet was exiled from the court for three years after this sermon, but he would return to thunder again. His was only the most eloquent voice; there were others who felt that the king must be an example for his subjects. At the other end of the scale there were several cliques of "ladies" who wished to oust La Vallière. The center of one of these was Olympe Mancini who could not forgive the intruder her victory. These ladies pushed one beauty after another into orbit around the king; they were unsuccessful for the moment, but victory might come in the long run. One of these women probably was responsible for the wicked song that passed around:

> Be lame but fifteen years of age,
> Have no bosom and few brains,
> Have parents whom God only knows:
> My faith, the first of all lovers will be yours,
> As the case of La Vallière clearly shows.

Louise should have shivered a little if she heard that song for fear that Louis might hear it, too.

The greatest problem for La Vallière was the one created by the two queens. Marie-Thérèse's opinion did not count for much, but Anne was a woman with more character. In these years her health was bad and her spirits depressed by the behavior of her two sons. She knew that all was not well in the household of Madame and Monsieur, and she knew that Louis was unfaithful to Thérèse. "These children! Ah, these children!" They were the source of sorrow. Louis would not give up La Vallière, but his mother's influence over him was too great for him to flaunt her wishes completely. Many times he left her chambers in tears, still maintaining his right to keep his mistress, but in the long run this situation boded ill for La Vallière. With all that was against her, Louise needed more brains, more personality, and more social skill than she possessed.

The secret may have been an open one, but it was still a secret. It was 1664 before Louis admitted that he could not in conscience make his Easter duty because he could not put aside his sin. The same Louis who had earlier upbraided his brother for eating meat on Friday, now reproached him for going to confession "simply because the Queen Mother wanted it"; Louis insisted that he would not be a hypocrite.[8] Nonetheless, it was not until October of that year that he "introduced" Louise to the court by bringing her to the gaming tables in the queen mother's apartment, and seating her at a table with Monsieur and Madame. Since Louise was well along with her third pregnancy, this seemed to be a daring thing to do. However, Louis had planned it well; the two queens were confined to their chambers by illness, so there was no chance for a scene. In the next few months, Marie-Thérèse nearly died as the result of a delivery, La Vallière gave birth to the little girl who became Mademoiselle de Blois, and Anne found the hard lump in her breast that warned her that death was not far away. As her illness developed, it became increasingly important to have the "secret" remain a secret.

There is good reason to believe that the break between Louis and La Vallière was postponed by the illness of the queen mother. A dying mother has a call upon her son, and both Louis and Louise were too sensitive not to recognize this fact. Thus she willingly stayed "out of sight" until after Anne's death, an arrangement that suited Louis' needs, too. But it took the mother two years to die. This was a very long time. It was filled with a dozen little crises, punctuated by three or four emotional bedside scenes where *adieux* were taken, only to become *au revoirs*. During all this time the secrecy of the affair made it seem that the court was all in order just as the queen mother would have it. Louis did everything possible for his mother: prayers were said in all the churches of the kingdom, forty-hour devotions were held, the remains of Saint Geneviève were carried through the streets of Paris and exposed to public view, medicines were imported from Italy, and Louis paid frequent visits to her bedside. The readers of the *Gazette* who followed the queen mother's last illness in great detail knew that the king was attentive and considerate. Before Anne died, Louis did persuade her to allow him to introduce Louise de la Vallière to her to prove that his mistress was, in fact, a lovely, pious girl. It was one further insult for poor Marie-Thérèse, but she was not yet forced to accept the king's mistress and his bastard children before the entire world.

Of course, it is not true that the court was hushed and serious for the entire two years of Anne's last illness. The round of balls, ballets, comedies, and other amusements continued; if an excuse was necessary, the presence of foreign ambassadors provided it. The gaming tables in the queen mother's apartments continued to be popular, and the court traveled about even when such traveling was painful to the sick woman. These were also the days when the court was in mourning for Marie-Thérèse's father, Philip IV, whose death affected the queens more than it did the king and his ministers. They later found it easy to wear the violet of mourning and still devise plans to cut up the inheritance of the Spanish crown.

Amid all this Anne prepared herself for death. The secretaries of state Guenegaud and Le Tellier helped her with her last will and testament, in which she naturally asked that she be buried beside her husband in Saint-Denis—and with a minimum of expense and formality. Among the items of the will there is a request for the reading of ten thousand masses for her soul at the expense of the executor, another for an endowment for the daily reading of a low mass at Val-de-Grâce in perpetuity. Her reliquaries were given to several people and institutions, but the ones that she had kept nearest to her in her chambers went to Val-de-Grâce. There were gifts of 20,000 to 90,000 livres to women in her entourage, a million livres to her granddaughter Marie-Louise of Orléans (the future Queen of Spain), and a request for the bounty of the king in favor of her domestics and for the

continuation of the building of the chapel at Val-de-Grâce.[9] She also prepared her soul for death with the aid of a humble priest vaguely resembling
Father Vincent de Paul, who had done a similar service for Louis XIII.
Anne knew well that a Christian death both edified those who saw it and
guaranteed the dying person salvation. She was too good a show-woman not
to see its advantages. But death humiliated Anne of Austria; she had always
been a fastidious person, anxious to be clean, fussy about her linen, careful of her body. Mazarin had often teased her about these traits. The
cancer that choked off her life affronted all these sensibilities and made
her last months both psychologically and physically miserable. When death
came, unquestionably she welcomed it.

The final act was dramatic. Anne "gave her blessing to the King, the
Queen, to Madame and Monsieur, with words so tender and so pressing
that they could only reply with torrents of tears. . . ." There are several
versions of Louis' behavior; obviously he was deeply moved by his mother's
death. At her bedside he called upon all to remember that this "great
Queen" had saved the kingdom when it was threatened by civil war—even
at her death he did not forget her part during the *Fronde*.

For Louis her death was both a shock and a liberation. Mazarin's
death had given him power, but as long as his mother lived he could not
escape her tutelage. He was tied to her by a host of strings and obligations,
by habits and memories, and unquestionably by real affection. His sobs at
the time of her death were probably more genuine and more deeply felt
than any he would ever again experience, even though much later he was
to see his dynasty threatened with extinction by the death of his son,
grandsons, and favorite granddaughter-in-law. On the other hand, Anne's
death allowed Louis to become a man; to shake the apron strings that had
bound him, to act on his own without worrying about what she would think.
Perhaps we do not see the real Louis XIV until after his mother's death.

Anne's death also freed the court of her control. Marie-Thérèse now
became *the* queen; Madame could now live her life more freely, even
though her own mother was to live about three more years. Anne's death
also marked the beginning of the end of the "reign" of Louise de la
Vallière. But all these things had to wait upon the funeral of the queen
mother. The house of Bourbon buried its dead with great pomp and circumstance, no matter what might be written in a will about a simple
funeral. Anne died at Paris on the morning of January 20, 1666, at 6:15.
Le Tellier read her testament, after which Louis and most of the court left
for Versailles. Her physicians, the members of her household, a number of
clergymen, two marshals of France, and a few others remained behind to

care for the body. Her heart, placed in a silver box, was sent to Val-du-Grâce; her entrails were sent to the Carmelite convent in Paris; her body, embalmed, clothed in the habit of a nun of the order of Saint Clair, was sealed in a leaden coffin that was covered by a mantle of black velvet and white silk. At one of the public services a scandalous contest for precedence broke out, involving loud talk, pushing, and elbowing, but this was characteristic of the French court. The ceremonies at the Louvre lasted until January 28 when the body was escorted to Saint-Denis. The procession included carriages loaded with all the members of the royal family except the king, all important members of the court and royal households; regiments of the French Guards, the Hundred Swiss, the Light Horse, with weapons reversed, followed by more carriages filled with clergymen, important nobles, representatives of the sovereign courts, diplomats, and others who came to the ceremony. At the Basilica of Saint-Denis the coffin was draped in mourning (these drapes were rented, and had to be protected from the crowds that had a tendency to steal them) and placed before the high altar. On January 29, the Bishop of Auch celebrated high mass, and on each day following, until February 12, one hundred masses were celebrated in the Basilica for the repose of Anne's soul, and fifty *écus* were distributed daily among the poor of Paris.

During all this time Louis remained at Versailles, where he received deputations from the sovereign courts, the University, the city government of Paris, foreign ambassadors, and many others who came to offer condolences. Here, too, there were contests over precedence, and poor Sainctôt, in charge of these ceremonies, had to be everywhere to see that all went smoothly. At the solemn ceremony of interment on February 12, everyone who was anyone—except the king—was in attendance at the great Basilica of Saint-Denis. It was an impressive ceremony, heavy with the pomp and tradition of hundreds of years of experience with such things. When it was all over, a splendid dinner was served for some two hundred and fifty of the most important participants, for it was a long way from Saint-Denis to Paris, and a trip without food would not have been very pleasant. In the following weeks every cathedral of France held some sort of a ceremony, always including a sermon eulogy, to mark the passing of the great queen.[10]

Even before Anne died, there were several women angling for the king. Primi says that there were many, and that "one should have some indulgence for this prince if he should fall, surrounded as he is by so many female devils, all seeking to tempt him . . . the worst are the families, fathers, mothers, even husbands" who push their women on him. The Duke of Enghien, writing to the Queen of Poland, says, "There are a thousand intrigues at Versailles among the ladies . . . what agitates their hearts is envy of Mademoiselle de la Vallière. . . ."[11] De la Fare more explicitly tells the names of the ladies who were trying to bring down the king. One of them, the Princess of Monaco, almost carried it off before the fair Françoise-Athénaïs finally managed to do it.

The lady who succeeded Louise de la Vallière was Françoise-Athénaïs de Rochechouart de Mortemart, wife of the Marquis de Montespan. If La Vallière lacked the brass to carry off the role of mistress, Athénaïs did not. Loret marked her when she first came to join Madame's household as "one of the most ravishing, most wise, most charming of all the ladies at Court. . . . She has, Oh reader, I insist, an air so modest and so sweet that one would call her . . . more angelic than human."[12] When she married, *La Muze* went on to warn her husband to "keep himself for her alone" and even suggested that he was not nearly good enough for her—a view soon shared by Athénaïs herself. Long before Louis actually took an interest in her, the Duke of Enghien wrote that court gossip had it that he was "thinking of her and indeed that she merited it for no one could have more wit or beauty than she. . . ."[13] Her family was one of the oldest of France; her father was a duke and peer; her brother Vivonne had been a childhood friend and favorite of the king, as well as a soldier-sailor in his armies. Like all her family she had brains, but she also had style, beauty, and impudence; she was proud of her charms and completely dissatisfied with her husband. Anyone who saw her portrait in the *Exposition Louis XIV* (in Paris, 1960) will understand why her contemporaries, as well as the king, found her beautiful. She had married the Marquis de Montespan in 1661 when she was just twenty; she had one son by him before losing all interest in this bizarre man. Thereafter she came to court with plans to try for the prize: the king.

Everyone knows that the best role for a lady who wishes to seduce a man is that of a close friend of the women in his life. Athénaïs became a close friend of the queen by her acts of piety, and she then insinuated herself into the confidence of La Vallière. The queen took La Montespan with her ladies and she soon became one of them; La Vallière was glad to have her around when the king visited, because she could joke and tease with him in a way that poor Louise could not hope to imitate. Before long Louis began to look forward to seeing her when he visited his mistress—perhaps more than to seeing the mistress herself.

As luck would have it, Madame de Montespan lost her mother about the same time that the queen mother died, so the two could console each other. Then she came down with measles and the king visited her bedside.

It has been suggested that during her convalescence Louis took a rather more personal interest in her. In the winter of 1666–67 the queen gave birth to a daughter who soon died, and Mademoiselle de la Vallière was pregnant; the Duke of Enghien wrote to the Queen of Poland that Madame de Montespan looked ravishing and clearly was in very high favor. Her husband could hardly have been unaware of the course of events, yet he went off to the south of France, leaving his wife to look out for herself.

Still, Louis' problem with the Marquise de Montespan was not a simple one. The king could take a gardener's daughter much as Jove would an earthling, and it might be noted that in this activity Louis resembled Jove more than Apollo—whose women seem always to escape as trees or something of the like. A king could even find a sex partner among the ladies of the court if the husband or family did not look or did not see: there was the lady, for example, who wore certain earrings when she was available; another who was "in and out" of the king's favor with her husband's permission, both of them emerging from the "in" affair loaded with riches and honors. There were many such passing "events" that must happen to a man besieged from all sides and somewhat susceptible to assault. Such little comedies were possible. But to make a married woman "mistress of the king" was another thing. In the first place, the Mortemarts were an important family that the king did not wish to offend, and although Monsieur de Montespan did not rate high, he could, as we shall see, be difficult. Moreover, the lady's ironic humor did not help much; she knew how to play with a man even when that man was the king. Louis probably did not know that her father hopefully watched the whole affair as an important business venture for the family, while her husband's debts suggest that perhaps he, too, saw it as a way out of his troubles. Somehow all these things had to be reconciled—and were.

However, there was still Mademoiselle de la Vallière to be cared for. Louis was never one to deprive a faithful servant of "place" without compensation; indeed, he had trouble forcing people to resign or sell their posts even when they were obviously unfit for them, so great was his respect for "acquired rights." Obviously Louise had "rights" to the place she occupied: the lovely little girl at Madame Colbert's who gave Louis so much pleasure in those days, as well as Louise's pregnancy, both emphasized her position. Surely she had to be paid. As Louis wrote to his son about Louise and her daughter, "I believed it rightful to assure this child the honor of its birth and to give the mother an establishment commensurate with the affection that I had for her during these six years." Naturally he did not tell the dauphin that the queen mother's death gave him freedom to act, nor that interest in another woman required this bit of "justice." On May 13, 1667, an act of Parlement registered the creation of the new duchy of Vaujours for the Duchess de la Vallière, and afterward for "our daughter Marie-Anne," who was legitimized. This was Louis' parting gift; it seemed to be a splendid one, but as a matter of fact, the duchy of Vaujours was not a rich apanage. The little Marie-Anne would have to look to her father for additional revenue. After thus buying off his mistress, Louis and the whole court departed for war. This was the time that Louise, left behind because of her pregnancy, suddenly realized her peril and hurried after the court to reclaim her place, only to be very coldly received by her lover. The queen's anger, La Vallière's humiliation, and Madame de Montespan's famous remark— "God keep me from being the mistress of the King, but if I am ever so unfortunate, I will never have the effrontery to present myself before the Queen"—are all renowned and well-explored landmarks in the story.

This was the time of Madame de Montespan. The court was not long in learning that the king had a new mistress, for unexplained absences were quickly noticed and gossipy tongues quickly spread the news. This time, however, it was a double adultery, for both Louis and Athénaïs had spouses whose rights were being trampled upon. The good people of the court, the kingdom, and Europe were scandalized; this was a very bad example for public morals. Posterity has shared this view and roundly condemned the sin of the king; not even the beauty of Madame de Montespan can be used as an excuse for the bad example that Louis gave to his court and his subjects. Louis himself must have realized this, for during many of these years the court spent much time at Chambord, far from Paris, where the scandal would not be quite as flagrant as it would have been in the capital city of the kingdom.

As it turned out, however, even after his mother's death, Louis did not escape from a secret affair. His mother could no longer interfere, but what of Monsieur de Montespan? When everything started, that gentleman seemed to be willing enough to let matters take their course, but then he reconsidered. In January 1668, Molière took the part of Amphitryon in his new play of that name. Amphitryon (clearly representing Monsieur de Montespan) was victorious in war, but his wife, Alcmène (Madame de Montespan) became involved with Jupiter (Louis) who succeeded in seducing her. Molière explains it all with the remark, "To share with Jupiter in no way brings dishonor!" There is little reason to believe that Monsieur de Montespan was greatly concerned about his "honor," but he seems to have been dissatisfied with his "rewards." In any case, he began to make scenes. Did Louis fail to offer him enough? Did he take a second look at his wife? It did not matter much which was true: he was the legal husband of Madame de Montespan, he could demand "his rights" as husband, and he could "claim" any children that she might have. This was an embarrassing set of circumstances: the King of France was no tyrant; he could not easily ride roughshod over the rights of his vassals. And yet the marquis was obviously making a fool of himself when he wore "horns," prepared statements about the biblical David that he was determined to present to the king, and in general made a nuisance of himself. Louis was no David; Monsieur de Montespan was simply arrested and sent to his estates in the south with orders to stay there.

This was all very well, but on his estates he could still cause trouble; he proceeded to hold a "funeral" for his wife and to act out the buffoon. His total behavior would not suggest that his wife's adultery was much different from his own except that hers was with the king, his with commoners, and yet he was a husband cuckolded and exiled. Surely he had a case. On the other hand, if the guilty lovers were resolved to continue their affair, there was only one solution that could deprive Monsieur de Montespan of his "rights": a court order separating him and Athénaïs and their property. One would think that such an order would be the simplest thing in the world to get if the king asked for it. Louis did ask, not once but many times; indeed, he urged action, but it took almost six years before Parlement could get around to issuing the edict that freed the adulterous couple of the dangerous, if foolish, Monsieur de Montespan.[14]

Nor was the wounded husband the only member of Athénaïs' family to object. While her father was pleased, her uncle the Archbishop of Sens let his ideas about it be known by sentencing a woman living in concubinage to public penance, and publishing the old canons against adultery in all the churches of his diocese. This included Fontainebleau! No one missed the archbishop's intention. Louis sent him an order not to leave his cathedral city; he went to Fontainebleau anyway, saying that the king could not prevent his doing his duty, and if he should try, he would excommunicate him. The court did not visit Fontainebleau again until after the archbishop's death. Apparently neither the church nor the Parlement was anxious to help the king in this embarrassing situation, and the church had not yet had its last word.

All this confusion spelled trouble for Louise de la Vallière. She was no longer the king's mistress in fact, but she had to seem to be his mistress to provide cover for the king's affair with Athénaïs. These two women found themselves willy-nilly bound together because there was no other way for Louis to manage; he could not recognize his new mistress, so the old one had to provide a front for the new affair. When he passed through the apartment of Louise to reach that of Athénaïs, Louis must often have meditated on the melancholy fact of having to hide his first mistress because of his mother, and then mask his second because of her husband. The wags of the court could not resist making light of it all with verses and song, one ending with the refrain, "But I know well that some day I will have two mistresses for one!"—another, "I want to do what the King does!" Very evidently the wits were of little help.[15]

There is a host of stories about this curious affair. From 1668 to the day when Louise entered the convent in 1674, France and Europe were treated to the spectacle of "three queens": Marie-Thérèse, the *de facto* queen; La Vallière, the mistress *en titre*; and Madame de Montespan, the mistress in fact. They rode together in the same carriage; they lived together in the court. Some were shocked at Louis' "brutality" toward his first mistress, and told stories that are so foreign to his character as to be quite impossible. But even though stories like the one that tells of his tossing a dog to comfort her distress may be untrue, his treatment of this girl was one of the most cruel episodes in his life. Poor Louise, rejected and ignored, had to watch her late lover pass through her rooms to reach those of the new favorite. Louis could not have found worse punishment for her had he tried. Those people who saw Louise's presence at court as evidence of the king's generosity had little feeling for her unhappy situation. But only a very few understood what was behind the sorry comedy. Louis simply could not publicly visit Madame de Montespan until the Parlement of Paris could get around to separating Monsieur de Montespan from his wife.

But why did Louise put up with this situation? Perhaps she could do nothing about it, but more likely at first she thought that she might get Louis back again. Then there were her two children: the boy was not "recognized" until 1669, and both of them had to be "provided for" before she could leave the court. Liselotte one day asked her why she put up with so impossible a situation. Louise replied, "God has touched my heart, has made it know its sin." Liselotte goes on to say, ". . . she thus thought it was necessary to do penance, and suffer that which was most sad for her, namely, to share the heart of the King and see herself despised." In February 1671, after her children had been "established," Louise tried to run away to the convent. Louis sent Lauzan to bring her back (this time he did not go himself). There were tearful sessions when the three "guilty ones" were together again, and finally Louise agreed to return. Bussy de Rabutin understood the situation; he wrote to Madame de Scudéry, ". . . I will even go so far as to say that it is to suit his own convenience and for political reasons that he [Louis] made La Vallière return . . ." (March 13, 1671). By spring of 1674, the Parlement of Paris was ready to issue an act legally separating Monsieur from Madame de Montespan. The lady generously allowed her husband to keep everything, including her dowry.

When this order was ready to be issued, Louise was free to leave the court. "Scarcely thirty years old," writes her most sympathetic biographer, "she had never seemed more beautiful. They wept, they admired her, they said obsequies, they said it was a triumph. Louise left the world in a way suitable to her loving and smiling nature, and the world had retained of her a gracious memory that still charms men today."[16] Her departure underlines the basic religious commitments of these seventeenth-century people; she entered a Carmelite convent and finally took the veil as Sister de la Misericorde. Bishop Bossuet, who had fought her as the king's mistress, was overjoyed by her action—"I am both delighted and dumbfounded by her conduct," he exclaimed; "I talk and she acts! Words are mine, deeds are hers!" Before leaving, she characteristically asked the king for pensions for her mother, her married sister, and her servants; she gave away some of her jewelry as souvenirs to friends; the rest went to her son and daughter. She said *adieu* to the king; visited the queen, and threw herself at her feet to ask for forgiveness. These were tear-stained partings. Madame de Montespan took her off to her apartments for a final meal. On April 14, 1674, she entered the convent; the next year on June 4, the Archbishop of Paris gave her the veil and Bishop Bossuet preached the sermon in the church of the Carmelites, Rue Saint-Jacques, Paris. Marie-Thérèse, Monsieur and Madame, Mademoiselle (Philippe's eldest daughter), La Grande Mademoiselle, Madame de Guise, Madame de Longueville, and a great number of other "people of quality" were in attendance, and "edified by the modesty and zeal of the profession [of faith]" (*Gazette*). Bossuet's sermon was aimed at the absent king who at this moment was facing another crisis with Madame de Montespan.

The last years of Louise de la Vallière's life were so edifying to her generation that there was expectation of miracles when she died, and a strong movement to have her canonized. She left a little book of "Reflections on the Mercy of God" that some believe she wrote and Bossuet edited.[17] Louise may not have written it, but she probably used the book in her devotions. "Is it too much, Oh my God," one of the stanzas exclaims, "in recognition of so many benefits, to repair the scandal of a life in which I only offended Thee. . . . Is it too much that I deprive myself of [the pleasures of the world] forever?" One day Louis himself would worry about such things, but not in 1675.

With La Vallière out of the way, Madame de Montespan appeared in full view as the mistress of the king. Louis never proclaimed her by this title, as he had La Vallière, but he recognized her children as his own, and openly escorted her here and there in full view of the court. This lady was one to make even a king proud of his conquest; she had the flair, beauty, and style to repair the deficiencies of poor Marie-Thérèse. At thirty years of age she "was beautiful as the day . . ."; "a surprising beauty . . ."; "even more blonde than La Vallière, she had a beautiful mouth, beautiful teeth . . . and a brazen air" (that last remark was by Liselotte, who hated her). She wore dresses made of "cloth of gold, with a double border blended with another sort of cloth . . . the divinest stuff ever invented by the wit of man . . ." (Sévigné). The artists loved to paint her in velvets, satins, gold lace, her figure revealed by the elegance of the drapery. Surrounded by her servants and courtiers, decked out in jewels and rich cloth, perfumed and rouged, she pushed the dowdy queen into the shade in her own court. And she did it all with an insolent air that proclaimed her own ancient lineage: the Mortemarts had the blood of Spanish kings in their veins; to their daughter, being mistress of the king was a sort of "marriage by left hand" that she earned by her blood, as well as by her beauty and brains. In any case, posterity will never forget the picture of de Montespan ". . . dressed entirely in French lace, her hair in a thousand ringlets . . . the pearls of Marshal d'Hôpital embellished as earrings, pendants of diamonds . . . a triumphant beauty." All this was very elegant, and it cost a lot of money—more than we shall ever know, for no good records were kept.

This lady was more than a doll dressed and rouged for the ball; she also had brains and a level of culture above many of the people around her. Like her brother Vivonne, who told Louis that "books nourished his brains just as the King's partridges nourished his body," Athénaïs was no stranger to books and literature. Indeed, Abbé Testu remarked that of the three daughters of the Duke of Mortemart, "Madame de Tianges talks like a person who dreams, Madame de Fontevrault like a person who speaks, Madame de Montespan like a person who reads." Mazarin had already impressed upon Louis the importance of patronizing literary and artistic endeavors in his court; Madame de Montespan reenforced this tendency by surrounding herself with artists, musicians, and writers. The artists did well by her, but some of the writers joined the pack as soon as her star collapsed—Racine should have blushed at least privately for his attack on the fallen mistress in *Esther*. Culture gave her the wit and the information needed to be a mistress of the king; she could amuse him in private with her ironic mimicry; she loved to "take off" the personages around her—savagely sometimes; she could hold her own in a witty conversation—her mocking sallies were famous. She needed all this to maintain her place in a court where there were many women only waiting for a chance to displace her.

She also had a disposition that sometimes erupted in violent torrents of words, and stubborn insistence on her own position as the only right one. How often she subjected the king to these outbursts we do not know; Madame de Maintenon, who took care of her children during these years, many times found her more than merely difficult; but the situation between these two women at this point in time may have accounted for the outbursts. Madame de Maintenon, as foster mother, enjoyed the love of the children, and felt responsible for their discipline; Madame de Montespan, as real mother, often found the children indifferent to her and tried to bribe or buy their love with food or favors that the foster mother did not think appropriate. Maybe under these tensions Athénaïs' disposition and self-control broke down more easily than when with the king. Even so, we do know that Louis had to take a great deal from this beautiful woman who captured his heart and his imagination.

While Athénaïs secured many favors for herself and her family, she was careful not to spread her influence too thin. A letter to a mother superior who had asked for her intercession recommends that the good sister discuss the matter with Colbert, and then goes on to say, "In that which concerns the affair of Sister Jésus-Marie . . . I ask you to say to her that it would be a pleasure to oblige her, but it is impossible. . . . I do not speak to the King about the affairs of private persons. I reserve this liberty for some communities [convents or monasteries], but I assure you that I do this only with reserve."[18] But she was generous with her own money, giving to hospitals and convents quite freely, and she continued to do so until her death: the Hôpital des Vieillards, the Ursuline Convent, the Hôpital de Sainte-Famille, the Maison de Saint-Joseph, and others owed much to her generosity. The gifts were probably not without ulterior motives. Like Louis, Athénaïs was concerned for her soul, even though she might find sin an agreeable pastime. To the superior of one of the convents that benefited from her bounty, she wrote, "I hope that you will remember me in your prayers . . . and that you will have the community do the same."[19] This is quite in character with another of her famous remarks. When the Duchess d'Uzès commented on her strict observance of the Lenten fasts, she exclaimed, "What, Madame, because I commit one sin must I commit others?" (Madame de Caylus).

There can be no doubt about Louis' involvement with Madame de Montespan; it was an affair of grand passion that lasted about twelve years. He sought whenever possible to please her, to do what she might wish of him. Even when he was off to the wars he did not forget to order new pleasures for her. Colbert, in his role as superintendent of the *bâtiments,* often received orders to continue work on her apartments, on the terraces outside her door, or for the "purchase of orange trees," or for other things. Colbert must "always ask her what she wishes."[20] Louis spent immense sums of money on her for jewels, clothes, her house at Clagny, for her "pin money" that went to the gaming table, charity, and the like. Of all the women who attracted Louis' attention, Madame de Montespan unquestionably was the most expensive package.

This also was the most scandalous affair of the reign. The manuscript copies of the *Amours de Louis le Grand,* as well as printed works purporting to tell the story (published always outside of France) provided reading that must have been bad for public morals in France, as well as for the image of the French court in Europe. The clergymen of the court and many pious people in Louis' entourage plotted to end this disorder. Two of the most eloquent clergymen of the century, Bourdaloue and Bossuet, as well as the young Fénelon and the Dukes of Beauvilliers and Chevreuse (who were sons-in-law of Colbert) formed the nucleus of a "party of moral order," soon to be joined by other clergymen and pious laymen. The blow fell during the Lenten season of 1675. Madame de Montespan sought to perform her Easter duty. She went to confession to a simple priest attached to the parish church of Versailles; such a man should make no difficulties for a great lady. But Father Lecuyer was a man of principles; he refused her absolution. The Curé of Versailles, ordered to admonish his assistant, refused to do so; there could be no absolution for an adulterous woman. At the same time, Louis' confessor found it impossible to find a time for the king to make his confession. Louis called in Bossuet for advice. Separation! A Lenten sermon by Father Bourdaloue eloquently called attention to the problems of salvation. Madame de Montespan was furious when Louis gave in; there was no help for it; she retired to her house on Rue Vaugirard, and Louis went off to the war in Flanders. The disorder was over. Or was it? Louis assured the queen, Bishop Bossuet, his confessor Father de la Chaise, and the Curé of Versailles that it was all over, that the disorder would end. During the next few months while Louis was in Flanders, Bossuet wrote to him often, exhorting him to remember the "promises he had given to God and man." It would be easier since the king was physically distant from the lady. "I do not ask, Sire," Bossuet wrote, "that you stamp out all in a moment a flame so violent . . . but strive to subdue it little by little . . . turn your heart toward God, think often of your obligation to love Him. . . ." Bossuet, muffled in a cloak to disguise himself, also visited Madame de Montespan to strengthen her resolution. She was occupied with "good works."

Louis gave the lady permission to go to Versailles before he returned from Flanders. It did not seem right to deprive the lady of the "delights" of the court and contact with her children just because the king had committed sin. Both Father de la Chaise and Bishop Bossuet were in despair. When Louis returned himself, the first person he met was Bossuet. "Say nothing to me, Monsieur, say nothing to me! I have given my orders." Louis and Athénaïs met in the presence of several ladies of unblemished character who were to act as chaperons. Madame de Caylus wrote, ". . . the King came . . . to Madame de Montespan's apartment . . . but he gradually withdrew her to the alcove of a window where they whispered together for a long time, wept and said the things that are usually said in such cases. . . . Finally they made a profound reverence to the venerable matrons and withdrew into an adjoining room, and thence came the Duchess of Orléans and later the Count of Toulouse." The memoirist believed that she could detect in the character and looks of the Duchess of Orléans traces "of this combat between love and religion." For the moment love won the fight: Louis had neither the will nor the character needed to repair his ways. There were to be two more children to legitimize, the sixth and seventh of the affair.

There can be little doubt that Louis recognized the bad example that he gave to his subjects. ". . . a prince," he wrote, "ought always to be a perfect model of virtue, it would be good that he avoid the follies common to the rest of mankind . . . nonetheless, if it should happen that we fall in spite of ourselves into some of these errors, it is important, at least, to minimize the consequences—to observe the precautions that I have always practiced . . . the first is that the time we give to our love affairs must not prejudice our political affairs, because our first object should always be the preservation of our *gloire* and authority . . . the second consideration, more delicate and more difficult, is that in abandoning our heart we must preserve our mind; that we separate the tenderness of a lover from the resolutions of a sovereign; that the beauty who gives us pleasure never has the liberty to discuss our affairs nor the people who serve us: these two things must be separate."[21] In this same vein Louis once spoke to a group of his courtiers and servants including Lionne, Le Tellier, Colbert, Villeroi, and others: "You are all of you my friends . . . whom I regard most in my realm, and in whom I have the greatest confidence. I am young and women generally have considerable influence over those of my age. I enjoin you all, therefore, that should you see that a woman, whoever she may be, has acquired ascendancy over me in the smallest degree to appraise me immediately of the fact. I shall need only forty-eight hours to rid myself of her and to set your minds at rest."[22] Clearly Louis was willing to excuse his behavior by saying that as a young man, he shared the foibles of men; he also seemed to believe that he was strong enough to avoid the consequences of the traps.

21

MATURITY: THE ROYAL FAMILY

THE KING WAS HEAD of the family, that is to say, the house of Bourbon, which included his own son's family; the cadet lines of Orléans, Condé, and Conti; the legitimized princely families descended from Henry IV; and his own legitimized bastard children. The king's authority over all these princes and princesses was considerable: the men acted out ceremonial roles at court, held offices in the king's household, and sometimes were given commands in the king's army. As might be expected, with the memory still green of the rebellions headed by princes of the blood during the regency of Marie de Médicis and the reign of Louis XIII, and of the *Fronde,* the king did not give these princes positions from which they could launch a revolt. Even a brother as harmless and as loyal as Philippe was refused the governorship of Languedoc because, as Louis explained to his son, the king "was persuaded by the disorders that we have so often seen in the kingdom, that it is a lack of foresight and judgment to put important governments in the hands of sons of France who, for the good of the state, ought never to have places of security other than in their brother's heart." Foresight and judgment—these were things that Louis tried to use in an effort to control the future. The princesses of the blood were even more slaves of the king than were their brothers; slaves bound by golden chains, perhaps, but nonetheless slaves who could be married abroad in the game of dynastic politics, to serve the king's policy. Two daughters of Gaston of Orléans were married to the Dukes of Tuscany and Savoy; a daughter of Philippe and Henriette, to the King of Spain. True, the Duchess of Tuscany revenged herself by making her husband miserable, and then by deserting him for a convent in France, but she could not refuse to do her cousin's bidding when he arranged the wedding.

One of these princesses was somewhat of an exception. Anne-Marie-Louise, Duchess of Montpensier, known in this story as La Grande Mademoiselle, several times refused to do the will of her cousin, and suffered only a temporary exile for her rebellion. As the daughter of Gaston of Orléans and Marie of Bourbon, Duchess of Montpensier, she had an immense fortune that both made her the richest heiress of all Europe and gave her freedom not enjoyed by her less fortunate half-sisters. She also was the target for royal fortune-hunters like Charles of England when he needed money to fight his way to his father's throne. La Grande Mademoiselle, however, had her own ideas: she wanted to marry a great king, the King of France or perhaps the emperor—she wanted nothing to do with adventurers or minor princes. We have seen her in this story at the cradle of her cousin Louis, at the Bastille where she fired on the king's troops, in exile after the *Fronde,* back at court again playing La Grande Mademoiselle. She rebuffed Turenne, when at Louis' request, he tried to marry her off to the ruffian King of Portugal; and she pushed aside suggestions that she might marry the Duke of Lorraine. She preferred to be La Grande Mademoiselle at the court of France, to visit her properties, to take the waters at Forges—all this better than the doubtful honor of a political marriage. The demands of her flesh seem to have been weak; she appeared content to remain an old maid and to allow her property eventually to be divided among her relatives. But at the age of forty-three (1669) she fell in love—love that became a *cause célèbre* and brought little glory to her cousin the king.

The crisis broke shortly after tragedy struck the royal family in the form of the death of Madame, Henriette of England. The latter had just succeeded in the negotiation of the famous Treaty of Dover, and was the toast of the family when she fell ill suddenly and died. Henriette was buried with all the honors due a royal princess, in the basilica of Saint-Denis, but even before she reached her tomb, men considered the question of her successor. Louis' remark—"There is a place vacant"—has become famous; he offered it to La Grande Mademoiselle who was some thirteen years older than his brother. After discussion, both Philippe and La Grande Mademoiselle decided that it would not work: he preferred to take a chance on a German princess, and she had already fixed her attention on another.

The object of her affection was one of the captains of the king's guards. This was no minor office; marshals of France were proud to be asked to purchase these places. Her "captain" was the Marquis de Puyguilhem (Péguilin), better known as Lauzun. Mademoiselle's memoirs dealing with the affair are charmingly naïve; indeed, it is difficult to believe that she could have been so simple. Her hero was six to eight years her junior and an entire universe away from her socially and financially. He had to make his way by his sword and his wits; she was the granddaughter of Henry IV. She managed to bridge the gap of age and station to allow him to understand that she loved him; with considerable caution, he long feigned not to understand, and yet managed to take full advantage of her naïveté; it was a dangerous situation for the captain of the guards. Lauzun was a man whom women liked. Some of his competitors for the favors of the ladies ruefully admitted that they could not understand how a "short, homely, greasy, dirty little man with a bald spot," who resembled more "a Tartar than a Frenchman," could have so much attraction. The descriptive words are from his enemies; he also was a bold, brave, vigorous fellow, gallant in war, masculine, virile, strong, and he knew much about women. He had his own way to make in the world. He attracted the king's attention enough to become captain of the guards; he became a duke and a favorite of the Queen of England, whom he served when the revolution of 1688 drove her from the island kingdom.[1] Once Lauzun also aroused Louis' ire to the point where the king threw his cane out of the window so that he would not use it on a subject, and finally Lauzun inspired enough fear for the king to send him to prison. No matter what anyone thought of him, he was a man of parts who several times managed to retrieve a personal catastrophy that would certainly have ended the career of many another. Saint-Simon, who became his brother-in-law, has left the world a saga of Lauzun's adventures; most of these stories must be taken with considerable salt, for "Péguilin" was not above telling the best of all possible yarns about his career.

Louis' first response to his cousin's demand for the right to marry this man was an amused acceptance of the idea; she was surely old enough to know her own mind. When three of his soldiers formally demanded the hand of La Grande Mademoiselle for their comrade in arms, Louis consented. How right was one of Lauzun's representatives who urged the couple to marry at once; how wrong was La Grande Mademoiselle's determination to have a court wedding. Time allowed the rise of opposition. The case was simple enough: the Duchess of Montpensier was a very rich woman —a very, very rich woman—and it would be a shame to have all that money slip out of the family into the hands of an "adventurer." When she began to endow her future husband with handsomely wealthy properties, the full meaning of her marriage stood revealed. Madame de Montespan had children who would need money; Philippe had a daughter who needed money; even the Condés, who were quite rich, could use more money; the properties, apanages, fiefs, and sovereign territories belonging to La Grande Mademoiselle had long been regarded as destined for the family. But even if there had been no money involved, the idea that she might marry Lauzun was shocking. She was of the blood of the Bourbons, and the Bourbons were not impressed by the pretty speech of the soldier who thanked Louis for allowing his blood to mingle with that of his subjects. The queen, whose flexibility was next to nil, was outraged; Condé refused to believe that it could be true. Madame de Montespan suggested alternative action. Under such pressures Louis had to reconsider.

After the event Louis wrote a memorandum in which he explained what had happened; this was the "official statement" to be given abroad. He explained that his cousin had wrung consent for the marriage from him by her tears and entreaties; that he agreed to receive the marshals who came to ask for her hand for Lauzun; that he only reluctantly gave that consent, "shrugging my [his] shoulders and saying that she was forty-three years old and could do what she wished." But the next day "reports came to me that my cousin said that she made the marriage because I wished it!" At that point Louis insists that he called her to him, and in the presence of witnesses, persuaded her not only to disavow having said any such thing but also to make a statement that would assure the world that the king had nothing to do with the marriage. Nonetheless, reports continued to flourish to the effect that the king, anxious to favor Lauzun, was forcing his cousin into marriage. "For this reason," Louis writes, "I resolved to break the marriage; . . . my reputation was involved." He went on to say that he called her to him again and "offered to lead her to the church himself" to marry any qualified person except Lauzun. "She shed tears and sobbed, threw herself at my knees as if I had stricken her in the heart. . . ." Louis also shed tears that he failed to mention in this memorandum. As for Lauzun, "he received [the news] with all the constancy and submission that I could ask for." Louis' story fits the facts fairly well; it simply leaves out some of the important details of family protests; there is no doubt about her tears—or Louis' for that matter—and it may well be that a "dry cough" (the Prince of Condé's) prevented the king from weakening at the critical moment. The king did not emerge from this scene in the story with any great *gloire;* but the worst was yet to come.

What happened afterward is open to several interpretations. However, the plain facts are that Lauzun gave back the lands and titles that had been bestowed upon him, and then like a bolt of lightning he was arrested and sent to the fortress of Pignerol in Italy, where he was kept in close confinement. At first he was not allowed even to talk with his fellow-prisoner Fouquet. Lauzun remained in prison for about a decade, and was released only after La Grande Mademoiselle had given the sovereignty of Dombes and the Comte d'Eu to Louis' bastard son the Duke of Maine. The king obviously "plucked" his cousin before returning her lover (whom she probably married about that time).

The money, however, hardly explains the harsh nature of Lauzun's prison sentence. Some have asserted that Louvois and Madame de Montespan, both of whom had old scores to settle with Lauzun, undermined his position and secured his arrest.[2] If they did, the best interpretation seems to be that they persuaded Louis that Lauzun was the kind of man who could lead a *Fronde.* With La Grande Mademoiselle's wealth and his bold character, rebellion might be possible. Louis, preparing to go to war in the Netherlands, far from his capital, may have believed that Lauzun, like Fouquet, was too dangerous to leave free while he was away, and that the two should share the hospitality of Pignerol. No matter what explanation is found, Louis does not come off very well. Lauzun did not initiate the love affair, and when the king decided against it, he accepted the decision "with all constancy and submission." To send him to prison was an act of tyranny that was not characteristic of Louis XIV up to that period; if it were, Louis would have fared much worse at the hands of history than he has.[3]

When Henriette died, a "place" was indeed vacant, and when La Grande Mademoiselle decided that she did not wish to become "Madame," French diplomacy cast about to find a suitable princess. The choice fell upon Elizabeth-Charlotte of Bavaria, Princess Palatine; she is known to us as La Palatine, or Madame, or simply as Liselotte. Some writers have suggested that the marriage was made with the idea of claiming a share of the Palatinate inheritance, which in fact did happen, but a glance at the documents that were used to establish these claims a decade later will show that at the time of the marriage the French had no idea about the complexities of German feudal law and no serious concern for the inheritance of the Palatinate. If we look at the marriage contract, it would seem that the jewels and vessels of silver and gold that the princess brought with her to France were of primary importance: the collar of pearls (fifty-four in number), the four watches (one set with diamonds), the bracelets, pins, earrings, and the silver and gold vessels were all carefully enumerated. Several of them must have been very beautiful.[4] But Liselotte was not a bejeweled beauty; she was a big-boned, broad-faced, buxom, outspoken lady—married to Monsieur who used rouge, wore ribbons and lace, and loved jewelry. He walked in mincing steps; she prescribed a two-league walk in case of illness. When Philippe first saw her, his question was the obvious one, "How can I sleep with her?" Her first question we do not know, but her voluminous correspondence, in which she was often brutally outspoken about her opinions, gives us the answer to many of the later ones.

La Palatine was to be a fixture in the French court for the rest of the reign. From her letters it is clear that she, like so many women, fell in love with the king; Louis did come off quite handsomely when compared with his brother. There is no indication at all that Louis ever responded to his sister-in-law's secret affection. Liselotte was the center of the small German circle in the court; she participated in all the court events, from the hunt to the balls. When her Heidelberg was destroyed by the king's order, she wept; when her son had to marry the king's legitimized daughter (by de Montespan), she suffered and carried on terribly; her hates seem stronger than her loves, and the historian is cautioned to use her letters carefully.

By the time Elizabeth-Charlotte arrived at court, the queen was almost in despair: her husband was unfaithful, and children of the mistresses flourished while her own died. Louis' legitimate children died one by one until only the eldest, the Grand Dauphin, remained. The little girls, named after the queen mother (Elizabeth-Anne, Anne-Thérèse, Marie-Anne), all died shortly after birth. Her second son, the Duke of Anjou, lived a little longer, but he died before reaching the age of three. These children were all buried with great pomp in the crypt at Saint-Denis; their deaths were a great tragedy to the queen, who understood that her most important role at court was the bearing of children to support the dynasty. It is difficult to measure Louis'. paternal feelings. In the *Bibliothèque Nationale* there is a little packet of letters[5] that he wrote to Madame de la Motte, the governess of his legitimate children. They are nearly all formal replies to her letters about the health of her charges: Louis expresses his satisfaction with the "perfect health" of his sons; with the fact that they had arrived at Compiègne where everyone knew "the air was better"; that the dauphin had been *sage* (an American father today would say "a good boy"); that the fever that "has given me room to worry" had now passed; that the king was satisfied with the good Madame de la Motte and wanted her to know it. The illness that took the life of the Duke of Anjou obviously caused Louis much concern. The first letter mentioning it came June 16, 1671—the king was well aware of the grave situation. He sent his personal physicians, continued to write and demand news, and finally went to Saint-Germain himself. The child died on July 12, 1671. But Louis was accustomed to death. If one follows the royal family from year to year it soon becomes evident that very few went by without death's striking someone in the house of Bourbon, mostly children under five. Visconti may not be far wrong when he writes that the royal children were killed by their physicians and surgeons who, prompt to bleed them, quickly ended their lives,[6] and yet we know that seventeenth-century children died easily even without the aid of physicians.

Louis took an interest in the education and the welfare of his son. His *Mémoires* were presumably composed as advice to the dauphin, and we find many other traces of the king's concern for the boy's spiritual as well as his secular education. The letters that passed between them, however, are stiff and formal. "I was very happy for the letter that you wrote me," he writes to the dauphin, aged eleven. "It appears you wish to see me and that you have some feelings for the things that concern my person, and the advantages of the church. Continue in this attitude and strengthen yourself in sentiments that are worthy of a dauphin and my son. . . . Your father hopes for nothing more than to see you worthy of that which you should someday become." His roundabout way of saying it may indicate that Louis is quite willing to see that day postponed. It certainly is a letter from a king to his heir rather than from a father to a son.[7] The letter that he wrote to Bossuet in May of 1676 is in the same tone: ". . . regarding my son, I recommend to you always to cultivate his mind with the necessary care for him to understand his duties toward himself, toward me, and above all toward God."[8]

The religious services that marked the dauphin's rise toward maturity were elaborately celebrated. His formal baptism in 1668 with the pope as godfather and the Queen of England as godmother (the Cardinal of Ven-dôme and Princess of Conti acting in their behalf) was a great display of pomp and ceremony. The château at Saint-Germain was gorgeously deco-rated and the little boy (six years old) was fêted by the great of the church, the state, and the army. It was an event to make him realize the distance between a king and other people, as well as to impress the world with the importance of this little boy in whose mother's name Louis was then making extensive (perhaps even extravagant) claims to territory in the Nether-lands.[9] After the ceremony came a banquet; the king and queen were served by dukes and peers of the realm; the dauphin probably went directly to bed.

With the testy old Duke de Montausier as his governor and Bishop Bossuet as his preceptor, the dauphin's education proceeded as well as could be expected. There were books of precepts prepared to bring him up as a Christian and as a king.[10] The young Louis copied some of these in his own hand, others he seems merely to have read. His most important surviving composition is a history of the Dutch War, *De Bello Batavico, anno 1672,* which was copied by a scribe and corrected by Bossuet. In this work the dauphin had troubles with capitalization that arouse considerable sympathy. Some of Bossuet's "sentences" that he had to copy obviously reflect the king, his father: "A general ought to endure cold, sun, and all the labors more than others, for he thereby wins his soldiers"; "One should not speak of love to young people for fear of exciting them in desires already too strong"; "A man born to high command ought above all to avoid ignorance"; "One should not listen to those who say that it is an act of courage to avenge oneself on one's foes. Nothing is more praiseworthy and glorious than to forgive and have clemency"; "Flatterers are incapable of being friends. They must be masters or slaves" (Plato); "One should not scorn reputation, but true *gloire* is always united with virtue." These and many more similar bits of wisdom were supposed to teach this boy to be a king.[11] No one will ever know whether or not he could have used all this wisdom, for his father outlived him.

As death cut down the number of legitimate children, those born out of wedlock became more important. As we have seen, Louis recognized both the mother and her children when Mademoiselle de la Vallière became the Duchess de Vaujours. Madame Colbert's little charges then came to court to take their rightful place as "children of France." Madame de Montespan's children created a different problem. As we have noted, until Parlement decreed her separation from Monsieur de Montespan, her children might be legally his. Thus they had to be hidden to prevent unpleasantness or scandal. There were three of these children when Louis decided to legitimize them in December of 1673 by the following formula:

Louis, by grace of God King of France and Navarre, the tenderness that nature gives us for our children and many other reasons which increase in us these sentiments, oblige us to recognize our natural children, Louis Auguste, Louis César, and Louise-Françoise, and to give them public recognition . . . we wish and intend that they should be named the Duke of Maine, the Duke of Vexin, and Mlle. of Nantes . . . by our power and authority we declare them legitimate. . . .

The mother of these children was not mentioned; everyone knew, however, who had borne them. Their Christian names associated them with their father, and in the case of the boys, with the mighty of the Roman past.

The arrival of these children had introduced into the entourage of the king a person who was destined to play a great role in the reign, the widow of the poet Scarron. There is much mythology around the life of Françoise d'Aubigné, a mythology buttressed by forged or altered letters as well as by loaded memoirs.[12] The fact of the matter was that even nameless children of France must be under the care of someone whose manners, language, and culture were those of the court and whose background would guarantee gentility. Madame de Montespan "discovered" Françoise, and that good lady had no qualms about caring for the bastard children of the king. It is not true that she negotiated with Louis himself before accepting the place; she needed something to do, and this was a splendid opportunity; she could never have guessed how splendid it was to be.

Françoise d'Aubigné was born in 1635 in the prison of Niort where her father was incarcerated for debt; a few years later she was taken to the islands of the Antilles where she lived until her teens when she again returned to France. Baptized a Catholic, she was briefly converted to the Huguenot faith by a relative (Madame de Villette), but reconverted by the sisters of the Ursuline Convent of Saint-Jacques where her mother had placed her on returning to France. Her prospects were poor; she had a reasonable education for a woman, but she was obviously doomed to live on the edge of respectability, even though her parents were noble, because there was no money for a dowry. Indeed, a poor marriage or the convent seemed her only prospects. At this point (she was just sixteen) she met the poet Scarron through a relative. He was many years her senior, a cripple, and anything but handsome, but he was willing to marry her without a dowry, and such a marriage seemed to her preferable to the convent.

Scarron was one of the important minor literary figures of the era; he wrote pamphlets for both Mazarin and Condé, poetry, and plays—none of these efforts turned out to be great literature, but he was literate, and in his house Françoise not only heard intellectual things discussed, but also met many important literary figures of the day. The marriage may not have been a very romantic one, but her education was enlarged by her life with Scarron. He died in 1660, leaving her at twenty-six a widow burdened with his debts. She managed to secure a little pension, but her prospects were slender. She was, however, received at the Hôtel de Richelieu and by the family of Marshal d'Albert, where she came to know people who lived in the larger world, and to discuss affairs of the court. Before she assumed the care of the king's children, she knew Madame de Sévigné, Madame de La Fayette, Madame de Coulanges, and others—a respectable, as well as cultured, group of friends. The person who cared for royal children had to be refined and genteel; Madame de Montespan undoubtedly felt that she was very fortunate to get Madame Scarron to assume the task: she was modest, educated, and capable of keeping a secret. Of course, Madame de Sévigné soon found out what her friend was doing. "We have found Madame de Scarron," writes our gossipy correspondent; "That is to say, we know where she is, for it is not so easy really to visit her. . . ."

Her charges came with regular succession: 1669, 1670, 1672, 1674. The first little girl died very young, but the others, with the exception of the Count de Vexin, lived to become adults. At first the children were separated, each with its own nurse, and Madame Scarron supervising the several households, but finally they were brought together in the house on the Rue Vaugirard with Françoise as mistress of the establishment. Apparently it was here that she first met Louis XIV who liked to visit his children; the eldest boy, the Duke of Maine, remained Louis' favorite throughout his life. We do not know much about this phase of the story; Langlois, who probably knew more about Madame de Maintenon than anyone else has ever known, says that there are "obscure points" about this period of her life. Louis seems to have taken a dislike to her at first: her language was a little pedantic and a little precious, and her mien so austere as to suggest that she might be a religious *dévote*—all things that Louis disliked in a woman. The stiffness of her talk as well as the fact that his mistress seemed to have no end of requests for "her friend," were both annoying, but in time he seems to have changed his opinion. She was attractive, she obviously loved the children, and she was virtuous. It may even be true that the king envied the pure love that the children enjoyed; and it may also be true that she put him off when he suggested an improper relationship.

There is a letter that Langlois accepts as authentic that would suggest that Louis made advances quite early in their acquaintanceship. But the date of the letter is not fully established. In it she writes, "This master [Louis] comes to see me sometimes in spite of myself; he returns without hopes but not rebuffed. You can guess that on his return home he finds someone to talk to; for my part, I am at ease knowing the rightness of my behavior." A recent biographer[13] has analyzed this problem at great length. Louis was only three years younger than Françoise; both were under forty; she was attractive; he was a man with a free and easy attitude toward women. Jove could carry off Europa whenever he found her. Once Louis lost his distrust of Françoise's intellectual stance, he could easily fall into an amorous mood. Although she evidently rejected his overtures, Cordelier argues that this was the real beginning of the affair between them. Naturally Madame de Sévigné also learned that Louis enjoyed visiting the widow Scarron: ". . . there is in the company of my friends a certain man [Louis] who finds her [Madame Scarron] so friendly and such good company that he is impatient of her absence . . ." (March 20, 1673). Louis undoubtedly was attracted by her calm intelligence—perhaps even by her virtue. In any case, when the children were legitimized, the widow Scarron went to court where she soon was to play an important role.

At court the relationship between the governess and the mistress changed for the worse. The two women were in more direct competition for the affection of the children, and the governess felt that the mother broke rules both of discipline and of diet to curry their favor. Furthermore, there is more than a suspicion that Françoise was a little jealous of the mistress' relationship with the king—if not jealous, she was critical of the scandal that it created and the danger to the souls of the two sinners. Difficult scenes between the two women became more and more common; after one of them, Françoise wrote to her confessor, "Madame de Montespan and I had a hot argument today. . . . I wept very much and she told the story to the King. . . . I do not dare to go directly to him because she would never pardon me for doing so."[14] Naturally Madame de Sévigné learned of these conflicts: "The perfect friendship between Quantova [Montespan] and her traveling companion [Françoise] has been converted in the last two years into perfect enmity . . . you ask whence it proceeds: from the friend's pride which makes her rebel against the orders from Quantova . . . she is willing to comply with the wishes of the father, but not of the mother" (August 7, 1675).

Françoise finally did speak to the king. "Do not fear a thing," she wrote to her confessor; "I think that I spoke to him as a Christian and as a true friend of Madame de Montespan. . . ."[15] There is another story that tells of the king arriving on the scene of a fight between the two women. Françoise seized the opportunity: "If your majesty will step into the next room . . . I shall tell you about it." According to the story, Louis was much alarmed at the possibility of losing the governess of his children, but what was his defense of Madame de Montespan? "Have you noticed how her [Montespan's] eyes fill with tears when she hears of a generous and touching action?"[16] In any case, Françoise let the king know that she would remain with the children.

It was during these years that Françoise became Madame de Maintenon. As she wrote, she had always wanted to own an estate (*terre*), and through the bounty of the king, she was able to buy the handsome château of Maintenon with its lands and gardens. This was a princely gift that provided her with a measure of security; however, she obviously had no intention of retiring from the court. Louis himself gave her the name when he introduced her as the Marquise de Maintenon; henceforth, Scarron was forgotten, and Madame de Maintenon began to emphasize the fact that one of her ancestors was a companion of Henry IV during the religious wars— he was a Huguenot.[17]

In 1675 when the crisis arose over Madame de Montespan's Easter duty and the king decided to send her away, Madame de Maintenon took the young Duke of Maine, who had become quite lame, on a trip to the south of France to try to find a cure. The progression was a triumphal tour; townspeople and nobility turned out to honor the king's son. Louis' letters are not preserved, but in Madame de Maintenon's correspondence there is evidence that he wrote to her during this trip. The subject of the letters undoubtedly was the health of the boy; yet Madame de Maintenon was surely pleased to have the royal attention. Furthermore, when she returned to court, her stature had grown considerably, for even Louvois now found it important to pay attention to her. Louis and the fair Athénaïs were again reunited, but Madame de Maintenon was making progress as "friend" of the king, and as Cordelier has pointed out, "friendship" between people of different sexes often "goes further than that." This does not mean that Madame de Maintenon used her relationship with Madame de Montespan as cynically as that lady had exploited her "friendship" with Louise de la Vallière. Françoise was a virtuous woman. From her letters we see that her interests during these years were centered on securing favors for herself, her brother, her friends; on the children under her care; and on her salvation. What part Louis XIV played in her fantasies we shall surely never know.[18]

The years 1676, 1677, 1678 were difficult ones for Louis. The fortunes of war were turning in his favor, but there were frustrations and dangers at every corner. With all Europe leagued against him and even England about to join his enemies, with economic disorders in the kingdom and consequent bread riots and threats of rebellion, with complaints over taxation, no one could be sure of the future. Louis never forgot that the Great German War (Thirty Years' War) and the war with Spain bred the dissatisfactions that had finally erupted into the *Fronde,* and he knew that such things could happen again. His physicians report that he had bad dreams, that he cried out at night, that he was sleepless; they gave him pills, enemas, and "medicine" (cathartics). Obviously the king was disturbed. His problem may have been personal as well as political. Louis was approaching his fortieth birthday, a period when many men seem to worry about themselves, and often act indiscreetly. Madame de Montespan did have two children during these years, but there is much evidence that Louis was also "unfaithful" to her many times. Madame de Sévigné, as usual, did not miss the symptoms; she wrote of "fresh game" and predicted an early end to the reign of "Quantova." The names of the women are well enough known; indeed, the court was filled with "beauties" who did not believe it sinful to seduce the king, or vice versa. Athénaïs was clearly in trouble; she fought back in every way that she could. However, she too was emotionally disturbed; this is the period when she began to squander huge sums on the gaming tables and to become fat. In the years that immediately followed her fall from favor, her gambling debts were tremendous, and her weight became excessive.

With the end of the war and the peace of Nymwegen it appeared that Louis was, in fact, Louis "the Great." The victory had been a limited one, but it was a victory, and the king "gave peace to Europe." Perhaps the new political situation demanded a new personal one; in any case, Madame de Montespan became a duchess. Her services recognized, a new mistress stepped into her place. Mademoiselle de Fontanges, not yet twenty, arrived at court with the intention of becoming the king's mistress. She was "beautiful as an angel, had an excellent heart, but was a stupid little fool" (Liselotte); she had the backing of her parents and the support of the anti-Montespan clique for her campaign; it was not long before she occupied an apartment next to the king's cabinet.[19] Not everyone was happy to see her "arrive." Madame de Maintenon wrote to her confessor, "Pray and have prayers said for the King, who is on the brink of a precipice." Madame de Montespan urged Françoise to try to become the king's mistress, too. Then there would be three: "Yes me [de Montespan] in name, that girl [Fontanges] in fact, and you [de Maintenon] in the heart." The statement speaks much about what was happening to the king. While he took the young girl for his mistress, his conversations with Madame de Maintenon became more and more frequent, to the point where she was being recognized as the "best friend" of the king. Obviously Louis knew that he must test himself, but he did not know what he really wanted.

Actually the Fontanges affair could not have great consequences. She was a fluffy little girl who did not have enough sense to curtsy to the queen whose bed she violated; who, set up as a duchess, had to have eight horses for her carriage (de Montespan needed only six); who flaunted her relations with the king both foolishly and shamefully. Louis was much taken with her body, but it is inconceivable that he could have enjoyed her company. She was so ignorant that he "seemed ashamed every time she opened her lips in the presence of a third party."[20] It is impossible to say how long she could have held the king's attention, for her career was cut short by a miscarriage that not only failed to produce a child, but wounded her mortally. Before it was understood how serious her condition was, people joked that she was wounded in the service of the king. It turned out that she lost her health, her beauty, the king's interest, and finally her life. She died in 1681 without creating much of a sensation. Louis however, seems to have been shaken by the whole affair; after her death, for all outward appearances his age of "gallantry" was over, and his life became regular. We shall see later what this meant.

It was about time for the king to regularize his life and end the scandal if he was to give a good example to the coming generation, for after the Treaty of Nymwegen, his son and his brother's daughter were ready for marriage. These were the two surviving children from the marriages of 1660–61; the dauphin was married to Marie-Anne, daughter of the Duke of Bavaria; Henriette-Anne, to the sickly King of Spain. Of the two marriages, the second was the more important for the dynasty, for if Henriette-Anne could gain some ascendancy over the mind and spirit of Charles II, the problems of the Spanish succession could be solved either by the birth of an heir to Charles II, or by the transfer of the Spanish crowns to a Bourbon prince in case of Charles's death. The Bavarian marriage was important solely as a means of securing the crown of France in the elder Bourbon line, for the Bavarian princesses could be expected to produce healthy children.

Henriette-Anne was married to Charles II by proxy. The Prince of Conti presented the ring, the thirteen pieces of gold, and answered the marriage questions. As soon as she was married, the Queen of Spain took her place on the high dais while a cardinal read the high mass. Afterward the Queens of France and Spain were sprinkled with holy water and saluted with the holy sacrament. At this point there was an unsightly contest for position between the Cardinal de Bonzi and the Bishop of Orléans to see which would have the right to present the king with the Bible for his kiss —the cardinal won. Louis took the oath to defend the Treaty of Nymwegen, and then there was a splendid banquet; the Queen of Spain ate at Louis' table with full royal honors.[21]

For all the magnificent decoration in the chapel (cloth of gold, velvet with gold fleurs-de-lys, Persian rugs, etc.) and the impressive ceremony involving cardinals, bishops, princes of the blood, and people of quality, the marriage was not a happy one. Everyone knew that Charles II was a dim-witted, sickly, unhappy man—hardly a suitable husband for the lovely daughter of Henriette of England. She would be isolated in the court at Madrid, surrounded by Francophobes and ill-wishers. It was a political marriage to introduce some French influence in that court, but even Henriette's parrot was strangled (probably because it spoke French) and she lived and died in Madrid under most sad conditions; there was more than a suggestion of poison at the time of her death in 1689.

The other marriage had first been proposed in 1670 when Louis was preparing for the Dutch War. The Bavarian house was a suitable family for an alliance with the Bourbons; even though they were only electoral princes, they had emperors in their history and they provided a nice counterweight for Viennese Hapsburg in German politics. Thus even during the war (1672–78), Cardinal d'Estrées secretly began negotiations for this marriage, and as soon as the peace came, Croissy went to Munich to finish them. It is an interesting fact that Marie-Thérèse, as mother of the groom, sent Croissy the full power to sign the contract of marriage.[22]

The first ceremony took place in Munich, January 25, 1680, when the bride's brother, Maximilian, married the princess in the name of the dauphin; the Marshal de Créqui was present to represent the king. She arrived in Strasbourg in the middle of February where the Duke and Duchess of Richelieu, who had been appointed heads of her household, met her and accepted the jewels that made up her dowry. Obviously the Bourbons were not expecting too much from their new relatives. Louis wrote to the Duke of Richelieu: "It may be that they [the jewels] will not have the value promised [100,000 *écus*] . . . but I do not want you to make any difficulties on this account." De Rochefort was instructed to ". . . accept the jewels without entering into any estimation of their value." Croissy had already warned the court that the princess was no beauty, but "her countenance and her manners had nothing that would not make her worthy of the honor that his Majesty destined for her."[23] If she was not beautiful, she was pious, virtuous, and well brought up. Before her marriage at the great church of Châlons, her desire to confess herself created some trouble, for although she did know several languages, she wished to confess in German. The nearest German-speaking priest came from Liège, and his experience had been confessing soldiers, not princesses; nonetheless, she was pleased with him. Then there was the French marriage ceremony: an officiating cardinal blessed the ring and the thirteen pieces of gold, after which Louis, Dauphin of France, officially married the Princess of Bavaria. That night the king and queen gave the bride and groom their night clothes and put them to bed. The next morning there was a solemn high mass with oratory, drums, trumpets, and artillery fire; the young couple approached the high altar and were blessed by the cardinal. Later in the day, in solemn audience they received felicitations from the Hôtel de Ville, the Academy, and other groups. It was all very wonderful, but Primi Visconti, who knew much about things, wrote: "The dauphin took a wife just as he took his lessons when he was a student . . . he has been raised in fear." This may be a little harsh, but he did forget to kiss the lady's hand when he was first introduced. His relations with his wife were more those of a son and mother than of a husband and wife; the dauphin never became fully mature.

Even after Louis' life no longer scandalized the world, the pious new dauphine was out of place in the French court. She would have nothing to do with the gaming tables, and she hated the hunt. She was shocked at the easy morals of the people about her. As her children came, her health deteriorated and prevented her from taking part in many functions. However, Marie-Anne was not without talents: she spoke several languages, danced well, enjoyed the theater and the company of the little German circle at the court. Her sad looks and bad complexion as well as her puritanical morals, prevented her from being really popular with the king, but the fact that she bore three sons assured her honor in the court. It is undoubtedly true that her early death left a very small gap in the court.

An interesting feature of the dauphine's household was the fact that after the Duchess of Richelieu, the next two ladies *d'atour* were the wife of the Marshal of Rochefort and Madame de Maintenon. The widow Scarron had obviously come a long way in a decade; none of the other important members of the household were of so humble an origin. His Majesty sometimes enjoyed talking to the dauphine, but he enjoyed much more the company of Madame de Maintenon. We can follow her progress in her own letters, in those of Madame de Sévigné, and in the memoirs of the period.

"Madame de Maintenon grows daily more in favor," wrote Madame de Sévigné; "nothing now but perpetual conversations between her and the King. . . . His Majesty frequently spends two hours at a time in de Maintenon's apartments, conversing in so friendly and natural a manner as to make it the most desirable spot in the world." A little later: "She has introduced him to a new land heretofore unknown to him, which is friendly intercourse and conversation without restraint or chicanery; he seems charmed by it." And later: "I am told that the conversations between his Majesty and Madame de Maintenon are becoming more frequent and more prolonged, that they last from six o'clock till ten; that the Dauphine occasionally pays her a short visit, that she finds them each sitting in an easy chair, and that they resume the threads of their conversation as soon as she leaves. . . ." Primi understood that Louis might be using her to edit his memoirs; everyone was aware of the new favorite. It is small wonder that Madame de Maintenon was now courted from all sides.

Louis needed a friend. He was in his early forties and his health was no longer as good as it had been. The mishaps that befell Mademoiselle de Fontanges undoubtedly shook him, and the ugly stories that were coming from the police department of Paris were even worse: his kingdom was scandalized by the accounts of sorcery, black masses, poisonings, and magic that were revealed by a royal tribunal. Now the daughter of Voisin, an old crone who had been executed a few years earlier for her evil deeds, was implicating the court in these ugly practices. Not only his court, but Madame de Montespan herself was accused of poisoning, of black masses, of buying love potions. Charges like these had already driven the Countess of Soissons (mother of Eugene of Savoy) from the kingdom, and had placed the Marshal of Luxembourg temporarily in the Bastille; these wretched people may have hoped, by implicating the powerful and important, to slip from the net themselves. The worst of it was that Madame de Montespan's maid had undoubtedly visited this Voisin, not to buy poisons but much as people today go to a fortuneteller, for these dealers in the occult and the wicked had many activities. Chief of police La Reynie and Louvois both seem to have believed in Madame de Montespan's guilt, but it was difficult to insist that the mother of the king's children was a poisoner and a dealer in magic. Colbert, whose family was now related by marriage to Madame de Montespan's, put one of his best men on the case. Colbert himself took the trouble to analyze the evidence carefully, and came to the conclusion that there was no truth in the words of the people who were accusing the king's ex-mistress.[24] The astonishing thing is that so many historians have been willing to accept the evidence against Madame de Montespan; she has always been the mistress "most disliked" by posterity. Louis, however, knew her very well; he also knew that the story that she had poisoned La Vallière, de Fontanges, and himself was false. Furthermore, he recognized that the evidence these people produced did not fit with the facts of the world in which he had lived for the past decade. The accusers had only hazy notions about life at the court, and an analysis of their evidence betrayed their ignorance. Louvois finally recognized that there was nothing in the story. Nonetheless, it was not a pleasant episode for the king. Poison, black masses, the occult: all this marred his reign; the accusations against his mistress brought the stain to the throne itself. He needed someone with whom he could talk.[25]

These problems alone could never explain Madame de Maintenon's rise to favor. Louis was undoubtedly troubled, but he also seems to have been a man who needed female companionship; his mother had been very important to him—he had visited her almost daily as long as she lived. Did he find in Madame de Maintenon a woman whose wisdom, courtesy, and conversational skills filled a deep need? Those who have tried to canonize Madame de Maintenon would have us believe that she was embarked on the mission to save the king's soul, that she reformed his life and morals, that she was curing the disorders of his court. This would make of her a sort of female Bossuet. It is quite inconceivable that Louis would have allowed her to play the role of moralist; that was the work of the clerics. Furthermore, her "conversations" with the king began when Louis was still very much involved with Madame de Montespan; they continued during the years when his life was at its most disorderly as far as women were concerned; she gained greatest favor at the very time that he was "gallant" with La Fontanges. This would not support the Maintenon myth. Nor should it, for it is clear from her letters that at this stage in her life Madame de Maintenon was no *dévote;* she was a virtuous woman, perhaps, but neither a religious fanatic nor a prudish moralist. Like many others, she disapproved of the double adultery, but she was not averse to caring for the fruits of this sin. Her favor with the king has to be found in her personal charm, her measured conversation, her emotional stability. Louis always remarked on her "imperturbability," her "stolidity." These were things he needed in a woman, and they were things he could not find in La Montespan or La Fontanges or the other gallant ladies of the court.

Later, when her influence was credited with reforming the king's life, the Bossuets, the Chevreuses, and others who had been shocked and offended by Louis' immorality, became her friends, but there is no evidence to suggest that the pious and moral people of the court pushed her into the position to "save the King's soul." When Madame de Maintenon became the king's "best friend" she was still only in her mid-forties, she enjoyed life at the court, she was interested in worldly affairs, she had good health and good spirits—she did not live solely on her knees before God. Her life had been regular and her reputation that of a virtuous woman, but this did not make her into a moralist or a reformer.

What was Louis' relationship to this lady? After 1681 he gave up his "gallant" behavior and to all outward appearances "returned" to the queen. From this date, however, Madame de Maintenon was never far from him. Even when the dauphine gave birth to the Duke of Burgundy, she followed Louis to the Loire rather than remaining with her mistress and her charge. The question of course is whether Louis merely wished to converse with his friend. Perhaps one should ask: Is it credible that Louis did become *sage* after 1681? Was he satisfied with his dull, weak queen? Could he throw off the habits and attitudes of two decades? As we have already seen, there is strong evidence that at an early point in their acquaintance Madame de Maintenon "evaded" an improper proposal from the king; at that time neither of them knew each other very well. At forty-five Madame de Maintenon was probably as attractive to Louis, who was now forty-two, as she had been when she was thirty-nine and he thirty-six. Her body was not worn out by childbearing, nor bloated by obesity; indeed, all the evidence that we have would indicate that she was a highly attractive woman, even though her portraits do not make her a great beauty. Through "conversations" they became "friends," but friendship between people of opposite sexes sometimes . . . Indeed, the question is, how long could she refuse Louis XIV?

Her most recent biographer (Cordelier) has probably assembled all the meaningful evidence that we will ever have, and has interpreted it with great psychological insight. There is no direct evidence, but there is much indirect suggestion, that she did, in fact, become Louis' mistress sometime in 1681. Her letters during this period, for the first time, fairly bubble with good health, happiness, contentment, light-heartedness. This does not necessarily mean that she was finding a new life; but her first marriage had not been much, and it is possible that life with the king was considerably more. This period, too, is the only one for which very few of her letters to her confessor have survived. Were they destroyed? There is the letter of 1682 in which she tells of her confession, and the subsequent "tears and tribulations." Langlois remarks that her confessor must have given her a hard time. Cordelier suggests that the churchmen were willing to look aside as long as there was no scandal; with the pious people of the court applauding her for her "conversion of the King," it would not be proper to have the agent of salvation appear in the role of Magdalene.

The queen benefited from Madame de Maintenon's influence, for that good lady urged Louis to pay more attention to his wife—and Marie-Thérèse was grateful. As Liselotte put it, ". . . as a good Spaniard, she was not averse to such labor. . . ." One of Madame de Maintenon's letters of 1682 to Abbé Gobelin, her own confessor, suggests both her own modest egotism as well as her understanding of Marie-Thérèse's inadequacies: "If the Queen had a director like you," she wrote, "there is no good that one could not have hoped for from the royal family, but she is troubled by a confessor who guides her on a route more proper for a Carmelite than for a Queen." We are permitted to wonder whether this queen could recapture her husband at this late date, and how Madame de Maintenon knew so much about the king's intimate affairs.

The king's life in 1683 presents a curious tableau. He still visited the apartments of Madame de Montespan nearly every day[26]—but always with other people present. He visited his wife, and apparently he had given up his gallant behavior. He spent long hours in conversation with Madame de Maintenon. No one can know how long this would have gone on, for the whole situation was suddenly changed. At the end of June the court returned from a trip to Franche-Comté and Alsace. The queen complained of not feeling well. Then a boil developed in her armpit. She became feverish, and her doctors began the process of bleeding her and giving her emetics. Liselotte may well have been correct in believing that they killed her; Marie-Thérèse died the last of July—after having been copiously bled by orders of her physician and surgeon. It is improbable that the relief of Vienna had anything to do with it.[27]

Louis was undoubtedly more surprised and shocked than sorrowed by this event. He made the appropriate remark:—"This is the only chagrin that she has ever caused me"—but he was soon over it. However, the death of the queen did create a new situation, and in fact, open a new chapter in the king's life. He was now free to marry again, for there was "a place vacant." He could marry a foreign princess, or one of the great ladies of his own kingdom, or he could find some other solution to the problem.

22

THE AGING LION: HUSBAND, FATHER, GRANDFATHER

WHILE Marie-Thérèse was alive she never seemed very important in the court; even though she was the queen, it was hard for anyone to take her very seriously. When she died, however, her husband and the entire court had much to do to be sure that all the pomp, tradition, and ceremony was properly observed. Louis undoubtedly was shaken by the passing of a person whose life had been so long associated with his own, but the shock was more the reminder of his own mortality than great concern over her fate. He soon recovered only to find himself involved in a round of ceremonial receptions and speeches from people who demanded to be noticed when they brought sympathy to their king. He had to be gracious; he had to carry off the role of king bereaved by the loss of his queen, long after he had fully recovered from the disagreeable experience of her death.

There was much to be done to tell the world that the Queen of France was dead. She was important as a ceremonial figure, and her demise was the occasion for elaborate obsequies: in addition to prayers and masses for the repose of her soul there had to be a state funeral to honor her name and to entomb her remains. The body was prepared for burial by a process similar to that used by Egypt's pharaohs. The heart, encased in a silver box bearing the inscription, "This is the heart of Marie-Thérèse, Infanta of Spain, wife of Louis the Great, fourteenth of the name, died 30 July 1683," was placed in the chapel at Val-de-Grâce near that of Anne, her beloved aunt and mother-in-law. The entrails were embalmed and likewise placed in an urn. The body, clothed in the habit of a Capuchin nun, was encased in a coffin of lead with the inscription, "This is the body of Marie-Thérèse, Infanta of Spain, wife of Louis the Great, fourteenth of the name, who died at Versailles Friday, 30 July 1683, aged 45 years." The coffin, draped in violet-colored velvet, surmounted with the queen's coat of arms, rested in state in a large room with two altars where priests said mass while monks from the monasteries of Versailles chanted the *De profundis* and other prayers. Four bishops came each day, the queen's chaplains stayed in the room most of the time, and the members of her household spelled each other in attendance of the corpse. The ceremonies lasted until August 10 when the body was taken in solemn procession to the Basilica of Saint-Denis for final burial.

Louis and the whole court went into deep mourning. This meant that everyone needed new clothes, that black and violet draperies were rented to decorate the chambers of the royal family and public reception rooms at the château of Fontainebleau where the king and court retired after a short stay at Saint-Cloud. Louis now appeared clothed in violet: his black hat had violet ribbons; the sheath for his steel sword was violet; his cape, and even his shirt, which could be seen only when he unbuttoned his surcoat, were violet. The rest of the court and all the officers of state except the chancellor[1] also appeared in mourning.

While the body of the late queen was prepared for the journey toward its tomb in the Bourbon crypt at Saint-Denis, there was much for the king to do. All sorts of people arrived at Fontainebleau to offer condolences: representatives from the sovereign courts, from the government of Paris, the University, the Academy, the diplomatic corps, and many others of less importance vied with each other to console the king and praise his dead wife. At the same time, from the pulpits of France there was an outpouring of sermons by clerical orators of varying degrees of eloquence, many of which were promptly printed and sent to the king. Some of them seem ludicrous; even the great Bossuet was forced to make much of the fact that in Spain she had been called both *Infante* and *Infanta*[2] for she carried the right to inherit the throne. While this was going on, funeral services were held at Saint-Denis, a near replica of those held for the queen mother almost two decades earlier, even to the problems of precedence and stealing that had troubled Anne's funeral ceremonies.[3]

Louis accepted the ceremonial role that a king must play under such circumstances, but it hardly corresponded to his personal feelings. His sister-in-law Liselotte wrote, "The King who loved his wife as much for the estime that she deserved, as for the great passion that she always had for him, was much touched to see her die, but Madame de Maintenon found means of consoling him within four days. . . . We were all much embarrassed and upset . . . several days later we went in the same carriage with him to Fontainebleau. We thought that he would be sad, impatient, in bad humor, and that if we did not appear sad, he would scold us. We were agreeably surprised to find in him gaiety that put us all in good humor." These words, written in 1716, probably cannot be taken completely at face value, yet there is little doubt both that Louis recovered soon from the shock of his wife's death and that Madame de Maintenon "consoled" him. The Duke of Rochefoucauld had been right in pushing her toward Louis as he left Versailles with the words, "This is not the time to leave him; he needs you."

Death opened a new chapter in the king's life. He was now free. He was only forty-five; many men at that age start a second family. Women had always pleased him—"almost all women except his wife." But a king's remarriage is a matter of state, and Louis never decided such questions without discussion in council. The pros and cons were reasonably clear: the dauphin's family was well started, with one son, and the dauphine pregnant again. There was little question about the succession to the throne. What of children of a second bed? Younger brothers of the first bed in France had often been troublesome to their elder brother when he became king; the history of France abounded with stories of revolts led by such princes. To be sure, the state that Louis was building would be less vulnerable than the French state of the Valois kings or even that of Louis XIII had been, yet it was not at all sure that revolt was impossible. At his supper on August 13, Louis announced that the council had been of the unanimous opinion that second marriages were unfortunate. A courtier remarked, "Sire, that is only for private persons." But Louis insisted that the inconveniences would strike all people without exception (Dangeau).

What about the king's private life? Could he continue the clandestine relationships with Madame de Maintenon if he married again? That lady undoubtedly asked herself the same question. For her there was one answer: if the king wished to remarry she must retire or run the risk of being exposed as a "sinner." During these first weeks after the queen's death she suffered from sleeplessness and *vapeurs* and *indispositions*. She was obviously worried about her future. It is inconceivable that she could have suggested to the king that he should marry her, the widow of Scarron. No. The suggestion could not come from her; all that she could do would be to ask permission to retire to her estate at Maintenon—a request that might force the king to consider seriously his own ideas about the future, about his private life, about this woman who had become so important to him.

Others were interested in the problem. Father de la Chaise; Louis' confessor Bishop Bossuet, court moralist and preacher; perhaps even the confessor of Madame de Maintenon. Two of the three, and perhaps also Bossuet, knew of the clandestine relationship between Louis and Françoise. As long as there was no scandal, they could look aside. They may also have realized that Louis was very fond of Madame de Maintenon. No woman since the death of his mother had been as important to him as a *confidente;* and she also satisfied his demands for a "companion." But could he go on with an *affaire* that had to be secret? Clandestine affairs and irregular living were bad, especially bad for a man who was both a father-in-law and a grandfather. The clergymen could point this out to the king, they could tell him that he could marry whomever he might wish, but probably they could not suggest the name of Madame de Maintenon even though they might wish to do so.

The decisions had to be the king's. While it was still in the air, he fell from his horse and dislocated his arm. Madame de Maintenon thought at first that it had been broken; she was at his side with womanly sympathy and comfort. Her letter is revealing; Louis was obviously both her hero and her king: "You no doubt know that after having been consoled over the loss of the Queen, we had to tremble for the King, and that we thought his arm to be broken. Happily it is only a dislocation, and thanks to God, it has been put in place so that there is nothing to fear. This accident allows us to see him as firm in pain as in every other action. There was little difference —in his *sang froid*—between him and someone who casually announces 'I told you that I broke my leg.' "[4] Can anyone doubt the sort of consolation that she gave him? Was it during these days that the idea came to him that he should marry her? Langlois placed the decision about this time, but there are no exact documents to establish the date. If his mother had been alive we undoubtedly would have a letter to her in his own hand explaining how clever he was to think of this way to solve all his problems; by marrying Françoise he could keep the woman who had become necessary to him, save his soul, and defend the security of his son's rule over the kingdom after his death. We can almost imagine the letter in the same exalted mood as the one that he wrote to Anne after the arrest of Fouquet.

When did the marriage actually take place? We do not know. Langlois[5] believes it was on the night of October 9–10, 1683; this is the earliest date suggested by any scholar. Louis Hastier[6] insists that she remained his mistress until 1697 when the marriage was formally celebrated, but even though his study is heavily documented, there is enough evidence that many people, including the papal curia, knew of the marriage by winter 1684–85 to make us prefer Langlois' solution. Boislisle, who was also an important authority, sets the date as January 1684.

We should follow a little the course of events through Madame de Maintenon's letters. At the time Marie-Thérèse died, Madame de Maintenon was quite excited over a recent gift from Rome of the remains of Saint Candide.[7] Naturally the queen's death momentarily interrupted her interest in the saint: the king became the center of attention. "Pray for the King," she wrote from Saint-Cloud, "he has more need for grace than ever to maintain a status contrary to his inclinations." Then came a little gift that the pope had sent to Marie-Thérèse before her death was known in Rome; Louis promptly gave it to Madame de Maintenon. She writes to a confidante, "the articles about Louis and Françoise . . . are follies." A little later she tells her brother that his fortune is made; that he does not have to worry about spending all his income. "Rejoice, dear brother, but innocently. . . ." This same letter discusses the roles of married people, and recommends that her brother be faithful to both God and his wife. In another letter to him she writes, "The reason that prevents your seeing me is so useful and so glorious that you should only have great joy from it." Soon she writes to a confidant, "I am delighted with the miracles of Saint Candide; you know how much I feel for him." Perhaps her happiness, which shines through the letters from that point on, indicates the nature of the miracle. Thereafter her letters to friends tell them that she "[dies] . . . with the desire to see [them], but . . . I no longer have time to look at myself. There is no indication that the court will leave here [Versailles] for six months . . . my happiness is perfect. . . ." One of her recent biographers, who agrees with Langlois that the marriage date was October 9–10, makes much of the fact that a few days later she asked her confessor to buy books for her bound in calf. What books? *The Imitation of Christ, Introduction to the Devout Life, A New Testament,* and several other religious books of the same character. Cordier remarks, "The beautiful *dévote* could now decorate her library [with pious works] and take up her prayers; she is no longer a 'favorite' and the stain [of sin] has been washed away." Perhaps he is right; this may be the conclusive bit of evidence for the early date.[8]

Who were the witnesses? We have no exact evidence, but probably Louvois, the Archbishop of Paris, and Father de la Chaise, who seems to have officiated at the service. In addition possibly de Bontemps, Governor of Versailles, and the Duke of Montchevreuil, a good friend of both Louis and Françoise. There may have been others, but not very many. The court suspected the marriage. A few knew for sure of its existence, but for years its reality was the "King's secret." Louis' brother Philippe learned of it when he surprised the king in Madame de Maintenon's bed.

A marriage between people in their late forties is difficult to assess. How did they feel about each other? Even in the "goldfish bowl" of the court this question could not really be answered. No one can doubt her affection for the king if the following letter is authentic, as Langlois thinks that it might be: "Sire," she wrote early in 1684, "one day of your

Majesty's absence is to me like a century. I believe that when one loves, one cannot live calmly without seeing the beloved person. For me, sire, my happiness, the pleasure of my life consists in your Majesty. I cannot again say what will be my destiny, but I tremble and am in continual emotion in writing this note. . . ."[9] The formal mode of address even in a letter so passionate, is in keeping with both the era and the king; Louis remained "The King" even to a mistress or a wife. We do not know what they called each other in their more intimate moments. It is quite unlikely that Louis felt the same passion for her, but his constancy to her, his concern when she was ill, a few charmingly friendly letters to her that have survived, and his obvious attachment for her company all argue that he found her to be a person necessary to his well-being. When the court returned to Versailles he gave her Madame de Montespan's apartment near his own, and sent the displaced lady to quarters on the floor below. From that day until his death she was never far from him for any long period of time.[10]

This does not mean that Louis allowed Madame de Maintenon to interfere with his affairs during this period, for if there is any one thing that can be said about him, it is that he tried not to be led by any of the women who shared his life. His mother, his mistresses, and his first wife were excluded from the affairs of state, and whatever influence his second wife was to exercise, it was not direct, nor was it decisive in the forming of royal policy—at least not until after 1700. Louis undoubtedly married Madame de Maintenon because she could play the role of mistress and wife at the same time. But his idea of the role of "wife" had been formed by his relationship with Marie-Thérèse; it was hardly one that would allow a woman to lead the king. And yet Madame de Maintenon's position was different from that of either Marie-Thérèse or of Madame de Montespan: Louis enjoyed her company, her conversation, her feminine ability to listen, as much as the favor of her bed. She unquestionably came to have considerable influence over his private life, and as we shall see later, perhaps even over some aspects of his public policy.

During the first years of her marriage all seems to have gone well, and Françoise, probably for the first time in her life, seems completely happy. In a few years, however, she came to find the court difficult and trying, "a strange country where men and women behave badly," but at first it and life around her seemed good. Her letters tell us that "the winter has passed with many pleasures . . ."; "It is fun to be at Chambord [in October] the weather is wonderful and the court is gay . . ."; "The King hunts in the daytime, in the evening there are other pleasures . . ."; "One day there is a ball, another there is a comedy." She obviously was in high favor with her husband; his health was still reasonably good. Yet she probably did not forget that Louis XIV had neglected one wife, dismissed three mistresses, and had skipped about with many women. Thus an occasional nagging fear that some day she might be disgraced crept into her letters. There seem to have been a few spats; what woman of spirit could live with Louis XIV, who believed that everything should revolve about him, and not have quarrels? But after tears, the difficulties were made up.

In this early period Françoise obviously takes great pleasure in her limited position and role at court; there is no evidence that she tried to influence the king's policy. The tradition that she is responsible for the revocation of the Edict of Nantes is simply untrue; although she advised her brother to buy up Huguenot lands and converted her Huguenot relatives, nonetheless her failure ever to join the rest of the kingdom in singing the praises of the king for destroying the "Hydra of Heresy" puts her with Catinat and Vauban in the disapproving minority.

In 1686 the king's health deteriorated badly; he was attacked at the same time by intermittent "fevers" and by an anal fistula that caused him much pain. Indeed there was danger for his life. About the same time Madame de Maintenon came to realize that hostility was rising against her in the court—particularly among the women; they could not forgive her position with the king. Madame, the Duchess of Orléans, and the dauphine, as well as a great number of other women who had hoped to "console" the king, began to show their unrelenting hostility. This made things difficult, for she was living in a court where rank and position were all-important. A handful of people knew that she was the king's morganatic wife, a larger number suspected it, but for all the world, she still was a simple marquise whose birth was humble enough to throw in doubt the possibility of the marriage. With a sick husband and a hostile entourage, she ceased to take so much pleasure in the court, and soon became carpingly critical.

Louis apparently encouraged her to take an interest in the education of young ladies as an outlet for some of her energy and intelligence. The result was the founding of the school at Saint-Cyr for the education of young women of good birth but small prospects. Neither Louis nor Madame de Maintenon liked convents as way stations for young women before marriage; they both believed that girls should have more education than was usual in a convent. Saint-Cyr was the answer; there, under her guidance, daughters of impecunious noblemen were given a Christian education, and the king provided money for dowries. We learn something about Madame de Maintenon from her *Maxims: to serve as examples to the Demoiselles of Saint-Cyr*. Her advice is to learn personal control, to gain knowledge and respect for others. Control passions and love God. A young woman must be prepared for many things, because no one knows where God will lead her. A woman must be modest, soft-spoken, retiring, yet she must know how to command, how to make her ideas felt by indirection, by modest use of her position, by influence derived from respect. There are one hundred and twenty-two of these maxims; if followed they would make a young lady into a refined, gracious, gentle, yet effective woman. Madame de Maintenon was such a person. But she also was a scold, a complainer, and often fickle in her personal relations—traits that she did not advise for her young charges. Her work and interests at Saint-Cyr are a whole chapter in her life. With Louis' patronage, the school gained fame, Racine was willing to compose plays for the girls to produce, and many men of good family were happy to find wives among its graduates.[11]

About the same time she also discovered that her husband had feet of clay, a revelation that comes to many a wife as she begins to see great need for improvement in the man she married. Many writers have asserted that after 1686 she sought to convert the king into becoming a *dévot*. This is hardly possible since she herself was not a *dévote* during these years. As she remarked in 1686, she was making no special austerities for Lent because she did not want to be like Marie-Thérèse, who often "behaved more like a Carmelite than a queen." But she did find things in her husband that she wanted to change. There were many things in the make-up of Louis XIV that made it difficult for an intelligent, sensitive woman to live with him. He was a hard man; he could not remember a time when most of the people around him were not looking at *the King,* when they did not assume that his will was theirs. He also was suspicious; the *Fronde* had taught him how little he could trust the surface texture of his fellow men and how much they are moved by selfish, personal interests. Mazarin had trained him to dissemble, to hide his feelings, his intentions, his aims, and to keep his own counsel while listening to others. He liked women for their loveliness and beauty and sexual attraction, for their conversation; but they were relaxation rather than serious companions in the business of ruling the realm. Madame de Maintenon could not forever be satisfied with so limited a role. She was also disturbed by Louis' religious ideas. Although no fanatic, she was a pious woman who took seriously the ideals of a Christian life. Louis' Christianity seemed to be little more than cult and superstition. Fénelon was undoubtedly echoing Madame de Maintenon when he wrote to Louis "You do not love God, you fear the devil!" Finally, Louis at this stage of his career had little feeling for his fellow man unless that fellow man served his interests; he mouthed words about the welfare of his people, but followed policies that led to wars and had nothing to do with their interests. Madame de Maintenon came to distrust and hate Louvois, his closest collaborator of these years, another hard man with little interest in the welfare of his fellows. She did indeed wish to reform the king, but how can one change a man over forty-five?

Who was Madame de Maintenon during these years? We have many pictures of the lady, especially those drawn by her enemies. All too often these pictures lump together in a single package the thirty-two or so years that she was married to the king; that is to say, the lady of forty-eight and of eighty are not separated. This of course is very foolish. At forty-eight she was still a vigorous, handsome woman interested in the life about her and not yet "bitten" with any ideas about her role in the state. The king in his mid-forties was also a relatively young man, passionate and amorous, still proud of himself, perhaps arrogantly so, and surely not yet punished by the disasters that were to stalk his later life. In this first period she was acquiring the enemies both in the court and out, in France and in the neighboring lands, who were to try to blacken her memory. They would make her out to be a female Tartuffe, a prude, a false *dévote;* in fact, there was such a fog about her reputation that it is almost impossible to see the lady who had married the king.[12]

Better than any of the scholars who have written about her, Abbé Langlois, who edited five volumes of her letters and studied her life most carefully, speaks about her lack of preparation for the role of wife to the king:

She lacked the general education and the special instruction that would prepare her for her role. It is enough to follow her to be convinced of this, and to pardon her with indulgence for her errors. Granddaughter of the Huguenot prophet, Agrippa d'Aubigné, daughter of an adventurer, born in the court of a prison, raised, abandoned—in America then in France—by an unfortunate mother and by protestant and catholic relatives, beggar, . . . married at sixteen to an infirm poet, widow at twenty-five, adulated in the hotels of Albert and Richelieu, governess of the children of Madame de Montespan, finally morganatic wife of the greatest King in Europe, she was deprived of tradition, race, ideas. She brought to it natural qualities, but at 48 years, she had become too individualistic. Without children, long without affection, she was not happy and she did not make the King happy. She would have been able to consecrate herself in intimacy and with self-denial, to a household . . . but the mechanism of life at court and with the King would not permit it. She had to hide her love, she felt prodigiously isolated beside the throne. Impulsive and spontaneous as she was . . . she had to dissemble, obliged . . . to act always by subterranean channels. The evils of her life barred exact discernment of people and things. She had a cushion by relating everything to herself. . . . In spite of the efforts of her

director, Fénelon, to correct her prodigious pride, he was too late. Her feminine
nature carried her to wish, without having the air of doing so, to control all in
the state and the church, in the court and the town. . . .[13]

At eighty-two Madame de Maintenon herself tells us, "It is a shame
that my education came so late, for I would have been spared the pain had
I known what kings and popes are capable of doing." In other words, she
admits her failure to "reform" the king's public life. Her effect upon his
private life is less problematical; Louis never again fell into the sexual
disorders that marked the first part of his adult life, but there is not much
evidence that Madame de Maintenon was really able to make him more
considerate of others or more truly pious.

This effort, combined with the strain of living in the court, sometimes
made Madame de Maintenon into a difficult woman. She scolded her
family, her friends, churchmen, and nuns, the girls at Saint-Cyr, and even
the king. She worked secretly against ministers who incurred her dislike,
and became fickle in her likes and dislikes of persons. Fénelon, for example, at first her favorite, fell into disfavor, like so many others who tried
to work with her. Her relations with the king were often strained during
this first decade or two of the marriage; indeed, several times she feared
that she might be disgraced. "I have not told you half of the troubles that
I endure," she wrote to the Bishop of Chartres, "Men are tyrannical, I am
convinced of it; they are not capable of friendship as women are. There
is none better than the King, but one must suffer from all, and God permits,
for my salvation, that I must suffer much."

For all these complaints, her life with the king was not, as clearly
noted, all tears and "vapeurs." Louis knew how to be gracious, and how to
make love. Most of his letters to her were burned, but one written from
Flanders in 1691 has survived; it surely was not unique. "I take advantage
of the departure of M. de Montchevreuil," he wrote, "to assure you of the
truth that pleases me greatly. It is that I cherish you always, and that I think
of you to the point that I cannot even express myself, and finally that, no
matter what affection you have for me, I have even more for you. . . . My
heart is made for you."[14] This sort of courting must have made up for
much distress. Almost all who write about her in these years insist that the
king was much in love with her, and we know that she had soft feelings for
her husband. When the gout forced him to leave the army besieging
Namur, she was happy! The gout was a minor ill compared with the dangers
from bullets in the trenches before Namur.

We shall see in a later chapter that Madame de Maintenon was the
only woman in Louis' life who was able even in a minor way to influence his

state policy, but this was not in the first decade or so of their marriage, nor was her influence ever very important except in church affairs, the traditional sphere for the activity of queens. What actually seems to have happened is that Louis found her useful; she was intelligent, she could obtain information, she was clever in negotiations, she knew how to write. Gradually he admitted her to a minor role in the "team" that he assembled to operate his government; not until he was near the very end of his life did she ever play a larger part.

Louis was also a brother, a father, a grandfather, as well as a husband. The royal family included the children of the king, legitimate and legitimized; his brother Monsieur (the Duke of Orléans) and his family; the Condés, the Contis, and the Vendômes (also legitimized by royal act); and the daughters of his uncle Gaston of Orléans. At a family gathering when a marriage contract or some such event was to be solemnized, there could be as many as twenty or more people present. Of these, his brother's family and his own were the most important.

Louis managed to keep good relations with his strange brother in spite of his dislike of Philippe's way of life. During these years (1680–1700) the Duke of Orléans was a short, fat man, grotesquely dressed with ribbons, jewels, and rouge; he did not grow old with dignity. His wife, Madame (Elizabeth-Charlotte), had also become fat and had lost none of her waspish disposition. There had never been any love between them, and she was able to sustain her life at court only by writing interminable letters to her German relatives, in which her dislike for Madame de Maintenon, her "Lutheran" hostility to the vices of the court, and her malicious gossip combined to give historians a slanted picture of the world about her. It is clear that she was in some way "in love" with her brother-in-law, whose way of life suited her better than poor Philippe's did. Elizabeth-Charlotte had to suffer two terrible blows from the king. The first came when the French armies invaded the Palatinate on the pretext of securing her inheritance, and then proceeded to destroy the beautiful palace high above the Neckar where she had been brought up as a child.[15] Even in ruins, this *Schloss* still reveals its former beauty. The second came when the king decided that her son, the Duke of Chartres, would marry one of his legitimized daughters. Madame could not see this daughter-in-law as anything but the bastard child of Madame de Montespan, whom she hated. It took days before she could face the world and accept the king's will. This marriage also caused some difficulty between the brothers, for the Duke of Chartres (the future Duke of Orléans and regent for Louis XV) regarded himself as dishonored, and proceeded to seek comfort in the arms of other women. When the Duchess of Chartres protested her husband's behavior, Louis asked his brother to interfere. Philippe's reply can easily be guessed; he simply reminded Louis of his own past. Several times, however, hot words between them could be heard beyond the king's chambers. As we shall see, this did not deprive the Duke of Chartres of Louis' favor.

Louis' son, the Grand Dauphin, very early revealed himself to be a man of little spirit and perhaps less intelligence. Bossuet did all that he could to educate this young man, but he was indolent, fat, and fatuous. Rigaud's famous picture of the dauphin and his family leaves little doubt about the artist's opinion of this poor man who as son of a king and father of a king, lived out his near meaningless life under his father's shadow. His marriage and the birth of three sons secured the succession, but few people took him seriously until Louis' illness for a moment threatened to make him king.

When the war broke out in 1688, Louis sent the dauphin to command the army besieging Philippsburg, and in the following years, Marshal Duras, Marshal Lorges, and Marshal Luxembourg at various times "commanded under the Dauphin's orders." Louis followed his son's military career closely. He was protective of him; when the dauphin tried to be brave, Louis ordered him not to go into the trenches again since he had "done all that is needed for his *gloire*." But he was not too happy to learn that his son's military activity was largely confined to long horseback rides. In many of his letters, however, he is kind to the young prince. He consoles him when it proved to be impossible to do very much against the imperials. On one occasion he writes, "I am convinced that you have a great desire to do something considerable, and I assure you that I hope for it as much as you do." On another, "I hope that you will have the pleasure of defeating them with your 1,000 horsemen, but I doubt that they will give you that pleasure. . . ." Another: "I gave your compliments to Madame de Maintenon. . . . She is much more nervous about the march of the armies toward each other than I am." When a campaign failed to accomplish much, Louis invited his son to come to see him: "I have made no plans for a trip to Fontainebleau . . . ," he writes, "but I will stop there as long as you wish with great pleasure. I find myself quite alone at Fontainebleau without you. I believe that there is not much to do where you are [with the army]. I propose that you come. . . ." In other letters he tells the dauphin about his hunting expeditions, one of which was spoiled by a terrible downpour of rain. The dauphin well knew that it took a very heavy rain to discourage his father's hunting. Louis also wrote to his marshals asking about his son's progress, and demanded from them all the news. "I take pleasure in your words," he wrote to Marshal Luxembourg, "about my son's application for the good of the army. . . . I am sure that you will not advise my son to do anything not apropos. . . ." He also read the dauphin's "orders for the march" and "orders for the camp"; Louis had always liked to supervise these things when he was with the army, and he knew how they should be written.[16]

Even so, the dauphin was afraid of his father, a fact that suggests that Louis was sometimes less kind and less understanding than he appears in these letters. The dauphin sought the intercession of Madame de Maintenon: "It appears to me that the King is satisfied with the way I am acting," he wrote to her, "I assure you that the greatest thing in the world is to please him. . . . I beg you to tell the King for me the desire that I have to please him."[17] After the dauphine died, the dauphin found Madame Choin, "his Maintenon," to console him. His first mention of it is revealing: "I am beginning to think about remarriage," he writes to Madame de Maintenon, "being young enough to feel that I would not be good (*sage*), and since I know that the King fears most in the world that I should fall into debauchery. . . ." He went on to tell her of his plans, but asked that she not yet inform the king. She could, however, "pave the way" for a request for permission. He adds, "I would rather die than do anything that would displease the King." A few years later he wrote to her, "I beg you to tell me sincerely if it seems to you that he is satisfied with me, for I only think of acquitting myself well in my duty. . . . I hope to find some occasion of meriting the esteem of the King and doing something that could be useful to the state."

In June 1694 he writes, "I am delighted that the King is at the Trianon, for he is happy there, and in addition his health is so dear to me that I cannot but be pleased when I hear of all the sickness that there is at Versailles. . . ." A Freudian might say more about this letter than an historian can allow himself to write.

The dauphine presented a very different problem. A sensitive, deeply religious young woman whose health was bad, and whose conscience revolted against the court's vices—which continued long after Louis had regulated his own life—this Bavarian princess never quite established herself in France. She liked to read, to take walks in the garden, to talk to the little coterie of German women in the court; she could not stand Madame de Maintenon and she hated most of the life around her. Only seldom did she please her father-in-law; but she did delight him once, when with her first pregnancy, she asked him for his portrait "so as to have it always before her so that her child would resemble him."[18] Her three pregnancies cost her heavily: her skin became sallow, her face drawn, and she died in 1690 still a young woman. Madame de Sévigné wrote, "There is the poor Dauphine, dead, very sadly. . . . She died the 20th of April. For six days the three [children] and Monseigneur watched her die. She asked pardon of the King for her lack of accommodation . . . and wished to kiss his hand. The King embraced her, his tears prevented him from speaking. . . . She placed her three sons before her and blessed them saying 'and you my little Berry [the third son, the Duke of Berry] even though you are the cause of my death.' " Tradition has it that Louis, at her deathbed, said to his son, "You see what is the end of the 'grandeurs' of this world. We shall become like her, you and I."[19]

While the dauphin never quite measured up to expectations, his children were a source of hope for the future. When the Duke of Burgundy was born, Louis called upon Madame de la Motte, who had taken care of the dauphin and his younger brother when they were children, to take charge of this grandson. But the letters that he wrote to her both while she looked after his own sons, and later his grandsons, give us small insight into the king's mind and feelings. Like all correspondence with people who served him, his letters to Madame de la Motte abound in expressions of confidence and gratitude, "The satisfaction that I have from your cares for all that concerns me . . ."; "[Let me] reassure you of the continuation of my esteem . . ."; "You know that I have great confidence in you, and that I send evidence of my pleasure as well as of my friendship . . ."; "I can find no room to question the care that you take . . ."; "For a very long time I have known the feelings that you have for all that touches my life. . . ." These may be formal expressions, but their repetition from one letter to another must have brought considerable satisfaction to the lady who read them.[20]

In these letters we find the king interested in the cutting of a tooth, in the child's first steps, in the diarrhea "which is not so serious in children," and in the fevers that were. Both Louis and Madame de la Motte must have long remembered the time the king was in the act of writing to her about his satisfaction over the apparent recovery of his second son, when a letter from her arrived, telling that the fever was mounting again. Louis' handwriting actually changes, revealing his emotion, for he well understood the course of these fevers and the clutching hand of death that reached to extinguish the life of children. Louis visited his son at Saint-Germain; unable to stop the course of the fever, he had to watch him die.[21] Happily none of the dauphin's children suffered this fate, but grandfather was always anxious for news—any news. Once when the Duke of Burgundy fell ill, he sent Fagon to him to be sure that the child had the best of possible care. "I am convinced," he wrote Madame de la Motte, "that you and M. Fagon have done everything necessary, perhaps even more. . . ."

At the time of Marie-Thérèse's death there were, in addition to the dauphin, six other children in the family, offspring of the liaisons with La Vallière and La Montespan. One of them, the Comte de Vexin, died soon, but the others, three girls and two boys, reached maturity. There are many stories about these children, some of them undoubtedly true, some probably false. The memoirists and letter-writers of the period usually stereotyped them with their mothers, whom they often much disliked. Only two of the six were without physical defects, but the king received considerably more pleasure from them than from his son and heir. Their presence in the King's entourage was probably the reason that Madame de Montespan was allowed to remain at court for a whole decade after she had no reason for being there.

Louis was much concerned about the future of his children, and determined to give them status in his kingdom. The last of them were legitimized in 1680 and 1681 and given the right to call themselves "de Bourbon." Like the earlier legitimization of La Montespan's children, these acts do not mention the mother, but in them the father assures the world of his affection for, and interest in, his offspring. This, however, was not enough; even the grant of titles and lands did not assure them the status that their father desired for them. In the case of the three girls, it was simple enough: by marrying them to princes of the blood, Louis could assure them and their children a place in the succession to the throne. What higher position could be given? Thus Marie-Anne (sole surviving daughter of La Vallière) married a prince of the house of Conti. Louise-Françoise married a prince of the house of Condé, and Marie-Françoise married the Duke of Chartres, Louis' own nephew. For the boys it was more difficult. At first Louis was of the opinion that men of their birth probably should not marry, but finally he did marry the Duke of Maine to a princess of the house of Condé; the Count of Toulouse was not married until after his father's death. Both of the boys were given high positions: the Duke of Maine became governor of Languedoc and also received much of La Grande Mademoiselle's property;[22] the Count of Toulouse became Admiral of France. Both these young men were inserted in the peerage table between the princes of the blood and the princes stemming from foreign sovereign houses, and before Louis died, he tried to place them in the line of succession to the throne. This obsession with the future of his children brought much criticism upon the head of the aging king.

The marriages of the daughters were important court fêtes. The Great Condé himself came to the wedding of Mademoiselle de Blois and the Prince of Conti; the old general wore his diamond-studded sword (*la famosa spada all'cui valore ogni vittoria certa*). Madame de Sévigné tells us that he also had shaved his beard and looked very dignified. This marriage seems to have been a love match, satisfactory to both parties. To assure their financial status Louis provided a dowry of 500,000 *écus* of gold, which was more than had been promised for Marie-Thérèse. Within a few years the Princess of Conti was a widow, and she remained a widow the rest of her life. She lived at court in great ease "with the air of a Venus who rules the skies . . . accompanied by graces. . . ." She was "completely ravishing . . . ," but her life seems to have been a bit hollow. The marriage between Louise-Françoise and Henri Jules de Bourbon, later Prince of Condé, had its problems. When Henri Jules died, six surgeons after an autopsy attested that his death was caused by "vice and the activity of liquor that had reduced the body to the extremity. . . ."[23] In his will, Henri Jules recommended his soul to God from whom he asked pardon for his faults. The last marriage, as we have already noted, caused considerable difficulty, for Madame did not want her son to marry a bastard. Louis tried to sweeten the pill by fixing the dowry at twice that given to the other girls, and by giving the couple the magnificent Palais-Royal in Paris. Even so, this marriage was not a very happy one. Perhaps Marie-Françoise actually did say that she wanted "the Duke of Chartres to marry her, not to love her"; in any case that is what happened.

Louis sent his legitimized sons off to war along with the Duke of Chartres in hope that they might learn the art well enough to command someday. Although they did not have the responsibility given to the dauphin during these years, we find the king following their careers with apparent interest. "I am sending my son, the Duke of Maine, to serve under your command," he wrote to Marshal d'Humières, "you know the feelings that I have for him and how much I hope that he will be worthy of the status that he has . . . you will have him do his duty. . . ."[24] The War Archives for the years 1690–96 contain a score or more letters of this sort as well as many short notes to the Duke of Maine and the Duke of Chartres when they were in the field. When the Count of Toulouse went to the Mediterranean to join the navy and learn the trade of admiral, his father also was anxious about his career at sea, even though he did not have much understanding for, or sympathy with, the navy.

The Duke of Maine was Madame de Maintenon's favorite. She had taken him to the south of France when he was a boy, hoping to find a cure for his lameness; he continued to be close to her throughout his life. Like the dauphin, he wanted her to intercede for him with the king, but he seems not to have been quite as afraid of his father as the dauphin was. There is one charming passage. Louis and his son were both with the army in 1691, and Louis would not listen to anyone's objections to his rashness. The Duke of Maine wrote to Madame de Maintenon, "He badly keeps the promise that he gave you not to allow himself to become fatigued . . . and he exposes himself; if I may say so, he acts like a young fool who has his reputation to establish and to prove that he is not afraid. I beg you to send him your advice, for he gets angry when we talk to him." In another letter to her he writes, "It seems that the King is satisfied with me; I would be happy to know this from you. . . ."[25]

The mother of four of these legitimized children, Madame de Montespan, remained at court until 1691. Primi Visconti tells us that he saw her descent from her carriage: "I was able to see that one of her legs was almost as large around as I am. . . . I must add that I have become somewhat slender." While she was at court, Louis visited with her almost every day, usually in the company of several other people. But these were difficult years for her. Of her children, only the Count of Toulouse (her only child without some physical handicap) was kind to her. But she could not leave the court. Permission to withdraw to a convent came in 1691 when she found herself deserted, and begged Bossuet to secure Louis' consent for her retirement. Louis gave it rather more quickly than she had expected, and immediately assigned her apartment to the Duke of Maine. Her last sixteen years were spent in prayers, alms giving, and good works; her penance was as complete as that of Madame de la Vallière, even though historians have usually not said much about it. Madame de Montespan, for all her youthful beauty and intelligence, had always had a bad press, neither her own generation nor those that have followed have forgiven her her adultery. Even Racine, upon whom she loaded honors and wealth, repaid her with the dramatic piece *Esther,* in which she is thinly disguised as the "Adulterous Vasthi, whose place I [Esther–Madame de Maintenon?] occupy." It has made no difference to anyone that Monsieur de Montespan was a sorry, bizarre creature whom few could ever love and none respect.

Just before Louis turned sixty, the Treaty of Turin not only brought the first step toward peace for Europe, but also a new personality into his entourage. When the Duke of Savoy secretly approached Tessé about the possible peace (1695), he gave him a portrait of his eleven-year-old daughter; early in November of 1696 this young lady, Marie-Adélaïde de

Savoy, arrived in France to become the bride of the Duke of Burgundy, a match negotiated at the time of the Treaty of Turin. This turned out to be an exciting event for the king and his wife. Louis went on ahead to meet the girl. "You will like her, she will please you . . . ," he writes to Madame de Maintenon. "She has the best grace and the most beautiful body that I have ever seen . . . her eyes are bright and very beautiful, her eyelashes black and adorable, her complexion . . . just as one would desire, the most beautiful black hair that one could possibly see and lots of it. She is thin as suits her age [twelve], her mouth is scarlet, lips large, teeth white and well set, hands well made. . . . She talks little, at least that I have seen . . . she has something about her face that is Italian, but she pleases and I have seen her through everyone's eyes. I am completely satisfied. . . . The more I see the princess the more I am satisfied!"[26] Were she his own granddaughter rather than his grandniece and granddaughter-in-law, Louis could hardly have found more compliments (let us admit trite ones) for her. She was a lovely girl, and she quite captured the old man's imagination.

Marie-Adélaïde was also a smart girl. When she was presented to the family a few days later, she was sweet enough, but not more than necessarily so, to her new father-in-law, to Philippe, and to his wife and the rest, but she threw her arms around Madame de Maintenon. Madame remarked, "You see how much she already is a politician." In effect Madame de Maintenon was to be responsible for her education, so much so that this little girl almost became the child of her marriage with Louis—for both the king and herself. She was a rejuvenating experience. We shall follow her career in the court in a later chapter. It turned out that this was the last warmth before the chilly winds that came with Louis' last war were upon him.

In the court of a king there were two kinds of life. The one was private, and even a Bourbon king had some private life; the other was public and engrossed much of the attention of the courtiers. In his later years Louis found the public life at Versailles confused and turbulent. Anyone who was well dressed could wander about the palace, and a great number of noblemen had patents from the king allowing them access to Versailles at all times. To evade some of this press of people, some of the confusion and disorder, Louis constructed first the Trianon palace a mile or so from the great château, and then developed the "retreat" known as Marly, a few hours away from Versailles. Marly was by all odds his favorite; it also was the only place where Madame de Maintenon regularly appeared publicly at court functions. While Versailles was a grand, imposing structure with a façade a fifth of a mile in length, Marly was a great garden with constructed waterfalls and fountains. In the center, with a prospect that allowed the King to see for miles and miles, was a charming little "cottage" perhaps thirty-five feet by fifty feet; on either side were a dozen smaller cottages, separate guest houses for invited members of the court.[27] Marly had some of the characteristics of a modern motel, but on a scale fit for a king. Everyone could be at Versailles, many people could go to the Trianon, but only those whose names were on the list could go for the weekends at Marly. A courtier would say to the king, "Marly, Sire?" But unless his name showed up on the list, he did not go. At Marly there were parties. Louis liked to have "auctions" similar to those that Mazarin had given in his day. All numbers were good for elegant gifts, and everyone would be satisfied. He also softened somewhat the rules about wearing a hat and other points of protocol, so that Marly became the place where even the king could relax a little.

The court also went to other palaces, but not as frequently as during the first half of the reign. Fontainebleau in October is beautiful, and any years that the king's health would permit it, the court went there for hunting and to enjoy the color of the forest. Only rarely after 1685 did the court return to Chambord, and Compiègne was only a stopover place when the king and court went to war in Flanders; it was the crudest of the royal residences.[28]

Saint-Germain was the usual home of the grandchildren, for everyone knew that the "air" there was better than at any of the other palaces except Compiègne. After 1689, however, it became the residence of James II of England. "You will be at home here," Louis told him, "and we can visit each other."[29] A king finds few people to talk to who are his "equals" either in rank or experience; although James's rule had been short, he nonetheless was a king. Louis also came to respect him as a man, almost as a saint. At the same time his courtesy, almost gallantry, toward James's lovely queen, Mary of Modena, made some wonder if his intentions were completely innocent. The court visited Vincennes less frequently; the Louvre only once in twenty years. Louis did not like Paris.

The public life of the court after 1684 is subject to several interpretations. If we are to believe Saint-Simon and Liselotte, the court functions were dull, uninteresting, even hard work. Madame de Maintenon also avoided them much of the time. But of these people, Saint-Simon was still too young or not at court, Liselotte too fat to enjoy the dance and often simply a "wall flower" for hours, and Madame de Maintenon too conscious of the hostility against her: none of them would have much fun at one of the *appartements* where everyone could dance, or play billiards or cards, or gamble, and at midnight attack the buffet where excellent and exotic foods made the tables groan. Some of the courtiers, however, were young enough to enjoy this activity. There were other formal events: reception of ambassadors or dignitaries, presentation of a cardinal's hat sent from Rome for the king to give to the new prince of the church, the baptism of a member of the family or a child lucky enough to have the king for godfather, and other such occasions were either solemn or gay depending upon the circumstances. Sometimes the king did not officiate, but the dauphin could carry off a procession of the knights of the Holy Spirit almost as well as his father.

There were other "occasions." The dauphin put on a carrousel that was supposed to be like the one his father had managed in 1662. But it was not the same, for Louis was the king and still very much alive, so the whole affair revolved about him rather than his unlucky son who had a back seat at his own show. While she was alive, the dauphine occasionally put on a party for a select group, including, of course, all the royal family. When the war began in 1688, and especially after it worsened in 1692 and 1693, the court still held receptions and such, but the number of parties tended to diminish and their sumptuousness became less extravagant.

In the years when the king's fistula made horseback riding difficult, Louis had to cut down on his hunting. Even so, year in and out, there was hardly a week that he did not hunt the stag or other large animals at least one day or perhaps shoot upland game birds and rabbits another. His second wife did not share his enthusiasm for the chase any more than she liked his insistence upon keeping windows open even when the weather was raw. "The face of a deer always touches me much," she wrote, "and I have a tenderness for them that makes me put their interests above those of the hunters." Her attitude, however, had no visible influence upon Louis' enjoyment of this sport; he hunted almost until the week he died. Madame de Maintenon complained often of drafts, while he was unhappy in a stuffy room; perhaps if she had loved the chase more, her husband's idiosyncrasies about open carriages and windows would not have annoyed her so much.

Many writers have insisted that after Louis' second marriage the court became hypocritically pious; the courtiers, taking their clue from the king, acted as if they were *dévots* and the gay life moved to Paris. Madame de Maintenon herself contributed to this tradition. In one letter she wrote, "I believe that the Queen had asked God for the conversion of the entire Court; that of the King is admirable, and the ladies, who seemed furthest from it do not leave the churches. Madame de Montchevreuil, Mesdames de Chevreuse, de Beauvillier, the Princess d'Harcourt, in other words the *dévotes* are not there more than Mesdames de Montespan, de Thianges, the Countess de Gramont, the Duchess de Lude and Madame de Soubise; simple Sundays are like Easter days earlier." It is interesting that she mentioned so many of the women who had had a longer or a shorter "affair" with the king.

The reader of the *Gazette* for these years would also gain much the same impression. The court and king seem to be completely involved with visits to churches, monasteries, religious processions, the king's washing the feet of the poor or touching the heads of the sick, or giving alms.[30] The *Gazette* seemed to be primarily interested in the "Most Christian King" playing out his role as the "anointed King of France"; it has contributed to the tradition of a pious but dull court that contrasts so nicely with the gay abandon of the first years of the reign when de Montespan was uncrowned queen. This picture, however, must be looked at more closely. In these years the *Gazette* was obviously no longer allowed to publish whatever it would; its pages were fewer and the long entries of previous decades were simply not included. When there were no stories from foreign correspondents or discussion of political, social, or secular affairs, these religious ceremonies become the most important events available.

Undoubtedly the court was more involved in religious affairs during these years than formerly, and yet as we noted, there were parties, and Louis continued to follow the hunt whenever his health would permit. His pleasures undoubtedly were simpler. A charming letter to Madame de Maintenon gives us a picture of the diversions of a man nearing sixty: "I will go for a hunt," he explains, "and will return about six-thirty to the gate of Saint-Cyr where I will meet my great carriage. I hope that you will come to join me there with such company as you would like. We will go for a stroll in the park. . . . If you will come to the garden gate this evening my carriage will take you to Saint-Cyr."[31] This little suggestion for a stroll in the park on a summer evening may not seem like much *divertissement* to the thirty-two-year-old Saint-Simon, but to Louis it was undoubtedly an agreeable way to spend an evening. We also know that during this period, Louis became enthralled with the game of billiards,[32] which may also be a game for an aging man. It is probable that the Duke of Beauvilliers gained favor in Louis' eyes more because of his wisdom, because he was the son-in-law of the great Colbert, and because he was an excellent billiard player, than because of his piety.

If one moved out beyond the immediate circle of the king, which seems to have revolved around his family and Madame de Maintenon's apartment, we find that the court had not so greatly changed since the earlier part of the reign. The gaming table was still the center of interest for many of the people who lived in "this strange land," and if the stories are correct, all gallantry did not end when the king regularized his own life. What we must see is that the court of Louis XIV, like any other institution, was fluid and changing. There were parties, theatres, gaming tables as well as receptions, installations, and the routine of the king's rising, dining, and going to bed. The courtiers still vied with each other to obtain the right to hold the royal candlestick in the evening, to attend the king at Marly, to enter his chamber in the morning for the *lever*. All this went on with regularity, except when the king's health prevented his acting out a public role.

In these years following his first wife's death, Louis' robust health began to fade. The king had seemed to be built physically to last a hundred years, and he actually did live to be seventy-seven. Perhaps without the attentions of his physicians he might have lived to be ninety, for he had a remarkable constitution. In his youth he had four serious illnesses: small pox, gonorrhea, a fever (probably typhoid), and in the early years of his personal reign, measles; in three of these his life was in danger. During the next twenty years, he had several bouts with real illness and some with hypochondria: dizzy spells, deaf periods, colds, general indisposition, and then attacks of fever that could have been malaria or something like it. He took pills, purgative bouillons, enemas of many and varied compositions, and submitted to bloodletting that often caused new disagreeable symptoms. His doctors always wanted him to go to the "pierced chair" ten to twelve times to be sure of complete cleansing; this often meant passing blood. He also suffered from bad teeth, rheumatism, and gout. The teeth were pulled, brutally so; for rheumatism there were ointments; for gout a limitation on his eating of meat. As we read the *Journal de la Santé du roi,* which is a "blow by blow" account of his health problems written by his physicians, we see these illnesses as essentially contests between disease and physicians, contests finally won by the latter who then received a new *gratification* for their effort. That Louis liked to have this *Journal* read to him[33] may indicate something about his personality, but it would be hard to define just what.

In the mid-1680's the king's health crowded news of the Hungarian war out of the pages of a little "newsletter" written at court. The writer was not always completely informed, but he knew that the king was in trouble.[34] In the late winter of 1684, Louis developed a rheumatic condition in his right arm for which his physicians ordered a lotion of oil, wine, salt, and vinegar. Soon it became evident that the teeth in his upper right jaw were bad and must be pulled. After the extraction the rheumatic condition disappeared, but a passage developed between his mouth and nose that allowed liquids to spray out of his mouth into his nose "like a spring." What was worse, it left a bad taste in his mouth and a bad smell on his breath. His physicians decided that the only cure would be to cauterize the passage. This was of course before the days of any effective anesthetic. On January 10, his surgeon Dubois applied the *bouton du feu* (a red-hot wire) fourteen times. "M Dubois," writes d'Aquin, "seemed more distressed than the King. . . ." D'Aquin knew that Louis would read the account many times; perhaps that is why he added words of praise for the king's decision to undergo the treatment. It was not enough. Four more times in January and early February they repeated the treatment before the passage healed.[35] Dr. David may be right that this was as dangerous as the anal fistula operation that followed.

In the terrible year of 1686, Louis developed an anal fistula, a passage beside his rectum joined to his large intestine; it grew inflamed and filled with pus; it became very painful. A newsletter written from the court explains that the king could not mount a horse; then that he could not take a walk; he was confined to bed. The dauphin had to take his place in ceremonies dedicating the statue in the Place des Victoires. The fistula started with a "tumor" that alternatively became hard and soft, that drained unpleasant matter; at first it was uncomfortable, then painful. Louis bravely tried to ignore it. He "touched" more than a thousand sick on Holy Saturday; on Easter Sunday he had to hear mass in bed. One day he would seem to be better, but always there was a relapse. Added to the discomfort and pain of the fistula, he also suffered more or less regular attacks of gout and fever. His doctors were apparently at their wits' end. They even suggested that the king should journey to take the waters at Barèges, a "curative spring" in the Pyrenees to which Madame de Maintenon had taken the Duke of Maine a decade before. This idea frightened the court very much, for to follow the king there would have been both uncomfortable and expensive. Louvois insisted on testing the spring; he sent four people suffering from anal fistulas to see what occurred when they "took the waters." Nothing happened. Madame de Maintenon keeps us informed about the attitudes of the physicians. In February she writes, "They tell us that the King's illness is getting better, but still threaten us with the scissors [an operation]." In April: "The King's troubles are not over. Those who treat him make me die of concern. One day hope, the next all contrary. . . ." "M. Fagon had a conversation with me this morning that has sorely wounded my heart. . . . He [the king] is gay and hopes to be healed." It went on like that all summer. One day Louis seemed to be better, another worse. On August 16, he awoke at three o'clock in the morning, "his teeth all chattering, a severe headache, his body frightened and prostrated, but not much fever." This probably had nothing to do with the fistula, but who knew that? D'Aquin ordered a strong purgative; Madame de Maintenon urged prayers.

The decision to operate came in the early fall. M. Félix, the king's surgeon, very carefully studied Galen's description of the operation for a fistula, and had a surgical instrument made according to the Greek physician's specifications. He then tried out the operation on as many people as he could find in the hospitals of Paris. Thus the surgeon, who before Louis' illness knew nothing about the operation, had become highly skilled by the time he operated on the king. As D'Aquin tells the story, on November 18, in great secrecy, "at eight o'clock in the morning in the presence of the Marquis de Louvois, me [D'Aquin], and M. Fagon, aided by M. Bessières [another surgeon from Paris], M. Félix introduced the probe . . . made especially [according to Galen's specifications], into the entire depth of the fistula up to the bowel which he joined with the fingers of his right hand, and pulling it from the bottom, opened the fistula with ease, and then, having introduced the scissors . . . he cut the intestine a little below the opening and cut all the ligaments in the intestine; a procedure that the King endured with great fortitude. An hour after the operation he [Louis] was bled in the arm. . . ." Obviously d'Aquin and Fagon did not want Félix to have all the credit for the king's recovery.[36] Louis' problems were not over when this first operation was completed. There had to be future sessions with the "scissors" before the fistula was finally removed and no new one created. In June of 1687 when the cure seemed complete, Louis expressed his satisfaction with his physicians and surgeon by a "gratification" of 150,000 livres for M. Félix, 100,000 livres for M. d'Aquin, 80,000 for Fagon, and 12,000 each for the four apothecaries of the king's household.[37]

When the court heard about the operation there was much excitement. M. Félix was besieged by people wishing to have the same operation; it was *la mode*—but some of them really did have anal fistulas. This did not distract from the fame that Louis had won by his bravery and fortitude.

In the following decade the king's health was not assaulted as violently again, but he did have bouts with gout and fever. Fagon, who succeeded d'Aquin as his physician, was less willing than his predecessor to allow the king to escape the lancet, even though bleeding did cause him discomfort and distress. The new physician, like his predecessors, was a firm believer in regular purgings and enemas as well as in bloodletting. Since he was the specialist, Louis submitted to his prescriptions, even though they cost him dearly. As Dr. Débrou remarks, "The intestines of Louis XIV were rarely in repose. Tormented by ceaseless purgings, concerned with digesting his frequent huge and often undigested meals, they [his intestines] suffered everything. And it was from his stomach and belly that came the vapeurs and dizziness that the physicians attacked with useless and harmful remedies."[38]

It is difficult not to sympathize with the aging king. His court still provided amusements of the concert, the theater, the gaming table, the *appartements* with dancing and heavy buffets, and the promenades in the park. He could still go on the hunt or visit Fontainebleau in the fall to see the color of the leaves, but his health was not what it had been. His teeth were bad, he could no longer eat the gigantic meals of earlier years, and the hunt tired him more than when he was young. His concern for his soul deprived him of some of the pleasures that brought excitement in earlier days, and we do not know whether or not his religious exercises and cere- monial parades brought much satisfaction. Some of his enemies, and per- haps the king himself, regarded these trials as the punishment for his sins; they were probably only the inevitable result of his life habits and of his age. The worst was yet to come: in the last decade and a half of his life, Louis tasted the chagrin and frustration of failure, defeat, humiliation, and met the tragedy of death's visits to those nearest to him.

VI

23

THE CULT OF THE KING*

"I HAVE EVERY REASON to be satisfied since the Very Christian King has treated me most civilly and others have done all that they can to give me pleasure. . . ." Thus wrote Crown Prince Frederick of Denmark to tell his father of his trip to the court of Louis XIV. His letters are a charmingly naïve account of the parties, balls, and court functions that seemed only slightly dampened by the war that raged in Flanders, the Rhineland, and Italy. He was extremely happy to have his princely rank recognized by the right to an armchair in the presence of the king and the dauphin even though he was "incognito." He visited most of the châteaus of the royal family, including the Palais-Royal, Marly, Versailles (for a *Mardi gras* ball), and on his departure Louis urged him to stop at the Condé château at Chantilly "where the gardens and the waters merit a visit." He must have been well treated, indeed handsomely so, for in one of his letters he tells his father that he has enough money, and needs no more. Surely this has happened to few enough tourists in Paris.[1]

What young Frederick saw was the court of France ensconced in the grandeur of the palaces built by its kings. When Louis came to the throne, the royal family had many châteaus both in the Paris area and down on the Loire. Some of them, like Fontainebleau and Vincennes, were old and had been remodeled many times; the most beautiful of them dated from the time of Francis I, particularly Chambord and Saint-Germain. There were palaces in Paris: the Louvre, the Tuileries, and the Palais-Royal that Richelieu had built and willed to the crown, and after the death of the dowager Duchess of Orléans (Gaston's wife), the Luxembourg Palace. At Compiègne and Versailles there were "hunting lodges"; the latter dated from the period of Louis XIII and was a delightful structure. There were other châteaus belonging to the houses of Orléans, Condé, and Conti, but the king's government had nothing to do with their upkeep.

Mazarin had believed that the king should build inside the walls of the great fortress of Vincennes, and indeed, the cardinal caused two pavilions to be constructed there and refurbished the chapel. But Louis' own first important construction was in Paris; in spite of his dislike for the city, he allowed Colbert to convince him that a great king should have an imposing palace in his capital city. The Palais-Royal did not quite reach the specifications, nor did the "new Louvre" built by Catherine de Médicis, Henry IV, Marie, and Louis XIII. What was needed was an important addition to the Louvre opposite the church of Saint-Germain l'Auxerrois and along the front of the river. Bernini came from Italy to help with the plans, but the final designs accepted were drawn by a French architect, Claude Perrault. These pavilions built by Louis XIV are still impressive for their monumental style as well as their excellent taste, but Louis probably had very little to do with it beyond giving his approval and supplying the money. When Colbert urged further construction in the city, the king was not interested. The memories of the *Fronde* and his own love of the open countryside combined to make him distrust and dislike the big city; he avoided visiting it for years on end.

Versailles was Louis' favorite project. The site seems first to have appealed to him in 1664 at the time of the party of the Enchanted Island, but the really important remodeling of the château did not begin until 1669–70. During the Dutch War the construction languished, but after 1679 it moved forward with a great pace. By 1682 Madame de Maintenon could write that Versailles had an "incomparable beauty," by 1687–88 the greatest part of the construction was complete—only the chapel remained to be built. Despite Saint-Simon and the other critics of Versailles, the great château remains as one of the important artistic accomplishments of our civilization. Louis built it at Versailles rather than at Vincennes to show the world that the King of France could build in the open. His soldiers were his defense; he needed neither walls nor moat to guarantee his security.

The cost of these palaces was enormous. In 1679 it ran as much as five and a half million livres a year; in 1685 it stood at more than eleven. Versailles, Madame de Montespan's little château at Clagny, and the Trianon (not as we see it today) cost almost a hundred million livres over a period of twenty-five years. We do not know how much this was in terms of the gross national product of the era because we have no statistics worthy of the name; it probably was not a much larger percentage of the national income than Francis I spent on Chambord, but that château also was a great effort at the time. The other royal châteaus had relatively little spent upon them, with the exception of Marly and Saint-Germain. The former cost about four and a half million livres; the latter absorbed about six and a half, first as the residence of the royal children, then as the home of the exiled King of England, James II. It is highly improbable that Louis was much concerned about these costs; he believed that great projects should be completed at whatever expense they might require. After all, a king like Louis XIV did not grub for his money like a merchant or a notary. Colbert, who often complained about expenses, also approved the construction of impressive châteaus that gave tangible evidence of the greatness of the king.

The emergence of Versailles can best be followed in the drawings of Sylvester and Edelnick, which give a pictorial history of the growth of this wonderful building. There were many details that were actually tried out in brick, stone, and plaster, only to be rejected as the characteristic forms of the château emerged. Le Vau, and above all, Mansard, were the most important architects; Le Brun was responsible for the decoration; Le Nôtre for the gardens and alleys and roads. These men were supported by the king and had plenty of time and money to work out the grand style of the palace. Versailles has to be seen to be appreciated; one can only say that the sumptuous public rooms, the apartments of the royal family, the halls and stairways, the rich baroque decoration, all combined to make it a palace fit for a great monarch and worthy of a rich and powerful kingdom. It was at once a home for the king, a reception hall for state occasions, an office building for the king's government, and a dwelling for hundreds of courtiers and royal officials who somehow managed to find living space in the rabbit-warrens of the *petits appartements.* The château, as it finally emerged, completely surrounded the original little hunting lodge of Louis XIII.

The garden and fountains and alleys of Versailles are every bit as imposing as the château itself, and they set a standard and a style that the western world will never forget. There were many fountains. One of the most charming was in the center of the Apollo-Diana garden circle depicting Latone with her children demanding the vengeance of Jupiter for the insolence of the peasants. As the god changes the peasants into frogs, the pool is filled with them in various stages of metamorphosis, each shooting water. The swamp fountain of the baths of Apollo, the fountain *renommée,* the dragon fountain with its grotesque fish and maidens, the three levels of fountains at the central stairs as well as dozens of smaller ones made the waterplay at Versailles a thing of wonder. Today it draws huge crowds who are enchanted by the magic qualities of the display. There was a zoo with animals from many lands. There were statues everywhere: Louis even dispatched warships to Italy to bring back the large blocks of marble for his garden statues. There was the rape of Persephone, a series for Spring, Summer, Autumn, and Winter, Diana, Venus, and other Greek and Roman deities, a faun seven feet high, satyrs of all sizes, nymphs, dancers, and magnificent bronze and stone vases with bas reliefs. Versailles represented the most conspicuous consumption of art since the great days of the Roman Empire.[2]

Louis has been severely criticized for spending so much money on the palace, for building the water works that cost much both in blood and treasure simply to provide visual satisfaction, for surrounding himself with so much grandeur and luxury when his people were so poor. These criticisms are surely justified in light of the assumptions of the men who made them, but Louis would have had difficulty understanding what his critics were talking about. He loved to build, he enjoyed his gardens—according to his upbringing, this was quite enough to justify the spending of so much money and energy. It would never have occurred to him that his palaces should not be decorated and his gardens cared for just because his people were poor; Louis had none of the "humanitarian" democratic sentiments of later eras, and little sense of "charity" embedded in the Christian thought of his own. If hard-pressed he might have come upon the nineteenth-century "trickle down" theory to justify his work. After all, Versailles did give employment to many, many craftsmen and artists with all sorts of artistic talents. However, it is even doubtful that he would have bothered to use any such argument to justify his constructions.

He might answer some of the criticism by pointing out that he allowed properly dressed citizens of Paris to walk in the gardens of the Louvre and Tuileries, and that anyone who was "decently dressed" could visit Versailles or Vincennes or Saint-Germain. Colbert opposed allowing the public to use the royal gardens, and when Louis overrode his objections, decided somehow to profit from their presence. Indeed, the practice of selling the concession for renting chairs in public gardens dates from Colbert's decision to reap some benefit from these visitors. The public was often troublesome; visitors walked on the grass, broke limbs from the trees, and made trouble for the gardeners; the registers of the secretaries of state contain numerous letters dealing with these problems.[3] It is surely true that the vast majority of the people of Louis' kingdom never saw Versailles, and yet before his death the palace was already a mecca for visitors from France as well as from foreign lands.

Versailles was both the residence of the king and the seat of his government. His ministers with their assistants, engineers, clerks, and agents, and the whole paraphernalia of government were housed in the château. Anyone who has visited Washington, D.C., with its miles of marble façades, its imposing office buildings, the Pentagon, and the palaces of government, who has seen the offices of a senator or a cabinet minister, will realize that Louis did not really house his government in the majestic style that twentieth-century men can afford. The king's apartments were adequate, and the state rooms sumptuous, but those of the courtiers and ministers were surely substandard. One would have to drop far down the ladder of hierarchy in Washington to find bureaucrats living under such conditions. Louvois would be astonished to see the Pentagon, of which his ministry was the prototype. On the other hand, it would be unfair to fail to say that Louvois, Colbert, and the other ministers of the crown did have sumptuous country châteaus and Parisian *hôtels* that were the result of the bounty of the king.

It is always a difficult question to discover how much the king himself actually knew about the work that was being done, how much he actually had to do with the plans. There can be little doubt that Louis loved to build. He took the same pleasure in the erection of handsome châteaus and beautiful gardens that other men take in the building of their houses and the care of their yards, but we do not know whether he took an active part in making the plans, merely approved plans presented to him, or in general outlined what he wanted, leaving the details to the architects of the *Bâtiments*. The *Bâtiments* was a bureau that supervised the royal châteaus, paid salaries of many kinds, prepared plans for rebuilding, new building, gardens, and many other such things.

Colbert, Louvois, Mansard (the only professional), and the Duke d'Antin in turn ruled this department during the reign of Louis XIV. It was an important post because the superintendent of the *Bâtiments* always had ready access to the king. But we do not know what part the king actually took in this area. Mansard's *Register* for 1699–1701 has survived in part, but it does not really answer all the questions. Obviously Louis was informed about much of the detailed work that needed to be done (cleaning statues with *eau forte,* repairing water systems, changes in the gardens at Marly and Versailles, etc.) and he may possibly have taken an active part in the projection of this work. However, it is impossible to know just what Mansard's formula "His majesty has ordered the pavement . . . etc." really means. Louis was probably merely ordering the *Bâtiments* to do what the superintendent proposed to do.[4] One thing that the *Register* does indicate is the fact that Mansard had many interviews with the king. The Duke d'Antin[5] gives us further evidence that underlines the importance of the position of superintendent, because of the opportunities he had to talk to the king. He also tells us that the professional personnel at the *Bâtiments* were pleased to be administered by a "man of quality" who, unlike

Mansard, did not interfere with their artistic plans and projects![6] The king was undoubtedly the kind of gardener who did not get his hands dirty or his nails black; he left that to the professionals who were expected to be "experts." But Louis was fond of his collaborators in the building of Versailles. There are touching stories: Many years after Versailles was completed, Louis, Mansard, and Le Nôtre—all old men—were being carried in chairs along the paths at Versailles and Le Nôtre with tears in his eyes said, "Sire, truly my good father would have wide eyes if he saw me in a chair beside the greatest king in the world." Mansard: "One must say that your majesty treats his mason and his gardener very well."[7] The words were probably never spoken, but they still seem to represent a truth about the relationship between the king and these two distinguished men. A further bit of evidence on Louis' love for his palace and gardens is the "Tour of Versailles," which he wrote in his own hand describing the "best way to see" the palace and gardens. It is an itinerary designed to show off the palace that a modern guide could still find useful.[8]

We cannot leave Versailles without reiterating that it had a purpose beyond being the residence for the king and his government. This great palace was a keystone in the new cult of royalty. In the preceding eras the great constructions were usually to the glory of God; even Philip II, when he built his great palace, made it a monastery with the chapel as the center of interest. At Versailles the bedroom of the king is the center, identifying the king as the highest power on earth, while the chapel is to one side. The imposing grandeur of the château was evidence of the wealth of the kingdom; and its construction without walls and moats was proof of the power of the king's government. Versailles was a challenge, a defiance flung out at all Europe; as impressive a display of the wealth, power, and authority of the French king as were his armies and his warships. Europe did not miss this. In the century after the construction of Versailles, châteaus at Vienna, at Potsdam, at Dresden, at Munich, at St. Petersburg, and the very plans for the city of Washington, D.C., reflected the influence of the grandeur of Versailles. A sovereign who wished to flaunt his power could do no better than to imitate Louis XIV.[9] Louis probably never dreamed of the fact that he had also built a monument that would become a lucrative tourist attraction for hundreds of years to come. He and his generation had the intention of housing the king, who was identifying himself with the kingdom in a way that would heighten his power and his authority in the world. We might note in passing that such magnificence is not easy to live with, and that Louis built Marly to escape from the *grandeur* that Versailles imposed upon him and his court.

If the royal châteaus were evidence of the king's power and importance, so also was the organization of the royal households. The king, the queen, the dauphin and dauphine, the king's grandchildren, the king's brother and his family each had a "household." These households included hundreds of people ranging from the two grand masters of France (the Prince of Condé and the Duke of Bourbon) who were paid 3,600 livres a year, a grand chamberlain (also 3,600 livres), four first gentlemen (3,500 livres), grand masters of the wardrobe, of the pantry, of ceremonies, etc., masters of the hunt, the stable, and the kitchen, secretaries of the chamber (usually held by a secretary of state at a stipend of 1,200 livres). And below these people, hordes of lesser servants of nonnoble origin did all sorts of work around the palace. Many of these people would hold appointments in more than one royal household, so that a top professional person like a doctor or a surgeon might have an income of over 10,000 livres; a secretary of state would have many times this amount. Besides the civil "household," there were clerical and military ones, each having officers of varying degrees. The *Maison du Roi* were the elite troops of the royal army.

All of these offices, from the captains of the guards, the chaplains of the king, the grand masters of "this and that," down to the clockmakers and valets and cooks' assistants, were venal. It was usual for a son to inherit his father's position by securing from the king during his father's lifetime a brevet assuring his succession. If the king wished to appoint a new face to a position, the new appointee had to buy the office from his predecessor at a figure set by the king. This was as Louis wanted it. He inherited his position and would pass it on to his son; he liked to have the same people about him, men who knew that they were destined from birth to carry on the family position in the royal society. By staffing the royal households with "people of quality" and ambitious nobles on the make, Louis could also assure himself that the wealthy of the land would have something to do and to talk about besides rebellion, and that they would fulfill their *métiers* under his supervision. When one remembers that the king also held the power of appointment to the clerical benefices of the kingdom, to hundreds, indeed thousands, of military and civil commissions, and to all these "household" offices, the picture of the court, watching carefully the news of deaths and rushing to the king to ask the dead man's place for themselves or their friends, becomes credible for there was a considerable turnover, in spite of the brevets of survival rights. To look at a three-month period at random, in the first quarter of 1686 there was a new maître d'hôtel and a new "ordinary" gentleman to the king, a new captain of the guards, a new lady and a maid of honor to the queen, a new chaplain to the dauphine, a new ensign in the queen's guards, a new ordinary gentleman to the dauphin.[10] A cross check of the lists of household officers in 1673 with those of 1699 reveals that the total number of people remained about the same; so did their pensions. It was possible, however, for an individual to make some progress, for there were several grades of each rank or profession, and the higher grades were paid more generously. Sainctôt, for example, moved from master of ceremonies at 2,000 livres (his successor got only 1,500 livres) to grand master at 3,000 livres.[11]

There was an elaborate bookkeeping structure to maintain the royal households, to pay for the soap, furniture, food and drink, and all the other things necessary to the king's well-being. There were problems in keeping all these things, and the people who managed them, under some surveillance. For example, while there was a great deal of food bought and prepared for the king's tables, the people who could eat there were carefully screened. It was a capital offense to steal from the royal household, yet some pilfering occurred. The king's valuables were regularly inventoried. One of the most interesting of these inventories was that of the crown jewels. In 1666 they were valued at just under five million; by 1683–84 they were up to a little over seven million. The eighteen large diamonds given the crown by Mazarin, the most valuable single item, were worth almost two million livres. The invoice included rings, pins, clasps, necklaces, brooches, earrings, pendants, cufflinks, shoe buckles, and other such personal jewelry; it is easy to see how Louis and his women could appear splendid before the world. One item seems to throw much light upon the problem of costs. When Marie-Thérèse died, the *argenterie* paid 297,500 livres for funeral expenses, mourning clothes for the royal household officers, and some 22,700 livres for gold embroidery made by the Daughters of Saint Joseph. This does not include money spent by French ambassadors abroad who also had to impress the world with the importance of the dead queen and splendor of their king.[12]

The most important offices in the royal households were occupied by great noblemen and their wives. There were about 250 individuals—men, women, and children—who were classed as people of quality: the princes of the blood, the dukes and peers, the very wealthy noblemen of ancient lineage (usually with the title *marquis*), important clergymen, and soldiers with high rank in the king's army or navy. Some of these people had family histories as old as the royal family itself, for indeed the kings of France were of this stock, but the majority were of more recent creation. There were considerable gradations among them. The peers and dukes took their position from the date of the creation of the title, the simple persons of quality from positions in the household, the church, or the armed services. Louis assured these people the respect due to their status in society; in court functions, at the grand sessions of Parlement, or simply in the social setting of the court, the dukes and peers shared the grandeur of the king; they were his "cousins," they acted as if they were set apart from the rest of humanity. Under Louis XIV they acted out roles that helped to create the *mystique* necessary to justify the power that the king did, in fact, exercise. Their roles, however, were purely ceremonial, for they were excluded from the realities of power. As Saint-Simon contemplated this situation, he reached the conclusion that Louis XIV was deliberately attempting to destroy the dukes and the peers of the realm.

Most of these people of quality owed their positions to recent kings; only a very few of them could actually trace their lineage deep into the middle ages. The kings of France had long since been encroaching upon the traditional feudal orders. None of the lay peers still ruled their provinces as quasi-independent lords, for the crown had absorbed their powers. However, in the sixteenth and seventeenth centuries a new feudality struggled to establish itself out of the disorders of the "religious" war and the rebellions of the first half of the seventeenth century. As men with enormous wealth, with governorships of provinces made hereditary in their families, these "great ones" of the land had dangerously threatened the king's authority. Louis XIV was well aware of the problem through his own experiences during the *Fronde*. Like his father and grandfather he strove to curb these "great ones." One of the most effective means was to cheapen their ranks by the creation of new peers, and by the encroachment upon their real powers as governors or as holders of great fiefs through the action of royal intendants dependent upon the king and directed by his ministers. In this way the new feudality could be curbed; at the same time, by bringing these great ones to court and domesticating them as servants of the royal households, Louis gradually weakened their will to rebel.

All of the bowing and scraping, the pretensions to grandeur, could not conceal the fact that Louis had separated real power from social prestige. Elizabeth-Charlotte saw this most clearly: "I am not ignorant to the point of not knowing what difference there is between the Elector of Brandenburg and Monsieur [her husband], but in order to prevent Monsieur from seeing that he is only in a way a slave of his brother, one gives him a huge idea of his grandeur, to which nothing can approach and which nonetheless is without any foundation, and is purely imagination." In another place she wrote, "I hold grandeur as purely chimerical when great power is not joined to it." But what was left to the great ones? They were offered social prestige, ceremonial importance, grandeur—if they would act out roles that would supply the *mystique* for their king's exercise of power. If they refused to accept the offer, they also gave up the royal favor that was translated into patronage, pensions, gratifications, and the *divertissements* of the court.

The memoirists of the era spent much of their time discussing the problems of rank. Saint-Simon, a duke whose father had been given that rank by Louis XIII, was particularly sensitive to slights or usurpations affecting his own status. It is he who has given us the notion that Louis excluded people of quality from his government and placed power in the hands of the "vile bourgeoisie," and he it is who is always jubilant when "justice" was done to people of quality by putting the "vile bourgeoisie" in their places. This idea, of course, is basically false. As we have seen, Louis' ministers were of the new race of professional royal servants; their lives, their ideas, their outlooks and their aspirations had little or nothing to do with the bourgeois class. Their children married the children of people of quality; Colbert's sons-in-law, the Dukes de Beauvillier and de Chevreuse, gained entry into the higher councils of the state. However it seems that Louis himself largely subscribed to Saint-Simon's value system, for we find him angry when Madame de Torcy, wife of the important secretary of state for foreign affairs, accidentally took a place at the table above her rank.

At another level Louis was even more insistent upon rank, namely in the diplomatic corps of Europe. He would not send an ambassador to the court of Vienna because the German Hapsburgs insisted upon giving the Spanish ambassador first place in their court. The fracas at London early in the reign was only the most dramatic of Louis' demands for first place in Europe. Indeed, in the correspondence in the Archives of the Foreign Ministry, the numerous letters dealing with this problem have the ring of the king's own words rather than simply the composition of his secretary. For example, we find him arguing with the Grand Vizier over precedence at the moment the Turks were about to attack Vienna.

All this emphasis upon grandeur, precedence, rank, and etiquette has led many historians to charge Louis with megalomania. At first glance the accusation seems quite correct, but a closer look will show that the king of France was really no different from the other monarchs of his age. They sought to fulfill their *gloire,* just as Louis did, and the contests over diplomatic rank were not single-sided affairs; other monarchs were just as desperately anxious to establish their places in the hierarchy. The squabbles over rank of the Diet of Ratisbon were notorious as one of the causes of the ineffectiveness of that institution. There can be no doubt about Louis' pride for his family and his kingdom; and this in effect meant personal pride, since the kingdom of France was centered on its king. But to see the ceremonial life of the court and the demands of his diplomats for recognition of their master's grandeur as megalomania quite misses the point. As Louis' power grew to the point where his officers could really reach into the provinces of his kingdom, and his soldiers could actually assure his government against revolt and rebellions, the *mystique* that has to accompany power had also to grow; this is the most important fact about the elaborate setting for the king.

On another level, the grandeur of the king was reflected in the music, art, and drama presented for the amusement of the court. Louis was the first king to have musicians directed by a conductor in the modern manner. Lully not only wrote music for his master, he also directed the musicians who played it; indeed, his death resulted from an accident that happened while he was directing the violins of the king.[13] The drama at court was often acted by courtier amateurs who fancied their ability to interpret the pieces of the theater, but Molière's troupe and others also played before the king, as the charming "Impromptu at Versailles" so cleverly testifies. The plays of Corneille, Molière, and Racine, as well as of other dramatists whose work is no longer known in our theaters, were frequently produced at court, in spite of the grumbling of some of the clergy who feared the influence of the theater. Louis also supported a "stable" of artists who produced under the direction of the "first painter to the king." Throughout most of the reign, Le Brun occupied this post. He and his co-workers have been criticized for their slavish adulation of their patron by men who failed to realize that they, like the builders of the châteaus and the gardens, were promoting the *mystique,* the cult of royalty necessary to Louis' government. Anyone who has seen a representative selection of Le Brun's paintings will quickly admit that he was a master painter as well as a courtier to his master.[14]

While music, art, and drama gave pleasure to the court as well as helped to make an imposing façade for the monarchy, the men of letters and of science also received the bounty of the king and responded by praising his reign. Voltaire long ago pointed out that Louis' government stands like a shining light as the patron of art, literature, and science, in striking contrast to the government of his archfoe William of Orange, who became King of England.[15] This is true. One has to wait until the establishment of the great American foundations like the Guggenheim, the Rockefeller, the Mellon, and others to see patronage of culture and science on the scale set by Louis XIV. Moreover the king's government was probably more im-

portant to the scientist and the artist than our contemporary foundations
are. For today a man of letters can make a living from his royalties; a
scientist, as a professor or an employee of a great corporation; and even
an artist or a musician, as a teacher; whereas in the seventeenth century
few such opportunities existed. Thus the king's bounty was very important.
The list of the recipients of Louis' pensions and *gratifications* sounds like
the roll call of the Guggenheim fellows: in one year there were three
theologians, eight linguists, twenty-five French and three foreign "men of
letters," five historians, one painter (most painters were employed by the
Bâtiments on regular salaries), one lawyer, six students of physics, four
surgeons and medical men, one botanist, one mathematician. Some of these
men were to become famous, others soon sank into decent oblivion. In 1669
Racine, Molière,[16] and Corneille were on the list; so were Perrault, Boileau,
Tallement, and Godefroy. De la Croix never missed it, for his studies of
oriental languages required money for travel. Many of these honored will
be known only to specialists in their fields. For some of them royal patronage was onerous; Racine, for example, had to accompany Louis on his
campaigns; his remark that he now understood that soldiers allowed themselves to be killed so freely because their lives were so bad, was not as much
of a joke as he imagined. He repaid Louis for taking him along by a *History
of the War* that reads like a fairy tale, but properly adds to the stature of
the king.[17]

Louis also sponsored academies of the dance, of painting, of science,
of letters; but one often suspects that he knew little or nothing about these
organizations. For example, he made only one visit to the observatory that
he "built and supported"; the tapestry commemorating that event does not
tell of its uniqueness. Obviously much of the king's sponsorship was the
work of his ministers, but it does not really matter whether the inspiration
came from the king, Colbert, one of the Le Telliers, or some other of
Louis' creatures—it was done in his name and the intention was to bring
prestige to the king and his regime. It was no accident that in the literary
quarrel known as the "battle between the moderns and the ancients," men
compared the age of Louis XIV with those of Pericles and of Augustus.
Louis' efforts to support science and culture obviously paid off in terms
of royal prestige, and as we shall see, his government needed his prestige
as a *mystique* to cover the extensions of power that accompanied the creation of the military-police state. When the king's power grew to the point
where another *Fronde* was simply out of the question, then also his prestige
and grandeur, the *mystique* that justified power, had also to expand.

However, the doings at court and in the capitals of Europe were known to only a few. The *Gazette* printed stories of court functions, but it had a limited circulation. Thus there was the problem of carrying the message to the people of the kingdom. They were feeling the imposition of power that came with the development of the bureaucratic, military-police state; they had also to accept the *mystique* that justified the king's assumption of this power over the kingdom. The solution lay in the profoundly royalist sentiments of the French. The clergy, the professors, the literate had long explained that God gave the power to govern to kings while He retained the authority to himself, and that He would hold the king responsible for his acts. The king was the "father of his country," the object of admiration— perhaps veneration—a consecrated figure with functions that made him godlike. Even the more violent pamphleteers during the *Fronde* professed loyalty and love for the king; he was the object of their desires. His role as a political agent, however, was not so clearly defined; there were many who believed that the centralizing tendencies of the royal governments were at least unfortunate and probably illegal. Since the last of the fourteenth century there had been a growing struggle in the kingdom between the decentralized sources of power (nobility, towns, guilds, etc.) and the centralizing tendencies of the monarchy. By Louis XIV's time this contest within the inherited pluralistic structure of politics had reached a crisis, a crisis that tipped the balance of force in favor of the central authority. This new balance had to be spelled out both in political institutions like the new army and the bureaucracy, and in the symbols and ceremony that gave to the people a visual apperception of political order. A most important factor in this vision was the image of the king in the popular mind.

The lives of most seventeenth-century men were lived out in a dull routine of traditional activity broken only by some colorful religious festival, an occasional arrival of a stranger, a troop of minstrels or players, a military cavalcade, or some such event. Thus the progressions of the court from one château to another that had long been the usual pattern of monarchy were "events" of importance in the lands through which the court moved. Anyone who has journeyed up the Nile on an excursion steamer, where he can see the seventeenth century juxtaposed to his own, will never forget the cries of the children and others who greet the weekly visit of the steamer as a contact with the outside world. How much more exciting must have been the cavalcade of soldiers and courtiers, the gay carriages, the wagons and mule trains, the fine gentlemen and bedecked ladies, with the person of the king as the center of attraction. A newsletter from the court in 1683 tells the story of the royal voyage toward Fontainebleau:

On the road from Chambor[d] . . . the King was loaded with presents of fruit
and flowers that the people brought to him and for which they were liberally
recompensed. One person . . . threw in front of the King's carriage the most
beautiful lamb that you have ever seen . . . but it fled so quickly that no one
could catch it. . . .[18]

It was a typical scene reflecting the popularity of the king—or perhaps the
vacuum in the lives of the people. Kings were well advised to travel from
place to place, to show themselves to the people, to allow the local clergy
to tell their parishioners that this was the king that God had given them.
It secured stability for their position and consent for their rule.

This was the age-old pattern. For centuries French kings had traveled
through their lands, giving justice, receiving the blessings of the clergy, and
the cheers of the people. During the reign of Louis XIV, in addition to this
well-established relationship, new patterns developed—a new cult that
associated the king more closely with the Godhead. This new cult foliated
in the form of festivals, fireworks, statues, fountains, palaces, expositions,
books, pamphlets, and religious services—all organized to glorify the king,
to raise his throne to the steps of heaven, to remove his person from the
ranks of ordinary human beings. Louis contributed to the process in numerous ways. For example, contrary to traditional usage, he refused to allow
his queen, the dauphine, or his granddaughters-in-law to kiss anyone outside of the senior blood lines of the Bourbon family; he spent millions to
erect the magnificent palace of Versailles; he allowed his courtiers to heap
adulations upon him beyond all reason; he tried never to appear in any
role except that of the king. This last effort of his has created problems for
historians, for he left hardly a scrap of paper from his pen that could be
called intimate. He always wrote *en roi*! "In his writing and his works,"
writes Grouvelle, who edited them, "one always feels the presence of the
diadem. We find almost no letters, no notes, not even to mistresses, nothing
intimate, nothing friendly. He was always on parade, always the king."[19]
But Louis did not create this image of royalty all by himself. His soldiers,
his ministers, his servants, his clergy, the magistrates, the Hôtel de Ville, the
University all joined to give a new interpretation to the role of king.

This generation of princes and statesmen stood on the edge of a past
that had been both difficult and disorderly; all over Europe the military and
political pluralism inherited from a yesterday had led to civil wars, rebellions, violence, contempt for the processes of law. Cloaked by religious
flags, by demands for the recognition of "liberties," or simply by a brutal
urge for pillage and plunder, these disorders had endangered the tranquillity
of the European world and the security of all men. The historian does not

have to journey far in the years 1600–60 to understand why Hobbes decided that the Leviathan was the only hope for society; such disorder could be cured only by power. A Henry IV might try to govern the kingdom in the manner of a guerrilla chieftain, but he had to realize that he shared his power with the men whose backs he slapped. Richelieu and Louis XIII could govern with erratic brutality, using picked panels of judges and the executioner to impose their will, but the headsman's sword cannot long replace the scepter if the king is not to appear a tyrant. This was the problem of the men around Louis XIV: they were willing to use force to give form to society, to break the will of rebellion, but they recognized that consent of the governed is most important for the ruler. Louis carefully explained to his son that it would be quite inconvenient to have to use force all the time to secure obedience. He had not read Machiavelli for nothing.

The vital forces of the kingdom seconded the royal will to restore order and break the political and military pluralism that had caused so much trouble in the past. The new army that Mazarin and his creatures were making was popular, for it could expel the "pillagers," as men called soldiers during the *Fronde*. The *Grand Jours* that invaded the provinces to bring malefactors to justice and peace to the land were welcome even though many of the criminals slipped through the nets. The intendants of police, justice, and taxation were well received when they began to inquire closely about the murders that passed as duels or accidents, the kidnappings that passed for elopements, and other acts of violence in the land. This was bringing order out of the *mêlée* and control over the pluralism that had created disorder. The new army and the bureaucracy were the agents of this action, but in addition there was needed a new image of royalty, a new *mystique,* and new sanctions for the power that it was exercising. This was the work of a propaganda that utilized all the vital forces of the kingdom.

A new image could be created only out of ideas that men already had or at least were in the process of acquiring. This was an age in which the literate of the population were familiar with classical antiquity and Byzantine practices. Ovid, Suetonius, and other Roman authors were widely read in excellent editions; in 1645 the publication of Byzantine antiquities provided insight into the practices of Roman emperors both east and west and added considerable underpinning to the basic assumptions of the supporters of monarchy from Luther to Hobbes and Bossuet. One has only to see the *feux d'artifice*[20] to realize that this generation understood that Caesar became a god in order to strengthen his position in society and cure its disorders; Augustus in the Pantheon, Hadrian identified with

Hercules, the deification of living emperors had become the common property of the literate world. The idea had long been established that kings ruled by divine right—this was the club that had beaten down the papal pretensions. Now was the time to identify this gift of God with the person of the king and thereby endow him with the authority to curb the lawless forces of society. This *mystique* seemed reasonable to a generation that willingly accepted theological assumptions, that believed in providential notions of historical causation; they could not be expected to know that their brothers, who were scanning the skies, who were studying the forces of nature, who were dissecting the human body, who were exploring the non-Christian world both past and contemporary, were in the process of destroying this theological orientation and of substituting for divine intervention a secular conception of the world. It is so often forgotten that Louis' entourage had every reason to believe in a theocentric world, and small reason to suspect that the elite of the next century would have little use for gods and would seek secular solutions and secular salvations for themselves and society. This may be why the late seventeenth-century men have so often been misunderstood. Let us listen to some of their voices and try to understand them in the light of their religious—rather than our secular—solutions to the questions before the world:

> God of Gods, Lord of Lords,
>> Save the king!
> God who established kings on the throne,
>> Save the king!
> God by whom kings rule,
>> Save the king!
> God who subjected people to kings,
>> Save the king!

FROM *Litanies pour le roi*[21]

. . .

Should anyone be astonished that God has blessed this regime that was consecrated to Him . . . that He has sustained its counsels which He inspired, that He has favored its enterprises conceived at the foot of His altars, that He has brought success to its projects of which He Himself was the author. . . ?[22]

. . .

Kings are the visible image of their invisible creator, and outside of His divine rights which we owe to the latter, all honors belong to the former by a new indispensable right . . . the sovereignty of an absolute monarch comes from God rather than from men . . . a true subject can never be faithful and obedient enough. . . .[23]

. . .

Yet while God has created all men according to His image . . . it is nonetheless true that it is in the person of kings that He has imprinted the most vivid colors and it is there that He carved the most perfect characters of divinity. . . . There is only one God in the world and in the kingdom there is only one king to whom alone one should render honor and duty . . . the power of kings is without limits. . . . God loves all his creatures, but not equally . . . one cannot doubt that, among all the mortal creatures, kings and monarchs are the most cherished by God. . . . [De Montmeran finds that God was also partial to France in giving the kingdom the most beautiful climate, landscape, and setting in the world and adds:] if God has poured so many benedictions on French soil, He has not been less liberal toward French kings. It is proper that a kingdom so favored of heaven should be ruled by kings filled with the grace and the gifts of heaven. . . .[24]

. . .

These sons of our Alcide
Issue of the blood of Gods. . . .[25]

. . .

Oh My God . . . Conserve for us this prince that you have given us through your love for us. Give him time to accomplish that which he plans for your glory. Cover him with grace as he covers us with his favors. . . .[26]

. . .

It is the order of the world established by Providence that places inferior things in subordination to superior ones. Whoever interrupts this order resists Providence and who resists Providence works for his damnation [Paul]. . . . Good or bad, pagan or faithful, one must obey princes; we are their subjects, they our sovereigns. Happy happy people whom God favors with a good king, who find their grandeur in his piety. . . . All men are the image of God but His true portrait is in the person of the sovereigns; their authority represents His power, their majesty, His éclat, their goodness, His charity, their rigor, His justice. They hold His place on their thrones, they speak in His name in their edicts, they exercise His vengeance in their wars and present in their persons the visible divinity. . . .[27]

. . .

Jupiter: This is the blood of Louis, victorious king under whom all Europe trembles and who sees nothing under the skies that equals him or resembles him. It is for him that I call you together.
Apollo: How many times have your fine verses not made Louis' exploits live, you have astonished eyes and are sad not to be able to follow [the king's activities]. . . .
[There follows a dialogue between Venus and Mars promising great things for Louis' grandson, then:]
Jupiter: "How much is the happiness, how much the prosperity, how much the *gloire,* how much the peace of peoples who live under the august power of Louis, of his son, and the young hero whose birth we celebrate [Duke of Burgundy]. Never has heaven seen so long a course of happy success and beautiful days. . . .[28]

All these people had a common need to identify the king with divine power; they required this image to support the power that the king was assuming over the land and the people. Louis accepted this status, for he too needed the identification; as Madame de Sévigné tells us, it was only when a misguided provincial published a thesis comparing the king with God in such a manner that "would indicate that God was only a copy" that Louis ordered the work burned. This was going too far!

Many of these voices have been those of clerics; but judges, town officials, university professors, and men of letters talked and wrote in the same tone. For example, Professor Fejaco from Caen wrote in 1685 that "the invincible, the magnanimous Louis gives happiness to France, destiny to Europe, and astonishment to the universe [Angels]. The glory of his name will extend to the extremities of the land. . . ." In this *panégyrique du roi* Louis emerges as a godlike figure whose achievements dwarf those of the heroes of antiquity. This was the slight effort compared with the anonymous *La mémoire éternisée de Louis le Grand* (Paris, 1683) in which some three hundred pages are needed to prove that there had never been a ruler like Louis: a "surprising prodigy of wonder"; the most "magnanimous of heroes"; "the most incomparable of monarchs"; "compassionate and generous" as a conqueror, and equitable and just as a king; a combination of "wisdom and valor" unparalleled in the world, to whom both France and the church owes "immortal obligations." A poem of Bernard, Sieur de Hautmont, is of the same genre; a naïve and tiresome account, it praised military, political, even engineering (water to Versailles) triumphs. A member of the Royal Academy of Arles dedicated his book to the dauphin, but it was a chant of praise for the king whom he compared with other figures in history meriting the surname "the Great."[29] Like the clerics, these men were picturing a king who could be associated with the deity, a king partaking of the qualities of God. Some critics have called these people Louis' literary valets; they certainly were the literary servants of a new image of the king that would clothe him with the authority to govern.

There was another type of propaganda that dramatized the identification of the king with God. When the court traveled through the land in former eras, it was usual for the king to be received and perhaps "harangued" by the local clergy; the royal family often spent the night in the bishop's palace. By the 1680's these local receptions often got completely out of hand. We know about many of them because local pride required that accounts of the reception of the king should be published and sold abroad and many of these pamphlets have survived to our day. In Louis XIII's time men were content with a speech, a poem, or a sermon, and perhaps a bonfire; now an extravagant *feu d'artifice* became the accepted pattern. In studying these elaborate designs we discover that the word "baroque" applies to them with the same appropriateness that it does to the settings for opera or theater during these years. There would be a stage, papier-mâché figures, inscriptions, fireworks, and of course descriptions explaining what the event was all about. On the trip north in 1680, one town after another welcomed Louis with a *feu d'artifice*. At Valenciennes the city magistrates begged pardon for failing to use the figures of Apollo and the Sun as the central theme; in their humble opinion, however, Hercules and his labors could epitomize the important works of the king. The elaborate tableau had a central figure of Hercules supporting the earth with the "labors of the god" on the four sides of the platform. They were, of course, the "labors of Louis XIV": fighting the hydra monster with three heads (Luther, Calvin, and Jansenius); cleansing the kingdom of revolt; giving peace to Europe. Lille was not to be outdone: its *feu d'artifice* showed the defeat of the giants (enemies of the king) and the granting of peace. When Louis reached Tournai he passed through an arch of triumph bearing inscriptions about "Louis the Great, the sun that gives light to the day . . . the sun that makes the birds sing." Marie-Thérèse was "the moon brightened by the sun" along with the other stars of the sky. One could extend such examples indefinitely. It is not necessary, however, to cite more of them to indicate the process of development.[30]

The person of the king was not even necessary for a celebration in his honor. After 1680 many occasions inspired townsmen to hold a pageant, to present a *feu d'artifice*. The birth of one of Louis' grandsons, the capture of Luxembourg, the occupation of Strasbourg, the revocation of the Edict of Nantes, all became occasions for the people to express their faith in the monarchy with oratory, music, and poetry. If the king could not be present in person, an account of the event could be printed and placed at the foot of the throne.[31] These publications are interesting evidence of the loyalty of the kingdom; they are even more evidence of the pressure of the royal intendants and their subdelegates upon the people of importance in the towns to persuade them to pay for such festivities; they are also probably evidence of the need for entertainment, an occasion to display local talents of oratory or poetry or music, surely a welcome release from rough labor and bleak, colorless lives.

By the mid-1680's papier-mâché and *feux d'artifice* were no longer adequate to express the ritual of admiration and adulation of the king. It seems that the Marshal de la Feuillade was the first to set a new pattern when he commissioned Sieur des Jordans to create a bronze statue of the king crowned with victory. It was an elaborate affair mounted on a pedestal surrounded by slaves and decorated by bas reliefs that recounted the victories of the king's arms.[32] Apparently much touched by this gesture, the king and council issued an *arrêt* ordering that the statue be placed in the street of the Fosses Montmartre where it intersected the new street then under construction, the rue des Petits Champs. All this called for a new square, and Mansard designed one causing the removal of houses belonging to Dame Hôtman, Sieur Perrault, and Sieur de Serre. The cost: 306,000 livres, paid by the Echevins and merchants of the Hôtel de Ville. Habitués of the *Bibliothèque Nationale* will recognize this as the Place des Victoires, but the present statue was put in place in the nineteenth century and, happily, is quite unlike the original.

When all was ready, a great celebration dedicated the statue and the place on March 16, 1686. It was marred a little by a squabble over precedence that broke out among the several sovereign courts, but all the important figures of Paris contributed to the celebration. Louis was ill; the dauphin took his father's place, reviewed the parades, listened to the oratory, and watched the show that included musket fire, drums, trumpets, and religious symbols. That evening there was a *feu d'artifice* at the Hôtel de Ville that represented Louis' victory over heresy (now a headless hydra), the bombardment of the Barbary pirates, the submission of the Doge of Genoa. Naturally there was more poetry and oratory.[33]

Not to be outdone by the marshal and Paris, other communities also demanded the permission to erect statues to the king. At Caen the city fathers, stimulated by the intendant Monsieur de Morangis, hired a local artist to make the statue and managed to hold their celebration on Louis' birthday, September 15, 1685, a full six months before the Place des Victoires was completed. The statue was of dubious artistic value, but the celebration—with oratory and artillery from the château and a parade of monks, university professors, bourgeois militia, and local nobility—was a brave affair; the Bishop of Bayeux presided, while local talent had a field day in French and Latin verse. Undoubtedly the fête brought joy to Caen and it may also have deepened the respect for the monarchy and its authority.[34] The account of the celebration at Poitiers naïvely admits that the intendant "suggested" the erection of the statue[35] in that city; this was probably the pattern everywhere.

At Ruel the Duke de Richelieu urged the erection of an equestrian statue of the king, and persuaded the merchants to pay for it, since they had "just recompense from the favors that they receive every day through the protection that he [the king] affords to commerce and the arts. . . ." How better could he say that the new exercise of power warranted new symbols of its authority? However, closer look would be needed to know whether the merchants paid for the statue as willingly as the account of the celebration seems to suggest. The city fathers at Paris, not content with having made a contract with the University for an annual eulogy to the king to celebrate the anniversary of his ascension to the throne,[36] erected another statue of Louis XIV in the temple of honor at the Hôtel de Ville and dedicated it with an elaborate *feu d'artifice*. It is interesting to note that this ceremony came on July 14, 1689, just one hundred years before another *feu* that has also many times been celebrated with oratory, poetry, and artillery fire.[37] There were many other statues that, happily, have not survived: one of the most elaborate celebrations came in 1699 when the equestrian statue was erected in the Place Louis le Grand, to commemorate the "victory" of Ryswick. The inscription proclaimed that the king "gave peace to Europe." It proclaimed that in spite of his wishes he had taken up arms to "defend religion and justice" and by those arms he had secured peace.[38] The text must have sounded a little hollow even to the men who wrote it, but it suited the patriotic needs of the kingdom.

What was Louis' part in all this? We shall never really know whether he encouraged this slavish adulation or merely tolerated it. There is, however, one story that seems to cast doubt on the picture of the king as an egotist seeking glory even when it is undeserved. When Pontchartrain proposed a plan for the reconstruction of the Place Vendôme at great expense, Louis remarked, "Louvois did almost everything in spite of me. All these gentlemen, the ministers, want to do something that will bring them honor before posterity. They have found the secret of making me appear before Europe as a man who loves all these vanities. Madame de Maintenon is witness of the chagrin that Louvois and La Feuillade caused me by these things. I wish henceforth to save myself from them and I want no proposals . . . except that my people shall be well nourished; I shall always be well enough housed."[39]

Before we leave these hymns of praise and celebrations, we should note that a study of this literature will call to mind the small-town, premotorized age of patriotic celebrations and ceremonies of July 4 or of July 14 (Bastille Day) and other such days that men set aside to instill patriotism and love for the Republic. The words in a society dedicated to popular sovereignty will be different from those used by men who believe that authority comes from God, but the impact is very similar. The orators who extolled the glories of the Republic, the heroism of its soldiers, and the faultless purity of its national policies were creating a secular deity out of the state, and their hearers were thrilled by their words and made more ready to obey the laws that were set above them. So was it when the clergy, the poets, the local dignitaries, and the chorus of singers from the cathedral gathered to honor the king and the kingdom by the erection of a statue or a celebration to thank God and the king for peace or some other blessing. The festive air, the excitement of the music, and the parade all helped to implant in the hearts of men the *mystique* that justified the exercise of royal authority. Men like Colbert, Louvois, Richelieu, La Feuillade, and others who inspired these events obviously did not need to do so merely to inflate the ego of the king. They knew that by involving the people of France in the cult of the king, the people would more freely submit to his exercise of power.

As is so often the case with Louis XIV, there is little direct evidence that will link the king as a person with the things that were done in his name or the processes that developed under the direction of his government. It is difficult to believe that Louis was personally responsible for the development of the *mystique* that raised the throne of the king to the foot of the throne of God and endowed his person with divine attributes; it is more likely that his creatures were responsible for this. By raising the throne far above the older centers of power, by placing the king in a unique and remote position instead of in the status of "first among equals" that had been true of the medieval feudal monarch, and finally, by identifying the person of the king with the vital forces in the kingdom, these men were preparing for the future state that would be able to exercise truly great power over the lives of its people. It would be interesting to know how much Louis was the author of this drama; perhaps he was merely a clever actor who took his clues from the men who were giving characteristic form to the emerging bureaucratic military-police state of the West. Unfortunately we shall never really know which is the case.

24

ONE GOD, ONE KING,
ONE LAW

THOSE WHO FOLLOW Louis XIV through the papers created by his government will quickly learn that the burden of work increased each decade at very near to a geometric ratio. Letters, minutes, orders, decrees, patents, grants, the registers of the household officials, and the correspondence of the secretaries of state all show the same pattern; the growing impact of the royal government upon the kingdom is reflected in an ever-increasing flow of paper. What could be cared for in 1661 by a secretary with an assistant and a few clerks, by 1685 required a small army of copyists, clerks, secretaries, and bureaucrats. The victory of the men of the pen over all competitors was complete. The secretaries and ministers who could be seen hurrying down the corridors of the royal châteaus to closet themselves with the king, exercised the power that formerly had belonged to princes of the blood, dukes and peers, marshals of France, municipal governments, and noblemen on their estates. Not all of the activity of these displaced persons had been usurped by the royal government, but enough had been to indicate the trends of the society that was in the process of becoming. The king himself was being slowly but surely subordinated to the procedures of his government; where his father had spoken of "my state," in the last twenty years of his life Louis XIV came increasingly to speak of "*the* state" of which he was the first servant.

In 1661 Louis ordered his collaborators not to sign or seal any order without his permission; by 1685 such an order, if literally obeyed, would have caused an impasse in the business of government. But by 1685 the king did not need to see every document; precedents had become established and bureaucratic procedures ironed out so that much business that formerly had required royal attention could now safely be cared for by a secretary. The king had enough to do in handling the important business of state, and the items of private affairs of his subjects that fascinated him; he could not look at everything. This fact becomes more and more apparent as we examine the flow of paper in the areas of foreign affairs, defense, commerce, police, religion, and the royal household. As the government's impact grew to include more and more of the life of the kingdom, the king, sometimes harassed by ill health, had to give much of the work to the team that helped him govern the state. Even a Louis XIV, who wanted to see everything himself, was brought to this situation by the growth of bureaucratic controls.

There was an enormous press of work for the government of the realm. These were the years when the great system of fortifications that rimmed the north and the east of the kingdom was built; guns, powder, magazines, soldiers, uniforms, and the whole paraphernalia of the emerging modern army came into the scope of the ministry of war. On the sea coast, in addition to the fortification of the great harbors, there were the naval arsenals where anchors, guns, rope, sails, and the host of other things needed for the new huge warships carrying 120 guns, were made or stored. The reports of the army of intendants, engineers, inspectors, clerks, and officers who were building these military institutions simply could not all come to the king's desk. Nor was that the end of the government's activity. This was the period when the chartered companies trading with Asia, Muscovy, America, the Levant, and elsewhere were burgeoning into important aspects of the political and economic society. Behind them was the whole economic structure that Colbert hoped to create to give France a primary place in the trade of the world. In another section of the château of Versailles the dispatches from French ambassadors, agents, and spies poured in telling of the activities and politics of France's neighbors, of the impact of French foreign policies, of the problems that were yet to come. Other servants of the king were concerned with religion, police and public order, the needs of the royal households, and the ceremonial activities of the court. Except for questions that particularly interested the king, many of these papers did not come to his desk unless the problems reached a stage of tension. Thus after 1680 it was surely possible that many things were done in his name without Louis' knowing much about them. Even today we cannot be sure whether his signature on many documents was written by him or someone who could sign his name even better than he could.

All this only underlines the fact that by the 1680's the business of the king's government had become the process of "mobilizing the potential power of the kingdom in the service of the state."[1] Louis' government was the first to create "modern" military institutions, and thus was forced to develop the financial and administrative structures to support them. Even though this was important business of the realm, with the rise of bureaucratic institutions much of it could safely be left to the attention of administrators like Louvois, Colbert, and the *cadres* that they were developing in the wake of their drive for power. Louis discussed their projects with them both privately and in council, but he left the details to those who managed the bureaus.

As the royal authority extended over the kingdom, it brought new business for the king and his government. We find Louis, for example, writing to municipal officers asking for the names of men who would be suitable replacements for a position vacated by death. In former years these officials were "elected" in a variety of ways, but now they more and more came under the supervision of the king. Louis was keenly aware of the importance of making good appointments, both to secure efficiency in government and to use political patronage properly. Even more common were the letters and minutes dealing with the extension of the police power. The countryside and the towns of France before the rise of Louis' police power were the scenes of much disorder. Murders, assaults, robberies, kidnappings were all too common and too often unpunished, indeed, unnoticed by local authorities. Such things were still not uncommon by 1680, but there was a definite effort to curb and control crime. Many other problems came before the king as highest judge of the land, but we often find him dismissing the request for royal intervention with the formula, "it is an affair for ordinary justice." However, we do see him acting in the role of "father of the country" to discipline errant sons at their father's request and to punish courtiers, noblemen, or others whose crimes did not come under the purview of the courts, as well as interesting himself in some spectacular crimes that came to his attention. The royal discipline was usually accomplished by a *lettre de cachet* by which the offender was summarily placed in a prison, a hospital, or a monastery for an indefinite period of time. In some cases the letter ordered the governor to treat the prisoner harshly, with close confinement and limited food; in others, softly and with kindness.[2]

It is not possible to list all the reasons for this royal discipline. Sieur de Forges refused to accept a court order: "This is rebellion . . ."; Sieur Parifort and Madame des Comptes committed "final extravagances," whatever that may have been; Abbé de Rochefort was imprisoned in a monastery "for no reasons, but simply to remain there separated from his parents with whom he is in difficulty." Most serious cases of violence seem to have been referred to the courts, but a courtier who displeased the king could receive an order to present himself at the Bastille for confinement, or an order to retire to his province. Such an order, as we have seen, could not prevent Monsieur de Montespan from coming to Paris when he became involved in a law suit there. In some cases where a nobleman's behavior required rebuke, the man might be ordered to present himself before the king. The Count de Roure obviously tried to avoid making the trip to Versailles, for the secretary wrote to him, "Your health allowed you to journey from Burjac to Montpensier; it will also allow you to come to Versailles. This is an order, you are to come within the month." In another case the secretary remarked, "You failed to obey an earlier order, I do not believe that you should risk his Majesty's displeasure in the future." It is impossible to know with how many of these cases Louis became personally involved, but the registers of the secretary of state suggest that many of them did come to the king's desk for decision.[3]

The king also considered pleas for clemency. The most usual, a stay of execution, often simply placed the poor wretch in the galleys for life instead of hanging him; it was becoming increasingly difficult to get enough oarsmen for the Mediterranean fleet. We also find such things as a stay of execution for a young woman until her baby was born; and sometimes there was an outright pardon.

With both the courts and the royal *lettres de cachet* sending men to the Bastille or other prisons, it was inevitable that some poor devils would land in prison and be forgotten. If a man had no friends at court or in the land who could petition the king for release, he might easily stay in jail all his life with no one knowing anything about it. To obviate this sort of injustice, we find the secretaries of state periodically ordering a survey of the people in prison. Occasionally cases of gross injustice would appear; during times of war we find that such surveys showed that a great number of the prisoners were foreigners accused of or suspected of espionage; at other times they were people whom "M. de Torcy [secretary of state] knows about" or whose crime "is well known," or occasionally, "who should be released." In some cases, such as the one when Sieur de la Motte was freed at the request of Count de Gramont, the prisoner was warned that if he "disobeys again he will go back to prison for the rest of his days."

In this role of judge, the king also often took cognizance of things that might cause disorder. The Curé of Vincennes had a young woman as a domestic servant; there was as yet no scandal, but the king ordered him to dismiss her. On the other hand, we also find Louis legitimizing bastards so that they could inherit their father's property and name and pass on their own property without fear of royal confiscation.

Some of the king's day must have resembled the work of his predecessors both in spirit and in action, but during the course of Louis' reign, the urge to create a state that could mobilize the power and the wealth of the kingdom for its own purposes, subtlely changed the emphases of many aspects of his activity. Nowhere was this more apparent than in his relations with the problems of the church and the religious life of the community. The more it became necessary for the king to impose his will, his collection of revenues, and his exercise of power upon the state, the more it became necessary also to have a social and political cement to supply his government with a consent of the governed. "One king, one law, one God" was an ideal increasingly important as the king needed more support from his people for his projects. In modern societies with their temporal secular orientation, this ideal of unity of spirit can be attained by education and propaganda vaguely subsumed under the heading of "nationalism." Seventeenth-century society still believed in God, in Heaven, in Hell; it made the church the custodian of the words for good and evil, and very naturally it regarded the religious beliefs and institutions as having paramount importance as cement for that society. Thus we find Louis' advisers urging that the religious minority, the Huguenots, be brought into the church of the king, and that the church of the king be subordinated to the royal power. In political terms this led on the one side to oppressive, tyrannical harassment of the reformed religious community,[4] and on the other, to an assault upon the papal prerogatives over the Catholic church that could have come to a schism separating the Gallican church from Rome.

Seventeenth-century Europe neither understood nor sympathized with the ideal of toleration. The religious wars had produced formulas for accepting the fact of religious diversity; the German solution of the Diet of Augsburg (1555) gave to the prince the right to determine the religion of his people; the French solution of the Edict of Nantes (1598) recognized that a prince could not force a sizable percentage of his subjects to conform to his religious beliefs. Neither of these was considered as more than an expedient. Both Catholic and Protestant recognized the prince's right to harass heretical minorities. Jurieu, the most important of the Huguenot ministers in exile, made the nice distinction that "he would allow a heretic to believe what he wished, but he would deprive the heretics' right to practice publically their religion" and above all deprive them of the liberty of "dogmatizing and seductively spreading their religion"[5]—this from a man who was in exile because of the intolerance of his king. Obviously it was not yet a time when relativist ideas produced a climate that would allow liberty for dissident minorities. In Protestant England the harsh religious codes put Jesuits and Puritans in the same jail; in Hungary Calvinists were brutally driven out of their homelands or even killed in "an effort to save their souls" and govern their lands. Louis XIV lived in this atmosphere; it is probably unfair to expect him to rise much above it.

The problem of toleration in France, as elsewhere, was rooted in the civil wars of the preceding generations. The Edict of Nantes was a treaty between the king and his Huguenot subjects, a treaty that had created a Huguenot republic within the kingdom. Henry IV had spent much of his time trying to whittle away some of the privileges that he had been forced to give; Louis XIII and Richelieu had carried the sword to victory and had taken from the Huguenot party its independent political and military power, but left the Huguenots their churches, their schools, and the right to practice their religion. This policy had been so successful that the Huguenots had become royalist to the degree that the *Fronde* saw them either neutral or in the king's camp; Huguenot intellectuals loudly supported the doctrine of "divine right" at a time when some of the Catholics questioned it. Even so, the Huguenots were not loved by the king's government. Mazarin had allowed the party to retain its synods and its national organization, and had counseled the young king to continue this policy, but Louis and his "team" were unwilling to recognize the existence of a "Gallican Protestant Church" as a nationwide institution, so after 1661 the national synods were no longer permitted, and gradually the Huguenot churches were forced to give up their central organization and become a series of decentralized communities, each largely independent of the others.

Louis' own attitude during the first years of his reign was one of simple tolerance, no more. As Colbert said, Henry IV loved the Huguenots, Louis XIII hated them, Louis XIV neither loved nor hated them. He himself summed up his attitude in his *Mémoires*:

I believed, my son, that the best means of reducing the Huguenots little by little . . . was not to press them with any new rigor, to recognize what had been accorded to them by my predecessors, but to allow them nothing beyond that and to reduce [their rights] by administration, to the smallest extent that justice and bounty would permit. But as to the grace dependent upon me alone, I resolved and I have punctually observed to do nothing to them, and by this bounty . . . to oblige them to consider from time to time . . . if there were not some good reason *to deprive themselves voluntarily of their advantages so that they would be like my other subjects* . . . [author's italics].

When harsh laws in England deprived Roman Catholics of their rights, Louis wrote to Charles II in April 1663:

You know with what gentleness and moderation the Catholic princes treat all those in their estates . . . who profess another belief. . . . As you love justice and since I have entire confidence in your friendship, I am convinced that you will consider carefully, and have some new regard for the recommendation that I bring to you in the interests of the Catholics in your kingdom. . . .

Nor was this simply propaganda; two years later he wrote to the Duke de Saint Aignan:

You have been prudent not to act precipitously on the stories that have been told you about the inhabitants of Le Havre belonging to the so-called reformed religion. Those who profess it are not less faithful than my other subjects; they should not be treated with less regard and kindness . . . if you find something [bad] among those of the said religion, be careful of making it a general affair . . . make it an individual case.[6]

There is no reason to doubt the king's sincerity. At this period a number of doughty Protestant soldiers, including Turenne himself, were ample evidence of the loyalty of the Huguenots, and others were to join the king's service both with the armies and the fleets. And yet Louis must have been suspicious of the dissident group. Ever since he could understand anything about politics, he had listened to speeches and sermons denouncing the heretics and urging him to cleanse the kingdom of the disorder. A book by Paul Hay, *Traité de la politique de France,* first published in 1666 but reissued in several editions during the next fifteen years, reflects the feelings, attitudes, and fears of the Catholic majority:

. . . diversity of belief, of cult, of ceremony divides [the king's] subjects and creates reciprocal hate and scorn between them from which conflict and war are born. . . . Contrariwise, unity of belief holds men together . . . one rarely sees that fellow subjects who pray to God in the same temple and sacrifice at the same altars do not fight in the same armies under the same flag. . . .[7]

This was a familiar doctrine; religious unity was social cement needed to give strength to the political community: one king, one law, one God. Bodin might insist that there are "goods" that transcend that of religious unity, but men trying both to build a state and to be sure of the subjects' loyalties to that state were willing to believe that they might be able to guarantee public tranquillity (Bodin's greatest good) and, with their new military power, suppress the divergent religious beliefs and cults to assure political unity. Hay went on to say of the attitudes of the Huguenots, "They are badly advised to make so much noise and such a parade about the Edict of Nantes; they extorted it with sword in hand. It is only an interim solution, waiting for them to become enlightened by the truth . . . for which they have had time enough already. . . ."[8] Like Louis in this same period, Hay does not urge the use of force "that might make them leave the kingdom as [the Spanish] made the Moriscos leave Spain . . . it would be prejudicial to the country. It would be lacking in humanity to chase the Huguenots this way; they are Christians, however much they are separated from the body of the church. . . ."[9] Nonetheless, Hay was sure that they would eventually be converted, and he left to Louis XIV "the *gloire* of cutting the last head of this hydra," even though it necessarily would take a little time.[10] Hay's advice to Louis was, first, to be sure that the Huguenot community had the opportunity to learn the truth—that is, to expose them to missionary activity; then, to prevent members of that community from holding any important position in the service of the state.[11] Those who would abjure the heresy, however, should be given every advantage. Finally, he urged that the Edict of Nantes should be strictly interpreted in matters of marriage, baptisms, property regulations, and the like, and that the reformed church should not be permitted to build new temples for worship nor its members allowed to live in towns not specified by the edict. This sort of harassment, he suggested, could make their heretical beliefs unprofitable.

Hay did not really suggest anything new, yet he did spell out more clearly the policy that the government had been groping toward ever since the registration of the edict by Parlement. Long before Louis' reign Huguenots had been seduced by pensions, *gratifications,* offices, and royal favors to change their religion. Henry IV had been the first to hold a "debate" between the leading intellectuals of the two religions; Louis XIV also brought men like Bossuet, a young, eloquent, and highly intelligent Catholic who was in charge of the dauphin's education, and Claude, the leading Huguenot spokesman, to a confrontation of ideas. The king urged the sending of missionaries to the Huguenots; some of them, like the young Fénelon, who would eventually have charge of the education of the dauphin's sons, were so eloquent that they made their hearers weep and accomplished many conversions. When the missionary departed, however, the local clergy often proved incapable of holding these new converts. In such cases the government added official pressure. Like Hay, he and his advisers believed that men who "sacrificed at the same altars" would "fight under the same flag," so by decrees and regulations they undercut the political and economic status of the members of the R.P.R. (so-called Reformed Religion) wherever they could. Two decrees of 1666 brought forth a strong protest against the "rude blows that struck like a clap of thunder . . ." from an anonymous Huguenot who was sure that the new regulations were illegal.[12]

To all this Louis added a further inducement. In the royal entourage there was an ex-Huguenot intellectual, Paul Pellisson, who among other things had helped the king prepare the *Mémoires* for his son's education; he suggested that many men would abjure if they were offered money, whereupon Louis provided him with a "conversion fund." The idea worked so well that the bishops of the kingdom were urged to the purchase of converts by cash gifts, offers of freedom from taxes for a limited period, and sometimes a royal pension. These were the inducements for conversion to Catholicism. While a great soldier like Turenne was converted by the eloquence and persuasion of Bossuet, many Huguenots who needed money, or an office, or simply wanted a little pension, might be converted by more materialistic arguments. The erosion was slow, but there was little doubt that the Huguenot party was losing ground. It was only a question of royal patience. But did Louis have that patience?

In 1677 the nuncio at Paris wrote to Cardinal Cybo, "Père de la Chaize assured me that the King was completely resolved to reduce the power of the Huguenot magistrates once this war is ended. . . ."[13] Not only the Huguenot magistrates came under greater pressure after the Treaty of Nymwegen, but also the whole Huguenot community. Their schools had been harassed; now some of them were closed on the ground that they were not provided for in the edict. The professors had already been under fire; now they were under further duress, so that in some schools where there had been six or eight professors, only one or two remained to teach everything. The Huguenot elite did not want to trust their children's education to a school with so little power, and as a result the whole community suffered. Huguenot booksellers were in trouble; Huguenot preachers were strictly regulated even to the clothes that they could or could not wear. Finally, the king's government began to limit the professions that a Huguenot could practice: the joiner's trade, the jeweler's craft, and the lawyer's bonnet seemed to have little to do with religion, but Huguenots could not practice these professions and many others. Nor could Huguenots become midwives or in any way assist with the birth of children, nor could a Huguenot doctor care for a Catholic patient. To give another side to the pressure, Jesuit missionaries were sent into the Huguenot towns to convert by eloquence where pressure did not succeed.

In 1681 Madame de Maintenon wrote, "If God saves the King, in twenty years there will not be a Huguenot in the kingdom. . . ." And a few days later: "The King is beginning to think seriously of his own salvation and that of his subjects. If God saves him for us there will only be one religion in this kingdom. This is the intention of M. de Louvois . . . more than that of M. de Colbert who thinks only of his finances. . . ."[14] The figure "twenty years" is the significant one; the attack on the Huguenots was designed to "erode" the party. If their schools no longer functioned; if their elite were seduced by money, by threats, by loss of professions; if their ministers found it difficult to carry on the pastoral work; then in time there would only be left a small hard core of people, separated from each other and relatively easy to contend with. A distinguished historian of the Huguenots believes that Madame de Maintenon's prophecy might well have come true had the government been willing to hold out for twenty years of pressure against the party.[15] Furthermore, as we pointed out above, leading Huguenot intellectuals like Jurieu might have regretted the severity of this policy, and yet they insisted that it was within the rights of the prince to adopt it. Unhappily for Louis' reputation among liberal historians, as well as for the well-being of his kingdom at the time, there were forces and personalities at work that changed the policy of severity to one of violence. As we shall see, it is hard to excuse Louis even though the change seems to have been inspired by Louvois and his father, Le Tellier, and though much of the disorder was kept from the king's knowledge. But before we investigate this new policy of violence, let us turn to the "Catholic" side of Louis' religious policies.

While the pressure on the Huguenot community mounted toward a fever pitch, another religious imbroglio developed serious proportions, pitting the ideals of the Gallican church against the will of the ultramontane papacy. Like so many questions where an institution as old as the Roman Catholic Church is involved, there were a number of facets to the problems that produced a conflict between Louis XIV and Innocent XI. There were several "Gallican" traditions in France. One was found most frequently among the bishops who believed that they were descendants of the apostles and that their sees had been founded by God. They recognized the primacy of the papacy, but insisted that the church was a decentralized institution with power at all levels. The assembly of the Gallican clergy was important to them, and they usually insisted that the ecumenical council of the church held primacy even over the pope. Another "Gallican" teaching found among the clergy, but even more definitely in the Parlement, the Sorbonne, and in the king's council, placed the Gallican church under the royal authority; the king was an officer anointed and consecrated by the church and given the secular government of that church by God. This tradition had been strengthened by the concordat that Francis I had made with Rome about the time that Luther was moving toward a break with the Roman Church. Like the bishops, the members of Parlement resisted the encroachments from Rome. They were willing to admit that Rome had final jurisdiction over matters of faith, but they insisted that any one pope might err. The church was infallible only because it was self-correcting; no one pope was infallible. The Parlement would not allow the introduction of a Roman inquisition into France, indeed not even the publication of a papal decree or writ without the consent of either the Parlement or the king's council. The decrees of the Council of Trent had not been proclaimed in France because of Parlementary opposition.

The French chûrch, however, often did find it advantageous to pass its problems on to Rome. The Jansenist controversy that had started in Richelieu's time went back and forth between France and Italy without a clear-cut decision. This was in part because the Jansenists would always agree that the propositions condemned were heretical, but they then would assert that these were not propositions that they had ever supported. Their lawyer briefs made condemnation difficult and supported the conflict between them and the Jesuits. Louis only wanted the question settled. He had a suspicion that the Jansenists were not friendly to the state that he and his bureaucrats were building, and he disliked the fact that they had aroused a divisive controversy in the church, but he probably never even tried to understand the complex problems of grace and salvation posited by their arguments.

On other occasions the Sorbonne acted with considerable independence vis-à-vis Rome. When the pope demanded that the censure be removed from a book supporting the doctrine of papal infallibility, Louis excused himself from acting, with a statement that he would be quite unable to interfere with the laws and customs of his kingdom. Both Rome and Versailles let the matter drop. It was often best to brush such problems under the rug where they could solve themselves or simply remain unsolved.

However, there was one problem that could not be so easily pushed aside. The King of France claimed the right to occupy and use the revenues of a bishop's see during the interval between the death of a bishop and the consecration and registration of the oath of allegiance of his successor. In practice Louis usually gave the money to the new bishop as a gift, but this did not alter the legal problem. This right was called the *régale,* and Louis XIV insisted that it applied to all bishoprics in his realm. As a matter of fact there were several bishoprics that had been added to the kingdom since the concordat that Francis I had made with Rome a century and a half earlier, and of these, two of the bishops resisted Louis' right to bring their sees under the rule. Both of these men were pious, scholarly clerics who insisted that they owed it to God to pass their sees on to their successors exactly as they had received them. By chance they both were also Jansenists, a fact that created an amusing situation, for the Jansenists were strongly Gallican, but the bishop's cause was defended by the ultramontane papacy, and the usually ultramontane Jesuits supported the Gallican position regarding the *régale* and attacked the Jansenist bishops and the pope who defended them.

The king's government seems to have been much surprised that Pope Innocent XI took up the cause of the two bishops, but when he did, Colbert accepted the challenge and declared himself ready to create a schism rather than surrender. The conflict between Innocent XI and Louis XIV was perhaps inevitable. The old pope looked back to the middle ages for his inspiration; he wanted to direct Europe on a last crusade that would rid Europe of Mohammedan power and reconquer the Holy Lands for Christendom. He reserved the conquest of Constantinople for the King of France, and proposed that the dauphin should be crowned king of a Christian state "guarded by God" centered on that city. Louis, more interested in the Spanish and Holy Roman empires than in the more distant one ruled by the Ottoman sultan, indicated an unwillingness to chase butterflies in the Levant. His attitude rankled the old pope even before the Ottoman attack in the Danube; as we shall see, after 1683 Louis angered him even more.

On another level Innocent did not recognize the fact that the papal authority had lost much of its power over princes, so when the controversy over the *régale* between the French king and the papal pretensions expanded, he wrote almost as a reincarnation of the medieval popes: "We will no longer treat this affair by letters, . . . we will not neglect the remedies that the power of God has given us." This sort of threat could not go unanswered; Louis called upon the assembly of the French clergy to express its "displeasure" with the papal letter. In the minds of the men who were building a state, the papal pretensions to authority in the affairs of the church in France were almost as disturbing as the pretensions of the Huguenots.

Innocent would not back down. The Bishop of Pamiers died, and a conflict immediately arose between the Jansenist majority in the cathedral chapter and the vicar general appointed by the Archbishop of Toulouse. Innocent excommunicated the vicar and announced that he could not withdraw his support from the Bishop of Pamiers "who is now in heaven"; the affair was perilously close to a break in the relations between Rome and Versailles.

The government called for an assembly of all the bishops who "happened to be" in Paris and the vicinity. Surprisingly enough there were fifty-two of them "available"—obviously not in residence in their sees. But these prelates were more embarrassed by the problem with which Louis presented them, than in their obvious truancy from their duties; they suggested that the question could be solved only by an elected general assembly of the French clergy. Unwilling to leave it to chance, Colbert, using the king's authority, saw to it that the "right" clergymen were elected. The Archbishop of Lyons, who should have presided but whose opinions were not "sound," was not on Colbert's list and did not come. Even so, Bishop Bossuet presented a compromise in his opening sermon that should have been satisfactory to both Rome and the king, and the assembly proceeded to send an explanation to Rome that could have ended the controversy. But the pope refused to open the brief for three days and then turned it over to others to consider. Colbert, and presumably the king too, decided that drastic measures were necessary to shock Rome into compliance.

The government took its case to the assembly demanding action that would punish the pope. The assembly then proclaimed the famous four articles of 1682. The first announced that kings and sovereigns are not under any ecclesiastical authority in temporal affairs, and they could not be "deposed either directly or indirectly by the authority of the Keys of the church." This harked back to the famous "Gallican oath" presented to the Estates General in 1614. As one clerical commentator remarked, it accepted the "render unto Caesar the things that are Caesar's" but forgot the rest of the quotation. The second treated the plenitude of the powers of popes over spiritual matters by reaffirming the decrees of the Council of Constance, which asserted the authority of church councils over popes. The third laconically insisted upon the rights of the Gallican church and its "rules, customs, and constitutions." This was vague enough to embrace anything; fo who knew what were those rules, customs, and constitutions? The last article recognized the right of the pope to pronounce upon questions of faith, but added that his judgment is not "irreformable"—in other words, that while individual popes could err, the process of decision-making would correct such error.

Neither Innocent XI nor Louis XIV really wanted a break; if either had really wished it, a schism would have come at this moment. The "eldest son of the church" knew that Rome was useful to him, that Innocent would not always be pope, and that his government had profited by its connection with the Roman Catholic Church. On his part, Pope Innocent also knew that the papal curia had need of the "most Christian King," even though the present occupant of that title might be difficult; in any case, another situation like the one that had developed in England would be most unfortunate. While Innocent continued to badger Louis about his attitude toward the advance of the Turks in the Danube basin and about French territorial aggression on the Rhine and in Italy, he saw to it that no real overt break did occur. Not until 1688, when Louis deliberately defied the pope in Rome itself, did Innocent come near to a break with France by his excommunication of Louis and his ministers.

While the storm within the Catholic church was developing, the pressure applied to the Huguenot community also increased. The migration of Huguenot intellectuals who could see no future for themselves in the kingdom began to assume large proportions, but in spite of the harassment, most of the Huguenots could not migrate. It was difficult to get out of France without a passport; moreover, what did the little people of the seventeenth century know about the world beyond their towns and villages? How could a man get his property out of the kingdom? Many people who had no intention of taking the king's money, or listening to one of his missionaries, decided to wait it out. After all, persecutions had occurred before, and in time the persecutors had always tired of their task. However, at this moment the government, or at least the war minister and some of his creatures, hit upon a method of "conversion" that had a terrible impact upon the unfortunate Huguenots: the quartering of troops upon those who would not abjure the heresy. These dragonnades have been described many times, and even if some of the more lurid accounts may be exaggerated, the total picture that remains is that of tyrannical action, violence, and injustice. Seventeenth-century soldiers were drawn from the bottom of the social heap; even when their officers attempted to keep them in some sort of discipline, they were dangerous to any population with which they lived. These soldiers quartered on Huguenot families were given much freedom to misbehave so that their unwilling hosts would "see the light quickly."

The responsibility for these acts has been fixed upon Louvois and his agents. Colbert died before they were fully developed, and it is probably true that he was opposed to such action, even though he seems to have encouraged, perhaps inadvertently, the first of the "mass conversions." It also seems nearly certain that Louvois kept much of the true picture of what was happening from the king. In the council meeting early in 1684 when the problem of conversions was discussed, Louvois pretended to side with the "moderates," but his actions, both before and after, were anything but moderate. These seventeenth-century men were not nineteenth-century liberals; Louvois and his father, who had become the chancellor, both hated the divisive effects of toleration, and like many of their Catholic contemporaries, they saw nothing wrong in using violence to "convert" heretics.

What was Louis' part in the picture? At this time, like his ministers, he was concerned with many problems of high policy: the annexation of Strasbourg and Casale, the orders of the courts of reunion, the threats of hostile leagues and alliances, the invasion of Europe by the Turks and the siege of Vienna, the pressure on the Spanish Netherlands and the making of the Truce of Ratisbon, the death of the queen and his remarriage—all these were big questions, and questions suited to Louis' interests. Yet is it possible that he could hear about the mass conversions, conversions that sounded like the miracles of the first Christian centuries, without asking why they happened? Thousands upon thousands of Huguenots abjured, either after the arrival of the dragoons or on threat that they would soon arrive. It seems that the king was given inadequate reports, that many of the accounts of violence were suppressed before they got to his table. And yet it is hard to believe, as, surprisingly, do Lavisse and many other historians who really did not like Louis XIV, that he could have been so innocent about what was happening in his kingdom. The lack of evidence is the greatest problem for an historical judgment.

By the time that there seemed to be no more "need" for the Edict of Nantes because "nearly all the Huguenots were converted," Madame de Maintenon seems to have become suspicious about what was happening. She remarks that it is improbable that all of the conversions were sincere, but she hoped that the children of these converts, raised as Catholics, would become sincere believers. If such could happen, the hypocrisy of the first generation would assure the salvation of those that followed. The argument may have appealed to her, but it must have been wormwood to many of the new converts. Surely she discussed the problem with her husband.

Why revoke the Edict of Nantes? With so few Huguenots left after the mass conversions, why was it worth outraging Protestant Europe by revocation? There seem to have been "good" reasons for the revocation. The first was economic. The "carrot"—that is, remission of taxes for a number of years, pensions, exemption from having troops quartered in the home, and the like—was all right as long as the number of ex-Huguenots was not very large. With the mass conversions, however, gross inequalities arose between the obligations of the new and the old Catholics. If all Frenchmen were to be under "one king, one law, one God," the burdens should be shared more equally. Another problem concerned the Huguenot pastors. What if they stayed in France under the "protection" of the edicts and secretly cared for their flocks? A shadow reformed church could exist beside the Roman Catholic one. If there were no Huguenot temples, no pastors, no church, then the new converts would not be tempted to relapse. Finally, there was Pope Innocent XI. He had criticized Louis for annexing Strasbourg, for the Gallican Articles, for not helping against the Turks, and for disrupting the crusade of the Holy League by the siege of Luxembourg—indeed for many other things as well. By revoking the Edict of Nantes, did not the eldest son of the church prove his devotion and merit papal blessing? He may have merited it, but Innocent did not give it to him.

The final text of the Edict of Fontainebleau states that war made it impossible to do anything about the so-called reformed religion until the Truce of Ratisbon gave repose and peace. It then explains:

We now see with the proper gratitude what we owe to God, that our cares have reached the goal that we sought, for the best and largest part of our subjects of the so-called reformed religion have embraced Catholicism, and now that, to the extent that the execution of the Edict of Nantes remains useless, we have judged that we can do nothing better to wipe out the memory of the troubles, of the confusion, of the evils that the progress of this false religion has caused in our kingdom . . . than to revoke entirely the said Edict. . . .[16]

The new edict provided for the exile of ministers who refused to abjure, for the destruction of temples, closing of schools, confiscation of foundations, and baptism by priests of those born into the false religion. Subjects who might try to leave the realm were threatened with the galleys.

This was a harsh edict, following up four or five years of brutal pressure on his subjects who had been nothing if not loyal ever since he came to the throne. It has been the most condemned action of Louis' entire reign, and yet when death overtook the king and funeral orations were preached to signalize his reign, this edict was the one action that was universally praised. If the flood of congratulation means anything, it also was probably the one act of his reign that, at the time, was popular with the majority of his subjects. Those men whose lives and homes and families and futures had been ravished by brutal soldiers or who had been forced into hypocrisy to avoid the worst impact of this tyranny, were not asked to preach sermons any more than they were expected to approve the policies that brought them back to the religion of their king. Le Clerc's poem suggests some of the argument in favor of the revocation.[17]

> In vain from all sides the chronicles of history
> And the charming concerts of the daughters of memory
> Attempt to transmit to the future centuries
> The eternal fame of your [Louis XIV] formidable name. . . .
>
> If this hydra that your hand has strangled
> Does not provide to your *vertu* the worthiest of trophies
> Then think of the cruel misfortunes that this sect has caused,
> See how it has divided your subjects,
> Consider in your heart its fatal practices.
> How much blood poured forth, how many tragic stories of
> The sacrileges of profaned altars,
> Priests scorned and degraded, temples destroyed,
> Blasphemies carried up to the sanctuary,
> By all this see what it had been able to do.
>
> To purge the state of an internal pestilence
> Louis saw that it was time to cut its roots.
> He broke the edicts by which our recent kings
> Allowed this serpent the right to speak
> From which never ceased to come its false maxims
> Infecting minds and fomenting crimes.

Outside of France, Louis' press was somewhat less laudatory. The Edict of Fontainebleau immediately evoked the response of the Edict of Potsdam by which Frederick William invited the oppressed Huguenots to come to Brandenburg. After the Treaty of Nymwegen and the subsequent pressure forcing him to give up his conquests on the Baltic, the great elector had been unwilling to do anything that might offend France, but he could not ignore the fate of his co-religionists. Much to the irritation of men at Versailles,[18] other German princes followed suit. An even more aggressive assault on Louis' action came from a host of publicists who had long disliked the Sun King and now happily seized upon this edict to attack him and his kingdom. It would be redundant to list here the books and pamphlets that followed the course of the persecution of the Huguenots. This stream of opinion only reenforced the hostility that the French policy in the Rhineland, in Luxembourg, and in Europe generally was evoking at this time. For example, the supposed exchange of ideas between a Frenchman and a Hollander found Louis' internal and foreign policies ever since the Treaty of the Pyrenees to be completely immoral. The Frenchman who defended the king sounds like a lawyer who knows in advance that he has lost his case.[19] Another sort of attack invites answers to questions from an "oracle": "What do you say to the fact that we are plucked . . . and reduced to misery and mendicity?" asks a Frenchman. The oracle replies, "It is for your salvation, poor blind people, for it is difficult for a rich man to get into heaven."[20] Other books pretended to copy a "catechism" by Monsieur Colbert, or announced that there were no limits to Louis' ambitions. The Pierre Marteau press, supposedly from Cologne, produced most of these books, but Anvers, Rotterdam, Leipzig, Amsterdam, Ratisbon, and other towns added to the chorus. These books and pamphlets are probably responsible for several myths about Louis XIV and his times. In them, Madame de Maintenon and Father de la Chaise were unjustly blamed for the Edict of Fontainebleau, as well as most of the other evils of the regime.[21] Another myth arises from the fact that the Huguenots who left France, following Jurieu's leadership, taught that they could only return to their homes when Europe, victorious in war over the French king, would force Louis to allow them to live peaceably in his kingdom. By hammering at this theme, and by working for a war against France, the Huguenots succeeded in selling later generations of historians the idea that somehow they brought about the war that broke out in 1688–89.[22]

The Edict of Fontainebleau gave Louis an enlarged field of activity to take up his time and energy. There were Protestants in his entourage whom he hoped to convert. One of the most important was Marshal von Schomberg. In February of 1686 Louis had two or three long conferences with him. It would be most interesting to have a record of these meetings. Did Louis try to convert the tough old soldier with theological arguments or simply with political ones? What was Schomberg's reaction? When the marshal refused to abjure, Louis allowed him to retire to Portugal.[23] His parting in March was difficult for everyone: the dauphin embraced him, the dauphine received him in her chambers and talked to him in German "most obligingly," and Louis showed much "chagrin." But Schomberg could not stay in Portugal either, for he was a Protestant now without the protection of the French king from the Inquisition. He soon went to England and then on to the United Netherlands, where he found employment for his talents in the armies of the Prince of Orange. He was killed a few years later in Ireland fighting against Louis' ally James II.

While Louis might personally try to convert a distinguished soldier, he depended upon others to carry the light to lesser persons who still remained outside of the church and unconvinced of the truth of Catholicism. On

October 29, 1685, the following message went to the intendants in the provinces:

> After so much happy success with which it has pleased God to crown the continued application and indefatigable cares of the King for the conversion of his subjects, you may well understand that his Majesty has nothing closer to his heart than the completion of this work, so agreeable to God and to his Majesty. [It went on to say that] the King believes that nothing could be better than to have those who are still in error to be instructed by the new converts to our religion; they should be most capable of drawing others to the light.[24]

This was to be a problem for a long time to come; the parish priests were often intellectually quite unprepared to hold the new converts, let alone to convert others. And when the government announced that it would not force people to abjure their private beliefs, many of those who recently had done so decided that it would be all right quietly to slip back into their old patterns. Thus arose the problem of "relapsed converts" that plagued Louis and his ministers for the rest of the reign. A whole series of edicts followed concerning the education of children, the right to live and to die as a Huguenot, the activities of Huguenot preachers who had been converted, and above all the punishment for "relapsing," or for trying to flee the realm. It was much better never to have abjured the heresy than to have been converted and then fallen back into the old errors. The Huguenot and ex-Huguenot with some sense for justice must have ground his teeth to see the king's name at the end of each decree with the formula "for this is our pleasure."

Some of the problems that Louis had to consider sound amusing today, although they were deadly serious at the time. When the declaration of April 1686 regulating people's dying failed to meet with much success, Louis issued an administrative order allowing people to die as they pleased "providing they do not make a big show of it. . . ."[25] When some of the ex-Huguenots understood that Bishop Bodeau had made a translation of the Psalms, they asked the king's permission to use it, since obviously the bishop would not be heretical, "But his majesty has forbidden M. Pellisson to send it to them for fear that they will sing the psalms in the village tongue and in private services outside the church."[26] Others of the new Catholics in the Paris area took to visiting the embassies of Denmark and Brandenburg on Sunday, obviously to worship in the chapel. Louis ordered their arrest and suggested that the officer should "take archers . . . to avoid any fears of the domestics of the embassies."

The migration of Huguenots to England, the Netherlands, and Germany caused Louis much pain. He sent agents abroad to try to persuade refugees to return. Those who asked permission to migrate might soon find themselves in prison with others who were caught before they could cross the frontier. Only the preachers were urged to leave; if they did not, they faced serious penalties. Those who did migrate suffered confiscation of their property in France, but there seems to have been a policy for the government to give such property to a Catholic relative of the emigrant. When no such relative was available, the property could be added to the royal domain or given to someone whom the king wished to favor, just as the small properties of bastards or foreigners who died in France were given to officers of the guard, courtiers, and even to artists; or the property might be given to a *hôtel Dieu* or a general hospital favored by the king.[27] Only occasionally do we find Louis granting permission to take property from the kingdom: the Duchess of Bouillon was given the right to take with her twenty-three items of silver vessels weighing about fifty marks.[28] This grace, however, seems to have been seldom granted.

The new Catholics were always under some surveillance. The king was most anxious that their children should be educated as good Catholics, and we find a body of correspondence dealing with this problem. When it was suspected that parents were secretly teaching their children heresy, it was not uncommon for Louis to order these children to be entered in a proper Catholic school. A letter of October 21, 1692, to the Marquise de Martel, illustrates the king's actions: Louis has resolved to put the son of Monsieur de St. Gilles in a college and his daughter in a convent, but Madame de la Rochegeffart, taking them in hand, had asked for grace because the girl's health was delicate. "His Majesty would prefer your house [Madame de Martel's] to a convent, but he has asked me to tell you that he would consent only if you agree to take particular care to raise this girl in the Catholic faith. . . ." Madame de Martel excused herself from the task, and the king ordered Madame de la Rochegeffart to find another suitable home. She suggested Madame de Puydu, but the king thought her to be too old. Finally Madame Cosne, recommended by the Curé of Saint-Sulpice, assumed responsibility for the girl.[29] It is curious that Louis seems personally to have been so much concerned with this sort of problem.

In the decade following the revocation, the prisons of the kingdom were crowded with new Catholics who had relapsed to heresy. A great number of the people whose "crime" came to the attention of the king seem to have been noblemen, or at least most of them seem to have had the particles *de, de la,* or *du* before their names. Unquestionably the relapsed nobleman was more "criminal" than a relapsed mason might have been, for Louis believed that the leaders of the society should set the pattern for the others. As Louis and his advisers watched the accumulation of disorder and difficulties that followed upon their attempt to force men's minds, they must have quietly asked themselves whether or not it had been wise to take such violent steps against the strong beliefs of these people. Later generations have been able to answer that question.

In the last decades of the reign, the effort to be sure that divisive elements did not win empire over the minds of the king's subjects led to more careful supervision of books and printers than had been customary earlier. The Parlement had long since assumed the right of censorship, and from time to time the officers of the crown also interfered to prevent publication of materials deemed dangerous. In other words, there was a strong tradition for control over press and book sales in the kingdom, but a tradition and serious effort to control are often two different things. It was the rash of books and pamphlets that burst forth after the Treaty of Nymwegen when the king's government began to put increasing pressure on the Huguenots almost simultaneously with the annexations of territory along the frontiers of the German empire, that first pointed to the need for greater control. Books printed abroad and books printed in France could both do great damage to Louis' reputation and authority. In August 1683, just after the death of Marie-Thérèse, an edict was promulgated to regulate both the printing and the selling of books. It was a formidable document. Professing as its objective the encouragement of good books, this decree bristles with threats of prison, fines, and loss of privilege for those who fail to obey its dictates. No one reading it will miss the fact that its intention was to see that books disagreeable to the king would not find their way into the kingdom. It regulated all aspects of the traffic in books: domestic printing, importation, and sales. It was followed by a second edict that created a company of binders and gilders of books so that these professions, as well as the printers, would be under supervision. It is interesting to see that one of the first men to be punished under the law was none other than Monsieur Saint Yon, physician to the king, who imported libels from Holland.[30]

The effect of this new pressure upon the printed word can dramatically be seen in the files of the *Gazette*. During the 1670's this journal had printed long articles from foreign correspondents as well as from publicists in France. Some of the former were so slanted against Louis and his government that the reader today has trouble believing that they were printed in times of war. By 1683, however, the *Gazette* began to reduce its size and to restrict the variety of its features. Stories about the court were almost limited to the king's religious and ceremonial activities, and stories about the army ceased to be published. The foreigner no longer had a platform for his views. In the next decade the *Gazette* became smaller and smaller until toward the end of the century for four or five years it ceased to be published at all.

The king's harassment of the printers followed the pattern of all attempts to control the written word. There were always people who would take the chance in order to put their views before their fellow men. Even while his armies were besieging Namur in 1692, we find Louis ordering one Godart, a bookseller at Reims, to cease forever from selling books because he had offered an offensive one for sale. A few months later the printers of Rouen were called up before a tribunal for their illegal printing, and Louis sent a secretary of state to Rouen to be sure that the trial was properly organized. These examples can be many times multiplied by even a cursory perusal of the registers of the secretaries of state.[31]

Even with these persistent efforts, the edict of 1683 did not function as well as the government had hoped, so that in 1701 another edict was proclaimed to "regulate the publication of books . . . [which have caused problems that] oblige us to seek proper means to re-establish order and discipline. This new edict prohibits the publication of any book without previous permission, which must be secured from the police judges or someone chosen by them to issue a permit. The printer must attach a seal to each book, and pay a fee. . . ."[32]

When one remembers that the king or his secretaries could imprison anyone suspected of disloyalty, or accused of talking against the royal authority, these efforts to regulate opinion take on their proper perspective. Louis wanted his regime to create a state with "one king, one law, one God," but it could be achieved only by the use of brutal force against the religious dissidents and much restriction of opinion of all kinds to prevent objectionable publications. Louis himself finally seems to have come to understand the futility of his efforts to control men's ideas, for in 1705 he wrote to his grandson, the King of Spain:

> I wish that one could stop the talk of which your majesty complains, but it is impossible to deprive the public of freedom to talk. They assume that right in all times and lands, and in France more than in others. It is best to give them only topics of which they can approve and praise. I hope that there will be frequent occasion to do this in the course of your reign. . . .[33]

This statement may well be the epitaph for his own efforts to regulate the thoughts and actions of his subjects. At the time that he wrote these words, the rising tide of hostile expressions against Louis and his government could not find publishers in France, but the songs and poems that passed from hand to hand in manuscript had become a formidable avalanche of criticism, criticism that neither the king, nor his ministers, nor his police could control. It is unlikely that he had any idea of the amount or the harshness of this literature that evaded his censors and his police. If he had, he might not have been as liberal in his advice to his grandson.[34]

Like other rulers who hoped to replace the pluralism in their lands by a formula like "one God, one law, one king," Louis encountered much difficulty, and in the end his efforts created disorder, suffering, and hatred, rather than the united kingdom of which he dreamed.

25

A POLICY OF VIOLENCE AND TERROR

AFTER THE Treaty of Nymwegen they called him Louis the Great. He had fought almost all Europe, and dictated the terms of peace, terms that joined a handsome province, Franche-Comté, to his eastern frontier, straightened and rationalized the frontier with the Spanish Netherlands, and forced Frederick William, Elector of Brandenburg, to return his conquests on the Baltic to Louis' sole faithful—but ineffective—ally, the King of Sweden. Anyone listening to Frederick William, could easily understand why Louis *le Dieudonné* had become Louis *le Grand*; the elector announced that henceforth nothing could be done in Europe without the consent of France, and forthwith petitioned for French alliance. Yet Louis himself must have had second thoughts. He understood that he had broken the coalition against France just in time to prevent England from joining it; he knew that the provinces of the Spanish Netherlands had eluded his grasp; and he remembered that his soldiers and sailors had been constrained to quit Sicily as well as the United Netherlands and the Lower Rhine. He knew too that the Dutch Republic still prospered, and indeed enjoyed more favorable tariff treatment in his kingdom than it had before the war began. He also realized that for all of Colbert's fiscal reforms, his kingdom was in a sorry plight financially, and that his canny minister was having recourse to "extraordinary fiscal measures" to keep the government afloat. France was the most populous, perhaps the most prosperous, kingdom in Europe; it had successfully confronted the coalition, but the peace was somewhat less impressive than Louis and his advisers had expected it to be when they invaded the Lower Rhine and the United Netherlands in 1672. Perhaps the dismissal of Pomponne, his soft-spoken foreign minister who had urged less adventure in foreign affairs, was as much in pique over Louis' own failure as in dissatisfaction with Pomponne's conduct of the business of state.[1]

Colbert and the two Le Telliers had cooperated in securing the disgrace of Pomponne, perhaps to draw their master's vexation away from themselves by providing him with a victim. Louis may have understood this, for he deprived the fallen minister neither of his pension of 20,000 livres nor even of his title as minister of state. As might be expected the dismissal had a very important effect on the king's policy. Pomponne's successor, Colbert de Croissy, brother of the "great" Colbert, was a short-tempered, irascible, cross-grained man who fitted nicely into the more adventurous programs advocated by Colbert and Louvois. There was no longer anyone in the king's inner circle to speak for the more subtle policy of Mazarin and Lionne who had believed in accommodation and negotiation wherever possible rather than aggressive confrontation. Louis might have thought that he conducted his own foreign policy, but he was a ruler always impressed by the opinions of men whom he considered to be "experts," and as the business of government became more and more complex, he was always associated with "experts" from the bureaus that he had created to operate his regime. Thus the king's image after 1679 becomes, like Louvois and Croissy themselves, more aggressive, more angry, more prone to violence; for the king was advised by men who believed that violence could command respect and achieve his goals. Louis never learned the lesson that politics and war are much too serious affairs to be left entirely in the hands of experts. Perhaps he failed to learn this because he never called "generalists" to his service or perhaps he did not call such men because he feared the breadth of their views, or could not find such men.

As one would expect, the policy that his ministers now urged was based more on the state's interest than on dynastic considerations. During the so-called Dutch War, two salient facts had emerged. The first was the importance of a defensible lineal frontier. The old frontiers made up of "provinces with their dependencies," and thereby complicated by irrational enclaves and feudal overlappings, had been satisfactory enough before the rise of the new armies and the new conceptions of political military power. A "province with its capital city" could be a satisfactory "gate" in Richelieu's parlance, but what was now needed was a frontier that could be defined and more easily defended by "lines" to prevent marauding enemy detachments from collecting "contributions" by invading the kingdom. Vauban had seen this in 1673 when he urged "by treaty or by a good war" that the irrational "*pêle mêlée*" of French and Spanish fortresses scattered here and there on the frontier should be made into a *pré carré,* a rational "dueling field," that could be defended without excessive costs. The Treaty of Nymwegen did away with much of the irrrationality on the frontier with the Spanish Netherlands, but no such rationalization occurred in Alsace. This led to the second lesson of the war, namely that Alsace created a serious problem for the defense of the kingdom; Croissy and Louvois argued that it could be solved if only the king occupied all the positions that had been ceded to him by the Treaties of Westphalia and Nymwegen. They had no trouble persuading Louis that the decision to do this was his own. What could be more agreeable to Louis XIV than to be sure that he actually ruled the territories that had been ceded by these treaties? It has even been argued that efforts to realize the treaties of Westphalia were the axis of his foreign policy throughout the reign.

Actually the intentions of the ministers went beyond mere treaties. They wanted to fix the frontiers of France so that they could be easily defended; and if the treaties failed to assure a defensible frontier, they were willing to evoke the armed power of the king to supplement the legal rights. The brusque manner in which Louvois forced the Electoral Archbishops of Mainz and Trier to evacuate the two little fortresses that they held in Lorraine after Louis had decided not to give that province to its duke, was an early indication of the brutal actions that were to follow. On the Spanish-Netherlands frontier Louvois did not hesitate to use soldiers to secure his king's "rights" in settling the Charlemont-Dinant clause of the treaty, and ended by keeping both of these cities rather than only one of them as provided by the treaty. The Spanish representatives on the commission that sat at Courtrai to determine the exact meaning of the frontier clauses in the Treaty of Nymwegen must have many times wondered why the commission had been called into being, for Louis' ministers were obviously bent on dictating all the solutions.

If the frontier with the Netherlands caused some difficulty, the frontiers on the Rhine and the Sarre-Moselle were much more complex. The Treaty of Westphalia was the problem. It had been deliberately ambiguous and vague about Alsace; the Hapsburg claims in the province had been ceded to the King of France, but nothing could be more ill-defined than those claims. The important Alsatian cities and the petty noblemen both believed that they were still under the empire rather than part of the kingdom of France; during the war, city gates all over Alsace had been closed to Louis' soldiers—and open to those of the emperor. Three times Strasbourg had been a "gate" for the German troops to invade the province. Back in 1664 Lionne had warned the king that any assertion of French rights would bring down hostility in Germany and endanger French leadership in the

Rheinbund, but this policy of "no interference" had endangered the security of the kingdom itself. Louvois and Croissy were less gentle, less diplomatic, less subtle than Lionne had been; they were determined to define the frontiers of Alsace to suit the needs of the state.[2]

Both Louvois and Croissy had had personal experience with the problems of these eastern frontiers. As minister and secretary of state Louvois was responsible for the administrative correspondence with the frontier provinces, including Alsace. He had visited the province many times, and had placed one of his creatures, de la Grange, there as intendant. He knew that the wartime governor, the bizarre Duke of Mazarin, had had no idea how to rule this province with its independent towns claiming to be directly (*immediatété*) under the empire; as a result Louis' authority in Alsace was everywhere in jeopardy. Colbert de Croissy had had even more intimate experiences with the problems of the eastern border. He had been president of the council for Alsace, intendant of that province, and president *à mortier* of the Parlement of Metz. He also had been ambassador to Ratisbon, Vienna, Clèves, Rome, and London. He had been in the Parlement of Metz when that court first started the inquiry into the territorial clauses of the Treaty of Westphalia, and he had made a special report on the "usurpations" of French territory by neighboring princes. Croissy, even though he was less bold, unquestionably was the man to work with Louvois on the problems of the frontier.

Most of the machinery needed to accomplish French aims was at hand. At Besançon and Metz there were Parlements and at Breisach a superior court; they claimed jurisdiction over the provinces of Franche-Comté, Alsace, Lorraine, and the three bishoprics of Metz, Toul, and Verdun. Where better to interpret the true meaning of the treaties? These courts could assume jurisdiction over the web of feudal claims, and the confusing, ambiguous problem of feudal "dependencies." When not one of the three bishops could produce a list of the fiefs properly under their sees, Louis created a special chamber in the Parlement of Metz to take the problem under consideration. As Louvois wrote to Croissy: "the Bishops of Metz, Toul, and Verdun, having explained to the King that most of their vassals refuse obedience to their lord, his Majesty has nominated a commission composed of thirteen judges from the Parlement of Metz, to adjust the differences between the bishops and their vassals."[3] Technically this was the only "chamber of reunion," though tradition has also lumped the work of the other two "sovereign courts" under this same name.

The ink was hardly dry on the Treaty of Nymwegen (September 9,

1679) when the Parlement of Besançon issued an order placing eighty-odd villages in the county of Montbéliard under French sovereignty, and ordering the noblemen who claimed these villages as fiefs either to recognize Louis XIV as their overlord or forfeit their claims. The most important nobleman was the Duke of Württemburg who would not do homage to the King of France. The next year the rest of the Comté, including the city of Montbéliard, followed the same path. One need only look at a map to understand what was at stake: the county of Montbéliard was the territorial link between Franche-Comté and Alsace; it could not be left in the hands of German princes without gross danger to both provinces. Naturally the Parlement found that it was a "dependency" of Franche-Comté.

While this went on at Besançon, the sovereign court at Breisach issued similar orders. The cities and noblemen of Alsace were summarily called upon to take an oath to Louis XIV—and with no mention of the empire or emperor. Louvois wrote to Louis, "I have alerted M. de Montclair [commander of the king's armies in Alsace] that the present state of your Majesty's affairs does not allow that one speaks of *immediatété* of the Empire in the oath. . . ."[4] Thus the royal army was at hand to see to it that these cities did open their gates: Colmar, Weissembourg, Haguenau, and other important Alsatian cities for the first time were really made a part of the kingdom of France. By August 1680 all of Alsace, except Strasbourg, had been forced to accept Louis as lord. It did not bother Louis that there was much discussion at Ratisbon; his courts and his soldiers had cleared up most of the frontier and territorial ambiguities of the Treaties of Westphalia and Nymwegen in a way quite satisfactory to his interests.

The chamber of reunion in the Parlement of Metz found bigger game than either of the other two. The frontier from Weissembourg west toward Luxembourg was a tangle of feudal principalities that allowed aggressive lawyers to find claims hidden within claims. It was not long before the "reunions" were pushing the frontier into Germany. Even Louvois felt that the chamber was moving too fast. "I have received your letter . . . to which was joined memoranda in which you have gone beyond the principles that I explained to you," he wrote to one of his creatures; ". . . I beg you to put yourself in the proper frame of reference; it is not a question of reuniting to the crown *in two months* [author's italics] the places that we believe to be dependencies but rather to do it in such a way that all Europe understands that his Majesty is not acting with violence and does not prevail through either military superiority or the *vertu* that has placed him above all the princes of Europe, but only to give justice to the churches whose lands have been usurped. . . ." Louvois did not say that the chamber should not examine the record and "find" what lands had ever belonged to the three bishops; he merely asked that the court proceed with less haste. The chamber at Metz annexed lands belonging to the Kings of Spain and Sweden, to the Electors of Mainz and Trier, and to a host of German princes and noblemen. It even discovered that Montroyal, an island far below Trier in the Moselle, belonged to the King of France; it was an excellent point for a fortification that could control traffic on the river and communications on the lower Rhine. But the most important "discovery" of this chamber (July 1681) was evidence that the county of Chiny, the most important fief of Luxembourg, had formerly been taken from the Bishop of Metz. Immediately the chamber issued an order demanding its return. After a little discussion with the Spanish officials, the French army "executed" the orders of the court. But this did not end the nibbling: Chiny formerly had had fiefs that had since been taken from it, so in August six more cities and a large number of villages were occupied. There scarcely remained anything of Luxembourg except the city fortification of that name, and obviously it too would soon fall victim to the chamber or to the French army, for as the soldiers occupied the lands around Luxembourg they quietly established a blockade, preventing food or supplies from passing to the fortress. A glance at the map will quickly explain why this fortification was important. It would be an anchor for the frontier lines from north of Weissembourg through Saarbrucken and Saarlouis to Luxembourg. The reasons for French action are evident enough, but they were not regarded as particularly valid by the princes and statesmen whose lands were being absorbed. To Europe it seemed to be violence and usurpation.

There were several ways of looking at these "reunions." Louis may actually have been convinced that he was merely asking for what was rightfully his. When the French ambassador to the German Diet asked him what he should say to people who questioned the proceedings, Louis simply replied, ". . . make only one general reply, that I intend to exercise my rights to all that belongs to me as a consequence of the Treaties of Westphalia and Nymwegen." He may have believed this, but Chamlay, writing years later, says "They [the courts] found several good and incontestable titles, others very doubtful, and rather than keeping within just limits which would have secured the greatest advantages for the King, they pushed things too far . . . so that in the Spanish Netherlands, . . . and particularly in the Empire . . . [they] aroused great umbrage."[5] Indeed they did. In Germany, and for that matter in all Europe, the sight of a French court assigning a territorial claim, and a French army executing the sentence, did not appear as an act of legality. What was even more difficult to take was the fact that a French army also invaded Flanders and laid waste the countryside when the Spanish governor refused to withdraw his troops from territories demanded by the court at Metz. The Spanish complained that this was not the way a Christian prince should act. They were yet to see how brutal Louvois could be in executing the "orders" of his master.

Not all of Louis' annexations during these years had the cloak of legality provided by his courts on the eastern frontier. In 1680 he reoccupied the principality of Orange on the Rhône River that belonged to Prince William of Orange, and when the prince's agent Heinsius came to Paris to protest, Louvois threatened to throw him into the Bastille.[6] The fortifications of the city of Orange were dismantled, the sovereignty assumed by the king, and the fief turned over to the Duchess of Nemours. The only justification that could be put forward was the fact that William was an enemy of the king, and was urging the re-formation of a grand alliance against France. There probably was another reason not discussed: Orange was a possible haven for Huguenot exiles and as long as it was under the Prince of Orange it could be a shelter for both hostile press and conspiracy.

But the most important arbitrary annexation was the city of Strasbourg. Men who remembered that during the late war Strasbourg had three times opened the route into Alsace for the imperial armies were probably not surprised when Louis' armies appeared before the city to demand its capitulation. The city government understood its peril a year or more before the ax fell; it asked to be allowed to become a "neutral city." The French did not see how it could be "neutral," since there was no war. While the other Alsatian cities one by one were being forced to admit their dependence upon the King of France and to recognize his sovereign rights, the Strasbourgers watched and nervously waited. There could be no help, for the emperor had no forces to send, and any move from Germany would have brought immediate reaction from the King of France. Toward the last of September 1681 the French forces in Alsace began to converge on the city. A cavalry unit seized the bridgehead, and Louvois summarily ordered the city fathers to come to his camp and sign a treaty of capitulation. On the evening of September 30, Louvois and Montclair entered Strasbourg and assumed control over the city. Upon hearing the news, Louis may have made the ironic remark that ". . . the security must have been complete since M. de Louvois slept there . . . ," but his letter to the minister was more gracious. "Tell the Barons de Montclair and d'Asfeld," he wrote, "that I am well satisfied with their conduct; I will not say anything to you of the satisfaction that I have for your cares in this affair since you must know that I am well pleased with you."[7] Indeed he might be, for Louvois had really arranged a *coup de théâtre*: the same day that he entered Strasbourg, another French army under Catinat entered Casale on the upper Po in Italy.

The French took over Strasbourg. Its bishop, von Fürstenberg, an agent of the French king for Germany, reconsecrated the handsome Gothic cathedral that was now returned to the Catholic church, and Vauban and Louvois surveyed the fortifications of both Strasbourg and Kehl (on the other side of the river) to assure the defense of their newest acquisition. The city was now a "gate" for the French to enter the empire, a "gate" barred to the imperials should they again seek to cross into Alsace. Toward the end of October, when the spiritual and physical installations were satisfactorily secure, Louis XIV and his queen, the princes of the blood, and a brilliant court of people of quality entered Strasbourg with great ceremony. The city had never before seen such magnificence. Louis held court, and remained in the city for three days. His subjects rejoiced while the churches of France sent *Te Deums* to heaven to thank God for His bounty. Unless the expressions of satisfaction were feigned, practically all literate France hailed the frontier annexations with great satisfaction. The criticisms all came from beyond the borders of the kingdom.

This thirtieth of September was a great day for Louvois. He had feared some eclipse of favor after the peace of 1679 no longer called for his military talents, but the "reunions," and now the annexations of Strasbourg and Casale, made him shine in the king's favor, made him "the indispensable man." He had timed it just right for a maximum effect. From Strasbourg he wrote to his father, "I await with great impatience the news from Casale where the troops of the King should have entered the same day that those of this province took possession of this place."[8]

The problem of Casale had been different from that of Strasbourg. Richelieu had established the French in Italy by acquiring the fortress of Pignerol. In 1680 the French ambassador to Savoy, the Marquis de Villars, suggested the possibility of acquiring Casale as a second point from which to control Savoy, as well as a fortification from which to harass the Spanish Milanese. Casale was the capital city of Montferrat, a little principality under the Duke of Mantua, who at that moment was a dissipated young man quite incapable of managing his own affairs. His mother, who had ruled, or misruled, during his minority, was also a bizarre creature, representative of the princely Italian families of the late seventeenth century. The family had lost its political meaning as foreigners took over control in Italy; self-gratification at the expense of his subjects was the only outlet left to the duke. Louis secured Casale by negotiation. Early in July 1681 the duke signed a treaty transferring the city to the King of France in return for 100,000 pistoles (about one million livres) and an annual pension of 60,000 livres. It was a stiff bargain, but it greatly increased French power and influence in Italy.

With the first "reunions," a tremor went through the empire, and the Diet at Ratisbon buzzed with excitement; as the reunions continued, taking territory from the Spanish and the Swedish kings, from the electors and princes in the Rhineland, the buzzing could be heard in all Europe. William of Orange, even before the loss of his principality on the Rhône, opened negotiations for the renewal of some sort of an alliance against France. The Swedish king cast about for aid when Louis annexed Zweibrücken (Deux-Ponts). When Luxembourg became the target, the King of Spain joined the outraged princes of the empire in looking to Emperor Leopold for leadership. William of Orange, an old enemy of Louis, sent his friend and agent Count Waldeck from court to court to discuss a new coalition against the aggressor. The political situation in Germany and in Europe, however, was very complex; it was not enough to sound a tocsin. After the experience of the last war some assurance of success was needed to create a solid alliance; but the power and diplomacy and money of France, the weakness of Germany, and the dangerous threat of a Turkish invasion of the Danube basin made the achievement of such a coalition improbable.

The Holy Roman Empire of the German nation was in full decay: the Reformation, the Thirty Years' War, and finally, the settlements of the treaties of Westphalia had corroded its strength; nowhere could this better be seen than at Ratisbon, where the Diet met continually, without accomplishing much of anything because of problems of precedence, divisions, and inner disorders. The emperor seemed almost helpless before this confusion; what power he had came from his position as a ruling prince on the upper Danube rather than from the imperial title that grew more hollow each year. And yet at this very moment there were forces being released that reaffirmed the *raison d'être* of the imperial power: while the French encroached on the western frontier of Germany, the Turks threatened to overrun all central Europe from the south. Up to this point in time Emperor Leopold I had appeared as a sorry figure; his children had died, his politics had failed; his cousin Louis regarded him as a priest-ridden, indecisive foil, perhaps not more dangerous than the redoubtable Elector of Brandenburg. In the decade that followed, this prince who had been sure that God had deserted his house, acquired the title Leopold the Great. He still lacks an adequate biographer, but he has found a secure place in the histories of this era of Louis XIV, William III, and Innocent XI.

The danger from the Ottoman Turks was complicated by the fact that rebellion in Hungary was endemic, and at the moment, Hungarian "malcontents" led by Count Tökölli and supported by French money, were willing to cooperate with the Turks in an effort to free their part of Hungary from Hapsburg rule. By chance this willingness coincided with the needs of the Ottoman Empire, which was sustaining itself against internal decay only by military action on its frontiers. This empire resembled nothing so much as a series of provinces governed by armies of occupation; it had no organic unity, no inner meaning to hold it together, and when it no longer expanded, its powers to resist decay soon melted away. The unsuccessful attack on the Danube in the early 1660's had sputtered to an end in the twenty-year truce with the emperor; the long war against Venice had resulted in the conquest of Crete; the forays against Persia had been inconclusive. In 1681–82 when the Hungarians appealed for aid against Emperor Leopold, the Grand Vizier Kara Mustapha decided that the time had again come to try war in Germany. There is even some evidence that he planned the creation of a sultanate on the upper Danube with himself as its ruler. With dismay the court at Vienna became aware of this intention when the emperor attempted to renew the twenty-year truce so that he could concentrate his attention upon French aggression in the Rhineland. Instead of a truce, the empire and the emperor had to brace themselves to meet a Turkish army, a mortal threat to the Danubian monarchy, and perhaps to all central Europe. Until this was settled, the questions raised by the French annexations had to wait.

In Germany at this moment there were strong forces unwilling to take a stand against the French, but quite willing to aid in defending the empire against the Turks. Louis' diplomacy had pensioned or subsidized the Dukes of Bavaria and Saxony and Brandenburg as well as the electoral bishops of the Rhine. These princes had even agreed to vote for Louis or his son in the next election for Holy Roman Emperor of the German nation. Without the aid of the Electoral Prince of Brandenburg, no imperial action against France was possible, and Frederick William would not move against France for he had taken French money and he believed that only with French aid could he achieve his ambition to conquer Pomerania and to establish a Brandenburg West African empire. He resented the growing pressure on the French Huguenots, but he would not break his alliance with Louis XIV. On the other hand, he was willing to fight the Turks.[9] The menace from Islam was a danger to all Christian Germany, or at least it seemed to be so, and thus for the first time since the mid-sixteenth century a Hapsburg emperor could go to the Diet asking for an imperial army to help him defend central Europe, the real task for which his house had been elected to the thrones of the Empire, Hungary, and Bohemia.

Thus, though Leopold hoped to fend off the Turkish menace by diplomacy so that he could deal with French aggression, he went to the Diet at Ratisbon early in January 1681 with a request for the creation of an imperial army capable of shielding central Europe against the Ottoman Empire. Though he did not mention it, everyone knew that once such an army would come into being, it could also be used against the aggressor in the west. Leopold proposed an army of 100,000 men; the Diet cut his request first to 60,000, and finally in April it agreed upon 40,000. Even this figure was somewhat ephemeral, for at the moment it would be difficult to build an army out of the troops available in the circles of the empire. Yet this act was very important, for it was the first real attempt to arm Germany in over a hundred years, and it gave meaning to an imperial war council, which, in time became an important institution. Leopold now had means with which to enlist princes of the empire as commanders of the army and counselors on the council, as well as the money with which to pay for soldiers. Louis and his advisers were contemptuous of the German soldiers—"caterpillars" they called them—but at the same time it was uncomfortable to see the empire develop armies under a war ministry that might in time do some of the things that Louvois and his father had done for armies of the kingdom of France.

While the Turkish threat and the rebellion of the Hungarian malcontents (also subsidized by France) occupied his attention, Leopold could not do more than protest when Louis annexed the imperial city of Strasbourg. But the temperature of the empire was rising; the Germans were more and more fearful of the aggressive "image" that Louis the Great presented to the world. In the winter of 1681–82 the French frontier nearly exploded when the Governor of Luxembourg, on short rations because of the unofficial blockade, sent out a sortie to break the French stranglehold by escorting a convoy of food into the city. Louis' reply was immediate. His soldiers occupied the territory around Courtrai where the frontier commission was ineffectively studying the problems of the Treaty of Nymwegen, and brutally devastated the countryside. It looked as if war with Spain was almost inevitable.

Then, with no warning, Louis suddenly announced that he was withdrawing his troops from around Luxembourg, leaving the settlement of his claims to the arbitration of the King of England. He explained his reason for this action to Marshal Créqui in a revealing letter in which he first pointed out that the Turks would invade the upper Danube next year, and "as I do not wish that those who *should* oppose the Turkish invasion *could reproach me* [author's italics] that my actions in the Lowlands to obtain my just rights, had made it impossible for them to wage war successfully for the defense of Christianity, I have resolved to end at once the business of the Lowlands by putting it to the arbitration of the King of England."[10] It would be hard to find a more cynically revealing statement of Louis' intentions. We know that the king and his advisers were convinced that Leopold could not build an army capable of standing up against the one that Kara Mustapha was assembling at Belgrade; we also know that Louis used every trick in his book to keep John Sobieski from allying with Leopold against the Turks, thus hoping to prevent the Poles from opposing the invasion. We also know that Louis had suddenly reversed his policy at Constantinople in a direction to encourage the Turkish invasion. Less than two years before, the French Mediterranean fleet had shelled Chios in an effort to punish an African corsair, and when the Porte had reacted by violent penalties taken on the person of the French ambassador, Louis had ordered his navy to attack the Dardanelles. Then the word came that the Turks were projecting a real invasion of the upper Danube, and Louis recalled his navy, apologized for the shelling of Chios, and assured the sultan that the Austrian emperor had shown so much ill will toward France that there was no possibility that French soldiers would save him this time if the sultan should attack. Louis was quite willing to have his ambassador reassure the sultan verbally, but he would put nothing on paper.[11]

Why did Louis lift the blockade of Luxembourg? Surely he was not at the same time a friend of the sultan and of those "who should defend Christendom" against the sultan's invasion. Louis wished to be free of blame for the debacle that he foresaw and tried to encourage, but he also would not become an out-and-out ally of the Turks as his forerunner Francis I had been. A corollary to these questions would be: Why did Louis not send troops in 1683 to defend Europe against the Turks as he had done twenty years before? When the pope asked him to join in the "crusade," he simply replied that princes did not fight "holy wars" any more, and furthermore it would only succeed in injuring French trade in the Levant. Obviously we must probe to try to discover what Louis' behavior in this crisis meant in terms of his vision of himself and the policy of his kingdom.

In any political situation there are usually several layers of policy. The Dutch War and the Treaty of Nymwegen proved to Louis how important it was to have sharply defined, defensible frontiers. States' interest in terms of defense and frontiers dictated the policies that led to the "reunions" and the annexations of 1679–82. Beyond this policy of states' interest, there was another with dynastic implications: the acquisition of the Spanish inheritance, or a part thereof, for the Bourbon family. This goal was important to a greater or lesser degree throughout his reign. Beyond this second layer, there was a third, perhaps less possible, less probable, but surely desirable goal in Europe, namely the acquisition of the crown of the Holy Roman Empire for himself or his son. Mazarin had toyed with this idea, and even attempted to secure Louis' election at the time that Leopold became emperor; Louis' interest can be seen in the treaties that he made with the Electors of Bavaria, Brandenburg, Saxony, and Cologne following the peace of 1679; each contained clauses requiring the elector to vote for Louis or his candidate to the imperial throne in the next election.[12] These clauses left the future in doubt, but they did act as a barrier against Leopold's naming a king of the Romans, and they left open the hope that a Bourbon might someday wear the imperial crown. As French ambitions grew, as the image that Louis and his ministers were creating became more and more impressive, this vision of a Bourbon prince wearing the imperial crown became more and more alluring to French statesmen. The Turkish invasion provided a superb opportunity to give it reality. The acquisition of that crown had not been a primary mainspring for Louis' policy before 1681, and after 1685 it never again was an important factor, but in 1682–83, the crown of the Holy Roman Empire seemed almost within his grasp, and Louis worked as hard as a Christian prince could to acquire it. There seems to be no other reasonable explanation for French diplomacy during these years, and Chamlay explicitly confirms our suspicions. If one considers the action of the French ambassadors to the German princes, to Poland, to the Ottoman Empire, and to the pope, it becomes evident that the King of France hoped soon to be the one power that could halt the Turkish horde that was about to overrun central Europe.[13]

Louis pointedly withdrew his blockade of Luxembourg so that those who *should defend* central Europe against the Turks could "*not blame* him for the failure." At the same time he promised the Turks that he would not assist *the emperor* if the Turks attacked him, and urged John Sobieski to keep Poland neutral. What Louis obviously expected was that the Turks would overrun the Hapsburg state complex, destroy all German confidence in the emperor, and actually invade Germany. If the Turkish army reached Bohemia, Bavaria, perhaps Saxony or Franconia, there would be only one resort for the German princes, only one power that could halt the Turkish thrust. Louis had promised not to aid the emperor, but that promise would not prevent the Most Christian King, the Eldest Son of the Church, from going to the aid of Christian Germany, with, of course, enormous benefits to that king.

Louis lifted the blockade of Luxembourg in the spring of 1682; in the summer of 1683 a Turkish army of 200,000 men marched up the Danube and besieged Vienna. All Europe watched anxiously. Marie-Thérèse said that she would gladly give her life to save the city, but her husband knew that should Vienna fall and a defeated German army be forced to retreat, then one successful battle could establish a French hegemony over Europe, more extensive and more powerful than his great-great-grandfather Charles V had ever had. Who conceived this policy? Was it Louvois, Croissy, or Louis himself? No Christian prince had ever before so cynically and so opportunistically used Islam against a Christian foe; not even the alliance that Francis I made with the Sublime Porte had such a Machiavellian intention. Well might Europe hail Louis as the "Most Christian Turk at Versailles."

Events took precedence over plans. When the Turkish army, under the banner with the horsehair plumes and commanded by Kara Mustapha himself, moved north from Ofen (Buda), Charles of Lorraine fought a delaying action while John Sobieski in Poland and the German princes in the empire prepared armies to meet the Ottoman hordes. Poland could not remain neutral when central Europe was endangered, and especially John Sobieski could not, for the reputation that led to his election to the throne was that of a warrior against the Turks. Even the urgent requests of his friend and protector Louis XIV could not prevent the Polish king from joining the forces of the empire.[14] Thus the central European peoples were enlisted under the imperial banner to block the flood tide of Islam. When the Turks reached Vienna they attacked a city defended by a tough soldier, von Starhemberg, who knew how to make a foe pay for every gain. In

Germany, Sobieski with about 20,000 Polish soldiers, mostly cavalry, and Duke Charles of Lorraine[15] with some 60,000 German troops prepared to raise the siege. Starhemberg held Vienna until the relieving forces reached the Kahlenberg, a hill several miles away, from which they descended upon the Turkish camp like avenging angels, and sent the whole Ottoman armament fleeing down the river toward Hungary. It was a glorious victory only a little marred by conflicts over the spoils of the Turkish camp, and claims and counterclaims about the importance of German or Polish soldiers in the battle. Western tradition, listening to his boasts, very often gives Sobieski full credit for the victory, forgetting that Charles of Lorraine, an able successor to Montecuccoli, commanded about three times as many troops as Sobieski did that day. A truer estimate gives to both Germans and Poles a share in the turbulent assault on the Turkish camp.

Europe watched with bated breath the march of the Ottomans, the vigorous defense of von Starhemberg, and finally the hammer blow of Lorraine and Sobieski. Nowhere was it more closely followed than at the French court; even the death of Marie-Thérèse only momentarily distracted attention from the events on the Danube. The Turkish army was a very large one, but it had neither the weapons nor the military skills that western Europe had developed since the Thirty Years' War. Even before the victory at Vienna, the French court came to realize that it not only was unlikely that their armies would be called upon to save Germany from Islam, but also probable that victory at Vienna would greatly enhance the emperor's prestige and make secure the imperial throne for his family. A new gambit had to be found to secure France its rightful compensations. A memorandum written by Chamlay several years later reflects the dilemma at Versailles: "Although the loss of Vienna would have procured great advantages for the king, both relating to his own *gloire*[16] and the interests of his state," he wrote, "His majesty, who was animated by another spirit, and who saw the general good of Christendom as more important than his own interests, learned with great pleasure of the lifting of the siege."[17]

Chamlay was one of the most important of the politico-military advisers in Louvois' bureau, and throughout the rest of the regime he had an important influence on policy. There can be no doubt about his knowledge of events, but his pious words, written probably a decade after the events, have little relationship to the feelings of the French king at the time when every advance of the Turkish army had been hailed almost as a French victory, and when his response to the coming imperial victory at Vienna was the reestablishment of the French blockade of Luxembourg and an invasion of the Spanish Netherlands. It is true that Louis immediately announced that he would be willing to end his military activity *if* the emperor and the King of Spain would be willing to *recognize his legal rights* to the territories that he had "rejoined" to his crown since 1679. It is difficult to find a more flagrant example of political blackmail; the emperor's victory at Vienna ended hope that the French army would become the "savior" of central Europe. The only recourse now left to the men at Versailles was to insist that they be paid before the Germans would be allowed to follow up that victory. The anonymous pamphleteer who told about Colbert's entry into hell after his death on September 10, 1683, seems to have reflected the real feeling of the French court. Colbert, arriving in hell, met Mohamet, who complained about the number of Turks being sent there by Starhemberg, Sobieski, and Lorraine; he was particularly upset over the defeat of Kara Mustapha's army. Colbert assured the Prophet of his own sorrow and that of the other ministers of the French king "who are also good Mohammedans." "We expect the siege of Vienna to be the fatal stroke, giving us all Germany," said Colbert; "I can see our chagrin now that I have the news!"[18] Even as late as 1683 the cultural and religious (ideological) differences between Christendom and Islam had the emotional force to make the term "Mohammedan" as pejorative as the term "communist" or "bourgeois imperialist" is in our twentieth-century secular society.

There was a voice that interjected another note into the picture of the year 1683. A few weeks after the Turkish defeat, Father Pierre Pièche mounted the pulpit to deliver a funeral oration for the dead Queen of France. Recalling her willingness to die to save Vienna, the good priest wondered why God had required this sacrifice. He was well aware that the physicians who attended her could not cure her illness, for God himself had taken her life in return for saving Vienna, and yet this seemed terrible. "Why," he asked God, "did You accept this sacrifice?"[19] Louis and his ministers did not attend the ceremony; they may not have realized this connection between the unexpected death of the queen and the defeat of the Turkish armies.

Louis returned his armies to the blockade of Luxembourg and invaded the Spanish Netherlands only a few days before the Turkish host was driven pell-mell from its trenches before Vienna. The French assumed that their demand was just. All that they required of the emperor and the Spanish king was a recognition of the legality of French annexations since 1679. The Spanish, however, had "paid" for peace at the end of the Dutch

War by giving up Franche-Comté, and they were in no mood to see so much more of the holdings of their king follow that province under French jurisdiction. When they heard that Vienna was saved, the Spaniards decided to force the emperor's hand by declaring war on France; it was a futile declaration unless the emperor and empire also declared war. The French response seems to have been the work of Louvois and his friend Chamlay; the French armies marched into the Spanish Netherlands and poured bombs into the border towns in massive bombardments that left whole areas of the cities in smoking ruins. At the same time, a French army commanded by Créqui undertook the siege of Luxembourg. Since Vauban organized the siege and there was no Charles of Lorraine and John Sobieski to raise it, Luxembourg was doomed.[20]

While the French army was terrorizing the Spanish Netherlands, Louis' navy brutally punished Genoa for its aid to the Spanish. Genoa was a free city; its people were often called the "Hollanders of the Mediterranean." Its political orientation was anti-French largely because it had long been the port through which passed all shipments to and from Spain, Milan, and Austria. When war broke out in 1683, the Genoese allowed the Spanish to recruit troops in their city, and outfitted and constructed galleys for the Spanish navy in defiance of a command from France not to do so. In May 1684, when the siege of Luxembourg held the attention of all Europe, the French Mediterranean fleet appeared before Genoa. Colbert's son, the Marquis de Seignelay, who now was secretary for the marine in his father's place, was on board, and Duquesne in command. Seignelay summoned the city to surrender; when it refused, the fleet began a tremendous bombardment that destroyed two-thirds of the town. The previous bombardments of Algiers and Chios were ineffectual attacks compared with the treatment given Christian Genoa. Seignelay thus proved to Louis that a Colbert could be as ruthless as a Le Tellier; he and Louvois both believed in the destruction of cities by fire as a means of terrorizing Europe into submission. At this moment Louvois and Seignelay *were* the face of Louis XIV, and as far as Europe was concerned, that face was opportunistic, brutal, ruthless, and tyrannical.

At Versailles, however, Louis smiled graciously at the world that he was terrorizing. He had just married Madame de Maintenon and probably did not notice the "image" that his ministers and warriors were giving him. He blandly assured the ambassadors at his court that he sought only "his rights." He had no intention of "embarrassing the emperor's fight with the Turks" if the emperor and the King of Spain would only recognize the annexations that he had made to implement the Treaties of Westphalia and Nymwegen. The Spanish king was "really doing harm to Europe by his declaration of war," thereby preventing German soldiers from fighting the Turks as they should. Finally, Louis offered to stop all hostilities if the emperor and the King of Spain would sign a twenty-year truce, provisionally recognizing the French frontiers as they existed. This would include Luxembourg. The truce would allow Germany to fight the Turks; this concession was Louis' contribution to their campaign. He did not insist on a definitive peace treaty since there was so much hostility to this idea in both Vienna and Madrid.

The decision before Leopold and his advisers was a hard one. Territory lost to Islam, many believed, would eventually be reconquered, but territory lost to France was forever lost; and yet it seemed important to strike in Hungary while the iron was hot. The Turks also were willing to make a new truce, but a pamphlet, written by one of Leopold's wisest servants, argued that the time was ripe for the conquest of Hungary, and that this conquest would give the Hapsburg Danubian state a power equal, perhaps even superior, to that of France.[21] To the voice of this bureaucratic statebuilder, Frederick William added another compelling reason for attacking the Turks rather than the French, when he announced that Brandenburg troops would fight on the Danube but not on the Rhine. Above the din of argument there was the voice of Innocent XI who had for so long awaited the chance to lead a crusade. Through his agent Marco d'Aviano, Innocent was building the Holy Alliance of the Holy Roman Empire, Venice, Poland, and—surprise added to surprise—Russia. The soldiers of this league were to be strongly supported by papal money as well as papal exhortations. While these arguments gained empire at Vienna, the war party in the Netherlands succumbed before French money and French threats. Some of the members of the General Estates were timid, some were venal; for these menacing gestures, for those bribes. The war party led by William of Orange did not have a chance. The last and probably most imposing argument was the fall of Luxembourg. It seemed that Frederick William was right: nothing could avail against France, so some sort of compromise had to be made.

The twenty-year truce signed at Ratisbon recognized tentatively gains made by the recent annexations, including both Strasbourg and Luxembourg. For the emperor this treaty was simply a truce that would allow his armies and his allies to turn their attention upon the Turks. He unquestionably hoped to reopen the armed debate of the Rhine as soon as he had settled that of Hungary. Louis was more realistic. He understood that twenty years is a long time, and that there would be many opportunities to change the truce into a peace. In the meantime his engineers could fortify the frontier that he had won, while his administrators and clergymen would integrate the territories into his kingdom. France was becoming a military, bureaucratic state; it was no longer simply a congeries of provinces and territories ruled by a single king. This fact changed the character of the annexations.

This truce marked Louis' only really successful conclusion of a military adventure. Neither the War of the Devolution nor the so-called Dutch War had been successful in light of French objectives when the wars began; the two last wars of the regime were to be nearly catastrophic failures. This little war of 1683–84 crowned four years of annexations by as near a successful *Blitzkrieg* as the seventeenth century was ever to see; it gave Louis unwarranted faith in the brutality policies advocated by his advisers.

The bombardments in the Spanish Netherlands were only the most dramatic evidence of French brutal policies; there were others equally cruel. When the Truce of Ratisbon was being written, Louis refused to allow the city of Genoa to make peace by that treaty. He required special amends. The French navy had destroyed a good part of the city by its bombardment, and Louis now demanded that the city humble itself before him as a striking and dramatic lesson to other cities that might think of disobeying a French command. When the Genoese hesitated, Louvois prepared an overland invasion of the city to complete the destruction that the navy had begun. While the French troops were assembling at Casale, the papal nuncio, who tried to intercede for the Genoese, had to hear the King of France haughtily declare that he did "not wish to take either the city of Genoa or any fortress belonging to it for fear of disturbing the peace that he had just given Europe, but that he would send his troops to desolate their land and to make a memorable example of his vengeance for all those who would dare to offend him."[22] If the Genoese wanted peace, the price was an ignominious journey of the doge and representative senators to Versailles to beg Louis' pardon. Unlike Gaifer Aga, the Algerian ambassador who had gone to Versailles the preceding year to ask pardon for the bombardment that Duquesne had given his city, the Doge of Genoa and his train had to pay its own way through France.[23] When they arrived at Versailles they were treated coldly "since it is natural that the king look with indifference upon a republic that has drawn his indignation upon itself and that has come to ask pardon from him. . . ." The audience took place on May 15, 1685. The king, surrounded by legitimate and legitimized princes of the blood and the high officers of his household, received the five Genoese. As the doge and the four senators approached, the king stood up and removed his hat; the Genoese made a deep reverence; then the king put on his hat, made a sign for the doge alone to put on his, the princes then put on their hats, and the doge read, in Italian, his speech of apology, begging the king's forgiveness. At the end Louis arrogantly assured him that he "would forget all that the republic of Genoa had done against his interests and its duty."[24]

This was a humiliating experience, but even worse was Louis' callous expectation that these Genoese gentlemen would now be happy to become temporarily courtiers at his court, and pleased with the progress of the Great King. As Sainctôt naïvely puts it, "It is natural that, having been received in his good graces, he [Louis] would give them the evidence of this change and that he would treat them with benevolence. . . ." How different was the "red-carpet" treatment given to the ambassadors from Siam. Sieur le Vachet, who spoke their language, met them at the frontier and escorted them to court. Everywhere cheap pictures of them were for sale, and the king had to give them a guard to keep back the crowd eager to see them. Their respect for royalty and their elaborate ritual much impressed the French. Sainctôt devoted forty folios to the account of their visit.[25] Siam, of course, had not "failed to do its duty" toward France. The head of the Siamese delegation assured Louis that as a result of his mission "all the Orient will soon and for centuries to come know of the incomparable *vertu* of Louis the Great."[26]

If he had any misgivings about the use of violence to achieve his ends, it did not prevent him from imposing his will on the Duke of Savoy and spilling over the violence of his soldiers against Protestants in this neighboring principality. For a long time the French court had treated Savoy as if it were an adjunct of the kingdom rather than an independent state. Louvois had even imposed one of his creatures upon Madame Royale, the regent, and Louis attempted to control both her and her son much as he managed his own family. At one point he went along with Madame Royale in a proposal to marry the duke to the Princess of Portugal so that he would leave the duchy of Savoy to her rule, but Victor Amadeus balked his mother's plan by pretending to be ill at the time the Portuguese came to carry him away. The most serious demands upon Savoy came after the revocation of the Edict of Nantes. The insistence that the duke should extirpate heresy from his realm just because Louis had revoked toleration in France is unquestionably one of the blackest pages of French domination over its neighbors. There were only a few Protestants in Savoy but they lived in mountain valleys near France where refugees from France might find asylum. The duke did not want to harm these poor people because they had never caused him trouble, but Louis forced him into a war against them in which French soldiers played the greatest role. When it was over the Protestants were herded into "concentration camps" where a majority died of illness connected with cold and malnutrition. There is no more heartless letter over the king's signature than the one that Louis sent to Savoy saying, "I see that illness has delivered the Duke of Savoy from the embarrassment caused by the necessity of guarding the rebels from the valleys of Luzerne; and I do not doubt that he easily consoles himself for the loss of such subjects who make room for better and more faithful ones."[27]

Louis' bullying treatment of Savoy was perhaps not different from his attitude toward other princes. He had refused "his permission" to Victor Amadeus to go to Venice for a pleasure trip, but this was not worse than his treatment of the Duke of Mecklenburg who came to Paris in September 1684 to enjoy the delights of that city as a tourist. Where did he live? In the donjon at Vincennes where Louis imprisoned him for three months because of his failure to live up to his agreement with the King of Denmark who was Louis' ally. This high-handed behavior has all the earmarks of Louvois' pattern of action, but it was authorized by the king. Rousset, after telling the story, exclaims, "To incarcerate the Duke of Mecklenburg like a debtor at the request of his creditor, to stop the Duke of Savoy from amusing himself in Venice: that no longer is politics, it is policing Europe. How did Louis XIV give himself the right for this; how long would Europe put up with it?"[28] A few years later Victor Amadeus married Louis' niece, but in revenge neglected her for another; Louis, with his own background, found it a little difficult to protest. And later still, when the young prince went to explore the "delights of Venice," and incidentally to meet several people who were obviously the creatures of the emperor, he neglected to tell Louis that he was going. It was no accident that the Duke of Savoy lined up against France as soon as it became clear that Louis had bitten off too great a mouthful when he invaded the Palatinate in 1688, or that he turned against the French in 1703 as soon as the War of the Spanish Succession began to go against France. Even though Victor Amadeus was the son of a French princess, was married to a French princess, and married his two daughters to Louis' grandsons, he, like William of Orange, never got over his hatred for the king at Versailles.

After the Truce of Ratisbon and the Edict of Fontainebleau, Louis could feel more secure in his title Louis the Great. His soldiers had won the *Blitzkrieg* that had been denied them in 1672; he had annexed the territories necessary to firm up his frontiers; and all Europe had recognized his power and feared his wrath. The vast majority of his subjects were as pleased with his conquests and his acts of terror as he was himself. Only the Huguenots who were being herded into the Catholic church by force and violence had serious doubts about the wisdom and glory of their king. Even so, he should have had some misgivings. Perhaps the anger that he showed when Eugene of Savoy and two princes of the house of Conti joined the imperial army to fight the Turks, and the attention that he gave to the progress of the war in Hungary and the Morea, is evidence of his concern for a future in which he might no longer be Louis the Great.

Had Louis looked about him, he would have seen that there was a growing chorus of voices expressing dislike and even hatred for the brutality of French policy. This rising tide of criticism and hatred for his regime was spreading all over Europe.[29] The Huguenot exiles in the Netherlands, the Dutch publicists perhaps in the pay of William of Orange, and a new crowd of German writers following the tradition established by Lisola, were swamping the presses with anti-French literature. Their books and pamphlets presented Louis as a tyrant at home and an aggressor abroad; in the Protestant press he appeared as a danger to the existence of the reformed religion; in the German Catholic press, as a Machiavellian opportunist whose word could not be trusted, whose policy was a threat to the safety of all Europe. At home, too, Louis should have given some heed to the small critical voices in poem and song. Traditionally in France, songs carried the critical word, sometimes softened by wit, sometimes not. In the early years of the regime, most of the songs were still good-natured criticisms: the poets allowed Louis to have his mistresses as long as they could suggest that he really had chosen second-rate goods; they allowed him his wars, as long as he won or seemed to win. But after 1683 there began a murmur that later would grow into a deafening shout of criticism. The multi-verse songs by Jean de Vert—the "Lanterlu, Lanterlu"—and others that in 1670 were good-natured, by 1685 had begun to have a bite.

> Now comes Louis the Great
>   With Madame de Maintenon,
> He says, making a slight bow
>   To the sweet little one,

> Indeed I sinned many times with Montespan
> > I sinned with that good wench,
> But with this one here,
> > I do my penance.[30]

This poem of about 1685 is still in the tradition of good humor; the bite in the domestic songs of this period was directed mostly against the ministers. Colbert was still remembered with few regrets, but Louvois was most detested.

> Here in the state of France
> > There is neither council nor generals
> For minister, an animal [Louvois]
> > The people live in indigence.
> Without justice or reason
> > One punishes or one rewards.[31]

By the time that the Spanish succession had pulled France into a terrible war, the king and the whole royal family came under attack.

> Some call him Louis the Great,
> > Others, Louis the tyrant
> Louis the bankrupt or Louis the unjust,
> > And this is about right
> Since there is no other reason
> > Than "we wish it and it pleases us."

> The grandfather [Louis] is a braggart,
> > The son [dauphin] an imbecile
> The grandson a big coward—
> > Oh what a handsome family.[32]

If Louis knew anything of this rising tide of criticism both foreign and domestic, his only attention was to suppress it by *lettres de cachet*. In the 1680's he had not yet been really punished by the world around him; he was still the Sun King, and the chattering complaints from beyond his frontiers could be dismissed as the croaking of frogs hostile to the sun.[33] Even though his health threatened to create serious trouble, life was still pleasant: Versailles was nearly completed, Marly had emerged as a wonderful retreat, and he was satisfied with his secret wife. In January 1686, before the fistula almost cost him his life, Louis planned a party at Marly for his family and intimate friends. The shade of Mazarin would have enjoyed the fun, for it was the sort of party that he liked to give. There was a booth in each of the four corners of the grand salon, one for each season of the year. With a nice understanding of symbolism, Monsieur (Louis' brother) aided by Madame de Montespan "kept" the winter booth; the Duchess of Bourbon (Louis' daughter) and Madame de Maintenon tended the spring booth. The Duke of Bourbon (son of Condé who was dying at Chantilly) had the summer booth, and the Duke of Maine and Madame de Tiange, the autumn one. Each booth had "merchandise" suitable to the season, and the "merchants" called to all passers-by to invite them to try their luck at games. It was a de luxe "midway." If the "players" won, they could carry off the merchandise—jewels, scarfs, knickknacks of elegant manufacture—without paying. The whole affair cost the king more than 60,000 *écus*. When the guests tired of the play, there were little cabarets where cocoa, coffee, and liqueurs were available, and after midnight there was a magnificent supper served at five tables. Only the poor dauphine was absent; she was pregnant and feared that she might lose her baby.[34] A party like this one may have helped to hide from his Majesty the fact that the French image in Europe was grotesque, distasteful, and fearsome.

26

DESCENT INTO
THE MAELSTROM

A SIGH OF RELIEF arose throughout Germany when the emperor signed the twenty-year Truce of Ratisbon. There would be no war on the Rhine. The humiliation of the Doge of Genoa, the pressure against the Protestants in Savoy, even the revocation of the Edict of Nantes could be ignored or explained away by men anxious to avoid a new conflict with France. But their optimism was ill-founded. In the mid-1680's Europe was menaced by a great political storm that would soon sweep across the land with iron hailstones, a storm with lightning that would start fires in the Americas, in Africa, and in India. The imperial armament seemed stalled in 1684 and 1685 when it failed to take Ofen (Buda), but this was only a pause in the march that would soon drive the Turks from both Hungary and Transylvania and grossly upset the balance of power in Christian Europe. This was to be the catalyst that would again start the war on the Rhine and bring into play political crises from England to Italy.[1]

There were many facets to this crisis. In England a Roman Catholic king mounted the throne in 1685 with the ambition to restore his religion to the kingdom; in the Rhineland the Protestant line of the house of the Palatinate died out, and a Catholic prince, who also happened to be the father-in-law of the emperor, became the new elector. While the crowning of these two princes seemed to indicate that Catholicism had won striking victories over the Reformation, the pope at Rome and the Most Christian King at Versailles drifted farther and farther apart in a crisis that finally became almost a war between Louis and Innocent XI. At the same time, the Bavarian Wittelsbach family, traditionally friendly toward France and related to the house of Bourbon through the marriage of the dauphin to a Wittelsbach princess, was slipping into the orbit of the emperor. The head of the family, Max Emanuel, married Emperor Leopold's daughter, Marie-Antonia, whose mother was the Infanta. Although she signed a waiver of her rights to the thrones of Spain in favor of her half brothers, Leopold dangled before the Bavarian elector both a command over imperial armies in Hungary and the governorship of the Spanish Netherlands, perhaps with full sovereignty, in return for an alliance. At Bonn, the capital of the electorate of Cologne where the Bavarian Wittelsbachs traditionally provided the electoral bishop, there was developing a contest for power between Egon von Fürstenberg, Bishop of Strasbourg and a French agent, and Joseph Clement, Max's younger brother. The young Wittelsbach prince was under proper age to become a bishop and had not yet taken even holy orders; still neither his family nor the emperor wanted to see his "rights" passed over in favor of Louis XIV's creature. Each of these problems grew more tense as the imperial armies reconquered the Danube basin.

At Versailles Louis and his ministers watched with anxious interest the shifting balance of power.[2] The king and his advisers blinded themselves to the reality by wishful thinking, for each spring they were sure that the Christian armies would bog down in Hungary. However, in the fall of 1686 there came a moment of truth: money from Rome, men from Germany, and the skills of the imperial commanders sent the Turks down the river in full flight, leaving Ofen (Buda) in Christian hands. The French ambassador at Constantinople tried to warn his king that some aid to the Turks was absolutely necessary if they were to stay in the war. Each new dispatch told of disorder in the Ottoman capital, of lack of money, men, and will.[3] By 1687 and 1688 the ambassador warned that unless France did something to save the situation the Turks would undoubtedly make peace; indeed, Leopold himself might impose peace in Constantinople. Vauban could assure Louvois and the king that the accounts from French spies with the imperial army provided ample proof that these soldiers could not stand up against the French army, and yet their victories in Hungary cast doubt on these assurances. The war was giving Emperor Leopold a vast new kingdom that he and his bureaucrats and priests were making into a source of power; it was also rebuilding the military forces of central Europe, perhaps not with the same genius that Louvois and his father had used in building the French army, but dangerously close to it nonetheless.

In the Germanies also, the reunions, the annexation of Strasbourg, and finally the dragonnades and the revocation of the Edict of Nantes had combined to erode the French northern diplomatic barrier against the Hapsburgs. Sweden, and then the Elector of Brandenburg, followed by numerous of the smaller princes, were slipping into anti-French coalitions and alliances. After he had defied Louis with the Edict of Potsdam by inviting French Huguenots to his lands, the powerful Elector of Brandenburg signed an alliance with Sweden, an agreement with William of Orange, and perhaps most important of all, an alliance with the emperor. At about the same time the young prince August of Saxony, eager to make a military reputation in Hungary, also renounced his late father's pro-French orientation to become the emperor's ally. With four lay electoral votes assured, Leopold could look forward to his son's election as king of the Romans,[4] which indeed did occur in 1688. French power in central Europe had deteriorated to the point that when John Sobieski fell ill in 1687, the French felt completely out-maneuvered and were almost ready to concede that Prince Charles of Lorraine, the emperor's candidate, would become the next King of Poland. Charles did not become king, for Sobieski outlived him; but a decade later Leopold's candidate, August of Saxony, did become King of Poland, giving further evidence of the growth of imperial prestige and power. In Germany and in the Baltic Louis was out-maneuvered; by 1687 his diplomacy was reduced to an effort to hold the Danish king as an ally and to secure the cooperation of the English fleet in support of his Baltic interests.[5]

The imperial victories on the Danube were coordinated with those of the Venetians in the Morea where Admiral Morosini and the German General Königsmark managed to take Athens (1687). These successes allowed the Italians to take a stronger stand against the French. The Venetians, who had never been particularly friendly, became more and more outspokenly anti-French, but the most dangerous postures were those of the pope and the Duke of Savoy. Pope Innocent XI did not wish a break with the French king, but he did want a change in both his foreign and domestic policies. He objected to the arbitrary imposition of the *régale* and to the doctrinal assertions in the Gallican articles, and he neither approved of the brutal methods of the dragonnades nor of the revocation of the Edict of Nantes, because these measures would bring reprisals upon Catholics living in Protestant lands. On the other hand, Innocent XI would not understand Louis' unwillingness to aid the crusade against Islam, nor his obstinate refusal to give up the *franchise* in Rome, which made it impossible for the papal police to punish criminals if they sought asylum in the properties of the French embassy. In Savoy, too, French influence was on the wane. The young duke could not forget the humiliations that he had received from Louis; he also understood that the emperor could grant him many a favor by giving him the imperial fiefs that were enclaves in Savoy-Piedmont. This would cost the emperor little while it gave the duke much. As the emperor's power grew with victory in Hungary, an agreement with Savoy against the King of France, who had always treated Savoy as a vassal, became more and more possible.

Leopold's advisers were well aware of the shifting balance of power; furthermore, it seemed to them that God Himself favored their victories when in early 1686 a great fire at Belgrade destroyed much of the grain needed to feed the Turkish armies. The Germans then realized that this would be the year of victory. Was it surprising that the emperor and his allies took a new look at the truce of Ratisbon and the imperial position in the Rhineland? Leopold's roving ambassador, Prince von Hohenlohe, visited one German court after another carrying news of victory in the east, and suggestions for a coalition or league to right the balance of power in the west. Three years earlier the French bombardments of cities had made opposition to the French king too dangerous to consider, but with Ofen (Buda) about to fall and the whole Danube basin open for invasion, the situation had radically changed. Furthermore, Louis' brutal actions against the Huguenot minority had outraged Protestant Germany so much that even cautious Frederick William of Brandenburg-Prussia was again now willing to risk the wrath of the Sun King. In March 1686 he reached an agreement with Leopold by which he increased the Brandenburg aid against the Turks and agreed to join with the emperor to check French aggression in the west. In July 1686 the princes of South Germany and representatives of the Kings of Sweden and Spain met at Augsburg and formed a league for the defense of the upper Rhine. Let us allow Dangeau to tell the story as it appeared in Versailles:

> . . . the ninth of this month a league was signed at Augsburg that seems to be directed uniquely against France. It is composed of the Emperor, the Kings of Spain and Sweden for their estates in the Empire, the Elector of Bavaria, the princes of the house of Saxony, the circles of Bavaria, Franconia, and the Upper Rhine. They say in the treaty that it is for the protection of Germany and the execution of the Treaties of Westphalia, Nymwegen and the Truce of 1684, but there are clauses by which the Emperor, if he wishes, can call upon them to declare war on France . . .

Dangeau goes on to list the military commitments of each of the participants, but does not point out that most of the troops mentioned were already engaged in the war against the Turks. Louis knew that this agreement was not immediately dangerous to him; as O'Connor remarks, "It was largely a paper alliance, viewed with much more detachment by Louis XIV than by many of the historians of his reign."[6]

While this League of Augsburg was not yet really a hazard for France, it was a straw in the wind pointing to a dangerous future. The following month (August) the three electoral bishops (Cologne, Mainz, and Trier) met at Bonn to discuss their role in the future of Germany.

The Elector of Cologne was in a difficult position. As a Wittelsbach prince he looked to Bavaria for leadership, but he had long been in the pay of the King of France, to whom he owed a very large sum of money, and his most important adviser was none other than William Egon von Fürstenberg, a well-known French agent. Nothing came of the meeting that could change the situation; at French suggestion the Electors of Cologne and Trier proposed a declaration opposing the formation of leagues or alliances in Germany, but the Elector of Mainz refused to go along. Thus Louis' diplomacy even failed to win a "paper victory" over the "paper league." The League of Augsburg was soon followed by other agreements much more dangerous to France.

While the bishops gathered at Bonn another rendezvous took place at Clèves between Elector Frederick William and William of Orange. Louis sent von Fürstenberg to talk with Frederick William before this meeting, in hopes of keeping him in the French camp. But by January 1686 the French-Brandenburg alliance was practically a dead letter, and the meeting at Clèves tied another knot in the network of alliances and understandings directed against France.[7] At Versailles, Louvois characteristically remarked that he would like to hang the Brandenburg elector, but the health of the king, threatened by the fistula, as well as the general political structure of Europe, prevented the French from making any strong reaction.

On September 2, Ofen (Buda) fell. Throughout Germany *Te Deums* arose from Catholic cathedrals to thank God, while Protestant and Catholic church bells rang and cannons boomed to announce the joyous news. In the pulpits all over Germany the clergy explained to their flocks that God had blessed the crusade, and James II in England announced that the credit for the victory, after God, should go to Innocent XI. Well might Christian Europe rejoice; Islam in the guise of the Turk had been a threat to central Europe for almost two hundred years; now that power was in full retreat, and it probably never again would lap against the frontier with tongues of fire. Europe could rejoice, but not the King of France. In June he had refused the Turkish request that he should mediate between the Porte and the Holy Alliance; in July he had given the Turks hope that France would create a diversion by making an alliance between France, England, and Denmark against the emperor. When Ofen (Buda) fell in September, Louis' health would not permit any adventure, and both the English and the Danish kings were uninterested in aid to the Ottoman empire. But if France could not act sharply to keep the Turks in the war, then some way had to be found to transform the twenty-year truce into a permanent peace, for once the imperial armies were free from war on the Danube, they might be used on the Rhine.

With characteristic vigor, the French struck out in two directions. The work on the frontier fortifications in the Rhine-Moselle area was stepped up to a point that aroused fears in Germany of an immediate invasion. On the other hand Croissy attempted to follow up the suggestion of the nuncio at Paris that Leopold was ready to negotiate a definite treaty to regulate the Rhine frontier. But the French *démarche* was clothed in the brutal framework characteristic of these years; it was an ultimatum delivered at Rome demanding the conversion of the twenty-year Truce of Ratisbon into a formal treaty of peace by April 1, 1687. A few weeks later the French ambassador at Ratisbon presented the same demand to the Diet, where no one missed the fact that the Turkish war was bringing pressures upon France as well as on the Ottoman Empire. Victory in the east made the Germans less anxious to compromise, or indeed, even to negotiate in the west.

The emperor was neither willing to give up the proposed Hungarian campaign for 1687, which promised great conquests, nor would he convert the truce into a peace. This stern imperial stance was most embarrassing for the men at Versailles. Louis' health was still in serious danger, so there was nothing to do but attempt to find a policy that would save face and still allow the French to back down from the ultimatum. They let it be known that a statement from Leopold assuring his respect for the truce would be satisfactory. Since this would cost him little, Leopold was willing to make such a statement. He sent a memorial to France assuring both the king and Europe that he would respect the truce of 1684 "even though a peace might be made with the Turks." "If this innocuous document," O'Connor remarks, "enabled the French to save face while retreating from an embarrassing diplomatic position, it did not veil the growing distrust and resentments that the Germans felt towards France in the wake of Louis' abortive peace efforts."[8]

During these years there were other complications in the Rhine-Moselle basins. In May 1685 Elector Karl von Simmern of the Palatine died without male heirs. In accordance with the Treaty of Westphalia, Philip William von Pfaltz-Neuburg followed him on the throne. While his predecessor had been well disposed toward France, the new elector, closely associated with the emperor both as a German Catholic and as his father-in-law, could not be expected to follow even a neutral policy toward France. The late elector's sister, Elizabeth-Charlotte, was the Duchess of Orléans and sister-in-law to Louis XIV. What were her rights to her brother's lands and property? No one knew. When she had been brought to France as a bride, the king merely wanted a friend on the throne at Heidelberg; no serious questions were raised about her dowry and there had been no thought given to a possible inheritance. Louis now sent one of his diplomats to discuss the matter with a learned German jurist at Frankfort. German law, it seemed, was complex; there could be no question about the alodial lands of the Rhine Palatinate: they were governed by the Salic law just as in France, but the elector also held other properties acquired since the Golden Bull of 1356. These incuded the Duchy of Simmern and several cities, among which Oppenheim and Kaiserslautern could be inherited by a woman, and finally, there was the elector's private property: tapestries, pictures, furniture, clothes, beer, wine, and foodstuffs that were not under the Salic law. Louis sent Abbé Jean Morel to Heidelberg to discuss Elizabeth-Charlotte's rights with the new elector. The outspoken abbé soon had everyone against him. It was now evident that neither the new elector nor the King of France had any intention of surrendering anything that either believed to be properly his. Louis understood that it would be very useful to have his brother installed at Simmern or Kaiserslautern as a German prince with the right to a voice at the Diet at Ratisbon, and Philippe, probably spurred on by Louvois, began to bluster about his future actions unless his wife's "rights" were respected. A bluster, however, did not help, for legal problems in Germany were tricky. Soon Louis realized that if he insisted upon his sister-in-law's rights the case could go before an imperial tribunal or the emperor's council. This, of course, would never do, so he announced that he would allow the pope to arbitrate the question. Elector Philip-William was most guarded in his replies. There were, he pointed out, feudal claims involving the emperor as overlord, and since the properties could revert to the emperor or to one of his relatives, it would be impossible to settle any questions without consulting the emperor. Finally, however, in January 1686, after the Germans realized that the pope would probably rule for them, they agreed to allow the pope to arbitrate.[9]

While this question was on the fire, another was developing down the river at Bonn. The Electoral Archbishop Max Henry was growing old and infirm, and there arose the possibility of making Bishop Egon von Fürstenberg his coadjutor. The problem was a complex one. For generations the Bavarian Wittelsbachs had furnished the candidates for the electoral throne at Cologne and Max Henry, very conscious of his family's rights, wanted to have a Wittelsbach prince follow him on the throne. At the moment there were, however, only two male princes of that line: Max Emanuel, Elector of Bavaria, who was soon to make a reputation for himself as the hero of Belgrade, and his teen-age brother Joseph Clement; but Joseph Clement was not yet a priest, nor was it at all certain that he wanted to be one. Furthermore, should Max Emanuel die or be killed before a son was born from his marriage with Leopold's daughter, Marie-Antonia, the young Joseph Clement would inherit the throne at Munich. It was well known that Bavarians were unwilling to see their rights passed over, and yet this situation created the possibility that another family might supply the candidate for the throne at Bonn. The Pfaltz-Neuburg family succeeded in placing a son, the Bishop of Breslau, in the cathedral chapter of Cologne, where he began to weave the political web that might make him Elector of Cologne.[10]

The French court had been quite content to have a Wittelsbach on the throne at Bonn as long as that family remained more or less Francophile. The dauphine was a Wittelsbach, and many years and a strong tradition had bound the courts of France and Bavaria together. But in 1685 Max Emanuel was moving away from this tradition; only the strongest French protest at Madrid had forced the Spanish to disavow Leopold's promise to place Max in power in the Spanish Netherlands; even so, the Bavarian elector married the emperor's daughter and accepted a command in the imperial armies in Hungary. Louis did not give up hope of recovering Bavarian friendship, but when Max signed the Treaty of Augsburg and joined the emperor's forces in Hungary with practically all his troops, Bavaria definitely slipped out of the French orbit.[11] But this was not the only reason for Louis' interest in the question of succession in the electorate of Cologne; the French also had a candidate for that throne.

When Mazarin had been in the Rhineland as an exile during the *Fronde,* he met two young German princes, the Egon von Fürstenbergs, whose intelligence and intricate understanding of German affairs caused him to recruit them to French service much as Richelieu had recruited him over twenty years earlier. These were years before there was a *mystique* of nationalism; the Egon von Fürstenbergs were noblemen, anxious to forward the interests of their family in any way possible, and Mazarin's suggestion that they serve France seemed most opportune. When Mazarin died, Louis in turn recruited them to his team, and for the next twenty-odd years they had much to do with French diplomacy in Germany. Their advice tended to urge soft-spoken negotiation rather than Louvois' brutal force, but they also knew how to make effective use of soldiers. During the Dutch War, William Egon von Fürstenberg was captured and jailed by the emperor; he was released by a special clause in the Treaty of Nymwegen.

Both William and his elder brother Franz were friends of Max Henry, and when the latter became Electoral Archbishop of Cologne, he summoned them to help him govern the electorate and the see of Cologne. Even before Mazarin knew him, Franz had been first minister and dean of the chapter of Cologne; later the two men served two masters, for Louis XIV also gladly gave them pensions and clerical positions. They, however, were really looking out for themselves and their families, and even though the emperor several times held out tempting offers they decided that their best interests were on the side of France. When Franz died in 1682, his brother William took his place at Cologne. In 1686, on the very day that Ofen fell to the imperial troops, Innocent XI, on the request of Louis XIV, elevated William Egon to the cardinalate, an honor that the archbishop Max Henry never achieved.

After 1685 William Egon, aided by French diplomacy and French money, began an intrigue to have himself named as Coadjutor Archbishop of Cologne, a position from which it would be easy to move onto the electoral throne in the event of Max Henry's death. This began a long process of intrigue and negotiation involving the Wittelsbachs at Munich, the Neuburgs at Heidelberg, the French court at Versailles, the imperial court at Vienna, and not least, the pope at Rome. William Egon had three trump cards: he had French money to give to his friends and well-wishers in the cathedral chapter that had to decide upon the question should there be a coadjutor; he had long managed the elector's affairs, so that he alone really understood them; and lastly, Elector Max Henry owed Louis XIV a very large sum of money that he had borrowed years before, and he feared for his reputation should he die before it was paid. Louis held out a bribe; he would forgive the debt as soon as his creature von Fürstenberg was named coadjutor archbishop. But there were strong forces opposed to that nomination; the imperial court did not want a French "creature" in control of an electoral vote; the Bavarian Wittelsbach "rights" seemed endangered enough to throw the weight of Bavaria against the nomination; and the papal court, where the nomination must be made, was almost at war with Louis. The crisis matured slowly. The cathedral chapter had to ask for a coadjutor before any candidate could be postulated at Rome, but since von Fürstenberg was so closely associated with the chapter, and so well informed about the inner political factions, early in January 1688 he was able to get himself unanimously elected as candidate for the post of coadjutor, but he could not have the office until his position would be confirmed by Rome. Innocent was reluctant to act. The problem was complex: the question of the rights of Madame, Louis' sister-in-law, to the inheritance of the Rhine Palatinate and this problem of the Cologne co-adjutorship came at the time when Innocent and Louis were at the verge of open war over the right of the *franchise*.

As we have noted, the *franchise* was the right assumed by the ambassadors to the papal court to grant asylum to anyone who applied for it in their compounds in Rome. Innocent was determined to suppress this practice, because police control of the city was impossible if criminals could so easily escape. All of the states except France agreed to his request, and when the Duke d'Estrées died in 1687, Innocent tried to force France to follow suit by announcing that he would not accept another French ambassador until Louis gave up this *franchise*. Louis' arrogant replies to the pope bear the marks of Louvois' pen, but Innocent would not be bullied for he knew that since he was right, God would help him and therefore that he would eventually win. Unfortunately the men at Versailles were equally adamant.

A new French ambassador, the Marquis de Lavardin, arrived in Rome supported by a hundred or more guards who were really soldiers; he took over the French embassy compounds and the surrounding streets. Innocent replied by forbidding any priests to say mass if de Lavardin was present; when a French priest publicly gave the ambassador communion, Innocent had no alternative to excommunication, for this was defiance of the papal authority in Rome itself. Since the ambassador was merely an agent, Innocent also evoked "the censure and the wrath of God" upon Louis and his ministers (November 18, 1687). This meant excommunication of the king and his advisers.

At Versailles the king's government anticipated some such action; before Louis had been informed of the excommunication, Croissy called in the papal nuncio to explain to him that the French king would take further reprisals if his Holiness should continue to prove intractable toward the new ambassador. The French king could always insist that the city of Avignon and the papal territory around it had been given to the papacy contrary to the laws of the kingdom, and therefore could be reannexed at any time. The recent annexation of Orange a few miles up the river from Avignon gave warning that the papal lands might suffer the same fate. At this point the papal brief excommunicating the king arrived at Versailles. How could it be presented to Louis? He refused to receive the nuncio unless the pope would receive de Lavardin. The impasse was broken in January 1688 when Doctor Amonio, a Roman cleric who practiced medicine, secured an audience with Louis to explain that the king and his leading ministers had been excommunicated for flaunting the pope's authority in Rome. Afterward the papal nuncio wrote:

> . . . the King listened attentively and with reflection to all that the doctor told him, and asked him to put down the major points in writing so that he might refresh his memory in the future. . . . He realized that Amonio had a mission to accomplish and held no ill-will toward him. . . . The King imposed the strictest silence upon him, making it clear that the life of Dr. Amonio depended upon it.[12]

Although he wanted it kept secret, Louis was less worried about this excommunication than Innocent thought he would be. The king explained to Dr. Amonio, "Cardinal Ranuzzi looks upon excommunications in the same way as they are looked upon in Rome, but we consider them otherwise." In the long years of the French monarchy's relations with Rome, it came to be understood that a king could not be eternally damned for political reasons.

The French answer to the papal action came in a speech made by the advocate-general of the Parlement of Paris, Monsieur Talon, condemning the excommunication of the French ambassador and calling for a council of the church. Innocent excommunicated Talon. It was war or schism—or both—depending upon the willingness of the king or the pope to push to that extreme.[13] Neither wished to go as far as an open break, but the situation was difficult for the French king; it was awkward to be deep in conflict with the pope at the very time that Innocent must pass upon both the question of the coadjutorship and the rights of Louis' sister-in-law to the property of the late electoral prince of the Palatinate.

In the meantime the situation at Cologne became more and more tense. Although Elector Max Henry was ill and no one expected him to recover, the emperor insisted that he did not need a coadjutor. Not even offers of military assistance for the Hungarian war could change Leopold's mind. The trial balloons sent up from Rome suggested that if Louis would become reasonable about the *franchise* and perhaps remove de Lavardin, then von Fürstenberg would be named coadjutor even in spite of the emperor's objections, but Louis called this suggestion "too unreasonable to demand attention." In the midst of the discussions, Max Henry died on June 3, 1688. Innocent remarked that he could not appoint a coadjutor to a "dead archbishop." The question of Cologne now was: Who will be the next electoral prince occupying the throne?

Max Henry's will left most of his personal effects to Joseph Clement, but did not stipulate anything about the succession. Louis was sure that von Fürstenberg could be elected if there was no outside pressure. The French announced, therefore, that 100,000 troops would enter Germany if any attempt was made to interfere with the election. Von Fürstenberg had control over the administration of the electorate; he was fortifying Bonn to prevent any invasion from north Germany; he had French forces nearby easily at his disposal. There seemed to be no reason why he could not secure the election to the archbishop's throne as easily as he had gotten the nomination as coadjutor. The summer of 1688 saw busy diplomatic action in Vienna, Munich, Heidelberg, Rome, and Versailles, while north German troops entered the free city of Cologne and more French troops moved into Alsace. The most important military action, however, was in the Danube basin where Max Emanuel, the brother of Joseph Clement, was about to besiege Belgrade. If the city should fall, territory that had been under Moslem rule since the fourteenth century would be recovered for Christendom. This was Innocent's greatest hope.

The election at Bonn came on July 19, 1688. Cardinal von Fürstenberg needed sixteen (two-thirds) of the twenty-four votes to win; Joseph Clement needed only thirteen (a majority). The Neuberg candidate withdrew, so that it was a contest between these two. The final vote: thirteen for the cardinal, nine for the Bavarian prince, and one vote each for two other candidates. Neither side won, so no one was postulated; the decision reverted to the pope.

Louis wrote a personal letter to Innocent XI to refute the charge that Cardinal von Fürstenberg was a French subject and therefore not eligible to become an elector of the empire: "So as to remove the incompatability which your Holiness may find in the Cardinal's holding the bishopric of Strasbourg, we propose that he be replaced by . . . the Bishop of Meaux [Bossuet], whom your Holiness has declared to be the scourge of heretics. . . ." He went on to assure the pope that there was danger of war if von Fürstenberg were not given the electoral throne. Emperor Leopold sent letters to the more important cardinals at Rome urging the nomination of Joseph Clement, and indicating that he would not tolerate an elector of the empire who was not satisfactory to him and especially not a creature of the French king. From the siege works around Belgrade, Max Emanuel's guns gave support to his brother. Innocent was very much in the middle of a thorny problem.

At this moment Louis dispatched to Rome the Marquis de Chamlay disguised as a Flemish gentleman; his mission was to attempt to influence Innocent's decision. Chamlay, one of Louvois' best friends and most important advisers, was a man of many parts: a diplomat, a military strategist, a superb officer in managing the movements of an army (*maréchal de logis*). He was instructed to make specific proposals: first, that von Fürstenberg should be confirmed as Archbishop of Cologne; second, that the pope send bulls in favor of the French bishops already nominated by Louis (there were some forty French bishops who had not been confirmed by the pope as a result of the conflict over the *régale*); third, that the pope accept the decision of the French Council of the Clergy (1682) concerning the *régale;* and fourth, that in exchange for all this, Louis would restrict the area of the French embassy quarter in Rome and limit the prerogatives of the *franchise*. Chamlay was also permitted to hint that Lavardin would be recalled after a decent interval. These proposals were first drawn up before the election when the French still believed that von Fürstenberg would win enough votes to be postulated. When the election misfired, Chamlay was allowed to add the proposal that Fürstenberg be made elector and Joseph Clement his coadjutor. Louvois also wrote to his friend urging him to "strongly exaggerate" the imminence of war between Louis and the emperor if the bulls were given to Joseph Clement. In another place Louvois told Chamlay to explain that "his Majesty would rather undertake a twenty-year war than to see the emperor absolute master of all the lands bordering his." Furthermore, Louvois asked how it could be possible to pass over a clergyman, sixty years of age, a cardinal who had served the church of Cologne for forty years, and accept a youngster of twenty who had not even been ordained? But the pope would not give Chamlay an audience; he could talk to Cardinal Cybo just as the nuncio talked to Croissy at Paris—nothing more. Even when Cardinal d'Estrées assured Innocent of his personal safety in case of an interview, the pope still adamantly refused.

Louis pretended to be shocked when his secret mission failed. Why did the pope refuse to see Chamlay? He stated publicly that the pope's action caused him much grief, indeed, that he "never would have believed that such a thing were possible." Of course he knew that "the Pope had an aversion for him, now it was clear that he was his mortal enemy. . . ."[14] Louis would not listen to the nuncio's protests that in France no secret agent could hope to see the king. Obviously Louvois was not the only unreasonable character at Versailles.

The pope gave the problem created by the election to an advisory committee, but there probably was never any real question about the decision. Joseph Clement was the emperor's choice; as the brother of Max Emanuel who was besieging Belgrade, and as a Wittelsbach prince asking for a see that traditionally belonged to his family, he obviously had all the advantages on his side. On August 26 the committee advised the pope to confirm Joseph Clement as Archbishop of Cologne.

As the summer wore on, Louis and his advisers at Versailles became painfully aware of the imminence of a severe diplomatic defeat in the question of Cologne. But this was only a small part of the problem on the council table when Louis met with Croissy and Louvois to decide his course of action. Much more dangerous was the situation on the Danube. Every letter from Constantinople told that the Turkish war effort was about to fold up; clearly when Belgrade should fall, and fall it must, the Turks would have no alternative to peace with Leopold, and peace on Leopold's terms. This would release the victorious German armies for adventures in central Europe. Although Leopold had given out the assurance that he would be loyal to the terms of the Truce of Ratisbon, no one around the table at Versailles had great illusions about the emperor's intentions. Leopold and the German princes, who for the first time in several generations were rallying to the imperial standard, were obviously anti-French, and would seize the first opportunity to retake the lands that they had lost to France. There were one or two other unknowns. William of Orange, a sworn enemy of Louis XIV, regarded himself as appointed by God to right the wrongs that Louis had committed against the "true religion" and against Europe, not to say anything about his principality of Orange that Louis had annexed. William was building an army and a navy made up in part of the refugees from Louis' dragonnades. Indeed, the army was commanded by Marshal von Schomberg who had drifted into the service of Louis' enemy. Was William directing this effort against France, or were these preparations being made for an attack on England? This was a very important and nearly unanswerable question.

Throughout Louis' reign England had been a problem. Charles II had accepted his money, but had not always been able to deliver the "goods" for which he had been paid; and at least twice during Charles's reign, England had lined up with the Dutch to force Louis to make peace. Charles had failed utterly to secure better treatment for Catholics in England and he had not excluded Huguenot refugees; he had been too good a politician not to realize that in England there was a very strong Francophobe sentiment and great fear of Roman Catholicism. He wanted to die in his bed and in England, so he hid his views and confused his policies to accommodate to the ideas of his subjects. In 1685 Charles's brother James II mounted the throne. Since he was a pious Catholic, the Test Act had prevented him from holding the office of Lord High Admiral, but it did not prevent his becoming king. His first Parliament generously gave him money for an army to suppress a rebellion led by the late king's bastard son, the Duke of Monmouth, but James was not a politician capable of taking advantage of this initial popularity. He soon began a forthright campaign to restore Roman Catholic worship in his kingdom and to put Roman Catholics and dissenters in high office by circumventing the Test Act through acts of indulgence. When a number of bishops refused to proclaim his edicts, he brought them to trial for seditious libel. These were God-fearing pious men who, as good Tories, believed in the divine right of kings; their trial seemed an act of tyrannical outrage. They were acquitted. The army, too, created problems, for James did not disband it after Monmouth's defeat, but rather appointed Catholic officers and recruited Catholic Irishmen into the ranks. Parliament objected, but could do nothing about it. A definite crisis arrived when James's young wife, Mary of Modena, gave birth to a son on June 10, 1688, just twenty days before the bishops were acquitted. This baby who appeared as a miracle to the Catholics, and to the Protestants as a fraud introduced into the queen's bed in a warming pan, raised the specter of a continuance of the Catholic monarchy in England and royal pressure for the eventual election of a Catholic Parliament that would legalize all of James's acts. As long as James's daughters, Princess Mary, the wife of William of Orange, and Princess Anne, the wife of a prince of Denmark, were his heirs, the Protestant succession was secure, but not so after the birth of James Edward.

The French ambassador in London had long been reporting this situation; he knew that a group of Whig politicians had been in contact with William of Orange, and that the army in the Netherlands was probably being prepared for an invasion of England. But James's attitude prevented Louis from taking any action, for while Louis regarded James II as his best ally, the feeling obviously was not completely reciprocal. James had not joined the League of Augsburg, but he also would not consider associating his navy with that of France to check the Dutch in the Baltic, and indeed when Louis did invade Germany in September 1688, James protested that this action was contrary to the Treaty of Nymwegen, and offered to join the Spanish and the Dutch to force him to retire; this just when William was preparing to invade England! Louis could not know exactly what William of Orange was going to do, but he also could not act to protect England from William without risking a ridiculous situation between himself and James. It was all very confusing; at Versailles, men remembered that a generation before had seen a long civil war in England, and reasoned that if William should invade the island kingdom, perhaps another long civil war would take both England and the United Netherlands out of the picture long enough for Louis to settle the eastern frontiers of his kingdom to the satisfaction of his clamoring soldiers and administrators.

Indeed, their clamors now came to dominate French policy. In 1682–83 visions of a universal empire with a Bourbon prince crowned at Madrid, Paris, and Frankfort had given substance to French policy. If it had turned out that France had become the defense of Christendom against the Turks, this dream might have come to fruition. But the victory of Christian arms at Vienna and the subsequent victories that pushed the Turks down the Danube and out of Hungary changed all that. It was Leopold rather than Louis, who became the dominant figure in the drama. His son Joseph was first crowned King of Hungary with a new constitution that made the crown hereditary in the Hapsburg family, and then elected and crowned King of the Romans, that is, successor to the emperor, at Frankfort. The Bourbon dynastic policy in Germany thus had failed. Louis recognized failure when he agreed to the ambiguous Truce of Ratisbon. Obviously French policy even in 1684 had been based upon states' interest rather than dynastic ambitions. By the Truce of Ratisbon the frontier desired by soldiers and bureaucrats, the frontier that was both defensible and rational, became the tentative frontier between the kingdom of France and its neighbors to the north and east. After the truce was signed, fortifications from Luxembourg to the Rhine and thence down to Switzerland sprouted out of the earth to consolidate these gains. The only trouble was that this frontier was not fixed by a definitive treaty of peace.

Thus after the conquest of Ofen, Louis tried to force Leopold to agree to such a treaty, but he had to be satisfied with the emperor's declaration of 1687, asserting that he did not plan to disturb the twenty-year truce "even though the Turks might make peace." In the summer of 1688, Max Emanuel was hammering at the gates of Belgrade. The French king needed a new policy, and it had to be a policy that would somehow change the Truce of Ratisbon into a treaty clearly fixing the frontiers. The line of the Truce of Ratisbon might not be enough, for if Leopold emerged from the Turkish war in firm control of both Hungary and Transylvania, the whole balance of power would shift drastically in his favor. In this case the French king should have some compensations to match his Hapsburg rival's gains. It would be better if somehow the Turks could be persuaded not to make peace. This could hardly be expected without French entry into the war.

What kind of a war could France support? The Dutch War of the preceding decade had been a great drain upon the resources of the kingdom; so great that Colbert had seen most of his fiscal reforms come to naught as he was forced to seek "extraordinary measures" to meet expenses. In the years after Nymwegen, the army, the building of fortifications, and the enormous funds needed for constructions at Versailles had continued the drain upon the treasury. Even before Colbert's death in 1683, there were many fiscal problems; after he departed from the scene, these problems became more acute. In other words, Louis in 1688 did not have great resources for a war; he could count upon his army and the supplies in his magazines for a short war, but a long one would be out of the question.

The army, however, was in excellent shape for a quick war. Louvois' genius for organization was extraordinary. In the period after Nymwegen he and his creatures had done much to improve the instruction of the officers, the organization of supplies and fortresses, the development of an engineer corps, even the rationalization of the weapons.[15] Louvois, however, was as arrogant as he was brutal, and his attitude rubbed off on many of the people who worked with him. As a result the men at Versailles underestimated their possible enemies. They were contemptuous of the German soldiers, a contempt that made them believe that only a short war would be needed to bring Germany to heel.[16]

The will-of-the-wisp that invited Louis to action was further strengthened by the memory of the campaign of 1683–84 that had so nicely ended with bo*h Spain and the empire accepting the French terms. This had been a *Blitz,* but it had been possible only because the emperor wanted to drive the Turks from Hungary. In 1688 the imperial armies were about to break the last defenses of the Ottoman Empire in the Danube basin. They might even drive on to the Sublime Porte itself. The situation was drastically different from what it had been five years before.[17]

Louvois' voice was not the only one heard in the king's councils. Croissy, for all his rough, irascible behavior, probably came down on the side of caution, but his nephew Colbert de Seignelay, who had built a fleet as strong as the combined Anglo-Dutch navies, who had conducted bombardments of cities as ruthless as any of those directed by Louvois, probably also came down on the side of war. Madame de Maintenon had not yet emerged as a force to be counted in high policy; through her and others Louis might have learned that there were many people who did not like the idea of war. However, the young men at the court, the soldiers who could win fame and fortune, and the bureaucrats who were emerging as important factors in the government probably largely favored the war. This time it was not dynastic interests that urged military action; the soldiers and bureaucrats were talking in terms of states' interests, defensible frontiers, and the balance of power in Europe. Their voices, added to those of the ambitious and warlike sons of the nobility, overrode the softer councils of cautious men. Furthermore, Rousset insists that "public opinion," for whatever that term might mean, overwhelmingly favored Louis' aggressive foreign policy, and approved of his entry into the war. This same public opinion changed when it became difficult either to win or to disengage from the conflict. This was to be more true in the war of the Spanish Succession, but after 1693 or 1694, it was also true of this first worldwide war.

It is not possible to fix the date when the decision was made to invade Germany nor to establish the protagonists who played out the drama, such was the secrecy in Louis' highest councils. Nonetheless, sometime toward the last of August, all the pieces began to come together. There had been no papal decision in the question of Madame's rights to a share of the Palatinate inheritance. It was becoming clear that the pope would not support von Fürstenberg's candidacy to the electorate of Cologne. Belgrade was about to fall, and without a diversion the Turks would surely make peace; there seemed less and less probability that the Truce of Ratisbon could be made into a peace; William of Orange's plans for invasion of England were far along, but was he going to England? Only a quick preventive war could clear the air and force a decision. There can be no doubt that Louis finally accepted this proposition, and yet the fact that it was not taken earlier in the summer when all these things were already well formed, suggests that the king did hesitate before committing himself and his kingdom to the adventurous policy demanded by the "war hawks."

Louis and his advisers obviously expected a short, limited war. One of his letters after another, as well as the proclamations in which he fairly shouted that he was the aggrieved party in the dispute, were all based on the assumption that there would be peace by January 1689. The only trouble was that no one believed him when he defined his war aims as reasonable and unpretentious, especially since the proclamations were interlarded with accusations and untruths that sounded like the sort of public proclamation that Europe had long since learned to distrust. Apparently Louis' objectives actually were limited, but hardly limited enough to satisfy his enemies if they believed that there was a chance to thwart him. He wanted to dismantle the imperial fortification at Philippsburg, which could become a "gate" into Alsace, since by spanning the river it would allow easy movement of the German armies westward over the Rhine. He wanted to secure Kaiserslautern, and several other cities formerly ruled by the Prince Palatine of the Rhine for his brother and sister-in-law as her share of the Palatinate inheritance. He wanted the confirmation of Cardinal von Fürstenberg as Elector of Cologne with Prince Joseph Clement as coadjutor. But

Europe—that is to say, the emperor and the German princes, the pope at Rome, and William of Orange in the Netherlands—was quite unwilling to grant these demands. Louis, Louvois, and a majority in the council believed that a show of force would succeed again as it had in 1683–84; they were convinced that a show of force would keep the Turks in the war and thus prevent the emperor from disengaging his forces in the Danube basin; in turn this would mean that there would be no possibility of the imperials opposing the French armies. Louis did not wish to become an ally of the Ottoman Empire, but he needed its support as a deterrent upon the German Hapsburgs. Thus the crumbling Turkish armies were undoubtedly a major consideration in the decision to go to war.[18]

The die was cast, and the drama began to unfold with the air of inevitability that so often marks such things. The French armies and their supplies began to concentrate in Alsace, and 6,000 French troops entered the electorate of Cologne at Bonn on September 10 only to be countered by an invasion of Brandenburger troops entering the free city of Cologne to strengthen the garrison. On September 15 at Rome, Cardinal d'Estrées read a long list of accusations blaming the pope for everything that had gone wrong, and on the same day French troops entered Avignon. On September 17 news of the fall of Belgrade reached Rome; fireworks, and *Te Deums* accompanied the confirmation of Joseph Clement as Elector of Cologne. On September 24, Louis published his famous manifesto explaining why he had recourse to arms, but promising to restore Philippsburg and Freiburg, minus their fortifications, if the empire would transform the Truce of Ratisbon into a definitive treaty of peace.[19] He proposed to occupy the territories that he believed belonged to his sister-in-law until that question was finally settled, and he demanded that Cardinal von Fürstenberg be named Elector of Cologne with Joseph Clement as coadjutor. At the end of the proclamation, Louis attached an ultimatum giving the German princes and the emperor three months to accept his demands. This phase of the war was to last nine years.

Better than most of the historians who have written about the French invasion of the Rhineland in 1688, Louis and his advisers understood that this action was an integral part of the problem of the balance of power that was becoming more and more acute with each new imperial victory over the Ottoman Empire. The French action was to have results beyond the imagination of the men at Versailles. The *Blitz* broke down, but more important than this failure was the fact that the attempted *Blitz* allowed William of Orange to transport his army to England where he and the Whig revolutionaries were to start that kingdom on its path to military and fiscal greatness. It was a fateful decision that was taken at Versailles those last days of September 1688, a decision that reverberated throughout the western world and transformed a war that had been localized in the Danube basin into the first European war that was fought in all parts of the world—really the First World War.

27

THE FIRST WORLD WAR: LOUVOIS

"YOU COMMAND MY ARMY. I am giving you the chance to prove your merits; go show them to all Europe so that when I die no one will notice that the king is dead."[1] With these words Louis sent his son to besiege Philippsburg. His father's illness had given the dauphin the chance to play out the ceremonial role of king in a procession of the holy spirit; now it gave him the opportunity to command a royal army. When the court learned that the dauphin went in the place of the king, many believed that Louis' illness would soon place that young man on his father's throne. For the moment, however, he was only to command an army. Under his orders were the Marshal-Duke de Duras, Turenne's nephew, and a brilliant cast of lieutenant generals including Boufflers, Catinat, and Montclair, and perhaps more important than all the others, Vauban and his engineers. The dauphin did not need to know much about war with these men "commanding under his orders."

This war was to be a *Blitz*. Neither the treasury nor the army was ready for a long war, but, as we have seen, Louis hoped that French intervention in the Rhineland would keep the Turks from making peace; it would also allow William to embark for England and thereby open a civil war, which Louis believed would last a long time and effectively tie up both England and the Netherlands. Civil war in England and the Holy War in Hungary would leave the German princes at the mercy of France. They would have no alternative; they would be obliged to accommodate themselves to French demands, to transform the Truce of Ratisbon into a cold peace and to recognize the French ambitions at Cologne and in the Palatinate. The intervention came none too soon. Belgrade fell on September 6, and only the invasion of the Rhineland prevented the war in the east from grinding to an end.[2]

As soon as the decision was finally made, the war ministry set its plans into motion. Everything was done quietly and secretly so as not to alarm and alert the victims. Wheat from as far away as Chartres; munitions and materials of war from the magazines in Alsace, the bishoprics of Metz and Verdun and Franche-Comté; soldiers and officers from all over the kingdom moved with as little disturbance as possible. Some of the officers did not even know where they were going until the enterprise was well under way, and the Germans were quite unaware of the dangerous threat that was hanging over their heads until the blow fell upon them.

The plan of attack was well conceived. The main army moved against Philippsburg, which was a natural target since it controlled the middle Rhine, and its capture would make Alsace secure against an attack from the north. While the main army was committed at Philippsburg, strong detachments fanned out to overrun fortifications in the Palatinate on both sides of the Rhine and to invade the lands far south of the Neckar and the Danube. These detachments had as their primary mission the imposition of contributions upon the German people from Baden to Hesse, thereby making them pay for a good part of the campaign, and forcing their lands to furnish food and fodder for the French armies. Louvois assured the king that this policy would encourage the German princes to be accommodating, and at the same time it would deprive the empire of the resources necessary for any serious resistance to the French invasion.[3] These raids did not achieve the objectives that Louvois claimed for them, but they did succeed in forcing the Germans to contribute both to the personal fortunes of the officers involved and to the coffers of the French army. The Germans, however, were aroused and angered rather than made compliant.

Philippsburg itself presented a thorny problem for besiegers. The fortification had been first constructed in the latter days of the Thirty Years' War to assure French possession of Alsace; with works on both sides of the river, it easily controlled the flow of traffic on the Rhine. The imperials had captured the fortification at the end of the Dutch War and even though they had done little to improve its works, the swamps more than its walls made it a formidable position. On the day that the French army arrived, the Governor of Philippsburg was so taken by surprise that he returned from a hunt to find the French army settling down before his fortress, and had to sneak into his own fortification by a trail through the swamp. But von Stahrenberg was a skillful artillery officer and a stubborn commander; his defenses, aided by torrential rains that turned the fields into a sea of mud, made the capture of Philippsburg in 1688 a major undertaking.

Louis, however, had not left the assault to chance. Duras' orders were precise: "M. de Vauban will be in Alsace on the 26th or 27th of this month [September]. His Majesty expects you to use his advice about the opening of the trenches and the details of the attack. Since you know his experience and capacity, *it is his Majesty's intention that he should not be contradicted* [author's italics]." No one up to this time had ever considered giving a mere engineer a high military commission, and Louis knew well that he had to be precise in his directions if Vauban's orders were to be carried out when a marshal of France was in overall command. During the Dutch War, Louis himself attended the more important sieges. If we are to credit a letter that he wrote years later to his grandson, his presence was necessary to see that Vauban "was not contradicted." He could not be sure that the dauphin would have the courage to confront a marshal of France with similar orders. Nor did the king leave it at that. He demanded letters from his son and Marshal Duras, from Boufflers, Catinat, and Montclair, and from Vauban, so that he and Louvois could keep informed about the progress of the siege. Failure to write brought a rebuke. "I am scandalized," Louvois wrote to Catinat, "at not receiving letters from you . . . His Majesty has much faith in your accounts and demands to know what you have written." If the king could not command in person, he wanted to follow the progress of the siege as closely as possible.[4]

The dauphin's part in the siege was not significant, but Louis showed great interest in his son's activity. "His Majesty is overjoyed," writes Louvois, "to learn how the Dauphin has conducted himself . . . and to see that the courtiers also receive letters that praise his goodness . . . and that everyone believes in his valor. . . ." "His Majesty reads his [the dauphin's] letters and admires the clarity and strength of his orders. . . ."[5] Madame de Maintenon also followed the young man's career; one of her letters reflects her personality as well as her attitude toward the heir to the throne: ". . . continue to act as you have begun and you will find everyone disposed to favor you on your return, and you will see what I have so often had the honor to tell you: your birth will bring you reverences, but your merits alone will attract esteem. . . ." There were a number of volunteers with the army, including princes of the blood and the Duke of Maine; letters from these young men seem to have not survived to tell their side of the story; nor do we have Louis' letters to them.

The rains made the siege longer and more difficult than Louis and Louvois had expected. As October wore on, a note of impatience appears in their correspondence, but they did not want their attitudes to cause any rash action. They were especially concerned about Vauban. In one letter after another they ordered him not to expose himself to any danger even if the siege were prolonged. Vauban had become the most important officer in the king's service. With him in command everyone knew that the fortress eventually had to fall; it surrendered on October 30 with the garrison being allowed to march off with full honors of war. The crusty old Duke de Montausier, the dauphin's governor, summed up the siege in a letter to that prince: "Monseigneur, I shall not compliment you on the taking of Philipps-bourg; you had a good army, bombs, and cannon, and Vauban. I shall not compliment you because you are brave, that is an hereditary virtue . . . but I rejoice with you that you have been liberal, generous, humane, and recognized the services of those who did well. . . ."[6] The king looked higher; in a letter to Louvois' brother, the Archbishop of Reims, he wrote, "I recognize that so fortunate a success in an advanced season and against a place so perfectly fortified, is visible evidence of the assistance of God, who has wished to preserve my son from the perils to which he was exposed. . . ."[7] According to Madame de Sévigné the news of the capture arrived on All Saint's Day during a sermon by Father Gaillard; the king, after a sign from Louvois, stood up and announced the fortunate news, and the good priest reorganized his sermon to fit the new situation.

The king's desire to establish his armies in winter quarters in the Palatinate and the lands below the Neckar made the early capture of Philippsburg important. Most of the cities had surrendered without a shot: Kaiserslautern, Heidelberg, Pfortzen, Heilbron, and many others simply opened their gates when the French army appeared. But Mannheim, Co-blenz, and one or two others refused to surrender without a siege. Mann-heim was the second target for the dauphin's army. The immediate center of interest, however, was farther down the river where Louvois, in spite of Vauban's objection that it would uselessly expend ammunition, ordered Boufflers to bombard Coblenz. The king, he wrote, wished to punish the Elector of Trier for refusing to surrender that city, which would allow the French to hold off any counterattack by the northern German princes. On November 7, Louvois wrote to his commander, "The King sees with pain that you have not started the bombardment of Coblenz . . ."; and a few days later, after hearing that Boufflers had reduced the city to ashes, "The King sees with pleasure that after having well burned Coblenz and having done all the damage possible to the palace of the Elector, you are marching on Mainz."[8] These letters are interesting since they seem to give both an indication about Louis' attitude toward the demolitions and burnings and evidence of the decay of French diplomacy.

Actually the vigorous defense of Philippsburg boded ill for the progress of the war. Louis' hope that the German princes would "accommodate

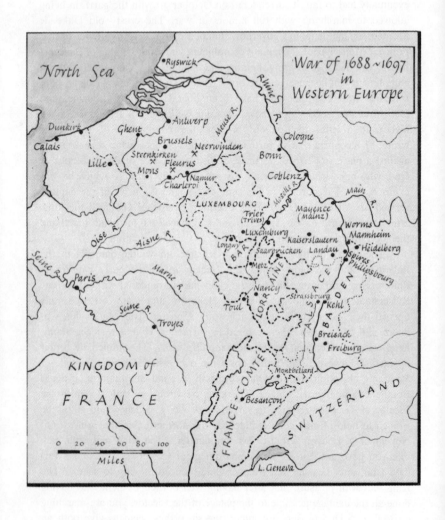

themselves" to his demands began to fade; indeed, by the first of November it was painfully evident that they were not going to pay attention to the French ultimatum demanding submission by January 1, 1689. On the contrary, the Brandenburg, Hanovarian, and Hessian troops were assembling on the lower Rhine; the Bavarians and Imperials were coming from Hungary. The war in Germany was obviously not going to end quickly. Moreover the situation in England did not turn out as expected. William's army landed on the English coast, but instead of encountering a stubborn resistance, they were received with open arms. Even Lord Churchill (Marlborough), who had been "loaded with honors and grants by the King" (*Gazette*), deserted James II and joined the invaders. James's queen and his son were soon exiles in France, and James himself followed them shortly thereafter. There would be no prolonged English civil war; indeed, William of Orange was soon to be in control of both England and the Netherlands with greatly increased prestige and power that permitted him to bring England into the war on the side of the coalition.

What could Louis do now? Somehow a peace had to be concluded or the kingdom of France might find itself in serious trouble. But how could the Germans be forced to come to terms, that is, to the terms that Louis had outlined in his ultimatum? They seemed more interested in waging war. Ominous decisions were in the making to force the German princes to accommodate themselves to Louis' terms. One of the first indications of the trend came November 2, 1688, when Louvois learned that Chamlay was discussing the fate of the Rhineland cities with a representative of the Elector of the Palatinate. "I do not know what has happened to your good sense," Louvois wrote to him, ". . . His Majesty wishes to be master of the fortifications [in the Palatinate] *to do with them as he pleases*."[9] The action that "pleased the king" proved to be fateful for the next year, for the next decade, perhaps for the next two and a half centuries.

The major decision was of course the destruction of the Palatinate; this was the most fateful of all the "atrocities" committed during the reign of Louis XIV. In the seventeenth century when a city expected to be besieged, the first act of the defenders was to demolish all buildings beyond the walls so that defending guns could have a free field of fire. Louis' France had in a sense become a fortress. The line from Huningen via New Breisach, Strasbourg, Fort Louis, Landau, and Philippsburg was a "wall" for the kingdom with the Rhine forming a part of the barrier. From Landau it turned west through Sarrelouis, Luxembourg, Montmedy, and on to the fortifications and works on the Spanish-Netherlands frontier. Late in October or early November, as the prospects of peace faded away, the men at

Versailles decided that the lands and cities beyond these lines on the Rhine
and the Moselle should be ravaged so that they would not serve as a base
for the enemy to act against France; they even suggested the demolition of
a number of exposed French fortifications that might be used by the enemy
if they were lost.

Louis and Louvois accepted this idea. Since a French garrison in Bonn
supported by the troops of Cardinal von Fürstenburg still held the lower
Rhine, the line from Trier via Mont Royal to Mainz would be held to
maintain communications, but the cities between this line and the French
frontier were marked for destruction. The same fate was reserved for the
towns and fortifications to the south of the Neckar. By destroying all food
and fodder as well as all houses that could be used by enemy troops, this
territory would not be a base for an attack on France. Furthermore, by
sending strong French detachments on deep penetrations into Germany to
collect "contributions," the German economy would be further debilitated.
Germany was not rich; if the Rhineland cities were demolished and her
peoples squeezed by the French army, the Germans would not be able to
fight effectively even if they should decide to make war rather than peace.
At that moment it looked like a good idea, and Louis agreed to it.

Louvois and his staff marked a list of cities and towns and châteaus for
demolition; Mannheim would be the key, but Tübingen, Heilbron, Heidelberg, Worms, Bingen, and a number of other towns were also to be completely wrecked. Mannheim was to be demolished so that not a "stone
remained on a stone"; Louvois even suggested that the stones from Mannheim buildings might be shipped up the Rhine to provide building materials
for Philippsburg. The king apparently had a few qualms about Heidelberg,
for he sent Vauban to see what should be done; "His majesty wishes not to
destroy completely the palace of the Elector . . . ," wrote Louvois when
he asked Vauban for his advice. By December 20, Louvois had a map that
marked all the projected demolitions and burnings: cities, towns, villages,
châteaus. The king intervened to save several chapels, but not the houses of
man.[10]

It is one thing to order the demolition of cities and towns and quite
another to accomplish it. In the first place, effective demolition would require an army of workmen and much powder; fire alone would make the
town only temporarily unusable. But even more important, the French
army was commanded by noblemen who had their own ideas about their
obligations to people who had surrendered without fighting, and considerable feeling about the fate of people without shelter in a German winter.
Moreover, the German cavalry was already beginning to appear on the

upper Danube early in December; this had not been part of the plans in Versailles. As the imperial army began to appear in the lands south of the Neckar, Louvois realized that the destructions were not going according to plan. In October, before the plans for demolition were made, these lands had been marked for French winter quarters, but the unexpected arrival of imperial and Bavarian troops made that impossible; perhaps these troops also had something to do with the failure to carry out Louvois' demolition orders. On December 17 he wrote to Montclair to recall that the king's intentions were to have "Heilbrom, Tübingen, and Eslingen destroyed so that they could not serve as quarters for the enemy." On the twenty-first he wrote to La Grange, "His Majesty sees with pain that one has not taken the measures needed to carry out his orders . . . in abandoning the lands between the Neckar and Tübingen." Three days later: "I am surprised to learn by your letter of the 21st . . . that one has not started the demolition on the pretext that there are more than 200 people [in Offenburg]. . . . I beg you to know that I do not want to hear of such things and that I want to know that the demolitions are going on. . . ." He added, "I am surprised not to have letters from M. de Montclair telling me that he has abandoned Heilbrom, Tübingen, Eslingen, and other places . . . after having put them in a condition that I ordered. . . . It is the precise wish of his Majesty . . . [and] his Majesty is not accustomed to see that one argues with orders that he gives, when they are so precise. . . ." A few days later to Montclair: "His Majesty recommends that you lose no time in blowing up the walls of Eslingen and in the other destructions; the king sees with chagrin that they have not yet been done. . . ." And a few weeks later (27 January): "It is annoying that you left Pfortzen in a condition that the enemies can establish a base there. The failure to execute orders that his majesty gave you on this point has not been agreeable to him. . . ."[11]

By January the letters from Versailles were more insistent: "You are informed that the intentions of his Majesty are to destroy the city and citadel of Mannheim and all its houses. . . . I do not doubt that you will execute this with all the diligence imaginable." Mannheim was completely destroyed and on the king's order its inhabitants were shot if they tried to return to the rubble of their city, but in several other cases the king's intentions were either not carried out at all or only partially so. Montclair proved to be "unable" to demolish all the installations below the Neckar, and his lieutenant Tessé allowed the inhabitants of Heidelberg to put out the fires that he started, but he did demolish the elector's beautiful palace on the hill above the river. D'Huxelles "failed" to destroy the castles in the neighborhood of Worms, and many other demolitions were only half done.

Louvois stormed, but the soldiers on the spot did not have the time, nor the men, nor the will necessary for complete destruction.[12] They did accomplish enough, however, to arouse the Germans against the French as they had never been stirred before.

Louvois and the king were not satisfied. "His Majesty is angry," wrote Louvois when he ordered Montclair to return to Heidelberg and complete the destruction that Tessé had failed to accomplish; "Everything must be burned." On the same day he wrote to d'Huxelles, "Let me tell you . . . that there is nothing worse than half executing orders that the King has given you for the destruction of those places to prevent the enemy from using them . . ."; and to de la Grange, "It is to be desired that the King's orders shall be better executed than they were at Heidelberg . . . ," with the added threat that "the King would remember" men who failed to obey.[13]

The tragic drama was not yet finished. Chamlay's vigorous mind continued to roam the problem of defending the kingdom of France, and as he saw the clouds gathering, he decided that Duke Charles of Lorraine would surely establish bases at Spier and Worms when he reached the Rhineland. He did not wish to be responsible for proposing the destruction of these ancient and famous cities, so he put the proposal in a letter that he wrote for the signature of the Marshal-Duke de Duras. The marshal had long since been accustomed to signing letters written by Chamlay; he signed this one without question. At first even Louvois had some hesitation, but finally he and the king accepted the proposal and ordered the destruction of Spier, Worms, and Oppenheim. When the marshal-duke came to realize what was really involved, he protested to the king, arguing that this act of violence would redound adversely to Louis' reputation. But by this time the German armies were moving into place, menacing the position of the French and Cardinal von Fürstenburg in Bonn. Undoubtedly Chamlay was right; the Duke of Lorraine would use Spier and Worms as a base. On May 31, 1689, Oppenheim and Worms were fired; Spier went up in flames the next day.[14]

The demolitions and incendiaries not only aroused the Germans, but also worked havoc with discipline in the French army. Just as in 1673, it proved to be impossible to ask troops to burn and then try to prevent their looting, and an army encumbered with loot loses its force. Cardinal von Fürstenberg's troops of German origin deserted to the enemy; the French commander in Bonn was killed; after Bonn, Mainz fell to the Germans leaving the French line of the Moselle in danger. The demolitions demanded more demolitions as the growing German power forced retreat.

The ancient city of Trier was in danger. Saint-Simon tells a story about Louvois' casually saying to the king that he had ordered the destruction of Trier; of Louis' violent reaction; of his threatening Louvois with firetongs; of Madame de Maintenon's intervention to prevent Louis from injuring the war minister. The story, like so much from the pen of Saint-Simon, is completely false. Chamlay did remark that it was a pity that Trier was located where it was, but even he could not suggest the destruction of that city with its churches, electoral palaces, Roman buildings, and ruins from the first century. Nor would it have been wise to ruin the city, for Trier was necessary as a base as long as the French held Mont Royal farther down the Moselle. What Louvois did do was to *threaten* the citizens of Trier with destruction *if* the German armies came too near. He did this in hopes that they would use whatever influence they might have had to keep the Germans at a distance.

As the Germans looked out over the blackened villages, ruined châteaus, demolished towns and cities, they "knew" that the dragonnades had been applied to Germany.[15] Everything the Huguenot refugees had said about Louis XIV must be true. A widely read pamphlet screamed "the French are cannibals" and "their king is a tyrant." Germany had never been so aroused. The Elector of Bavaria, whose sister was the dauphine in France, was as angry as the emperor and the men who had signed the Treaty of Augsburg. This may have been the time when that fateful movement, German nationalism, was born. Was Louis responsible? There is not a shred of evidence that the king ever objected to his minister's orders for the incendiaries and demolitions, and there is much evidence that he was fully aware of what was being done. The few times that he intervened were to save a chapel rather than a town or a château.[16] If such useless destruction really is a "war crime," then Louis must share the responsibility; if this particular episode of destruction really is responsible for the rise of German resistance in 1689 and for German nationalism in the years that followed, then this burden of responsibility is great indeed.

Some French historians allege that the Germans first committed this sort of atrocity when the imperial army invaded France back in 1636–37 and excuse the burning of the Palatinate in this way. But this leaves it open for the Germans to justify their doctrine of "frightfulness" because of French behavior. Americans, too, have fallen back on these burnings to justify Sherman in Georgia and perhaps the atomic bombs over Japan. Like those of Louis XIV, these measures were taken to force the enemy to "accommodate" himself to demands for peace. The justifications will always seem a little hollow to the people who saw their relatives murdered, their lands blackened, and their cities destroyed.

German unwillingness to agree to a peace was only part of Louis' problem in 1689. The situation in England went from bad to worse; James was driven from the kingdom, and his attempted return via Ireland was a complete fiasco. James had been a good Lord of the Admiralty, but he was a poor politician. He did not know how to organize Irish loyalty or how to use French assistance. His invasion of Ireland only resulted in a disaster for him and his followers, and in the enthusiastic intervention of England in the war against France. The English were henceforth to call this struggle the War of the English Succession, and the new government of England that emerged from the "Glorious Revolution" knew how to mobilize the wealth and power of the kingdom to fight that war.[17]

In central Europe too, men organized for war. The so-called League of Augsburg was only an agreement between princes with territory in Germany. In September 1689 the emperor and the United Netherlands signed a treaty of alliance at Vienna by which they undertook to force France to return to the frontiers of Westphalia and Nymwegen. The Dutch also agreed to support Leopold's claims to the Spanish inheritance. In March 1689, Marie-Louise of Orléans, Charles II's French wife, died in Spain under circumstances suggesting poison; six months later Marie-Anne von Neuburg, Leopold's sister-in-law, became the new Queen of Spain, and in June 1690 Spain joined the Treaty of Vienna. About the same time the Duke of Savoy, who greatly resented Louis' tutelage, also joined the alliance in the very face of a French army. William brought England into the war when James, supported by the French, invaded Ireland.

So by the summer of 1690 Louis was faced with a coalition that included all his neighbors, and except for a tenuous relationship with the Ottoman Empire, he did not have a single ally. His consolation: France did have a powerful army; the French fleet was the largest in the world; and while his enemies were united in their dislike of France, they were quite disunited in their arms and aspirations.

The king's attitude to the events of 1689-90 cannot be followed in letters, but the reorganization of his government would seem to indicate that Louvois lost some of his prestige and influence during this year. In rapid succession there came changes: Le Peletier, who had been associated with the Le Tellier faction, gave up the office of comptroller general of finance and was replaced by Pontchartrain (Phelypeaux); Seignelay, Colbert's son, who had been secretary of state for the navy and commerce, was made a minister and invited to join the council; Colbert de Croissy secured the *survivance* of his office as secretary for foreign affairs for his son the Marquis de Torcy (who later married a daughter of Pomponne). Thus the Le

Telliers seemed to lose to the Colberts and their allies. This did not diminish Louvois' authority in the ministry of war, but it did temper his influence in the councils of the king when men who would advise a less high-handed approach to politics had the king's ear. Henceforth France's king could be expected to speak a little more softly.

Indeed, France was clearly in trouble. The Dutch War, followed by the years of expensive construction at Versailles and Marly, the long list of pensions and gratifications, and the rapidly increasing cost of government, had left the treasury in a weakened condition. Louis knew in 1688 that there was not money for an extensive war, but once he had engaged in the conflict there was no easy way to disengage. Pontchartrain had to find financial "expedients," none of which could solve the real fiscal problem. One of these personally affected the king and many of the people of quality in his court. Seventeenth-century kings and noblemen had beautifully worked vessels and plateware of silver and gold for table service; these pieces were mentioned in every marriage contract between people of importance, and they became heirlooms in the families. The king ordered that his silver and gold plate be sent to the mint to be made into coins, and his court had to follow suit. Madame de Sévigné gives us a little insight into the shock and sorrow that this caused among the ladies of her acquaintance. Unhappily, much of the value of these pieces was in the wonderful artwork of the goldsmiths and silversmiths, and at the mint this was simply lost. The King of France sought many expedients for finding money; unfortunately for him, he was never able to find the treasure chest that the English king discovered after 1688 in the cooperation between Parliament, the treasury officials, and the money interests of London. In France the excise field was already heavily burdened, and any debts had to be the king's debts; Louis had no Parliament that could create debts for the people of France.

The year 1690 not only saw the completion of the coalition, but also several brilliant military actions; none of them, however, proved to be decisive. The first of these battles was fought in Flanders with the Marshal-Duke of Luxembourg in command of the king's armies. This choice probably also was indication of Louvois' loss of influence, for he and Luxembourg had been poor friends ever since the latter had been thrown in prison on a charge of poisoning at the time of the Voisin incident. Luxembourg's orders were to prevent Prince von Waldeck from invading France; he was given freedom to decide what should be done. After several weeks of maneuvering, the two armies confronted each other at Fleurus (July 1, 1690). Waldeck set out to defend himself by the classic confrontation of a fortified line of battle; Luxembourg decided upon a maneuver that allowed him to attack both of Waldeck's flanks. For a few hours the issue was in doubt, but the engagement ended in a complete French victory.[18] The king immediately sent off an account to the Sultan of Turkey by special boat; this victory might hearten the Turks and encourage them to fight.

The battle of Fleurus was followed by a complex exchange between Louis and Louvois that throws some light upon the relationship between the two men. Louis refused to allow Marshal d'Humières to take advantage of the battle by attacking the Spanish army opposite him, but he did agree (July 3) to a siege of either Charleroi or Namur by Luxembourg's army. Louvois tells us that he immediately started the preparations for a big siege. The very next night at the king's supper he presented Louis with a draft of the proposed orders. Louis, however, noted that since the Elector of Saxony had just joined the imperial army opposite the dauphin and Marshal de Lorge, the dauphin's army might be at a disadvantage. French strategy was based on the assumption that interior lines provided the means of confronting a coalition whose forces were greater than those at French disposal. By detaching parts of an army not threatened and sending it to the support of the one threatened, the French could meet the challenges of their superior foes. The coming of the Saxon army to the Rhine would require that part of Luxembourg's army should be detached and sent to the support of the dauphin. Louvois tells us that, over his objections, Louis insisted that this be done. The king wanted to be sure that nothing "disagreeable" happened to his son's command. Louvois had the task of announcing the news to Luxembourg. "His Majesty knows," he wrote, "that this order [detaching part of the army to the Rhine] will mortify you, but he expects you not to murmur since he thinks it to be for the good of his service."[19] Boufflers took the detachment to Germany, and the siege of Charleroi was put off to another year.

There are several interpretations of this event. Rousset thinks that the king lost his nerve just as he seems to have lost it the next year at Mons. It is possible, however, that Louvois himself was responsible for the decision; he could have orally presented the matter in a way to make the king reject the proposed siege to prevent Marshal Luxembourg from gaining too great influence. Louvois had had his troubles with "famous and prestigious soldiers" when Turenne and Condé were alive; he may not have wanted to see a man who had become something of an enemy in a similar position. This thesis seems even more credible when, after Louvois' death, we find Louis practically forcing Luxembourg to besiege Charleroi after the battle of Neerwinden. However, it could even be that there really are not unexplained motives for this action in 1690; he may merely have been fearful for the safety and reputation of the dauphin. He probably had read Chamlay's letters in which his son's "warlike" stance did not appear exactly warlike, and had lost hope for his military career. In any case Luxembourg's orders were summed up by Louvois on July 23: "His Majesty hopes that you will save his country and this ought to include the conservation of his army which is of great importance to him." A week later he added, "Being convinced that you have the same desire to attack the enemy that you had at the opening of this campaign, his majesty would have given you the order to seek out M. de Waldeck by all measures open to you, but in view of the state of things in Ireland, his Majesty repeats to you again . . . that you should fight M. de Waldeck and M. de Brandenburg only when you have a great advantage over them . . . his Majesty completely approves that you should await them in a strong position and profit from bad mistakes that they make."[20] Were these the words and ideas of the king or of the minister?

Another French victory followed on the heels of the battle of Fleurus when Admiral de Tourville, with orders "to seek out and fight" the Anglo-Dutch forces, fought the battle of Beachy-Head. Louis, who was not a naval enthusiast, exclaimed, "I now find myself master of the Channel after having defeated the English who prided themselves for several centuries on being its masters . . . even though they were supported by the Dutch." As usual Louis gave God credit: "Wishing to thank God for His protection and so that the divine favor will continue to be given to the justice of my arms, I am going to ask the bishops and archbishops of my realm to sing *Te Deums*."[21] But there was no follow-up of that victory; indeed the death of Seignelay, which made Pontchartrain secretary of state for naval and commercial affairs, even though he knew nothing about them, followed closely, and marked the beginning of the decline of the French navy. Within two years the mastery of the Channel was out of French hands.

There was another victory before the summer ended. Catinat defeated the Savoyard-Imperial forces at Staffarde on August 18. The victory would have been an annihilation of the enemy had it not been that the young Eugene of Savoy skillfully covered the retreat. This was the first time that Eugene battled with the soldiers of his erstwhile monarch; it was not to be the last. The victory, however, accomplished practically nothing, for Catinat did not have enough troops to follow it up with a siege, and he was soon obliged to withdraw his little army back to France for winter quarters.

Perhaps the most important result of the French victories of 1690 were the solid checks that they gave the forces of the anti-French coalition;

still, neither victories on land nor on sea had actually broken the front against France. Nor did the honeyed suggestions that France had only limited war aims and therefore would make a reasonable peace have any more effect on Louis' enemies. Early in 1691 William of Orange called a conference to strengthen the grand alliance and to make plans for the humbling of his enemy. At Versailles a similar council of war decided to make a dramatic stroke of French power while the enemies were assembled at The Hague, a stroke that might unhinge the coalition. Louvois made a tremendous effort to bring together an even larger army than had been assembled the year before. The plans prepared a double stroke: the siege of Mons in Flanders and of Nice in Italy. Furthermore, both of these sieges were planned to come very early in the season—long before the coalition could put an army in the field. Thus by the middle of March, William, surrounded by the electors and princes of Germany, by representatives of Spain, Sweden, Savoy, and the emperor, received word that the French were investing first Mons, and a week later, Nice. It was a dramatic coup, but it did not have the effect that the siege of Ghent had had back in 1678, for the coalition was still new and its members were determined to hold together. One or two of the lesser princes listened momentarily to French agents, but none of them was ready to bolt the alliance.

Louis himself commanded the armies at Mons. He went to war accompanied by members of his court, but the ladies stayed at Versailles. He was now fifty-four, he had suffered from serious illness, from bad teeth, from overweight, but in the spring of 1691 he was in better shape than he had been for several years. His physical condition however, was only part of his problem: with age Louis seems to have lost some of his nerve. The outcome of the siege was a foregone conclusion; Vauban directed the operations and there was no possibility that the allies could mount an army capable of interfering with the assault. Nonetheless Louis worried about an attack from a relieving army. There were rumors that the Prince of Orange was coming with a big force. A peasant said that he had seen the allied army at Hal. Vauban insisted that it was impossible and other witnesses denied the report, but Louis could not be calmed. He demanded that more troops be moved to Mons; in spite of Louvois' protests, the frontier fortification cavalry were set in motion and stationed in the vicinity of the siege where they consumed food and forage needed by the rest of the army. There apparently were other points of conflict between Louis and his war minister during the course of the siege. Saint-Simon's story about the placing of troops is probably untrue, but Dangeau was undoubtedly right when he reported that disagreements led to "a little anger"—his account is often an understatement. The war was already going badly and we can be sure that both Louis and his minister realized their peril, a realization that led to recriminations and arguments.

As might be expected, even though the power of the coalition was growing, Mons capitulated. Dramatically enough, April 8 saw the French in control of both Mons and Nice, and the chiefs of the coalition had only wry explanations to make. One section of the *feu d'artifice* in Paris that celebrated the victories portrayed the figure of Hercules on a mountain with the League of Augsburg buried under an avalanche; another showed the sun rising over a dead lion; another portrayed the assembly of enemy princes at a table with the caption "All their plans are pure fantasy."[22] Louis, however, returned to Versailles despondent and dissatisfied. Rousset insists that it was his chagrin over his own loss of nerve. This may be the case; in any event, he refused to allow any deputations to present compliments on the victory at Mons.[23]

Louis' pessimism was firmly grounded; the victories at Mons and Nice proved sterile, for the allies did not show any signs of accommodating themselves, and the French armies could not follow them up with other striking successes. Luxembourg devastated the encampment site of Hal, and Boufflers bombarded Liège, but these acts of violence had no political results. Chamlay argued that the victories should be followed by a field battle that would destroy the enemy army, perhaps invade the empire, and thereby force a conclusion to the war, but Louvois argued that if anyone were to attack, it should be the Prince of Orange. It is hard to know who made the decisions. Louvois wrote the letters and used the king's authority wherever he needed it: "it is his Majesty's intention . . ."; "His Majesty orders . . ."; "His Majesty wishes . . ."—these were the formulas. They probably confirmed the king's assent to his minister's policy; they may also have expressed the king's own wishes. Louvois decided that a bombardment of Brussels might force the issue, but Luxembourg and Vauban argued against it. Vauban pointed out that while none of the bombardments had ever won an inch of territory, all of them were expensive in powder and shot.

While the war in Flanders languished, in Italy one of Catinat's detachments undertook the siege of Coni, but the French commander lost his nerve when he heard that Eugene of Savoy was coming with relief; he raised the siege even though a strong French force was on its way to support him.[24] There is a charming story, probably another bit of *Treppenwitz,* that tells of Louvois announcing the news to the king with tears in his eyes. Louis rebuked him, "You are broken by this little thing. I can see that you are used to success. For my part, I have seen the Spanish troops in Paris: I am not crushed so easily." Too bad that this conversation probably never occurred; it should have, for it presaged the coming difficulties of the French armies.

On July 16, 1691, a Monday, Louvois was working with the king when he suddenly became ill. Louvois had not been really well for some time, but this was a sudden attack. He left the king's chambers, sought the aid of a physician, and was dead in a matter of hours. "He died," wrote his son, "more quickly than anyone could believe. A half hour earlier he complained of difficulties in his stomach. One bled him on the right side and he seemed somewhat comforted . . . ; he asked to be bled on the other side; his doctor refused because of his extreme weakness. . . . M. Fagon [the king's physician sent by Louis] entered the chamber; he began to tell him where he felt sick, but a moment later he said that he was fainting. He asked for me . . . and said that he was dying. After these last words, his head fell on his shoulders, this was the last moment of his life. . . ."[25] Barbézieux was sure that his father was poisoned, but the evidence does not support it. The supposed poisoner was freed as clearly innocent, and the autopsy indicated that Louvois died of a "pulmonary apoplexy," whatever that might have been. He was much overweight; he worked very, very hard; and his personal life was irregular: he probably died of "natural causes."

This death broke an association of almost thirty years. When Louis first worked with Louvois it was a young king working with his junior; as time went on, Louvois' skill, his vast knowledge of affairs, his dominating personality gradually changed this relationship to one in which the minister usually was in a position to convince or even to dominate the king. Louis recognized his minister's great ability as an organizer, an administrator, a tremendous worker; no one knew better than Louvois how to harness the intendants, engineers, clerks, and soldiers into a team effort. He provided Europe with its first picture of a war minister and chief of staff who could organize a bureau and a campaign. His father, Le Tellier, and before him Sublet de Noyers, had created the basic plan of the "modern army."[26] Louvois was the administrator who could direct the flow of food, fodder, and materials of war so that this weapon could be used; he also learned how to bring the captains who commanded the armies under the king's control. Louvois further exercised great influence over the formation of policies requiring the use of this army. Louis recognized the work of his minister, and believed that he himself used it for his own aims. The king had difficulty distinguishing between his own "intentions," and the "intentions" of the men who surrounded him and operated his government. In any case Louvois spent his life in Louis' service regulating the war office, the construction of palaces, direction of mails, and general administration of the kingdom. He had much to do with the foreign and domestic policies that made Louis XIV's reign often seem ugly, brutal, and mean.

Saint-Simon, who hated Louvois even more than he hated Louis, tells us that Louvois was on the verge of disgrace at the time of his death. He even asserts that if he had not died, Louvois would have been arrested. These stories apparently came from Chamillart who was closely associated with the king a few years later. It could well be that, after Louvois' death, Louis came to realize how much influence the war minister had exerted over him, and with that realization, had come to be angry with him; Dangeau's evidence also would suggest this.[27] However, it is almost inconceivable that Louis in 1691 had any idea of disgracing or arresting a war minister who knew how to manage the army. Louis understood that his kingdom was in trouble; the death of Louvois meant deeper trouble. His arrest would have been a catastrophe, for Louvois had many friends and creatures in the army and the war office who would have had to suffer a similar fate; it could have caused the loss of the war then and there. Saint-Simon also speaks of Louis' unconcern about his minister's death. But the fact that Louis as a public figure seemed to take little notice of the death of his collaborator of three decades meant only that the king knew he must act out his role as king. The state, he once said, would go on when he died; naturally the state must go on even though a great servant were dead. Louis well knew that he had suffered a loss, that his affairs were in danger; but he also knew that the expression "the king is dead, long live the king" was applicable to all who served the state. When the minister died, there was nothing to do but hail his successor.

28

THE FIRST WORLD WAR:
LOUIS

THE DEATH OF Louvois removed a powerful figure from the king's entourage, opening a great gap in his government; it also removed a screen that had prevented us from seeing the king. "Only with great displeasure can I tell you of the unexpected death of the Marquis de Louvois . . . ," Louis wrote to his commanders, and then went on to urge them to have great care that this event should not bring misfortune to the state. Well might he be concerned; for almost three decades Louvois had been a pillar of strength who had carried the weight of the war office on his shoulders. It would be difficult to replace him. The dead minister's son, the Marquis de Barbézieux, had the right to succeed his father, but he was only twenty-three years old, and while he had been his father's assistant, he obviously could not direct the marshals of France. Louis called de Chamlay[1] to him from Germany, and offered him the opportunity to purchase the office. Chamlay had been one of Louvois' most trusted advisers. A specialist on the problems of military geography, he knew Germany and the Netherlands better than anyone. He also was a bold strategist and an expert in the arts of war. But Chamlay would not deprive his dead friend's son of his inheritance; he suggested a compromise whereby Barbézieux would become secretary of state for war while he, Chamlay, would become a confidential military adviser to the king. This arrangement meant more responsibility for Louis than he had ever assumed: he now had to write the letters to the commanders in the field and oversee the work of the secretary in the ministry of war. Unhappily this latter task was as real as the former, for in these first years of office, Barbézieux, while competent enough, was not as responsible as his father had been. His behavior even led Louis to think of removing him from his post.[2]

Thus began a new routine that was to last for the next two decades. Louis assumed an active role in the direction of military policy; he sought the advice of "experts"—Chamlay, Vauban, and several younger men whose work in the engineer corps, as intendants, or as officers in the field brought them to the king's attention. With their advice Louis wrote to his commanders in the field at length on military policy, and finally evolved the military programs of action to be adopted. Madame de Maintenon was quite right when she said that the king had the full burden of the war on his shoulders.

Louvois' death also brought changes in the political direction of the state. Twelve days later Louis invited the Duke de Beauvillier and Pomponne to join his government in the capacity of ministers of state. The Duke de Beauvillier was a son-in-law of Colbert; he already had high offices in the king's household as well as being chief of the council of finance; he was the governor of the Duke of Burgundy, a friend of Madame de Maintenon, and a member of the pious little group at the court that wished to purify manners and morals. Pomponne, of course, was the minister who had been dismissed from the foreign ministry in 1679 because he talked "too softly" when defending the king's interests. He was the father-in-law of the Marquis de Torcy (also a Colbert) who had the right to succeed his father, Colbert de Croissy, as secretary of state for foreign affairs. Both Pomponne and Beauvillier could be counted upon to urge a less adventurous policy than Louvois had charted; both would advise the king to be moderate in his ambitions and programs.

One of the first acts of the post-Louvois government was an effort to come to terms with Spain, and thereby to break the coalition. Early in August 1691 Louis asked Cardinal Janson-Forbin to get in touch with Cardinal Salazar in Rome to see what could be done to bring peace between the Catholic powers. While the orders made much of the need for understanding between the Catholic monarchies, the undercurrent of the question of the Spanish succession was also much in evidence. Louis was "sure" that the Spanish king would not choose anyone to succeed him on the throne "except M. le Dauphin, who is the only legitimate heir." He did suggest, however, that if the problem of the unification of the two crowns under the dauphin caused concern, it would be possible to pick one of his younger sons to be king; indeed, "one could find means and conditions by which the Duke of Anjou or the Duke of Berry could be sent to Spain so that they could be brought up according to the maxims of that monarchy. . . ." Louis went on to urge the cardinal to explain that France would not try to govern Spain the way the Germans would if they succeeded in placing an archduke on the Spanish throne.[3] Nothing came of the suggestion. Cardinal Salazar was in close communication with the Austrian Cardinal Goetz, and the Spanish government, dominated by the German queen, was unready to make peace on terms that Louis might suggest, and even more unready to consider naming a Bourbon as successor to Charles II.

The failure of the Janson-Forbin *démarche* did not prevent Louis from trying to make contact with Madrid through the intermediary of Father de la Blandinière, whose order was domiciled both in France and in Spain. The good priest was instructed to try to appeal to religious unity as well as to sow seeds of doubt about the intentions of the allies in the Spanish Netherlands. Who could trust a man (William of Orange) "who had dethroned his own father-in-law and broken all laws human and divine?" Obviously the Dutch and the English meant no good for the Spanish in the Low Countries. The instructions went on to deal with all phases of the problem, but they never came to anything; it was too late to use the ideal of religious solidarity as an issue for ending the war. The war was not a religious war, and nothing that Louis could say would make it one.[4] Obviously the king had to depend upon his soldiers to win the war, and with Louvois dead, this meant that Louis himself would play a large part in the direction of the conflict.

Louis assumed the task similar to that of an American chief of staff or a German quartermaster general. That is to say, he assumed responsibility for overall direction of the war effort: the allocation of troops, the collection of intelligence, the movement of detachments to meet enemy threats, and with the cooperation of the war minister, the recruiting and training of troops, and the organization of supplies. It was a formidable task, but Louis now had thirty years of experience behind him—more than anyone in his entourage. He still had to rely upon the advice of experts and specialists, but he was no longer as dependent upon them as he had been earlier in the reign. He knew his officers and how to distinguish among them. For example, his letters to Marshal Luxembourg, heavy with the prestige of the battle of Fleurus, were very different from those to the Marshal de Lorge, whose measure both Chamlay and the king had taken and found somewhat lacking. To Luxembourg he wrote, "I have every confidence in you and agree to whatever you believe apropos to the good of my service . . ." ; "I take the affairs of my army to heart . . . worry about what might happen . . . [but] when I give you my thoughts I know that I teach you nothing"; "I am convinced that if I did not send you my thoughts you would do as well or perhaps even better, but *amour propre* makes one believe that what one says is useful. . . ." For all this apologetic tone, Louis did write enough to let Luxembourg know his intentions. But to Marshal de Lorge he was much more direct. "I am upset to see my army where it is . . .

if I did not give you positive orders it was because I do not like to decide these things that I do not see myself, but after having seen your letter . . . you should cross the Rhine to use up the supplies and forage of Germany and to save Alsace. . . ." Or again: "I am convinced that you always follow orders and the things that conform to the good of my service." Obviously Louis was convinced of no such thing, but wanted Lorge to understand what was expected of him. Noailles on the Spanish frontier, who was as near to being a personal friend as Louis allowed anyone to be, had much freedom of action: ". . . study carefully the state of affairs and send me accounts so that together we can plan the next campaign . . ."; or even playfully: ". . . if there is as much desertion from the enemy army as you say, it will soon be reduced to nothing since it was so small when the campaign began. . . ."[5]

In all his political and military correspondence Louis demanded full and exact information; he insisted upon being informed of the bad news as well as the good. When Luxembourg failed to tell him that several standards of the guards had been lost at the skirmish of Leuze, Louis came near to scolding the marshal for the omission. He also strongly insisted on discipline. Indeed, the transformation into disciplined soldiers of the marauding bands that fought the earlier wars must in part be credited to Louis XIV. For him the discipline was almost an end in itself.[6]

Louis' military ideas reflected the ideas of his advisers in the war ministry. Like any careful strategist, he insisted that his commanders must always take up positions that would give them an advantage in case they had to fight; indeed he usually demanded that they must not give battle without good "expectations for success." By 1691 the mid-century military ideas of a Turenne or a Condé had largely given way to conceptions of the lineal frontier developed by Vauban, Louvois, and others. In place of the fluid military situation in which armies maneuvered more or less at will from one fortified position to another, the commanders now had to think about the "lines" that largely coincided with the political frontiers. These lines were established by rivers, field fortifications, and entrenchments punctuated here and there by larger fortified positions or towns. The armies were deployed along these lines in such a way that they could use the fortified positions to prevent the enemy from invading the kingdom, levying contributions, and stealing food and fodder. At the same time they tried to establish advanced positions that would allow their own detachments to raid the enemy territory for contributions and supplies, thereby saving the king's frontier provinces from both friend and foe. This lineal conception of the frontier was in the process of fixing the boundaries of Europe on a new basis. Whereas it had been customary to think of the frontier as the frontier province "with its dependencies," now the notion of a military frontier created for the defense of the kingdom gave new form to the boundaries of states.[7]

In the discussions of frontier "lines" and "fortified positions" it may appear that Louis and his advisers had well stabilized and precisely formulated conceptions about the conduct of military operations, but in actual fact the king's direction was often a haphazard affair. While the officers in the field were in fact limited in their activity by the number of troops and the amount of supplies that the king and his minister of war put at their disposal, they were not often hampered by specific directions for the use of these troops. Louis may have recalled Turenne's complaints during the Dutch War when Louvois' orders became too precise, but it is more likely that he recognized, as he so often said, that he was not in a position to know the conditions in any one of the theaters of war as well as the officer in command. Thus, rather than detailed orders, Louis contented himself with a statement of his "intentions," and usually left the details of execution to his commanders. Only now and then did the men at Versailles try to impose ideas upon the men in the field, and even then the commander was usually given veto power.

One such occasion affords us considerable insight into the "hand to mouth" nature of policy-making during this period. In the late fall of 1691 Monsieur de Verger, an engineer stationed at Dunkirk, sent the king a memorandum in which he proposed a surprise attack on Ostende to prevent the English from using the port for the landing of troops. His proposal was buttressed with carefully worked out suggestions for the attack. The plan appealed to Louis and his advisers, so the king sent it on to Boufflers who was in command of a detachment strengthening the field fortifications of the lines on the northern frontier. Louis explained to Boufflers the nature of the project: the number of troops, the type of transportation, the methods for a surprise attack (even down to the use of many drums to confuse the defenders), and the precautions necessary to allow a safe withdrawal in case of failure. De Verger's proposed date for the assault, December 17, seemed satisfactory because the tides and the moon would combine to favor the attacking forces. Boufflers immediately raised objections, but Louis ordered him to consult with Vauban for "I am anxious that this affair should succeed, but I would not like to lose a great number of men. . . ." Boufflers and Vauban worked over the plans; Villars, then a coming man, also was called in to reconnoiter the ground. Their care impressed the king. Louis wrote, "One could not be more satisfied with the application and care that you have taken. . . ." But as so often when the commanders considered a project thrust on them from Versailles, their care and application resulted in the decision that the plan was not feasible. Louis was no doctrinaire. When he saw the reports and objections prepared by his soldiers, he quickly retreated from his earlier position. He wrote to Boufflers, "I am convinced that you have as much desire as I have to do something advantageous to the state and glorious for yourself . . . that is why I praise above all your wisdom. I take great pleasure in giving command of my armies to men enough in control of themselves to prefer the good of the state to my advantage or their fame." In the next letter: ". . . I am well satisfied with you and the sincerity with which you have spoken, continue to do the same. Tell me always what you think is useful to my service." The king's replies both to a proposed attack and to the objections, are in keeping with his character. He respected the advice of the "expert," he liked advice from men with ideas, and he did not insist upon his own fixed notions in face of apparently sound objections.[8]

The strategy for a campaign, however, was not open to the same discussion, for as in the lifetime of Louvois, the war ministry allotted troops and supplies in relation to the projects that were expected from the commanders. This fact had been the key to Louvois' ascendency over the "famous soldiers" who commanded the armies; their activity was always limited by the forces placed at their disposal by the war ministry. In the winter of 1691–92 a grand plan evolved to bring the king's enemies to their knees. On one side an expedition made up of French, English, and Irish soldiers assembled at La Hougue where the fleet was prepared to transport them to England. James II believed that there would be a considerable commitment to his cause once he established himself on English soil, and that he could reconquer his throne. At the same time, another army, under the command of Louis himself, prepared to besiege Namur. This mighty fortress on the junction of the Meuse and the Sambre would give the French control of a large triangle of land in the Spanish Netherlands. Its capture might inspire the Dutch to make peace, but if not, Namur in French hands would be an important pawn at any future peace conference. It is hard to know how much of these plans was Louis' own idea; probably very little, but he did approve of the plans and agree to "command" the siege operations so that Vauban's orders would be carried out without interference from anyone who might outrank him.[9]

Louis joined the army in Flanders on May 17, 1692; by May 30 he was ready to invest Namur with an army of 130,000 men to make the siege and protect the operation from interference by the enemy. Madame de

Maintenon and much of the court went along with the king, and found quarters at Dinant, a few miles up the Meuse from Namur. She found the accommodations poor, but her anxiety for the safety of the king outweighed such considerations. Indeed, she was happy when an attack of gout forced him to leave the siege and to join her at Dinant. It may well be that she was right in saying that Louis, "in the midst of this prodigious power, places all his confidence in God," but she, like any soldier's wife, knew that a stray bullet could kill her husband if he were in the besieging trenches. As the *Gazette* described the siege for its readers, Louis played a large role in the operation. In point of fact, however, he left the task in Vauban's hands.[10]

Namur fell the last of June. Louis may have been right in ordering *Te Deums* of thanksgiving for the victory, for Namur was as near an impregnable fortification as one could find, but even he seems to have neglected the work of his engineers when he wrote to a correspondent, "the *gloire* for so great a victory belongs to God alone, Who has wished to confront all Europe with visible evidence that He continues to protect the justice of my arms."[11] This statement, however, is characteristic of the king; when he was victorious he believed that God protected him; when the balance of power shifted against him, he was sure that God had withdrawn His protection.

While French arms were successful at Namur, the proposed descent on England was a failure. The battle of La Hougue in itself was not a drastic defeat for the French fleet, but in the weeks following much of the French navy was either put out of commission or destroyed. Colbert, and after him, his son Seignelay, had built a navy powerful enough to contest the narrow seas with the combined fleets of England and the United Netherlands, but after Seignelay's death, there was no one in the naval ministry who really understood the navy or its needs. Indeed, Pontchartrain who succeeded Seignelay, protested that he did not know enough to direct the navy, but Louis, who had little interest in the navy himself, would not listen to him. The failure of the French fleet to keep its superiority was of course as much the result of renewed efforts on the part of France's enemies as of the mismanagement and neglect of the navy in France. In spite of William's preoccupation with the war in Flanders, the English statesmen were more willing to spend money on the fleet than on soldiers. But it matters little where the blame should be placed; the facts were that after the battle of La Hougue, in subsequent actions the Anglo-Dutch navy bombarded French coastal cities, interfered with French commerce, and controlled the seas both in the Atlantic and the Mediterranean. Chamlay pointed out several years later that the enemy's naval power had even stalled French efforts to take Barcelona. Thus not only did the descent on England fail to come off, but also France's war efforts on the continent were injured by the failure to keep command of the seas.[12]

When Louis returned to Versailles after the capture of Namur, spies soon had the story that William of Orange was planning to recapture the fortress as soon as he could assemble his army. Naturally Louis was not ready to see his recent conquest taken away from him; he wrote to Marshal Luxembourg, ". . . my intention is that you should march with speed and approach him . . . and fight him before he can establish his trenches [before Namur]. . . . I will not prescribe the route; you know better than anyone the best way to fall upon him. . . ." When Luxembourg demurred that William was too strongly fortified to attempt a frontal attack, Louis wrote, ". . . you should approach the enemy and try to make them attempt a gambit from which you can profit. . . ." Luxembourg did not need much urging, but he did wait until the situation seemed to favor his arms. He joined battle at Steinkirke on August 3; the issue was not completely decisive, but William did leave the field in French hands, along with a number of his cannons, standards, and a large quantity of supplies, and the battle ended the threat to Namur.[13]

This battle also climaxed a long controversy in the French war office. Louvois had rigidly opposed the replacement of the musket and the pike by the fusil and bayonet as the basic weapons for the French infantry, even though the experience of the imperial troops on the Danube pointed to the need for this change. Thus at Steinkirke there were still pikemen in the French army at a time when the pike had ceased to be a very useful weapon,[14] and the enemy had the fusil that gave them firepower much more effective than the French musket. Luxembourg sent his son to explain the battle to the king. Without Louvois to interfere, Louis made up his mind quickly. "Look into it," he wrote to Luxembourg, "to see if you believe that it would be most useful to the good of my service either to have the infantry entirely armed with fusils or to leave the situation as it is. Talk to the old officers and tell me what they think best . . . if you believe that it would be good to arm my infantry with them, tell me and I will order that they be distributed in the quantity that you desire."[15] This was a characteristic decision. Louis asked for expert advice when a situation indicated need for a change, and then tried to follow the best advice he could get. Unlike Louvois, he did not *know* what was the best weapon for infantry.

Another interesting result of the battle of Steinkirke was the king's insistence that Luxembourg should bombard Charleroi. The project was originally conceived by Chamlay to prevent the enemy from using Charleroi as a base for winter quarters, but Luxembourg was reluctant to follow Chamlay's plan. Things looked different in Flanders than they did in Versailles; there was not enough forage, the enemy was too strong, a military promenade would be better. But Louis insisted, and finally Luxembourg gave in and sent Boufflers with a detachment to bombard the town.[16]

The next year's campaign (1693) was the critical one for the French. The kingdom was already dangerously threatened by the economic distress that had followed bad harvests, and the king's government was beginning to be severely pinched by lack of money, even though new fiscal policies were attempting to tap a larger flow of revenue.[17] The king and his advisers, realizing that the war had to be won this year or it might well be wholly lost, decided to probe in three directions: in Flanders Louis and Marshal Luxembourg would confront the Prince of Orange; in Germany Marshal de Lorge would attack Heidelberg; and in Italy Marshal Catinat would contain the Duke of Savoy and try to defeat him. Lorge, with a fine army under his command, got off to a head start, but by the middle of May he seemed to bog down before Heidelberg. The correspondence is clear indication of the urgency felt at Versailles. This had to be the year of victory. Barbézieux wrote to Lorge, "I must tell you that [the king] . . . will be much displeased to have an army as strong as the one that you have this year become useless. . . ."[18] A few days later Louis wrote to him, "I count on you: if they [the Germans] approach you, try to fight them. This year it is essential that you do something with *éclat* to bring esteem to my troops in Germany and make them feared." In any case he later wrote, "try something, rather than do nothing."[19]

Meanwhile, the army assembled in Flanders was one of the largest and best that France had yet put into the field. It was under the king's command with Marshal Luxembourg "commanding under his orders"; there was every reason to believe that it would be able to overwhelm the coalition forces at William's disposal. Before this army could be thrust into Flanders, however, news came that Heidelberg had fallen, and that the German armies were in full retreat. A council of war was held at the Abbey de Saint-Denis in Flanders, at which it was decided to detach a large body of troops from the army in Flanders and to send them to the Rhine under the command of the dauphin to see if the Germans could be forced to sue for peace. This is the occasion that Saint-Simon uses to prove Louis' "cowardice"; he was sure that Louis failed to use his fine army against William because he was afraid of the issue of battle.[20] But Saint-Simon did not know whereof he wrote. Louis' letters to his brother, to

Catinat and others, show clearly that he was overruled by the council of war, and persuaded of the wisdom of sending the dauphin to Germany with a large detachment of troops. "I must tell you," he wrote to Philippe, "of the resolution that I took yesterday upon receiving the news of the capture of Heidelberg . . . to send my son with a large army into Germany to compel the princes of the Empire, and perhaps the Emperor himself, to accommodate themselves to me. I will admit that I had hopes of doing something extraordinary here [in Flanders] . . . but I finally gave in because of the arguments presented to me as well as the movement of my own reason. I sacrificed the pleasure of my own desires and personal tastes and all that could flatter me, for the good of the state. . . . I was convinced that this gambit would more effectively secure peace than any other that I could take. . . ."[21] From this it becomes clear that the council believed that the war could be won in Germany; Luxembourg may also have wanted to send the king back to Versailles, for he assumed that no field battle should ever be fought as long as it was necessary for the commander to worry about the personal safety of the king. It has also been suggested that Louis' health had something to do with the decision, but this is quite inconclusive.[22]

Louis obviously pinned his hopes for peace on the campaign in Germany. With Lorge and Boufflers to help him, the dauphin presumably could force the issue. The king's orders were concise and to the point: seek out the enemy army commanded by Louis of Baden, and force him either to fight or to flee.[23] Unhappily, however, Louis of Baden proved to be a commander quite capable of looking out for himself and his army, while Lorge was not an aggressive commander who could force his opponent out of a fortified position. The dauphin, for his part, spent much of his time riding horseback;[24] Lorge and Boufflers spent theirs trying to find a solution of the German war. Nothing came of it. The king urged his commanders to take Heilbron and thereby force Louis of Baden to fight, but the dauphin explained to his father that the situation was such that the cavalry could not be used, and that the French infantry was always at a disadvantage because of Baden's fortifications. It was most disappointing. When the French finally retreated, Louis had to be content to congratulate his son because "the enemies are not trying to trouble your withdrawal," and by September, when it was clear that no victory was to be had in Germany, he wrote to his son, "I hope that next year you will repair that which you could not do in this campaign . . . you must not have remorse because you could not have done it better."[25]

While the dauphin was unable to bring off a victory in Germany, Marshal Luxembourg had better luck in Flanders. A few days after the council of war at the Abbey de Saint-Denis, Louis wrote to Luxembourg, "I hasten to repeat to you that you should approach the enemies as quickly as possible; I leave it to you to fix the time . . . recommending only that you take precautions that nothing disagreeable happens to my army." A few days later he added ". . . fall on their rear guard . . . if you cannot do this I will know that it is impossible." Then fearing that Orange might break through the lines, "These are measures that I offer to you to prevent the enemies from entering Flanders and for allowing my army to support itself in their territory without ruining my own. . . . If the occasion presents itself to fight, especially if [it is] a position where my cavalry can act favorably, you may take it." By the end of July, Louis wrote, "If you can find the opportunity to fight the Prince of Orange, you will not do me a greater service, especially if it is a cavalry action. . . ." Five days later (July 29) Luxembourg gave battle near Neerwinden; the action was not completely decisive, but it was a French advantage. Louis wrote to his marshal, "It is a pleasure to give orders to one who obeys them as you did . . . ," and Luxembourg replied graciously that it was easy to obey a king whose orders were so clear and concise.[26]

After the victory, the men at Versailles proposed a siege of Charleroi, and Louis sent Vauban to organize the operation. It was one thing, however, for Vauban to direct a siege under the orders of the king and quite another to do so under Marshal Luxembourg. The marshal proposed objections. He argued that there was not enough forage, not enough money; a promenade or a bombardment should be enough. Louis remained firm; "I still think that you can besiege Charleroi . . . I have not given you positive orders, being content to let you know my thoughts." Later: "I am sure that having considered it . . . you will decide to besiege Charleroi." Again: "I am not interested in promenades to Angheim, Hermes, Huies . . . it is solely a question of Charleroi . . ." Finally Luxembourg gave in, and Charleroi did fall. "I have always believed that you could take Charleroi," Louis wrote, "because of the knowledge that I have of the wretched condition of the enemy army. . . ." Nor could he resist crowing a little —"I do not see how the Prince of Orange can show himself in England if he allows Charleroi to fall . . . but he is accustomed to this sort of disagreeable surprise."[27]

During the late summer of 1693 the war in Italy also came to a climax. Earlier the Duke of Savoy had raided French territory, causing much distress to the inhabitants, and by July he was besieging the French fortress of Pignerol. Louis ordered Catinat to take reprisals by a raid into Savoy with harsh treatment of the duke's subjects, but Catinat did not believe that he had enough troops for a serious aggressive action. However, Louis urged him on: ". . . I want to repeat to you that you cannot do anything more agreeable to me, in addition to the deliverance of Pignerol, than to carry considerable advantage over the enemy, which will convince the Duke of Savoy of the necessity of accommodating himself to me . . . this is not a precise order to attack . . . since if things seem impossible or dangerous to you it is not my custom to order thus, particularly for those whom I hold in esteem. . . . You are to do all that is humanly possible to give the enemies a check."[28] Marshal Catinat obeyed very well; he defeated his foes in a bloody battle at Marseille (Marsaglia) and forced the Savoyards to lift the siege of Pignerol. Louis wrote to him, "I cannot tell you of the signal satisfaction that you have given me. . . . I will only say that it is proportional to the important services that you have rendered to me. . . ." He then went on to hope that the battle would result in "reestablishing peace in Italy and even in Europe . . . that this action will force the Duke of Savoy to ask for peace. . . ." A few days later he still purred his satisfaction with Catinat: "It makes one see the difference between people who know how to act and those who act without reflection. . . ."[29] The year surely was one of "victories."

It soon became obvious, however, that these victories of 1693 were not going to force the "enemies" to a conference table. While his armies were trying to find a solution on the field, Louis had also been working hard diplomatically to unhinge the coalition that had risen so formidably against him. French agents in Rome tried to work through the Holy Father and the Spanish and Austrian cardinals to find a formula for peace and for the settlement of the Spanish succession in the case of Charles II's death. Louis wrote that he "would prefer a good peace through the interposition of the Pope to all the advantages that [he] could hope for or foresee by the continuation of the war."[30] This was undoubtedly true, but no peace could be had, for Emperor Leopold, secure in the treaty with his allies in which his "rights" to the Spanish succession were guaranteed should Charles II die during the conflict, wanted no peace that was not advantageous to him. And the Spanish government simply replied that "the ministers of the Catholic King . . . should not talk about peace because it can only be arrived at in conjunction with the Prince of Orange and the Dutch."[31] Louis' victories in Flanders and Italy did not shake this refusal to consider separate negotiations.

Louis, however, did not give up his hopes. "The success of my arms," he wrote, "upon which the benediction of God continues to rain, has not erased from my heart the desire that I have to make a good peace."[32]

Madame de Maintenon reflects this same attitude in a letter to Madame Brinon: ". . . our victories give me most pleasure in that they have not altered the heart of the King in his good intentions for peace; he knows the misery of his people; . . . one [Louis] searches for means to comfort them and his only hope is that God will show our enemies the folly of their hopes of defeating France. We will always defeat them because God is on our side."[33]

All France knew that the kingdom needed peace. The harvests had fallen far below expectations; the kingdom was in severe economic trouble. The rest of Europe was also hurt by the weather conditions that blighted the harvest, but with the economic power of England and the Netherlands, and their control of the sea, it was possible for the coalition to meet the crop failures in the west by bringing grain from the Baltic. The coalition would not come apart as long as there was money for subsidies and a good hope that the growing power of the allied armies would soon be much greater than that of the French.

With the failure of this peace offensive, Louis and his advisers had to plan for war in 1694. It was a bleak prospect that became bleaker as the evidence of economic distress in the kingdom piled into a mountainous realization that there could be no thought of an aggressive campaign; there was not enough money to hire carts to move whatever food and fodder would be needed, even if they could have bought it. How could anyone prepare for an attack? There was no alternative; the French armies would have to stand on the defensive, and try to hold off their foes until a break could be made in the diplomatic armor of the coalition.

Lorge was left in Germany where he knew better than anyone the terrain and the problems of warfare. The dauphin and Marshal Luxembourg would guard the frontier to the north where William of Orange might try to force the lines. Catinat in Italy and Noailles in Spain would try to hold their positions. Philippe again was put in command of the coastal defenses in hope of preventing further naval bombardments that were destructive to life and property. France was on the defensive.

Louis pretended not to be surprised at the growing power of his foes' armies, but his letters breathe anxiety over the course of the war. Since his son was "in command" of the army in Flanders, Louis felt quite justified in giving instructions in detail. His letters to the dauphin are almost a textbook on the problems of logistics, safety of convoys, management of the troops, and general superintendence of the army. The king had not been at war most of his life without learning the jargon of soldiers; he seems pleased to be able to share his knowledge with his son, whose replies were always respectful, always obedient. It would be interesting to know what that young man really thought about his father's letters. The dauphin was not too bright, but even so he must have resented his father's explaining obvious things. Louis felt it to be necessary to tell his son how to keep a good supply of bread, how to guard the rear of his troops, how to keep track of his enemy's motions, how to maintain discipline. It may be that the dauphin was happy when his father praised him for the "correct placement" of his camp, and yet he must have known that others than himself had made the decision.[34]

By the middle of July, when no action of any kind had yet taken place, the dauphin wrote to the king expressing hopes that he might somehow earn a reputation during the campaign in which one of his opponents was his own brother-in-law, Max of Bavaria. Louis was quick to reply, "I hope more than you that you will be able to acquire much *gloire,* but since you ought always to think of the good of the state, I do not doubt that you will conduct yourself with wisdom and prudence."[35] The sharp tipping of the balance of military power against the French armies is evident in this letter. Louis no longer urges even Marshal Luxembourg to "approach the enemy," to "fall upon his rear," to "fight when there are reasons to believe in your advantage." In 1694 his concern was rather that the lines might be broken, that the enemy might invade the kingdom. "The strength of the enemy does not surprise me," Louis wrote. "I have watched them prepare for a long time, but I hope that by your good conduct, you will stop them from doing anything prejudicial to the good of my service."[36]

The campaign went badly. Huy fell to the enemy; Dunkirk was seriously damaged by a naval bombardment; and the war in the Mediterranean was stalemated. "I am inconsolable," Louis wrote to Noailles, "to find everywhere difficulties and obstacles that I cannot overcome."[37] Perhaps it was the obvious impossibility of doing anything constructive against the enemy that summer which allowed him to take a personal interest in the affairs of his sons (the Duke of Maine and Count of Toulouse) and nephew (the Duke of Chartres), who were with the armies in Flanders and Germany, and to write personal letters with court gossip and stories of his own hunting for the dauphin. More of this sort of correspondence has survived for 1694 than for any other year of the reign.[38]

While Louis had not yet come to the conclusion that God was against him, his opponents were quick to argue that their victory was assured by Providence. A broadside printed in Holland published a letter supposedly written by a priest of the oratory in France to a Huguenot friend: "One must be stupid and insensible not to recognize the hand of God . . . in the course of this war. We have seen blood flow day and night . . . the land uncultivated and sterile . . . we have been denied His blessings . . . there is even a lack of bread for children. It seems that God has loosened the furor of His three avenging angels on this kingdom."[39] Louis, however, could find hope in the fact that the harvest of 1694 was nearly normal; he ordered his bishops to hold forty-hour devotions in all the churches to thank God for "the harvest that has repaired the sterility of the last two."[40]

In the winter of 1694–95, however, Louis and his advisers became even more anxious to try to find some gambit that might persuade his foes to make peace. Then Marshal Luxembourg died early in January leaving a great gap in the military command; it was uncertain whether Villeroi and Boufflers could fill his place in Flanders and even more questionable whether they might bring off a victory. The king fixed on Italy for decisive action. If Catinat could go on the offensive, the Duke of Savoy might be induced to make peace and this would fold up the entire Italian front, but as the fiscal picture for the coming year became clear, Louis had to write to Catinat canceling the plans because he could not find the "large sums of money necessary to obtain carts" needed for any offensive. "The state of the finances," he wrote, obliged him "in spite of [himself] to stand on the defensive again for the coming year."[41] In the meantime the enemy's powers were waxing stronger each day. An imperial army was on the way to join the Duke of Savoy for a siege of Casale, and perhaps also of Pignerol; in Flanders the imperial and the Anglo-Dutch armies were preparing for a siege of Namur, and perhaps a break in the lines defending the kingdom. How could the French reply to this? Chamlay's only resource was the bombardment of Turin and later of Brussels; Vauban once said these bombardments could not add an inch of land to the king's domain, but Chamlay believed that such savagery might force the enemy to be accommodating.[42] The experience of the devastation of the Rhineland apparently had taught neither Chamlay nor the king anything about the psychological effects of wanton destruction.

While the soldiers marked time, waiting for the foe to organize the direction of the war, the diplomats feverishly sought to find a way to ease the crisis. The reports from the secret mission that had gone to Turkey in 1692 gave little hope for assistance from the decaying Ottoman power, but Louis continued to urge Castagnères de Châteauneuf to keep the Turks from making peace. The king's attitude toward the Ottoman Empire is most curious: he would not make a treaty of alliance with the Moslems, but he easily justified working with them through a sort of double-talk that made it seem that it was the emperor rather than himself who was to blame for

Franco-Ottoman cooperation.[43] While there was little to hope for from the east, the prospects for negotiation in the west seemed brighter. In 1677–78 peace had come when French diplomacy succeeded in separating the patrician party in the Netherlands from William of Orange. Louis hoped to repeat the procedure. His first contact was made through an agent of the Polish king in Amsterdam, an Italian named Mollo; he was followed by Saint-Germain, Baron d'Asfeld, and finally by Callières, who carried full power to negotiate. But these negotiations seemed always to break down just when there was some hope of success. The fact of the matter was that as long as Heinsius was in control of the Dutch government, there was really no chance that he would listen to proposals for abandoning the cause of his friend William III. All that these negotiations accomplished was the exploration of the ambitions and hopes of both sides of the conflict.

At this juncture an agent of the Duke of Savoy, disguised as a peasant, made contact with Tessé who was second in command on the Italian front. For more than two years there had been half-hearted secret negotiations between agents of the Duke of Savoy and Tessé, who enjoyed disguises and secret meetings enough to make him an excellent diplomat for negotiations in Italy. Up to this point, however, the negotiations had come to nothing. The trouble was that the Duke of Savoy was not able to decide whether he could get more from his allies or his enemies. He had ambitions: the iron crown of Milan, the French fortresses of Pignerol, the marriage of his daughters to French or to German princes, and a number of lesser things that might fall his way if he played his cards right. Up to this point there had been no crisis and therefore it had not been necessary to decide, but in 1695 an imperial army under Eugene was preparing for the siege of Casale and the emperor was urging the Duke of Mantua to order his subjects to revolt against the French garrison there. This prospect gave the Duke of Savoy second thoughts about the imperial influence in Italy. What would happen if the Imperials took Casale? The Duke of Savoy decided that it would be to his advantage to have Casale dismantled and neutralized, and thus, because of its geographical location, at the mercy of Savoy. The duke's agent therefore proposed that the French should surrender Casale without waiting for a siege, on conditions that the fortress be dismantled and turned over to the Duke of Mantua.[44]

Louis' first reaction was negative. The Duke of Savoy was slippery; he had not come through in earlier negotiations; what would be the French advantage of surrendering the fortification? However Tessé was allowed to continue the discussions. Louis was much interested to learn that the duke urged the agreement because he "feared the Emperor's power in

Italy." This interest was further quickened when the duke sent a portrait of his eldest daughter. Louis pretended not to know what might be "in the air," even though the marriage between the Duke of Burgundy and the Princess of Savoy had been suggested at least two years earlier. Barbézieux wrote to Tessé, "The King has seen the portrait of the daughter of the Duke of Savoy that the Sieur Grupel gave you. His Majesty was surprised . . . this does not appear to have any connection with the affair at hand [dismantling of Casale]. . . . If things take another turn. . . . His Majesty will explain his feelings about this. . . ." Tessé returned with the suggestion that perhaps the Duke of Savoy would like a picture of the young Duke of Burgundy. Thus did the prospects for peace in Italy begin to reveal themselves.[45]

The negotiations were secret and difficult. The Duke of Savoy was a bizarre man whose moods and ambitions, fears and maneuvers, were a continuous challenge to Tessé's skill as a negotiator. Finally, however, they did reach an agreement about Casale, and in July 1695 the governor surrendered after a *chamade*[46] from the drums of the Savoyard army. The terms were those agreed upon by the duke and Tessé: demolition of the fortifications before the French garrison returned to France and then the city to be turned over to the Duke of Mantua. Louis was disturbed to find that the terms did not include neutrality in Italy for the remainder of the year, but fortunately there was no reason for his fears; the war in Italy came to a halt with the surrender of Casale.

Further negotiations between the duke and Tessé had to wait until the duke attempted to come to an agreement with the Spanish. He, as much as Louis, was aware of the fact that the succession to the throne of Charles II was really the big problem of the hour, and he hoped to get "his share" of the inheritance. When he understood that the Elector of Bavaria had been made Governor of the Spanish Netherlands, he attempted to get the governorship of Milan as an hereditary office in his family. As a result of these efforts, the negotiations with France languished until the first week in February 1696. Months later, when the Treaty of Turin was ready for signature, Tessé gave Louis a picture of these negotiations: "I have come, Sire, from a voyage to the most difficult, most suspicious, most indecisive prince that could ever be. Not, Sire, that I did not find him decided to follow his true interests in attaching himself to your Majesty, but the means by which he did it . . . and the circumstances that accompanied the events leading to the signing of the treaty . . . after having made and remade the same thing twenty times . . . I feared that your Majesty would not understand that I had business with a prince who wishes and does not wish, who accords and does not accord . . . who retains with one hand what he lets go of with the other. . . ." Tessé goes on for pages pouring out the troubles that made the negotiations so difficult.[47]

Even though the Treaty of Turin was enormously favorable to the Duke of Savoy in that it left him largely in control of the French gains in Italy made during the preceding three-quarters of a century, it was difficult to get his signature. The French even contemplated bombarding Turin to jolt him into action. The treaty was secretly signed the last of June 1696. In the following month the duke very skillfully disassociated himself from the Imperials by revealing piecemeal the treaty by which he had duped his allies. On October 7, 1696, the emperor recognized that he had been out-maneuvered in Italy by signing the Treaty of Vigevano that neutralized Italy. Since it meant surrender of French territory and influence in Italy, Louis signed the Treaty of Turin "with regret." However, the marriage contract of September 15 between his grandson and the Princess of Savoy, and the very humble and submissive letter from the duke the next day partially removed the sting of the fiasco that had overtaken the Italian policy initiated in Richelieu's time.[48]

While these negotiations were going along, the war in Flanders and Germany became more and more threatening to France. Every report produced more evidence that the enemy was stronger than the French and undoubtedly would try some adventure. Villeroi came up with a suggestion to unite his and Boufflers' armies for an attempt to crush William's forces before the Imperials could come to his assistance. The king's reply shows how much events had changed his attitude since 1692 and 1693: "This would be to my taste, and I would hope that you could defeat them," he wrote on June 23, 1695, "but the more I think of their strength . . . and of how the Duke of Würtemberg could force our lines at Ypres, the more I am convinced of my opinion that it is important to think of defending my country, and [to do this] . . . to conserve my troops. . . . If in holding the lines, one loses a great many troops, one can hope that the enemy will lose considerably more. . . . One must defend my country foot by foot." When Villeroi protested the decision, Louis wrote, "You have my last letter on this subject. . . . I pointed out my intentions . . . not believing it for the good of my service to change orders that I have given you."[49] The orders were to strengthen and hold the lines and thereby to prevent the enemy from invading the kingdom to impose contributions. "You must apply yourself," Louis wrote, "to be sure that they do not penetrate my lands," and again, "You must regulate your action by their movements. . . . I am convinced of the opinion that it is important to think of defending my country and conserving my troops the best ways possible. . . ." Clearly the king was afraid; small wonder that he was willing to give up advantages in Italy to secure peace.

Soon it became evident that the enemy planned an assault on Namur as a first step in undoing the French conquests earlier in the war. Louis ordered Boufflers to throw himself into that city with a strong detachment, while Villeroi would command the army of observation. Thus if William did attack Namur it would be a hard nut to crack, and would perhaps tie down enough of his forces to give Villeroi an advantage. But even this was not certain. The Anglo-Dutch naval forces prowled the Channel and bombarded French cities, and in the Rhineland and Spain the French forces only barely held their own. The balance of military power was indeed turning dangerously against the French armies.

When the Electoral Prince of Bavaria invested Namur, the tension at Versailles mounted to a fever pitch. Louis and Chamlay struck out in several directions to find a suitable reply, but Villeroi, commanding in the field, found their proposals for investing Nieuport, or fighting the Spanish army, quite impossible. "No one is more aware of the good intentions of M. de Chamlay than I," wrote Villeroi; "In justice he owes me the same admission [for my intentions], and I do not doubt that he will accord it after I have explained my thoughts. . . ." Louis had to give up one project after another. Finally he wrote to Villeroi, "I leave you the freedom to do all that you think a propos for the conservation of my lines." Again: "When I ordered you to attack Nieuport, my intention was not that you should undertake this enterprise without the appearance of possible good results. . . ." The tightening grip on Namur, the bombardment of the Channel ports, the threats of invasion whipped the king's anxiety high; his letters are evidence of the pain these reverses were causing him.[50]

There could be no countersiege to secure compensation for the imminent loss of Namur, but Chamlay did come up with a plan to punish the enemies for their audacity: a bombardment of Brussels. In connection with this project, Louis made an interesting overture, perhaps the first proposal for the recognition of "open cities." It was not accepted, but its existence gives us insight into the king's mind. Villeroi's proclamation read as follows:

The King, filled with bounty for his subjects and attentive to contribute to their defense, seeing that the Prince of Orange sends the fleet to the coasts of France to throw bombs into the maritime cities trying to destroy them without gaining any advantage, has believed that it is better to restrain the hostility that the Prince of Orange shows in every encounter against his subjects than to try to take reprisals, so his Majesty has ordered me to bombard Brussels and to declare that it is done with great sorrow and that if one would agree not to throw more bombs in the maritime cities, the King would not throw any into cities belonging to the princes at war against him, reserving, however, the liberty to do so in the case of cities under siege. . . .[51]

Since this bombardment of Brussels was the only reply available to the siege of Namur, Louis was determined that it should succeed. "I repeat to you again," he wrote to Villeroi, "that if the enemies put themselves in front of you, and you see an apparent certitude of being able to fight them, do not hesitate to march at them even if you have not yet accomplished the bombardment of Brussels." This is more aggressive than Louis had been for over a year; it reflects his tension over the siege of Namur.[52]

The bombardment of Brussels did not save Namur, but Boufflers directed the defense of the place so well that it cost the enemy two whole months to capture the city, and even then, Boufflers was able to surrender and save his 6,600 men just before an assault that probably would have overwhelmed him. These troops were allowed to march to Dinant with full honors of war, while William arrested Boufflers and sent him off to Maestricht. In Versailles this was regarded as more evidence of William's bad faith; but since the negotiations between William and Louis were finally made through Boufflers, other interpretations can be placed upon the action. Louis praised his marshal for the valorous defense of the fortification, elevated him to the rank of duke, and when he returned from captivity, wrote to him, "If you wish to command an army, you may . . . but after the fatigues that you have suffered if you think that you need a rest . . . I will permit you to come to me to tell me about the siege. . . ."[53]

In the first six months of 1696, when Louis was concerned about the ratification of the Treaty of Turin, the French armies in Flanders faced an ever-growing concentration of troops with unusual optimism. Louis at first thought that his marshals would have forces roughly equal to those of the enemy, but by the end of May, as evidence piled up, he had to recognize that his armies would be outnumbered. Under such conditions he could only give orders for defensive action. He wrote to Boufflers early in June, ". . . it is not for the good of my service to risk anything. I recommend that you keep my troops on enemy soil to supply them, but that you establish yourself in such a manner that if they wish to fight you it will not be with any advantage [to them]. . . ." Toward the end of June, Villeroi again came up with a proposal for uniting his and Boufflers' armies for a battle with the Anglo-Dutch under William. Louis replied, "I do not believe that I can permit you to try the gambit that you propose, at least not yet. . . . I fear that when you leave [Flanders] the Prince of Vaudémont will come with his forces to ravage the country . . . he could go beyond the Sambre and Meuse and destroy the forage for my troops. . . ." Louis could only reiterate his intention that his commanders should defend themselves so that the enemy could not "fall on one of my armies" or take "one of my fortifications" or "otherwise invade the kingdom."[54]

Louis' hesitancy to undertake any general action, even if his generals thought that they might win a victory, probably reflects his knowledge of the negotiations between his agents and the Dutch. As we noted, more than a year earlier French agents had opened a discussion with representatives of the General Estates; by the spring of 1696 they had progressed to the point that Callières, acting for Louis, and Boreel and Rijkvelt, representing the Dutch, seemed to be near an agreement. In the early stages of the negotiations, Louis tried to limit the talks to the problems affecting the French and the Dutch, even to the exclusion of England, for he hoped to separate politicians in the General Estates from the Prince of Orange; by spring of 1696 this effort had proven to be impossible, and the negotiators were discussing the whole panorama of problems that must be considered in the making of peace. The most difficult of these were the recognition of the Prince of Orange as King of England and the subsequent status of James II in France, the Dutch demand for a barrier against French future aggression, the question of the French tariffs on Dutch commerce, and the big problems of the territorial settlement in the Rhine-Moselle areas where the reunions as well as the conquests of the current war created a host of questions. The Dutch negotiators' attempts to sustain the emperor's rights in the Rhineland, particularly to the city of Strasbourg, caused much friction in the negotiations. Louis was not willing to give up that city, and surely not if it were to remain a fortified point on his frontier that would open the kingdom to invasion from beyond the Rhine. There was much discussion of "equivalent" fortifications—Philippsburg, Kehl, Breisach, Landau, and others—but the emperor apparently insisted upon the return of Strasbourg, and wanted to discuss the question of the Spanish inheritance.[55]

By the spring of 1696 Louis had succeeded in establishing the principle that the conditions of a new treaty would be fixed within the framework of the Treaties of Westphalia and Nymwegen, and the Truce of Ratisbonne. Nonetheless the negotiations were far from any conclusion. A memorandum from the Dutch on May 11 indicated that there may have been some meeting of minds, but since the Dutch still refused to give up the emperor's demands for Strasbourg or William's insistence that he be recognized as King of England *before* the conclusion of peace, as well as a number of less important issues, it hardly seemed worthwhile to call a peace conference.[56]

Then the news of the Treaty of Turin burst like a bombshell over the whole discussion. The Duke of Savoy not only got what he wanted from Louis, but also placed his erstwhile allies in a very difficult political and military situation. William did not forgive him this act of "treason" as long as he lived. This treaty, however, started the rush for peace. The Dutch negotiators announced that they were ready to go to a Congress to attempt to reach a peace; they accepted the King of Sweden as the mediator. They were willing, they explained, to negotiate within the boundaries set by the treaties of Westphalia and Nymwegen. Unhappily the emperor would not confine himself to this pattern. He wanted to discuss the Spanish succession as well as Lorraine and Alsace. Louis also was anxious to go to a conference, but unwilling to accede to the emperor's demands. The French negotiators were instructed to temporize. "Avoid anything," Louis wrote to his ambassador, "to give hope of my renunciation, and that of my son, to the succession in Spain. No mention is made of it in the Treaty of Aix-la-Chapelle nor in that of Nymwegen. You must hold to the terms of these two treaties . . . and if they make demands . . . you will 'regret' not having information from me on so novel a proposal." The attitudes of both the King of France and the emperor gave little assurance for successful negotiation; nonetheless the powers agreed to meet at Ryswick and attempt to write a treaty.

The negotiations very soon became a diplomatic quadrille that went round and round without producing anything. Both sides presented memoranda, demands, proposals. However, it seemed obvious to the Venetian ambassador that the French and the Dutch had long since come to agreement, and sooner or later they would force agreement upon the others. As a matter of fact it was the general demand for peace that was forcing all the combatants to seek agreement. The war and the economic distress of the decade had been so harsh that everywhere men were ready for peace at almost any price. Thus the sparring at Ryswick was only the outer form of the process that was making the peace, and it would be fruitless to follow the proposals and counterproposals that took up the time and attention of the disputants and of the Swedish ambassador who acted as mediator.

When the time for fighting returned in 1697, William took the lead. He knew that he must either win the war on the field or secure peace at the conference table, for in England also there was a strong demand that the conflict should end. Rather than try for a military decision, he seized the initiative for a political agreement with Louis. His friend and confidant, Bentinck (Lord Portland in England, Benting or Bienting in the French documents) arranged for a conference with Marshal Boufflers.[57] Bentinck explained his king's willingness to make a treaty that would end the war between France on the one side and England and the Dutch Netherlands on the other if Louis would agree to conditions. This was the break that Louis needed; if he could separate the emperor and Spain from the maritime powers, then a general peace would have to follow. Louis announced to his marshal that he was happy to see that the "Prince of Orange desired to return to my good graces" and went on to assert that "the conditions that I offer for peace show that I put the tranquillity of Europe above my own advantages." Louis, however, was quite unwilling to drive James II from his kingdom even to gain "the firm and durable peace" or to "prevent a new war in the future." He insisted that William must accept his assurance that neither he nor his subjects would assist the Stuart pretenders in any plot against William's throne in England. While William was worried about the Stuarts in France, Louis worried about returning the principality of Orange to William; it could become a haven for Huguenot exiles from France and the center of plots and propaganda against the French kingdom. When William and Louis reached agreement on these questions through the efforts of Boufflers and Bentinck (Mylord Portland), the Treaty of Ryswick could be written and signed. William and Louis agreed that it was not wise to put clauses covering their particular problems in the formal treaty, so the document signed at Ryswick does not contain important compromises and concessions involved in the settlement. The problems of Orange, of the Stuart parties plotting against William, of the French tariff reduction, were all left to private agreements.

At first neither the emperor nor the King of Spain would sign the treaty that, while it did surrender most of French gains since the Treaty of Nymwegen, including the duchy of Lorraine, did not transfer Strasbourg to the empire. However, without the support of the Anglo-Dutch navy, the Spanish were unable to stand up against the French invaders who now took Barcelona, and the emperor had to recognize that he could not successfully fight the French on the Rhine as well as the Turks on the lower Danube. The treaty was not exactly what he wanted, but the emperor could preen himself on a considerable victory over his French brother-in-law, since obviously the Ottoman Empire would soon have to make a treaty leaving all of Hungary and Transylvania in his possession. Moreover, he had already reaped important fruits of his victory: his son Joseph had been named King of the Romans as well as annointed hereditary King of Hungary, and his candidate for the Polish throne, August of Saxony, carried the day over the Prince of Conti supported by Louis XIV. Eugene's coming victory over the Turks at Zanta and the subsequent Treaty of Carlowitz consolidated the newly won power of the Danubian monarchy. The balance of power in Europe definitely tipped in the favor of the emperor. It is small wonder that Vauban considered the peace of 1697 to be a humiliating disaster for his king.[58]

Louis, however, tried to make the best of it. In August 1697 he wrote, "The happy success with which it has pleased God to favor my enterprises during the course of this war has produced the first overtures . . . for peace. . . ."[59] Whether he actually believed that his arms were so successful is open to considerable doubt if one reads his military correspondence, and yet he obviously wanted his subjects to believe that things were going well. When the treaty was finally signed he wrote to the Archbishop of Paris in an open letter for publication, "The happy success with which Heaven has favored my arms in the course of this long war, has never separated me from the sincere desire that I have for a peace that has always been the single aim . . . of my undertakings." He went on to say that he abandoned some of his ambitions to contribute to the repose of Europe, and now "God, favorable to the designs that He has always inspired in me, has opened the eyes of the allied powers, who, disabused of their false hopes, and touched by their veritable evils, have accepted the conditions that I have so often offered them. . . ." On the day that a *Te Deum* was sung in the Notre Dame to celebrate the peace, a great *feu d'artifice* in Paris provided a secular celebration to match the religious one. The theme was "Louis XIV gives peace to Europe." Hercules figured in the first scene while pedestals on the corners honored RELIGION, JUSTICE, COMMERCE, and THE ARTS. With a rainbow, the sun changed the impact of the worst of storms.[60]

While *Te Deums* and *feux d'artifice* suggested that the treaty should be celebrated as a victory, a private letter of the same week probably more closely reflects the king's true feelings. He explains that his subjects "waited without impatience the return of peace, so necessary to flourishing regimes, but in the midst of the prosperity of my army, the losses of private individuals seemed to me to be like my own, and the general confidence in my measures for the recovery [of peace] forced me to redouble my efforts to heal their misfortunes. . . . *I sacrificed the advantages that I gained in the war . . . to [the needs] of public tranquillity . . .* [author's italics]."[61] He recognized here that victory escaped him but tried to make it appear that because of the distress of his kingdom, he had freely consented to a peace that cost him much. This is quite in line with Louis' ability to deceive himself when the facts became too brutal to face directly.[62]

The Treaty of Ryswick, when taken with those of Turin and Carlowitz,[63] emphasized the great changes that had taken place in the structure of European politics since Nymwegen. Louis had had difficulties disengaging his kingdom from the conflict of 1672–78, but after 1676 there had been little danger that the enemies would be able to impose their will upon him and his kingdom, and when the peace was written, it was a modest victory for France. But after 1693 the situation changed drastically: Louis was hard pressed by a Europe that was rapidly learning as much about the organization of war as the French knew it, and each effort to disengage seemed to leave the possibility of peace farther and farther away. However, just as in 1678 the break between William of Orange and the bourgeois politicians in the General Estates gave Louis the chance to break the coalition, so in 1695–96 the defection of the Duke of Savoy and the subsequent Treaty of Turin made peace possible. Louis should have reflected that in both cases it was luck that allowed him to disengage from the war; perhaps he did, for, as we shall see, in the following few years he desperately tried to prevent another one.

29

THE SPANISH INHERITANCE*

THE TREATIES OF Ryswick, Turin, and Carlowitz, the election of the Imperial candidate to the Polish throne, and the weakened condition of France all pointed to the fact that there was a new balance of power in Europe. Whatever may have been Louis' ambitions between 1680 and 1688 for the establishment of a Bourbon hegemony on the continent, a realistic look at the world of 1697–99 imposed a plan of limited action upon the court of France.[1] Perhaps it was fortunate that Louvois and the crusty Colbert de Croissy were dead, for France needed ministers like Torcy, Pomponne, Pontchartrain, and Beauvillier who spoke softly and urged caution. And Louis, much chastened by the recent war, was ready to listen to their reasonable arguments. Unfortunately, the march of events was such that even soft words were not necessarily a guarantee that the kingdom could enjoy peace; for peace would require that Louis give up much more than any King of France would be willing to surrender.

The problem was the Spanish inheritance. Charles II, against all expectations, was still alive, if only marginally so. Had he died during the late war, the Archduke Charles would have mounted the throne as Carlos III, for the western powers had signed a treaty (1689) with Emperor Leopold assuring his son's succession to the thrones of Charles II; but once Europe was at peace, it would not be easy to ignore the Bourbon claims to the inheritance. Indeed, Leopold himself had recognized that his sister-in-law Marie-Thérèse had some rights to the inheritance when he signed a "partition treaty" with Louis just before the Dutch War, and Louis never tired of reiterating his wife's claims to her father's thrones. Even though he knew that Louis would insist upon Bourbon "legitimate pretensions," Leopold seems to have believed that the German-born Queen of Spain would look out for his interests in Madrid, and that the treaty of 1689 would guarantee them in Europe so that his son Charles would indeed become Carlos III of Spain.

The question, however, was more complex than that. Unlike the

Lands of
The Spanish Crown

Spanish Territories also included
portions of N. and S. America as
well as the Philippine Islands

North
Sea

Baltic
Sea

SPANISH
NETHERLANDS

LUXEMBOURG

Luxembourg

Atlantic
Ocean

K. of
FRANCE

MILAN

Genoa

Pisa

TUSCANY

Adriatic
Sea

NAVARRE

K. of PORTUGAL

ARAGON

CATALONIA

CORSICA

Rome

Naples

K. of
NAPLES

Madrid

C A S T I L E

K. of SPAIN

BALEARIC IS.

Majorca

SARDINIA

GRANADA

Mediterranean

Sea

K. of SICILY

French throne, the thrones of the Spanish inheritance could all be inherited by, or through, a female in default of the male line. With Charles II the male line of the Spanish Hapsburgs was coming to an end; the next in line, presumably, were the heirs of his sisters, Marie-Thérèse the elder and Margaret-Thérèse the cadet. Marie-Thérèse, however, had waived her rights when she married Louis XIV. But renunciation was conditioned upon the payment of a dowry that was never paid, so the French insisted that it was not valid. Nor was the unpaid dowry the only argument for the rights of her heirs; as we have noted, it was a real question whether or not a princess could waive the rights of her unborn children. The testament of Philip IV reiterated the waiver by disinheriting his eldest daughter in favor of her sister, the empress of the Holy Roman Empire. For her part, Margaret-Thérèse left only one living heir, her daughter Marie-Antonia, who on her marriage to the Elector of Bavaria Max Emanuel, a Wittelsbach prince, had waived her rights to the Spanish throne in favor of her half-brother Charles. Marie-Antonia in turn was survived by one child, Prince Joseph Ferdinand, who was still a little boy in 1697. The waiver imposed upon Marie-Antonia was highly questionable, and never recognized in Spain. However if the two renunciations were valid, then the heirs of the daughters of Philip III would be next in line, since all the heirs of Philip IV would be excluded by the renunciations. Philip III had two daughters; Anne, the mother of Louis XIV and Philippe of Orléans; and Marie, the mother of Leopold I. Anne also had been obliged to renounce her rights to the Spanish thrones when she married Louis XIII, so only Leopold carried unrenounced rights to the throne; but as in the case of Marie-Thérèse and Marie-Antonia, the renunciation imposed upon Anne was also open to serious question. If one moved farther back along the lines of the Spanish Hapsburgs, the Duke of Savoy and several other princes could find claims, though not equal to those of the Hapsburgs, Bourbons, and Wittelsbachs.

Who had the best claim? Even if this question could have been answered easily, succession would have created problems for Europe, but the question itself depended upon interpretations of the waivers. If Louis XIV were correct in asserting that his wife's renunciation was conditional on the payment of a dowry, then there was no question about the authority of the Bourbon claims. And yet Philip IV had specifically disinherited his eldest daughter in his testament. What of the claims of Joseph Ferdinand, the Wittelsbach prince? His mother had been forced to renounce the rights that she had from her mother so that the rights of Leopold's sons could be asserted, but no court in Spain had ever acknowledged this action. If one moved back to the daughters of Philip III, what of the claims of the house of Orléans? Philippe was Anne's second son and could claim through her the right to the throne on the grounds that the French and Spanish thrones should not be united under one head. It was all very perplexing and especially so since the other powers in Europe would have something to say about any sudden enlargement of the power and prestige of either the Austrian Hapsburgs or the French Bourbons.

Louis fully recognized that the problem was as much a political question as a legal one. This was true for the kingdom of France as well as for the balance of power in Europe. What did he want from the Spanish inheritance? What would Europe allow him to have? At one time Louis dreamed of a Bourbon election to the throne of the Holy Roman Empire and to the thrones of Spain, but in 1697 he was well aware that Europe would not tolerate such an accumulation of power. And it was also a question whether such a situation would be in the interests of the kingdom of France. The source of French strength was obviously grounded in the relative homogeneity and the territorial unity of the kingdom, and this might suffer if the thrones of Spain were added to the French throne. Parts of the Spanish inheritance, however, would be of great benefit to France. The Treaty of Nymwegen and the courts of reunion had done much to make firm the frontiers of the kingdom, but these changes would have been small compared with the possible acquisition of the Spanish Netherlands, Luxembourg, and control over Milan, Naples, and Sicily, particularly if the latter Italian lands could be exchanged for Lorraine, Savoy, Piedmont, and Nice. If this could be accomplished, France would emerge powerful and rich, but it was a very real question whether Europe would ever agree to any such growth.

It could be assumed that the Dutch and the English both would object to French control over the Spanish Netherlands. After the Treaty of Ryswick the Dutch garrisoned a line of fortifications in these provinces, the barrier forts, to assure themselves that France would not take them. Dutch objections to French control of Luxembourg were only slightly less strident, for they believed that their control over the Maas below Maestricht would be in jeopardy were the French established in Luxembourg. The emperor had strong feeling about the French in Milan and the Anglo-Dutch commercial interests were such that French control of Naples and Sicily would work to the disadvantage of their Near Eastern trade. In truth, there was no part of the Spanish inheritance that could fall to France without some one of the powers objecting. Perhaps with care, however, a compromise could be worked out.

Louis had one other possible course of action. If the Spanish could be persuaded to send for one of his younger grandsons, either the Duke of Anjou or the Duke of Berry, to be brought up in Spain and to learn Spanish *maximes,* perhaps most of Europe would have no objection to his mounting the throne on the death of Charles II. The emperor, however, would surely object to any such project just as Louis himself would object to an Austrian archduke in a similar role. It was a vexing question to solve in a manner that would not relight the flames of war that had so debilitated Europe in the preceding decade.

What of Spain? The French had been cut off from contact with Madrid for almost a decade, and had no exact information. Louis knew that the queen, a sister-in-law of Emperor Leopold, was supposed to have considerable influence over the dim-witted king. There were soldiers in Spain under German officers, and there was a "German" party in the court. Furthermore, Charles II, like other monarchs of his era, had strong feelings for family and dynasty. The mere fact that the dauphin in France probably had more Hapsburg blood in his veins than Charles himself could not make the dull king forget that the dauphin carried the name Bourbon and that his succession to the throne would introduce a new dynasty. Charles II preferred a Hapsburg. Moreover, all his life Charles had suffered from the depredations of his brother-in-law whose armies had carried fire and sword into the territories of the Spanish crown and whose diplomacy had wrenched from his sovereignty lands bordering the kingdom of France. Although Charles never forgot his charming French wife, Marie-Louise of Orléans, he had a strong aversion for France. Louis was probably correct in believing that if it were up to Charles II, the Austrian archduke would become the universal heir. On the other hand, there was a strong anti-German party in Spain that perhaps could be used in French interests.

Louis sent one of his soldiers, Marquis d' Harcourt, to be his ambassador in Spain. His instructions were to report the situation in the Spanish court, and to warn the Spanish that the French would react if either German soldiers or the archduke were introduced into the Spanish territories. Louis explained that the marquis was not to threaten the Spanish, and yet he went on to say, "I have thirty battalions and three thousand cavalry placed in a manner so that they could assemble quickly if it becomes necessary. The magazines are filled on the frontiers of Catalonia, and will suffice if it becomes necessary to invade that province, and if it is apropos to invade Navarre, it will not be difficult to provide that frontier with the necessary munitions and supplies in a very short time." Unlike

England and the United Netherlands, where tight-fisted representatives of the electorate refused to support large armies in peacetime, Louis did not disband his armies after the Treaty of Ryswick. He knew that the Spanish succession might well require soldiers for its solution; he also knew that the emperor's armies engaged in the Turkish war would soon be free for any action. Louis was prepared for conflict, but the disastrous war that had just ended had been a heavy drain upon the physical and human resources of the kingdom, and he understood that his greatest need was peace. Snatching the Spanish crowns from under the emperor's nose might give satisfactions, but it would also probably cause "the powers of the league to reunite to prevent . . . [Louis'] harvesting so great an inheritance. . . ." And this was something that he wished above all to avoid. There were several possible ways, but the best procedure seemed to be some sort of a partition of the Spanish empire between the several heirs. Perhaps partition could draw the dragon's teeth.

But whom should he approach? Leopold had once signed a "partition treaty" with him, but that was long ago. Since then he had conquered Hungary and Transylvania, he had written a treaty with his allies assuring his second son the Spanish throne, his elder son had been elected King of the Romans, and his complex of Danubian crowns had become a great power in the world. Leopold believed that the whole of the inheritance would fall to Archduke Charles, so why should he negotiate a partition treaty? William of Orange, on the other hand, could be expected to be more approachable. After his wife's death, his popularity in England continued to fall to new lows, and he could not really count on the island kingdom to support him in any adventurous policy on the continent. The United Netherlands, too, was enjoying the fruits of peace, and like England, wanted no new war. Obviously if a compromise could be reached, William III was the man to help achieve it.

When William sent his close friend, Mylord Portland, to be his ambassador to the French court, the French concluded that this was to be an opening move in the discussion of the Spanish succession. Mylord Portland ("Beintig" in the Boufflers-Bentinck negotiations) was an experienced diplomat and high in the councils of both the English and the Dutch governments. However, when he came to France, he seemed to be preoccupied with one problem and one alone; namely, the status of King James II and the exiled court at Saint-Germain. Mylord Portland's instructions were to have James and the English refugees expelled from France. It was out of the question; Louis would as soon expel his own brother.

On March 9, Mylord Portland made his formal entrée, and in the language of diplomacy expressed his king's hopes to live in good relations with the King of France. Louis replied that ". . . if his master wished, we would be able to do important things." The following exchanges were formal and banal. Five days later Pomponne and Torcy had a long conference with Portland, suggesting partition as the solution for the Spanish succession.[2] Portland was noncommital; he had no instructions. Three weeks later Louis tried to open the subject with him, but Portland explained that William had been surprised by the proposal and needed time to consider it. Early in April they tried again, but Portland obviously was not prepared to talk. Louis decided that he must transfer the negotiations to London where his ambassador Lieutenant General Tallard could discuss the problem directly with William. On April 11, 1698, William finally broke his silence. His proposals were not what Louis had hoped to hear, but with good will and patience, a compromise seemed possible.

The negotiations between William and Tallard continued all summer and well into the fall before a treaty could be agreed upon (October 11, 1698). Historians have often asked why Louis had so much confidence in Tallard, whose command in both 1703 and 1704 was something less than brilliant. It may be that these months of negotiation, in which the future marshal showed himself to be a man with calm nerves and good judgment, established his position in the esteem of the king. In any case, a treaty was agreed upon that gave most of the inheritance to Prince Joseph Ferdinand. The Austrians were to get Milan, and the French, Naples, and Sicily.

Actually, the decision that made the treaty possible was Louis'. There seemed to be no territory that William would willingly allow to pass to France, and Louis found himself continually forced to back off from "his legitimate expectations." Finally he wrote to Tallard, "I consent that my son's share shall only be the kingdoms of Naples and Sicily, the fortresses of Tuscany Finale and Sardinia, that the Archduke shall have the Milanais, and the Electoral Prince [Joseph Ferdinand] the rest of the monarchy. . . ." Why was Louis willing to reduce his claims? These are questions that are difficult to answer, but if we believe his own words, it was unquestionably his fear of the revival of the league against France and another disastrous war.

I have examined with great attention [Louis wrote] all the problems that one could foresee either by suspending the negotiations with the King of England or concluding them. The first seems to me to be the greater [danger]. In breaking with that Prince we would indirectly decide to force him to enter relations with Bavaria, and the other princes of the Empire . . . it would be easy for him to draw out their ideas . . . [and] treaties could be signed during his stay in Holland. . . . With a league being formed [against France] before the death of the King of Spain, it would be impossible to support the legitimate rights of my son to this succession . . . without causing a new war in Europe as great as the last one.[3]

There can be no doubt about Louis' sincerity in this statement. Mazarin had warned him against war that might evoke a coalition against him, and his experiences from the War of the Devolution to the Treaty of Ryswick sharply underlined how dangerous such coalitions could be. Although he was convinced of the justice of his claim, Louis wrote, "It is certain that the disposition of the people of Spain and the measures that I have taken would give me just hopes for a successful outcome of the war, but one knows this when one begins [a war], *and one does not know the finish* [author's italics]. Nothing is more assured than the evils that it would bring and the suffering of my people. . . ." The entire correspondence around these treaties shows Louis to be aware that any considerable growth in French power would immediately cause a "tremor" in Europe, and that a coalition against France, the greatest evil imaginable, would probably follow. Unquestionably this fear of a war was most important in his decision to find a solution for the problem through partition.

There was, however, another factor responsible for Louis' reasonableness. He "knew" that Charles II would name the archduke as his universal heir. His Hapsburg blood, his German queen, his hostility to France all guaranteed that the archduke, or perhaps Joseph Ferdinand, would be the heir designated by any testament made by Charles II. Whether he believed that Charles had the right to designate his successor or not, Louis knew that the king's will would have important influence in all the lands of the Spanish crowns as well as in Europe itself. A treaty of partition, however, could undo some of the work of such a testament. It is impossible to know what Louis' attitude would have been had he known from the start that Charles would finally name the second son of the dauphin as his universal heir, but we might guess that he would have moved more slowly in the question of partition.

The partition treaty of October 11, 1698, named Prince Joseph Ferdinand as the principal heir to the Spanish thrones. When the terms of this treaty became known in Spain, the court was appalled at the idea that Spanish Italy should be divided between Austria and France. Even the queen joined in forcing Charles II to make a will naming Joseph Ferdinand as his universal heir. It all turned out differently. The little Bavarian prince journeyed to the Netherlands where his father was governor; then he sickened and died (February 6, 1699). Charles II took some satisfaction out of the fact that he had outlived his heir, but Europe as well as Spain was again confronted with the necessity to act if a great war were to be prevented.[4]

Louis again turned to William for further negotiations, and after convincing him that Max Emanuel could not be introduced as King of Spain without military action, Louis himself found the solution that might have had a chance of success. There had been much talk of "equivalent" territories. Louis wrote to Tallard, "The division of the Spanish monarchy is now reduced to two parts . . . the change it involves does not remove the resolution that I have taken to prefer the tranquillity of Europe to my own advantages. . . ." Then he went on to say, "I know how much Europe would be alarmed to see my power raise itself above that of the house of Austria. . . . But the power of the Emperor is much enlarged by the submission of the German princes and by the advantageous peace that he has just made with the Porte [Treaty of Carlowitz]. . . . It is to the general interest that if his [power] becomes great, mine should always be in condition to counterbalance him." He then went on to suggest that the archduke might have most of the inheritance that had been given to the Bavarian prince, leaving Italy and some little scraps along the Pyrenees frontier to the dauphin. The idea that Milan, Naples, and Sicily might be the equivalent of Spain, the overseas empire, and the Spanish Netherlands may seem strange until one realizes that French control of Italy would prevent close cooperation between the Hapsburgs at Vienna with those at Madrid. Louis' proposal seems based on a deep understanding of the military realities of the day.

These new negotiations, however, were more troublesome than the earlier ones, because neither English nor Dutch politicians wanted to see the French control all Italy. The unfolding of this problem is a difficult and often perplexing story of diplomatic maneuvers that we cannot follow in detail.[5] In the course of the negotiations the French agreed to try to exchange Naples, Sicily, and Milan for Lorraine and the territories of the Duke of Savoy. This would both relieve the fears of the Anglo-Dutch merchants about the Mediterranean and provide France with more solid frontiers. Naturally a treaty between the kings of France and England could not actually exchange Milan for Lorraine, but article 4 of the treaty provided for such an exchange. William and Louis signed the treaty provisionally on June 11, 1699. When the treaty was put before the General Estates of the Netherlands new objections were raised—so many that Louis could begin to wonder if his "allies" were actually willing to have a partition treaty. Nonetheless, the Dutch signed the treaty on March 15–25, 1700.

Louis, too, had second thoughts about the treaty. "The share that I consent to give the archduke," he wrote, "is so great that [considering] the power that I have to sustain the just rights of my son, one would have difficulty understanding that I should leave such important states to the House of Ausria if I had not already made it known that the conservation of the general peace is the first aim that I put before myself." Throughout the discussions of this second treaty we find Louis insisting that he placed the "tranquillity of Europe" above the "just rights" of his son, that he wished to preserve the "peace so needed by my subjects" and to prevent bloodshed. This note had run throughout the entire course of the negotiations. Such talk fooled no one. Louis had just experienced the disaster of a war against a great coalition, and he wanted to avoid another such war at almost any cost.

There was another reason, unspoken, but always near the surface, and obviously very important in the considerations of the French court. As long as Louis assumed that Charles II would name the archduke as his heir, he needed the legality of the partition treaty and the support of the maritime powers if he were to get *any* advantage from the succession. Even down to the last moment, when all evidence pointed to his grandson Philippe as the universal heir, Louis could not really believe it would happen. He wrote, "The King of Spain has always opposed the legitimate rights of my son. The mastery of the Queen over his mind and the attachment that she has for the Emperor's interests have been such that it is not surprising that I demand assurances before listening to any proposition [that Philippe would become Charles' universal heir] so contrary to the conduct of the King of Spain throughout his life." These words were actually written after Charles was dead, but before the news had reached France.[6] We may be permitted to wonder what Louis' previous attitude would have been had he known that Philippe of Anjou would be the heir.

Emperor Leopold made the same assumption about the testament of the dying Spanish king; namely, that it would name the archduke as the universal heir. Furthermore, he apparently could not believe that William III would lead the Anglo-Dutch forces against him on the side of France. The men at the Viennese court had been shocked when the Queen of Spain sided with the cabal that forced Charles to name Joseph Ferdinand as heir, but after the Bavarian prince was dead, they could not believe that she would allow Charles to name a Bourbon prince. In addition to their expectations, the emperor's refusal to sign was also based upon generalized dislike for the terms of the treaty. Count von Harrach explained to Villars, ". . . M. the Archduke is master of nothing when he is King of Spain, the Indies, and Flanders. The Spanish could expel him and the Indies could give themselves to whomever they wish, and Flanders the same. . . . When we do not hold Milan, the Archduke is painted on canvas. . . ." Like Louis, the men at Vienna realized that Milan was a crucial point on the map. With Milan, the Austrians could control northern Italy and the route to Spain; without Milan, the two Hapsburg states would be separated effectively, and thereby greatly weakened. Count von Zinzendorf told Torcy that "he would be much displeased to sign such a treaty since he knew how disadvantageous it would be for his master. . . ." Even so, the Austrians did ask what Louis would do in case the apple should be given to his grandson. Torcy assured them that "as soon as the treaty is ratified, no offer would prevent his Majesty from doing exactly what he promised to do." But the Austrian court would not ratify; in Vienna they gave the excuse that it was unseemly to divide up Charles' property before his death. They did, however, suggest that perhaps Louis and Leopold could make a treaty, but since their suggestions for the French share fell upon Flanders and the Indies, the French believed that all the Austrians wanted was to bring France at odds with the English and Dutch, neither of whom would ever consent to such a proposal. No matter; up to the death of the Spanish king, Leopold refused to sign the treaty.

The emperor's refusal to sign and the evident coolness with which the treaty was received in the rest of Europe more than ever convinced Louis that he must be prepared to seize the dauphin's share as soon as Charles II should die. However, he continued to negotiate with the Duke of Savoy, the Duke of Lorraine, with the other Italian princes, with the German princes, and the King of Portugal. But only one of these, the King of Portugal, signed the treaty before Charles II's death, and he did so with so many obvious reservations that it would have been unwise to count on Portuguese help to enforce it. The Dutch and the English also gave Louis reason to believe that they were only halfhearted in their support. William did not have an English army at his disposal, and the Dutch were anxious not to become involved in another war. William's remark that he had "made the treaty to avoid a war" and did not intend to "go to war to implement the treaty," does not suggest much willingness to act vigorously to protect the interests of the King of France. All of this gave Louis pause, especially when he knew that Leopold was strengthening his position in Germany for war. Late in October Louis wrote, "This response [the emperor's refusal to sign] makes me see that the Emperor does not wish to . . . assure the continuation of peace. The desire that I have to maintain it is still the same, my intention is . . . not to undertake any enterprise during the life of the King of Spain, but if he [the emperor] forms some designs against the peace, and I find out that he intends to execute them, he ought not to think that my forces will remain unused. I have reason to believe that, joined to my allies [England and the Netherlands], it will be enough to maintain the complete execution of the treaty, and I am far from admitting any change in the conditions for the choice of a third prince [if Charles refused the throne as offered by the partition treaty, then according to the treaty another prince would be chosen to occupy it] . . . it is up to the Emperor to prevent this choice by accepting the treaty. . . ."[7]

This letter and many other similar indications seem to prove that Louis fully intended to stand by the partition treaty. Indeed, on November 1, the very day that Charles died, Louis wrote to his ambassador in Constantinople, "For some time the health of the King of Spain has been reduced to such an extremity that news of his death has already been spread about, but even though he lives the peril seems the same, and the events foreseen by the treaty [of partition] are on the point of happening. The Emperor still refuses to subscribe to the conditions . . . however, everything is prepared in such a manner that if the King of Spain dies, I can confront those who wish to oppose the execution of the treaty and put myself in possession of the part I have reserved for my son. My troops are on the frontiers of Spain, and I have sent the Marquis d'Harcourt as commander. I have others on the Rhine front, I have others in Dauphine and Provence. Finally my ships are armed at Toulon and ready to sail at my order, and the Dutch are prepared in the future to join their navy with mine and to enter the Mediterranean as soon as I deem it necessary. You may spread about news of our dispositions if the death of the King of Spain causes a war. . . ."[8] It was not clear that Louis would have much help from his "allies"; nonetheless, he seems to have been ready to enforce the treaty by military action. This letter was written with knowledge of the rumor that Charles had signed a will giving the thrones of Spain to Philippe of Anjou, Louis' grandson, but a careful reading of this document seems to indicate that the king still believed that, in spite of all the rumor to the contrary, Charles II would nonetheless make Archduke Charles his universal heir. Obviously he still thought on November 1, 1700, that he must use his army to assure his son's rights to Spanish Italy. Louis was never sure until the ambassador arrived with the offer of the throne that Charles would not somehow make his will in favor of the archduke.

In Spain the story of the last days of Charles II sounds more like an account of a *Walpurgisnacht* than the history of the court of an important European state. Superstitions of all kinds came to the surface; exorcism of bad spirits, macabre visits to the tombs of dead kings and queens, terrible pressures on the credibility of a dull and sick man who happened to be king. Poor Charles II standing at the end of his line presents a pitiful picture of a dynasty in complete decay. The realization that Europe was discussing a treaty that would partition his empire caused him much distress. When the death of Joseph Ferdinand removed the only compromise candidate, leaving the Bourbon and Hapsburg princes face to face, poor Charles became the center of a storm of intrigue that forced him, much against his will, to name a Bourbon prince as his heir.

There was a pro-Hapsburg party in Madrid, but since the great question of the hour centered upon the problems of partition, the Hapsburg party was doomed to lose. The proud Spaniards could not accept the idea that the crowns of their empire should be divided between the heirs. Although within the several Spanish kingdoms men acted as if they were independent, the empire had so long been a unit that the men who benefited from it could not believe that it could be otherwise. War was a lesser evil than partition, but if it had to be war, the Spaniards wanted to be sure to win. This made the question simply, "Which of the two families could defend the integrity of the Spanish Empire?" The emperor was far away in central Europe and had no naval forces of his own. The King of France was in the very center of the Spanish empire: his armies could reach the Netherlands, Italy, and Spain with ease, and he had a navy that could deny the sea to his Hapsburg rival. There was no other conclusion: the Bourbon claimant had to be the heir. It took time to drive Charles to this decision. A letter from the pope, the pressure of princes of church and state in Spain, and the demands of the high officers of his government all drove the king to make a will giving his thrones to Philippe of Anjou. The choice fell upon this second son of the dauphin in hopes that, by this separation of the thrones of Spain and France, the will would be acceptable to a Europe that feared any growth of French power, and to a Spain that feared French domination.

Once Charles' opposition was overcome, another question emerged, "Would Louis accept the throne for his grandson? Or would he insist upon the partition provided for in the treaty?" When Spanish agents tried to get an answer to this question they could not get a response. Since Louis apparently did not really believe that his grandson would be the choice, he would not allow himself to be drawn into a false move that might jeopardize the negotiations for the Treaty of Partition. When Charles died on All Saints Day, 1700, the Spanish court knew only that Philippe of Anjou was designated as their next king; it did not know whether or not he would accept.

The testament that Charles signed on October 2, 1700, is a long involved document with 59 articles, but article 13 was the critical one. It annulled the renunciations imposed upon both Anne and Marie-Thérèse and fixed the succession to the Spanish throne first upon Philippe of Anjou, and after him upon his brother the Duke of Berry; if these princes should die or refuse, then the next in line was Archduke Charles, second son of Leopold I; should he die without heirs of his body, then the Duke of Savoy would be next in line. The will provided that a regency government should assume command in Spain until the new king would arrive. The selection of a French prince was popular in Spain where there was a strong anti-German tradition, and d'Harcourt was undoubtedly correct when he assured Louis that his grandson would be welcomed by all sections of Spanish society. But the fixing of the succession upon the archduke in case of French refusal made the selection a "golden apple" that could not fail to create discord, since King Charles' will and the Treaty of Partition were now confronting each other in a way that, if war were to be averted, demanded greater diplomatic dexterity than any of the principals possessed.

Charles died on November 1, 1700; the testament was read immediately and the regency council dispatched an envoy to France to announce the decision. If the French should refuse the thrones, then the envoy was to proceed to Vienna and offer them to the archduke. The news reached Fontainebleau on the ninth of November. It confronted Louis with the most important decision of his reign.

Louis had known for some time that his grandson might be named heir to Charles' thrones, but even as late as October 31, the day before Charles' death, Louis was far from any decision. "I see that from all sides one confirms that which you wrote to me about the disposition that he [Charles] made by his testament in favor of one of my grandsons," he wrote to Blécourt in Madrid. "Nothing makes it more evident than the secrecy that they keep on this subject with the Emperor's ministers, and at the same time by the fact that some of those who witnessed the signature

of the Testament have assured you of this disposition. *But since I cannot change the resolutions that I have taken on the simple news that you give me, it will be necessary to await the declaration. . . . There is even much chance that if the health of the King should improve one would make him change the dispositions that he made in his extremity . . .* [author's italics]."
In this letter there is, of course, the suggestion that the king *might* be willing to change his mind about the partition when the news finally could be confirmed, but there is still the suspicion that somehow the archduke would be named as the heir no matter what rumor might say to the contrary. In that case the treaty would be necessary to support any French claims. Obviously he had not yet made up his mind what should be done in the case that his grandson was named universal heir.

Nor had he made up his mind when the Spanish ambassador formally announced the news. "We shall see": this was the formula that the king had used all his life when confronted with a problem that required counsel. The Spanish envoy, however, was astonished to hear "We shall see" as the answer to an offer of twenty-two crowns. Nonetheless, the simple fact that Louis did not immediately explain to the ambassador that he had treaty obligations respecting the disposition of the Spanish inheritance must mean that he had considered the possibility of accepting the "splendid gift" if it were offered him.

The problem was discussed in council. The dauphin, the Duke of Beauvillier, Torcy, and Pontchartrain sat with the king; later he talked to Barbézieux and several others who were involved with his government. Obviously there were two very different considerations. From the view of the interests of the kingdom of France, the partition treaty offered the most solid gains. For by acquiring provinces on the frontier that would allow greater defense, with the archduke as King of Spain, the situation would not be much different than it had been; the states' interests would be served. Thus from the point of view of states' interest, the possibility of establishing a Bourbon dynasty in Spain was not very important, for such a dynasty would undoubtedly become "Spanish" in interests, or it could even become a drain on France because of its military weakness. On the other hand, from the point of view of the dynasty, of the Bourbon family, the possibility of a Bourbon prince on the throne of the Spanish Hapsburgs was a brilliant prospect, and the dauphin, usually as apathetic as he was fat and dull, spoke fiery words in favor of accepting this "splendid gift."[9]

Were the arguments inherent in the pros and cons to be decisive, it is hard to say which course of action would have been adopted, but there were other considerations. All his life Louis had spoken out strongly in defense of his pledged word; this was the theme of one of the most vigorous passages in his *Mémoires* and it had often been a theme of his discussions. Could he keep his word and accept the thrones? This was a subtle question. One of the secret clauses of the treaty allowed the emperor two months to sign the treaty after the announcement of the death of the Spanish king. If he had failed to sign by that time, another prince would be chosen to take over the archduke's share of the inheritance. Should Louis accept the throne for his grandson, would a delay of two months before Philippe arrived in Spain make it seem that Louis had kept his word? The problem was even more complex than this. If he should refuse the thrones, the Spanish envoy would proceed directly to Vienna and offer them to the archduke. Could he believe that Leopold would also refuse because of the treaty that he had not signed? "I do not expect any consent from the Emperor," Louis wrote on November 10, "for, after having refused to subscribe when nothing seemed to oppose the execution of the treaty, he will consent still less when he can assure himself that the refusal of my grandchildren would give the Archduke a right founded upon the testament of the Spanish king." In other words, Louis believed that Leopold would not sign the treaty, and that if the succession passed to the archduke, he would accept it. In such a case the dauphin's share could only be had by war.

Nor was the probable Austrian attitude the only one that upset the king. Before the death of Charles, Louis had offered the Duke of Savoy the duchy of Milan in exchange for his lands on the French frontier. By all counts this was an exchange advantageous to the duke, but the duke had held back and refused to sign. Louis now thought that he saw this as a policy aimed at France. He wrote, ". . . there is reason to believe that the Duke of Savoy, seeing himself the immediate successor to the Archduke, will line up with the Emperor to obtain execution of the testament and the favor of the Emperor as soon as my grandchildren will have abandoned the new right that they could obtain from the testament."[10]

And what of the attitude of the English and Dutch? The English army had been disbanded; the Dutch had promised to send a squadron to the Mediterranean, but it had not arrived. Louis suspected them of being lukewarm in their urging the emperor and others to sign, if, indeed, some of the Dutch diplomats had not actually been disloyal to the treaty. In this discussion we are not interested in the question whether or not, in fact, the English and Dutch intended to help Louis maintain the treaty; the sole point of importance was Louis' belief about their action, and it is certain that he was not at all sure of either their loyalty or their aid.[11]

There was another final consideration that Torcy insists was of greatest moment. If the thrones were refused, the French kingdom would have to fight a war against the emperor and the Spanish kingdoms to secure the dauphin's rights. In this war the French would be the aggressors hammering at the gates of a neighboring state. If the thrones were accepted, there would probably be a war in which the emperor would be the aggressor, but France would be allied with Spain defending rights recognized in the Spanish empire. In either case it seemed likely that the Anglo-Dutch military forces would be either neutral or only halfheartedly engaged, for the martime powers were most anxious for peace. Louis guessed correctly that they would recognize Philippe as king so long as the French and Spanish crowns were not held by the same prince. Since there would be war with Emperor Leopold either way, it seemed better to fight with Spain as an ally than as an enemy. Louis did not like the idea of sending his armies against a state that had only recently generously offered to accept his grandson as its king.

The court left Fontainebleau on November 16 to go to Versailles. Only a few in the king's entourage actually knew that the young prince, his grandson, was to become Philippe V of Spain, for Louis wanted the secret of his decision kept until he was ready to announce it formally. His hesitation may have stemmed from doubts about the wisdom of the decision, or he may have had attacks of conscience for a reversal of policy that he had followed for over two years. In any case, he wished to announce his action to the governments in England and the United Netherlands before he made it public in France.

The scene was a memorable one. The Spanish ambassador entered the king's cabinet at Versailles, and Louis announced to him that he could salute Philippe V as his king. The ambassador fell to his knee and addressed the boy in Spanish, a language that Philippe did not know. Then Louis called in the courtiers and announced, "Messieurs, behold the King of Spain. His birth called him to the crown. All the nation hoped for him and demanded of me that which I give them with pleasure. This was the command of heaven." The Spanish ambassador, kissing the hand of his king, exclaimed, "What joy, the Pyrenees no longer exist, they have been leveled and now we are one." Like so many things attributed to Louis XIV, this speech was not his. He well knew that the Pyrenees were still there.

Nineteenth- and some twentieth-century historians have criticized Louis severely for his bad faith. They fail to notice several things about the drama. In the first place, Louis behaved *en roi* as a king of his times. What we know about Leopold I, or Frederick William of Brandenburg-Prussia, or Charles IX of Sweden, or August of Saxony-Poland, or indeed any of the princes of Europe, probably including William III, whose case may be a little different, would indicate that under these circumstances, it is highly probable that they would have acted the same way. The confusion of states' and dynastic interests, much condemned by nineteenth-century scholars, was common in the seventeenth century. Louis was not wiser than others of his era. The second point that is often overlooked is the fact that Philippe's trip to Spain was arranged so that he did not cross the frontier into his new kingdom until the expiration of the time set for Leopold to sign the treaty. Since Leopold prepared for war rather than signing, Louis watched his grandson mount the throne of Charles II probably believing that he had fulfilled his pledged word.[12]

30

THE WAR OF THE TWO
CROWNS: FIRST YEARS

"EVERYONE SEEMS DELIGHTED with the Spanish affair. Our young King received it with the gravity and coolness of a king of eighty years. . . . Some very wise men believe that there will not have to be a war and that we would have had a long and difficult one, ruinous for France, if one [Louis] had insisted on the execution of the treaty. The Emperor has confirmed the King in the opinion that he has done the right thing for he [Leopold] refused to sign that treaty. God governs all, one must abandon oneself in that thought."[1] Obviously Madame de Maintenon was worried, but like most people at Versailles she hoped that the decision had been the correct one. Yet the threatened war was only one problem of the inner circle at Versailles. "Sadness is mingled with joy," she wrote as Philippe prepared to leave for Spain. The young king was only seventeen; since his mother's death he had been more or less intimate with the king and Madame de Maintenon. ". . . you know how much the French love their princes." She wrote, "The King, full of goodness, cannot see his grandson leave him for-ever wihout tears. . . . One pretends that he will visit his lands . . . and that in going to Flanders we will see him again, but [Louis] believes that the Spaniards will want him to have an heir before making voyages. . . ." She then went on to say, "The King does not believe that he should marry an Archduchess [as suggested by the testament of Charles II]. He leans toward the Princess of Savoy who is past twelve, and we are assured that she has a body as beautiful as the Duchess of Burgundy [her sister]. This is important for a woman and for the children that one expects. . . ."[2]

In these first months after the death of Charles II, second thoughts about the wisdom of the decision and the perplexing questions of a possible war caused Louis to restrain the young king in several ways in order to show Europe that it would still be possible to settle the succession to the thrones of Spain by the Treaty of Partition if Leopold was willing to do so. Philippe did not sign himself with the traditional Spanish flourish *Yo el Rey,* he did not alter the constitution of the government provided by the testament of Charles II, he did not present himself at the Spanish frontier until Emperor Leopold had had more than the two months that the treaty provided him before his failure to sign would be construed to be a final decision. Many princes of Europe were less tactful than the king. Max Emanuel recognized his nephew as King of Spain on November 26, and he was followed in rapid succession by the rulers of Darmstadt, Savoy, Poland, Brunswick, Malta, and Danzig, all before Philippe left Versailles. The English and Dutch quite properly held back, but in the following spring they, too, recognized the *fait accompli.*

Louis' apparent hesitancy to burn the bridges that might allow a compromise obviously indicated an ambivalence, but his actions in the few months following the scene at the Spanish frontier when Philippe and his brothers made their tear-stained farewells, show that he believed that Charles II had implemented the will of God by giving the throne to Philippe. The "magnificent gift" probably could not really be refused no matter what it cost, but Louis did not subsequently need to antagonize Europe by words and deeds that threatened the peace.

The first of Louis' indiscreet acts was an official recognition of Philippe's place in the line of succession to the French throne. This famous document was drawn up in December 1700, and registered in Parlement the first of February 1701—well after Leopold's period of "grace." The arguments, the diction, and the word choices in this document betray the fact that Louis either dictated it or carefully edited it before registration. The proclamation is a flaming defense of the doctrine of divine right in contrast to the new "English" doctrine that assumed succession to the thrones to be subject to the will of men. Since succession was the will of God, Philippe could not be deprived of his rights to the throne in France simply because he accepted the one in Spain. Louis fairly shouted that men must accept "God's impenetrable judgments" rather than "place confidence in their own strength . . . that successions to thrones are dependent upon His bounty and the things that He wishes to give." Thus, the melancholy fate that overtook the Spanish house of Hapsburg could be repeated for the house of Bourbon should this be the Will of God, and men must accept these decisions of God. The document went on to say, "If it should please God that our dear and well-beloved grandson, the Duke of Burgundy, should die without male heir, or that those from a good and loyal marriage should die before him . . . in which case our grandson, the

King of Spain . . . would be the true successor to our crown and estates . . . to deprive him of that right would mean an injustice that we are incapable of committing, and an irreparable prejudice to our kingdom. . . ." How better could he tell Europe that all the waivers, all the paper documents in the world could not counter the will of God? Then following a theme that Louis had repeated all his life, he went on to say that God "wishes that the kings He chooses to lead His people should foresee distant events that could produce disasters and bloody wars, [and] . . . that they should use the light that His divine wisdom has given them to prevent these [disorders]." Thus he argued, "we accomplish His designs when, in the midst of universal rejoicing in our kingdom, we consider the possibility of a sad future which we pray to God to prevent from happening." He failed to say anything about the separation of the crowns of Spain and France should Philippe be called to wear the latter.

French historians favorable to the king assert that it was quite unnecessary for Louis to assure Europe that the crowns of France and Spain would not be worn by the same man. Just as the Grand Dauphin and the Duke of Burgundy resigned their rights to the throne of Spain when Philippe mounted it, so would future princes "adjust" the will of God so that the burden would not be too great for one man. It is all well and good to argue this way, but such talk does not change the fact that this proclamation was a bold, brash, arrogant challenge to the Europe that had written the partition treaties, and particularly to William of Orange and the men who had placed him on the English throne. It not only defied their policies but also boldly asserted that God, not Europe, would decide the fate of the Bourbon succession in both Spain and France.

There was a flurry of resentment when this document was registered in Parlement, but in both England and the Netherlands there were strong forces anxious to prevent war. The years following the peace of Ryswick saw an explosion of commerce and prosperity that men did not wish to jeopardize; indeed, there were many people in England who argued that the testament was actually a better solution for the Spanish succession than the partition treaty would have been, since France did not acquire more territory when a French prince became king of the Spanish empire, while the treaty would have importantly aggrandized Louis' kingdom. Such talk did not please William; "I am pained to the bottom of my soul," he wrote to Heinsius, "to see the majority in this country . . . rejoice that France preferred the Testament to the Treaty." But there was little that he could do, for the English Parliament had deprived him of most of his army and showed no willingness to change this decision. In the Netherlands there was an army, but hardly one to challenge the power of France, so there was nothing for William to do but watch the course of events, perhaps to influence them a little by "talking" to his friends on the continent.

Did this give courage to the King of France? Or was it simply that he lost his sense of proportion and judgment when he saw his grandson established on the Spanish throne? Unfortunately we do not know what happened. Perhaps Louis saw himself again as the Sun King who could give law to Europe. In any case his next move was shocking for both the Dutch and the English. After the peace of Ryswick, Dutch soldiers occupied the great fortifications in the Spanish Netherlands. These troops were under the command of the governor Max Emanuel of Bavaria, but were paid for by the Dutch as a "barrier" to the ambitions of France. For more than a half-century French policy had threatened the Dutch by its obvious ambition to control the Spanish Netherlands; Mazarin, Turenne, Colbert, and many men of lesser light had urged the King of France to annex these provinces. Now that Louis' grandson was King of Spain, it would be possible for France to acquire them. The first move was made in concert with both the Spanish government in Madrid and Max Emanuel in Brussels. Six days after Philippe crossed the frontier into Spain, French troops suddenly appeared at each of the "barrier fortifications." The Dutch soldiers, completely unprepared, were disarmed and imprisoned. Marshal Boufflers and Max Emanuel had managed the maneuver without a slip. Since Spain and the United Netherlands were not at war, these soldiers were sent home, but in small groups so that they could not make any reply to the *coup de force*. The French ambassadors in Europe piously explained that the move would contribute to peace by preventing the United Netherlands from using these forts as bases for an attack on France, and that in any case, since the United Netherlands had not yet recognized Philippe as king of the territories, surely they could hardly expect to be allowed to occupy his cities. Finally, Louis assured Europe that his soldiers would withdraw as soon as Philippe could raise troops to take their places in the fortifications. Of course this was double talk, and no one missed it.

The peace party in the Netherlands began to melt, but it was still strong enough to demand that some effort be made to negotiate. Louis, however, was not only unready to negotiate; he was also preparing another blow. The Spanish empire was the first upon which "the sun never set," but by the opening of the eighteenth century, with its mines exhausted and its colonists discouraged, it was no longer the rich prize that it had been a century or so earlier. Nonetheless, there was still a market for slaves, manufactured goods, and some items of food and drink; it was a market that French traders shared with those from England and the United Netherlands. Once Philippe was safely established in Madrid, his government gave special privileges to the French traders to the prejudice of their rivals. The cry that went up from the Anglo-Dutch commercial classes made more rapid the melting of the peace parties in both countries. William III must have enjoyed the sight, for he knew that Louis would not negotiate away his gains.

The prospects for peace were fading rapidly, but the politicians in England and the United Netherlands could not break with France without one more effort to solve the mounting crisis. The Dutch government presented the French ambassador with a formidable document listing what amounted to the conditions requisite for peace; at the same time the English ambassador at The Hague also gave the French ambassador a memorandum adding further English conditions. At the head of the list was the suggestion that the ultimate fate of the Spanish empire must be determined by negotiations that would include the emperor as well as the English and Dutch governments, or a suggestion that would leave Louis at the conference with three of his enemies on the other side of the table. The note went on to insist that French soldiers must leave the Spanish Netherlands and allow the Dutch to return, and that the Spanish government must cancel all special advantages that had been given to French merchants in its empire. It went on to require that the French recognize all treaties between France and the Netherlands signed since 1646, and finally, that both the King of Spain and the King of France solemnly bind themselves and their successors to respect all these requests. The English memorandum added the condition that English troops must be allowed to garrison Ostende and Nieuport, a suggestion probably not too welcome to the Dutch. It would be hard for Louis to agree to these formidable conditions, especially since his armies were strong, while the Anglo-Dutch forces were practically nonexistent and also since his soldiers and those of his grandson occupied the territory under dispute. Could he be forced to give up his advantages in return for peace?

Actually the French had already decided to risk the anger of the maritime powers, and these demands for reconsideration were unable to alter their decision. Louis believed at this point that Anglo-Dutch politicians would bluster, but that in the end they would accept the *fait accompli*. Had they not recognized Philippe as king? And would not war endanger their prosperity? And even if the Anglo-Dutch governments should declare war, the two crowns of Spain and France would defeat them.

He replied to the Dutch that he would be happy to renew the Treaty of Ryswick in all its articles if this would contribute to the security of their state, but he went on to say that he would have nothing to do with their outrageous demands beyond publishing them so that people in both France and the United Netherlands could judge the intentions of the men who made them. As for the English request, if William wanted to say anything to the King of France, "he can send his orders to his ambassador, to me, or speak to Count de Tallart." Hardly a reply to stave off war; the Sun King had spoken.

It was exactly what William was waiting for; the emperor, already at war with France, was clamoring for the renewal of the Grand Alliance, and now in both England and the Netherlands the war parties gained the upper hand. During the summer of 1701 the coalition that had fought the last war began to reassemble in order to restrain the unbridled ambitions of the Bourbon king. On September 7, 1701, a treaty was signed by which the United Netherlands, England, and the emperor undertook to secure their "rights" in the Spanish empire, even though it should require war; the allies invited other princes to join them to prevent the house of Bourbon from destroying the balance of power in Europe. The fact that a war between Sweden on the one hand, and Denmark, Poland, and Russia on the other, had already broken out in the north, limited the aid that could be expected from that quarter. But Eugene of Savoy's successful campaign in Italy promised that the new Grand Alliance would be able to place bounds on the arrogance of the King of France.[3]

The council that had accepted the throne had understood that it could mean war, but a war in which the two crowns would be allied. Moreover, Louis could expect to enlist the aid of Philippe's two Wittelsbach uncles—Max Emanuel of Bavaria by veiled promises about the Netherlands, and his brother the Electoral Archbishop of Cologne by other promises. The Duke of Savoy sent his younger daughter to Spain to be queen, and joined his forces with the French to keep the Imperial armies out of Italy. The King of Portugal also joined the Franco-Spanish forces, albeit a little reluctantly. What better situation could a soldier-king wish to have? He and his allies occupied all the real estate under dispute. With Bavaria and Cologne deep in the empire, it should be easy to bring the German princes to their senses, and with Savoy, Spanish Milan, and Sicily occupied, the forces of the Grand Alliance seemed to be checkmated in

Italy. If the armies of the two crowns could successfully stand on the defensive, there was nothing for their opponents to do but make peace.

Louis felt so defiant that he went out of his way to insult William III whom he considered the author of the coalition rising against him. The aged James II was on his deathbed; he had received extreme unction and communion and was preparing himself for the end. As the *Gazette* tells the story, "The King went to see him and declared in the presence of the Queen and the noblemen of the two courts that if God takes his Britannic Majesty, he, Louis, would recognize the Prince of Wales as King of England, Scotland, and Ireland. All the English expressed their gratitude and joy at this occasion by their acclamations and their tears. . . . James spoke to his wife and his son, pardoned those who had caused him evil and finally quietly died. . . ."[4] This was the story that Louis wanted given to the world, but in fact, the *Gazette* simplified the story greatly. Louis visited Saint-Germain on September 6, and was greatly moved by the Queen of England's plea for her son who soon "will return to the state of a private individual." Louis told her that any action concerning her son would require council consideration, but that he had always had great respect for James II, whom he regarded as a saint, as well as for her and for her son. A council was held the next day to decide what should be done. The chancellor and most of the ministers opposed recognition of the Prince of Wales on the ground that it was contrary to the Treaty of Ryswick, but the king and the Grand Dauphin supported it on the ground that William might be king *in fact,* but that the Prince of Wales was king *en droit.* James and his queen learned the news of the decision to recognize their son as king on the thirteenth; James is supposed to have said, "I pray God that He care for you in this world and in the next. . . ." James died September 16, and a few days later the Prince of Conti, in the name of the King of France, recognized James Edward as King of England. The pope and the Prince of Modena (his mother's relative) followed suit.[5] James died on September 16 after the treaty of the Grand Alliance had already been drafted and signed. Louis' action was therefore not responsible for England's entry into the coalition, but it did help to make Englishmen more enthusiastic for the war.

Emperor Leopold did not wait for his cousin to arouse the maritime powers before opening hostilities. It was a shock for the French when Eugene spilled over the Alps and into Italy; they had boasted that the Imperial army would have to learn to fly if it wished to get past Marshal Catinat's defenses. Even with forces inferior in number, this grand nephew of

Mazarin, whose request to become a soldier had years earlier been spurned by Louis, soon had Catinat in trouble. The soldiers of the king "fought with incredible valor"[6] but they were forced to retire in the face of the enemy. Catinat complained that he always ran into strong fortifications whenever he approached Eugene. He did not account for the fact that in the skirmishes between the two armies his detachments were usually beaten. In early July the town of Capri changed hands several times, but finally the French withdrew after losing fourteen officers. Louis was much disturbed. "I trust," he wrote, "that my soldiers did their duty. . . . I have ordered Marshal Catinat to assemble all the troops under his orders and attack the enemies while they are between the Po and the Adige. . . ." In the actual instructions he added that Catinat should "take precautions and not hazard an unfavorable battle."[7] This last admonition was enough to make Catinat cautious; as Tessé remarked, "without precise orders to fight, I am convinced that anyone always seeks reasons for doing nothing. . . ." Louis needed to find another general. Villeroi had been a competent officer under Luxembourg, and after the latter's death he had shown himself to be capable of command. The king had vetoed his more daring suggestions only because he had been sure that the treasury and the balance of power between the armies no longer would allow any risks. Louis and Villeroi had been boyhood friends, and the elder Villeroi had been Louis' governor. Who better could be sent to Italy to punish the "little abbé's" presumptions?[8]

Villeroi hurried to Italy, anxious to carry out the king's orders. From Milan he wrote, "It is important that I shall be seen in this city to persuade people that your Majesty disapproves of the past conduct of the campaign." A few days later he assured Louis that "the dispositions are favorable for our enterprise . . . your Majesty can wait with calm and tranquillity." Louis purred his satisfaction, "A happy victory will change the face of the Italian war." Villeroi replied, "Believe me, sire, that days and nights pass in an effort to obey you; whatever is not impossible will be done. . . ."

Louis needed a victory over Eugene to assure the continued loyalty of Italy to his grandson's regime. These people in Italy had no particular love for either Bourbon or Hapsburg; they only wanted to be on the winning side. On September 7, not knowing that the battle had already been fought, Louis wrote to Villeroi, "I cannot tell you how pleased I am to have you in command. . . . I have reason to believe that you will finish the campaign gloriously, but take care of yourself, you know how necessary you are to me. . . ." Villeroi in the meantime had joined the army; the

Duke of Savoy, Marshal Catinat, and the Prince of Vaudémont were under his command as he marched to fight Eugene. He found him at Chiari.

When Louis received the letter that Villeroi wrote to him on September 2, he must have reread it several times before he understood what had happened. "I have the honor to tell the king of an action that we had with the enemies," Villeroi wrote. "I would have hoped that it could be more decisive. If the enemies had not been entrenched and reinforced by walls, the affair would not have lasted very long; we hope to find more favorable occasions later. . . ." As he started the account, it seemed to announce a victory; he then went on to say that when his army approached the Imperials, he had explained to his fellow officers that he had precise orders to fight. Apparently no one in the French camp understood that the forces in front of them were more than a small detachment of Eugene's army, when in fact the whole Imperial army was there. The council of war decided to attack, even though "the enemies had worked three days on their position." The engagement was a disaster; the Imperials drove back the French with a withering fire that took heavy toll. Villeroi finally concluded that he must call off the attack before committing all his army, for he hoped to be in position to continue the campaign with forces superior to the enemy's. But there were pages and pages of confused explanations before these facts finally emerged.[9]

As Louis read this letter his heart must have been in his mouth, for gradually the story unfolded of the French army attacking a strongly fortified position and being cut to bits with terrible musket fire. Villeroi's naïve remark, "I believe that it will be necessary to seek other means to attack the enemy in places more accessible where we can fight on a wider front . . . ," told the awful story of Chiari. Who was to blame? Villeroi did not blame himself or his fellow officers; all fought valiantly. But the Italians were sympathetic to the Imperials; "Everyone is against us here, we never get good information and the enemy is alerted to all our moves." It was the Venetians who had given the walled town of Chiari to Eugene. At Versailles the full extent of the carnage became clear with Villeroi's letter of September 4: 88 officers, including a brigadier, were killed, and 203 wounded. This latter number soon climbed to 250, and many of them died. There were nearly 3,000 casualties in the ranks. In the letters that followed, the death toll grew rapidly as fever attacked the wounded.

A part of Louis' reply to Villeroi's letter should be quoted, for it is highly indicative of the character of the king: "I see by your letter that you attacked the enemy trenches with twenty battalions . . . on the assurance

that the enemy had retreated leaving only a detachment of infantry . . .
that this attack was made on the advice of the Duke of Savoy and the
unanimous agreement of the generals. It would be desirable that you had
better advice . . . but with what you had been told there was no other
gambit to take. . . . I cannot praise too much the valor of my troops and
the work of the generals . . . the Duke of Savoy should not expose himself in the future. I understand that Marshal Catinat was in great danger.
. . ." Louis then went on to urge Villeroi to work closely with Catinat and
"not again to attack the enemy without advantage." He then returned to
Villeroi's reiterated statement that he had gone to Italy with the king's
orders to fight. Louis' self-justification is gentle: "I ordered you to seek
out the enemy, to keep as near to them as possible, to give battle, but that
order *ought to have been carried out with prudence* [author's italics]."
Villeroi was an old and faithful friend as well as a loyal servant; Louis
could not break such a man. "I have great confidence in you," he wrote,
"let me know . . . what you think best to do next." At the same time he
wrote to the Prince of Vaudémont urging him to use the Spanish soldiers
effectively.[10]

As the casualty lists came to Versailles, Louis began to understand
the extent of his losses, and more importantly, the military problem that
was emerging with the rise of Eugene of Savoy to command new well
drilled and equipped soldiers similar to those that Louis and Louvois had
first introduced on the battlefields almost a quarter-century earlier. "The
number [of casualties]," Louis wrote, "is much greater than you had indicated. . . . I am hurt to lose so many brave men in one affair. . . . The
more the enemies take precautions, the more you should watch them. . . ."
He went on to regret the pro-Imperial attitude of the Italians, but he added,
"You should be cautious and risk nothing with people who know how to
profit by everything and who entrench themselves before you." A few days
later he reminded Villeroi that he must not fight without "advantage." "If
you do otherwise, I lose my troops, the reputation of my arms suffers,
and the King, my grandson, will lose Italy."[11]

As usual Louis recovered his natural optimism quickly. He still had
hopes that Eugene could be driven out of Italy, for he believed that his
armies still had "enough superiority over the enemies to attack them," a
fact that he hoped would influence Italian opinion. It turned out otherwise.
The morale of the Franco-Spanish troops was poor, desertion was heavy,
while that of the enemy was good and became better as Eugene skillfully
pinned down the French. By mid-October all French optimism for the

campaign was gone. Louis ruefully admitted, "It seems that the enemy troops have shown great courage . . . the difficulties of the terrain cause me much distress. It seems almost impossible for you to attack with advantage. You must lead the troops with prudence. . . ." It was disheartening, for by October Louis was well aware of the fact that next year's campaign would be fought on the broad field of Europe rather than simply in Italy. Even so, he expected to have "a considerable increase in the number of troops in Italy . . . and," he added, "I have difficulty believing that the Emperor will be able to increase his army equally."[12] It was to take great reverses to cure this optimism.

Unfortunately for Villeroi the campaign was not over; he was fighting Eugene, and Eugene was first of all a man of war. Villeroi settled down comfortably in Cremona to wait until the next April when a new year could begin. Eugene planned a bold move. On January 31 by a ruse, he thrust himself and a body of picked troops into Cremona and kidnapped Villeroi. Louis was shocked, but recovered when he realized that at least his soldiers had expelled the invaders. It could have been worse. He sent letters of congratulations and promotions in rank to the men who had prevented Eugene from capturing the city when he took Villeroi.[13] The *Gazette,* forgetting its previous statements about the wretched condition of the Imperial troops, gave a blow by blow account of the battle in the city streets and added cryptically, "One will find few examples of a similar victory." Wags soon had a poem that has followed Villeroi ever since.

> *Français rendez grace à Bellone*
> *Votre bonheur est sans égal*
> *Vous avez conservé Crémone*
> *Et perdu votre Général.*

The Cremona affair was hardly over when the death of William of Orange gave hopes that there would be no war in the west. William fell from a horse on March 4; he could not hold anything in his stomach, and by March 18 his doctors discovered "that his nature was not strong enough to withstand the evil,"[14] and he died the following day. The succession in England had been fixed by an act of Parliament. The second daughter of James II, Princess Anne, wife of a prince of Denmark, became Queen of England. It was not clear what would happen. She had had a host of children, but all of them were dead. The Act of Succession named the grandchildren of Elizabeth, Electoral Princess of the Palatinate, daughter of James I, as her heirs, but Anne had scruples about the divine right of kings that made her wonder if her half brother, the Stuart pretender, should not occupy the throne. For a moment the men in Versailles breathed in relief; perhaps there would be no war after all. It was another hope without foundation. Queen Anne was a dull woman, but in 1702 her confidante was Sarah Churchill, the vigorous wife of Jack Churchill, Duke of Marlborough, who had been in William's confidence during all the negotiations for the Grand Alliance. He, with his aristocratic friends and relatives and the Whig chieftains in Parliament, had no intention of calling off the war. Indeed, without William it could be fought more effectively, for William was a poor soldier, while Marlborough, who had studied war under Turenne, was to become one of the great soldiers of the era.

By the middle of April Louis was resigned to the fact that there would be a war, but maintained enough optimism to believe that it would be short. How could the enemy hope to win with the Franco-Spanish forces in possession of most of western Europe? He sent a large army down the Rhine to Cologne to contain the Anglo-Dutch armies. So sure was he of success that he placed his grandson the Duke of Burgundy in command. Marshal Boufflers served "under his orders," and Boufflers had orders from the king to seek out and fight the enemy. "You know," Louis wrote him, "the consequences a happy opening campaign . . . could have on the enemy, and the effects that it might produce on the princes of the Empire who are on the point of declaring themselves." And he believed that a successful campaign was possible, because the French army was composed of veteran troops that had served in the last war, while the enemies would be largely green *levées* recently recruited. Thus would England pay for the disbanding of William's army.

Louis watched the events on the lower Rhine with very great interest because his grandson was "in command." The talented young Duke of Burgundy was the apple of his grandfather's eye. There was little hope that Louis the Grand Dauphin would ever be more than a fat, dull man, but Louis of Burgundy was alert, well-educated, and intelligent. He might even learn the art of war and some day really command a royal army.

A lightning bolt that misfired in Italy gave the king much to worry about; Eugene attempted to kidnap Vendôme, who had gone there to command the troops after Villeroi had been kidnapped. What if someone should try to take the Duke of Burgundy? The escort that accompanied the young prince to the front was almost an army, and Boufflers received exact instructions to keep him safe from harm. "You know," Louis wrote to him, "the love that I have for him [the Duke of Burgundy]. . . ." He also demanded full news about his grandson's progress. "I am interested in everything that he does," Louis wrote, "I should not doubt his courage, those of his blood have never lacked it, but the manner with which it is shown, and the satisfaction of the troops [with the young duke] have given me something that I cannot express. . . ." Grandfathers the world over take pleasure in their grandchildren.[15]

One of Louis' legitimized sons was also with the army on the Rhine. The Duke of Maine could not be given the "command" of the army, but Louis hoped that if the Duke of Burgundy should settle down to a siege, the Duke of Maine might "command" the army of observation. Naturally the Duke of Burgundy was supposed to be the star. "You can guess my impatience," Louis wrote to Boufflers, ". . . I hope for the fame of my arms and that of the Duke of Burgundy that it will be possible to attack the enemies. It would be glorious for him to win a considerable advantage."

Unfortunately for the aging king, his hopes were doomed to frustration. Marlborough kept the French off balance, and slowly but surely drew a net around the whole position in the lower Rhineland. It was not a question of attacking him; he had the initiative.

By the end of August it began to penetrate to Versailles that the war was really going badly. Louis warned Boufflers, "If they take Venlo, then Guedre will be lost, and in the end you will be driven from the whole territory of Cologne. . . ." There had to be something to do. He sent Vauban to help, and wrote letters encouraging action. The young Duke of Burgundy wrote often, but by September without optimism. The horses were in wretched condition and could no longer be used for any extensive action. This was always a great problem of war in these years; there simply was never enough forage to keep the army in good condition. But the Anglo-Dutch horses had more to eat than the French horses. The young duke understood what was going to happen and decided to leave before he could be implicated in the disaster. It was a "surprise" for his grandfather. "I had not expected that the Duke of Burgundy would leave the army so promptly. I was sure that he would not do anything without having . . . seen my latest intentions. I fear that his departure will have a bad effect on my troops and give confidence to the enemies who will be sure that my army is in no condition to attempt anything against them."[16]

The worst was yet to come. Marlborough pinned down the French forces and then proceeded to besiege and capture them without giving them a chance to surrender and march out with the honors of war. This was a predatory pattern that the French did not at first understand. Louis watched the fighting with a fascination bordering on horror. "I knew when you said that all general officers felt that it would be impossible to aid Venlo that the whole province was lost, but I convinced myself that you could save Liège. . . ." A little later: "If they take Liège, the Elector of Cologne will have to come to terms with them . . . this would put them in position to begin next year's campaign with the siege of Namur, perhaps Luxembourg, and then the frontiers of my country. . . ." Later still: "I see that they are going to attack Liège . . . your orders are to save it. Your troops seem to be inferior to those of the foe. I do not hold you to attempt a battle with questionable results to save Liège, for there could be worse losses than Liège. . . ."[17]

The campaign moved swiftly. Roermonde capitulated. The Elector of Cologne declared his neutrality. The French fell back to the Moselle with an army needing everything. Villars won a victory over Louis of Baden at Friedlingen, but this could not soften the blows that were falling on poor Boufflers. By the middle of October Marlborough was before Liège. Louis wrote plaintively, "You know the pain the siege of Liège causes me and the importance of that fortification for the war." Then musing about possible outside aid, "It would seem desirable that the advanced season would have checked their plans. . . . It is a long time since anyone has seen conquests as rapid as these. . . ." The next day: "I tell you I have been pained to see that nothing seems able to stop their rapid conquests. They are in position to take whatever they attack. . . ." Louis was ready to write off Liège, but he began to think about his army. "My intentions are that you save my troops [in Liège]. . . ." But Marlborough never gave them a chance to surrender; he stormed the fortress and made the garrison prisoners of war. Louis was truly worried; "I have lost at Venlo, Roermonde, Stevinswert, and Liège more troops than the enemy lost at Fleurus, even though that victory was complete . . . and this without counting the losses of supplies and munitions of war and not counting what it costs to fortify these places, which amounts to great sums. . . ." His only remaining wish was "that this unhappy campaign should end so that next year could start with hope for success.[18]

The campaign of 1702 was not so unfortunate on the other fronts. Villars stood off Louis of Baden on the middle Rhine and finally brought him to a battle at Friedlingen on October 14. It was strikingly different from the contests between Louis of Baden and de Lorge during the last war; Villars won a clear-cut victory, and his troops hailed him as Marshal of France, a title that Louis confirmed as soon as he heard the story.[19]

In Italy Vendôme had replaced Villeroi after Cremona. His problem proved to have two faces: Eugene's army continued to be dangerous, and the Duke of Savoy, in spite of the fact that two of his daughters were married to Louis' grandsons, was secretly negotiating with the enemy. Vendôme had to watch him as well as Eugene. The Italian war was a thing of maneuvers and skirmishes, until August 15, when a pitched battle occurred at Luzara. Both sides claimed victory, and *Te Deums* were sung in Vienna and in Paris to thank God for His blessings. Louis was indignant at the behavior of his cousin Leopold who "noised around" that his forces had won the battle.[20]

While the Duke of Burgundy failed to cover himself with much glory in the lower Rhineland, his brother the King of Spain had a similar lack of success in his new kingdom. Louis had sent Philippe to Spain expecting that the young king with his Spanish counselors, a few "experts" from the French treasury, and a bit of advice now and then from grandfather or his ambassador, would be able to govern the Spanish kingdoms. Louis recalled how he himself had "taken over" at Mazarin's death; he seemed not to realize that Philippe was still in his later teens and that the machinery left by Charles II was not the same as that which Mazarin had left for him. Poor Philippe was appalled at the idea of trying to govern Spain. Confronted with the task, he did exactly what many teen-age boys do when given problems beyond their ability: he simply looked the other way and refused to see the job. Adults often call this behavior "laziness," which is exactly the word that Louis used to describe his grandson's action. Madame de Maintenon, with more insight and perhaps less false confidence, wrote, he "is old enough to be a king, but not yet old enough to have a will of his own."[21] Louis had to ask: how could a Bourbon prince refuse to rule?

At this point another personality was introduced into the Spanish court: Marie-Louise of Savoy. She was still under fourteen when she married Philippe, and the marriage started off with a fight. Grandfather had insisted that all of her Savoyard friends be sent home and replaced by Spaniards. She was so indignant that she refused to allow Philippe in her bed the first two nights of their marriage. It began a relationship that lasted all their lives, in which she had the upper hand. Marie-Louise was a stronger person than her husband; or perhaps Philippe was a man always to be ruled by women, for his second wife had the same advantage over him that Marie-Louise had exercised.

Grandfather Louis sent a sage letter to his grandson explaining how one manages a queen. This letter tells us much about Louis' ideas concerning royal marriages; it had little or no effect on Philippe's.

I awaited with impatience news of your marriage. Your letter and Louville, whom you sent to me, have told me about it. He speaks to me of all the good qualities of the Queen. She can make you happy if she makes good use of them. I hope for it even though she began badly. I attribute what she did to bad counsel, and you ought to see by this example how important it was to send away the men and women whom she brought with her. She has intelligence, and she will see that she ought to care uniquely to please you. I am sure that she will apply herself to this as soon as she controls her own behavior, but it is necessary for your happiness, and for hers, that she diabuse herself of the ideas that someone has given her of governing you. I believe that your Majesty will not tolerate it. She knows well enough the dishonor that such feebleness brings. One does not pardon it in individuals. Kings, exposed to public view, are even more scorned when they allow their wives to dominate them. You have before your eyes the example of your predecessor. The Queen is your first subject. In this role and in that of your wife, she ought to obey you. You ought to love her. You will not love her as you ought if tears have enough power over you to make you agree to things contrary to your *gloire* ["duty" in this case]. Be firm from the beginning. I know that the first refusals will cause pain; that they are repugnant to the sweetness of your nature, but do not fear to cause the Queen these slight chagrins for they will save her real ones in the course of her life. It is by this conduct alone that you can prevent outbursts that you cannot stand. Will you allow your subjects [and] all Europe to witness your domestic differences? Keep the Queen happy in spite of herself. If it is necessary, constrain her from the beginning. She will be obliged to you in the end, and the violence that you do her now will be the most solid marks of your affection for her later. Reread, I beg you, that which I have set forth in this letter. . . .[22]

Louis must have forgotten Molière's *School for Wives,* or if he remembered, he refused to believe that a prince of his blood could not handle any situation. It turned out that he knew practically nothing about these two young people who very quickly fell deeply in love with each other, shamelessly admitting the spell that sexual attraction had spun over them. This was not all. At fourteen Marie-Louise had more understanding and skill about affairs than her husband would ever acquire, and as we have seen, she quickly established her dominance in the marriage. In most marriages the tasks are divided according to ability; unhappily Marie-Louise was the queen, when she should have been the king. Louis watched this situation develop with unbelieving eyes. Had he not warned the boy? How could a woman rule her husband? He had had many women, but none of them had dared to try to rule his head.

The whole situation in Spain was unfortunate. Louis found himself engaged in a war to save that kingdom from partition, and yet he could get little or no help from Spain; the burden of the war fell on France, and the Spanish were quite unwilling to have it otherwise. When he sent French tax administrators to try to bring some order out of the Spanish chaos, there was a cry that France was trying to load the Spanish with taxes beyond their ability to pay; when he recalled his administrative officers, there was a protest that France was abandoning Spain. He was damned if he did help, and damned if he did not. But the big problem was Philippe's failure to take hold of the government; decision after decision about Spanish affairs had to be made in Versailles; indeed Louis had the load of governing both kingdoms squarely on his shoulders.

The situation in Italy also required attention. The Italians in Naples and Sicily as well as in Milan were largely indifferent to the fate of the crown. Hapsburg or Bourbon: neither had much solid support in Italy. Louis knew that a king who could make himself visible to his subjects could command considerable loyalty: thus Philippe should go to Italy. The suggestion was unpopular. The Spanish were outraged that Italy should seem more important than Spain, and Philippe did not want to leave Marie-Louise! Again grandfather had to play the role of carping critic, demanding that his grandson do his duty. How could he put his personal desires above his duty? How could he admit to the world that he did not want to leave his wife? Philippe finally did go to Italy and "covered himself with glory," which is to say that he was exposed to bullets, but he could not forget Marie-Louise. He became "ill" for his queen, but refused to look at any of the girls that his advisers produced as temporary substitutes. No matter what grandfather might think, he finally returned to Madrid and Marie-Louise—after all, he was only eighteen.

With Philippe in Italy or in Spain it mattered little; the Spanish government could not or would not carry its share of the costs of war. Nor would it consider allowing Louis to annex the Spanish Netherlands so that France could recoup a little of the burden it was carrying. The Spanish believed that the war was being fought to save their empire, not to partition it. Even French assistance in guarding the Spanish treasure fleet did not accomplish all that Louis hoped for. The fleet arrived safely only to be destroyed at Vigo Bay by a daring Anglo-Dutch raid. Louis even had trouble with the French "advisers" whom he had sent to look out for Spain; each of them tried to jockey for a stronger position, with the result that there was more confusion. It was not easy to govern a land that had had bad government for almost a century; it was especially not easy to do so from Versailles. Louis must often have wondered whether he had not made a serious mistake when he attempted to assure Bourbon succession to this curious throne.

In January 1703, Villars visited Versailles to receive the king's congratulations and to plan for the coming campaign. The king told him of all of his griefs from the movements of the armies in Flanders and in Germany, of his chagrin to see them driven out of the Rhineland without a battle—that he was "as much a Frenchman as a king, and that that which affects the reputation of the nation is more on [his] mind than anything else." He went on to explain that "usually toward six o'clock in the evening Chamillart comes to work with me, and for more than three months, he has told me only about disagreeable events. The hour of his arrival is always marked by movements of my blood."[23] Well might his blood pressure mount. In Flanders his armies faced the Anglo-Dutch forces behind lines only recently traced and fortifications of obsolete design. This war, Louis noted, was not like the last one: "Then my frontier was studded with fortresses and my armies were superior to those of the enemy. Now the fortifications of the Spanish Netherlands are poor and can only be defended by my armies, and those of the enemy are stronger than mine."[24] It was simply a question of whether Boufflers and Villeroi could build lines across the Netherlands before the foe broke into the provinces. In Spain, the weakness of Philippe's government invited treason and encouraged Portugal to change sides in the war. In Italy, Vendôme faced the Imperial army but could not advance because large detachments of the French forces there had been sent to southern France to put down a Huguenot revolt. In Germany, Louis of Baden, still licking his wounds from the defeat of Friedlingen, was busy constructing a line of field fortifications beyond Kehl, to shut the French out of Baden and south Germany. Louis decided that Kehl, on the other side of the Rhine from Strasbourg, should be taken as a gauge for entry into Germany, and gave Villars orders to besiege the city.

As Villars tightened his grip on Kehl, Louis began to think of the vicious war that Marlborough had fought the year before, especially of his policy of making prisoners of every garrison. "The affair of Liège," he wrote, "and the conduct of the English and Dutch forces toward prisoners . . . makes me desire to find a chance to show my resentment," but on second thought he gave Villars the power to allow a treaty of capitulation rather than accept the casualties that would result from storming the fortification. Kehl was allowed to surrender and its garrison marched off with the "honors of war."[25]

The conquest of Kehl was not part of a "grand design for 1703"; *no such design existed even as late as the middle of March*. Indeed, Villars had recrossed the Rhine with the bulk of his army before the men in Versailles realized that the Germans might be preparing for an assault on Bavaria. Cologne had been forced out of the war in 1702; was it Bavaria's turn now? Louis had long shown a reluctance to send an army "over the mountain [Black Forest]," for Bavaria was a very, very long distance from Paris in 1703; in many ways it was farther than Zanzibar is from Paris today. But when he realized that the Germans were concentrating a large army "with which [they] will attack and force [Max Emanuel] to accept the conditions that the Emperor will grant, or drive him entirely from his estates," Louis was willing to send troops to the upper Danube. Max Emanuel, he optimistically believed, was the "ally to whom I owe much . . . who can make the Emperor tremble . . . and who can give law to the Empire and procure the peace so necessary to Europe." But in 1703 Max Emanuel was in grave danger. Louis wrote to Villars, "I do not see how I can do anything but put you in condition . . . to join him or to approach the Prince of Baden so that he cannot divide his forces without exposing himself to defeat. . . . My intentions are that you take the necessary measures with the Elector of Bavaria to join him. . . . I need not tell you that upon this junction depends the success of the war which would be more difficult to sustain . . . if I should lose an ally who . . . might secure for me a peace as glorious as it would be advantageous. . . ."[26]

Villars was a competent commander. He bypassed the German lines and reached Bavaria with an army of 48 battalions and 60 squadrons; added to the Bavarians, this was a force capable of undertaking some enterprise. And indeed he and Max immediately got together on a grandiose plan to make an assault on the hereditary Hapsburg lands. The project called for one attack from Bavaria, and another from Italy over the Brenner Pass, and the cooperation of the Hungarian rebels whom Louis subsidized to the tune of 600,000 livres a year.[27] If Vendôme would cooperate with 20 battalions and 25 squadrons, Max and Villars believed that they could force the emperor out of the war. When the plan was presented to them, Louis and his advisers at Versailles quickly agreed to it and sent the necessary orders to Italy. At the same time detachments from the other armies moved into Alsace to take the place of the troops that had gone with Villars, so that the Prince of Baden could not invade that province while the French army was in Bavaria. Marshal Tallard was to command this Alsatian force, and shortly afterward the Duke of Burgundy joined him in hopes of winning an easy victory; everyone believed that the

Germans would have to strip their forces to the bone along the Rhine to meet the threat to the emperor's lands in central Europe.[28]

However, the pincer movement did not get started before Villars and Max Emanuel fell to fighting with each other. Villars had known Max since the days of the Hungarian war; he recognized him as an excellent drinking and "partying" companion, but thought somewhat less of his skill as a soldier; before long he was treating the "conqueror of Belgrade" with near contempt.[29] The difficulty was that Max could not or would not stay with the plans that he and Villars had made. Villars' letters began to sizzle. Even by the end of May there was serious trouble between the two men. Louis wrote to Villars, "I cannot recommend strongly enough . . . not to be haughty with a man of his birth and rank. You should be firm in important things, but present them frankly and you will gain more influence over his conduct than you can by other means." Villars had trouble following Louis' sage advice; he was no psychologist—only a soldier who saw things going badly. By the end of the summer Louis reprimanded him, "That is no way to talk to a man of his rank!" What happened was that Max took off on a personal project against the Tyrol leaving Villars with inadequate troops to meet the German army in central Europe. Had Vendôme sent his troops over the Brenner, it might have saved the day, but these troops did not arrive. Villars was no diplomat anyway, and when he saw his plans go astray in the Tyrolese mountains while his own army was seriously in danger because of Max's irresponsibility, he became more and more irascible. Louis still hoped for "a revolution in Germany . . . your arms will force the Swabian and Franconian circles to ask for neutrality, and the other German princes will . . . seek similar proposals." The thing wrong with Louis' hopes was that Villars was in danger of being thrust out of Bavaria entirely while Max's invasion of the mountains came to nothing.[30]

Even had the Franco-Bavarian armies succeeded in their part of the plans, there remained the problem of Vendôme's cooperation. When Louis ordered him to send the detachments over the Brenner Pass, he countered with the news that the Imperial army had been considerably reinforced in Italy. Louis was indignant. "It seems to me," he wrote, "that the Emperor would be better advised to keep his troops near himself, to fortify the corps of von Schek and von Stirum and the Prince of Baden, to conserve his own estates rather than to employ them in Italy in a way as ruinous to himself as to me [sic!]."[31] Clearly Leopold was not cooperative; perhaps Louis misunderstood the plans that Eugene was making. Moreover, Vendôme had another problem. The year before, there was rumor of negotiations between the emperor and the Duke of Savoy; now these rumors were becoming more and more persistent. Louis hoped that they were unfounded and continued to urge his commander to send troops over the Brenner Pass. All summer Louis wrote with high hopes for the success of the "pincer movement." Not until the sixth of September did he realize that Vendôme had no intention of weakening his army in Italy to help Max and Villars defeat the emperor. Vendôme, with one excuse after another, simply sabotaged the project. It had not been of his making, nor did he have any confidence in it. Vendôme also was a proud Bourbon, and it always proved difficult to control his behavior. Louis did, however, reply with a severe letter:

One could not be more surprised than I to see . . . that you have taken upon yourself to defer the execution of an order which would have been of such great importance that you have reason to be upset the rest of your life for having contributed to a disarrangement . . . that you cannot repair. Do you think when I give you an order as precise as the one that you received, that I do not have reasons stronger than yours for sending it? You allow yourself to be engaged by what is before you, and I see those things that are in the distance which can have effects and which cause me to make resolutions suitable to one who is charged with the weight of government. . . . I ran the risk of losing my army [Villars' danger from the Prince of Baden] and that of an ally who can alone contribute to the maintenance of an honorable war and open to me the route to a peace. The conquest of the Tyrol would have been easy. . . .[32]

The pincer movement failed, but Max and Villars were able to force Louis of Baden to give up Augsburg, which he had taken while the elector was in the Tyrol. The king, more gracious than his commander in the field, wrote to Max, "My brother, I am never surprised about the advantages that my troops win when you are at their head, and I am convinced that led by you, and inspired by your example, they will be invincible."[33] The skirmish to which Louis referred took place near Höchstadt about one year before that village was to be made forever famous.

Vendôme, in the meantime, probably escaped the wrath of the king because the Duke of Savoy actually did change sides to join the emperor. Louis ordered Vendôme to disarm the Savoyard troops while he lulled the Savoyard ambassador in Paris with friendly words. When all was ready he sent the treasonous duke a letter: "Monsieur, since religion, honor, interest, the alliance, and your signature mean nothing to you, I am sending the Duke of Vendôme at the head of my armies to explain to you my intentions. He will give you only twenty-four hours to make up your mind." There actually was no reason for surprise at Savoy's treachery; the French had seen it coming for a long time.[34]

In another theater, the campaign of 1703 provides us with important insights into Louis' role as soldier, as ruler, and as grandfather When Villars crossed into Bavaria, Tallard moved into Alsace with orders to prepare some suggestions for the use of the army under his command. He immediately suggested the siege of Breisach; its capture would ssure the communications between Alsace and Villars in the upper Danube. This proposal suited the king, but even his early letters suggest that Tallard had not fully considered what would be involved in the siege. "The secrecy that you ask for as essential does not depend upon me," Louis wrote; "I do not see how you can do it without the aid of intendants and others to help with the preparations. . . . Marshal Villars has all the artillery officers with him, you have no engineers, no surgeons, no munitioners, no magazines. I know that the cities on the river will furnish you part of these things. . . ."[35]

As Tallard's plans matured, Louis realized that the army in Alsace could provide his grandson with excellent experience and almost certain "fame." Villars and Max would occupy the Germans so that there would be little chance for them to attempt to relieve the siege of Breisach. "I am sending the Duke of Burgundy to Alsace to command my army," he wrote to Tallard, "You must not doubt that he is sensitive to the fame that he will acquire by . . . the conquest of Breisach. I place myself in your hands for the project that should be attempted . . . if you actually decide upon Breisach, do not forget that the Rhine rises during the season of melting snows."[36] This last remark shows that Louis sensed the really important problem of the siege, which, as we shall see, Tallard overlooked.

In the letters that followed between the young Duke of Burgundy and the king, we find the same attempt to build up his confidence that we see in Louis' letters to the young King of Spain. Louis reminds him that he *is* in command, that he should give *his* orders, that he must learn to exercise authority. This does not mean that he should act without counsel; Louis never forgot that counsel was essential for wise action, whether the question was politics or war.[37]

As Marshal Tallard and the young duke shaped their plans, Louis suggested several times that it might be better to besiege Landau, but both his grandson and the marshal insisted upon preparing for the siege of Breisach. Louis finally agreed, hoping that the campaign would cause the enemies to be "fatigued beyond their power and discouraged by their lack of success" and thus come to "demand peace, which alone can reestablish the tranquillity of Europe. . . ." Then toward the last of June, Marshal Vauban passed through Versailles; he had a torpedo for Tallard's project. Louis' letter tells the story: "I have your letter in which you and the Duke of Burgundy have decided to besiege Breisach on the basis of the permission that I gave you on June 22. I understand your reasons for preferring this to Landau . . . they leave me no room to doubt that you have examined the inconveniences that you might encounter of which the only important one is the depth of the water in the moats. . . . Marshal Vauban who knows it, because he fortified it, insists that it is not possible to take it until the floods of the Rhine have receded, and that if the Duke of Burgundy attacks it before the end of August or the beginning of September, he will receive an affront. He tells me that during the present season the locks are not necessary, that the water of the river covers the earth . . . one will find water a foot or two deep all around like a swamp. . . . [He says] it would be better to attack Freiburg or Landau . . . than to hazard without hope of success an enterprise of this consequence that involves the *gloire* of the Duke of Burgundy. . . ." Louis went on trying to soften the blow; he was not one to cut the ground from under a faithful servant without giving him some ego-satisfaction: "You know the confidence with which I give myself to anything that you think proper for the good of my service. It is still the same. . . . I cannot, however, put aside the experience of a man who has served me so long and so well as the Marshal Vauban."[38]

This letter is precious evidence of Louis' feelings of insecurity in face of the military experience of the "experts," as well as of his attitude toward the men who served him. He knew that his own knowledge was not enough to direct great military enterprises; he sought the best advice that he could find, or that he knew how to find. It also is evidence of the "hit and miss" military planning of the regime. Louis' confidence in the man in command of his army led him to expect that man to prepare projects for the use of the army. These plans were discussed and criticized at Versailles, but it usually took the counsel of a man as prestigious as Marshal Vauban to force a change in plan. Louis' veto power over his marshals' projects was real, but rarely used. The other striking thing about this letter is the fact that Louis reassured Tallard rather than relieving him of command; his feckless plan should have warned Louis that his marshal might be an excellent diplomat—as indeed he was—but only a mediocre soldier. The next year this fact became clear.

Breisach did fall in the early autumn of 1703. Louis sent Vauban to Alsace to be sure that there would be no mischance. By this time Vauban's prestige was so great that it was no longer necessary to insist that his commands be obeyed; indeed the king's correspondence almost indicates that Vauban was doing Louis and his grandson a great favor to take the fortress for them. An autographed letter in the hand of the king explains to the

Duke of Burgundy the proper relationship between the commander of the army and Vauban, that is, the relationship that had existed between the engineer and Louis himself during the previous wars when they campaigned together. The commander should ask Vauban what would be needed, and then be sure that Vauban lacked none of the things that he asked for. Louis assured his grandson that in his day Vauban had never lacked necessary supplies or men.[39]

The fall of Breisach assured communications with Bavaria, but it was hardly enough to compensate for the failure of Villars' plan to force the emperor out of the war by a great pincer movement against the hereditary lands. The most unfortunate result of that failure, however, was the conflict that raged between Villars and Max Emanuel. Villars decided that his usefulness with the army in Germany was so jeopardized that the king should relieve him of his command. Reluctantly Louis did so and sent Marshal Marchin, a man with fewer talents but a softer tongue, to join the Bavarian elector. Villars was given the task of suppressing the Huguenot revolt in the south of France, and so was far away at the time when his vigorous and daring personality might have saved the French king great distress in the campaign of 1704 when the initiative again was definitely in the hands of Louis' enemies.

31

FROM BLENHEIM
TO OUDENARDE

IN 1703 LOUIS WATCHED HIS HOPES FOR victory vanish in the misty hills of the Tyrol and on the plains of Italy; two of his allies deserted him leaving the lines of communication with Milan endangered by the Savoyard army at Turin, and the kingdom of Spain open to attack from Portugal. At the same time, the Huguenot rebellion in the south of France expanded into a major conflict. Nor were there any compensations to balance this disarray of Louis' hopes and purposes. The French failed to interest Charles XII of Sweden to attack Brandenburg-Prussia, whose ruler now appeared in his new title of king in Prussia, and the Turks refused even to consider effective aid to the Hungarian rebels against the emperor. They recalled too well the last war. It was all most distressing. There seemed to be no good move that could end the war, or even to slow it up enough to encourage negotiations.

Furthermore, Louis' troubles with his grandson's kingdom became worse and worse. Spain could not be made to carry its part of the load, and in the Spanish court, intrigues involving the French agents in Madrid as well as Spanish courtiers, and even the young royal couple itself, all combined to haunt the king's waking hours. A little later Louis almost wept thinking about it: ". . . I am sustaining with great difficulty the entire weight of the Spanish monarchy. Anyone would rightfully be astonished to see what I have been able to do the last four years . . . the Spanish seem indifferent to things concerning their affairs, and fail to produce resources of their own. It would seem that I want, needlessly, to exhaust my own kingdom to sustain a nation that seems hurrying to its own destruction. . . ."[1]

While the men at Versailles were trying to make some sense out of their war effort, the situation on the Rhine suddenly changed drastically and wrested any semblance of the initiative from their hands. A massive movement of supplies up the Rhine with great depots of war equipment established at Coblenz cast an ominous shadow of the coming Anglo-Dutch campaign. The year before, the conservative Dutch politicians had kept Marlborough's aggressive projects well in check, but in 1704 he had plans to free himself from their constraint with a bold stroke of force that might even end the war. The French could not tell where the blow would fall: from Coblenz he could aim at the Spanish Netherlands, at Alsace, or at Bavaria, and until his plans became clear, the French armies were frozen in their defensive stance from the Channel to the middle Danube. It would have been folly to move without knowing where the Englishman planned to strike.

Even when Marlborough's columns had passed Coblenz, it was not safe to react strongly to his march, for he could easily double back against Luxembourg or the Netherlands. On June 4 the enemy cavalry passed Mainz; a few days later the lead columns passed the Mannheim-Heidelberg area. There were still the alternatives—Alsace or Bavaria. Then came news that Eugene was marching up to the Danube with another Imperial army. It became suddenly clear: Marlborough, Eugene, and the Prince of Baden were planning an assault on Bavaria. The year before Louis had sent Villars with a powerful army to prevent the emperor from destroying his last remaining ally. As another such attempt appeared in the offing, Louis' letter to Marshal Tallard fairly breathes anxiety: "If he [Marlborough] . . . passes into Franconia, you and Marshal Villeroi should come together with a plan to prevent all the forces of the Empire from uniting with the Dutch and the English and falling upon the Elector, who would be unable to resist them. . . . I await your proposals to assist an ally who is so necessary to me, and whose forces, joined to my own, have occupied the attention of all the Empire." A few days later, his tone was even more insistent: ". . . there is not a moment to lose," he wrote, ". . . act powerfully, gathering all the troops that you can, and employing them in such a manner that they will force the enemy armies to divide their efforts."[2]

In the meantime, at Versailles, Chamlay and his colleagues in the war ministry came up with a project. Louis had suggested preventing the Anglo-Dutch forces from joining the Imperials; Chamlay's plan was designed to compel Marlborough to return to the Rhine by breaking his lines of communication with the Netherlands. He proposed that Villeroi from the Spanish Netherlands and Tallard from Alsace should converge upon Marlborough's rear, occupying a broad belt of territory between Stuttgart and Heilbronn. This would place the Englishman in a most dangerous position and force him to give up the invasion of Bavaria. The memorandum was carefully supported by a discussion of the movements of troops in that area during the last war as well as a careful analysis of the problems of supply. It ended upon a note of urgency: there was no time to lose.[3]

But neither Villeroi nor Tallard liked the plan, and their objections finally overruled it. Then Lieutenant General Legall,[4] who had a considerable knowledge of south Germany, came up with a proposal to send Tallard to the upper Danube where he could be in close communication with Marchin and Max, and to have Villeroi move into Alsace, thrusting part of his army over the Rhine to the upper Neckar. This, in effect, would move the whole French defensive stance eastward, leaving only detachments in the Spanish Netherlands to watch the Dutch garrison forces opposite them. It was less bold than Chamlay's proposal and presumably easier to accomplish. In his letter to Tallard, Louis attached Legall's memorandum and supported it vigorously.[5]

Legall's proposal had another advantage. As the crisis unrolled, Louis realized that in addition to the danger of losing Bavaria as an ally, there was also the hazard that Marchin's army might be captured or destroyed in the process. The French were not at all sure that Max Emanuel would not "accommodate" himself to the emperor in face of the armies advancing from both the Rhineland and the Danube. In such a case, Marchin would need immediate support. By sending Tallard into the upper Danube and Villeroi across the Rhine at Strasbourg to the upper Neckar, there would be enough French troops to insure Marchin's retreat. Louis' orders to Tallard gave him an army of 40 battalions and 50 squadrons to move into the upper Danube region, but he suggested that it might be better not to join this force to the armies of Max and Marchin unless the Anglo-Imperials united for an attack on them. By keeping Tallard as an independent link between Villeroi and Marchin, Louis hoped to maintain an escape route for his army if Max Emanuel should make a separate peace, and at the same time to have the necessary forces available to save Bavaria should the occasion for a battle arise.

Then came the news of the Franco-Bavarian defeat at Donauwörth (The Schellenberg). The casualties on both sides were heavy, but the battle both opened the way into Bavaria for the Anglo-Dutch armies and gave Marlborough a new line of communications into central Germany. While Tory politicians began to criticize Marlborough for the "butcher's bill," the French were shocked to see the imposing gains that the enemy had made. Villars did not help much when he wrote to the king that a year earlier he had suggested strengthening the old Swedish fortifications at the crossing at Donauwörth, and added that it was not done because Max was surrounded by "fools and *fripons*."

What would happen now? Everyone knew that a "secret" agent of the Elector of Brandenburg (king in Prussia) was in the Bavarian camp. Savoy and Portugal had deserted Louis the year before; as Louis sorrowfully watched events in Bavaria, his stilted language betrays his feelings: "I do not know how to doubt that the Elector has made his accommodations. I am not even able to be surprised because of the position that he has put himself in by allowing the Emperor to pass the Danube. . . . Nothing now can prevent the Emperor from making himself master of Munich, taking the Electress and her children prisoners and all that [the Elector] regards as most precious. I would like to believe that he could have prevented this passage."[6]

Louis considered the possible results of Max's treason. If the Bavarian elector should "accommodate" himself to the emperor, Marchin and Tallard were to converge on Ulm where together they would have 77 battalions and 150 squadrons; even though some of them had suffered severely at Donauwörth, this would be a formidable army. His letters brim with advice for "saving his army" in case the near future should produce a "disagreeable situation."[7]

While preparing for Max to desert the Franco-Spanish crowns, Louis did all in his power to hold the elector in line. On the morrow of the battle at Donauwörth, he sent Legall to Max's camp to explain to him how Tallard and Villeroi were moving toward the Danube, and to suggest that even though the enemy might cruelly devastate Bavaria, if they could not capture the great Bavarian fortress and major cities, they would be forced to retire in confusion as soon as fall should set in.

Max finally made up his mind: with the possibility of becoming hereditary governor, perhaps even lord, of the Spanish Netherlands dangled as bait before him, he decided to stay and fight for his nephew's cause. Louis was pleased, and perhaps also surprised: "He has taken the extreme gambit; he is determined to sacrifice his country to the fury of his enemies and he now thinks only of putting himself in condition to join you [Tallard] and have a force equal or superior to theirs and to seek out and fight them . . . wherever he finds them." Max and Marchin had been forced to "hole up" in a fortified camp, while Marlborough, Eugene, and Louis of Baden had had a field day in Bavaria; when Tallard arrived with such massive reinforcements Max believed that he could meet the enemy on at least equal terms. Louis was not so anxious for a battle. He knew that all the Franco-Bavarians needed to do was to hold their defensive positions, and he reasoned that when Tallard joined Max and Marchin, the Franco-

Bavarian armies "will be so numerous that the enemy will not dare to attack them in any place," and if the foes did not win a victory, they would have to retreat.[8]

This line of reasoning was undoubtedly sound, for the Anglo-Imperials could not hope to winter in Bavaria unless they were masters of both the important fortifications and the countryside. However, this fact really meant that once the armies under Tallard and Marchin joined Max Emanuel, the die was cast, for Eugene, Marlborough, and the Prince of Baden would have to find a place to fight, or retreat. Neither Versailles nor London and The Hague could have any influence on the action, for they were far, far away; indeed, decisions taken on the Danube could not be known in Versailles or London for a week or more, and by that time the situation would be greatly changed. The men in the field were not equally anxious to fight. Louis of Baden had had all he wanted at Donauwörth, and was quite willing to settle down to besiege Ingolstadt while Marlborough and Eugene observed the enemy. In the French camp, Marshal Tallard was so worried about the safety of the king's army that Max and Marchin came to regard him as an "old woman." On the twelfth of August the two armies camped within six English miles of each other: the Anglo-Dutch-Imperials at Münster, the Franco-Bavarians on the high ground beyond the Nebel creek between Blenheim and Lutzingen. Even today a visitor to this site has difficulty believing that the Franco-Bavarian position could be successfully attacked. While the Nebel is not much of a river, it still is four to six feet wide and the high ground rises sharply fifteen to twenty feet on the Blenheim side. Tallard and his fellow commanders believed themselves safe, and went to bed knowing that the enemy would have to draw off. Yet at seven o'clock the next morning the soldiers massed in the fields on the other side of the creek left no doubt about the enemies' intentions, and by that night the Anglo-Dutch army was in possession of the field as well as of a host of French officers and soldiers, including Marshal Tallard.

There are many accounts of this battle of Blenheim, and this is not the place to tell it again; Louis was far away when his armies were so roughly mauled by the ruthless soldiers who were creating a new kind of warfare. All we might note is that the French officers, scores of them, who were penned together after the battle, all were asking "What will the king say?" It was more than a week before the king knew that anything had happened.

Tallard's letters explaining that he had joined Max and Marchin arrived at Versailles about the time that the Anglo-Imperials were preparing their blow.[9] The first letter telling about the battle came from Jean

Schmid, a Strasbourger who often did intelligence work for the war department, but it was badly written and quite incomplete. Then came an avalanche of letters via the posts from Basel and Rhine cities to members of the court assuring mothers, fathers, sisters, and wives that their loved ones were unharmed and safe. It was a cruel way for the king to learn of the disaster. On August 21 Louis wrote to his commander, "the news from Basel and various points on the Rhine . . . and the large number of letters from officers of my troops who are prisoners of war, leave me no room to doubt that there has been an action at Höchstedt in which the enemies have had a considerable advantage. . . ." In spite of evidence to the contrary, Louis still had hope: "I do not know how it is that I do not have news from you [Tallard] nor from M. de Marchin . . . in waiting I still hope that the situation is not as bad as the enemies have asserted."[10] Two days later, still without a report from his commanders, Louis dictated a letter to Marchin: "I have no room to doubt that the infantry of the army of M. de Tallard and our regiments of dragoons have been cut to pieces. . . ." He then crossed out "cut to pieces" and substituted "entirely defeated and taken prisoners of war."[11] Still no official news: Tallard was a prisoner, and Marchin and Max were heavily engaged trying to bring some order out of their retreat.

Louis understood what was needed; he ordered Villeroi to move the heads of his columns into Germany to make contact with the retreating Franco-Bavarians. Nor did he forget Max Emanuel who, he feared, might now make his peace with the emperor. Louis sent him word that he and his soldiers would be welcome if they would cross the Rhine and continue to fight at the side of the French until it would be possible to make a general peace assuring Bavaria and its elector the advantages that they merited. Finally, in a musing mood in which a bit of his optimism still came through, Louis expressed the hope that "M. de Marlborough would give him an opportunity for revenge."[12]

Louis had become accustomed to seeing his plans fail; he had even come to accept the loss of a fortress or even of a province, but this was the first time that one of his armies had been defeated and so badly used that it lost its ability to fight. It also was the first time that the enemy had captured one of his marshals[13] and hundreds of his officers in a single action. It was a catastrophe. All Bavaria was lost, and with Bavaria all hopes of forcing Germany to come to terms melted like snow in May. Now the enemy was in position to put real pressure on Alsace or on the Spanish Netherlands, pressure that could endanger the kingdom itself. Louis worried over the battle. What had gone wrong? By the middle of September as the evidence came in, he concluded that ". . . the dispositions were badly made, that [his] officers did not know the terrain that the troops were to occupy . . . we must," he added, "hope for more happy opportunities, and that the enemy will not gain other advantages from this battle beyond that of forcing me to recross the Rhine and to abandon Bavaria."[14]

Fortunately for him, the Anglo-Imperials were sobered by the victory; at first there were great shouts of joy, but when their casualty lists came through, there was again grim talk about Marlborough's "butcher bill." The French underlined their enemies' losses by publishing a propaganda broadside that must have been inspired by the king, for its diction is often much like his own, in which the names and station of hundreds of Anglo-Dutch-Imperial officers who were either killed or wounded are listed. Some twenty-four German officers of high noble rank were on the list of killed; it took three pages to list them all. Louis could not know it, but these casualty figures were to "chain" Marlborough's ambitions for more than a year to come.[15]

The action in Bavaria adversely affected other theaters of the war. Vendôme had to give up plans for the siege of Turin, and the armies in Flanders were completely on the defensive. In the Spanish waters near Malaga there was an important naval battle that Louis tried to make into a victory, since his legitimized son, the Count of Toulouse, commanded the French fleet. "The enemy," he wrote, "thought only of defending themselves . . . my son frustrated their ambitions."[16] But neither *Te Deums* in the cathedrals nor *feux d'artifices* in the public squares could hide the fact that Toulouse had to retire, leaving the English in position to capture Gibraltar. The only real "victory" was won by Villars against the Huguenots in Cévennes, but that was a victory over Frenchmen.[17]

Louis was sixty-six years old, his teeth were nearly all gone, his health poor, his spirits low. He felt that God was punishing him for his sins, for his arrogance, for his pride. Madame de Maintenon shared his tears and his conviction that Divine Providence no longer protected France. He had flashes of optimism when he talked of the coming campaign, but they could not last long as he contemplated the blows that had fallen upon him. The English were at Gibraltar, and Tessé's attempt to drive them out was a complete failure. In Italy Vendôme talked about a siege of Turin, but rumor had it that Eugene would again be in command in Italy, and if he were, it might be difficult to punish the Duke of Savoy. But the greatest worry was the long semicircular front from Breisach near Switzerland to the Spanish Netherlands and the English Channel. Louis did not know that Marlborough was accompanied by men who were not going to let him risk the army in another battle like Blenheim; he knew only that Marlborough was a dangerous opponent, a bold, predatory soldier who threatened the kingdom of France itself. In 1705 Louis defended this long front with three armies; Marchin, Villars, and Villeroi (supported by Max Emanuel) were in command. They were ready to send detachments to each other whenever the handsome Englishman seemed bent on attacking a particular sector of the front. In the meantime Louis prayed that God would forgive him, and hoped that his dispositions would be able to meet the dangerous enemies pressing his frontiers.

Tessé's failure to dislodge the English from Gibraltar was only part of Louis' worries about Spain. Philippe simply could not seem to take over his task as king to satisfy his grandfather. The letters between the two men are filled with Louis' admonitions and assurances. While he would write, "It is not suitable to your rank that you make detours to explain your true sentiments . . . it is better to put aside contradictions and speak as master than to . . . talk so ambiguously," he also would assure the young king of his deep affection for him and his faith in his future ability to rule. In letters to Tessé, however, he often enough revealed his dissatisfaction with Philippe and his worries about Spain. It was becoming possible that the archduke would arrive in Spain, and then there was danger that Spain would overthrow the Bourbon monarchy and recognize the Hapsburg prince as king. All contacts with the young couple were not so formal or political; we find in the correspondence that Louis is pleased that "the Queen of Spain is well-satisfied with the dresses that the Duchess of Burgundy has sent her" and little notes of affection between grandfather and his grandchildren. Indeed, in reading the letters of this fateful winter when the English fixed their hold upon Gibraltar and the Straits, it seems that Louis did not realize the full meaning of this move. His France was a "land animal," and even the memory of what had happened during the final years of the last war when the Anglo-Dutch fleet controlled both the Atlantic and the Mediterranean seems not to have alarmed him.[18]

As always Flanders was the most important front. Louis wrote to Villeroi the middle of May 1705: "The situation in Flanders requires great precautions on your part to avoid having a combat forced upon you. You understand . . . the smallness of the advantages if you should win, and the terrible results of losing." The king's war plan demanded that his armies establish themselves strongly behind the lines, and that detachments should be ready to rush to the support of any sector of those lines that might be threatened.[19] When his spies discovered that Marlborough had decided to attack Alsace where Villars was in command, Louis immediately detached troops from Villeroi and Marchin, including the elite *Maison du Roi,* to strengthen Villars, whom he assured that he "had every reason to expect . . . [Villars] to make good use of [them]. . . ." His letters brim with confidence, but occasionally a phrase like "I have difficulty convincing myself that he [Marlborough] will dare to attack you in the advantageous camp that you occupy . . . it would only be at great disadvantage to himself . . . exposing himself to the loss of his best troops in his army without hope of success" gives us the feeling that after Blenheim he did much whistling in the dark.[20]

This time, however, the king was right. Marlborough approached Villars' camp, reconnoitered it several times in person, and decided that there was better game in Flanders. Louis of Baden pulled back to the Rhine, and Marlborough took his army to join the troops on the frontiers of the Spanish Netherlands. The French apparently had won the first round of 1705.[21]

As Marlborough moved toward Flanders, Louis detached troops from Villars' army to join the one commanded by Villeroi. Villars himself remained behind; "I did not send the Marshal de Villars to Flanders, even though I will be obliged to send the best part of his troops there . . ." wrote Louis, "because he could not serve there with agreement. I have reason to believe that the Elector of Bavaria would be pained to see him."[22] Louis' loyalty to Max Emanuel was a great handicap to the successful conduct of the war; political factors obviously were more important than purely military ones. It is evident, too, that he understood Max's limitations, for when Chamillart wrote to Max that with the reinforcements he was sending to Flanders the army would be in shape to "make war honorably," Louis crossed out that statement and wrote "in condition to sustain the defensive honorably." He did not want Max Emanuel to rush into an action to revenge the defeat of Blenheim.[23]

Marlborough never gave Max the chance to fight; he struck the lines near the present village of Waterloo and broke through. The whole French position crumbled. Max Emanuel wrote to the king: "In spite of all the precautions that we took to guard the lines . . . the enemy surprised the barrier between Wanghen and Espen, and at four o'clock in the morning broke through. It was not discovered until five o'clock. When I was alerted, I went with the Marshal de Villeroi with all diligence, but too late to remedy the situation, for we found a great number of the enemy army had passed through in spite of the charges that were made without success because the enemy forces were superior to those that we could oppose against them. The army was too spread out to attempt a general engagement. . . ."[24]

In the next few days it became clear that Max's carelessness was responsible, and that the results of the breakthrough were catastrophic. The French army had to retreat in great haste and disorder across the front of the Anglo-Dutch forces. Had Louis seen Marlborough's frustration when the Dutch commissioners refused to sanction a general attack, he would have understood better why his army escaped destruction.

What Louis did understand was that his army was in dire danger; he may also have understood that Max was to blame, but he could not remove him from his command. To Villeroi he wrote, "However much convinced I am of your vigilance and the care that you have taken to be alert to the movements of the enemy, it is nonetheless quite disagreeable to see them past the lines in the center of the Netherlands, and at several important places, with my army obliged to retreat precipitously in front of them to avoid defeat. . . ." He went on to ask what would become of the lines that should have been guarded; perhaps "it might be necessary to abandon this type of warfare [defensive lines] which seems to suit neither the genius of the nation nor the army that you command." It was hard for him to understand why, with an army as large as Marlborough's, his commanders could not do better. However, with the lines broken, there was nothing to do but to wage war "as we did in the past [Turenne's days] holding the countryside and seeking advantage by making excellent defensive camps . . . not exposing ourselves to a general conflict but also avoiding too great caution since the enemies will profit if they see caution." "It seems to me," he added a few days later, "that your future action should show the enemy your strength without seeking to fight them."[25]

The French officers finally fixed the blame on Max and the Bavarians, but nothing could be done about it. Louis' faith in Villeroi was quite unshaken: "You must always tell me truly what happens without fear of hurting me by disagreeable news. . . . I have let you know well enough what my feelings are toward you, and what I think of those unhappy days of the 17th and 18th on which I know that *you* took all the precautions that were expected of you. . . ." When Marlborough failed to make much of his advantage, and finally retired from the Spanish Netherlands, Louis was jubilant: "I am overjoyed to learn that the great bragging that they made . . . ended in a shameful retreat . . . the manner in which this affair ended is glorious for you and for the Elector. . . ."[26]

The little satisfaction that he got from the fact that Marlborough was "chained" by the timid Dutch commissioners was dissipated by the stale-mate in Italy that prevented Vendôme from starting the siege of Turin, and in Spain by the Anglo-Dutch-Imperial landing at Barcelona that allowed the archduke to appear as Charles III. Furthermore, the costs of this war were ruinous. Every day it was more and more evident that France would not be able to carry them without more help from Spain, and yet who knew whether Spain might not accept Charles III rather than pay for the war? In public Louis kept the proud pose of confidence, for he knew that a king must act like a king, but in the apartments of Madame de Maintenon the tears that were to flow so freely in the next few years already coursed down his cheeks. How far would God go in his punishment for the sins and the arrogance of the king?

In the spring of 1706 optimism again ran high on several fronts. Villars and Marchin were sure that they could invade Germany from Alsace and perhaps force some of the German princes out of the war. Vendôme was sure that he could hold off the Imperials while Feuillade besieged Turin and settled the score with the Duke of Savoy. In Spain the Franco-Spanish armies were preparing to besiege Barcelona in hopes of throwing the archduke into the sea. This time Louis himself was less sanguine than his soldiers. He wrote to his grandson, "The defense of Barcelona will be stubborn, but its conquest will bring closer the end of the war. The outcome is in the hands of God, *we must await with sub-mission whatever he wishes to do for the good of Europe.* I, however, will never forget to give you tender proofs of the friendship that I share with you." God might decide to depose Philippe, but his grandfather would never disavow him.

How right he was to be fearful of the future. In May, Villars' limited success in the Rhineland was completely canceled by a terrible defeat in Flanders that forced the French to evacuate the whole of the Spanish Netherlands. Louis had given Villeroi and Max a mighty army of 96 bat-talions and 150 squadrons to "reestablish the confidence of the inhabitants of the Spanish Netherlands." He believed that Marlborough would not have a larger one. What must have been his reaction when he got Villeroi's letter of May 24 announcing the battle of Ramillies? "I have the honor to inform your Majesty of the unlucky day of the 23rd. The army started to move at the break of day . . . and the combat lasted until half past six in the evening. We marched all night to reach Louvain; the beginning of our retreat was in good order, but the end was in great confusion." The letter then went on to describe the battle. Poor Villeroi; the king's orders had allowed him to be a bit aggressive, so when Marlborough's army approached him on May 21 he sought and found a suitable defensive position from which to bar the progress of the enemy. According to his story, by May 23 he and Max were ready; the enemy had the alternatives to attack or to retreat. The unlucky marshal's account of the battle then proceeds to explain how the foe attacked on his side of the line only to be repulsed. In this first stage of the battle it seemed to Villeroi that the French would surely win. Then ". . . one came to tell me that our right wing had been absolutely defeated. I went there and saw a disorder even greater than had been indicated. The Elector arrived there too. Since I had been near the village that had been attacked [on the left], I had not seen the action that occurred on the right. The Elector also had not seen it. . . . Now I saw the enemy squadrons established on the terrain that had been occupied by our right wing, and our right wing was exposed . . . the enemies again attacked Ramillies making themselves masters of it . . . there was no other possible action than seeking a way of retreat. At first it was made with great order . . . later the disorder was great . . . by good fortune the enemy did not follow us closely and our troops reached Louvain. . . . I cannot yet tell your Majesty the extent of our losses. You will see by the numerous officers killed and wounded that the action was rude. It is sure that the enemy lost more men killed and wounded than we did. . . ." It was a long letter and it takes only a little imagination to see Louis bowed and broken by this terrible news.[27]

Louis' first thoughts were for the safety of his army. He urged both Max and Villeroi to work desperately to reestablish it as a fighting force, for this would be the only way "to prevent the enemies from profiting too quickly from the advantages that they won." He also detached large bodies of troops from the army in Alsace to fill the places of those that were lost, even though this act condemned Villars to the defensive. Villeroi asked to be relieved from his command because he lacked the confidence of the troops, so Louis called Vendôme from Italy to take his place. However, he persuaded Villeroi to stay with the troops until Vendôme should arrive, and tried to smooth the marshal's wounded feelings of defeat and discouragement by kind words. When Villeroi finally came to Versailles the king met him with, "*Monsieur le Maréchal,* one is no longer lucky at our age."[28]

Ramillies had adverse effects on every theater of the war. Villars' plan to invade Germany had to be called off, and since Vendôme was needed to bring some order to the army in Flanders, the plan to besiege Turin was much less certain of success. Louis' letters to his soldiers seem to lack buoyancy; he was soon to be seventy and his physical state matched the disorders that were plaguing his armies; his words sound defeatist, discouraged, desperately worried, and yet he tried to keep a close watch on the course of the war and the actions of his commanders. Only in Italy was he willing to take a chance; he felt sure that Eugene could be kept beyond the Adige River while another army besieged Turin. Even when he knew that reinforcements were going to Italy from Hesse and perhaps from other parts of Germany, he would not believe that Turin could be relieved. The treacherous Duke of Savoy had to be punished.[29]

The siege of Turin was begun by an army under the command of the Duke of Orléans, Louis' nephew and son-in-law, with Marshal Marchin "under his orders" to be sure that all went well. Another French army stood on the Adige to "watch" Eugene. Then things began to happen. As recruits spilled over the Alps from Germany, Eugene made a large detachment from his army and began to move. As Eugene slipped around behind it, the French army of observation was pinned down by the arrival of more German troops from over the Alps. Eugene's detachment was not as large as the army before Turin, so at first the men in Versailles were not disturbed, but when he captured the troops sent to "amuse him," the fever of excitement began to rise. The king wrote his son-in-law explaining how important it was to finish the siege of Turin before Eugene could arrive, but when he saw that this probably could not be done, Louis accepted the idea that the answer to the Imperial threat was "to continue the siege and give battle to Eugene if necessary . . . ," and Louis was "convinced that the results would be happy."[30] This suited Eugene. He and the Duke of Savoy surveyed the French position around Turin, and decided to attack.

What Louis did not know was that the French defensive lines around the city were not complete. The French commanders did not believe that Eugene would ever reach Turin, or if he did, that he could do anything but observe the fate of the city, since the detachment that he commanded was so small. But Eugene and the Duke of Savoy, pooling their troops, stormed into the French lines. At the last moment Marchin sensed his danger, and even predicted his own death, but by that time it was too late. The French army was routed, Marchin killed, the supplies captured. It was a terrible shock at Versailles, for all at once not only the army that had been before Turin was in terrible trouble, but the army in Lombardy was now also in danger from two fronts.[31]

For the first time Louis seemed to be at a loss to know what to do. He turned to Vendôme in Flanders whose years of service in Italy should give him good ideas. "The defeat," Louis wrote to him, "has determined

me to ask you what you would do, what orders you would give
. . . should we join all the troops that are in the lands of the Spanish
King and in the lower Po valley to form a single army, or would it be
better to settle them in the strongest fortifications and abandon the open
country to the enemy? . . . I am convinced that in a situation as embarrassing as the one we are in, we must redouble our zeal to block the enemies'
plans . . . but my uncertainty about the conditions . . . and about what
has happened prevents me from making plans. . . ."[32] Unhappily Vendôme
could not help either, for the situation in Italy was in Eugene's hands.
In Louis' letters to the Prince of Vaudémont and the French commanders
in Italy, his hopes for recovery of the Franco-Spanish position in Italy faded
as news poured into Versailles. It took a little time, however, for him to
realize that the enemy actually did have a force superior to his own, and
that their morale was high, while the French troops were discouraged,
bedraggled, and frightened.[33]

By December 1706, the Franco-Spanish cause was surely at low ebb:
practically all of Spanish Flanders was in enemy hands, all of Italy was
lost, and in Spain it seemed possible that Philippe might soon be thrust
out of his kingdom. Only the great fortifications of the French frontier
seemed to guarantee that the kingdom would not be violated. But the
kingdom itself was also in serious financial difficulties. France had carried the
ever-mounting cost of the war for five years, and the strain was beginning
to tell. An old man and an old woman wept bitter tears in Madame de
Maintenon's rooms. The King of France kept a proud façade when he
stalked among his courtiers in the public rooms of the palace of Versailles;
but it was difficult to keep it up, for everyone understood how desperate
was the situation of the kingdom. Especially did his foes understand and
thus they spurned all the proposals for peace that were tentatively offered
by agents of the French king. Would not the year 1707 give France a
final blow that would force her king to accept the conditions that were
presented to him rather than those that he might suggest?

However, the blow did not strike in 1707; indeed for a moment the
war seemed to turn in France's favor. Part of the respite was due to the
other war, which was raging in eastern Europe between Charles XII of
Sweden and his "personal foes," Peter of Russia and Augustus of Saxony-
Poland. Charles XII dramatically appeared in the middle of the German
empire to break Augustus. Would his armies leave Germany or would they
aid France? Charles's camp at Altrandstadt became a Mecca for the
soldiers and diplomats of the western world. Marlborough visited him; the
new emperor, Joseph I, acceded to all his demands for toleration of the

Lutheran party; indeed he said that he was lucky that the Swedish king had not demanded that he become a Lutheran himself. Louis' hopes that the Swedish army might somehow help France were doomed to failure, first because of Charles' prejudices against France, and second because of his determination to "punish" Peter of Russia for his "sins" against Sweden. No matter whether Charles wished to help France or not, his very presence in the empire did slow up the Anglo-Imperial drive in the west until after the Swedish army departed for Russia—and Pultava.

There was another source of advantage for the Franco-Spanish crowns in the treatment that the Dutch gave to their Flemish "cousins" when the French were driven out. There was little love between the United Netherlands and the Spanish Netherlands, and the former regarded the conquest as an opportunity to recoup some of the costs and the losses that they had suffered through this war. The result was that the townsmen in Flanders were soon regretting the expulsion of the French, and when the opportunity arose, they were quick to help Vendôme recover the losses of 1706. In Spain, too, the allied victories turned somewhat to the advantage of the Bourbon cause. Archduke Charles was a Roman Catholic, but the armies that were trying to secure his title as Charles III of Spain were largely Protestant; some of them were French Huguenots, some English or Dutch Calvinists, some German Lutherans, but nearly all of them regarded Spanish Catholicism as superstition or worse, and did not hesitate to show their contempt. When an army reached Madrid commanded by a French Huguenot, the Earl of Galway, for the first time in the course of the war, the Spanish came out of their stupor, and money and recruits became available for the armies of Philippe V. Moreover his queen, who had long been more popular than he, was pregnant; her condition and the behavior of the enemy caused both peasants and noblemen to join the Bourbon cause. By the time that Berwick (Roman Catholic Englishman, bastard son of King James II) won a battle over Galway at Almansa, Philippe was started on the way to achieving independence from his grandfather's tutelage and control over his kingdom. A male child was born in September, and shortly afterward the Spanish besieged and took Lerida.

Louis' reactions to the Spanish situation are interesting. When Philippe wanted to command the army himself, his grandfather discouraged such action: "Your true *gloire* consists in securing the good for your kingdom . . . in council. You know that I would not advise you contrary to the best interests of your kingdom. . . ." When the young queen asked Louis to give her son his name, Louis replied, "You can easily judge that I do not hesitate to grant your request. . . . I hope in giving my name to the

prince . . . to be able to communicate to him the wisdom and other qualities of his father and mother. . . . I hope that God will continue the gifts
that he has given you." After the child was born, the queen wrote, "The
King and I will raise him, if it is possible for us, to fulfill all his duties to
God and man. We will teach him that he owes you an obligation that he
must never forget."[34] By November, Philippe's power had grown to a
point where, when he urged his grandfather to join him in an assault on
Sicily, Louis' answer shows how the roles of dependence were beginning
to shift. The plan was a "good idea . . . but unhappily I am not in the
position that you are to contribute to this enterprise . . . as you must
know from other sources."

For the year 1707 Louis concentrated his greatest effort to provide
Vendôme in Flanders and Villars in Alsace with power to resist the terrible Marlborough; the other fronts were proportionately weakened. Both
of these men succeeded beyond the expectations of Versailles. Vendôme
was able to reenter the Spanish Netherlands, and with the connivance of
the townsmen, one fort after another fell to the French army. It was not
entirely Vendôme's genius; Marlborough was again "chained" by timid
Dutch politicians who feared the "loss of the entire war in an afternoon's
battle." In Germany, too, Villars made a broad sweep reoccupying the
"lines of Stolhofen" and levying contributions deep into Franconia and
Swabia. Louis was delighted.

I do not know how to praise too much the disposition that you made to become
master of the lines of Stolhofen, and the way it was done and the lucky success
of the movement. I await with impatience details. . . . You remember that the
great advantage that you can draw from this expedition *is that of allowing my
army to supply itself at the expense of the enemy and to oblige them to fortify
considerably their forts to oppose you.* If they do not put themselves in condition to check your progress, I am convinced that you will take contributions
from as far away as you can go. You can make them pay the arrears of the
past and, not content yourself with letters of exchange, you will make them
pay most of it in silver and gold and you will take hostages for the rest. . . .[35]

While the French were moderately successful in Flanders and
Germany, the allies decided to attack in the Mediterranean area. By June
it began to be apparent that they had designs upon one of the French
Mediterranean harbors, probably Toulon or Marseilles. By the second
of July, Louis informed Marshal Tessé of the probability of an invasion
and supplied him with memoranda by Chamlay and Catinat discussing the
necessary reactions. Tessé set out immediately to fortify Toulon where the
defensive works were in very poor condition, and at the same time plans

were put under way at Versailles to assemble an army to defend the threatened points effectively. By the first of August, Louis was optimistic about the success because of the "incredible diligence" of his marshal: "According to all the rules of war the fortification ought to be in a state of complete security . . . [and] if they start a siege, I will have an army to give you, independent of the one that you have employed for the defense of Toulon. . . ."[36] Before the siege began he sent Tessé a blank commission for him to fill out to appoint someone to command in Toulon in case Monsieur de St. Pater, whom Tessé had placed in command, should be disabled. Louis also began to draw troops for this battle in the south from Spain, Alsace, and Auvergne; he even called up the militia from Grenoble. This siege of Toulon, he wrote, is a "rash and impracticable act . . . it will cost them dearly!"

The enemy did come to Toulon—Eugene and the Duke of Savoy, and a sizable Anglo-Dutch naval force—but they found that Tessé had, in fact, fortified the city so that it would not be an easy mark, and that the French soldiers fighting on French soil proved valiant and brave. Louis, almost seventy years old, still with a great deal of energy, wrote to all commanders for aid, urging rapid marches toward Toulon, finding money and materials to support Tessé's battle with the invaders. "It is enough to give you an idea of this new war and the danger it would be to allow Prince Eugene and the Duke of Savoy to establish themselves in my kingdom at the gate of Languedoc. . . . ," he wrote, demanding detachments from Spain. By August 14 he decided to send his two grandsons, the Duke of Burgundy and the Duke of Berry, to command, in hopes of stimulating even greater efforts in his army. The young Bourbon princes, however, did not arrive in time and they were not needed; Tessé, with the aid of reinforcements that the king sent him from all parts of France and Spain, forced the enemy to lift the siege. It was a victory heartening to the kingdom as well as to the king.[37]

Louis happily wrote to his commander, "I have news of the enemies' retreat . . . you have just saved, by your care and the extreme diligence with which you have used my troops . . . the port of Toulon, the marine of the Levant, a post which could have given my enemies an establishment from which it would have been quite difficult to drive them during the rest of this war. . . . I have reason to believe that the measures you took, on the retreat of the Duke of Savoy and Prince Eugene, will cost them dearly. . . ." The troops that he had borrowed from the Spanish front returned to Spain, but in such poor condition that they could not be used any more that year. These troops, however, along with those from Alsace, had been the backbone of the effort that saved Toulon, and Louis showered presents and pensions upon their officers as well as upon those in the city whose "valor had matched the arrogance" of the invaders.

The next spring the French armies in the Spanish Netherlands continued to make progress against the enemy; the cities of Ghent and Brussels both surrendered, giving Louis some hopes that this year of 1708 would bring an "honorable peace." There was one vexing problem. The army was under the command of the Duke of Burgundy and the Marshal Vendôme, whom Louis had placed at the very top of the roster of French marshals because of his Bourbon blood and his successes as a soldier. Several years earlier there would have been no trouble, for then the Duke of Burgundy was only learning the art of war. But by 1708, this grandson of the king and presumptive heir to the throne, was beginning to have ideas of his own about warfare. He found Vendôme a little too careless, a good bit too rash, and surely too ambitious; Burgundy, like his grandfather, was a cautious man who had already had experience dealing with a dangerous enemy. A conflict began to appear between him and Vendôme, a conflict that soon was laid upon the king's desk in a dozen subtle ways. Burgundy presumed upon his grandfather's affection to present his side of the case in private letters. Louis, anxious not to offend Vendôme and yet undoubtedly drawn to his grandson's side of the argument, tried to get the two men to resolve their differences without his interference. He did tell Burgundy that "it is not possible to succeed if you do not in the future act in concert with the Duke of Vendôme."[38]

Even so the French were doing nicely in Flanders. The army was as large or larger than the Anglo-Dutch field army under Marlborough and there were detachments to the south that could be hurried to the support of these forces. Louis' optimism ran high. "The march of the army . . . and the good order that you have maintained," he wrote to his grandson, "gives me great pleasure. It ought to impress the enemies and make them know that the superiority that we have over them should convince them to end the war, which will only last as long as the people and the commerce of the Netherlands will tolerate it." Toward the last of June, however, a note of caution enters the letters. Prince Eugene was marching an army to the Rhine; it was not clear whether he would move into Alsace or the Spanish Netherlands. Marshal Berwick, with a large detachment, marched to counter Eugene. The way this news was treated by all parties concerned reflects the fact that Eugene's military genius was much feared even though he had been forced to give up Toulon the year before—perhaps even because of it, for Eugene was breathing fire in his desire for revenge.

Louis' urgings that his grandson "take precautions . . . against the negli-
gence of some officers who are so careless . . . ," that he "maintain the
discipline of the army" now were increased. Even so, he really did not believe
that Eugene would join Marlborough "because of the difficulty of providing
sustenance for so great a number of troops and the impossibility of using
them usefully."[39]

However, without the king's permission, Eugene came on! At Oudenarde he and Marlborough caught the French armies in a difficult maneuver and forced them to fight. By dusk the French found themselves within
a horseshoe of fire. Vendôme was sure that he could turn the tables on
them and wanted to fight it out another day; the Duke of Burgundy lost his
nerve and ordered a retreat. The months of controversy that were to follow
never solved the question of which one was right.[40]

As usual the commanders both gave the king a slightly watered-down
account of what happened. Soldiers seem always to minimize their losses,
at least in the first reports. Perhaps they themselves are not completely
aware of the situation. Thus Louis could still be a little optimistic in the
first days after the battle. He wrote to his grandson:

I have received two letters . . . that inform me of a battle fought near Oudenarde. It now seems that it was stubborn . . . and the losses greater than I had at
first believed . . . the confusion of the retreat was great and I am displeased
that the first chance that we found was not a more happy event. Do not lose
courage. We must reassure our officers and troops by our discourse and our
good countenance. . . . We still have such a considerable number of troops that
we find ourselves, after separating those battalions that suffered much, with an
army stronger than the enemy have ever had, . . . without the junction of
Prince Eugene, we would have had nothing to fear. . . .[41]

Two days later, when he could better understand what had happened,
we find the king dictating a long list of instructions and suggestions for his
grandson. This is a remarkable document for a man of seventy; it shows us
that Louis had forgotten none of the problems of making war in Flanders.
It also contained sage advice for the young Duke of Burgundy: "It is of the
greatest consequence for the good of my service that you urge the Duke of
Vendôme to act with more precaution, and to work with you in all things,
that you give him your confidence, and for his part, that he does things that
will merit it. . . ." At the end of the letter Louis returns to the admonition
that he had given every commander since 1661: "Keep the troops in an
exact discipline and hold, by your own conduct and your attention to the
needs of the bourgeois [of Ghent], the zeal and good will of the inhabitants

of that city." He did not yet believe that the disaster of Oudenarde would have the same unhappy results that had followed Blenheim and Ramillies.[42]

The king's hopes for successful action even though the army had been defeated at Oudenarde were destined to be blasted. Eugene and Marlborough were not to be checked; they did not have great superiority over the French, but they did have a close cooperation between their armies that was completely lacking on the French side. As the Anglo-Imperials pushed their campaign on to the point where they were ready to lay siege to the powerful fortress of Lille, Louis had to watch the controversy between Vendôme and his grandson cripple the efforts of his soldiers. He sent Chamillart to Flanders to try to bring harmony to the army; he sent Berwick to join the Duke of Burgundy; he wrote letters of sage advice. But he could not prevent Eugene from drawing siege lines around Lille. Nor was that the end of his troubles. As the Anglo-Imperials pushed on toward Lille, they were able to send detachments into northern France to exact contributions; for years Louis' soldiers had done this in Germany and the Spanish Netherlands, but it was another story when the enemies were laying exactions on French towns and villages. "Your unhappy day will be even worse," Louis wrote to Burgundy after Oudenarde, "if the enemies are able to live off of the land and maintain themselves using the canals and rivers." Two weeks later the evil was upon him. "We have learned," he wrote to his grandson, "of the harshness with which the enemy execute their demands for contributions and all that which they do *contrary to the laws of war* . . . [author's italics]."[43] It had been good when Villars sent his horsemen into Baden and Franconia, but Louis was now horrified to see sweeps of 600 to 1,000 enemy cavalrymen imposing contributions upon his subjects.

Soon the siege of Lille blanketed everything except the smouldering controversy between Vendôme and Burgundy. Louis placed the defense of the fortification under the old Marshal Boufflers who proved himself to be as doughty a soldier as he had been years before at Namur. Indeed the fate of the city was by no means settled when Eugene drew his lines around it. Lille had been fortified by Vauban and it was a natural site, since the whole defense system could rest on rock. Furthermore, for all Eugene's genius, he was not Vauban, and his style was better expressed in an open field battle. Finally, with Boufflers defending the city, the assault used up a large number of men; this meant that Marlborough's army was not really superior to the combined French forces that he was expected to "observe." Indeed if the armies under Vendôme and Burgundy could have acted more effectively, Marlborough would have been in trouble. It took his genius, and perhaps his fearful reputation, to maintain the field army that protected the siege.

Before Lille fell, there was much fighting over the supply lines that provided Eugene's army with food, fodder, and munitions. Some of these skirmishes would have passed as a full-fledged battle a century earlier. The tension at Versailles ran high during these battles; Louis was worried about Lille, about the contests between his most famous marshal and his grandson, and about Burgundy's safety. He wrote, ". . . my attention should . . . be to see that you serve as usefully as you can . . . you should take opportunities to animate the officers and troops by your presence . . . without exposing yourself unnecessarily to danger . . . and since you have not yet acquired everything that long experience [with war] will teach . . . I am sending Marshal Berwick to be near you and assist your judgments. . . ."[44] A week later when there seemed a possibility that a full-fledged battle might develop between his armies and Marlborough's, Louis held back. The object of the two armies, he wrote, is to take or to save Lille and we "can save the fortification without committing the fault of a battle which would take place too far away from [Lille] to force the enemy to abandon the enterprise." Indeed it might be better to allow Eugene to take Lille rather than to lose a battle that would ruin the army. By early September Louis still hoped that the city would be relieved. "Nothing," he wrote, "could be more advantageous to the good of the State. I pray to God that He will assist you and conserve you in what you are doing." By the first week in October, he admitted that if the English army could keep open the supply line from Ostende, Boufflers would soon be forced to retire to the citadel. But Boufflers held on, and by October 23, Louis wrote, "As the season begins to advance, the nights become cold, sustenance for cavalry disappears. If the enemy insists upon remaining in the country, you must take measures to care for the cavalry. . . . Marshal Berwick can be of assistance to you along with old cavalry officers. . . . The foe is in the same situation as you are. . . ." By the end of October, Boufflers surrendered the city and retired to the citadel. He held out until December, but finally had to surrender (December 9). When the campaign was over, he was the only officer who emerged from the battle with his reputation intact. The others had disgraced themselves by unsightly conflicts that did the king's service little good.[45]

As the disastrous campaign ground down to its conclusion, Louis apparently became convinced that the war could never be won. A letter to his grandson the King of Spain toward the last of November, when he expected every day to hear that Boufflers had surrendered, rather sadly remarked, "I have always labored to maintain you in the rank that it pleased God to place you. You see that up to now I have made the utmost efforts to keep you there and I have not asked whether the good of my kingdom demanded it. I have followed the suggestions of the tender love that I have always had for you and you can be assured that it will lead me as long as the state of my affairs permits. . . ." He went on to tell Philippe how public opinion blamed the generals and his brother for "the unlucky successes of the war." While he insists that the "public deceives itself," he is nonetheless discouraged.[46] He could not know that the terrible winter just ahead would almost complete the ruin of his kingdom.

32

THE PEACE THAT FAILED

On MAY 12, 1709, the Cardinal Archbishop of Paris celebrated a high mass in the church of Sainte Geneviève; the next day came a formal demand for a procession of the relics. On May 15 the English Pretender and his court heard high mass in the church, and that night amid tolling of bells and blaring of trumpets the *châsse* of Sainte Geneviève was brought from its traditional resting place. The next morning, following the king's orders and most of the Parisian clergy, the singers of the Notre Dame, and a host of important people assembled for the procession. The Cordeliers, the Jacobins, the Augustinians, the Carmelites, and the barefooted brothers of the Notre Dame marched with the relics of the saint. Next came the priests of the Oratory with the relics of Saint Magloire, and the Benedictines with those of Saint Martin des Champs and the *châsse* of Saint Paxent. Then came the clergy of the collegial churches and the monks of Saint Opportune and Saint Honoré with crosses and reliquaries, followed by the clergy from Saint-Germain l'Auxerrois and from Saint-Martin with the *châsses* of Saint Landré and Saint Clément. Finally, after a press of barefooted friars, came the cardinal archbishop and other princes of the church. Next came the members of the sovereign courts with archers, and the city government with soldiers and guards. Bells tolled, trumpets fanfared, drums rolled as the procession marched through the streets of the city to the great cathedral where the cardinal archbishop celebrated a pontifical high mass. The ceremony took the greater part of the day.[1]

The relics of the saint were never paraded without good reason, and it may be that never before nor afterward were the provocations so great. The kingdom was in dire danger. While enemies hammered at its gates with fire and sword, a terrible winter—frost that killed men, animals, and even the grain in the fields, the vines and the trees—had created a famine that would slay more men than the war had killed. All winter hungry women wrapped in shawls and blankets had gone to the church to petition Saint Geneviève for relief. Presently the king himself called upon her powerful aid to save the kingdom. Now, if ever, her intercession with God was important.

France desperately needed a peace that the enemy was in no hurry to grant. The enemy armies were growing stronger, their cause more prosperous each year, and with strength came appetite for the spoils of war. After Blenheim, Louis put out feelers for peace; after Ramillies and Turin he was even more anxious for peace, but as he wrote to his grandson in Spain, "Negotiations are not happy when not seconded by the events of war." Clausewitz was not the first to learn this unfortunate fact. Louis knew that to make peace from a position of weakness he must agree to the partition of the Spanish crowns. As early as 1706 he wrote to Philippe, "I dislike as much as you do the necessary division of your estates . . . ," but then, and every year after, he was confronted by the ever-growing desperateness of the situation in France, a situation that demanded relief from the war. "You say that you fear my ministers [who were demanding peace]," he wrote to Philippe in 1707. "It would be easy enough for me to impose silence on them . . . but I cannot, I dare not silence the voice of my people which will be raised to God if I neglect them." But even with great concessions, Louis was in the unhappy position of wanting a peace that his enemies would not give. In 1707 he hoped that the limited success in Spain and at Toulon, as well as his voluntary withdrawal from Italy, would suggest peace on the basis of a division of Spain's empire that would leave Spain to the Bourbons, and the Netherlands and Italy to the Hapsburgs, but the emperor and the archduke would hear nothing of it. In fact, they forced the pope to recognize Charles as "the Most Catholic King" and persuaded their allies that no solution would be possible that left a Bourbon prince in Spain. One agent after another went from Versailles to talk peace only to taste bitter failure.

The campaign of 1708 had been a disgraceful failure; it was bitter satisfaction to celebrate as a victory[2] the *delayed* loss of Lille; it was bitter to face the fact that the Duke of Burgundy's reputation had been badly marred and the usefulness of the Duke of Vendôme placed in jeopardy. Madame de Maintenon, undoubtedly mirroring the opinion of her husband and the government, wrote to the Princess des Ursins:

Without doubt you know that the end of our campaign has been pitiful, and that the enemies have the audacity to besiege Ghent because they hope that they will have as much success there as they had in the assault upon Lille. Marshal Bouffler's defense has made us understand how bold this enterprise was, since he gave our armies four months to raise the siege and during those four months we were able to succeed only in small enterprises; a greater effort would have had the same success.[3]

There is little doubt that this was Louis' opinion as well as hers. Both his grandson and Marshal Vendôme were in disgrace: Burgundy asked to be allowed to return to his regiment as a simple officer; Vendôme's predicament was even worse, for now his enemies loaded upon him the loss of Turin as well as the failures of 1708.

M. de Vendôme [wrote Madame de Maintenon] will not go out [to the army] any more, at least not this year, and I doubt that the life that he leads will allow him to serve in the future. We have all been deceived by that man, and the King was badly informed about what happened in Italy. We owe to him the entire loss of the siege of Turin. . . . After [Turin] he conducted this beautiful campaign of the past year that reduced us to the state that we are now in and he set the Abbé d'Alberoni, an Italian and his creature, to dishonor the Duke of Burgundy . . . this same M. de Vendôme decided upon the siege of Barcelona [which failed]. I have always had the attachment for him that I believed he had for the King, but the things that he allows his household to do against the Duke of Burgundy are quite opposed to such an attachment."[4]

One ray of hope came from the campaign of 1708. Marlborough opened a discussion for peace with his nephew Marshal Berwick, and about the same time an agent of the Duke of Holstein-Gottorp, who was resident at The Hague, brought news that the Dutch would be willing to talk peace. This man, Herr Petkum, had tried to open peace talks in 1707, but now he seemed to have a good basis upon which to act. The French greedily followed both of these leads, even though Berwick was highly suspicious of his uncle's motives.[5]

Indeed, Louis had little alternative to following any lead that might come. Even before the terrible winter freeze made peace absolutely imperative, there was not enough money available to continue the war with any hope of success. Cliques were developing at Versailles, and Louis' ministers were united in their demand that peace must be negotiated at once. Chamillart's letters were now those of a tired, defeated man,[6] and the other ministers were hardly less hopeful. A little group of well-meaning people were gathered around the dauphin in hope of using his influence; another group, nicknamed the "Seigneurs," was with the Duke of Maine; others met with the Colberts. Madame de Maintenon tells us that everyone had ideas about peace, indeed, that every young woman in the court had ideas about the crisis and presumed to know what the king should do. Undoubtedly she exaggerated, but there was much more talk about public policy than would have been tolerated before. A parody on the Lord's

Prayer circulated through the court along with songs mocking the king and his ministers.

Our father who art at Versailles, whose name is no longer hallowed, whose kingdom is no longer large, give us our daily bread which is lacking everywhere! Pardon our enemies who defeat us and not our generals who allow it to happen. Succumb not to the temptations of de Maintenon and deliver us from Chamillart.

The song of the day called Louis a braggart, his son a fool, and his grandson a coward. These were hard days for the king.

While the situation in France drifted toward an abyss, Philippe's position in Spain turned for the better. After the victory at Almansa, the archduke was driven back to Barcelona, leaving Philippe in control of most of Spain. The reconquest of Aragon allowed Philippe to make radical changes in the constitution. Result: a centralization of power and a considerable increase in the Spanish king's revenues. Furthermore, the scandalous behavior of the Protestant soldiers with the archduke caused pious Spanish Catholics to welcome Philippe as a Catholic king. Thus by 1709 Philippe was at the head of a government that had an army and a treasury and loyal subjects; he had not been in so good a position during any of the previous years of his reign. Now, if ever, he might shake off the controls that his grandfather had over his policy. When he learned that Louis was ready to negotiate a treaty that would partition the empire and drive him from Spain, he attempted to open separate negotiations with the Dutch. His letters to the Count de Bergeyck, a Flemish gentleman who acted as his agent for peace, are striking evidence of Spanish intentions to separate their policy from that of France. The Dutch, however, would not listen to them.

By early 1709 the pattern of politics that would finally dominate all the negotiations for peace was beginning to assume firm contours. The war against France was a victory for the allied armies, especially since famine clutched at the throat of that kingdom. But the war in Spain most surely was something less than a victory for the Anglo-Dutch-Imperials. It was several years before everyone recognized the meaning of this paradox, which was in fact the dominant factor in the negotiations for peace. Philippe seems to have understood. He wrote to his grandfather that he would never leave Spain alive, that the blood in his veins would not allow him to give up the "throne that God had given him." It makes no difference who spurred Philippe into acting like a king;[7] his decision to do so was important. Louis, on the other hand, with a hungry, ragged, bootless army and an empty treasury, could only answer, "I praise the sentiments of your Majesty . . . but knowing that my kingdom cannot hope to sustain much longer the weight of this war . . . it is necessary to end it at whatever price. . . . Do not be surprised if you hear of the conditions being proposed at the conference in Holland." A few weeks later he added, ". . . if I consent to conditions of peace as disagreeable to me as they are to you, I accept them only with the view of saving you some part of your estates. . . . My subjects are now reduced by famine to the point where it is no longer permissible to negotiate."[8] Philippe's kingdom was not quite in this desperate condition.

In the early months of 1709, Louis was facing the hardest decisions of his life. He knew from contacts with the Dutch agents that any terms for peace would be harsh. He hoped to save Naples, Sicily, Sardinia, and the Tuscan ports for his grandson, even at the expense of considerable French sacrifices on the Flanders frontier and in Alsace. When Rouille left for The Hague in the middle of April 1709 to negotiate the terms for peace, he carried fifty-odd folio pages of instructions explaining how the king wanted him to fight for each concession, but in case after case he was allowed to give in if he could not reach a compromise.[9] However, when the French diplomat reached the Netherlands, he discovered that Petkum and Bergeyck had not known the full extent of the enemies' pretentions. The escalation of terms began. First came the agents of England and the emperor with demands; then Eugene and Marlborough arrived in person with new conditions; then the German allies, the Savoyards, the Portuguese began barking their requirements. And what was the worst of all was the fact that each new report from France telling of the famine, the revolts, the lack of money, grain, and military supplies, and the mutinous spirit of the French army, gave these pretentions new validity: the allies were sure that Louis must accept any and all conditions that they might wish to propose.

Torcy's *mémoires* tell us of a meeting of the council *en haut* in which the ministers' reports confirmed the allied opinion that the French were unable to reject *any* terms. The king's tears, usually reserved for his wife's chambers, flowed freely as he accepted the seemingly inevitable:

> The King did not waiver an instant [writes Torcy]; he had taken the ultimate resolution. Sensibly affected by the distress of his people, he thought that he could not purchase peace for them too dearly.
>
> God was pleased to humble him before he chastised the pride of his enemies. The King, submissive to the orders of providence, consented to make new sacrifices without knowing whether they would be accepted. . . .

In the last sentence Torcy has captured the basic problems of the hour; Louis was ready to submit to the will of God, but could he placate his enemies? His letters to his grandson are dotted with expressions such as "God decides the fate of battles . . ."; "God will decide upon the justice of your [Philippe's] cause"; "We must submit to God's will . . ."; "I hope that God will make you triumph over your enemies. . . ." There can be no doubt about Louis' belief in providential causation in history; he saw it all as God's march through the world. At this point in time he also accepted his wife's opinion that God was punishing him and his kingdom. Her sentiments in a letter to the Princess des Ursins were undoubtedly also those of the king: "You are right madame to say that we must recognize that whatever happens to us comes from God. Our king was too glorious, He wishes to humiliate him to save him. France has been too much enlarged, perhaps unjustly, He wishes to establish frontiers more just . . . our nation was insolent and lawless, God wishes to punish and to reduce us. . . ."[10] But if God punished France, would he not punish the king's enemies as well? In this hard spring of 1709 it seemed that He would not. It also seemed that there was no alternative to submission to any demand that they might make. At this point it was decided that Torcy himself must go to the Netherlands to find what actually were the limits of these demands, for every letter from Rouille brought new conditions, new escalations in the terms for peace.

Louis could not know that the conditions that would finally be proposed to him would be impossible to accept. The allied statesmen well understood that they had not yet subdued the Bourbon power in Spain, but when they saw the depths to which France was reduced by war and famine, they were determined to attempt to win at the conference table points that they had been unable to win on the battlefield. In a very real way they almost had to win Spain at the conference table, or face a serious problem at home. For if France should obtain peace while England and the Netherlands had to continue the war to place the archduke on the Spanish throne, there would be many people in both England and the Netherlands who would criticize and cause trouble. There was one further point: even if France should be given peace before the conquest of Spain, the allied armies would need to march across France to subdue that kingdom. This led to the new extreme demands that France surrender her most important frontier fortifications as a pledge of good faith for a two-month truce during which Philippe must leave Spain. If he refused, then the French armies would be required to join the allies in driving Philippe out of Spain or to face reopening of the war in Flanders. In spite of his instructions to find peace at almost any price, Torcy could not agree to such terms; he left Rouille in the Netherlands to continue the discussions and returned to France. When he stopped off to visit Villars and his army, now on the Flanders frontier, both the commander and the secretary of state for foreign affairs knew that somehow, some day, a military decision must be sought. When he reached Paris he was pleased to find that the tired, defeatist Chamillart had been replaced as war minister by Voysin, an able and vigorous administrator who was willing to try to find the money and supplies that Villars would need to continue the war.

The negotiations for peace had been accompanied by preparations for war; it would have been folly to act otherwise. The campaign of 1708 had gone badly: as we have seen, Berwick, at odds with Vendôme, was sent to Alsace; and both the king's grandson and Vendôme retired from the campaign in disgrace. Louis asked Boufflers to take command of the army in Flanders and, if possible, prepare to stop the coming attack. But Boufflers was an old man and the problems were enormous. Then the temperature began to drop, rivers froze over, men and animals died of the cold, and Boufflers became ill with a chest ailment. Greatly concerned, Louis sent his own physician to care for him and listened to his brave willingness to sacrifice himself. Finally Louis wrote, "The confidence that I have in you made me hope that you would be strong enough to head my army in Flanders . . . the heavy work and desperate fatigue . . . and the illness that you have had since your arrival in Flanders have caused me to believe that your strength will not match your will. . . ."[11] It was a hard decision to make: Louis believed that Boufflers' defensive skill might save the kingdom, but he could not put such responsibility upon the shoulders of an old and sick man.

Who would command? Only one other Marshal of France had the reputation for victory requisite to the task: Villars. It had been impossible to send Villars to Flanders as long as Max of Bavaria was there, and when Max went to Alsace, Villars had to be transferred to Italy. The bad blood between these two men meant that they could not work together, and Louis had to accommodate his ally. As long as Vendôme was successful in Flanders, there was no reason for transferring Villars to that front, but with Vendôme in disgrace and Boufflers ill, Villars was the obvious man to oppose Eugene and Marlborough. A recent biographer[12] of Villars insists that Louis feared to use Villars because of his irascible disposition, his rash boldness as a soldier, his failure to keep the affection of his immediate subordinates who did not like the sacrifices that he demanded any more than the brutality of his address. These factors may all have been important, but most important of all was the fact that between 1704 and

1706 Max's presence in Flanders meant that Villars could not be used there, and between the battle of Ramillies and the fall of Lille, Vendôme still had both the prestige and the confidence that made him a natural for command. When Boufflers became ill, Louis ordered Villars to go to Flanders to take his place.[13]

Villars had worked with Boufflers in Flanders during the latter years of the last war; he had had personal experience with the problem of the lines: his first act was to build new ones that would protect the kingdom. The engineers went ahead marking the route, the soldiers followed building fortifications of earth, stone, and fallen trees to close the gaps between the rivers and canals. These lines, if defended by determined men, were enough to give any commander pause before attempting to breach them. Villars also lived up to his reputation as a hard taskmaster. The troops under his command were far from the storybook "spit and polish" regiments; they were ragged, shoeless, hungry, poorly armed, badly disciplined, and prone to desert. Indeed, only the fact that there was more bread in the army than in the villages kept many of them from taking leave without permission. Villars was fortunate in that his enemies gave him time to whip the army into some kind of shape. Perhaps Eugene and Marlborough put off starting their campaign for 1709 because they were so sure that Louis would be forced to accept the peace terms offered to him that they saw no reason to risk battle. In any case, they were slow in starting, and by the time they were ready to invade France, Villars' lines and the army were both much better prepared to meet them than anyone would have believed. Rather than risk a fight at the lines, Marlborough decided upon a siege as the opening gambit of the campaign.

When Torcy returned to France with the impossible terms, he wrote, "Had I the power to sign, I would have broken off relations rather than bind your Majesty to such conditions." He spent several days with Villars explaining the presumptions and arrogant terms for peace; Villars held a review, informed his soldiers of the conditions, and fairly shouted to the world, "Soldiers, the only hope of the King for an honorable peace rests with your bayonets. . . . We shall give no quarter and ask for none . . . !" Louis, too, thought the terms impossible. He could not be asked to use his army to drive Philippe from Spain. The council *en haut* decided that the negotiations had failed. The dauphin and the Duke of Burgundy, who now joined all such deliberations, were most emphatic that they would never agree to a war against Philippe. However, several of the ministers, and eventually Madame de Maintenon herself, reached the conclusion that if only by war against Spain could France have peace, then France must fight Spain. In June 1709 their position was overridden when Louis agreed with his son and grandson.

Let us follow the course of his reasoning. On June 3, Louis wrote to Villars:

I know that the Marquis de Torcy has informed you of all that happened at The Hague . . . it would be impossible for me to accept conditions which would only give suspension of arms for two months, and which would oblige me to join my armies to those of my enemies to dethrone the King of Spain or to recommence the war against them, after having put them in possession of the most important fortification on my frontiers. . . . If I can find the means to pay my troops and supply them, I will order Monsieur de Rouille to declare that I cannot accept the proposals. . . .

On the day before, he wrote to Philippe:

I have not answered your letters between 22 April and 20 May because I waited from day to day for news of the negotiations for peace. [He had been willing to surrender Spain to the archduke—hardly suitable news for his grandson.] . . . I have asked M. Amelot to inform you of my enemies' excessive pretentions . . . and how they are supported by the confidence that they have in their strength. . . . I am obliged to oppose them, and consequently to recall my troops currently in Spain. . . . Their departure . . . will increase the zeal and faithfulness that the Spanish have for your Majesty, for your defense will henceforth be committed to the nation. . . .[14]

On June 9 he wrote again to Villars:

I have been forced to decide to continue the war. My enemies are willing to consent to peace only on conditions that do not depend upon me, and which would not be less dangerous than the war. . . . I have revoked the offers that M. de Torcy made. We must prepare this campaign so that it will end in a manner that the enemies will not have the right to propose such terms. . . .[15]

On June 12 he wrote to the Cardinal Archbishop of Paris an open letter to be printed and distributed broadside:

I have regarded as one of my first duties the employment of my efforts to procure peace for my people at a time when the evils of war are not the only ones that it has pleased God to inflict upon my kingdom. But no matter what were the offers that I have made to my enemies. . . . I have seen by their replies that, confident in their strength, they have consistently opposed their wills to my efforts for the peace of Europe. . . . The results of this campaign will decide; it is completely in the hands of God. . . . It concerns His cause since our holy religion is being attacked by our enemies. . . . I have reason to believe that it will please Him to give new evidence of His divine knowledge of the purity of my intentions and the sacrifices that I have resolved to make for the peace of my people. We must, however, implore His mercy as much with confidence as with humility. . . .[16]

On the same day he wrote to the governors of his provinces:

The expectation of a quick peace was so generally diffused throughout my kingdom that I think it my duty, in return for the fidelity which my people have shown me . . . to give them the satisfaction of knowing the reasons which still hinder them from enjoying . . . repose. . . .

In order to establish a general peace I would have accepted terms much opposed to the security of my frontier provinces, but the more I have shown myself ready and disposed to remove all suspicions . . . the more they have multiplied their pretentions insomuch that, by gradually adding new demands . . . they have shown that their only intention was to enlarge the states which border France [at the expense of my crown] and to open an easy way for themselves to penetrate into the heart of my kingdom. . . .

. . . . they limited to two months the time wherein I must execute the treaty, and pretended to oblige me to deliver the strong towns which they demanded of me in the Netherlands and in Alsace. . . . They refused on their part to enter into any other engagement than to suspend acts of hostility until the first of August, reserving to themselves the liberty of renewing the war if the King, my grandson, persisted in the resolution to defend the crown which God had given him. . . .

Such a suspension of arms, more dangerous than the war itself, retarded peace . . . for I was not only obliged to continue the same expense of maintaining my armies, but my enemies, after the term of suspension, would have attacked me with new advantages by reason of the strongholds that I was to deliver into their hands. . . .

I shall take no notice of the insinuations they have made to me to join my forces to those of the confederacy and to compel the King my grandson to descend the throne. . . . It is shocking to humanity to believe that they would entertain any thoughts of engaging me to enter such an alliance. . . .

It is therefore my intention that all those who for so many years have given me proofs of their zeal in contributing by their labor, their property, and their blood to support so burdensome a war, should be informed that the only return that the enemy pretended to make to my offers was a suspension of arms, which limited to two months, would have procured for them much greater advantages than they could expect from the confidence that they put in their troops. As I put mine in the protection of the Almighty and as I hope that the purity of my intentions will draw down the Divine blessing upon my arms, I believe that my people . . . should know."[17]

He also prepared a propaganda harangue calling upon the people of France to "save the fatherland." The Revolutionaries of 1792–93 did not do much better:

I have conducted this war with hauteur and pride worthy of this kingdom. With the valor of my nobility and the zeal of my subjects, I have succeeded in the enterprises that I have undertaken for the good of the state. I have given my attention and my efforts. . . . I have taken the measure that I believed to be necessary to fulfill my duty and to demonstrate my love and affection for my people by winning for them a peace that would assure tranquillity for the remainder of my reign. . . . I have considered proposals for peace and no one has done more than I to secure it. . . . I can say that I have done violence to my character . . . to procure promptly a peace for my subjects even at the expense of my personal satisfaction and perhaps my *gloire* . . . but up to now my most important enemies have sought only to distract me, and have used every artifice . . . to deceive me as well as their own allies whom they oblige to make the great expenditures demanded by their unbridled ambitions. . . . I can no longer see any alternative to take, other than to prepare to defend ourselves. To make them see that a united France is greater than all the powers assembled by force and artifice to overwhelm it, at this hour I have put into effect the extraordinary measure that we have used on similar occasions to procure the money indispensible for the *gloire* and the security of the state. . . . I come to ask for your councils and your aid in this encounter that involves your safety. By the efforts that we shall make together, our foes will understand that we are not to be put upon. The aid that I ask of you will oblige them to make a peace honorable for us, lasting . . . and satisfactory to the princes of Europe. This is the aim of my thoughts . . . the happiness and well-being of my people has always been and will always be to the last moment of my life, my most important and serious consideration.[18]

No reader needs to be told that Louis gives himself virtue that he did not always merit, but at seventy-one he had not lost his skill as a propagandist and a politician. The striking difference in tone between the letters that were simple administrative correspondence and those intended to arouse his subject's will to resist, well illustrates the king's political skills.

The decision to fight brought with it many other problems: it was imperative that grain for bread for the army be found in quantity, even though the famine might be worsened as the cities and towns were stripped of their slender supplies. There is a series of letters in the National Archives dealing dramatically with the spread of the famine as the army's needs gobbled up the grain. At the same time Villars' letters to the king and the war minister show that there was never enough bread for the troops; some days there was none at all. Yet the army continued to labor on the lines. "I am humble," Villars wrote to Madame de Maintenon, "when I see the backbreaking labor men perform without food." The king and his ministers did everything they could do to pour supplies of all kinds into Flanders where the military decision would be made.[19]

While Torcy was in the Netherlands, both Eugene and Marlborough openly boasted that no French army could withstand their power; if the King of France would not grant peace, they would march to Versailles and impose it upon him. The actual campaign, however, turned out differently. They scouted Villars' lines only to decide that the casualties might be too great if they tried a frontal assault. Then they settled down to besiege Tournai. Louis and Villars were both jubilant. While Villars assured the king that he could rest securely with his army in Flanders, Louis wrote, "This [siege] is enough to discredit them in Holland and with their other allies who know by the conditions that they dared to publish [no peace without Spain] . . . it is up to them to produce a peace. . . ." He fairly exudes his satisfaction with his soldier whose field fortifications had constrained the enemy: "I count much upon your wise dispositions and the precautions that you have taken to reduce their vast projects to this one effort. . . ." Tournai was strongly fortified; both Louis and Villars were sure that Surville, its defender, could keep the enemy occupied during most of the campaign.[20]

Villars did not allow the enemy to settle down peacefully for a siege. With strong detachments he attacked their outposts, killing and capturing a large number of troops, and forcing Marlborough to withdraw soldiers from the besieging army to increase the size of his army of observation. Louis praised his soldier, and encouraged him to maintain a strong defensive position. But when Villars suggested that a surprise attack on Brussels might throw the enemy off balance, Louis insisted that the first objective of the army was "to prevent the enemies from entering my kingdom" and he went on to warn Villars "not to quit the posts and the camp . . . that provided entire security . . . and always to be situated so that you will not be forced to fight unless you enjoy a great advantage . . ."[21]

In the opinion of the men at Versailles that summer, the chances of war could be summed up something like this: if Villars should give battle and lose, the kingdom would be open to invasion and the foes could impose their will; if he should win, the French would be unable to follow up the victory with any degree of success. In other words, a defeat would be absolute, a victory only qualified. But as the month of July began to run out, Villars' problems with supplies grew worse each day, and his letters began to have an insistent note demanding either peace, or a battle that would take the pressure off his army. In his mind there was no choice, since "the proposals that the enemy make for peace are all to their advantage. They are sure of the surrender of Tournai . . . and then they can use their army for another enterprise. . . ." Louis softened a little and toward the first of August he wrote, ". . . in case of a new enterprise on the part of the enemy, I would give you the freedom to attack and fight them if you believe that you would be able to do so with some advantage. I still think it is better not to be forced to seek an opportunity to fight. . . ." Villars continued to tell Louis and Voysin that there was no wheat for bread; he drew up a long memorandum explaining how he was defending the lines, but in another letter he noted that it was dangerous to the state to allow the army to go without bread. A successful battle alone would end the threat from the foes. He also demanded that the king send him reenforcements from Alsace and the troops that were coming from Spain, since "it is here in Flanders that the fate of the kingdom will be decided." When Voysin told him that the peace conditions were still unacceptable, Villars wrote, "Since the peace will not come, there is nothing to do but recommend ourselves to the Holy Mother and strike hard!"[22]

The marshal finally got his permission to fight. Perhaps it was his exclamation, "God help us, but the more I think of the problem of food, the more I find that we must either have peace or a battle . . . it is a miracle to maintain the army without food . . . and it is dangerous to the state." The time of Louis' capitulation can be marked by the fact that he sent Boufflers, now somewhat recovered of his health, to Flanders so that there would be two men on the battlefield capable of commanding the troops. We have seen that in every case where a battle was in the offing, Louis tried to prepare for possible accidents; with a rash man like Villars in command, this was even more important than ever, for Villars was not afraid of enemy bullets. Boufflers was a good choice. Villars had served under him during the last years of the late war, and the two of them, good friends, believed that the other marshals of France were all duds. It may be that each had some reservations about the other, but they never expressed them openly. Boufflers willingly agreed to serve under his younger colleague, and Villars welcomed him to Flanders. There were still some reservations at Versailles: "The gambit of seeking out and fighting," wrote Voysin, "is still regarded here as one of extremity. His Majesty is convinced that you will not do it unless you are forced in some way and see that you will be able to fight with advantage. . . . But," he finally added, "the King leaves it entirely in your hands to do what you believe yourself forced to do; be it to seek out or to avoid combat, not doubting that you will take the one most useful to the state." If we did not know how Louis treated soldiers who lost battles, this could be considered as a letter saying "Go ahead, but at your own risk!" However, Louis never once took reprisals upon the men who unsuccessfully commanded his armies in battle. This was, then, an honest permission for Villars to decide what was best.

At this moment the siege of Tournai seemed about to come to an abrupt end because Surville was ready to surrender. Villars thought his action to be a coward's choice and demanded reprisals against him. Tournai fell, and the Anglo-Imperial-Dutch army again was ready to move.

Villars was a bold soldier. When he saw Eugene and Marlborough move toward Mons, probably to undertake another siege, he decided that the time had come for a battle. "I have the honor to inform your Majesty," he wrote on September 8, "of the resolution to assemble the army and seek a battle. . . . M. de Boufflers is here to testify that, if we attack, it will be with good reason; if we do nothing it will also be true that a brave man will be witness that we have done our best." Versailles held its breath![23]

Villars had a reputation for rash acts, perhaps deserved, but at Malplaquet he challenged the two greatest soldiers of his age only after carefully preparing his position and studying the field. It was his foes who behaved rashly; they could have fortified themselves in front of Mons and taken the city at their leisure leaving Villars to chew his nails, but instead they decided to test their fortune on the field. The two armies came within cannon-shot of each other on September 10. "Your Majesty's army," wrote Villars, "began a battle at ten o'clock this morning . . . a brisk cannonade lasted from ten o'clock until the fall of night, and we now remain within musket-shot distance apart. It ought to please your Majesty . . . that the entire army has shown much ardor, the troops never marched so well and in such good order, the valor of the soldiers and of the cavalry inspires everyone. . . . I would have preferred a cavalry action, but our dispositions are so good that if the enemy attacks, with the aid of God we shall disperse them." The next evening, with a serious bullet wound in his leg, Villars again wrote to the king, explaining how the battle had begun. It was a long letter in which he assured Louis that even though the French army withdrew from the field, it was not defeated, and that the enemy had suffered enormous losses. He praised Marshal Boufflers who took over when his own wound made it impossible for him to command. Boufflers wrote the same day. He suggested that Villars' wound forced the withdrawal of the army, it was a "misfortune that forces me to tell of the loss of a new battle, but I can assure your Majesty that never has a misfortune been accompanied by so much *gloire*. . . ."

The first impression at Versailles was that of gloom, another battle lost; another commander covering up the disaster. This had been the pattern of the war since Chiari. But in three or four days it became apparent that the French army was still very much in existence and ready to fight again, that the enemy had lost many more flags and standards than the French, and that many more of their men were dead or wounded. The Dutch losses were terrible: of 80 regiments there were not enough men left to make up 18. The Dutch dead were piled on the field in heaps. The enemy losses were at least a third more than the French losses, and probably much more than that. But the French army also had its casualties, for this was the bloodiest battle of the century; men had to wait until Borodino for another like it. Boufflers wrote to the king, "The bad success will not cost your Majesty an inch of land . . . and it will make the enemy respect your troops and become a little more docile."

As the gloom began to lift at Versailles, Louis turned his attention to his army, urging Boufflers to whip it back into shape as quickly as possible, and then ιo his soldiers: "I have lost some brave officers," he wrote, "and I am much disturbed by Marshal Villars' wound, which I fear might be dangerous." It was dangerous, even though Villars played it down, assuring the king that it would soon heal. Before the fever nearly took his life, he wrote, "I would have preferred a cavalry action to an infantry battle, but . . . the dispositions were so good that I had reason to hope for success. The truth is that I hoped to be attacked . . . your Majesty must understand that there were terrible losses for the enemy . . . and, sire, if God gives us the grace to lose another similar battle, your Majesty can count on his enemies being destroyed."[24]

By September 20 the news from Flanders clearly indicated that the enemy had been so mauled that there probably would be no danger of another effort to invade the kingdom. Louis expressed his gratitude to Villars by making him a Peer of France.

It was cold comfort, however, to learn that the bloody battle of Malplaquet had caused much distress in England and the Netherlands, for the Anglo-Imperials went on to besiege and capture Mons. Boufflers could do nothing to stop their progress, nor could the king's government do anything about the economic distress in the kingdom. Every letter, every council meeting, every evening with Madame de Maintenon, Louis heard that peace was an absolute necessity, and that the Anglo-Dutch slogan "no peace without Spain" meant that he would have to sacrifice his grandson's interests to secure peace. The Imperials were quite unwilling to consider any treaty that would divide the Spanish inheritance; the English and Dutch were convinced that it would be unsafe for their commerce if a Bourbon prince remained on the throne of Spain and ruled the Indies. Louis and Madame de Maintenon, confronted with the disasters that were overtaking the French army and kingdom, decided God's will demanded Philippe's abdication. They could not understand why the young king was unwilling to forget the scandal caused by the Duke of Orléans' rash words about his "rights" to the Spanish throne, when neither of them was destined to have it.[25]

The king's policy almost seemed to anticipate "God's will" in Spain. He demanded the return of French soldiers, he ordered his ambassador Amelot, who had virtually been First Minister of Spain, to withdraw from the council and then replaced him with a man quite inferior in both knowledge and skills. At the queen's urgent request, the soldiers were allowed to stay until the fall of 1710, but Louis ordered their commander, Marshal Bezons, to avoid any battle. This order prevented Philippe from winning a victory over inferior forces, but he could get no response from his protests. Louis would not even allow Philippe to take the French troops into Spanish pay either directly or via the subterfuge of desertion and reenlistment. Like his ministers, like Madame de Maintenon, Louis had reached the conclusion that Spain was lost to the Bourbons. It was not easy to tell Philippe that all was lost. "If your Majesty will reflect on what I have done for you," Louis wrote, "it will be easy to understand the displeasure that it causes me not to be able to continue the assistance that I have given you up to now. I hope that the measures that you take for conserving your crown will succeed. . . ."[26] A few weeks later after a council meeting where only the dauphin and the Duke of Burgundy defended a policy of aid to Spain, Louis again wrote, "I cannot hide from you the fact that peace becomes more necessary every day, and you must not be surprised if I accept the offers that my enemies seem about to make. . . . Do not be deceived by the feelings that I have for you," he cautioned, "I believe that I show my feelings by warning of what I am forced to do."[27]

The situation in France deteriorated almost by the hour: poverty, hunger, and death stalked the countryside, and Villars assured the government that everything pointed to a disaster for the army, since both officers and men were deserting to save themselves from starvation. There was no money, no credit, no magazines, and no way to secure these things. Perhaps the worst of all was the fact that Villars' wound had not really healed, so that he might not be able to command the army, but even if he could, his confidence in the future was slight. There again were terrible alternatives: an immediate battle that would risk the fate of the kingdom in an afternoon, or peace at any price.[28]

Louis' enemies still regarded the preliminary articles for a general peace that had been the basis for discussion the preceding year as the only route to a peace treaty. This document left no part of the Spanish inheritance to the "Duke of Anjou," as it referred to Philippe V, and it would obligate the French to join in driving him from the throne in Spain. Would the enemy be willing to discuss alternatives? Louis resolved never to make war on Spain, but he accepted the council's suggestion that France might offer to pay a subsidy to the enemy to assist them in making war against Spain. Perhaps this would satisfy their foes. As for the Spanish inheritance, the council returned again and again to the proposal that Philippe be given a kingdom made up of Naples, Sicily, Sardinia, and the Spanish posts on the Tuscan coast. What of the other terms? The Dutch wanted a "barrier" made up of fortifications facing France in the Spanish Netherlands, they also wanted commercial advantages; the English wanted colonial and commercial advantages; the Germans, whose contributions to the war were less than those of their allies, had extravagant claims that would have deprived the kingdom of France of all its gains since 1648, and if Louis should insist upon the return of Bavaria to its duke, even Alsace, as it was considered in 1648, must also be surrendered. Torcy called these barbarous terms, proposed by men "inflated by unexpected prosperity procured for them by their allies. . . ."[29] By the spring of 1710, however, Louis was ready to concede almost everything. He would not send Rouille back to negotiate; this time the choice fell upon Abbé Polignac and Marshal d'Huxelles, who arrived in the Netherlands the first of May to try to find an honorable peace. Before this conference of Gertrudenberg was over, Louis did offer to surrender Alsace as well as several large towns in Flanders, but he could not agree to the demands made of him regarding Spain.

Almost the same day that Polignac and d'Huxelles arrived in the Netherlands, Louis had a final meeting with Villars to discuss the conduct of the war. It was a hard decision to make, but Villars left no alternative; the French army was in no condition for an extended campaign, and so it must seek a battle almost at once, leaving the issue to the "God of Battles." Villars himself believed that peace, even if it required war with Spain, should be negotiated, but that it might be possible to deprive the foe of the "right to make arrogant demands" if a battle could be won. Louis again reluctantly agreed to stake the fate of the kingdom on the issue of a single battle, and Villars went off to Flanders to take command.[30]

As a result of improved harvests, the French army was not as badly off as Villars had believed it would be, and more important perhaps, Marlborough was not willing to risk another Malplaquet. In Villars, he discovered a soldier even more ruthless than he was himself, and he had no intention of giving this wild man the chance of victory, or even to lose a battle like Malplaquet. The Anglo-Imperials fortified their camp and settled down to besiege Douai, and Villars could not force them to test their fortune by a clash of arms. He immediately began to give orders and suggestions for the defense of Douai and looked about for some way to lift the siege. Now it was Villars who became cautious. He asked the king for orders; Louis' reply was quite in character:

> . . . it is not possible for me to give precise orders from this distance. I have explained to you my ideas, and you know well the reasons that make me hope to be able to oblige my enemies to raise the siege of Douai. Their army would have small chances to retreat if you should succeed in defeating them while they still await some troops that have not yet come up . . . they must have at least 20,000 men in the trenches . . . if there is a time when I have an interest in fighting them, it seems that it ought to be during this siege of Douai . . . however, if you find the enemy too well posted to be able to attack them without too much risk, or if you cannot fight them without believing that there are reasonable hopes for success, it would be rash to engage in a disadvantageous battle, and it is not my intention to give you such an order. I put myself entirely in your hands. . . ."

But Marlborough would not let Villars lure him into another battle, and even with the king's permission, Villars was too wise to attack a strongly fortified position.[31]

The siege of Douai was prolonged into June. Louis' main concern was to be sure that the garrison surrendered soon enough to assure its right to leave the city with the honors of war and rejoin the rest of the army. Since fortification was doomed anyway, the soldiers were more valuable than the time that they might buy. What would be the foes' next objective? Obviously they had given up the plan to march on Versailles and impose peace; they seemed to be committed to attempt to take one after another of the great fortifications that guarded the kingdom. Would the next assault be against Valenciennes or Bethune? If the former, "you should not hesitate to march against them," Louis wrote to Villars, ". . . fight them before they have time to establish themselves." For all his reputation for rashness, again it was Villars who remained cautious; he was in no hurry to hand Marlborough an easy victory. Douai capitulated the last of June, but the garrison was saved. Villars wrote to the king, "It seems to me that the enemies ought to seek a general engagement; we will neglect nothing to make it very dangerous for them, and I hope that God will give us the grace to confound their pride. . . ." But why should Marlborough risk giving Villars a victory? Every bit of information that came from France confirmed the belief that Louis must finally accept the terms of peace that were offered to him. There were negotiations going on at Gertrudenberg that should give the allies a great deal more than they could possibly win by a battle.

This conviction turned out to be the undoing of the grand alliance. In his *Mémoires,* Torcy undoubtedly proclaims Louis' faith in Providence: "God," he writes, "designed a larger inheritance for the descendants of St. Louis, while he hardened the hearts of their enemies." The allies were so sure that Louis had to make peace that there was hardly an end to the escalation of their terms. They wanted to cut France back to the frontiers before 1648, they would listen to no partition of the Spanish empire in favor of Philippe, and they made impossible demands upon Louis to assure themselves of the Spanish inheritance. His plenipotentiaries wrote to the king: ". . . the allies reject absolutely the proposal that we have made to aid them in their war against Spain [the subsidy proposal]. . . . They do not even wish to unite your Majesty's forces to theirs to force the King of Spain to surrender his crown, but that your Majesty alone either persuade that prince to consent, or depose him within two months, at the end of which if it is not done, the truce will be broken and the war will recommence . . . the only favor to which they will agree is to allow the troops that they have in Portugal and Catalogna to assist the conquering of Spain in order to give it and the Indies to the Archduke . . . but when the two months expire, their troops will no longer act and your Majesty will be obliged to finish the enterprise alone. . . ."[32] This, in addition to demands requiring the cession of Alsace if the Electors of Bavaria and Cologne were to be restored, and the mountain of commercial concessions in favor of England and the United Netherlands, was piled upon the council table at Versailles. The king, his son and grandson, and his ministers had to decide. They could not accept these terms, but they had to reject them in a way that would allow all Europe to know that France's enemies were responsible for the continuance of the war.

Louis wrote to one of his ambassadors, ". . . it seems to me that peace is farther away than it has ever been. My enemies are no longer content to ask me to join with them to dispossess the king, my grandson. . . . They require that I act alone against him, and . . . after having delivered my fortifications according to the preliminaries [for peace], that I conquer Spain and the Indies in two months. This time expired, they declare that they will recommence the war if the Catholic King is still on his throne. . . . An impossible demand."[33] It gave hope to the King of Spain. Philippe wrote to his grandfather, "I learn with pleasure of the rupture of the negotiations that were going on in Holland. . . ." A little later he again assured Louis that he, as King of Spain, would consent to no terms that were contrary to his honor, his *gloire,* and the obligations that he owed his faithful subjects.[34]

In the meantime, the enemy was probing for another fortress to be-siege, and Louis was anxious to prevent their doing it, even if it meant a battle. "You wrote me that the enemies have retired toward Holchin to move against Bethune," he wrote on July 22. "If they turn towards you, it is not at all necessary to avoid fighting them since their army is still . . . reduced by the number of troops that they will be obliged to leave at the siege, and that will deprive them of their superiority of numbers. . . . You can even make a march with the intention of fighting them and attacking according to the orders that I previously gave you. . . . I put myself en-tirely in your hands well knowing that the outcome of a battle is always uncertain. . . . I do not wish you to attack if you judge the chances are not about equal . . . but I believe that in choosing your terrain carefully, you should march at them rather than await them because this conforms more to the spirit of the nation, and my troops will be more anxious to fight if they are inspired by the [here Louis struck out the word *gloire,* and added] audacity of the attack, rather than if they believe that they are simply defending themselves." This letter alone should refute the traditional idea that Louis was unwilling to take the chance of a battle.[35]

Perhaps the king's desire to have Villars give battle was heightened by the fact that the marshal's wound was troubling him so much that he asked to be allowed to leave the army in September to try curative baths; without him in command a battle would be hazardous. Louis was gracious about it, but obviously disturbed:

What bothers me the most is the state of your health and the fact that you believe it necessary to visit the waters at Aix-la-Chapelle next month. You know that I depend entirely upon you for the command of my army . . . it is of extreme importance for this campaign. I strongly hope that your wound will allow you to put off the water remedy until next year, but no matter the need that I have for your services, if you must go . . . I will consent so as not to deprive you of the necessary aid and comfort, and to put you in better condition to command my armies in the next campaign. . . .

Early in September when it was time for Villars to go, Louis again wrote him:

I had strongly hoped that you would have been able to finish the campaign, but I agree with the good reasons that make you desire to take the waters this season. I desire the complete recovery of your wound too much not to consent to anything that will contribute to it. You may leave the 20th of this month and I believe that it is more prudent for you to go to Bourbonne rather than to baths at Aix. I have chosen Marshal d'Harcourt to command my army for the rest of the campaign. . . .[36]

Louis had hoped that Marlborough would not try any further "enter-prise," but the allied strategy intended to strip France of íts defenses, so the English turned upon Aire after taking Bethune. The king's informers told of great losses and much sickness in the English camp, and Louis be-came hopeful that Aire might be saved. He wrote to Marshal d'Harcourt urging him to put the army "in condition to march and attack the enemy . . . the usefulness of this would be so great for my service that I believe that it would be well worth the effort. . . . Nothing would better reduce my enemies to more reasonable terms and nothing would encourage my troops and nothing would be more glorious for the nation than to force them to abandon the siege of Aire after sixty days. . . ."[37] At seventy-three Louis had not lost his sense for morale building, for propaganda values, or for political advantage. He well understood the relationship between military action and political possibilities.

The slogan "no peace without Spain" produced another result that the allies had not expected. When the conferences in the Netherlands failed to bring peace, Louis felt free to send Vendôme to Spain. Philippe had seen Vendôme in action in Italy, and the Spanish soldiers believed that he was a great general; no matter that he was in disgrace in France after the cam-paign of 1708, he was still a daring, bold commander. Louis allowed him to take about 8,000 French soldiers from the south of the kingdom to stiffen his army in Spain. It was none too soon.

In the early summer of 1710 the emperor (Joseph I) and his allies prepared a new campaign in Spain: 14,000 Germans, 4,000 Englishmen, 1,400 Dutchmen, 1,400 Portuguese, and about 3,000 Spanish Carlists made up the army to secure Charles III his throne. It was a formidable force, even though the command was divided among several generals. Philippe's army, badly commanded and discouraged by a rumor that the Bourbon king was only seeking a face-saving operation to give him an excuse for giving up the throne, was defeated first at Almenara where only the conflicts between the German and English commanders prevented their destroying the little Spanish army, and then again under the walls of Saragossa, which action opened the road to Madrid. Starhemberg warned against the occupation of Castile, but his advice was unheeded and the Carlist forces advanced to the capital. Pushed out of Madrid, Philippe wrote to his grandfather that he was willing to be "submissive to the will of God" and Louis assured him that "one conforms to His wishes by seeking means to remedy the misfortune with which it has pleased him to afflict you." This was the right advice, for Vendôme was coming, and he soon would have an army worthy of the name.

The people of Madrid did their share. They remembered the Protestant armies that had occupied the city a few years earlier; many of them left the city, and of those that remained the important ones refused to have anything to do with Archduke Charles and his Protestant soldiers. As Vendôme collected an army, the Carlists' position became more and more untenable. Charles' soldiers lacked food, munitions, supplies; they began to loot and then to raise more antagonism from the Spanish population. Soon Vendôme was aided by guerrilla bands that cut off stragglers, interrupted supplies, and made life difficult for the enemy. The Carlists had to retreat from Madrid.

Vendôme, shaking off his usual lethargy, followed on their heels, not even allowing Philippe to share in the victory celebration at the capital. The allied army was in trouble and its commanders' inability to act together compounded the trouble. Vendôme caught Stanhope off guard at Brihuega (December 9). The fight was short but sharp; the English commander and some 4,000 of the best troops in the Carlist army were made prisoners before Starhemberg could come to their rescue. Vendôme then turned on the German commander. At Villa Viciosa the Spanish army revenged itself for the defeats earlier in the summer. As Philippe wrote to his grandfather, "The debris of the enemy army retired in much haste . . . licking their wounds." Aragon again was under Philippe's control. Finally only Barcelona remained under the archduke, and soon he would have to give up that city as well. Philippe's queen sent the first news of the victories to the old king at Versailles; she was not sure that her husband would be pleased that she made the announcement "taking away the pleasure of sending . . . this agreeable news first, but," she wrote, "he will pardon me." Louis never wrote with much emotion, but even under his precious circumlocutions, this time he seems to purr his satisfaction: "The importance of the events that you have informed me about would assure you my joy even if you did not know of my tender interest in your *gloire* and your successes. . . ."[38]

The victories adjusted the balance of power, and in London men now began to see clearly the folly of the slogan "no peace without Spain." Just before Christmas, Torcy received a letter from England saying that the United Kingdom would no longer insist upon the restoration of the Hapsburgs in Spain, "provided France and Spain will give us good security for our commerce." This letter told volumes about the prospects for the future. An important change was developing in England. Marlborough's wife, Sarah, lost her hold on the English queen, and the Tory party began a march to power. The ministry was attacked piecemeal: first Marlborough's son-in-law, Sunderland, lost his office; then on August 8, 1710, it was Godolphin's turn to surrender his post. Marlborough's days as chief of the coalition were soon to be ended. Vendôme's victories in Spain only further underlined the trend. When Torcy heard the news from Spain, he wrote, "No matter what, never has a victory been more complete and this day will change the face of affairs in Spain and at the same time those of Europe."[39] He could not know that on the heels of ministerial change in England and Philippe's victory in Spain was to come the death of Emperor Joseph and the election of the Archduke Charles to the imperial throne. Within a few months the political climate of Europe changed drastically in favor of Louis XIV. He would be obliged to give up some of his pretentions, but the peace that he could now make would be negotiated rather than dictated.

33

PEACE FOR EUROPE

"WHO COULD HAVE FORESEEN," exclaimed Torcy, "that the prosperity of the alliance so formidable for France and Spain, was at an end, that the Supreme Being who fixes the boundaries of oceans and calms the impetuosity of the waves . . . should stem the torrent of so many victories. . . ?" A few pages later he added, ". . . the peace was not the work of human policy; God had reserved for himself the manner and the time for restoring it to afflicted Europe. . . ."[1]

Many in Louis' entourage had long since believed that God was punishing France and the king, that there could be no doubt about the reason for the allied successes: France and the king had been too great, too proud, too arrogant, and God wished to humble both of them. God alone could have so hardened the hearts of the foes as to make it impossible to disengage from the conflict; every request, every *démarche* of the king had been met by impossible conditions, outrageous demands.[2] When the tide turned it was natural for men to believe that God's justice was satisfied with the trials that He had inflicted upon France and that He would now show his vengeance, as well as his justice, by also punishing the "enemies."

The shift of events was dramatic, so dramatic that a generation that believed in Providence could not fail to see it as the work of God. In Spain the Anglo-Imperial armies had assumed the offensive during the spring of 1710; in a matter of months they had piled up impressive victories that carried them into the city of Madrid itself, while Philippe V was again almost a refugee in his own kingdom. Then the tables turned abruptly; the Archduke Charles and his soldiers had to retreat before a growing Spanish army that supported the Bourbon king. After Vendôme arrived to command Philippe's armies, the retreat turned into a rout; two important victories in December 1710 drove the archduke back into Barcelona, leaving most of the Spanish peninsula in Philippe's hands. By January 1711 Louis could write to his friend Marshal Noailles, "The happy events that have occurred in Spain since last month should deprive the enemies of hope . . . to become master of the country. . . . The affairs of the King, my grandson, are now in better shape than they have been since the beginning of the war. . . ." To Philippe he wrote, ". . . if you can chase them from Spain, I trust that the advantages will not be less useful to my kingdom than they will be for your Majesty. After the battles that you have won, I find that in Holland and in England, peace is more desired than ever before."[3]

While Vendôme's victories underlined the fact that the allies were not to win the war in Spain, events in London transformed the situation in Flanders. A Tory victory, supported by the queen, resulted in a change in power in England. The Marlborough-Godolphin ministry had been attacked piecemeal; then in the late summer of 1710 the Tories took control of the government. Marlborough's days as commander were numbered; his influence on English policy was at an end. Feelers for negotiations were in order, for the Tory party was anxious for peace, even though it might mean deserting England's allies. By January 1711, when Vendôme's victories in Spain had proven that the peace terms offered a year and a half before were unrealistic, secret agents began to prepare for a meeting between English and French negotiators. Then came a stroke of thunder: Emperor Joseph died of smallpox, leaving no male heir to inherit either the thrones of the Danubian monarchy or the imperial dignity, and his brother Charles, the archduke who claimed the throne in Spain, became Charles VI, Holy Roman Emperor and ruler of the Hapsburg states in central Europe. Who in England or the Netherlands would be willing to spend treasure and blood to assure him the Spanish throne as well?

Louis, recognizing that Emperor Joseph's death changed the political climate of Europe, immediately urged his grandson to write to the archduke suggesting ways for peace. Philippe's long letter to Charles, whom he calls the King of Bohemia (sic!), was predicated on the idea that Roman Catholic princes should now cooperate, that their common interests stemming from their religious convictions transcended all other considerations, that they must give a peace to Europe satisfactory to their church. Philippe seems to have been quite serious in this suggestion, for he writes to his grandfather, ". . . a Catholic prince ought to consider the preservation of his religion as more important than his personal aims or achievements. . . ."[4] Needless to say, his letter evoked no response from Charles, who had set his heart on becoming King of Spain and wanted no change of plans. Nonetheless, the political world in which he was the emperor was different from the one in which his brother had ruled the Holy Roman Empire.

When these prospects for peace began to materialize, Louis was seventy-three years old. His health was poor: indigestion, gout, "vagabond" aches and pains, and a general feeling of weakness indicated that he would not much longer be King of France. He still went on the hunt—in a carriage; he still acted out the ceremonial role of king, but it was often interrupted by indisposition. What part did he have in forming the peace negotiations? It is quite obvious that Torcy directed French policy, but it is also evident that he consulted the king. The sessions in Madame de Maintenon's chamber, discussions with Torcy, Voysin, and the others both in council and separately, were daily events, but it is hard to believe that Louis did much more than approve proposals or at most make tentative suggestions. The letters signed by the king during these last years sound more like the writing of Torcy or Voysin than of the king, and yet in them there are ideas and phrases that are characteristic of Louis XIV.[5]

The negotiations with English diplomats got under way in the spring of 1711. Father Gaultier, a Catholic priest resident in London, was the first important contact, but soon the discussions involved other agents as well. There were many problems to solve. The English were primarily interested in securing for themselves colonial and commercial advantages from both the French and the Spanish overseas empires, as well as the possession of the naval bases in the western Mediterranean. They also wanted assurance that the thrones of Spain and France would not be joined. Naturally these were problems that affected the court at Madrid as well as the one at Versailles, but the English wished to negotiate with Louis' government alone, so he had to secure his grandson's consent for any concessions that had to be made for Spain. As the discussion progressed, everyone understood that Philippe's government would be forced to accept the partition of the Spanish empire, leaving only Spain and the Indies as his part. To Louis' surprise the Spanish seemed to accept this and were even willing to surrender Gibraltar and Port Mahon to the English, as well as to grant them participation in the colonial slave trade. Louis suspected, however, that further concessions might be required, so he secured from Philippe the unequivocal right to negotiate concerning the Spanish empire. Louis wrote:

I hope that you will not regret this confidence . . . in me, and that you will find that I will make good use of the power that you have given me. If I engage you in conditions that you have not foreseen, you will find that they are essential, and that it was necessary to grant them to overcome the stubborn opinion that the English maintained to obtain concessions in the Indies. There are times when it is important not to allow events to escape . . . thus do not be surprised if I interpret your powers without consulting you. . . .[6]

Louis went on to explain that both France and Spain needed peace, and that for his part, Louis would be "happy to see [Philippe] solidly established on the Spanish throne." Other things, not as important, could be given up.

The negotiations took months of patient discussion, but finally late in September 1711, the Anglo-French conversations resulted in the statement of "seven propositions" that could be the basis for a peace treaty. These were: 1) the recognition of Queen Anne and the Act of Succession that regulated the English throne; 2) guarantees that the thrones of Spain and France would never be united; 3) suitable satisfactions in the peace for all parties engaged in the war, and particularly the assurance of the commerce of England and Holland; 4) Dutch occupations of the fortifications to secure the Dutch "barrier"; 5) a protective barrier for the empire and Austria against France; 6) demolition of the fortifications of Dunkirk; and 7) in the negotiations "one will discuss in good faith . . . all the pretensions of the princes and states engaged in the war, and nothing will be omitted to attempt to regulate them to the satisfaction of all parties concerned." The assurances that this document gave to England's allies were too vague and amorphous to inspire much confidence in the hearts of either the Dutch or the Germans, but they suited well the interests of England.[7]

While the diplomats were discussing the prospects for peace, the campaign of 1711 simmered down abruptly. In Spain, Noailles and Vendôme stripped off the outer defenses of Barcelona, but they did not try an assault on that city, even though the archduke left Spain to secure the crowns in Germany. In the Flanders theater, Villars and Marlborough, both with orders not to bring the war to a pitched battle, simply maneuvered to take a fortress or two. Early in April the two armies came face to face at a crossing of Sensee; it was awkward for a moment, but soon the soldiers stacked arms and began to fraternize. Villars and the pretender to the English throne even crossed the stream and visited Marlborough's camp. Villars' supplies and equipment were still in relatively short supply, but he now had food, and he chafed a bit under the regime of inaction. Louis, however, ordered him not to "risk anything that might expose the troops to a disadvantage," and on April 26 added, "I do not believe it to be àpropos for you to seek to fight the enemies . . . the present conjuncture does not require that we risk any considerable action."[8]

Louis the politician was obviously speaking for Louis the soldier. He had so often found it next to impossible to disengage from a war that he neither wanted adventures in Flanders that might interrupt the course of peace negotiations nor a military disaster that might place him at a disadvantage at the council table.

He was, however, willing to risk action in Germany. When it became more evident every day that the emperor, and perhaps the German princes, were not going to associate themselves with the Anglo-French peace negotiations, Louis detached a strong force from his army in Flanders to send to the Rhine. He hoped that Maximilian and Marshal d'Harcourt would be able to attack the German lines and create an attitude among the German princes a bit more conducive to peace. It worked out otherwise. Prince Eugene sent German troops to match the French reinforcements, and the stalemate on the Rhine-Sarre-Moselle front continued. By the end of July, when Louis had given up hopes of acting in Germany, he detached troops from Alsace to support Berwick against the Savoyards. He was particularly anxious about this front. The Savoyard cavalry threatened to range as far as Lyon, but even more important, the Duke of Savoy was demanding French territory along his frontier as a "barrier." This was territory that Louis had "always considered to be [his] domain," and he was quite unwilling to give it up unless he had to do so. However, none of the frontiers flared into much violence in 1711, for Europe was tired and the war was waiting for a peace settlement.[9]

But when the delegates met at Utrecht to negotiate a peace, it became immediately evident that only the English and French were sincerely attempting to come to terms. As the imperial delegates explained their position, everyone knew that they were there only to disrupt the congress; the Dutch were hardly less intransigent than the Germans. The smaller states were sure that they could get much more out of France if Eugene could be allowed to continue the war and dictate terms in Versailles. Furthermore, it seemed that everyone at the conference was looking over the Channel to see what was happening to Queen Anne who was old and sick. If she should die, Prince George of Hanover would become King of England; he was Marlborough's friend and companion in arms and under his rule the Whig party would surely again come to power and reverse the action of the Tory statesmen. Even the English delegates had to keep this possibility in mind; a reversal in England could cost them their heads as well as their offices if they made an unfortunate peace.

Then came the series of deaths at Versailles that shook the whole structure of the Anglo-French negotiations. The Duke and Duchess of Burgundy and their eldest son suddenly died, leaving a second son, a child of two, who himself barely recovered from the same disease that killed his parents and brother, as the dauphin. He was the only "life" between Philippe V of Spain and the throne of France. The preceding year the death of the Grand Dauphin, Louis' only living son, had caused a ripple of anxiety to pass over the discussions between London and Versailles, for a cardinal point in any peace between Louis XIV and his foes had to be the separation of the two crowns. With the Duke of Burgundy and his two sons as next in line, the dauphin's death had not seemed so important, but when only a sickly little boy remained between the throne at Versailles and the King of Spain, it was a problem of a very different sort. Louis well realized that there was great danger in the situation. When his son had died, he wrote a letter of simple dignity[10] that accepted the death as a family matter. Louis had lost a son; Philippe, a father; Spain had lost a strong advocate of French support for Spanish pretensions, but there was no need for Europe to become alarmed. However, the terrible blows of February and early March 1712 that snuffed out three lives so near the throne was a very different matter. Louis' letter to Philippe on March 11, 1712, shows that in addition to family grief, these events involved high politics of Europe:

The bad news repeats itself and each week I must tell you of some new misfortune. I have just lost the Dauphin, my great grandson and eldest son of your brother. I had little hope of saving the Duke of Anjou, now the Dauphin, but he has more happily come out of the same illness that had attacked him at the same time as his brother. We do not know the secrets of Providence, but your Majesty is now regarded by all Europe as the next heir to my crown, and this general opinion will increase the difficulties of the peace. I am convinced that in the midst of these terrible events, you feel more tenderness than ever toward your family, and if it is possible that you will take an even greater interest in the kingdom that apparently will someday be yours. I pray to God that he will care for you, and I can assure you that my consolation will come in giving you evidence of the true and tender feelings that I have for you.[11]

Everyone was embarrassed by the problem, because it was difficult to find a suitable response. The English government struck out in several directions, for obviously a solution must be found if the men who now governed England were to be safe after the death of the queen. None of their suggestions, however, seemed viable. Torcy's argument, obviously developed in conjunction with the king, pointed the problem as the French saw it:

France could never consent to become a province of Spain, and Spain thinks the same vis-à-vis France. Therefore it is a question of finding solid measures to prevent the union of these two monarchies. But it would fail completely to satisfy this objective if . . . the fundamental laws of the realm were contradicted. According to these laws the prince nearest to the crown is the necessary heir . . . he succeeds, not as heir but as monarch of the kingdom . . . by the right of his birth alone. He does not owe the crown to the testament of his predecessor, to an edict or decree, nor to anyone's generosity, but from the law alone. This law is looked upon as the work of Him who has established all monarchies, and we are convinced in France that God alone can abolish it. No revocation therefore can put it aside, and if the King of Spain gives his renunciation for the good of the peace or by obedience to his grandfather, one fools oneself in accepting it as an expedient capable of preventing the evil that it proposes to avoid.

This is Louis' doctrine of divine right stated in the same terms that it had been ever since he first denied the validity of his wife's renunciation of the Spanish throne. But in England, where the queen sat on the throne in defiance of such a law and where the succession had been fixed by an act of Parliament rather than by "divine right," statesmen would have nothing to do with this theory. If there were to be peace, France must find some viable solution.

Louis' first proposal was that the will of Charles II should be followed. Thus Philippe could rule in Spain until such a time that he should inherit the throne of France. If he decided to accept the French crown, he would renounce the Spanish one for himself and his children; it then would be offered to his brother the Duke of Berry. If the Duke of Berry should refuse, then, since Philippe had proclaimed the descendants of Anne of Austria to be next in line, the crown would be offered to the Duke of Orléans, grandson of Anne and Louis XIII. Europe could guarantee this line of succession by the treaty of peace. But the English would hear nothing of this proposal. They were not willing to allow Philippe to retain the choice of accepting or rejecting the French throne in case it should come to him, even though he might assure the world that he would give up the Spanish throne if he accepted the French one. Nor were they willing to consider a "European guarantee" that the thrones would remain separate, for only by a war could the "guarantee" be implemented. Thus the choice before Philippe, as his grandfather saw it, came to this: Philippe must either abandon at once the Spanish throne, and come to live as a private person in France in order to enjoy "the rights to the succession to the French throne that perhaps might never develop, or renounce the rights to the French throne and retain . . . the thrones of Spain and the Indies. . . ." "My intention" wrote Louis, "is not to give any advice on this choice to my grandson"—a decision that he could hardly keep.

Philippe hesitated. At the court in Madrid men very often indulged in vague hopes and extravagant dreams. Philippe wanted to secure the throne of Spain for one of his children, the throne of France for another. Louis ordered his ambassador to let both Philippe and the queen understand that he was willing to fight the war to assure their hold on the Spanish throne, but that it "is not just to ruin my kingdom to retain for them the right either to unite the French and Spanish thrones, or to divide them beween their children." Louis went on to say that the choice had to be made and that he "had difficulty believing that a prince who has ruled for eleven years, who loves his subjects and who has received so much evidence of their faithfulness could decide to abandon them to lead a private life awaiting the uncertainty of succession. . . ." Louis concluded in a postscript, "the peace will be absolutely destroyed if the King of Spain does not renounce his rights to my throne and if the Duke of Berry does not renounce, at the same time, his to the crown of Spain. It only remains to decide whether I want peace at this price or a continuation of the war. . . ."[12] Even this did not bring a decision from Madrid. Louis was faced with renewal of the war in Flanders on a grand scale and he could no longer depend upon Vauban's defensive shield, for most of his fortifications had been captured. He knew that Eugene was telling everyone that the allies would dictate peace in Paris. Louis wrote to Philippe, "Every moment is precious at this conjuncture of events, I cannot urge you enough of the importance . . . of your decision. I hope that you will put me in position to make a glorious peace, saving the crown that you have on your head, which has already cost so much blood and expense."[13]

In Spain there were still dreams. Philippe wrote his grandfather on April 22, expressing his willingness to give up the succession in France, but he insisted that the English should grant him considerable advantages for this concession. What he wanted was the assurance that he would be given all the Spanish inheritance except the Spanish Netherlands: the Milanais, the Tuscan ports, Naples, Sicily and the Islands, as well as Spain and the Indies. Philippe's naïveté can be seen in his letter to his grandfather:

I pride myself that you will recognize, and all France as well, by the gambit that I am taking that I contribute . . . to the peace more than anyone in the world could believe possible, and that I have not been, nor am, nor will ever be the cause of the common misfortunes that we have suffered in this war or that can happen to us in the future.[14]

Letters from Versailles attempted to dispel the clouds of mist that surrounded all thinking at Madrid: it was folly to believe that Europe would allow Philippe to come to France as king with his eldest son as dauphin, while the child yet unborn remained in Madrid as infant ruler with Philippe or his queen as regent. It was also folly to expect the English to try to secure Italy for Philippe. It was folly not to decide quickly to stay in Spain as king rather than to return to France as "expectant" heir. Louis may have once thought that he would give no advice, but his and Torcy's letters to Philippe, to Bonnac, to the Princess des Ursins abounded in urgent advice bordering upon absolute orders.[15]

At this moment the English came up with a proposal that much appealed to Louis. Let Philippe cede Spain and the Indies to the Duke of Savoy. In return the duke would cede Savoy, Piedmont, Montferrat, and Nice to Philippe. These territories added to Sicily would form a kingdom for Philippe to rule until he might be called to become King of France. Were he to become King of France, Sicily must be ceded to the Austrian Hapsburgs, but the other territories bordering France would be added to the kingdom of France. Here was a return to the ideas of the partition treaties that gave France territorial advantages from the breakup of the Spanish empire. Louis' letter to Philippe took on a soothing tone:

I assure you that in spite of the disproportion of the estates [Spain and the Indies for an Italian kingdom], I have been sensibly touched by the idea that you could continue to rule, and that I could still see in you my successor, and that you could visit me from time to time. Think of the pleasure that you would bring me to allow me to rest assured about the future. . . . If the Dauphin lives I would leave him a regent accustomed to command, capable of maintaining order in my kingdom and able to smother cabals. . . . If this child dies, as his feeble complexion seems to indicate, you would follow me in the succession according to the order of your birth. . . . I would have the consolation of leaving my people a virtuous king, capable of ruling them, and whose succession would unite to the crown the considerable estates of Savoy, Piedmont, and Montferrat. I avow to you that I am much pleased with this idea, but principally so because of the sweetness of the proposal that I would pass the rest of my life with you and the Queen . . . to instruct you in the conditions of my affairs. . . . I can imagine nothing comparable to the pleasure that you would give me if you accept this offer.

If your feelings . . . for your subjects are pressing motifs for remaining with them, I can say to you that you owe me these same feelings, that you owe them to your family, your fatherland, before owing them to Spain. I ask you therefore the favor, and I will regard it as the greatest happiness in my life, that you resolve to come to me and conserve your rights that you will . . . one day regret if you abandon them.[16]

We may be permitted to wonder whether Louis was completely candid in this letter; the prospect of adding so much of northern Italy to the French crown must have appealed to him and his advisers at least as much as the pleasure of seeing his grandson.

This clearly was a request that Philippe should accept the English proposal; the French ambassador at Madrid, de Bonnac, further elaborated the king's wishes, but the young King of Spain and his wife had become Spaniards. Philippe felt at home at Madrid; he was quite sure that he would be much less so in France. Furthermore the French throne was still a gamble rather than a sure offer. After much deliberation he answered his grandfather:

> . . . too many reasons are opposed to it for me to accept. It seems to me that it would be more advantageous for France that a branch of our family should reign in Spain than to put the crown on the head of a prince whose friendship is not assured, and this advantage seems to me more considerable since it is not certain that one day would see the unification of Savoy, Montferrat, and Piedmont with France. I believe therefore that it is greater evidence of my affection for you and your subjects if I stand by the resolution that I have already taken . . . rather than to follow the plan suggested by England. By this I will give peace to France and I will assure her of an ally . . . which otherwise might one day join her enemies. . . . At the same time I take the gambit that seems to me most agreeable to my *gloire* and the good of my subjects, who have so strongly contributed by their attachment and zeal to the maintenance of the crown on my head.[17]

This reply was not exactly what Louis wanted, but it did remove the roadblock obstructing the peace with England. He wrote to his grandson, "I have lost no time making your decision known in England. This will make the peace possible. Now you must draft the act [the renunciation] . . . required of you. . . ." The English action had already been taken—overhastily, perhaps. When Bolingbroke learned that Louis had presented Philippe with the alternatives of the crown of Spain and the Indies or the Italian crown proposed by the English, he concluded that his government could be satisfied with either one, and therefore wrote to Lord Ormonde, who had taken Marlborough's place as commander of the English army in Flanders (May 10–21, 1712), "It is the Queen's positive command to your grace that you avoid engaging in any siege, or hazarding any battle, till you have further orders from her Majesty . . . ," and in a postscript he added that the court of France would also receive this order so that the English commander could talk to his French counterpart to arrange details.[18] This action was taken a week before Philippe had made his decision. The fact that Versailles knew about it before any of England's allies gave rise to considerable recrimination against Bolingbroke and the Tory government in England.

Louis, however, was not concerned that England's allies were dismayed by Bolingbroke's action. He saw it solely as a way to disengage from the war. His letter to the Archbishop of Bourges is an interesting act of faith; he *knew* that he could end the war only when God was ready to give him that grace. "I regard the present disposition toward a reestablishment of general peace as the work of God, and my cares to advance it will be useful only inasmuch as they please Him to finish what He has Himself begun. I am convinced that you will do me the favor of ordering prayers in your diocese to obtain from the divine bounty that the conference [at Utrecht] . . . will produce a good so necessary to Christendom. . . ."[19] The reign of *le Dieudonné* that started with *Te Deums,* public prayers, novenas, and other such pious recognitions of God's will and God's action on earth, never lost its faith in His Providence as the mainspring of history.

The solution of the crisis that the deaths of Louis' grandson and great grandson had created came none too soon, for Louis' position had been desperate when the crisis flared up and threatened to end the negotiations. Even though his armies were better prepared to fight than they had been two years before, they still were no match for the combined forces that the allies had assembled in Flanders. If the English remained loyal to the coalition, Eugene's boast that he would impose peace upon France at Versailles was a distinct possibility. Louis' advisers were of mixed opinions: some wanted to move the king and court to the Loire for safety. This Louis would not do. Villars met with the king in the early spring of 1712 to discuss the coming campaign. Louis, shaken by the deaths in his family and the dangers that threatened his kingdom, could not hold back his tears, but his resolution was firm. He would not withdraw to the Loire. If the enemy should break through the defenses, he would join the army and seek death in battle rather than surrender ignominiously. Villars probably did not report the king's words exactly as he said them, but the stand is unquestionably the king's, clearly within the range of his character as we know him. His life was too near its end for humiliation; such a death could guarantee his honor and his *gloire.* Villars, somewhat shaken by his interview, returned to the army in Flanders resolved to beat off the enemy.[20] Luckily for him, Bolingbroke's order of the May 21 came in time to save the army and the kingdom.

Even after the Duke of Ormonde separated his forces from the allied army, Eugene still had a slight superiority of number over Villars, for the German troops that had been in England's pay decided to remain with their comrades rather than withdraw with the English army, as Eugene, seeking to rebuild the coalition without England, prepared to break into France. He opened his trenches before Quesnoy early in June, and made plans for moving on to Landrecy as the next and final obstacle in his road to complete victory. Villars could not seem to find a way to halt his progress. Eugene's communications to his base at Marchiennes were well fortified by the lines that Villars himself had built several years before; Eugene referred to this route as "the road to Paris." There was no weak spot for

Villars to attack until after the English army actually left Flanders in the middle of July.

The king's correspondence during this month of July and August of 1712 is striking proof that at seventy-four Louis still followed changes in the military situation with characteristic vigor. He knew that Quesnoy could not be saved, but he was determined not to let Eugene take Landrecy. When Villars informed him of his plans for action, the king immediately answered:

I strongly approve . . . you have done well to explain to the principal officers of my army that I have given you orders to attack and fight the enemies in case that they should undertake the siege of that fortification [Landrecy]. . . . I expect from your zeal for my service that you will omit nothing that will be practicable. You know how important it is to save that fortification and I hope that my troops will behave with the same valor that they have shown on so many occasions. . . .[21]

This letter was hardly finished when a letter from Villars came explaining the difficulties he was encountering in this plan to attack Eugene. Louis immediately replied:

My intention is not to push you into an act that is impossible, but [to do] . . . all that is possible to bring aid to Landrecy and to prevent the enemies from making themselves masters of that fortification. . . . Your letter does not exactly explain the disadvantages of attacking the enemy between the Sambre and the branch of the Priche. I am convinced that the enemies will not fail to take advantage of the time that you give them. The situation demands the most prompt determination. You can take your moves from my previous orders . . . that I confirm . . . without asking for further ones. . . . It is up to you to determine both the time and the place for action and to make the best arrangements to insure success.[22]

These are not the words of a timid, tired old man; they can be duplicated in orders that Louis sent to Luxembourg, to Catinat, to Villeroi, to Vendôme, to Tallard, to Berwick, and to Villars from 1691 onward.

Actually Villars had decided upon his objective, but he wished to assure surprise. For over a month there had been suggestions that the weak link in the foe's communications was the field fortification at Denain where the troops that Lord Albemarle commanded, some 20 battalions and 20 squadrons, no longer defended the line. Villars prepared to fall upon this point in the line with his entire army. The move was made with complete secrecy: the French army did not know its destination until the very last moment when commitment was imperative. On the morning of July 24, a mass assault overran Denain, killed or captured most of the defenders, and then regrouped in time to maul seriously the relief forces that Eugene managed to pull together. It was a complete success. Eugene's communications with his supply base were cut and the balance of military power in Flanders shifted drastically in Villars' favor.[23]

The king's letter to Villars on July 27 is both a hymn of praise, and a correct assessment of the importance of the battle: ". . . the number of general officers captured indicates how complete was the victory and that the defenses of the camp were completely overrun." Eugene's siege of Landrecy would now be raised. Louis the politician, who understood that men live by recognition as well as by bread, continued ". . . my troops have shown a courage that I cannot praise enough; I recognize in this action the valor of the nation. . . . I am also sorry to have lost so many officers and soldiers, I regret the death of M. de Tourville [who would undoubtedly have become a marshal of France had he lived] and I hope that the wounds of the Marquis de Meuze and the Marquis de Jensac will not be as dangerous as first believed. . . . All general officers who have commanded and who marched in the first rank have given evidence of their zeal and capacity. . . ." This last was an understatement; hardly a man in the first rank of the attack survived; there were a little over 2,000 casualties, nearly all of them in those companies that took the first volley from the defense of Denain.

Louis now lost no time in urging Villars to assume the offensive. It should be easy to raise the siege of Landrecy and to begin that of Douai, both of which would be of utmost importance in the negotiations at Utrecht. Let us listen to the words he wrote to Villars:

Nothing could more favorably advance and assist the negotiations for peace . . . than to recover this superiority that my troops have had for so long but which they unhappily had lost for the last several years. The powers that now are negotiating, and that seemed resolved to create a new league, will now become more tractable when they see evaporate all the hopes that Prince Eugene had promised them. . . . This is the fruit that I hope to harvest from the very important service that you have just rendered for me [Denain].[24]

When Eugene seemed a little slow in grasping the fact that he must fall back to a defensive stance, Louis became impatient:

. . . It does not seem to me that the Prince Eugene has decided to raise the siege of Landrecy and this makes me believe that he is determined to succeed in this enterprise that alone can maintain his control over the spirit of his allies. I have explained to you in my last letter the essential reasons that I have for seeking out and fighting the enemy rather than risk the loss of that fortification. These reasons are still valid and I do not believe it necessary to give you further orders. . . .[25]

A few days later:

> You ought to find some means to force the Prince Eugene to raise the siege
> . . . there does not appear to me any better way than by cutting his communica-
> tions with Mons which is the only place from which he can draw supplies.

Louis was most upset that Eugene continued the siege:

> After the advantages that my troops just won, there will not be enough profit
> from them if the Prince Eugene can continue the siege and make himself master
> of a fortification that could give him easy access into my kingdom. . . .[26]

Villars, however, did take advantage of his victory. An assault on
Marchiennes on July 30 was a complete success; the French captured huge
magazines of food, military supplies, and a hundred new cannons. Eugene
had to give up his hold on Landrecy, while Villars went on to recapture
Douai, Quesnoy, and Bouchain in quick succession. The king's letters began
to bubble with satisfaction.[27] When the campaign neared its end, he wrote
(to Villars):

> This is a return of prosperity; it is very agreeable to see: in less than three
> months after the defeat at Denain; the conquest of Marchiennes and the con-
> quest of three strongly fortified cities. . . . [He went on to add] I believe that
> I cannot better recognize the important services that you [Villars] have rendered
> me than to mark the personal satisfaction that I have from them by giving
> you the government of Provence which has become vacant by the death of
> the Duke of Vendôme. . . . I send you orders to march my troops into the
> places where they will pass the winter and then . . . you must let nothing
> prevent your leaving them so that you can come to be with me.[28]

Louis had made Villars a marshal of France, a duke, a peer, and now
he made him governor of one of the most important provinces of his kingdom. His gratitude was well placed. Villars' victories in the summer and
fall of 1712 brought about a general desire for peace. Only the emperor
still refused to negotiate. The Treaty of Utrecht could now be written.

The Anglo-French negotiations were conducted at Versailles or London before being transferred to the diplomats at Utrecht for incorporation
into the treaty; they were complicated because both parties had a "protégé"
whose interests often created more problems than those of the principals.
Louis' protégé was the Electoral Prince Max Emanuel of Bavaria. His
record as a soldier during the war had been somewhat less than brilliant;
indeed, on several occasions Louis expressed the wish that Max would take
more care and interest in his role as commander, and Max's very presence
had made it impossible to use Villars in any theater where the Bavarian
also held a command. But Max and his brother the Archbishop of Cologne

had been faithful allies, the only faithful allies in this long war—indeed, except for Philippe's Spain and Sweden in the Dutch War, the only faithful allies that Louis had ever had. Just as he rigorously supported the Swedish "rights" against Brandenburg in 1678–79, so Louis attempted to defend the "interests" of his client in the negotiations at Utrecht. In fact, the king's correspondence with his grandson for the preceding half-dozen years is sprinkled with demands that Philippe should recognize Max as sovereign prince in the Spanish Netherlands. He alternately begged and threatened his grandson until at last the Spanish did send the necessary papers, but neither the English nor the Dutch would recognize Max as ruler of the Netherlands. When Louis proposed it again shortly after the opening of the conference at Utrecht, he was only to be met by shocked stares. In the course of the negotiations with the English, Louis suggested that Max might be given Sicily as an alternative to the Spanish Netherlands, but he was unable to get anything more than simple restoration of Max's Bavarian estates in central Europe, and of his brother's at Cologne. In 1712–13 Louis had no levers comparable to those with which he forced Frederick William to return his conquests of Swedish territory after the Treaty of Nymwegen, so the Bavarian princes fared less well than the Swedish king had on that earlier occasion.

The English "protégé" was none other than the Duke of Savoy. Although he was the grandfather of both the heir to Louis' throne and the heir to Philippe's crowns, there was little love lost between him and the Kings of Spain and France. However, with the English backing his claims, the "treacherous" Duke of Savoy was assured of a good share of the spoils, even though it might take the threat of reopening the war to force Louis to grant the terms. The Savoyard emerged from the peace with all his former estates intact, with a "military" frontier along the Alps next to France, with sovereign rights over Sicily, which he later traded for Sardinia, and recognition of a place in the succession to the thrones of Spain and the Indies immediately after Philippe V and the heirs of his body.

The Spanish king also had a protégé: the Princess des Ursins, who wanted sovereign rights over a territory in the Spanish Netherlands. This little affair nearly broke up the conference of Utrecht, because her hold upon the King and Queen of Spain was almost complete, and she was quite willing to wreck the conference rather than give up her pretensions.

This is not the place to retell the story of the negotiations for the peace of 1713–14. They were the work of many people besides the king, and were developed at the conference table at Utrecht and in the chambers of ministers and rulers all over Europe. Legrelle, who probably knew more about the French negotiations than any other historian, gives Torcy credit for much of the work:

We do not fear to proclaim [that] the true leader of the orchestra in this immense cacophonic political drama which lasted from 1701 to 1713 was much more the grandson of the cloth merchant of Reims than the grandson of Henry IV . . . the young minister worked through the dispatches, studied the questions, prepared projects, sustained them in discussion before the King, who decided or referred the question to Torcy, better informed. . . .

As for Louis' part, especially after 1712, Legrelle finds "a king who hesitated, embarrassed himself, contradicted himself, and enfeebled by his private and public misfortunes, allowed simple sentimental considerations to balance reasons of state, in a word, [a king] who no longer knew what he wished."[29]

If Louis no longer had a firm grasp upon the issues of politics, Torcy was strongly aided by a crowd of bureaucrats and diplomats who understood the political problems, as well as the military-political situation of the kingdom. Legrelle calls our attention to Callières and Pecquet, who were the chiefs on the king's "cabinet" and in the bureau of foreign affairs, as well as to a dozen others who aided the process of peacemaking. The Marshal-Duke d'Huxelles, the Abbé de Polignac, and Mesnager, a career diplomat with robe background, represented the kingdom at Utrecht with Polignac as the real chief of mission. In 1713 these men, rather than the seventy-five-year-old king, were the face and the brain of France. While Villars commanded the armies that forced Eugene back upon the Rhine, these men made peace with England, the United Netherlands, the King of Prussia, and the Duke of Savoy. Emperor Charles, still hoping that somehow he could place himself on the throne in Spain, adamantly refused to make peace until the next year, when the round of settlements as well as the military situation clearly indicated that he could not hope to benefit by further resistance. The peace on the Rhine was made by Villars and Eugene, after mutual exchange of their instructions, at Rastatt.

The Spanish were almost as difficult as the emperor. The testament of Charles II had as its primary objective the prevention of partition for the Spanish empire; it was with bad humor that Spanish statesmen watched the peace develop into the last of the "partition treaties." Their empire was divided up among the many participants in the war, leaving Philippe V only the Spanish crowns and the Indies. This was not the way the men who surrounded Philippe V wanted it, and they tried several gambits to modify the terms. Louis had only one strong lever to force them to agreement: military assistance for the siege of Barcelona. Even though the

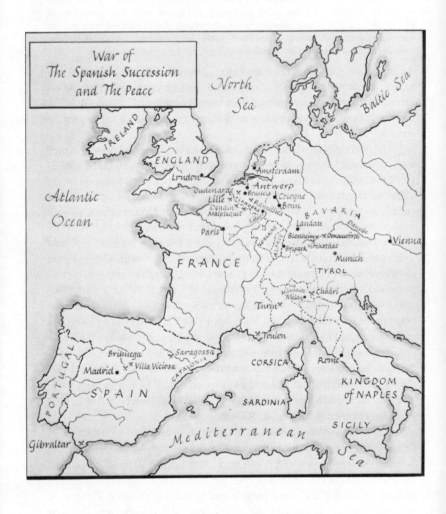

War of
The Spanish Succession
and The Peace

North
Sea

Baltic Sea

IRELAND

ENGLAND

London

Amsterdam

Antwerp

Oudenarde × Brussels
Lille × Ramillies
Denain × Cologne
Malplaquet Bonn

BAVARIA

Landau

Blenheim × Donauwörth
Brisach Hochstädt

Vienna

Atlantic
Ocean

Paris

FRANCE

Munich

TYROL

Milan × Chiari

Turin ×

Toulon ×

PORTUGAL

Brihuega ×
Madrid ● × Villa Viciosa

Saragossa ×
CATALONIA

SPAIN

CORSICA

Rome ●

KINGDOM
of NAPLES

SARDINIA

SICILY

Gibraltar ×

Mediterranean
Sea

English abandoned the Catalans and it was obviously impossible for Charles to aid them, they refused to return to obedience to Philippe on the terms offered them, namely that they lose their special privileges and accept a position exactly like the other kingdoms of Spain. Philippe needed his grandfather's military aid to reduce them to obedience by force. Thus when the Spanish refused to sign the treaty with the United Netherlands, Louis wrote to his grandson, or at least signed a letter that Torcy probably wrote:

I have several times called your attention to the prejudice that your delay in making peace with Holland is causing your interests. . . . Since I have acted [by the French treaty with Holland] according to your intentions and powers, it is well founded for me to demand that you fulfill my promises . . . everyone abroad believes that you have confidence in my advice—so much so that no one would ever believe that the reasons you give [for not signing] . . . could prevent your making peace if I sincerely urged you to do so. It is so important to destroy suspicions that the enemies of the peace have spread about my secret intentions, that I tell you that I will not give you any new aid until you have signed the treaty with Holland.[30]

The Catalan question has been a "hairshirt" for English historians ever since the peacemakers of 1713 abandoned these wretched people to the tender mercies of their "rightful" king. They find it nearly impossible to defend the English action.

During the year 1714 the bundle of treaties needed to end the war was finally completed, and Louis was allowed about a year to contemplate the peace that he had given his subjects, or, to put it in his idiom, the peace that it pleased God to grant to Europe. Torcy was undoubtedly expressing the king's own feelings when he wrote:

God has crowned the Christian courage of this King by maintaining Philippe V, his grandson, on the Spanish throne in spite of the efforts of a formidable league and the unheard of successes that resulted from the alliance of so many princes. The simple statement of the truth will make manifest the marvels of Providence and prove that it alone has conducted and maintained this prince on the throne of Spain which it had destined for him from all eternity. . . .[31]

Although the Spanish empire was partitioned and France had lost territory both in North America and along the frontiers of the kingdom, a Bourbon prince still held the throne of Spain, and France had not suffered the losses and indignities that had been threatened in 1710. No one should doubt the king's sincerity when he ordered *Te Deums* in all the cathedrals of France to thank God for His blessings. However, France's enemies could also thank God with equal fervor, for He (or they) had set limits, strict limits, to the expansion of the realms of the Sun King.

34

THE LAST ACT

WHEN LOUIS REACHED SIXTY the court prepared to see him die and cliques formed around his son and his grandson as men tried to assure places for themselves in the future. But Louis lived on: sixty-five, seventy, seventy-five. In spite of his doctors, in spite of his penchant for exposing himself to all sorts of inclement weather, in spite of his gross eating habits, in spite of boils, gout, worms, headache, dizziness, bouts of fever, bad teeth, and other evils that plague old age, his general health remained remarkably good. If we compare it with the standards of his era, it was excellent. He did become corpulent, but not like his brother and son. Perhaps Fagon was right when he explained that Louis suffered from "melancholic" rather than "coleric" *humeurs,* and therefore required him to change from the white wines of Champagne that d'Aquin had ordered, to the heavier red wines of Burgundy. But neither d'Aquin nor Fagon was able to limit his meals to control his gout and digestive disorders. He lost most of his teeth, but not his appetite. By the time he was seventy-five, people were beginning to wonder if he would live forever.[1]

Although these years were filled with severe trials brought on by war and terrible tragedy within his family, Louis seems not to have lost his zest for life. At seventy he was still lusty; so much so that Madame de Maintenon found it difficult to respond to all his needs. He was vigorous in other ways as well. We find him presiding over councils, arguing with ministers, following the hunt in a carriage, promenading in the garden with the ladies, arranging family parties at Marly, and acting out the role of head of the family at the signing of marriage contracts and other family occasions. He attended mass, reviewed his troops, touched the sick, played godfather to children of ambassadors and others who had his favor. Up to the very last he played out the ceremonial role of king as only a superb actor could handle it.

Behind this façade, however, his health did leave something to be desired. Fagon's registers reveal that he underwent an endless number of purgings, enemas, and bleedings, and that he swallowed quantities of medicine of dubious value. At least every five weeks he took "medicine" that sent him to the chair twelve to fourteen times a day; he was plagued with worms, probably the familiar ascarids usually associated with eating improperly washed salad. He had vapeurs in his stomach and intestines, suffered alternately from constipation and diarrhea; he had an irregular pulse; he had "sand" the size of a grain of wheat in his urine. Fagon tells of his being confined to his rooms often enough to suggest that his life was much less regular than Saint-Simon would have us believe. Yet on the other hand, as we watch the king in the midst of his activities, we also become convinced that Fagon made his illnesses more important than they really were—perhaps to make them more interesting when the story was reread to his Majesty, and therefore to make Fagon's ministrations appear the more important.

As we have seen, these last ten to fifteen years of the reign were complicated by great and vexing questions of peace and war, but this did not prevent Louis from interesting himself in the myriad domestic questions that also came to his attention. A simple perusal of the registers of the secretary of state responsible for religious affairs shows that the conversion of the Huguenots had an important place in the king's business long after 1685. In his correspondence we find him asking about relapsed converts, about refusals of the Roman Catholic sacraments by men on their deathbeds, about the reeducation of children, about the marriages of wards with Huguenot backgrounds, and about the sticky problem of trying to persuade émigrés to return to France. His Catholic subjects also were often difficult. Robberies in churches were not uncommon and too many people committed "nuisances" in church buildings. On March 10, 1700, Barbézieux wrote, "His Majesty, having learned that his ordinances and those of the kings, his predecessors, touching the respect due churches are not being executed, and that indecencies and scandal become more numerous day by day, and that people of both sexes seem to have entirely forgotten their important duties, ordains, and orders that the edicts, ordinances, *arrêts,* and legislation on this subject should be executed punctually. . . ." That same week Louis also learned that in many dioceses of the kingdom, bishops "have neglected to hold processions on the day of the Assumption instituted by the late king in 1638. Since he had thus placed the kingdom under the protection of the Holy Virgin, it is His Majesty's intention that this procession shall be held. . . ." The copy of the ordinance of 1638 reveals that this had been the occasion when Louis XIII asked for the intervention of the Mother of God to have his unborn child be a son.[2]

Other problems were less easy to solve. Frenchmen (ex-Huguenots) too often visited foreign embassies on Sunday, obviously with the intention of attending church services. Some of the embassies sold meat in their courtyards without paying the tax, and even on Fridays. In a letter to the chief of police in Paris the secretary notes that "There is no reason to doubt that they [the ambassadors] will not obey the King's orders, but it will be nonetheless good for you to keep an eye on the situation. . . ." On another level, in 1712 we find the king asking all his bishops if they think it wise or necessary to "execute the pious intentions of our dear and well beloved Cardinal de Noailles" who ordered doctors to suggest the administration of the last sacraments to patients whose illness could cause death.[3]

The king's interest did not stop with religious affairs. Under Fagon's prodding he issued orders for demonstrations by the professors of medicine in the medical herbs section of the Royal Gardens. The registers testify to his continued interest in the Collège Mazarin (College of the Four Nations) and the several faculties of the University. It is questionable that his granting sons of professors the right to inherit their fathers' posts contributed to the prestige of the University or to the teaching of the students. His own and his predecessor's ordinances against dueling were obviously very important to him, for we find Louis time and again insisting that they be respected. He regarded this legislation as one of the most important acts of his and his father's governments. These were only a few of the many items that came to his desk; perhaps these minutiae somewhat distracted his attention from the discouraging news that came from his soldiers and diplomats. In any case, we can conclude that Saint-Simon's testimony is undoubtedly correct when he wrote, "He [Louis] enters into the immediate needs of the troops, clothing, arms, exercises, discipline . . . in a word, all sorts of small details. He concerns himself not less with his châteaus, his civil household, his expenditures for the table. . . ." The duke was sure that this indicated a mediocre mind; perhaps it did, but it also was the pattern of life to which Louis had become accustomed ever since Mazarin's death, and he was quite unable to break free from it before he died.

At the turn of the century, however, subtle changes began to appear in the court and the government of the kingdom. With the king over sixty, it seemed wise to invite his heirs to take part in the council; first the dauphin, and then his son the Duke of Burgundy, were admitted to the inner circles of the government, so that if the king should die, the transfer of power would not be difficult. The fat, indolent dauphin had few ideas of his own, but he became the center of a cabal that tried to instruct him and apparently did cure him a little of his fear of his father. Madame de Maintenon wrote, "The Dauphin listens and speaks more; he even carries complaints that he hears to the King. After which he says, 'I have spoken' . . . thus giving more blame to his father."[4] He also caused some little distress in the family by taking a violent dislike for his own son, the talented, but overly-pious and priggish, Duke of Burgundy. After the fiasco at Oudenarde and the disastrous campaign that followed, the dauphin openly and loudly took up the part of Vendôme against his son. It did not help Vendôme much, but it did distress the Duke of Burgundy's friends. As might be expected, that young man also attracted a coterie of men who saw the future of the kingdom in him. The most famous of these were the Dukes of Chevreuse and Beauvillier, Saint-Simon, and of course, the Archbishop of Cambrai, Fénelon. These men were a cut above the ones who surrounded the dauphin, but since Louis outlived both his son and his grandson, their hopes were all equally doomed to frustration.

If the dauphin and the Duke of Burgundy played a minor part in the government during these last years, the same cannot be said for Madame de Maintenon. However, in light of the tradition fostered by the writings of Saint-Simon, the Duchess of Orléans, and others who blamed the lady for all the evils that beset the reign, it is important to take a closer look at the actual part that she did play. We should start by reiterating the fact that although Louis did use her as a member of his "team" to seek out the names of clergymen worthy of high office, and occasionally did discuss with her personalities and problems of the court, before about 1700 he did not allow her any part in important decisions. One has only to read her letters during the 1690's to see her frustration: she was learning much about the secret affairs of state, and her fingers fairly itched to have a part in them, but Louis had no intention of giving over affairs to a woman, not even to one as intelligent as his wife. Madame de Maintenon understood this thoroughly, and despite her headaches, she was careful not even to ask for anything unless her case was excellent, for as she wrote, it is better "not to accustom the King to refusing requests."[5]

The limited influence that she had during these years was not always happy. Her personal friends were few and her contacts with most of the court were formal. She was friendly with the Dukes of Chevreuse and Beauvillier, both of whom had married daughters of the great Colbert. At their houses she met Fénelon, who later became responsible for the education of the dauphin's sons. Under similar circumstances she met Madame Guyon, whom she introduced both to her circle at Saint-Cyr and at the court, but when the Quietist controversy flared up, Madame de Maintenon quickly withdrew her support from Madame Guyon, whose pathetic letters she simply did not answer. Fénelon gallantly stood by Madame Guyon until Rome condemned her teachings and the support of them. It was unpleasant, but politically not dangerous.[6]

More distressing was the fact that her candidate for the episcopal throne in Paris became involved in the Jansenist controversy. The previous archbishop, Harlay, had been unfit for his high office because of his personal life; Archbishop Noailles, whose family was closely allied to Madame de Maintenon, got in trouble because he refused to "wash himself clean" of the taint of Jansenism by condemning certain propositions in Quesnel's *Réflections morales sur l'Evangile*. It was most embarrassing. Finally Rome condemned the book and the whole Jansenist movement by the bull *Unigenitus* in 1713. Louis, who hated theological disputations and friction in the church, took terrible revenge upon the Jansenists by destroying their church at Port-Royal, perhaps because they had been *Frondeurs* as well as heretics. But he could hardly blame his wife for the part played by Archbishop Noailles.

One striking enigma of this period remains unsolved. Did Madame de Maintenon try to persuade the king to recognize their marriage publicly and thus make her queen? The evidence is unclear. Did Louis actually put the question to his confessor? Did the Jesuit suggest that Fénelon should give the answer? Did Fénelon beg to be excused, for no matter what answer he might give, it would ruin him? Someday these questions may be answered. Cordelier, the most recent biographer of Madame de Maintenon, has created a psychological model of the lady which, he insists, proves that no such request could ever have been made.[7] Louis Hastier takes the evidence and argues that the marriage was at stake, but not the recognition of the marriage. In his account Madame de Maintenon was simply the king's mistress until the last years of the 1690's when he finally decided to marry her.[8] No matter what the truth was about her ambitions, Louis obviously had no intention of recognizing the marriage publicly. Louis XIV had very strong feelings about the absolute importance of rank by birth; he, like the rest of his family, placed high value upon blood. He could marry Madame de Maintenon secretly to regularize his life, to save his soul, or simply to have agreeable companionship, but it is quite inconceivable that he should recognize a woman with her humble background as Queen of France. If she actually did have hope of this recognition, the fact that she was not proclaimed queen indicates the limitations of her influence.

There can be little doubt that the part played by Madame de Maintenon in the affairs of state before 1700 was slight. However, after the turn of the century this picture slowly changed and Madame de Maintenon was consulted more frequently and given a larger part in the consideration of affairs, although she never selected the king's ministers, nor did she take their place in Louis' government. Louis Bertrand insists that her role was largely that of helping Louis be sure that his ministers were not hoodwinking him. According to this thesis, Louis developed the custom of working with his ministers in her chambers so that she could help him to evaluate their sincerity and honesty. Were these young men "putting something over" on the old king? Four eyes could observe their actions better than two. This picture of the two old people suspiciously watching the men who served the state has much to recommend it, for we do know that Louis had little confidence in men's motives and much belief that they should be watched. But with no real evidence to support the thesis, it must remain an inference.

What we do know for sure is that much of the business of state was conducted in Madame de Maintenon's presence, and that often the king actually called upon her to join in consultation. We also know that she often demurred, and that when she did hazard advice, she was careful not to oppose what she believed to be her husband's intentions—at least not in the presence of a minister. It is very possible that in their private conversations her clear vision and articulate speech may have made a deep impression upon him.

On her own confession, however, sometimes she talked plainly to the king:

Princes never want to look at misfortune; they are accustomed to having these things hidden from them. I find myself driven by my conscience, by the love that I have for the King, and the true interest that I take for all that concerns him, to tell him the truth, not to flatter him, to make him realize that people often deceive him and give him bad counsel. You see how it saddens me. . . . I wish to please him, but I am obliged to do it. I often cause him sorrow when he comes for consolation. . . .[9]

It may have been her disinterested advice, her calm approach to problems, her obvious concern for his interests that gave her Louis' confidence. He spoke of her "stolidity," and obviously came to value her advice. Her own account of "her day" toward the end of the War of the Spanish Succession tells us much about her place at court and her relations with the king. Her chambers were filled with people in the morning, after mass, and again after the noon meal when the king and the Duchess of Burgundy usually visited her along with the others. But of the afternoons she writes:

When the King returns from the hunt, he comes to my apartments; he closes the door and no one enters any more. There I am alone with him. It is necessary to soothe his troubles if he has them, his sadness, his vapeurs; sometimes he

weeps tears that he cannot control. . . . Then comes a minister, often bringing
bad news. The King works with him. If he wishes a third in council, he calls
me; if he does not want me, I go away a bit . . . while the King works, I have
supper, but it is only once in two months that I do so on my own time. I know
that the King is alone or depressed or, indeed, when M. Chamillart is nearly
finished, he calls me to hurry. Another day he wants to show me something so
I am always hurried. I always eat quickly [we should note that she was a chronic
complainer to others, but not to the king]. After that, as you can guess, it is
late, I have been up since six o'clock in the morning. I have hardly been able
to draw a breath all day. I begin to feel tired, I yawn. . . . I am beginning to
feel my age. The King realizes this and sometimes he says: "you are all in, you
must go to bed. . . ." My women undress me, but I sense that the King has
something to say to me. He waits until they go; or waits for another minister to
come in, and he is afraid that they [the women] will hear. This worries him and
me too. What do I do? I hurry until I make myself sick . . . you know how
I hate to be rushed . . . finally I am in bed and I send my women away. The
King comes and stays by my bed. . . . I am in bed but I need something for I
no longer have a beautiful body. . . . The king stays with me until he goes to
supper. About a quarter of an hour before supper M. le Dauphin and the
Duke and Duchess of Burgundy come in. At ten or a quarter past everyone
goes out. I am alone and I take the comforts that I need, but often worries and
fatigues prevent my sleeping. . . .[10]

We get further insights into the expanding role played by Madame de
Maintenon through the extensive correspondence that she carried on with
the Princess des Ursins during these years. These letters had one objective:
they were an important tunnel into the affairs of the court at Madrid. Louis
got his information about the government and the army from his ambassadors and soldiers, he got further news by his correspondence with
Philippe, but only in these letters between Madame de Maintenon and the
princess could he learn of the more intimate affairs of the young king's
household. The princess, for her part, also benefitted, for Madame de
Maintenon had to give her reciprocal information about the affairs of Versailles. At many points in their correspondence these two women stood at
opposite poles in their own ambitions and policy, but the letters continued
to be exchanged, for they were too valuable for either of them to give them
up. In her general correspondence, however, Madame de Maintenon was
careful not to overstep her role; for example, when the French ambassador
at Madrid, the Duke d' Harcourt, attempted to exchange letters with her,
she answered, "I do not understand how you found time to write me two
letters . . . and I beg you not to write again except about private affairs,
or to reassure me a little about the war. . . ."[11] She understood that
Louis did not want her to by-pass the secretary of state for foreign affairs.

There was another area where her influence obviously was important.

All the younger men in the royal family wrote to her to intercede for them with the king. The dauphin, the legitimized sons, the Duke of Burgundy, all urged her to tell the king how anxious they were to please him, how much they wanted him to be satisfied with them, how good were their intentions. These princes obviously knew what they were doing when they asked for her favor. The Duke of Burgundy's letters are most interesting. He alone of the princes had no fear of his grandfather—until the disaster of Oudenarde, at which time his letters, too, showed the same anxiety that characterized the others. Undoubtedly Madame de Maintenon discussed these letters with her husband; we wonder whether she softened the king's irritations with the inadequacies of his descendants.[12]

We should return again and again, however, to the fact that Louis did not give the direction of his affairs over to his wife, no matter what some of the memoirists might say. We find her often disturbed by the king's policy. "God is in wrath," she writes, when really it was probably Madame de Maintenon who was "in wrath." She had not been raised to rule, and she could not accept the distress of the people, the casualties in the army, the disorders in the kingdom that caused suffering, as easily as Louis could. Louis had always been king; he was a hard man who could order brutal repression of a rebellion without worrying about the results. He did not like to see the casualty lists grow, but they did not bother him as they did his wife, who worried "about the poor people for whom nobody cares" or the "sufferings of the brave men that one loses. . . ." Against the backdrop of her womanly concern, Louis' attitudes often seem hard and callous. It is quite clear that the contemporary songster was unjust when he wrote:

> One could without being satirical
> Even find this regime comical.
> See how this holy whore
> Directs this whole empire
> If we were not dying of hunger
> We could die of laughter.

She did not actually manage the state any more than she was responsible for the famine that so distressed the kingdom. The poet grossly misunderstood the king's concern that no one—and certainly not a woman—should rule him.

As Louis grew older the court also underwent changes. It had always been a "strange land"[13] where intrigue, envy, and all the lowest motives that man can have regulated life, but during these years to many it also became dull, and affairs that should have brought pleasure became a *corvée*. Some complained that because of the king's piety the gay life migrated to

Paris. Much of this talk is undoubtedly true. Louis' age, the reverses of the war, the problems with his family, all contributed to gloom. In the inner family circle, the young Duchess of Burgundy seems to have brought a little pleasure, but the court was undoubtedly as bad as Saint-Simon says it was. As a matter of fact, Louis and his wife were also alienated in their own court. Let us listen to some of Madame de Maintenon's complaints about manners that were undoubtedly also the opinions of the king:

> I tell you, Madame, the women of these times are insupportable; their senseless, immodest dress, their tobacco, their wine, their overeating, their grossness, their laziness; all this goes against my taste. It seems to me that I can no longer put up with it. I like women who are modest, sober, and happy, capable of serious conversation and witty répartées . . . whose hearts are good and conversation elevated, and yet simple enough to tell me that they recognize themselves in this portrait. . . .[14]

Louis had other troubles with the court. He even had to give up listening to the choral singing that he liked, because there was so much criticism of this old-fashioned entertainment. The gap of fifty years between the king and the young men around him was difficult to fill; at sixty-five, Louis seems to have forgotten what it had been to be twenty.[15]

During these last years of the reign, death stalked the court and the kingdom; one by one the men and women who had shared his youth dropped aside, leaving young and unfamiliar faces in their place. Louis also was growing old, but death seemed to pass him by in its hurry to strike down those around him. Often the names of the men who held high office in his household remained the same, since he had given his faithful servants the right to pass their positions on to their sons, but the age gap between the king and those around him grew with every year. By 1710 there was hardly anyone left who had seen the brave days of 1661. Some of Louis' tears that flowed so freely these latter days in the chambers of Madame de Maintenon must have been for the men and women who were no longer alive. In public he had to carry off his disdain for the ravages of time; even if the king should die, the cry must be "long live the King!" but in private the tragic facts of life and death could bring tears and regrets.

His own immediate family could not escape the blows. In March 1701 the dauphin suffered a stroke that nearly ended his life. He was a man with an enormous appetite who bulged at every seam; for a while no one believed that he would recover, and many accepted the *Te Deums* that were sung to thank God for his life as evidence that God indeed had saved him. Early in June 1701 it was Philippe's turn, and he was unable to stave off his fate. This strange brother ate like an ogre, perhaps to comfort himself for the emptiness of his existence; when his stroke came there was no return. A pen portrait of Philippe, prepared for Anne of England when the war began so that she could know her foes, treated him thus:

He is a good enough prince who does neither good nor ill. He loves the people who love him more than they esteem him. He is two-thirds as tall as his brother . . . but very fat. He wears a black wig, his nose and rouge on his cheeks almost obliterate his face. He does not appear to approve of the policy of persecution of religious dissenters of which he never speaks. He does not lack bravery as was evident at Mont Cassel . . . he knows ceremonials better than anyone . . . never has anyone loved himself more than he does . . . his affections do not go to women whose gallantry seems common to him, nonetheless he affects their manners . . . his make-up resembles the ladies more than a general of the armies.[16]

The author should have mentioned that Philippe disapproved of his brother's secret marriage, and resented the fact that Louis forced him to marry his eldest son to one of the king's legitimized daughters. Poor Philippe, a homosexual whose rouge, jewels, ribbons, and lace brought smiles to many faces, could not reform himself no matter how his brother might urge it. When he died, the sale of his personal jewels brought more than a million livres; the invoice, more than two hundred pages of manuscript, listed rings, pins, charms, earrings, studs, buttons, and the like, set with pearls, rubies, diamonds, and other precious stones. It was a fabulous collection made by a fantastic man who had been an important part of the court of Louis XIV.[17]

Philippe's death was a shock to Louis, partly because only a few hours before, the two brothers had been quarreling over the behavior of Philippe's son toward his wife, Louis' natural daughter. Philippe loudly taunted the king about his own behavior toward Marie-Thérèse; Louis shouted back. A servant had to call attention to the fact that everyone in the hall could hear them. Philippe returned to his own château at Saint-Cloud; a few hours later, after eating and drinking heavily, he suffered a stroke. When Louis learned that his brother's condition was really serious, he hurried to Saint-Cloud, but too late to make any contact with the dying man. There have been many accounts of the death of Philippe, but the one in the *Gazette* was obviously the one that Louis wanted his subjects to read; in this account there is no mention of conflict between the brothers, and much discussion of Louis' fraternal and pious concern for his brother's family. The king ordered 21 high masses and 680 low ones to be said immediately for the repose of the dead man's soul, and before the body was finally entombed at Saint-Denis, he ordered an additional 1,500 masses to be read at the Basilica.[18]

The death raised questions about the status of Philippe's son, whose conduct had occasioned the last fraternal quarrel. Would the king endow him with his father's titles and wealth, or would these be reserved for a prince in the direct line of succession? The Bourbons had twice given the title Duke of Orléans to cadet sons: should it now go to the Duke of Berry rather than to the Duke of Chartres? And what about the dead man's wife, Elizabeth-Charlotte, whose time was largely spent in letter-writing but whose life would be blighted if she were sent from the court? Louis' problem was not as difficult as it might seem. The children of the Duke of Chartres were *his* grandchildren, and in time he would marry one of them to his grandson, the Duke of Berry. Thus he had no scruples in recognizing his son-in-law as the "First Prince of the Blood," a title heretofore belonging to the Condés, and in giving him his father's titles and wealth. The new Duke of Orléans was already a wealthy man, for at the time of his marriage he had been given an enormous dowry, as well as the Palais-Royal in Paris; now with his father's wealth added to his own, his house became the richest family in France, perhaps in all of Europe. Elizabeth-Charlotte was also well treated; Louis left her in possession of her pensions, her household, and her position at court.[19]

For all the king's efforts to provide his brother Philippe with *grandeur* and importance, this unfortunate man was at best never more than a grotesque decoration of the court, at worst a burden, perhaps even a disgrace, to his brother, the king. Louis' son, the dauphin, was hardly more: indolent, fatuous, and dull, only the saving grace of his bourgeois morals kept him from outraging the pious people about him. Like his father he enjoyed the hunt, but that was about the only way in which this disappointing son resembled his father. The king's grandsons were the hopes for the future. Their Bavarian mother died when they were still young, but her blood apparently thinned out the over-concentration that occurred when Louis married his own first cousin. Of her sons one seems to have been very able, a second was reasonably intelligent but "weak-willed," the third took after his father and grandmother.

The eldest was the Duke of Burgundy, a talented young man who tried hard to prepare himself to be king. His preceptor, Archbishop Fénelon, gave him an excellent education, and the king's soldiers tried to teach him to command the army. He was married to the lovely Marie-Adélaïde of Savoy who was the favorite of both Louis and Madame de Maintenon. Louis' letters to this grandson while he was with the army are filled with sage advice about the art of war, particularly the part that a prince could usefully play while he was nominally in command. His letters to Boufflers, Tallard, and Vendôme are filled with concern for the young prince's safety as well as for his opportunities to promote his reputation. Time and again he tells his marshals how much this young man means to him, how important he is to the kingdom. Anyone reading these letters quickly understands that Louis hopes to see this young man take command of the kingdom as a soldier-king. He always tried to buttress the young prince's self-respect; for example, during the campaign in Alsace in 1703, when the young Duke of Burgundy was still very much an amateur at war, Louis even changed the wording of letters prepared for him by the secretary to make them read *as if he* (Louis) *really believed* that the young duke, rather than the marshal who "commanded under his orders," was in command. He spoke of his "giving orders to Marshal Tallard," of his "commanding the troops" to move to this or that position. He also always took pains to let this grandson know how much he trusted him, how much he believed in him, how sure he was that he would succeed. The Duke of Burgundy responded to this treatment by adopting an easy, familiar approach to his grandfather—until, as we have noted, after the battle of Oudenarde and the disastrous campaign of 1708 when we find him writing to Madame de Maintenon with the tone of fear and deference toward the king that was characteristic of the other princes.

Louis' relations with his second grandson, the King of Spain, provided the material for an excellent book on the relations between the courts of Spain and France in 1700–15,[20] and could also be used to extract at least one further book on Louis' conception of kingship. As we have already seen, when Philippe married Marie-Louise of Savoy, his grandfather tried to tell him how important it was that a husband establish empire over his wife. Louis' astonishment and chagrin grew by leaps and bounds as he learned how Philippe fell under his wife's rule. It was impossible even to persuade Philippe to stay in Italy because he wanted to be with Marie-Louise. There are no letters more amusing than those in which the old king tries to force his grandson to do his duty as king and forget the pleasures of his young wife. It was probably this experience that almost convinced Louis that Philippe would never learn to govern on his own.

The letters that he sent to Madrid are filled with sage advice about government as well as about the best ways of dealing with people. At times Louis had to use rather strong threats to secure obedience, "Do you want my counsels, or those that will ruin you?" In another, we find the old king trying to bolster his grandson's ego by assuring him that he had great confidence in his judgment. Again, after finding Philippe to be of little use on the battlefield, Louis urged him to believe that a king can better do his duty in the council, where he could secure money, troops, and political support, than on the field directing his forces. These letters are filled with advice about ways to thank faithful subjects, ways to secure obedience and support, ways to pick good personnel to manage the state. Philippe was under his grandfather's domination until the famine and military disasters of 1709 forced Louis to recognize the possibility that Spain could be lost to the Bourbons. Then Philippe, fortified by his wife and the Princess des Ursins, took over control of the Spanish kingdom and became free of his grandfather, but not from the women who were his companions.

Louis advised both of these grandsons of the necessity for plans and projects that could control the future, but he also warned them that failure might come anyway. "It is not enough to see what we should do if we defeat the enemy," he wrote. "It is also necessary to prepare ourselves for all events with the spirit of submission and resignation. . . ." God, he pointed out, "is the arbiter of battles," and Christian princes must be prepared to accept His strange decisions with Christian piety. The letters to both young men were studded with the king's belief that the course of events represents the will of God, that in effect, history is God's intention manifest on the earth. These were years when Louis was experiencing the impact of God's will, perhaps of his wrath.[21]

If Louis wrote any letters to his third grandson, they seem not to have survived. They probably would not have been of much interest anyway, for the Duke of Berry was an unenterprising fellow who several times did get a chance to go to war with his elder brother, but never to play an important part. He seems much better suited to run errands for his sister-in-law and her ladies than to learn the soldier's art.

The two elder grandsons were married to the two daughters of the Duke of Savoy: Marie-Adélaïde and Marie-Louise. Their father's betrayal of the Franco-Spanish crowns caused some consternation in the family circles, and both girls wrote to their father urging him to "return to his duty." The wily duke, however, hardly knew his daughters, both of whom had left his palace at an early age. He had never forgiven Louis XIV for the humiliations that he had suffered in his youth, but more important, he was sure that the Grand Alliance would win, and that he would gain much from his association with its members in the war. Thus, as we might expect, he paid little attention to either his daughters or their children.

On the other hand, the great-grandfather at Versailles was much interested in the arrival of new princes and princesses; many grandsons were needed to assure the succession to the two crowns. When the Duchess of Burgundy was delivered of a child, Louis was at hand to give her his compliments; he wrote letters to all Europe carrying the good news. When the Queen of Spain had a son, he wrote both to her and her husband. "You should judge my joy when I learned of the birth of the Prince, your son," he wrote Philippe, "Now I only want to learn of the health of the Queen, and to have you give me pleasure by assuring me that she is as well as her condition will allow. I thank God, and I have ordered public prayers in all my kingdom. I hope that your Majesty will follow this by a Christian education . . . suitable for a king."[22] The baby was the Prince of Asturias, heir to the throne of Spain.

Like the births of the three children of the Duchess of Burgundy, these Spanish infants cost their mothers dearly, for both of the Savoyard princesses suffered poor health and complications before and after the arrival of their children. This problem was responsible for one of the stories told by Saint-Simon to illustrate the selfishness of the king. The Duchess of Burgundy was pregnant, and the doctors refused to allow her to accompany the king to Marly for fear of a miscarriage. Louis would not go without her for she was the life of any party at Marly, but he was much irritated with the whole affair. The misfortune occurred anyway; the duchess lost her child. The Duke of Rochefoucauld announced in Louis' presence that this might mean that she could not have any other children. According to Saint-Simon, Louis angrily replied, "And what is that to me? Does she not already have a son? And should he die, is not the Duke of Berry of an age to marry and have some? What does it matter to me if I am followed by one or the other? Are they not all my grandchildren?" Then he went on to shock the duke, "Thank God that she did miscarry since it had to be that way; now I will not be prevented from making trips by the protests of doctors, I shall come and go as I wish." Saint-Simon explains that this scene proves that Louis loved only himself.[23] This may be true, but one wonders at the boorishness of the Duke of Rochefoucauld who taunted a seventy-year-old man who was carrying the burdens of a war that could not be won, as well as the illness of a princess who was about the only light left in his life. Perhaps Louis answered him as he should have been answered, if indeed the quotation has any validity at all.

The Duchess of Burgundy did have another son. On February 15, 1710, Louis wrote to Philippe:

My family is increased by the birth of a prince of whom the Duchess of Burgundy was happily delivered this morning. I have given him the name Duke of Anjou that you carried. I hope that he will make himself as worthy as you did of my affection, and that a more fortunate time will come when I can convince your Majesty that my affection for you will never grow less.[24]

The next year found the king rejoicing that the Queen of Spain was pregnant again; he added, "I hope for you and for her that her health will be as good as we all desire it to be." There was always the lurking danger that births would cause the mother's death; in the seventeenth century, this danger was very real.

The month of April 1711 brought the first of the tragic series of deaths that darkened the king's four last years. On April 11, the Duke of Maine wrote to Madame de Maintenon about the smallpox epidemic and his worries for the king's health. Then the dauphin caught the disease and died almost immediately.[25] The king's letter to his grandson Philippe, a son of the dauphin, is one of the classic documents of the period.

I have lost my son and you have lost a father who loved you as tenderly as I loved him. He deserved all my love by his affection for me, by his continued efforts to please me, and I looked upon him as a friend to whom I could open my heart and give all my confidence. However I might find some sort of comfort to bring to you for this affliction that you experience no less vividly than I. It is nonetheless only from God that I can hope for the support necessary to carry this burden. I beg Him to console your Majesty, and if the assurance of my love can aid you, believe that I hold for you the same tenderness, and that the only pleasure that I can enjoy is to discover in you the same feelings that my son gave to me in the course of his life.

Philippe's reply was almost as moving. He wrote:

The sole consolation that I can find in the loss that I have just experienced is to see your Majesty's desire to merge your grief with mine. . . . Like you, I feel the need to have recourse to God in this sad conjuncture since from Him alone can come the strength and constancy necessary in such misfortune. . . . I beg you to take the place of my father. . . . I take pleasure in finding in you the same goodness, the same tenderness, and the same feelings that I have already received . . . and your Majesty will always find in me the same veneration, the same respect, and the same attention, that I have always had and that will never be effaced from my heart. . . .[26]

The king's letter was in a classic simplicity, in French it is almost like organ music, quite unlike his usual circumlocutions and awkward expressions. In his *Mémoires,* Torcy claims the authorship of the letter. We do not know who wrote Philippe's. This was an era when men thought that the emotions they ought to have should be expressed in elegant language. What they actually thought may have been quite different. Philippe had not seen his father in a decade and had little correspondence with him; Louis had seen his son, but not as a tower of strength or a source of satisfaction.

The dauphin's death was a shock to the cabal that surrounded him; their hopes for the future collapsed. Perhaps the tears of his half-sisters, the Princesses of Conti and Condé, were as much for their lost hopes as for the unhappy man who had died. Since smallpox was recognized as a contagious disease, the corpse was quickly sealed in its leaden casket and moved to Saint-Denis for quick burial. The religious ceremonies, the public prayers, and the laudatory sermons took weeks to be accomplished, but the court had little to do with most of this, the king even less.[27]

Madame de Maintenon tells us that her husband was much moved by the dauphin's death, but also that now he was happy to have the Duke of Burgundy as the dauphin, and his lovely wife as the dauphine. But by 1711 the Duchess of Burgundy was in trouble: a tumor probably located on her uterus was causing her distress. It was, however, not this tumor that was soon to remove both her and her husband from the earth, thus creating a personal and a political crisis for the old king.

Perhaps we can best follow the events of this tragedy in the letters that went from Versailles to Madrid early in 1712.[28] In the middle of January, Madame de Maintenon wrote that the Duchess of Burgundy regretted her lost youth and worried about her present illness, but, she went on, "she is right to be happy, she is well married, much loved by the King and the Dauphin [her husband], and truly, she brings pleasure to the Court." On February 7, her letter to Madrid is filled with the terror created by an epidemic of measles: young and old are dying from this disease, and the Duchess of Burgundy has come down with it. The duchess "has taken a fourth dose of opium, chewed and smoked tobacco, and feels better," but with others dying, it was frightening to see her ill. On the fourteenth, Madame de Maintenon could not write; her niece Madame de Caylus sent a letter to the Princess des Ursins telling of the death of the Duchess of Burgundy. The king and his wife were prostrated for "all is death here; life has gone from this place. This Princess loved everyone, charmed everyone. . . . We are all deaf and dumb from our loss and each day we feel it more vividly." The king is in "despair and we fear for his health"; as for her aunt, she "is overwhelmed by grief." At the end of this letter, Madame de Caylus hints at worse things to come, for she announces that the Duke of Burgundy now has the disease, and he also is in danger. He died on February 18; his eldest son, a child of five, died on March 5; and his other remaining son missed death only by a narrow margin—for several months his death was expected, for he could not seem to recover from his illness. On March 27, before the death of the first child, Madame de Maintenon wrote, "It is true, Madame, that I am sad; no one ever had more reason than I to be so: there is no more joy, no more activity. The King does all that he can to console himself but always sinks back to his grief . . . however his health holds up, and he does not fail to do his work. . . ."

Louis had done everything to save his grandchildren. He had even ordered the opening of the coffin of Sainte Geneviève to seek aid from heaven. When the Duchess of Burgundy died in spite of this intercession on high, Louis closed all theaters and spectacles, even the fair, for public mourning; he ordered a hundred masses a day at Saint-Denis for fifteen days for the repose of her soul. When the Duke of Burgundy came down with the disease, he ordered midnight masses so that the public would not be alarmed; after the young duke's death, he ordered masses and public prayers throughout the kingdom. His church seems to have consoled the old man when all else failed. The letters to his governors, mayors, bishops, and archbishops asking for prayers testify to his grief and anxiety.[29] A sample can be taken from the letter to his friend Bishop Noailles, "In the last six days," he writes, "I have lost my grandson and granddaughter; a blow so staggering and so unexpected has caused me the greatest possible affliction. . . ." He went on to ask for masses and public prayers. There can be no doubt about the reality of his grief; Villars tells us that the king passed through the court dry-eyed, but when he was alone with the marshal, "he did not feel the same constraint. . . . His heart opened in face of all this domestic misfortune and he said: 'There are few examples of what has happened to me. . . . I lost almost within a week a granddaughter and a grandson, and then their son—all of them with great expectations, and all tenderly loved. God punishes me; I have merited it, and I will suffer less in the next world. . . .' "[30] This is a remarkable revelation of the king's beliefs about his plight, as well as his faith in God's part in it. The Duke d' Antin, who also lost his eldest son in this epidemic, underlines this same point when he tells us that the king dearly loved the Duke and Duchess of Burgundy, and that "his Majesty had need of all his courage and all his religion to sustain the terrible loss. . . ."[31] He was undoubtedly correct; Louis was finally left with no other consolation than his faith in God, and Madame de Maintenon would not have suggested any other recourse.

Neither the king nor his wife could believe that they would ever be comforted; the Duchess of Burgundy had been a bright spot in the winter of their lives. There was, however, some hope that the Duchess of Berry, who was also Louis' granddaughter, might bring some joy into the family circle by becoming the mother of a new Bourbon prince. In July 1711 her first pregnancy had resulted in the birth of a daughter who lived only a few hours. In the fall of 1712 she was pregnant again, and early in 1713 she gave birth to a male child, the Duke of Alençon. Louis was both great-grandfather and great-great-grandfather to this prince; he sent letters announcing the birth to everyone of importance in the kingdom and in Europe, while *Te Deums* sent his thanks to God from every cathedral in France. A few weeks later the child was dead. It seemed that the pall that hung over these last years would not rise.[32]

The next spring the Queen of Spain died. She had never actually met her husband's grandfather, but the fact that she was the sister of the Duchess of Burgundy added to the lively correspondence that had passed between Versailles and Madrid for more than a decade, almost made her a personality in the French court. Louis' letter, however, reflects the lack of intimacy:

I received the news of the death of the Queen of Spain, my granddaughter. You will understand how touched I am . . . the personal worth of this Princess and the affliction that her death will cause my grandson the King, both bring me to regret her loss and to pray God that He will provide the King, my grandson with the consolation that he needs.[33]

Louis could not have guessed that a new queen, the Italian princess Elizabeth Farnese, would appear in Madrid before the year was over. Nor could he have ever guessed that she would immediately banish the Princess des Ursins and establish an empire over Philippe V more complete than his lovely first wife had ever achieved.

A month after the death of the Queen of Spain, the Duke of Berry was injured in a hunting accident, and died without leaving an heir. Would God never forgive Louis' past transgressions? Only a few years before, his throne was buttressed by a son, three grandsons, and four great-great grandsons. Now the dauphin was a little boy of five and Louis' only other direct descendants were Philippe V of Spain and his two sons, who had been declared ineligible to succeed to the French throne by solemn international agreements. The Duke of Orléans, Philippe's dissolute son, would mount the throne in case the dauphin should die, but under conditions that might lead to civil or international war. A recent biographer of Louis XIV insists that these last years were happy ones for the old king because the war was over; he somehow failed to understand that personal tragedy with almost Shakespearean grandeur stalked the waking hours of an old man who was sure that all that happened to him was the judgment of God.[34]

Nor was the haunting fear for his own fate all that troubled these unhappy years. Louis had always worried about the future of his legitimized children. It had been easy enough to take care of the girls: by marrying them to the Princes of Orléans, Condé, and Conti, their offspring became princes of the blood in line for succession to the throne. But the two boys, their father's favorites, could not so easily be cared for. He could be sure that they had money, but he also wanted to have their children share honors and positions worthy of descendants of Louis XIV. This was not easy to accomplish, for both the princes of the blood and the dukes and peers of the realm regarded these legitimized princes as somehow tarnished by their irregular births.

Louis finally found a plan that suited his wishes, but that raised cries of anger from most of the "people of quality" in his kingdom. In July 1714 he called a delegation from Parlement to meet him at Marly, and explained "that after serious reflection he had resolved to change the status of the Duke of Maine and the Count of Toulouse, giving them the right to succession after the legitimate princes of the blood." This also gave them a new and important status in Parlement when that body met in formal session. He justified this action on the grounds that "in case God in His anger wished to take from France all those who remained of the legitimate princes of the august house of Bourbon," then the issue of these two princes would be available as heirs to the crown. Louis obviously was not sure that God's anger had been appeased; his critics, remarking that these two princes were the issue of the king's sins, could not believe that God would like the situation any more than they did. But Louis was the king, and he insisted upon the registration of his decrees: the first in July 1714, with another buttressing it in May 1715. Most of the dukes and peers were shocked; the Duke of Maine, however, graciously replied to Monsieur Lipp's speech at the time of the registration, assuring the Parlement of his loyalty and affection. He probably guessed that the edict might some day be annulled, as of course it was. The most eloquent pages of Saint-Simon's *Mémoires* describe the scene in Parlement after Louis' death when the regent secured the act depriving these two princes of their father's gift.[35]

As much as the status of his sons, the problem of the coming regency bothered the old king. The little dauphin was a charming, sober child, a "precious Dauphin," wrote Madame de Maintenon, but he was only a child, and so for the third time in a century a Bourbon king would have to start his reign as a minor. There would be a regency, and regency governments had always encountered serious problems. When the Duke of Berry died, the Duke of Orléans was the obvious candidate for the office of regent, and he surely would be so recognized by Parlement. This fact caused concern: in the first place, according to the Treaty of Utrecht, he also was the next in line to the throne, and history and myth had many stories of treachery and foul play when an uncle was both guardian and heir to a small child who was king. Even if this problem did not exist, the Duke of Orléans' dissolute character was enough to create doubts. He had been a valiant soldier, but he also was a libertine who feared neither God nor the devil nor the moral law; an unbeliever, a man of violent actions. Should such a man have charge of the education of a child? He might make a good regent, for he was a clever politician and a strong man, but the king wanted to be sure that his great-grandson's reign would be secure.

All his life Louis XIV had tried to control the future by making careful plans. At the end of his days, he had not lost the belief that a prince can evade difficulties by facing them before they arrive. Unhappily, as we have seen, he was not always wise enough to form the right plan, and often the future turned out to be somewhat different from the model that he and his advisers created. This time he sought to fix the future government of the kingdom by a testament, even though he knew that his father's will had been put aside and that no dead King of France could control the actions of a living one. Nonetheless he could try to provide for the personal safety of his successor and the wise direction of his government.

The testament begins with a long preamble in which Louis gave all credit to God for the blessings that had come to the kingdom, and expressed regret that war had prevented him from giving the consideration to his people that he had wanted to give. Then he announced that a regency would guarantee peace and prosperity for the future, and named the Duke of Orléans as regent with the provision that he respect the decisions of a regency council composed of the regent, the Prince of Condé (as soon as he reached twenty), the Duke of Maine, and the Count of Toulouse, the chancellor, Marshals Villeroi, Tallard, Villars, and Harcourt, the four secretaries of state, and the comptroller general of the finances. This council must assemble four to five days every week, with seven members constituting a quorum; it should consider questions of peace, war, appointments, and domestic affairs. A majority vote would make decisions mandatory for the regent. If the testament were not challenged, this council presumably could effectively control the regent.

The council was also to be responsible for the welfare of the young king, but the Duke of Maine was specifically entrusted with his education, and Marshal Villeroi was named as his governor. If the Duke of Maine should die, the Count of Toulouse would take his place; if Marshal Villeroi should die, Marshal d'Harcourt would become the governor. The officers of the king's guard were required to give their oaths into the hand of the Duke of Maine who was thus responsible for physical security as well as the intellectual development of the little king. By this testament, Louis hoped to erect walls of safety around both his kingdom and his great-grandson; there could be no changes in the will unless they were written in the king's own hand.

It is not important to follow all the legal arrangements by which Louis attempted to force his testament upon his successors. The document was deposited in Parlement with an "edict for the disposition of the Testament" early in August 1714. This edict explains how God, for His own reasons, had taken, in turn, the dauphin, the Duke and Duchess of Burgundy, and their eldest son, leaving a child as heir to the throne. Thus a regency government was inevitable, and the testament would regulate the constitution of this government. The rest of the edict was a sort of legalistic incantation designed to prevent anyone from putting the testament aside. At the end of the document the king urged the regency to hold fast to the church, for "during our entire reign, our principal application was always to preserve the purity of the Catholic religion in our kingdom, and to ward off all kinds of innovations. . . . We made every effort to unite with the church those who were separated from it . . . we exhort the Dauphin to continue. . . ." The other policy that he specifically urged upon his successors was the edict against dueling, "that we have issued as most useful for attracting the blessings of God to our posterity and the kingdom, and for the conservation of our nobility." And finally: "Our intentions that the disposition in the edict of last July in favor of the Duke of Maine and the Count of Toulouse shall always be respected."

Apparently the more he thought about the young king's safety, the more worried he became. At last he decided that Villeroi was a sterner character than his good-natured son, and added a codicile (April 13, 1715) in which he ordered that immediately upon his death, the guards must be placed at the disposition of Marshal Villeroi who should take the king to Vincennes where "the air is good," and he might have added, the walls strong. On the way, the king should stop to visit Parlement, and witness the opening of the will and testament of Louis XIV. Perhaps at the suggestion of Madame de Maintenon, who understood children a little better than Louis, this codicile also ordered that Madame de Ventadour should accompany the king as a "governess to whom he is accustomed." The last and final codicil (August 23, 1715) came only a few days before Louis died; it named the Bishop of Fréjus, Sieur de Fleury, as preceptor, and Father le Tellier as confessor of the minor king.[36]

During these dark days Louis wrote the famous letter of Louis XIV to Louis XV giving the child advice that might help him govern the kingdom.

The letter does not have the calm assured tone that characterized the *Mémoires,* written a half-century before for the instruction of his own son. This letter is troubled by the uncertain and insecure feeling that life is transient, that death is the common companion of all men. Louis urged his heir to cling to the Duke of Maine and his family for security in France, and to keep in close alliance with Philippe V and Spain as "the sole means of conserving the balance of power in Europe." But it is clear that he was as much concerned for the personal life of this child as for the security of the kingdom. He urged his great-grandson to hold firm to the Roman Catholic Church and its teachings, and to "live as a Christian even more than as a king. *Never draw down upon yourself the wrath of God, who visibly protects the kingdom, by any disorder in your morals* [author's italics]." A king's first duty is to give a good example to his subjects, as a father should give to his family. Finally "Love peace . . . remember my son that your most striking victory always costs most dearly when it must be paid for by the blood of your subjects." Madame de Maintenon must have felt great satisfaction to hear so many of her ideas presented as advice for the next King of France.

The old man was right to expect death to be following him, but in the first six months of 1715 things were so little changed in the manner of his life that when death came, it was really unexpected. He went in his carriage to follow the hunt, he listened to music, attended the theater, promenaded in the gardens, held council meetings. It was as it had always been. Then in the second week of August he found himself in physical pain that soon localized in his leg. A dark spot appeared and quickly spread. The Duke d'Antin tells us that Fagon was the last to realize that the king was going to die. This, of course was nonsense; Fagon knew about death, he also knew that he must encourage the king and his wife. As the gangrene spread to cover the entire leg, Louis, as well as the court, knew that the reign was almost over. The king accepted his fate with great patience; he was resolved to die as a hero and a Christian.

There are many stories about the last days of the king. Louis' generation was one schooled to die dramatically, and the man who had played out the role of king so well for more than seventy years could be counted upon to finish the story with the proper flourishes. Several of the deathbed scenes can be retold without burdening this history. He received his courtiers with a little speech that may actually have run something like this account that Dangeau has left us:

Messieurs. I am satisfied with your services, you have faithfully served me with a desire to please. I am distressed not to have better repaid you. I leave you with regret. Serve the Dauphin with the same affection that you have served me; he is a child of five years who can suffer many vexations, for I recall to have suffered many during my childhood. I am leaving you, but the State will always remain. Be faithfully attached to it and let your example serve all my other subjects. Be united and in accord; this is the unity and strength of a State . . . follow the orders that my nephew gives you; I hope that he will always do good. I hope also that you will do your duty and that you will sometimes recall me to mind.

The most famous of all the scenes came when the old king of seventy-seven said goodbye to his five-year-old successor:

Soon you will be King of a great kingdom. I urge you not to forget your duty to God; remember that you owe everything to Him. Try to remain at peace with your neighbors. I loved war too much. Do not follow me in that or in overspending. Take advice in everything; try to find the best course and follow it. Lighten your people's burden as soon as possible, and do what I have had the misfortune not to do myself.

This speech, like the others, is well within the frame expected of a dying man who was a ruler. It is the sort of pious advice that old men have given to children for many, many generations; it strips reality of all its complexity, making it seem that a man could somehow control his destiny and actions for the good of mankind. Louis may no longer have remembered how the things that overtook his reign actually happened. It seemed so easy for an old man simply to say "do good, wish well, act righteously." In any case this was what was expected of him, and Louis would not die without doing his duty.

His farewells to his nephew, the Duke of Orléans, and to his personal servants were of the same order. He did what was expected of him. An old actor like the king could not have heard the countless stories of death scenes without properly acting out his own. Louis was probably grateful that his final illness came with measured tread leaving him time to fill in the lines and finally accept the inevitable. It may be that in these last hours, his moments alone with Madame de Maintenon produced the tears and regrets that might be expected. They also were probably marked by the exchange of personal feelings between these two who had shared more than forty years together. But just as she helped him burn his private papers and as she expurgated personal notes from her own correspondence, Madame de Maintenon has not left us the account of her last private hours with her husband. Perhaps it is just as well that the world knows that this man, who better than any other always managed to act out the title role of king, should be allowed to die as a "hero and a Christian," without revealing his simpler feelings and emotions.

We are told that his last words were the Roman Catholic formula, "now and at the hour of my death, help me, oh God." He sank into a coma the afternoon of August 31 and died without recovering consciousness on the morning of September first, just five days before his seventy-seventh birthday.[37]

The funeral of the king, with masses, chants, processions, and all the other trappings that we have seen at royal funeral services, gave a dramatic conclusion to his reign. The last act was played out at Saint-Denis with a solemn high funeral mass, and with the chanting of the *De Profundis* as his casket was lowered into the Bourbon crypt, where it remained until the Revolutionary mob desecrated all the royal tombs three-quarters of a century later.

NOTES

BIBLIOGRAPHICAL NOTE

THE *mémoires* of the period are well known; I cite them by author only: Mme. de Mottevillc, Mlle. de Montpensier, Dangeau, Spanheim, de Sourches, etc.

My bibliographical article, "The Reign of Louis XIV, a selected bibliography of writing since the War of 1914–1918," *J.M.H.*, XXXVI, pp. 128–144, and the excellent bibliographical sections in *Clio, le XVIIᵉ Siècle* make it seem unnecessary for me to append any considerable bibliographical material to this study. I have usually cited other authors only when taking a direct quotation because I did not want to burden the book with a too elaborate scholarly format. Exception has been made in the case of recent studies by U.S. scholars because it is only in the last two decades that much serious work in this field has been undertaken by students in the United States. I am, however, like all students, deeply indebted to the labors of my many predecessors in the field.

ABBREVIATIONS IN FOOTNOTES

A.A.E.   Archives des Affaires Étrangères

A.M.G.   Archives du Ministère de la Guerre

A.N.   Archives Nationales

B.Maz.   Bibliothèque Mazarine

B.N.   Bibliothèque Nationale

Baudrillart   A. Baudrillart, *Philippe V et la cour de la France, 1700–1715*, Paris, 1886.

Legrelle   A. Legrelle, *La diplomatie française et la Succession d'Espagne*, 6 vols., Paris, 1895–99.

Lettres (Geffroy)   *Madame de Maintenon d'après sa correspondance authentique* (A. Geffroy, ed.), 2 vols., Paris, 1884.

Lettres (Langlois)   *Madame de Maintenon, Correspondance* (M. Langlois, ed.), 5 vols., Paris, 1933–39.

Mémoires   *Mémoires de Louis XIV* (Charles Dryss, ed.), 2 vols., Paris, 1860.

Mignet   *Négociations relatives à la Succession d'Espagne sous Louis XIV* (Mignet, ed.), 4 vols., Paris, 1835–42.

Œuvres   Louis XIV, Œuvres (Grimoard and Grouvelle, eds.), 6 vols., Paris, 1806.

Rousset   C. Rousset, *Histoire de Louvois*, 4 vols., Paris, 1862–64.

Saint-Simon (Boislisle)   *Saint-Simon, Mémoires* (Boislisle, ed.), 43 vols., Paris, 1879–1930.

I

1. LOUIS LE DIEUDONNÉ

1. *Lettre du roi, escrite à Monseigneur l'Archevêque de Paris* (1638).
2. Anon., *Le Bonheur de France* (1639), p. 6. In the B.N. there is a large collection of pamphlets dealing with the satisfaction of the kingdom over the birth of Louis XIV. Sermons, poems, speeches, and essays of all sorts congratulated France on the birth of Louis le Dieudonné.
3. D. Motteville, *"Anne d'Autriche." Divers portraits à Mademoiselle de Montpensier* (1659), p. 247.
4. *Mlle. Andriéa à Mme. de Sencé, 9 avril 1639,* A.A.E., France, 833, fol. 95–96.
5. Charles Dreyss, *Mémoires de Louis XIV pour l'instruction du Dauphin* [henceforth cited as *Mémoires*], vol. II (Paris, 1860), p. 18. See also P. Erlanger, *Monsieur, Frère de Louis XIV* (Paris, 1953).
6. The tradition, still honored by many historians, that Louis XIII was ruled by his cardinal minister, had a wide acceptance in the latter seventeenth century. The very idea that his father had not acted out his role as king was distasteful to Louis XIV, and led him to dislike the memory of Cardinal Richelieu.
7. B.N., ms. franç. 16630, fol. 175.
8. Cf. Pierre Blet, "Richelieu et les débuts de Mazarin," *Rev. H. Mod.* (October 1959); G. Dethan, "Mazarin avant le ministère," *Rev. His.* (1962), pp. 33–36.
9. *Declaration du Roy sur la Régence de la Règne Verifiée en Parlement le 21 avril 1643.* In the introduction of this curious document, now in the B.N., Louis XIII identifies God with the work that he and Richelieu had accomplished in the preceding two decades.
10. There is a stone marker at the site of the battle of Rocroi, but it is almost impossible to reconstruct the battle because of the forest that now occupies most of the field.

2. THE FORMATION OF THE REGENCY GOVERNMENT

1. Ralph E. Giesey, *The Royal Funeral Ceremony in Renaissance France* (vol. 37 of *Travaux d'Humanisme et Renaissance,* Librairie E. Droz, Genève, 1960).
2. *Arrest donné par le Roy Séant en son Lict de justice en sa cour de Parlement de Paris, 18 mai, 1663,* Paris chez F. Leonard.
3. Cf. Georges Dethan, *Gaston d'Orléans, Conspirateur et Prince Charmant* (Paris, 1959).
4. In 1645 Chancellor Séguier said to the parlementarians ". . . that there [was] no minority in kings with respect to power and authority, no deficiency nor disqualification, that the queen was obliged to conserve her authority and that she would rear her son in the memory and resentment of the injury [parlementary rejection of fiscal expedients] inflicted on his authority" (Talon [Michaud ed.], p. 142). Anne said the same thing—that she would maintain her son's authority and transfer it to him unimpaired on the assumption of his majority (Ormesson, *Journal,* I, p. 273; cf. E. H. Kossmann, *La Fronde* [London, 1954], p. 43).
5. At this time Mazarin had no family in France and was totally dependent upon the crown for wealth and advancement; later his sisters and their children came to France to share his fortune.
6. Mazarin, *Lettres du cardinal Mazarin pendant son Ministère,* Chéruel ed., vol. I (Paris, 1872), p. 321.
7. Henry de Campion, *Mémoires* (1807 ed.), pp. 235*ff.*

8. Herbillon, *Anne d'Autriche* (Paris, 1939), pp. 210–11; the B.Maz. has a fine collection of these songs in manuscript copy (ms. 2194*ff.*).

9. Soviet historians are making much of these rural revolts. They have at their disposal the papers of Chancellor Séguier, acquired by Catherine II, that have proved to be a goldmine of information about rural discontent. The Marxists' conclusions, however, often seem a little forced. For the most recent analyses of the literature on this problem see Leon Bernard, "French society and popular uprisings under Louis XIV," in *French Historical Studies*, vol. III, no. 4, pp. 454–74.

3. THE BOY-KING

1. P. H. Chérot, S.J., *La première jeunesse de Louis XIV, 1643–1653* (Paris, 1892). This is a very valuable book because it prints in full letters by Louis' confessor to Rome and elsewhere.

2. B.Maz., ms. 2117.

3. Louis' translation of the *Gallic Wars* is to be found in the manuscript division of the B.N. It is surely as good a translation as is usually made by secondary school sophomores. But we do not know how much help he had in polishing it, so we cannot judge his work. If this is all the Latin he knew, he probably would have had trouble with Cicero or Virgil.

4. P. H. Chérot, *op. cit.*, p. 49; B. Capefigue, *La vie de St. Vincent de Paul* (Paris, 1827), pp. 272, *passim;* G. Vauthier, *Anne d'Autriche et l'église du Val-de-Grâce* (Paris, 1916).

5. *Gazette*, 1647.

6. *Harangue de M. Talon . . . 15 janvier 1648*, B.Maz, ms. 2117.

7. Madame de Motteville's observation was undoubtedly correct. A year or two later when the court moved through Normandy, Louis' confessor wrote:

> "All went well here . . . it is a gift of grace to see the King . . . in France that is the most important and the most sought-after grace . . . such is the majesty of our Prince, in spite of his dozen years, such is his bounty and the ease of his humor, joined to the gracefulness of his body and the sweetness of his appearance that I know no philter more powerful for the enchantment of men's hearts. All Normandy could not see enough of him. (P. H. Chérot, *op cit.*, pp. 57–58).

4. THE "FRONDE" I: PARLEMENTARY, 1648–49

1. B. F. Porshnev, *Die Volkaufstände in Frankreich vor der Fronde* (translated from the Russian by M. Brandt, Leipzig, 1954); cf. also Mousnier, "Recherches sur les soulèvements populaires en France avant la Fronde," in *Rev. d'H. Mod.*, vol. V (1958), pp. 81–113.

2. B.Maz., ms. 2117, pp. 262–86.

3. L.S.D.T., *Manifest du Roy* (Paris, 1648).

4. The victory at Lens was also highly useful to French diplomacy at Westphalia; it was one of the most important events forcing the emperor to accept the treaty.

5. B.Maz., ms. 2117, p. 306.

6. M. Chéruel published this section from Mazarin's *Carnets* in *Rev. Hist.*, vol. IV, 1880, pp. 103*ff.* We are deeply indebted to him for transcribing Mazarin's almost completely illegible handwriting. The passage quoted here was written in August 1648.

7. There are several good contemporary accounts of Anne's and Mazarin's position on the concessions of October 1648. Anne refused to have the royal declaration mentioned; she considered it ruinous to royal authority. Mazarin thought similarly, and immediately prepared to violate its terms. See Motteville (Michaud, ed.), p. 218; Mazarin's *Carnets*, vol. X, quoted in Chéruel, *Minorité de Louis XIV*, vol. III, pp. 91–92, and in Perkins, *France Under Mazarin*, vol. I (Boston and New York,

1886), pp. 445–46; Letter from Mazarin to Le Tellier, October 23, 1648, Chéruel, *op. cit.,* vol. I.

8. The University of Minnesota Library and the Newberry Library (Chicago) both have fine collections of these pamphlets of 1848–52. C. Moreau has provided us with a checklist of these pamphlets, and a volume reproducing characteristic ones: *Choix de Mazarinades* (Paris, 1853).

9. Cf. Kossmann, *op cit.,* and A. L. Moote, "The Parliamentary *Frondes* and Seventeenth-Century Robe Solidarity" in *French Historical Studies,* vol. II, no. 3, pp. 330–55.

5. THE "FRONDE" II: THE PRINCES

1. Cf. below, ch. 8, pp. 85*ff.*
2. B.N., ms. franç. 14120, Sainctôt.
3. Chérot, *op. cit.,* pp. 94*ff.* Cf. de Motteville, Année 1651. She gives a complete account of the events of September 7 and 8 including her version of the more important speeches.
4. There is an interesting anonymous manuscript account of the second *Fronde* in the library of the University of Michigan, DC 124-M.53.
5. Dethan, *op. cit.,* has a good analysis of the problem of Gaston's role in the *Fronde.*
6. *Louis XIV to the Duke of Orléans, August 29, 1652,* B.N. Bal., 349, fols. 21–23.
7. B.Maz., ms. 2158, 137.
8. B.Maz., ms. 2195 (10).
9. B.N. Bal., 349, fols. 36–37.
10. L. André, *Michel Le Tellier et l'organisation de l'armée monarchique* (Paris, 1906) and *Michel Le Tellier et Louvois* (Paris, 1942).

6. THE EDUCATION OF THE KING: I

1. M. Druon, *Histoire de l'Education des princes dans la Maison des Bourbons* (Paris, 1897), "Louis XIV." John B. Wolf, "The Formation of a King," *French Historical Studies,* vol. I, no. I.
2. Péréfixe, *Henry IV* (Paris, 1659). Cf. also Péréfixe's *Institutio principis* (1647).
3. B.N., ms. franç. 4926 (3858).
4. The B.N. has a remarkable collection of these sermons; taken together they make an impressive picture of clerical attempts to influence the mind of the king.
5. Father Paulin, candidly comparing Anne with Blanche of Castile, mother of Saint Louis, wrote, "What is enough to bring up a good man and a great king, is not enough to make a saint."
6. De Motteville, "Anne d'Autriche," *Divers Portraits,* 1659.
7. One of them, Vivonne, was the brother of Madame de Montespan, whose later career as Louis' mistress may have earned her brother his marshal's baton. In his *Carnets* Mazarin tells of removing another young man from the king's entourage because of his "perpetual flatteries [which] might make the King feel displeasure against those who tell him the truth." Cited by G. Lacour-Gayet, *L'Education politique de Louis XIV,* p. 124.
8. B.Maz., ms. de Mazarin, III, fol. 305.
9. Godeau, *Catéchisme royal* (Paris, 1650, 4° Lb37–1711).
10. Cf. *Gazette* and numerous pamphlets in the B.N. telling of the event.
11. *Ibid.*
12. Most of the tapestries are still in the museum at Reims.
13. There are many accounts of the consecration. Cf. B.N., L b 37, 3211–20. The titles of a few of them: *Le véritable journal de ce qui s'est passé au sacre du roi Louis XIV dans la ville de Reims depuis le 3 juin à 9 . . ."* (Paris, 1655); *Sacre et couronnement du roy Louis XIV* (Paris, 1654); *La Pompeuse et magnifique*

Cérémonie du sacre du Roy Louis XIV (Paris, 1655); *Les cérémonies faites et observées au sacre et couronnement du Roy Louis XIV en la Ville de Reims le Dimache 7 juin 1654* (B.N., Rés., 8° Lb37 3215A, Z 2284 T.163·).

7. THE EDUCATION OF THE KING: II

1. Mazarin's printed letters cited above. The collections of manuscript copies in the B.N., the B.Maz., and the A.A.E. are still a mine of information not completely worked out. But to use them fully, the scholar should be able to transcribe the *Carnets* (B.N.), which is a formidable task for anyone, no matter how great are his linguistic and paleographic skills.

2. Péréfixe, in the dedication to his *Henry IV*. This, like the other quotations of advice to his son, is taken from Louis' *Mémoires*.

3. The reader will not miss the idea that God is proud of his place in the hierarchy just as the king must be of his.

4. In the Dutch War Louis' moral right to the territory he demanded was shaky, but the Dutch Republicans did not have the same moral right to sovereignty that other princes possessed. Louis' ancestors had been their rulers by grace of God, whereas the Dutch governed themselves by virtue of a rebellion against royal authority.

5. Dreyss, *op. cit.* Dreyss had published most of these "notes" that seem to be the basis for the framework of the *Mémoires*. To understand the problems that they raise, one has to call for the big carton of papers themselves in the *Salle des Manuscrits*. By skillful detective work, Paul Soninno ("The Dating and Authorship of Louis XIV's Memoirs," *French Historical Studies*, vol. III, no. 3, pp. 303–37.) was able to revise some of Dreyss's conclusions.

6. *Divers Portraits*, 1659.

8. THE YOUNG KING: FAMILY AND COURT

1. "Fragments des Mémoires inédites de DuBois, Gentilhomme Servant du Roi," *Bib. d'école de Chartres*, vol. II, series 4, pp. 22–23.

2. Victor Cousin has transcribed and printed a series of these letters: *Madame de Hautefort et Madame de Chevreuse* (Paris, 1856), pp. 469–83.

3. For the codes used in the royal correspondence, cf. B.N., Bal., fol. 329.

4. Victor Molinier, *Notice sur cette question historique: Anne d'Autriche et Mazarin étaient-ils secrètement mariés?* (Paris, 1887). Molinier analyzed the evidence and reached the conclusion that they were married; but he was unable to find any registration of such a marriage, nor any dispensation from Rome, nor statements by direct witnesses. Yet circumstantial evidence points to marriage. My own studies support this thesis.

5. Cf. *Lettres du Cardinal Mazarin, La Paix des Pyrénées* (Paris, 1845), as well as Chéruel's collection, *Lettres du Cardinal Mazarin pendant son ministère*, 6 vols. (Paris, 1872–90).

6. Cf. C. Rousset, *Histoire de Louvois*, vol. I (Paris, 1862), p. 11.

7. Cf. B.N. Bal., 329 and 349, fols. 36, 37.

8. We should note the different attitude toward gambling in the sixteenth and seventeenth centuries from that in our own society: "People had no objection to allowing children to play cards and games of chance, and to play for money. One of Stella's engravings devoted to the subject of *putti* [frescoes depicting naked children] at play gives a sympathetic picture of the child who has lost all his money. The Caravagesque painters of the seventeenth century often depicted bands of soldiers gambling excitedly in taverns of ill fame; next to the old troopers one can see some very young boys, twelve years old or so, who seem to be enthusiastic gamblers. A painting by Sébastien Bourdon shows a group of beggars standing round two children and watching them playing dice. The theme of children playing games of chance for

money obviously did not shock public opinion as yet . . ." (Philippe Ariès *Centuries of Childhood* [New York, 1962], p. 71). Ariès missed one of the most charming pictures depicting children gambling—Murillo's beggar boys in the Munich Gallery.

9. The B.N. has a fine collection of prints depicting hunting parties.

10. A.A.E., France, 871, fol. 33, May 14, 1650.

9. THE MANCINI CRISIS

1. Chéruel, *Lettres du Cardinal Mazarin*, vol. VIII, pp. 455–520.

2. This material on the king's health is taken from the *Journal de la Santé du Roi Louis XIV*, J.-A. Roi, ed. (Paris, 1861).

3. Marie Mancini, *Apologie, ou les véritables mémoires de Marie Mancini, connétable de Colonna écrits par elle-meme* (1678), B.N., Lm 27–4627. The authenticity of this most interesting little volume has been questioned; however, if it was not written by Marie Mancini herself, it was obviously written by someone who knew her and her career very, very well.

4. *Le Grand dictionnaire des précieuses*, vol. I (1660), Livet, ed., B.N., Rés. 2034.

5. Mancini, *op. cit.*, pp. 23–24.

6. *Ibid.*, p. 27.

7. Mazarin's letters in manuscript are to be found in many places. The collection in the B.N. is the most complete; there are slight differences in the texts of several of the letters found in different depositories, such as is in the B.N., Fonds Dupuy; in the bound volumes of Mazarin's correspondence in the B.Maz.; and in the Archives of the French Foreign Ministry. The first publication of them was in a volume entitled *Lettres du Cardinal Mazarin, La Paix des Pyrénées*, (1845) whose editors did not understand many of the code words in the letters. Chéruel's *Lettres du Cardinal Mazarin*, vol. IX, contains most of the important ones for the Mancini crisis. Chantelauze, *Louis XIV et Marie Mancini* (1880), publishes several not in Chéruel. There are also several others in Perey, *Le roman du Grand Roi,* and Robiquet, *Le coeur d'une reine.*

10. THE LAST ACT UNDER MAZARIN

1. *Recueil des Portraits et Éloges en vers et prose dédié à S.A.R. Mademoiselle,* 2 vols. (Paris, 1659). Another edition called *Divers Portraits,* 1 vol., p. 22.

2. *Ibid.*, pp. 265–68.

3. *Lettres du Cardinal Mazarin* (edition of 1845), pp. 195–96.

4. *Traité de paix entre les couronnes de France et d'Espagne avec le contract du marriage* (Paris, s. d.), A.A.E., France, 4240.

5. This document can be seen at the N.A., K 118 B no. 97.

6. The volume containing copies of these documents, preserved in the Archives of the French Foreign Ministry, is an instructive lesson in the problems that need to be regulated at the end of a great war.

7. Mignet, *Négociations relatives à la Succession d'Espagne*, vol. I (Paris, 1835), pp. 33–34.

8. *Louis to the Duke of Orléans December 9, 1659,* B.N. Bal., 349, fol. 53.

9. Mignet, vol. I (Lionne, August, 1656), p. 35.

10. *Nouveau Journal historique contenant la rédaction véritable de ce qui s'est passé au voyage du Roy et de Son Eminence et aux cérémonies du mariage de sa Majesté* (Paris, 1660), 8°L 37 b 3392; *Nouvelle Relation contenant l'entrevue et serment des roys pour l'entière exécution de la paix . . . et les cérémonies du mariage* (Paris, 1660), 8° L b 37 3395. The series 8° L b 37 3391ff contains a half-dozen or so of these accounts. The *Gazette* also carried the story in detail.

11. B.N., ms. franç. 4240; *Cab. d. Et.* Oa, 22.; *Ordre général et particulier de la*

marche . . *pour entrée de leurs majestez dans leur bonne ville de Paris* (Paris *s. d.*); *La Marche royale de leurs majestez à l'entrée triōmphante de la Reine* . . . (Paris, 1660); *Explication des diverses générales et particuliers des tableaux, figures* . . . , etc. (Paris, 1660); *Description de feu d'artifice* . . . (Paris, 1660). In the B.N. 8° L b 37, 3380*ff.* there are a dozen or more of these pamphlets explaining the symbolism of the papier-mâché figures, the banners, the fireworks, etc. Paris had a festive air from August 26–29, 1660.

12. *Lettres pattentes portant don fait par le Roy à Monseigneur le Cardinal Mazarini, à Toulouse, décembre 1659,* A.A.E., France, 908. This is a remarkable document which endows Mazarin with a truly princely gift of lands and titles.

13. B.N., Clair., 499. no. 393*ff.*; N. A., O-23, no. 327*ff.*

14. These letters are scattered in several places; some are published in *Lettres de Louis XIV aux Princes de l'Europe* (Paris, 1755); others are in the B.N., Nov. Acq. Franç., 2038; others at the A.A.E., France, 414.

II

11. THE NEW GOVERNMENT:
THERE SHALL BE NO MINISTER-FAVORITE

* Of the memoirs, those of Madame de Motteville, de Brienne, de Choisy, and the *Journal* of d'Ormesson are the most useful. P. Clément, *Lettres . . . de Colbert,* and his *Histoire de Colbert,* vol. 1, and *Les Mémoiraux du conseil de 1661* (Boislisle, ed. Soc. d'hist. d. France) are all valuable. Of the studies, Jules Lair, *Nicolas Fouquet,* 2 vols. (Paris, 1880), P. Viollet, *Le roi et ses ministres* (Paris, 1912), and finally, Georges Mongrēdien, *L'affaire Fouquet* (Paris, 1956) should be consulted. There is place for a study on Fouquet in English. The scholar who does the work should visit Vaux-le-Vicomte so that he will not uncritically repeat the story of Louis' jealousy. The gardens at Vaux are worth a visit anyway, for the present owner has done everything possible to restore them to the condition of 1661.

1. Orest Ranum, *Richelieu and the Councillors of Louis XIII* (New York, 1963). This is an informative analysis of the actual functioning of French government under Richelieu.

2. *Mémoires,* vol. II, p. 524.

3. L. André, *Michel Le Tellier et Louvois,* (Paris, 1942), p. 293.

4. There can be no other explanation of the packet of letters concerning Fouquet during the long years of his imprisonment: Louis had to fear the man or he would never have gone to such lengths both of persecution and of attempts to discover his "secrets." This fear, rather than envy, was the cause of Fouquet's disgrace. A.N., K-120, *passim.*

5. The story of the king's jealousy is probably quite untrue. While Vaux-le-Vicomte is a beautiful château, it did not compare with Chambord, Fontainebleau, the Luxembourg, the Tuilleries, the Palais-Royal, or Saint-Germain—all royal châteaus in 1661. The gardens at Vaux were something new, but such gardens were not impossible for the king either from the point of view of money or artistic talent; it was simply that Le Nôtre's gardens were "new" in the France of 1661. They were to become the "mode" in the next three decades.

6. Cf. *Mémoires,* vol. II, p. 524.

7. Thus Lavisse and other historians who dislike Louis and chide him with the fact that he "conspired secretly" against his finance minister because he was "afraid" to use "his power," simply miss the point.

8. *Lettre du roi Louis XIV Écritē à la Reine Mère relative à l'arrestation du Surintendant Fouquet.* Found in the papers of M. Rose; 8° L b 37 4677.

9. A.N., K-120, *passim.*

10. The disgrace and trial of Fouquet inspired many a story to be told in back corridors and a great number of poems that circulated in manuscripts were sung at odd moments. The following is only one example of many; it had some thirty verses of about the same quality as those quoted:

> À la venue de Noël
> Chacun se doit bien rejuir
> Car Fouquet n'est point criminel
> On n'a pas le faire mourir
>
> Saint Hélaine fort l'emporta
> Quand il se met à rapporter
> Et le beau premier protesta
> Qu'il le falloit decapiter.
>
> Dieu s'écria Monsieur Pussort
> Qu'il est profond, qu'il est savant
> On peut, on trouvet un plus fort
> Pour regir le senate normand
>
> Ayez pitié, grand Colbert,
> De Fouquet qui soupire
> Nous l'avons vu comme vous
> Peut-être vous verrons nous
> Bien pire, bien pire, bien pire

These verses were taken from a manuscript in B.Maz., ms. 2193, 110. Barbier and Vernillat published a slightly different version in their *Histoire de France par les chansons, Mazarin et Louis XIV,* vol. II (Paris, 1956).

12. THE COLLABORATORS OF THE KING

* For this chapter consult the two books by L. André, *Michel Le Tellier et l'organisation de l'armée monarchique* (Paris, 1906) and *Michel Le Tellier et Louvois;* C. Rousset, *Histoire de Louvois,* 4 vols. (1862); C. W. Cole, *Colbert and a Century of French Mercantilism,* 2 vols. (1939); P. Boissonnade, *Colbert et le triomphe de l'étatisme* (1932); C.-G. Picavet, *La diplomatie française au temps de Louis XIV (1661–1715): institutions, mœurs et coutumes* (1930). There is place for a study on Hugh de Lionne, and much material in the A.A.E. to document it.

1. See the number of *XVII Siècle* (1960) dedicated to this problem and Philippe Sagnac, "Louis XIV et son administration d'après des ouvrages et travaux recents." *Rev. d'hist. pol. et Const.* (January 1939), pp. 23–47.

2. *Mémoires,* vol. II, pp. 240–41.

3. The important and excellent study by Rousset was responsible for the confusion; André has filled in the picture.

4. B.N., *Recueil Cange, Salle des Rés.,* 30 (21).

5. L. André, *Michel Le Tellier et l'organisation de l'armée monarchique;* Rousset, *op. cit.;* Hans Delbrück, *Geschichte der Kriegskunst im Rahmen der politischen Geschichte,* vol. IV (1920); and André Corvisier, *L'Armée française de la fin du XVIIe Siècle au Ministre de Choiseul,* vol. I (Paris, 1964).

6. Louis' letters abound in consideration of problems of discipline. *Œuvres,* and A.M.G.-Al, *passim.*

7. Cf. B.N., *Recueil Cange, Salle des Rés,* and A.M.G., series Al.

8. The adjectives are from C. W. Cole's pen; they seem most appropriate. *Colbert and a Century of French Mercantilism,* vol. I, p. 300.

9. Colbert, *Lettres* (Clément, ed.), III[1] and III[2].

10. A. Chéruel "La politique extérieure de Louis XIV au début de son gouvernement personnel," *Rev. d'Hist. Dip.,* vol. IV (1890), pp. 161–73.

11. The wits of the court had to have their say about the king's choices. Here is an example of the many poems harpooning king and court (B.Maz., mss. 2194, 358–64):

> L'attelage du soleil
> N'aura jamais son pareil
> Il est de quartre chevaux
> Precédés de deux cavalières
> Qui ne sont ni bons ni beaux—
> Le Tellier, Louvois, Colbert et Lionne,
> Mme. de Montespan et Mlle. de la Vallière

12. See the excellent studies by Herbert H. Rowen, "Arnaud de Pomponne, Louis XIV's moderate minister," *Am. Hist. Rev.*, LXI (The Hague, 1956); *The Ambassador prepares for war, 1669–1671* (The Hague, 1955); and the brilliant introduction in his *Pomponne, Relation de mon ambassade en Holland 1669–1671* (1955).

13. THE 'MÉTIER' OF THE KING

* For all the writing that there has been about the fact that Louis undertook the *métier du roi* as his primary task, there is very little written on it. The little article by Louis Madelin, "Comment le Roi Soleil dirigeait ses Ministres," in *Historia* (March 1953), is the only recent publication. Most authors assume that everyone knows how a king acts *en roi;* this chapter should provide an introduction to the problem.

1. By 1700 Louis XIV usually referred to "the state" rather than "my state," but he still spoke of "my service" and "my army."

2. *Lettres de Louis XIV aux princes de l'Europe* (1755), p. 64, and *passim; Œuvres*, vol. V, pp. 20, 204, and *passim*. This statement should be put beside another in the *Mémoires* in which Louis insists that all the goods of all his subjects belong to the king. He obviously meant that the king had the right to tax rather than to confiscate. La Bruyère may have heard that such an idea circulated in the court, for he wrote: "To say that the prince is absolute master of all the goods of his subjects, without regards, without question, without discussion, is the language of flatterers. . . ." Louis was no tyrant, but he did have lofty ideas about the powers as well as the duties of a king.

3. *Mémoires*, vol. II, 427.

4. *Relation des divertissements que le roi a donné aux Reines*, (1664) p. 6.

5. *Mémoires*, vol. II, pp. 436–37.

6. Primi Visconti, *Mémoires sur la cour de Louis XIV*, J. Lemoine, ed. (Paris, 1909), p. 31.

7. B.N., ms. franç., 2038–35.

8. It is also a pleasure to try to account for the king's zealous curiosity; the Freudian interpreter would certainly have the most fun with it, but other viewpoints so abound that no mere historian would dare to take sides.

9. A.A.E., France, 414. fol. 157.

10. Boislisle, *Le Cabinet Noir sous Louis XIV* (Paris, 1876); E. Vaille, *Histoire générale des Postes françaises*, vol. IV (Paris, 1950).

11. *Mémoires*, vol. II, 88–90.

12. B.N., ms. franç., 25747, 25748, 25749, 25750. A.N. Series O, A.M.G., A¹.

13. *Œuvres*, vol. IV, p. 211.

14. A.N., 2038 and 2039, *passim;* Series O¹, *passim; Lettres de Louis XIV* and *Œuvres, passim;* B.N., *Recueil Cange*, 30 and 31, 1660–74, *passim*.

15. A.N., series O. The four volumes edited by G.-B. Depping have long been a source for this sort of information: *Correspondance administrative sous le règne de Louis XIV*, 4 vols. (Paris, 1850–55).

16. Many of these orders were printed, signed by the king, undersigned by a secretary. The B.N. has a very large collection of them: *Catalogue général des livres imprimés de la Bibliothèque Nationale, actes Royaux*, vols. III and IV (Paris, 1950).

17. P. Clément, *La Police sous Louis XIV* (Paris, 1866).

18. B.N., Cab. des E., A22.

19. *Mémoires*, vol. II, pp. 225–26.

20. A.N., K 120, fol. 155.

21. N.A., series O¹.

22. *Lettres de Louis XIV*, May 22, 1662, 1755, p. 89.

23. Some of this material can be found in B.N., ms. franç. 25747–25750; *Salle des Rés., Recueil Cange, premier boit K;* A.N., series O¹.

24. L. André has given us enough about this problem to warrant a thorough-going study: *Michel Le Tellier et Louvois.*

25. The *Bienfaits du Roi*, B.N., mss. franç., 7655–7658, are especially revealing.

26. A recent biographer tries to make him into a "reluctant soldier," but with no great success because his scholarship is so faulty. W. H. Lewis, *Louis XIV, an Informal Portrait* (New York, 1959).

27. Sainctôt's registers, B.N., mss. franç., 14117, 14118, 14129.

14. HIGH POLICY

* The impressive, if not too well organized, bibliography in L. André's *Louis XIV et l'Europe* (1950) with my bibliographical article (*J.M.H.*, vol. XXXVI. no. 2, pp. 127–44) makes additional citations unnecessary. The reader who wishes more evidence should, of course, consult G. Zeller, *Histoire des Relations Internationales, Les Temps Modernes, De Louis XIV à 1789* vol. II, (Paris, 1955).

1. De la Vaux, *La France invincible, ou discours remarquable et diésintéressé touchant les moyens de rendre la France tranquille et heureuse* (Paris, 1661).

2. B.N., Clair, 485, fols. 6, pp. 53–54.

3. *Œuvres*, vol. V, pp. 67–68.

4. P. Sonnino, *Louis XIV's View of the Papacy, 1661–1667* (Los Angeles, 1966).

5. De la Serre, *Les Éloges de la voix publique présentée à sa Majesté très Chrétienne, Louis XIV à l'honneur des héros de son armée triomphante en Hungrie*, B.N. ms. franç. 6946. Louis' letters to his commanders are to be found in his *Œuvres*, vol. V.

6. *Lettres de Louis XIV*, Louis to Conti, October 25, 1662. The main burden of the letter is a request for two million livres from Languedoc where Conti was governor. See also Le Maire, *Le rachat de Dunkerque par Louis XIV* (Paris, 1924), and Saint-Léger, "L'acquisition de Dunkerque et de Mardyck par Louis XIV," *Rev. d'H. Mod.*, vol. I, pp. 233–45.

7. Cf. "Memoire on Lorraine of 1662," A.A.E., France, 415.

8. Treaty of Montmartre, February 6, 1662.

9. At the time that Louis forced the Duke of Lorraine to live up to his agreement, he wrote a letter to his aunt the Duchess of Savoy that is very characteristic of the king who always was concerned about the fate of his officers. "Dear Aunt, If I merit some praise for the reduction of Marsal, it is because I saved the blood of a large number of noblemen whom it would have been necessary to sacrifice by a siege—the praise you give me is evidence of your friendship . . ." (A.A.E., France, 414, fol. 293).

10. *Œuvres*, August 25, 1661, vol. V, p. 46.

11. L. Mignet, *Négociations relatives à la Succession d'Espagne sous Louis XIV, 1662–1679*, 4 vols. (Paris, 1835–42).

12. A. Aubery, *Les justes prétentions du roi sur l'Empire* (Paris, 1667), Lb 37-3556.

15. THE WAR OF DEVOLUTION

* As we noted in the preceding chapter, André's bibliography is quite complete for international relations and war. In addition to Max Immich, *Geschichte des Europäischen Staatensystems von 1660 bis 1789* (Paris, 1905), we should also call attention to the latest German handbook and bibliographical guide covering war and high politics, Walther Hubatsch's *Das Zeitalter des Absolutismus, 1600–1789* (Braunschweig, 1962), in which there are references to studies that are important, but peripheral to the central theme of this study. For the wars of 1667–68 and 1672–78, and later for the great conflicts of the last part of the reign, the student should know the seven-volume work of the marquis de Quincy, *Histoire militaire du règne de Louis le Grand* (Paris, 1726). Any student working in the Archives of the War Ministry will have come upon his "tracks" in the documents.

1. Zeller, *op. cit.*; André, *Louis XIV et L'Europe*. Meineche, F., "Der Regensburger Reichtag und der Devolutions krieg," *Hist. Zeit.*, vol. 60 (1888); Emerton, *Sir William Temple und die Tripleallianz vom Jahr 1668* (1877); Mignet, *op. cit.*, vol. II; K. Feiling, *British Foreign Policy (1660–1672)* (London, 1930); Rousset, *Histoire de Louvois*, vol. I.

2. *Traité des droits de la reine très chrétienne sur divers états de la Monarchie d'Espagne*, Imprimerie royale (Paris, 1667), 270 pages.

3. Quotations from Louis XIV's *Mémoires* have been widely used for indication of the king's own feelings or opinions.

4. B.N., Nov. Ac. franç., 23611, fol. 28.

5. *Lettre à M. L'Archevêque de Paris, juillet 11, 1667*, B.N.

6. *Œuvres*, vol. III, pp. 78, 84–85.

7. An article in the *Rev. d'Hist. Dip.* (Oct.-Dec. 1965), by Jean Bérenger, "Une tentative de rapprochement entre la France et l'Empereur: Le traité de partage secret de la Succession d'Espagne du 19 janvier, 1668," provides an interesting analysis of both the general problem of the rights to the Spanish crowns and the particular question of the first Franco-Imperial treaty of partition.

8. *Mémoires*, vol. II, pp. 350–51.

9. *Ibid.*, pp. 164–74, 245–76.

10. A.M.G., Al-228, Vauban to Louvois, October 13, 1668.

11. Quoted in C. Barthémeny, *Erreurs et mensonges historiques* (Paris, 1879), pp. 19–20.

16. THE DUTCH WAR: ASSAULT

* In this study the so-called Dutch War is treated in the following three chapters, but there is no reason for treating the bibliography this way. In addition to the works cited in the preceding three chapters, there are a number of classics that should be consulted. Waldteufel, *La politique extérieure de Louis XIV, conquête de la Hollande* (Paris, 1898); there are classic studies on DeWitt by A. Lefevre-Pontalis and N. Japikse, on Louis' relations with Brandenburg, by G. Pagés, and on the problems of the involved Spanish Succession in this war by Mignet and Legrelle; Keith Feiling's, "Henriette Stuart, Duchess of Orléans, and the origin of the treaty of Dover," *Eng. Hist. Rev.*, vol. XLVII (1932); E. Fremy, "Les causes économiques de la guerre de Hollande, 1664–1672, *Rev. d'Hist. Dip.* (1914), pp. 523–51; as well as the works of Rowen and Elzinga cited below. See also the issue of *XVIIᵉ Siècle*, Nos. 46–47 (1960) dealing exclusively with the foreign policy of Louis XIV. For the other recent studies see my bibliographical article cited above.

The war also has a literature. Condé and Turenne both have many studies devoted to their exploits. The André bibliography is complete enough for an introduction to the problems of military action. The reader of the three chapters that follow will quickly realize that there is a place for a modern study on this war.

1. S. Elzinga, *Het voorspel van den oorlog van 1672: de economisch-politieke betrekkingen tusschen Frankrijken en Nederland inde jaren 1660–1672* (Haarlem, 1926)

and his "Le prélude de la guerre de 1672" *Rev. d'Hist. Mod.,* vol. II (1927); he blames Colbert for the war. Cf. H. Rowen's book *The Ambassador Prepares for War,* in which Colbert's role is minimized.

2. Rousset, *op. cit.,* vol. I, p. 147.

3. These adjectives represent the views of the French court; a more friendly attitude would give a more gracious picture of von Beuningen.

4. One of the most interesting "histories" of this war, *La précise historique des campagnes de Louis La Grand,* was written by the noted dramatist Jean Racine. It has all the elements of an heroic poem or a traditional fable, and should be consulted on the origins of the conflict; for Racine undoubtedly explained it as Louis wished it to be told. "The United Netherlands," he tells us, ". . . carried the commerce to the Indies where it almost destroyed the power of Portugal; it treated as an equal with England . . . whose vessels it burned in the Thames. . . . Blinded by prosperity it failed to recognize the hand that so many times strengthened and supported it. Leagued with the enemies of France, it pretended to give law to Europe, and prided itself on limiting the conquests of the King. It oppressed Catholics . . . it opposed French commerce in the east. In a word, it failed at nothing that could bring down a storm that would inundate it. . . . The King, tired of these insolences, resolved to punish them. He declared war on the Dutch . . . and marched against them. . . ." An elegant edition of this work was published by *Les amis de l'imprimerie nationale* (Paris, 1953). The poetic language of this "history" should make it a classic in seventeenth-century literature.

There were many such works. While Racine's is the most elegantly written, the one by de Vertron, *Dictionnaire historique ou l'histoire de Louis le Grand* (B.N. ms. franç., 4927), is perhaps the most astonishingly uncritical. The dauphin's *History of the Dutch War (De Bello Batavico, Anno 1672)* will be cited later in the chapter. These books, intended for the eye of the king, perhaps to secure a pension for the author, have contributed to the idea that Louis himself was completely egomaniacal. In his own correspondence, however, we very often find Louis attributing his successes to "the bounty of God" and the bravery of his subjects while these "histories" made, or seemed to make, everything depend upon the king.

5. Racine explained the war thus: "The King, tired of these insolences, resolved to punish them. He declared war on the Dutch . . . and marched against them. The vigor of his march astonished them. However criminal they were, they did not believe that punishment would follow so swiftly. . . . They could hardly believe that a young prince, born with all the graces of body and mind . . . in the midst of pleasures . . . would be able so easily . . . to go far from his kingdom, and to expose himself to the fatigues of a long and troublesome war with uncertainty of its success . . ." (Racine, *op. cit.*).

6. In 1659 he had crossed over into Spain incognito, but officially he never left the French side of the Isle of Pheasants.

7. A.N., K-119, fol. 15.

8. A.N., K-119. fol. 20.

9. Rousset, *op. cit.,* vol. I, pp. 348*ff.*

10. A.A.E., France. 279, fol. 34.

11. The Duke de Longueville was Condé's nephew; he left no legitimate heirs, but he did have a natural son. At the request of the Duchess de Longueville, Louis legitimized this child with the name Charles Louis, bastard of Orléans; A.N., 01–16.

12. *Œuvres,* vol. III, p. 198.

13. Mignet blames Louvois for the decision in *Succession d'Espagne,* vol. IV, p. 33. Pomponne obviously believed that the Dutch conditions should have been accepted, and at the time he advised this course of action; see *Mémoires du Marquis de Pomponne,* vol. I, "Angleterre," *passim.* But obviously a preponderance of his advisors urged Louis to insist upon harsh terms.

14. Racine, *op. cit.,* p. 8.

15. *Ibid.,* p. 10.

16. Cf. *Gazette,* August 14, 1672, pp. 349–60.

17. B.N. (1672) 8 ye 3318.

17. THE DUTCH WAR: THREAT OF DEFEAT, 1673–75

1. In light of the military situation at the moment when the French attack bogged down, it is very difficult to understand how Turenne and Condé, both of whom had had thirty or more years of experience with warfare, could have allowed the release of these soldiers for a nominal ransom.

2. A.N., 2039 [361]; *Œuvres*, vol. III, p. 251.

3. The B.N. has a wonderful collection of pamphlets describing the fêtes, religious and civil, that celebrated the victories of the king. It also has a surprising number of the sermons and speeches delivered at the time. See also *Journal de la santé du roi Louis XIV de l'année 1647 à l'année 1711, écrit par Vallot, d'Aquin, et Fagon,* ed. J. A. Le Roi (Paris, 1862).

4. *Œuvres,* vol. III, pp. 287*ff.* A.M.G., Al-281, p. 282 *passim;* Rousset, *op. cit.,* vol. I, pp. 227*ff.* If the letters in the Archives of the Ministry of War are an indication of his concern, it was only after 1673 that Louis began to become really worried about the military situation. Before that time he seems to have left much of the decision to his military advisers, particularly to Turenne and Condé. The failure of the campaign of 1672 taught him much about war and soldiers.

5. The *Gazette* during the first decades of the reign is a very interesting document; it must have made easy the work of spies as well as of propagandists among the enemies of the king. It is also very useful for the student of the period. In the latter years of the reign, however, it became a colorless official publication and has little or no value to the historian.

6. *Œuvres,* vol. V., Louis to Louvois, December 25. 1672, p. 204. See correspondence dealing with the destruction of the Palatinate in 1688–89, A.M.G., Al-824.

7. June 7, 1673.

8. *Œuvres, op. cit.,* vol. III, p. 410.

9. A.A.E., France 2789, fols. 87-103.

10. A.M.G., Al-1667, July 29, 1703.

11. A.A.E., France, 297, fol. 145.

12. A.M.G., Al-379, pp. 284-89; *Œuvres,* vol. III, pp. 488*ff.*

13. A.A.E., France, 297, fols. 18*ff,* and France, 938, fols. 278*ff.*

14. The B.N. has a large collection of pamphlets like the one to the Capitouls of Toulouse, 8° L b 37 4736; some ask for prayers, many for *Te Deums,* all are pervaded with a sense of providential force in history. These were not written by the king, but they do reflect the same spirit and ideas that we find in his personal letters.

15. B.N., ms. franç. 10261, fol. 45.

16. Primi Visconti, *Mémoires,* p. 102.

17. A.M.G., Al-379, Louis to Turenne, May 21, 1674.

18. A.M.G., Al-380, June 10.

19. *Ibid.,* July 4.

20. *Ibid.,* July 22.

21. The correspondence is in A.M.G., Al-381 and 400.

22. He was with the English regiment attached to the French army.

23. A.M.G., Al-380, Louis to Turenne, June 22.

23a. Saint-Abre, whose wound much disturbed the king, wrote to Louis on June 24: "Sire, my son and I lost our lives in the same battle. . . . I have all my life lived as a man of wealth, but that was possible only because of my friends. I leave six children. . . . I hope that your Majesty will have the goodness not to abandon them to the evil state of my affairs. I can assure your Majesty that up to the last day of my life, which apparently will be tomorrow, I would die for your Majesty." A letter like this was not uncommon; the king was the "social security" for his soldiers, and the hope for their heirs. Louis was not unmoved by such appeals. A.M.G., 380, June 24.

24. A.A.E., France 297, fol. 158.

25. The present author "followed" the king's army through the "Spanish Netherlands" in the summer of 1963. Some of the "camps" had become large towns,

most of the forests were located differently than in 1675, the roads were somewhat changed, and the names of some places altered, but it was possible to find the route of march and gain much insight into the problem of moving an army in the late seventeenth century.

26. This sweep is well described in a beautifully illustrated manuscript history of the campaign preserved in the B.N.—ms. franç. 7891—probably written by Chamlay, which gives exact description of the movements of the French army. It is amusing to note that this was the year of saints in the passwords: Saint Francis and Narbonne; Saint James and Madrid; Saint Michael and Rouen; Saint Étienne and Bordeaux; Saint Peter and Rome; etc.

27. See book III, ch. 21.

28. The letter of congratulations for this victory went to Vivonne, the brother of Madame de Montespan and boyhood friend of the king. *Lettres de Louis XIV* (1755), pp. 213–14.

29. The life and death of Turenne in the *Gazette*—pp. 703–26—is worth reading for an understanding of the shock caused by his death.

30. Turenne was actually buried in Saint-Eustache where his family built an enormous tomb out of all proportion to the rest of the church. When Louis learned of this he ordered La Coste to destroy part of it and rebuild the rest so that the marshal "will rest in a situation that will mark the honor that his service has earned him" (N.A., K 122, fol. 12). It might be noted that La Coste was one of the important architects in the *Bâtiments,* and was responsible for the development of the rococo style.

31. A.M.G., 1A-433, 434, 451, 459.

18. THE DUTCH WAR: LAST PHASE

1. Vauban returned from an inspection trip of the frontier between France and the Spanish Netherlands. His critical advice was, "Seriously, Monseigneur, the King ought to consider making his *pré carré* [field marked out for dueling]. This confusion of friendly and enemy fortifications, stuck pell-mell, the one with the other, does not please me at all." A.M.G., A1-337, January 19, 1675. Also quoted by Rousset, *op. cit.,* vol. I, p. 430.

2. *Œuvres,* vol. IV, p. 75.

3. B.N., ms. franç., 7892, pp. 8*ff.*

4. B.N., ms. franç., 7892, pp. 8*ff.*

5. Louvois to Le Tellier, May 19, A.M.G., A1-499, fol. 153. Cf. also *Gazette,* pp. 379–81, where this account is printed almost word for word.

6. Louvois to Le Tellier, A1-499, fol. 166.

7. Saint-Simon (Boislisle), vol. X, pp. 3408*ff.*; vol. XX, pp. 12*ff.*

8. *Lettres historiques de M. Pellisson,* vol. III (Paris, 1727), 44*ff.*

9. A.M.G., A1-508, p. 41.

10. *Mémoires,* pp. 284*ff.*

11. Rousset, *op. cit.,* vol. II, p. 226.

12. The letters between Louis and Louvois are to be found in A.M.G., A1-500, 501, *passim.* We cite here only a few that seem most revealing both of the problem of war that summer and the king's attitudes toward them.

13. *Ibid.*

14. July 27, A.M.G., A1-501.

15. Even today the visitor to Maestricht can easily follow the problems of the besieging and the relieving armies.

16. Mme. de Sévigné, Paris, August 5, 1676.

17. *Lettres de Louis XIV,* pp. 212–14.

18. There can be other explanations for these absurd claims about the "actions of the King," his "incredible foresight," his "attention" that won all victories, and the like, but the present author, after reading pieces ranging from the beautifully bound manuscript history of this war (probably written by Chamlay) to the

numerous little pamphlets, histories (Racine), the accounts in the *Gazette,* the poems of praise, etc., has reached the conclusion that the people who wrote such things believed that the king's ego needed bolstering. It is hard to see that any other explanation can be given for the official history intended for Louis' own edification. The author must have thought that the king was terribly insecure, that he needed assurance. Surely this author *knew* that Louis was aware of what had happened and did not need his history to refresh his memory—therefore he was trying to give the king "an interpretation" that might soothe Louis' troubled doubts. If the author actually were someone in the war ministry, this thesis becomes more and more plausible, for a Chamlay knew Louis XIV and his reactions better than a publicist or a contemporary historian would know him.

19. A.M.G., Al-544 fol., p. 89, *passim.*
20. *Lettres de Louis XIV* (1755), 216 18.
21. These letters are in A.M.G., Al-544. Fol. 145 bis. is particularly interesting, for in it we see Philippe paying his court to the powerful war minister: ". . . seeing you serve the King makes me ask for your friendship and assure you of mine."
22. A.M.G., Al-545, fol. 71.
23. A.M.G., Al-545, fol. 91.
24. A.M.G., Al-544, fol. 107. See also the accounts by Racine, *op. cit.,* and the author (Chamlay?) of the history of the campaign prepared for the king (B.N., ms. franç. 7892). The *Gazette* also has a complete account of the battle. Although he wrote about it, Racine was not with the king on this campaign. When Louis rebuked him for not being with him, he said that he and Boileau "are two bourgeois who have only city habits" (Sévigné, November 2, 1677).
25. B.N., ms. franç. 7893, no. 19.
26. Philippe Erlanger, *Monsieur, Frère de Louis XIV* (Paris, 1953), pp. 171*ff.*
27. Cf. book IV, ch. 5, 6; book V, ch. 2–6.
28. *Œuvres,* vol. IV, p. 117.
29. Visconti, *op. cit.,* pp. 221–23; Pierre Goubert, *Beauvais et le Beauvaisis, 1600 à 1730* (Paris, 1960) and *Cartes et Graphiques* (Paris, 1960)—this work analyzes closely the cost of living in an important province of France. In it we can follow the successive crises that shook the kingdom.
30. A.A.E., France 297, fol. 187.
31. The ladies encountered considerable distress: rain, mud, bad roads, and poor accommodations. Rousset, *op. cit.,* vol. II, pp. 488*ff.* Mlle. de Montpensier, *Mémoires.* Racine, who was there, remarked to the king, "Sire, we are no longer surprised at the extraordinary valor of soldiers; they are right to hope to be killed in order to end so miserable a life."
32. B.N., ms. franç. 10331, fols. 83–84.

III

19. THE COURT OF APOLLO

* The court of Louis XIV has been the subject for many articles and books. Indeed, it is hard to say anything new about it. One of the recent books on the court is by the distinguished Duke de la Force, *Louis XIV et sa Cour* (Paris, 1956). One of the best contemporary accounts is the *Mémoires sur la Cour de Louis XIV* (ed. J. Lemoine, Paris, 1909) by Primi Visconti. Saint-Maurice, *Lettres sur la Cour de Louis XIV* (ed. J. Lemoine, Paris, 1930), *Le Grand Condé et le Duc d'Enghien, Lettres inédites à Marie-Louise de Gonzague, Reine de Pologne sur la Cour de Louis XIV* (ed. E. Magne, Paris, 1920), and of course, the gossipy Madame de Sévigné are also valuable. In addition there is a wealth of material on the court. Madame Taillandier's *Le Grand Roi et sa Cour* (Paris, 1930), Funck-Brentano, *La*

Cour du Roi Soleil (Paris, 1937), and Jules Mazé, *La Cour de Louis XIV* (Paris, 1946) may be representative of the more popular literature providing a setting for the king's regime. This chapter is largely based upon contemporary materials available in the B.N. I have used these materials in an effort to capture the feeling tones of the period.

1. The first medal using Apollo is from 1653; see *Medailles sur le Règne de Louis le Grand* (1705), p. 69.

2. As we have seen, these people of quality sometimes managed to upset the military table of rank established by the king; their social prestige created a "shadow hierarchy" behind the military one. This accounts for Louis' promotion of officers whose status was dependent on the war minister or on officers who actually were of royal blood, like Vendôme, Orléans, or Berwick. In the early years of the reign, however, the great nobles still commanded the armies.

3. In the B.N. there are numerous printed works as well as manuscripts from this period dealing with these matters; the Sainctôt registers (B.N., ms. franç., 16633*ff.*, 14120*ff.*) will be used often in this account.

4. After the death of Louis' brother Philippe, the Prince of Orléans became the "first prince of the blood" and entitled to be called Monsieur le Prince. Then Condé became Monsieur le Prince de Condé.

5. For an example of this right, see N.A. K122[10], K120B[16]; B.N. ms. franç. 6679 fols. 467*ff.*, 14118 fols. 4–17.

In presence of	Dauphin Dauphine Children of France	Grand-children of France	Prin-cesses of the blood	Princes of the blood	Cardinals	Duchesses Princesses of foreign houses Spanish Grandees	Dukes Princes Spanish Grandees	Women of Quality	Men of Quality
King	Tabouret	Tabouret	Tabouret	Stand	With King, Stand	Tabouret	Stand	Stand	Stand
Queen					With Queen, Tabouret				
Dauphin Dauphine Children of France	Armchair	Tabouret	Tabouret	Stand, then Tabouret	Tabouret	Tabouret	Stand	Stand	Stand
Grand-children of France		Armchair	Chair with back	Chair with back	Chair with back	Tabouret	Tabouret	Tabouret	Stand
Princes, Princesses of the blood	Armchair for all							Seated	Seated

Chart taken from Henri Brochet, *Le rang et l'étiquette sous l'ancien régime* (Paris, 1955), p. 29.

6. Book IV, ch. 23, *infra*.

7. In addition to the usual *mémoires* of the court, one should look at the superb collection of etchings made by van der Meulen and his associates and preserved in the B.N., C. des E., Al-10 f., which allow us to "see" the progress of the court through the land, as well as its life in the royal châteaus. It also contains pictures of the king on campaign in the wars.

8. Lemoine and Lichtenberger, *De la Vallière à de Montespan*, (Paris, 1902), p. 38.

9. Translation by the author; perhaps more exact than poetic.

10. Hautecoeur, *Louis XIV, le Roi Soleil* (Paris, 1953), p. 18.

11. Lemoine and Lichtenberger, *op. cit.*, and J. Lair, *Louise de la Vallière et*

la Jeunesse de Louis XIV, (Paris, 1881), both contain descriptions of these parties. *La Muze Historique* and the *Gazette,* as well as numerous pamphlets like *Les Divertissements de Versailles* (Paris, 1672), provide much contemporary evidence. Madame de Sévigné tells the story of Vatel's suicide; it is probably as correct as any.

12. There were several "programs" for the Carrousel and then pamphlets describing its course. The *Gazette* and *Muze Historique* both carried accounts. There is a beautiful collection of etchings of the event in the B.N., C. des E., Aa10, and a complete account of the whole show, *Le Grand Carrousel du roi, ou la course de Bague ordiné par sa Majesté* (Paris, 1662), chez Cardin.

13. The winner of the tourney was her brother, and the poet exclaimed, "France burns with love of his name which she wishes to eternalize" (*La Muze Historique*).

14. The red leather-bound manuscript from the library of the Duke de Coislin is one of the most interesting accounts of this party (B.N., ms. franç. 16635). See also ms. franç. 19188, fol. 217. There was a printed account sold in Paris, *Relation des divertissements que le roi a donné aux reines dans le parc de Versailles* (Paris, 1664). Naturally the *Gazette* carried the story.

15. B.N., ms. franç., 16633; see also ms. franç. 14120.

16. A.N., 0–20, fol. 239.

17. Cf. book V, ch. 34, p. 597.

18. Cf. B.N., ms. Clair. 1229, and *Gazette* for contemporary accounts.

19. B.N., Sainctôt's registers, ms. franç. 16633, 14120.

20. A.N. K541 #29, July 2, 1663. In the K series there are many similar accounts. Louis also often witnessed the marriage contracts of his great nobles; the details of dowry, jewels, clothes, and property make these documents very interesting reading.

21. The list of royal visitors in these first two decades is not so very long, for princes rarely trusted themselves beyond their own frontiers. Louis never left the kingdom except in company of his army. However, there were some visitors:

1661, the Duke of Lorraine

1662, Prince Bernard de Weimar

1663, Crown Prince of Denmark (incognito); Louis wrote a charming letter to his father about the son's visit.

1664, the Duke of Meckembourg (or Meckeemburg; there are several spellings of this), who was given the Order of the Holy Spirit.

1669, the Duke of Tuscany (incognito)

1672, the Duke of Neuburg

1673, the Duchess of York

After that date the war closed in and ended visits for some time (Sainctôt, III, ms. franç. 14119, fols. 179–217 passim).

22. To get a better view of seventeenth-century ceremony we might follow the king to the *lit de justice* of 1669. By 5 A.M. the Hundred Swiss and the French guards were posted from Porte St. Honoré to the Palace of Justice. About 9 A.M. the king, accompanied by the chancellor, the Duke of Tuscany (incognito), the Duke of Guise, a company of ambassadors headed by the papal nuncio, and a host of people of quality—all arrived at the Porte-Saint-Honoré and marched to the Sainte-Chapelle to hear mass. From there they went to the grand chamber, accompanied by the beat of the drums of the Hundred Swiss, a parade of dignitaries including princes, dukes, officers of state, and soldiers. The king sat on the throne while the chancellor harangued the company. At the same time, Monsieur visited the chamber of accounts and Monsieur le Prince the court of aides. After the *lit de justice* the king dined at the Tuileries (B.N., Sainctôt register, ms. 14117).

The baptism of the dauphin, March 24, 1668, provided another round of ceremonies. The château of Saint-Germain was elaborately decorated for the occasion, with the bishops, dukes, marshals, and others dressed in full regalia. The dauphin was in bed fully dressed so that the noble ladies could "awaken" him and lead him to the chapel where the choir was singing the *Veni Creator.* The Bishop of Orléans, surrounded by six other bishops, officiated. The cardinal legate and the Princess of Conti were godfather and godmother. The king and queen watched from a little distance. After it was over, there was a state dinner with the king and queen in the center, the other guests were set at each side, two places away from the royal couple, seated on folding chairs and served by the gentlemen of the king. The account of the festivities makes up twenty-four folio pages of manuscript. (B.N., ms. franç. 16633, 6387). When the ʾking entertained a cardinal legate at dinner, the legate was served on a platform two places below the one for the king; both had armchairs. The king was served by his grand master of the horse, the cardinal by the general controller of the king's household. They were assisted by other gentlemen and twelve *maîtres d'hôtel (ibid.).*

23. The B.N. has a large collection of the registers of the masters of ceremonies. These documents have not been ransacked for the information that they can produce (mss. franç. 16633, 14117, 14118, 14119, 14120).

24. Madame de Sévigné speaks of the "divinely" furnished apartments of the king. Visitors to Versailles or other royal châteaus are often surprised at the barrenness of the chambers; they forget that these are just the rooms with only a suggestion of the grandeur of their former furniture and *objets d'art.* In 1960 the *Musée des arts décoratifs* had an exposition, *Louis XIV, Faste et Décor,* in which they brought together things that furnished the rooms of Louis' châteaus: furniture, tapestry, candlesticks, table services, paintings, architects' designs. The show underlined the grandeur of "baroque" art and furniture. In the Louvre there is a permanent exposition of Louis XIV rooms that is often overlooked by tourists, but well worth attention. One has actually to *see* the furnishings to understand what Madame de Sévigné meant by "divinely furnished—all is magnificent. . . ." See also her letter of March 18, 1671, in which she tells how the king punished M. de S—— for cheating at cards. "The King," she writes, "disliked having to dishonor a man of the quality of M. S—— . . . but since for two months all those who played with him were ruined. . . ."

25. The Duchess of Orléans, Elizabeth-Charlotte, *Correspondance Complète,* vol. I, Lb 37–4554, p. 15.

26. Visconti, *Mémoires,* p. 35.

20. THE YOUNG KING: HIS WIFE, MOTHER, MISTRESSES

* Louis' affairs with women very naturally have attracted the attention of many writers and of a few serious historians. The Bussy-Rabutin, *Histoire amoureuse des Gaules* exists in numerous manuscript copies and has been printed in many editions. The two-volume edition by Sainte-Beuve (1868) is probably the one to start with, even though several of the eighteenth-century editions are more complete. J. Lemoine and A. Lichtenberger, *op. cit.,* Jules Lair, *Louise de la Vallière et la jeunesse de Louis XIV* (Paris, 1881), P. Clément, *Madame de Montespan et Louis XIV* (Paris, 1868) and A. Houssaye, *Mlle. de la Vallière et Madame de Montespan* (Paris, 1896) seem to be the base for most of the subsequent writings. A few authors have been able to add here and there to the story of La Vallière and the "high career" of Montespan, but mostly the problems arise from interpretations. Maurice Rat, *La Royale Montespan* (1959), Gonzague Truc, *Madame de Montespan* (Paris, 1936), and G. Mongrédien, *La vie privée de Louis XIV* (Paris, 1938), could be consulted. See also my bibliographical article *J.M.H.,* XXXVI, pp. 127–44.

1. M. Fléchier, *Oraison Funèbre . . . à Val-de-Grâce* (1683, 8Lb37-3814).

2. Père Pièche, *Oraison Funèbre . . . à Saint-Sauveur* (1683, 8Lb37-3819).

3. The B.N. has almost two dozen of these "funeral eulogies" as well as Bonnaventure de Storia's *La vie de Marie Thérèse* (8Lb37-3825, 1683). They make instructive reading, but hardly a complete picture of the queen. B.N. series 8Lb37, 3814–3834.

4. De Storia, *op. cit.*, pp. 69–70. Today we would understand that Louis' children by his "first first" cousin probably suffered from genetic handicaps.

5. Cf. A.N. K-120, B.69 for some of her accounts.

6. Visconti.

7. The B.N. has three or four of these manuscript accounts in which there are minor differences; it, along with more of Bussy de Rabutin's works, has been printed under the title *Histoire amoureuse des Gaulles,* the Vallière affair under the subheading: *La France galante, le palais-royal ou les amours de Madame de la Vallière.* There are many editions of this work (B.N. ms. franç., 19188, fols. 180*ff.,* 13774, fols. 15*ff.*, 15113, fols. 34*ff.;* also Rés. Lb37, 3523 D).

8. Ormesson, *Journal,* vol. II, pp. 47–48.

9. B.N., ms. franç., 4385, fols. 270–76.

10. In the B.N., consult ms. franç., 16633, fols. 1–34. The B.N. also has a host of funeral sermons for the queen; the accounts in the *Gazette,* and a large number of the B.N. pamphlets would provide a complete picture. See also A.N., K-118 B.

11. Émile Magne (ed.), *Lettres inédites à Marie-Louise de Gonzague, reine de Pologne sur la Cour de Louis XIV* (Paris, 1920), p. 330.

12. *La Muze Historique.*

13. Mange (ed.), *op. cit.,* p. 309.

14. Almost a decade later Monsieur de Montespan had a law case before the Parlement of Paris and Louis was constrained to allow him to come to Paris to fight it. He was a continuous threat to Louis, who wrote to Colbert: Monsieur de Montespan "is a fool whom you will do me a pleasure to watch closely." And again: "he threatened to see his wife and he is capable of it . . . the results are to be feared. . . . See that he leaves Paris as soon as possible" (*Oeuvres,* vol. V, pp. 576*ff.*). Obviously the King of France was not all-powerful over his subjects.

15. B.N., ms. franç., 19.188.

16. Lair, *op. cit.,* p. 293.

17. De Genlis, *La duchesse de la Vallière* (Paris, 1843). Later the librarian of the Louvre, Dumas Himard (1852) proposed the theory of collaboration with Bossuet.

18. *Lettres de Madame de Montespan et al* (Le Roi, ed.), (L7 K4901, Versailles, 1860), pp. 45–46.

19. *Ibid.,* p. 46.

20. *Œuvres,* vol. IV, pp. 514–35, *passim.* On June 5, 1675, Louis wrote to Colbert from his camp at Latines, "Madame de Montespan has written me that you do very well the things that I have ordered you to do [for her], and that you always ask her if there is anything that she wishes. Continue to do this always. She has written that she visited Sceaux [Colbert's château] and that she had a very pleasant evening. I have advised her to visit Dampierre and assured her that Madame de Chevreuse [Colbert's daughter was married to the Duke of Chevreuse] and Madame Colbert would welcome her there with a good heart . . ." (*Œuvres,* V, pp. 536–37). Both Sceaux and Dampierre still merit a visit by anyone interested in seventeenth-century châteaus. The park of Sceaux is particularly beautiful

21. *Mémoires,* II, pp. 314–15.

22. *Mémoires de Charles Perrault,* (Avignon, 1759), p. 28.

21. MATURITY: THE ROYAL FAMILY

1. A.N. O^1–36, May 2, 1692.

2. Cf. the mémoires of Saint-Simon, La Grande Mademoiselle, and Segrais.

3. For details of Lauzun's imprisonment see letters in A.N.—K.-120, A.

4. A.N., K.-542, fol. 9.

5. B.N., ms. franç., 10261.

6. Visconti, *op. cit.,* pp. 315–16.

7. B.N., N. Ac. franç., 4385 fol. 33.

8. *Lettres de Louis XIV* (1755 ed), p. 212.

9. Sainctôt's registers are quite complete. B.N., ms. franç. 14117, fols. 261ff.

10. B.N., ms. franç., 19, 916, fols. 1–21; 36–46, ms. franç. 12839, fols. 47–161; Clair., 485 fols. 229–73.

11. B.N., ms. franç. 2839, fols. 60ff.

12. Marcel Langlois in his biography *Madame de Maintenon* (Paris, 1932), and in his five-volume edition of her letters [*Madame de Maintenon, Correspondance* (Langlois, ed.), 5 vols. (Paris, 1933–1939)], which unfortunately was never completed, gives the most authoritative statement about Madame de Maintenon. His bibliographies should be consulted.

13. Cordelier, *Madame de Maintenon, une femme au Grand Siècle* (Paris, 1955).

14. .*Lettres* (Langlois, ed.), vol. II, no. 41, July 1674.

15. *Ibid.,* vol. II, no. 68, April 5, 1675.

16. *Souvenirs de Madame de Caylus* (Paris, 1886 ed.), p. 61.

17. *Lettres* (Langlois, ed.), vol. II, no.'s 49, 64, *passim.*

18. There is an amusing story in the mythology that tells of a woman of the people who thought that Madame de Montespan had "purchased the place of Madame de la Vallière." In the king's government all places were venal; so why not that of mistress of the king?

19. Brevet of April 11, 1679, A.N., O¹, fol. 23. A lampoon of the day insists that Marsillac, who introduced Mademoiselle de Fontanges to the king, was given the charge of Grand Veneur (director of the royal hunt) for "having put the beast in the ropes." *L'Esprit familier de Trianon ou l'aparation de la Duchesse de Fontanges* (*s.d.*), pp. 10–11.

20. De Caylus, p. 29.

21. B.N., ms. franç., 14120; *Gazette* (1679), pp. 433–48.

22. A.A.E., France, 425, fol. 18; see also B.N., ms. franç., 14120, fol. 260ff., and the curious little book *L'Alliance sacrée de l'honneur et du virtu au mariage de M. le Dauphin avec Mde. la p. de Bavière* (Paris, 1680), pp. 80ff.

23. A.A.E., France, 425, fol. 16.

24. These documents are very interesting and instructive to the historian. Colbert, *Lettres, Instructions et Mémoires de Colbert,* P. Clément, ed., vol. IV, pp. 407–30.

25. The best bibliography for the affair of the poisons is to be found in Georges Mongrédien's *Madame de Montespan et l'affaire des poisons* (Paris, 1953) which, incidentally, conclusively buries Madame de Montespan's supposed guilt. Pierre Clément's book on Madame de Montespan (*op. cit.*) was the first modern history of the lady; it tentatively accepts the possibility of her guilt; Funck-Brentano, *Le Drame de Poisons* (Paris, 1899) is a strong affirmative of this guilt. Jean Lemoine, *Madame de Montespan et la légende des poisons* (Paris, 1908) produced the strongest defense of the lady, and actually no really serious scholar has believed in her guilt since this book. Mongredien's book, however, is the most recent complete discussion.

26. Madame de Montespan remained at court for almost a whole decade after she no longer was the king's mistress. Her position was perhaps not as ambiguous as that of Mademoiselle de la Vallière earlier, but it was difficult. There can be little doubt that she suffered much. When she left the court she spent the remainder of her life doing "good works" and "atoning for her sins." She died in 1707. Curiously enough historians always tell the story of La Vallière's "atonement," but most of them ignore Montespan's.

27. Cf. book IV, ch. 25, pp. 145ff.

22. THE AGING LION: HUSBAND, FATHER, GRANDFATHER

1. The highest officer of justice, as the embodiment of the state's authority, never went into mourning; he had to be ready to meet the demands of the king's subjects.

2. In Spain, male children of the royal family were called *Infante,* females *Infanta.* Naturally Bossuet used the French forms of the two words.

3. The documents relating to this funeral are most complete; they should interest historians who are concerned about social and economic history, as well as those involved with ceremonial and political problems. See the series O1–1043 and K-120 B in the A.N.; the Sainctôt registers in the B.N., ms. franç. 16633, have some 154 pages devoted to the ceremonies, and there are over forty printed items in the B.N., L 37 B 3786–3826. In addition, there are at least twenty printed sermons for the dead queen in which she appears as a saint, as a great queen, as a remarkable woman. Many of the harangues and speeches of condolence given to the king were also printed and can be found in the B.N.

4. *Lettres* (Langlois, ed.), vol. II, no. 325.

5. Langlois, *Madame de Maintenon* (Paris, 1932), pp. 123–31. In his edition of the *Lettres,* vol. II, pp. 66*ff.,* Langlois is more precise than in the biography; and in his essay, "Madame de Maintenon et le Saint Siège," *Rev. d'Hist. Eccl.,* XXV (1929) pp. 33–72, even more so.

6. Louis Hastier, *Louis XIV et Madame de Maintenon* (Paris, 1957), *passim.*

7. There was a lively traffic in "remains of martyrs" during these years; Saint Candide was only one of several Roman saints who thus came to France. Cardinal Gaspard de Carpeigne's letter explains, "To all those who see these present letters let us certify that for the greater glory of God all powerful and for the veneration of the saints, we have made a gift to the very illustrious and very excellent Dame Françoise de Maintenon, of the body of Saint Candide, martyr for Jesus Christ taken by us from the cemetery of Saint Pontien." The grant allows her to "expose the relics for the veneration of the faithful." She could and did give parts as relics to friends for their edification. *Lettres* (Langlois, ed.), vol. II, no. 507, *passim.*

8. This material has largely been taken from *Lettres* (Langlois, ed.), vol. II. Cordier also relies heavily on the same source.

9. *Ibid.,* vol. III, p. 48, for discussion of this letter. It may have escaped being burned by being stolen.

10. When Madame de Montespan was dislodged the Marshal-Duke de la Feuillade is said to have remarked to her, "You have been dislodged, Madame, but by my faith, not without trumpets!"

11. Madeleine Daniélou, *Madame de Maintenon éducatrice* (Paris, 1946); C. Dumoulin, *Receuil des instructions que Madame de Maintenon a données aux Demoiselles de Saint-Cyr* (Paris, 1908), B.N. ms. franç. 15353, fols. 19–27.

12. Madame de Maintenon's enemies were legion. Madame (Elizabeth-Charlotte, Duchess of Orléans) could not think of enough bad things to say about her, and Saint-Simon waspishly seconds her efforts to defame the lady's character. Others took up the cry. After the revocation of the Edict of Nantes, she was blamed for the brutalities of the French army in the war following 1688. The B.N. has a very large collection of the books and pamphlets, mostly from Amsterdam and Cologne, that blackened her reputation and attacked the king; the B.Maz. has a large collection of the poems and songs of this period in which she appears as a sort of evil spirit. Some of these have been published in P. Barbier and F. Vernillat, *Histoire de France par les chansons, Mazarin et Louis XIV* (Paris, 1956).

Much of this literature is dull, repetitious, and badly written. There are attempts to make it exciting by details of sex and intrigue, but somehow even these passages lack force today. In the late seventeenth century, however, these books were titillating experiences. Some of the titles give clues to the contents. The following are examples of their literature: *Le Tombeau des Amours de Louis le Grand en les dernières Galanteries* (1695), *Les Intrigues amoureuses de la cour de France* (1685), *Le Divorce royal ou la Guerre Civile dans la famille du Grand Alcandre* (1692), *Scarron aparu à Mme. de Maintenon* (1694), *La vie de la Duchesse de la Vallière* (1695), etc.

13. Langlois, "Madame de Maintenon et le Saint Siège" *Rev. d'Hist. Eccl., op. cit.,* pp. 71*ff.*

14. *Œuvres*, vol. VI, p. 21.

15. Cf. *infra*, book IV, ch. 27, pp. 452*ff*.

16. The AMG series A1 has many of these letters scattered through its volumes. A1-824 to A1-1261 particularly should be consulted.

In December 1699, when the dauphin learned that the king had raised his allowance (*menus plaisirs*) to 3,000 livres a month, he asked Madame de Maintenon to thank the king. His gambling debts were not mentioned. Cf. *Bienfaits du Roy* (1699), B.N. ms. franç. 7665, p. 18.

17. This theme runs like a red thread through a little collection of his letters. *Lettres de Louis XIV, Mgr. Le Dauphin et autres à Madame de Maintenon* (Paris, 1822).

18. B.N., ms. franç. 10265.

19. A.N. O1-1043. Madame de Sévigné's letter is dated April 26, 1690. With the death of the dauphine, the court went into mourning, but not the king. The princes of the blood were in mourning for one year. B.N. ms. franç. 16633, fols. 531*ff*.

20. B.N., ms. franç. 10261 *passim*.

21. The letter is fol. 101 in B.N., ms. franç. 10261.

22. But when she died, La Grande Mademoiselle made Philippe, Duke of Orléans, her "universal" heir. There were legal problems because her half-sisters, the Condés, and the Guise family all had claims to her property, which was scattered throughout Europe (A.N., K-543).

23. A.N., K-562, fol. 49; K 543, fol. 96.

24. *Œuvres*, vol. IV, p. 14.

25. There is a little package of the Duke of Maine's letters to Madame de Maintenon between 1680 and 1711 in the A.N., K-121. The tone of these letters is formal, but they reflect a close, friendly relationship.

26. *Lettres de Louis XIV et le Dauphin . . . à Madame de Maintenon* (Paris, 1822) B. N. Rés. Z 3266, p. 4.

27. The buildings at Marly are all gone, but the park is still visited as one of the beauty spots of the Paris area.

28. Louis is credited with the remark: "At Versailles I am housed as a king, at Chambord, as a prince, at Compiègne, as a peasant." The present palace at Compiègne is of eighteenth- and nineteenth-century construction.

29. In January 1689 Louis gave James 150,000 livres as an outright gift, and a pension of 50,000 livres a month. B.N., ms. franç. F, 659, fol. 12*ff*.

30. Madame de Maintenon writes that the "King said that his alms were only new burdens on his people, that the more that he gives, the more he takes from them; his alms are without merit since he does not take them from himself . . . ," again "all my alms are a sort of luxury, good and permitted . . . but without merit." Langlois, *Madame de Maintenon, op. cit.,* p. 141.

31. In a slightly different form this letter is reproduced in *Œuvres*, IV, p. 27, and Langlois' *Lettres*, vol. V, p. 307.

32. This game was played somewhat differently from modern billiards, yet it seems to have had some of the same fascination of the modern game. There are several etchings showing the king and members of his immediate entourage around the table.

33. Much of what follows is taken from this famous Journal published under the title *Journal de la Santé du roi* (Paris, 1862); from Dr. Débrou's essay "Comment les médecins soignaient la santé des rois de France," *Mémoires de la société d'agriculture et science d'Orléans,* vol. XXXIX, (1899); and from Th. David, *Les Dents de Louis XIV* (Paris, 1887). It is time that someone equipped with modern medical and dental understandings reexamine the evidence. Dr. Débrou's medicine was probably closer to d'Aquin's than to ours today.

34. B.N., ms. franç. 10265, *passim*.

35. *Journal de la Santé du roi,* p. 163.

36. *Journal de la Santé du roi,* p. 174. See also Langlois' *Lettres,* vol. III, *passim*.

37. B.N., ms. franç., 7659, fols. 60, 67.
38. Dr. Débrou, *op. cit.*, p. 67.

IV

23. THE CULT OF THE KING

* The best way to get an understanding of the development of the new *mystique* of royalty at the climax of the period when kings ruled by divine right is to read through the mass of contemporary material that flooded from the presses of France. The B.N. has hundreds of these items listed under the L 37 b 3700–4100 series. They range from items like the *Explication du feu d'Artifice dressé devant l'Hôtel de Ville par ordres de Ms. Les Prévosts des Marchands et Echevins, pour la naissance du Prince que nous vient de donner Mme. la Dauphine* (1682) [L 37 b 3768], and *Explication des figures de grand feu. Tiré devant le Louvre sur la Rivière de Seine le jour de St. Jean, 25 Août* [L 37 b 3776], to *Éloge du Roi pour les Prières de Quarante heures prononcé en l'église Royal de Sainte Oportune par Monsieur Mace* (Paris, 1692) [L 37 b 4005], or *Le Parfait monarque ou les augustes charactères et héroiques vertues de Louis le Grand, appliquées à l'histoire de sa Majesté prouvées par les poètes, vérifiées par l'Écriture* . . . par M. Espitalier (Chartres, 1697) [L 37 b 4112] and *Panégyrique de Louis le Grand en forme de thèse théologique, Juin 1685*, par Philibert Madon [L 37 b 3868]. It would be useless to give more titles, and yet without sampling deeply into this material, it is easy to miss the assumptions of the men who wrote these pieces and to make the mistake of crediting to them ideas and beliefs of later secular eras. This literature not only gives insight into assumptions but also is one of the best windows to the psychology, attitudes, and public commitments of these people; out of it emerges my thesis that the deification of the person of the king in this theocentric era was accomplished in much the same way and with the same intentions that secular societies of the nineteenth and twentieth centuries have deified the state. In the past this material has been too often dismissed as simple toadying to the enormous egotism of the king; students will be able to find in it many other things once they disabuse themselves of the idea that it was merely the work of literary valets who cannot be taken seriously.

1. Kongehusets Arkiv, Denmark, Christian V breve Kronprins *Frederik [IV] 1690-erne;* B.N. ms. franç., 6679, fols. *55ff.*

2. There are so many books on Versailles, that it is not profitable to cite any one of them. The drawings mentioned are to be found in the B.N., Cab. d. E., HC-17.

3. A.N., series O-1 Register of the secretaries of state; for the *Bâtiments* see Jules Guiffrey (ed.), *Comptes des Bâtiments du Roi sous Louis XIV,* 5 vols. (Paris, 1881–1901).

4. A.N. "Régistre où sont écrits les ordres que le roi a donné à M. Mansard . . . ," O1-1474.

5. Madame de Montespan's first and only child by Monsieur de Montespan. Louis paid no attention to him until after Madame de Montespan's death.

6. This suggests that the professional personnel of the *Bâtiments* had more freedom under d'Antin than under Mansard. The king's influence surely did not change. *Mémoires de duc d'Antin* (Paris, 1821), pp. 70ff.

7. *Dictionnaire Historique* (Paris, 1820), Louis XIV.

8. B.N., Cab, d. E., Ve 1318 Rés. It has been printed in B. Champigneulle, *Mémoires de Louis XIV et divers écrits* (Paris, 1960), pp. 227–33.

9. Louis Réau, *Le rayonnement de Paris au XVIII Siècle,* Paris, 1946.

10. B.N., ms. franç. 6759, January–April, 1686.

11. There are many records of these offices from which interesting studies in social structure could be distilled. Cf. B.N., ms. franç. 7659, 7688; ms. Clair. 814, fols. 177–267; A.N. O1-715, 176; KK 2041; and many others. There are also annual printed lists of the royal households.

12. There is need for a good study of the royal households and there is a mass of manuscript material available. A.N., O1-23, fols. 327ff.; K-1198; B.N., ms. Clair., 499, fols. 393–453.

13. While conducting, as was his custom, by tapping a heavy staff on the floor, he smashed his toe, and the infection that followed took his life.

14. The LeBrun exhibition at Versailles in 1963 was an imposing display of the master's skill and artistry.

15. Voltaire's letter to Mylord Hervey quoted in *Dictionnaire Historique, Louis XIV.*

16. Molière's charming poem *Remerciement au roi* is delightful evidence of the esteem that this critic of manners and morals had for Louis. No doubt it was conditioned by the king's favor, and yet it has a valid ring.

17. Cf. Book II, ch. 16, *passim.*

18. B.N., ms. franç. 10265, fol. 70.

19. Louis IV, *Œuvres,* vol. I, p. 201.

20. These were elaborate tableaus made of wood, metal, and papier mâché, representing gods, heroes, mythological creatures, fauna, and flora in an architectural setting; the tableaus were theatrical in organization, to dramatize or recognize some event. The final act usually included fireworks. The B.N. has hundreds of pamphlets describing these *feux d'artifice.*

21. *s.d., c.* 1670, Paris.

22. Abbé de Drubec, *Oraison Funèbre* (September 1, 1667).

23. De la Serre, *Les maximes politiques de Tacite ou la conduite des gens de cour,* vol. I (Paris, 1664), pp. 7, 25, *passim.*

24. De Montmeran, *Le Temple* (Paris, 1661), pp. 1, 2, 43, 45, 60, 65, *passim.*

25. Caption on a picture of the dauphin and the Duke of Anjou (Louis' two sons) *c.* 1671, B.N., Cab. d. E., a22.

26. *Panégyrique du Roy,* 15 septembre (Caen, 1685), B.N.

27. M. Mace, *Éloge du roy pour prières de Quarante heurs* (Paris, 1692).

28. C. Perrault, de l'académie française, *Le bouquet des Dieux pour la naissance de Msg, le d. de. B.* (Paris, *s.d., c.* 1681.)

29. M. Vertron, *Parallèle de Louis le Grand avec les Princes qui ont été surnommés Grands (s.d., c. 1680).*

30. *Description des feux d'artifice 'faits à l'honneur du roy à Lille, 1680; Hercule soutenant le ciel; entrée du roy à Valenciennes, 1680; Au Roy; visite du roy à Tournay, 1680;* the B.N. has many more of the same sort. The appearance of ridiculous exaggeration of the *feux d'artifice* is paralleled in the adulations of followers of some twentieth-century dictators who also are trying to justify their power by a certain *mystique.*

31. The birth of the Duke of Burgundy produced a sheaf of such pamphlets. The account of a *feu d'artifice* for that event, *Inscriptions, devices, et l'emblèmes au feu de Jove* (1682), or the *Réjouissances faites dans la Ville de Dijon* (1682), are only samples of this literature. In all of them "the blood of Louis XIV" is identified with the heavens—either with God or Jupiter.

32. Part of this monument is preserved in the Louvre.

33. There are many printed accounts of this event, but the most complete seems to be in the B.N., ms. franç. 16633, fols. 455ff.

34. *Récit de ce qui s'est fait à Caen, 15 septembre 1685* (Caen, 1685); *Panégyrique du roy* (Caen, 1685).

35. *Relation de ce qui s'est passé à l'érection de la statue du roy dans la ville de Poitiers, 25 août 1687* (Poitiers, *s.d.*).

36. *Contrat de la Ville de Paris avec l'Université pour faire un Éloge du roy le 15 mai de chaque année, le jour de l'avènement de sa majesté à la couronne* (Paris, chez F. Leonard, 1685).

37. *Statue de Louis le Grand, placée dans le temple de l'honneur; dessein du feu d'artifice* (Hôtel de Ville, Paris, 1689).

38. *Cérémonies observées pour l'érection de la statue équestre du roy, 1699;*

Le portrait du roy par les inscriptions du piedestal de la statue équestre dans la Place Louis le Grand, 1699.

39. *Nouveau Dictionnaire Historique* (ed. 1804), p. 6. The citation is obviously a paraphrase of a letter from Madame de Maintenon to the Archbishop of Paris, July 28, 1698. "M. de Pontchartrain proposed yesterday that the king demolish all the buildings on this place of the Hôtel Vendôme and rebuild according to a design by Mansard. The king replied that M. de Louvois had done such things in spite of him, that all these gentlemen, the ministers, wish to do things that will bring them honor in the future; they found means of presenting him [Louis] to the public as a lover of all these vanities," Geffroy, vol. I, (Paris, July 28, 1698), p. 308.

24. ONE GOD, ONE KING, ONE LAW

1. In *The Emergence of the Great Powers, 1685–1715* (New York, 1951), I have developed this theme more completely to show how the wars and threats of wars during these years forced all Europe to develop political institutions that could "mobilize" this power. See also my essay "The Emergence of the European States System" in *Chapters in Western Civilization,* vol. I (New York, 1961).

2. Cf. A.N., O-1 series.

3. This material comes from the registers found in the A.N., series O^1-1ff. In these registers we can see much of the daily business of the realm pass in review.

4. In French documents the "*religion, prétendue réformél, R.P.R.*"

5. Jurieu, *Le tableau du Socinianisme* . . . (The Hague, 1690), p. 426.

6. *Œuvres,* V, p. 375; *Lettres de Louis XIV* (1755), pp. 170–71; B.N., ms. franç., 7045, Fonds Colbert, 3242, no. 2.

7. *Traité* (edition of 1670), p. 63.

8. *Ibid.,* p. 74.

9. *Ibid.,* p. 76.

10. *Ibid.,* pp. 66–67.

11. This is exactly what the English did by the "Test Act."

12. *Observations sur les déclarations du roi données à St.-Germain en Laye le 2 avril 1666* . . . (Paris, n.d.), pp. 133; see *Édits, Déclarations et arrests concernants La Religion P. Réformée 1662–1751,* Leon Pilatte, ed. (Paris, 1885).

13. Cited from Vat. Archive, Nunz. di Francia, Vol. CCCXXXII, fol. 64. Georges Guiton, *Le père de la Chaize,* vol. I (Paris, 1958), p. 236.

14. Langlois, *Madame de Maintenon,* p. 44, and *Lettres* (Langlois), vol. III, p. 131.

15. Madame Elizabeth Labrousse, one of the most sensitive and intelligent of the students of this problem, suggested this in a public lecture at the University of Minnesota (spring 1965).

16. Text registered in the *Chambre des Comptes,* A.N., K 120-b no. 16. See also F. Puaux and A. Sabatier, *Études sur la révocation de l'édit de Nantes* (Paris, 1886); O. Douen, *La Révocation de l'édit de Nantes à Paris* (Paris, 1894); and P. Bert, *Histoire de la révocation de l'édit de Nantes à Bordeaux et dans le Bordelais* (Bordeaux, 1908).

17. Le Clerc, de l'Académie Française, *Le Triomphe de la Foy* (1686), B.N., Ye 25851. In the translation, the author hopes that he develops the poet's ideas better than he represents his poetry.

18. Newsletter from Versailles (December 5, 1685, B.N., ms. franç., no. 10265) gives a graphic account.

19. *Entretien d'un Français avec un Hollandois sur les affaires présentes* (Cologne, 1683).

20. *Prédictions sur la destinée de plusieurs princes* (Anvers, 1684).

21. An example of this literature is *Le Prince assis sur une chaise dangereuse* (Cologne, 1689). The Marteau press actually was domiciled in Holland.

22. *La France toujours ambitieuse et toujours perfide* (Ratisbon, 1689) is a good example. The French kings do not keep their word to their neighbors or to their own

subjects, and are willing to ally with the Turk or the devil to achieve their ends; the book hammers this theme for 259 pages to the conclusion that war with France is just and inevitable. The other myth, that the migration wrecked the French economy, is exploded by W. C. Scoville, *The Persecution of the Huguenots and French economic development,* 1680–1720, (Berkeley 1660).

23. Von Schomberg first went to Portugal because he had been sent by Turenne to command the armies of the Portuguese king during the war of liberation against Spain. He was a tough soldier of fortune in the mold of the great captains of the Thirty Years' War.

24. B.N., ms. franç, 6557, fol. 244.

25. A.N. O¹-43, fol. 30.

26. B.N., ms. franç., 6557, fol. 245.

27. The O¹ series shows that these gifts were very frequent following 1686. Examples of gifts to charity hospitals: April 1688 gift of the property left by testament of Sieur de la Quierre for the education of R.P.R. ministers was given to the charity hospital of Châteauneuf; the consistory property of Plessis-Morly to the *hôtel dieu;* the consistory property of Bionne to the general hospital and the *hôtel dieu* of the city of Orléans. A.N. O¹-32 fols. 108, 110, 111.

28. A.N., O¹-32 fol. 143.

29. A.N., O¹-36, fols. 214, 216, 217, 229.

30. A.N., O¹-27, fols. 241–256, 256–262.

31. A.N., Series O¹-27*ff.*

32. A.N. K-121-B, fol. 364.

33. Louis to Philippe, September 6, 1705, A.M.G., Al-1890, fol. 112.

34. Pierre Barbier and France Vernillat published a representative sample of this literature in *Histoire de France par les chansons* (Paris, 1956). Vol. II deals with Mazarin and Louis XIV. However, to get any idea of the extent of this literature one must look up the manuscripts in the B.N. and the B.Maz.; both the number and the several versions of each poem provide insight into the anger that Louis' wars and repressions aroused. A recent study by Lionel Rothkrug, *Opposition to Louis XIV: The Political and Social Origins of the French Enlightenment* (Princeton, 1965), deals with this opposition on a more profound level.

25. A POLICY OF VIOLENCE AND TERROR

1. Madame de Sévigné wrote that Pomponne was dismissed "*because he was* Minister of Foreign Affairs in 1679. He had respect for the powers, and language too humble for a king who was not unfortunate." June 7, 1679. Cf. Rowen, H, "Arnauld de Pomponne, Louis XIV's Moderate Minister," *A.H.R.,* LXI (1956).

2. This thesis is difficult to document; it emerges from my studies, particularly those in the Archives of the War Ministry.

3. Chamlay, *Mémoire sur les événements de 1678 à 1688,* A.M.G., Al-637.

4. Louvois to Louis XIV, September 17, 1679, A.M.G., Al-632.

5. Chamlay, A.M.G. Al-1183.

6. Rousset, discussing this incident, remarks ". . . Twenty years later, as heir to the influence and the hates of William, Heinsius found himself to be the first official of Holland and a chief in the Grand Alliance, it was not on Louvois that he avenged himself . . . it was on Louis XIV and on France. . . ." Rousset, III, p. 211.

7. Louis to Louvois, October 2, 1681; A.M.G. Al-663.

8. Quoted by Rousset, *op. cit.,* vol. III, p. 54.

9. Brandenburg policy is most complex. At one point Frederick William hoped to replace Sweden in the French Alliance system. Cf. Andrew Lossky, *Louis XIV, William III and the Baltic Crisis of 1683* (Los Angeles, 1954); G. Pages, *Le Grand Electeur et Louis XIV* (Paris, 1905); Ferdinand Fehling, *Frankreich und Brandenburg, 1679–1684* (Leipzig, 1906); Wolf, *The Emergence of the Great Powers, 1685–1715* (New York, 1951), Bibliography.

10. Louis to Créqui, April 1682, B.N. ms. Franç. 10265, fols. 22–23.

11. Cf. A.A.E. Turquie, vols. 15 and 16; Hongrie et Transylvanie, vols. 3–7 *passim;* and Pologne, *op. cit.,* pp. 71–73.

12. S.F.N.Gie, "Die Kandidatur Ludwigs XIV bei der Kaiserwahl vom Jahre 1658 mit besonderer Berücksichtigung der Vorgeschichte," *Abhandlungen zur mittleren und neueren Geschichte,* vol. 61 (1916), pp. 1–108.

13. See also quotation from Chamlay's *Mémoire, op. cit.*

14. At one point in Sobieski's career, Louis offered him French nationality and asylum; at another Louis became Godfather to Sobieski's son. A.N., 2039, 5020, (369).

15. Whose lands Louis was holding as a result of the treaty signed by Charles' uncle two decades earlier but never recognized by Charles, the rightful heir.

16. This can only refer to the possibility that France would "save" Germany after the defeat of the imperial army.

17. Chamlay, *Mémoire,* A.M.G. A¹-1183; also cited in Rousset, vol. III, p. 233.

18. *Entretien dans le Royaume des Ténèbres* (1683), pp 18–19.

19. Pierre Pièche, *Oraison funèbre de Marie-Thérèse* (Paris, 1683), pp. 39–40.

20. The policy of bombarding cities to force a foe to yield was a terrorist measure that became popular with many French military theorists during the last two decades of the seventeenth century; Vauban was the only important French soldier to raise his voice against it. Louis unquestionably agreed to these bombardments, whether they were against the "pirate cities" on the African coast, Genoa, or the cities of the Spanish Netherlands. Later when bombs began to fall on French coastal cities, he changed his mind and attempted to persuade his foes to recognize a policy of "open cities."

21. *Osterreich über alles wann es nur will* (1684).

22. Dangeau, May 1685.

23. Gaifer Aga received the King's pardon and concluded a treaty with France ending the depredations on French commerce. B.N., ms. franç. 14118 fols. 117*ff.*

24. B.N., ms. franç., 16633, fols. 389*ff.* and 14117, fols. 754–63.

25. B.N., ms. franç. 14118, fols. 133–73.

26. *Harangue faite à sa Majesté par les Ambassadeurs du roy de Siam,* Paris, January 14, 1687.

27. Louis to d'Arcy, November 8, 1686, quoted by Rousset, vol. IV, p. 28.

28. *Ibid.,* vol. III, p. 287.

29. Every important library in Europe has exemplars of this literature, most of it of little value except as indication of opinion. Much of it is anonymous. A sample might include: *Unvorgreiffliche Bedanken über des Königs in Frankreich gegenwärtige Kriegs-Praeparatorien und Vorhaben* (1680), in which Louis is likened to the Turks; *Entretien d'un François avec un Hollandois sur les affaires présentes* (Cologne, 1683), in which Louis is presented as tricky and dishonest, an ally of the Turks; and *Sighs of Enslaved France* (1686), by a Huguenot author. Pierre Barbier and France Vernillat have published a few of the songs in *Histoire de France par les Chansons* (Paris, 1956), but anyone wanting to see the extent of this literature should consult the manuscript collections in the B.N. and the B.Maz., which have very large collections of them in manuscript.

30. B.Maz., ms. 2165, fol. 212. These translations by the author are more accurate than poetical.

31. *Ibid.,* fol. 260.

32. *Ibid.,* fol. 39.

33. Cf. Commire's amusing *Le Soleil et les grenouilles, addition aux fables de Phèdre, tirée de la bibliothèque de Leyden,* B.N., Yc 10233.

34. B.N., ms. franç. 10265, fols. 98*ff;* a newsletter dated January 9, 1686.

26. DESCENT INTO THE MAELSTROM

1. Cf. Wolf, *The Emergence of the Great Powers, 1685–1715* (New York, 1951).

2. Cf. Ph.D. thesis in University of Minnesota library by Frank R. Place, *French Policy and the Turkish War, 1679–1688;* this is a most interesting account of the problem.

3. The dispatches written by Giradin and Fabre after the death of Guilleragues are most revealing. A.A.E., Turquie, vols. 18–21.

4. The emperor elect.

5. Janine Foyard, "Les tentatives de constitution d'un 'Tiers party' en allemagne de nord (1690–1694)," *Rev. D'Hist. Dipl.,* 79th year (Oct.-Dec., 1965), pp. 338*ff.*

6. John T. O'Connor, Ph.D. thesis, *William Egon von Fürstenberg and French Diplomacy in the Rhineland Prior to the Outbreak of the War of the League of Augsburg in 1688* (University of Minnesota, 1965), p. 132. See also R. Fester, *Die Augsburger Allianz von 1686* (Munich, 1893).

7. Note: It is most curious to note that with the emperor, Frederick William talked only about French aggression, but with William of Orange he revealed his deeper fears of a "Catholic League" in which France might have a leading part. Frederick William died before the storm broke in 1688 revealing the fact that religion had little or nothing to do with the political structure of the period.

8. O'Connor, *op. cit.,* p. 152.

9. Max Immich, *Zur Vorgeschichte des Orleansschen Krieges,* (Heidelberg, 1898), is still a valuable account of this problem.

10. There is a large literature on this problem; the most recent study, and the only one that has extensively used the archives of Paris, Rome, and Vienna, is John T. O'Connor's Ph.D. thesis, *op. cit.* It also has the most complete bibliography.

11. It was at this point that Villars appears in Munich as Louis' agent and joins the elector in the campaign in Hungary, but Villars was unable to detach Max from the circle of Louis' foes. Cf. *Mémoires du Maréchal de Villars* (Paris, 1884), vol. I.

12. Ranuzzi to Casoni, January 19, 1688, Vat Arch. *Avvisi.* vol. 179a, fol. 90. Quoted by O'Connor, *op. cit.* p. 210.

13. The excommunications are discussed by Jean Orcibal, *Louis XIV contre Innocent XI, les appels au futur concile de 1688 et l'opinion française* (Paris, 1949).

14. Quoted by O'Connor, *op. cit.,* from Vat. Arch., Nunz di Francia, vol. 177, fol. 444.

15. But Louvois made two mistakes: he refused to allow the traditional musket to be replaced by the fusil; and although the bayonet was introduced, it did not completely displace the pike. The German armies in Hungary were more advanced.

16. See Rousset, vol. III, pp. 288–349. See also the A[1] series in the A.M.G. for the 80s. Much of this material is very difficult to use because Louvois' hand-writing is often unclear.

17. Cf. Wolf, *op. cit.,* ch. II.

18. Louis' famous letter to his ambassador in Constantinople on the eve of the war is striking evidence of his point of view. He was willing to urge, even to en-courage, Turkish military action, but he wanted nothing "on paper" to connect him with this action (cf. Wolf, *op. cit.,* p. 34). Villars's *Mémoires* provides evidence on the problem of the declaration of war. After discussing the probability of an invasion of England by the Prince of Orange and the importance of the Turkish war, he writes: "The Court was quite undecided which gambit it would be best to take; to support James about to be attacked or to prevent the Turks from making the peace that seemed about to be concluded, and which the next moment would bring down on us all the forces of the Emperor and Empire; upon his return from Forges, where he had been for several days to take the waters, M. de Louvois decided upon the second gambit . . . nothing was more important for us than to make a diversion to keep the Turks in the war. . . ." (Villars, *Mémoires, op. cit.* vol. I, p. 101). Villars should have known, for he had been a French agent attached to the imperial army in Hungary and undoubtedly was kept *au courant* of the affair. His crediting Louvois with the decision is more or less confirmed by the evidence in the War Archives and fully accepted by Rousset, vol. IV, ch. X. In other words, Louis accepted his ministers' recommendations; he did not form the policy.

19. The introductory statement of *Mémoire des Raisons* by which Louis explained his action is revealing: "Those who will examine the conduct of His Majesty since the outbreak of the war in Hungary without passion and with no other interest than the public good will have good reason to be astonished since, even though he was alert to the Emperor's long established plans to attack France as soon as he could have peace with the Turks, His Majesty has waited until this hour to prevent this, and far from using the pretexts that the rules of good policy would suggest to him for checking the aggrandizement of that prince, he has even been willing to sacrifice for the good of peace, the just reasons that they have so often given him for employing the forces that God has put in his hands as much to take from the Court at Vienna the means of harming him as to check the injustices and violent usurpations of the Elector Palatine . . . and to dissipate quickly the leagues and preparations for war, that have finally forced him to take up arms on the banks of the Rhine and to attack the fortifications which would give the Emperor easy possibility to recommence and sustain war against France. . . ." The *Mémoire* is a long one listing all of Louis' grievances and demands. The entire document is to be found in B.N., *Recueil Cangé,* vol. 33, fols. 174–81.

27. THE FIRST WORLD WAR: LOUVOIS

1. Dangeau, *op. cit.,* September 22, 1688.

2. The count of Turn und Taxis, who came to Versailles to announce the victory that the dauphine's brother had won at Belgrade, was coolly received in France even though the emperor sent him to "announce a victory for Christendom," (*Gazette,* 1688), pp. 480, 491, 526.

3. One of my students, Mr. Ronald Ferguson, is just finishing a Ph.D. thesis on this problem of "contributions." It will be available in the University of Minnesota Library probably under the title, *Blood and Fire: Contribution Policy of the French Army, 1668–1715.* He has told a most interesting story largely taken from National Archives and the A-1 series in the Archives of the French Ministry of War.

4. These letters are in A.M.G., Al-824.

5. Louvois to Saint Pouenges, October 23, 1688, A.M.G., Al-824. There are numerous letters of this sort.

6. Sévigné, *op. cit.,* December 1, 1688.

7. *Quelques lettres de Louis XIV* (Paris, 1862), p. 10.

8. Louvois to Boufflers, November 7 and 14, 1688, A.M.G., Al-824.

9. A.M.G., Al-824, no. 217.

10. A.M.G., Al-871, fols. 175ff.

11. A.M.G., Al-871, fols. 177, 192.

12. A.M.G., Al-871, fols, 209–382.

13. A.M.G., Al-872, fols. 27, 39, 40.

14. A.M.G., Al-876, *passim.*

15. Hubert Gillot, *Le règne de Louis XIV et l'opinion publique en Allemagne* (Paris, 1914). Gillot points out that the Germans called the French *Huns* in 1689. For a more recent study, cf. Kleyser, Fr., *Der Flugschriften Kampf gegen Ludwig XIV zur Zeit des Pfaltzischen Krieges,* (Munich, 1935).

16. A.M.G., Series A¹, pp. 871, 872.

17. Cf. Wolf, *op. cit.,* pp. 103–20.

18. A.M.G., Al-937 and 938.

19. Louvois to Luxembourg, July 4, 1690, A.M.G., Al-938.

20. Louvois to Luxembourg, July 23 and 31, A.M.G., Al-938. The "events in Ireland" were the battle of the Boyne and James's subsequent flight from the island. The battle was hardly more than a skirmish, but it ended the chances of James' holding Ireland as well as the life of Marshal Schomberg who has played an important role in this story.

21. A.M.G., Al-956, fol. 186.

22. *Explication du feu d'artifice dressé devant l'Hôtel de Ville* . . . *le 25 Avril 1691*, executed by Sieur Dumesnil and Sieur Caresme (Paris, 1691)..

23. Rousset, IV, pp. 468–69.

24. A.M.G., Al-1030–1060, particularly 1047, 1089, 1977.

25. Quoted from A.M.G., Al-1033, by Rousset, IV, pp. 497–98.

26. This army was standard for Europe until the French Revolution.

27. When Louvois' body was moved from the Invalides to his tomb at the Capucin's, Plâce Vendome, at midnight April 16, 1699, Louis is supposed to have remarked, "C'était un homme insupportable." Madame de Maintenon called him ". . . a rude, hard man, attached to the King and the State, but presumptuous and so contrary that he became insupportable to his master . . . he would have slipped into disgrace without the war." *Lettres* (Langlois, ed.), V, pp. 407–08.

28. THE FIRST WORLD WAR: LOUIS

1. We have met this interesting man earlier. His papers and letters bulk large in the Archives of the Ministry of War, but outside of a little, quite unimpressive account by A. de Boislisle, *Le Marquis de Chamlay* (Paris, 1877), there is practically nothing written about him. His papers, of course, have been used by historians, but even so they have not been exploited as effectively as they merit.

2. A letter from Louis to the Archbishop of Reims, Barbézieux's uncle, should be quoted in part: "I know well what I owe to the memory of M. de Louvois, but if your nephew does not change, I will be forced to take action. I will be hurt if I have to do so. He has talents, but he does not make good use of them. He too often gives parties to the princes in place of working, he neglects business for his pleasures, he makes officers wait too long in his antechamber, and speaks to them with arrogance and harshness . . ." (*Œuvres*, vol. IV, p. 24).

3. A.A.E., Rome, 341, fols. 126–31.

4. Cf. A. Legrelle, *Notes et documents sur la paix de Ryswick* (Lille, 1894), pp. 9–17.

5. A.M.G., Al-1060, *passim*.

6. Cf. A.M.G., Al-1089. Throughout the A.M.G. series, Al, we find this concern; see also many letters in *Œuvres* dealing with discipline.

7. Cf. the letters of the king in A.M.G., Al-1052, 1060, 1089, 1104, 1105. See also Boufflers' account of the lines from Lille to Ypres and the accompanying map, A.M.G., Al-1052 (Nov. 25, 1691). Pieter Geyl found that the frontier between the Spanish Netherlands and the United Provinces was drawn by the military facts of the revolt. In this case, however, the rivers, rather than tactics, made the military solution a natural process. Only along the Rhine could a river clearly define the frontier of France; the new structure of warfare, however, made the line possible.

8. A.M.G., Al-1052 (Dec. 2–Dec. 18, 1691).

9. Vauban had just been made a lieutenant general, but he was out-ranked by other lieutenant generals with earlier commissions and by the marshals of France.

10. *Lettres* (Langlois, ed.), vol. IV, p. 725*ff; Gazette* (Paris, 1692), pp. 251–314.

11. *Quelques Lettres de Louis XIV* (1862), p. 23.

12. A.M.G., Al-1143, 1204. De la Roncière, *Histoire de la Marine*, vol. V (Paris, 1932); Toudouze, *La Bataille de la Hougue* (Paris, 1899). See also Wolf, *op. cit.*, pp. 45*ff.*, and its bibliography on naval affairs. Since Louis was never deeply interested in the navy, its story is largely neglected in this volume. The works of René Mémain give an indication of the possibilities for further research.

13. A.M.G., Al-1142. The letters between Louis and Luxembourg are most interesting evidence of Louis' willingness to accept a battle when he trusted his general. They are much more aggressive than Louvois' letters had usually been.

14. The pike had been the "queen of the battlefield" over a century earlier and the "thrust of the pike" was a decisive factor. But the development of firearms gradually outmoded this famous weapon. By the late seventeenth century, pikemen

were simply defenders of the musketmen against hostile cavalry; there was no one on the battlefield less dangerous than the pikeman, who had to stand and be killed by bullets while he waited for someone to attack his pike. The battle of Steinkirke was one of the last battles in western Europe in which pikemen were still in the battle line.

15. A.M.G., Al-1143, no. 88.

16. A.M.G., Al-1144 (August 1692). This exchange of letters shows Louis supporting his adviser in Versailles against the commander in the field. His insistence was never peremptory, but it remained firm.

17. Cf. Wolf, *op. cit.,* pp. 170–97.

18. A.M.G., Al-1219, May 15, 1693.

19. A.M.G., Al-1219, May 15 and June 10, 1693.

20. Saint-Simon, *Mémoires* (Boislisle, ed.), vol. XXVIII, pp. 20*ff.*

21. A.M.G., Al-1201, June 2, 1693.

22. Fagon in *Journal de la Santé du Roi* (Paris, 1862), pp. 205–06, tells of an attack of "rheumatism in the neck" that started the last of May—after a bleeding, the king suffered "vapeurs . . . [and] indisposition for the rest of the voyage." He suggests that the return to Versailles was caused by this illness. Madame de Maintenon, however, writes "The King is well, I am delighted that interests of state have forced him to return to Versailles." Lavellé, *Lettres historiques,* vol. I, 1856, p. 302.

23. A.M.G., Al-1219, June 10, 1693.

24. The dauphin kept Madame de Maintenon informed about the campaign, obviously as a channel to his father. Before he arrived in Germany with the detachment (July 2), "I pride myself that when I will have joined Marshal de Lorge I will carry out the King's projects and that he will have reason to be pleased with me." July 8: the dauphin hopes that "I will find some opportunity to merit the esteem of the King and to do something that will be useful to the good of the State." August 17: after she tells him that the king understands why he did not attack the Prince of Baden, "You could not give me greater pleasure than to write to me that the King is satisfied with me and understands. . . ." *Lettres de Louis XIV, Mgr. le Dauphin . . . à Madame de Maintenon* (Paris, 1822), pp. 25–33.

25. A.M.G., Al-1219, September 2. Father de Loinnière, who also saw the dauphin's campaign bog down before Heilbronn, explained the problems in terms of German valor and skill. "It must be admitted," he wrote, "that the Germans have always been regarded as an invincible people. The Romans . . . after having triumphed over the most powerful peoples of the world, had the shame of fleeing from this redoubtable nation. . . . Today they are even more redoubtable than formerly, since the war that they have so long sustained against the Turks, has given them the opportunity to join to their valor a vast military experience. . . ." (Abbé de Loinnière, *Panégyrique ou Portrait de M. de Dauphin,* 1693). Louis' own estimate of the Germans—"the caterpillars"—was somewhat less flattering, but the failure of his armies must have given him pause. Unhappily we have no indication of his feelings about it at this moment.

26. These letters are to be found in A.M.G., Al-1201, 1205, 1206.

27. These letters are in A.M.G., Al-1201 and 1208.

28. A.M.G., Al-1220, September 26, 1693.

29. A.M.G., Al-1220, September 26-October 13, 1693.

30. A.A.E., Spain, 76, fol. 186*ff;* Rome, 358, *passim.*

31. A. Legrelle, *op. cit.,* pp. 181*ff;* A.A.E., Rome, 358, fol. 226.

32. *Œuvres,* vol. IV, pp. 415–16.

33. *Lettres* (Langlois), vol. IV, no. 814, Oct. 14, 1693.

34. A.M.G., Al-1256, 1257.

35. A.M.G., Al-1257 (July 23, 1694). The dauphin continued to write to Madame de Maintenon. July 19: "I am delighted that one [the king] is satisfied with me; my only ambition is to find means of pleasing the King." August 5: "I can assure you that no matter how much I wish to acquire fame, I will never order anything . . . without hope of success. . . ." August 25, after telling of outmaneuvering

the Prince of Orange: "I compliment myself that the King will be satisfied with us. . . ." *Lettres de Louis XIV, Mgr. le Dauphin . . . à Madame de Maintenon,* pp. 35–42.

36. A.M.G., Al-1259, no. 10. Not all the intelligence reports were immediately available. There is an amusing letter from Louis to Vauban, July 8, 1694, in which, after thanking Vauban for the pamphlets that he has sent, Louis adds that he had not replied earlier "because I wished to know what these pamphlets contained, but I have not yet found anyone who understands Flemish well enough to translate them." A.M.G., A-1 1257, fol. 49. Obviously there is place for a study of the intelligence services of these armies.

37. A.M.G., Al-1271, August 28, 1694.

38. A.M.G., Al-1258, 1259, 1089, *passim;* and *Œuvres,* vol. IV, pp. 450–58.

39. *La politique françoise demasquée* (Utrecht, 1695), pp. 2–3. This was only one of many such broadsides. Some of them take the form of conversations between the dead. In *Le triomphe de la Ligue, ou La France à la veille de Soucrier à la Paix* (dated Paris, 1694 [sic], but probably printed in Holland), Innocent XI and Mazarin meet in hell and discuss religion, war, and politics. Mazarin is revealed as a wicked Machiavellian hated in France and the world; Innocent as a bad Catholic; but Louis XIV emerges as the villain with his confessor de la Chaise and Madame de Maintenon as evil spirits.

40. *Gazette* (1694), p. 395, A.M.G., Al-1259.

41. A.M.G., Al-1326, no. 1.

42. A.M.G., Al-1236, nos. 87, 117, *passim.*

43. A.A.E., Turquie, 25, 26, 27, 28. These papers are very revealing of the political structure in the Near East as well as of Louis' propaganda offensive. They should be studied by scholars interested in the problems of Persia, Russia, and the Levant.

44. A.M.G., Al-1326, fol. 44*ff.*

45. A.M.G., Al-1326, fol. 180*ff.*

46. A *chamade* was a specific drum beat to call a fortress to surrender.

47. A.M.G., Al-1372, July 1, 1696, fol. 4*ff.* 11.

48. Legrelle, *op. cit.,* has examined the complex negotiations in the A.A.E., Turin vols. 95 and 96. When these are added to the documents in the A.M.G., Al-1326, 1327, 1330, 1370, 1371, 1372, the French side of the negotiations become clear.

49. A.M.G., Al-1309, nos. 81, 131.

50. A.M.G., Al-1310, nos. 37, 38, 39, 54, 55, 64, 93, 100, 110, 136, 155.

51. A.M.G., Al-1312, fol. 71–72.

52. The bombardment was a savage affair. Red hot bombs systematically set fire to one section of the city after another, forcing the inhabitants to flee and allowing no let-up to check the blaze. *Relation ou description du bombardement de Brusselles . . . August 16, 1695,* B.N., ms. franç., 18,540, no. 15. Louis was well pleased with the action, especially since Villeroi retired without loss of any of his guns. A.M.G., Al-1312, nos. 133, 181; Al-1313, 55, 106.

53. These documents are in A.M.G., Al-1313, nos. 53, 119, Al-1314, nos. 4–22. Boufflers' defense of Namur establishes his reputation as a commander who understood the art of defense. Without a visit to the city of Namur it is almost impossible to understand the problems involved in besieging the fortification. The rivers strictly limit the attacking forces to a small front, and even there, the rocky ground and the sharp upward slope of the terrain give great advantages to the defenders.

54. A.M.G., Al-1356, fol. 221, is a long letter to Villeroi discussing all possible gambits and reiterating the need of defense action. This defensive posture did not prevent him from being happy when a skirmish turned to his army's advantage. "I believe that you will not be angry to hear the news that I just received," he wrote to Madame de Maintenon; "M. de Vendôme with 1.200 cavalry has just defeated the German cavalry to the number of 4,500. . . . The one unfortunate thing was that Longueval was killed" *Lettres* (Langlois), vol. IV, p. 68.

55. Most of the documents for these negotiations are to be found in A.A.E., Hollande, 162, 163.

56. Legrelle, *Notes et documents sur la Paix de Ryswick* (Lille, 1894), p. 55ff. A.A.E., Hollande, 163, May 3 and May 13, 1696.

57. The answer to Legrelle's question about the whereabouts of the letters that Louis sent to Boufflers in response to his first contacts with Mylord Portland (Beinting) can be cleared up (Legrelle, *Notes. . . . sur la Paix de Ryswick op. cit.*, p. 88). They are bound in A.M.G., Al-1357, and dated July 12 and July 16, 1696. Somehow these copies of the letters sent to Boufflers were misdated and therefore bound with the letters of the preceding year. The letter of July 12 is almost word for word the same as the letter dispatched to the plenipotentiaries at Ryswick the preceding day. A.A.E., Hollande, 168, July 11, 1697. I have no idea where or how \Grimblot found these two letters for his *Letters of William III and Louis XIV and of Their Ministers* (London, 1848).

58. Cf. Wolf, *op. cit.*, pp. 49–53.

59. *Quelques Lettres de Louis XIV;* Louis to Governor of Berry, p. 24, Lb37–4534.

60. *Lettre du roy à M. l'Archevêque de Paris, 12 novembre 1697* (Paris, 1697); *Dessein du feu d'artifice, 16 novembre 1697* (Paris, 1697).

61. *Quelques Lettres de Louis XIV*, pp. 27–28; Lb37–4534.

62. A striking example of this self-deception is to be found in the correspondence between Louis and his agents in Constantinople in which he consistently projects upon the emperor his own feelings of guilt for his association with the Turks. A.A.E., Turquie, 28, 30, *passim*. Perhaps this self-deception was augmented by the unrealistic words of many about him; for example Monsieur Vittement, rector of the University of Paris, lectured before the king, praising him for making peace "in the midst of victories" and for not being like other princes "insensible to the tears of their subjects" and only "making peace when all other resources are gone."

63. Cf. Wolf, *op. cit.*, for an analysis of these treaties and insight into the emerging balance of power in Europe.

V

29. THE SPANISH INHERITANCE

* The partition treaties have been the subject of much research. The most important study of the French side of these negotiations is A. Legrelle, *La diplomatie française et la succession d'Espagne,* 6 vols. (Paris, 1895–99). I have relied heavily upon this work, but I did check the critical documents in the Archives of the Ministry of War and of Foreign Affairs. For a short concise account, see M. A. Thomson, "Louis XIV and the Origins of the War of the Spanish Succession," *Transactions of the Royal Historical Society,* series V, vol. IV, pp. 111–33.

1. Wolf, *The Emergence of the Great Powers 1685–1715* (New York, 1951) pp. 49–53.

2. "Relation de ce qui s'est passé dans la visite que M. de Pomponne et M. de Torcy ont rendue à Mylord Portland par ordre de sa majesté," A.A.E., Angleterre, 174, 82–92.

3. A.A.E., Angleterre, 176, Louis to Tallard, July 15, 1698.

4. Naturally the charge of "poison" was heard when Joseph Ferdinand died, but all indications are that his death was "natural." This was an era when half the children born did not reach twenty years of age.

5. Cf. Legrelle, vols. II and III.

6. *Ibid.,* vol. IV, p. 141.

7. Louis to Villars, October 20, 1700, A.A.E., Autriche, vol. 175. A "third prince" might be the Duke of Orleans or the Duke of Savoy.

8. A.A.E., Turquie, vol. 33, Louis to Monsieur de Ferriol, November 1, 1700.

9. The Marquis de Sourches (Chamillart?) writes of the council of November 11, 1700, "This was the council in which the King wished to stand by his word in the succession treaty. Monseigneur stubbornly insisted that he ought to accept the crown of Spain for the Duke of Anjou, and maintained it so strongly that the King finally gave in."

10. A.A.E., Holland, vol. 190, Louis to Briord, November 10, 1700.

11. Cf. Legrelle, vol. IV, ch. 5.

12. Both before and after the decision to accept the throne, the French discussed the question in pamphlets and books. For obvious reasons the overwhelming bulk of this literature favored the acceptance of the throne. Much of this literature was probably "inspired," or at least encouraged, by the court. In 1699 a book that had been first published in 1666 written by George d'Aubusson, argued that the fundamental laws of Spain demanded the Bourbon succession, that the Spanish would not object to a foreign prince, issue of a princess, for "the laws of the kingdom . . . declared the crown hereditary for the Infantas in case of a failure to produce an Infant." *Défense du droit de Marie-Thérèse d'Autriche . . . à la succession des couronnes d'Espagne* (1666 and 1699). The B.N. has a large collection of the pamphlets indicating that the French were also well aware of the pieces published in England and the Netherlands. The following titles are only a small sample: *Réponse aux libelles répandus dans le public au sujet de la succession de la Monarchie d'Espagne* (s.d. probably 1701); *Réflexions sur les mouvements de l'Empereur au sujet de la succession d'un prince français à la Monarchie d'Espagne avec une démonstration de la nullité de ses prétentions sur l'Espagne, Milan et les Pays Bas* (Mons, 1701); *Examen de deux grandes questions: la première ce que le roi de France fera au sujet de la Monarchie d'Espagne; la seconde quelles mesures doit prendre l'Angleterre*, trans. from English (London, 1701)—the writer was alarmed at the rise of French power and feared for the balance of power that assures peace and justice; *Remarques sur la Succession du duc d'Anjou*, trans. from English (London, 1701)—a legal and historical argument showing that Louis was wrong to accept the throne; *Réflections sur divers écrits concernant la succession à la Monarchie d'Espagne* (Ville France, n.d.) also argues that the decision was morally, legally, and politically wrong. Louis probably never heard of any of these or the scores of other such documents, so we shall not bother to look at them in any detail.

30. THE WAR OF THE TWO CROWNS: FIRST PHASE

1. *Lettres* (Langlois) vol. V, no. 1400.

2. *Ibid.,* vol. V, no. 1405.

3. See Wolf, *op. cit.,* pp. 54–59, for a discussion of the problems created by this War of the North and the subsequent organization of European balances of power.

4. *Gazette* (September 24, 1701), pp 454ff.

5. A.N., K–121B, fols. 35ff.

6. *Gazette* (July 23, 1701).

7. Louis to Vaudémont, July 17, 1701, A.M.G., Al-1515.

8. Louis' letter to Villeroi on August 4, 1701 (A.M.G., Al-1485), speaks of a letter from the Prince de Vaudémont telling of the progress of the enemy and the indecisiveness of the French. He went on to say that with 40 squadrons and 20 battalions, "I cannot accommodate myself to M. de Catinat's slowness . . . if he had chosen his tactics well, the war would not be in the middle of Italy. . . . I believe that it is to the good of my service to send you to command my troops. You know how important it is for the beginning of a campaign to be fortunate, and that the solutions in Italy depend upon the duration or the end of the war. I will leave M. de Catinat with you. I am convinced that with a body of troops so superior as the ones that I have in that land, you will not miss any occasion to act. . . . Come to me at Marly . . . it is of greatest importance that I give you instructions. . . ." The instructions were to seek out and fight Eugene. Leaving Catinat with the army is also

typical of Louis' action: he liked to have a second officer capable of commanding the army on a field where a battle might be fought, in case the first should be killed.

When Eugene had asked to be allowed to be a soldier, Louis insisted that he should become a priest; his nickname at Versailles was "the little abbé"; events were to change it simply to "Eugene."

9. A.M.G., Al-1515 no. 123–24, A1511, September 2, 1701.

10. A.M.G., Al-1507, September 11, 1701.

11. These Chiari letters are scattered through A.M.G. Al-1507, 1511, and 1516. Catinat must have felt justified for his caution as he read the king's letters.

12. A.M.G., Al-1507, September 22, 28, October 19, November 12.

13. On February 13, Louis wrote to Villeroi in prison, "My cousin, I would desire nothing more for the glory of my troops and my own satisfaction than to have you share the honor that they have earned by the defense of Cremona. I am touched by your fate. You know for a long time the friendship that I have had for you; it will not diminish by your absence and I will never forget that which you have a right to expect from a good master. . . . I pray God . . . ," etc. (Boislisle, ed. *Saint Simon,* vol. X, p. 471). Villeroi was ransomed the next year for 50,000 livres. This may well be the highest ransom ever paid up to that time.

14. *Gazette* (April 1, 1702).

15. These letters are in A.M.G., Al-1555.

16. See A.M.G., Al-1556, especially fol. 75.

17. *Ibid.,* and Al-1557, fols. 115, 116.

18. A.M.G., Al-1557, fols. 134, 176, 199.

19. A.M.G., Al-1582, *passim.* Louis' correspondence would indicate that he was much less interested in this theater of the war than in the struggle for the lower Rhine or Italy. His contempt for the German soldiers was not completely realistic.

20. A.M.G., Al-1556, fol. 291; 1557, fol. 78.

21. *Lettres* (Langlois ed.), *op. cit.,* vol. V, no. 1398.

22. A. Baudrillart, *Philippe V et le cour de France* (Paris, 1890) vol. I, pp. 85–86. This famous book is still much worth reading; its findings have passed into the literature.

23. Villars, *Mémoires,* vol. II, p. 48.

24. A.M.G., Al-1667, fol. 189.

25. A.M.G., Al-1639, fol. 46; 1675, fol. 85.

26. A.M.G., Al-1675, fols. 133, 154.

27. A.A.E., France, 310, fol. 146.

28. A.M.G., Al-1676, *passim.* See particularly no. 87, Louis to Villars.

29. A.M.G., Al-1676, 1640, fol. 43, 105*ff.*

30. A.M.G., Al-1677 no. 22, 25, 117, *passim.*

31. A.M.G., Al-1685, no. 118.

32. A.M.G., Al-1686, fol. 26.

33. Comte de Jametel, *Lettres inédites, 1680–1714* (Paris, 1898), no. xxvii.

34. *Œuvres,* vol. IV, pp. 135, 136; A.M.G., Al-1507, 1512, 1513, 1514, 1515. On January 4, 1704, Louis sent a letter to the pope to explain the reasons for his declaration of war on Savoy. This letter, printed in several languages and broadcast over Europe, expresses the king's astonishment and anger at the duke's treason; it also is an excellent example of French propaganda techniques, and corresponds closely enough to Louis' own literary style to make us sure that he at least edited it. *Lettre du Roy au Pape contenant les motifs de la guerre de Savoye* (L 37 b 4237); *Brief von dem König van Vrankryk an den Paus Behelfendende des motiven den Tegenwoordigen Oorlog me Savoyen* (L 37 b 4237 bis.). The propaganda literature of the reign would make an interesting study.

35. A.M.G., Al-1666, fol. 98.

36. A.M.G., Al-1640, fol. 137.

37. A.M.G., Al-1666, fol. 256*ff.*

38. A.M.G., Al-1667, fol. 6.

39. A.M.G., Al-1667, July 29, 1703; order in the hand of the king.

31. FROM BLENHEIM TO OUDENARDE

1. A.A.E., Spain, vol. 147, fol. 61.
2. A.M.G., Al-1749, fols, 197, 211, 218.
3. A.M.G., Al-1749, no. 316.
4. Baron René François Le Gall who had become lieutenant general in 1703.
5. A.M.G., Al-1750, no. 18.
6. A.M.G., Al-1750, no. 89.
7. A.M.G., Al-1750, no. 89, 96, 111.
8. A.M.G., Al-1750, 111, 127.
9. A.M.G., Al-1750, no. 130.
10. A.M.G., Al-1750, no. 131, 134, 138, 1731; fols. 36ff.
11. A.M.G., Al-1751, Louis to Marchin, August 23, 1704.
12. So great was the disorder, that the letter Louis wrote on August 21 to Marchin was never delivered; it returned to the war office unopened. These letters are to be found in A.M.G., Al-1750 and 1751; a few have been published in Louis' Œuvres, vol. IV, pp. 163ff., and in Jametel, Lettres inédites (1898), p. 81ff. His letter to Max Emanuel is quite typical of Louis' efforts to keep good personal relations even though it must have cost him much, for Max was partly responsible for the disaster: "You can be sure," he wrote, "that I will remember all that you have sacrificed to contribute to keeping the crown of Spain on the head of my grandson who is the legitimate owner. . . ." Max's presence with the army in Flanders was destined to cause further problems, for it prevented Louis from using his best general (Villars) there because of the feud between the two men.
13. Villeroi had really been "kidnapped" at Cremona.
14. A.M.G., Al-1751, September 13, 1704, Louis to Marchin.
15. Liste exacte des officiers de Considération fait Prisonniers sur l'Ennemi à la Bataille de Höchstädt (1704). In the B.N.
16. Quelques lettres de Louis XIV (Paris, 1862), pp. 43–44. See also Lettre du roi à M. le Cardinal de Noailles, 17 Septembre 1704 (Paris, 1704), in which Louis ordered Te Deums for the victory.
17. A.M.G., Al-1796 and 1797.
18. A.M.G., Al-1890.
19. A.M.G., Al-1835, no. 20.
20. A.M.G., Al-1828, no. 42–44, passim.
21. A.M.G., Al-1828, nos. 53, 54.
22. A.M.G., Al-1844, no. 172.
23. A.M.G., Al-1829, no. 1, July 9, 1705.
24. A.M.G., Al-1836, Elector of Bavaria to Louis XIV, July 19, 1705.
25. A.M.G., Al-1829, 1836, July 1705.
26. A.M.G., Al-1837, nos. 37, 217.
27. A.M.G., Al-1936, fol. 210. The battlefield of Ramillies today is difficult to untangle since later generations have drained swamps, cut forests, and lost interest in the events of 1706; indeed, the visitor will be told of a little skirmish of 1939 rather than the largest cavalry charge of all times. There is an account and map of the battlefield in the B.N., Ramillies (L 37 b 4307).
28. Louis has been heavily criticized for his faith in Villeroi; the critics expect more from the king than he could do. Villeroi and his father were Louis' close friends, and Louis was not one to break a close friendship. His letter of June 30 answering Villeroi's agreement to wait with the army until the arrival of the Duke of Vendôme is quite in character: "Your letter of the 28th confirms the opinion that I have always had that you would forget yourself if it were for the good of my service. Your presence is necessary in Flanders until the arrival of the Duke of Vendôme. . . . Until then I recommend that you pay attention to everything and give the orders that you believe necessary for the good of my service. . . ." In his heart Louis probably thought that he, rather than either Max or Villeroi, was to

blame; it was God's mysterious will that was being executed, and Villeroi was not responsible for God's decisions. (See A.M.G., Al-1937, no. 63, 139, 270, Al-1933, fol. 50, 78.)

29. A.M.G., Al-1963, fols. 233ff.

30. A.M.G., Al-1933, September 6, 1706.

31. The whole story of Turin unfolds in the two volumes A.M.G., Al-1963–1964.

32. A.M.G., Al-1933, fol. 100.

33. A.M.G., Al-1964, *passim.*

34. A.M.G., Al-2051, fols. 64, 87.

35. Louis to Villars, May 28, 1708, A.M.G., Al-2015, no. 26.

36. A.M.G., Al-2042, no. 1. When Eugene opened his lines around Toulon, Tessé set up his camp so that it was practically impossible for the imperial army to invest the city. Louis was delighted. "I will not tell you what to do," he wrote, "it is up to you to see for yourself what you can do in so difficult a conjuncture in which you will find yourself embarrassed at times . . . but you will cover yourself with honor and *gloire,* if contrary to all expectations, you will be lucky enough to frustrate the enemies' projects." After discussing Tessé's plans, Louis added hopefully, "It will cost them dearly to make themselves masters of that fortification. You should continue to furnish them . . . all the obstacles that your position will allow . . . [your position is the only one] that will oblige them to stay on the Vallette coast without being able entirely to invest Toulon," then went on to tell Tessé that saving Toulon would have an important psychological effect on the army and all France. A.M.G., Al-2042, no. 34.

37. The story unfolds in the documents A.M.G., Al-2041–2042.

38. These letters are most interesting; the conflict between Vendôme and Burgundy that became almost open war after Oudenarde was already a serious affair some time before that battle.

39. A.M.G., Al-2075, July 3, 1708. As the reader already knows, this is typical of Louis' optimism and willingness to deceive himself. Time and again similar patterns emerge.

40. There is an interesting contemporary account of the battle, obviously written by someone with the Anglo-Imperial armies, and yet quite dispassionate. *Relation de la Bataille d'Oudenarde, 11 Juillet 1708* (L 37 b 4331). The list of French officers made captives was—Liste des oficiers [sic] françois qui ont été pris à la Bataille d'Oudenarde le 11 Juillet 1708.

41. A.M.G., Al-2075, July 16, 1708. B.N., ms. franç. 10267; Louis to the Duke of Burgundy, July 18, 1708.

42. A.M.G., Al-2075, July 18, 1708, 25, 27, 30; B.N., ms. franç. 10267, fols. 6–11.

43. A.M.G., Al-2075, August 1, 1708. B.N., ms. franç. 10267, Louis to Duke of Burgundy, July 18, 1708.

44. A.M.G., Al-2075, August 22, 1708, Louis to Burgundy.

45. A.M.G., Al-275, August 22–December 9, 1708; see also B.N., ms. franç., 10267, *passim.*

46. A.M.G., Al-2106, November 26, 1708.

32. THE PEACE THAT FAILED

1. *Relation de ce qui s'est passé en decouverte, descente, et procession de la châsse de Sainte Geneviève faite le seizième mai 1790,* N.A. K 122 fol. 4.

2. The letters are to be found in A.M.G., Al-2083 and 2084.

3. Madame de Maintenon to Madame the Princess des Ursins, December 23, 1708, Geffroy, *op. cit.,* II, p. 185.

4. *Ibid.,* March 18, 1709, pp. 199–200.

5. Berwick, the natural son of James II and Marlborough's sister was the half-brother of the Pretender. Should James Edward come to the throne in England,

Marlborough wanted to be in his good graces; thus we find him at several occasions playing up to the English court in France. These peace probings may also have been related to Marlborough's desire to hold off the French until Eugene could establish his position around Lille.

6. Chamillart revealed the desperate condition of France to the Dutch with the suggestion that they could not afford to allow France to be defeated. He hoped that they would react as they did after 1646 toward Spain.

7. Philippe was not a man of decision, but his wife and the Princess des Ursins pushed him into this stance that saved his kingdom for the Bourbons.

8. A.M.G., Al-2179, nos. 21, 27.

9. A.A.E., Holland 217, fols. 109–60.

10. Geffroy, *op. cit.,* II, p. 185.

11. A.M.G., Al-2146 Louis to Boufflers, January 1, February 15, February 20.

12. Claude C. Sturgill, *Marshal Villars and the War of the Spanish Succession* (Univ. of Kentucky, 1965).

13. A.M.G., Al-2150, nos. 185, 243, 266.

14. A.M.G., Al-2179, Louis to Philippe, June 2, 1709.

15. A.M.G., Al-2151, Louis to Villars, June 9, 1709.

16. B.N., Rés. *Recueil Cange,* XXXVII, 211ff.

17. *Correspondance de Louis XIV avec M. Amelot 1705–1709* Girardot, ed. (1864), pp. 51–52. See also "Appendix" in *Mémoires de M. de . . .* [Colbert de Torcy] *pour servir à l'histoire des négociations depuis le traité de Riswick jusqu'à la paix de Utrecht,* 3 vols. (Paris, 1756–57); English trans. 2 vols. (London, 1757).

18. A.A.E., France 297, fols. 214–15.

19. A.N., KK-1003; A.M.G., Al-2151 and 2152; De Vogüé, *Madame de Maintenon et le Maréchal de Villars, Correspondance inédite* (Paris, 1856).

20. A.M.G., Al-2141, July 1 and 2, 1709, and *passim.* It is interesting to recall that when the French army besieged Tournai in 1667, Louis wrote to d'Humières who was conducting the siege, "Since it is a remarkable action to take the fortress of Tournai, and since it does not matter to take it one day early or one day later, I wish that you shall conserve as much as possible the troops who will attack it. . . ."

21. A.M.G., Al-2151, July 1709, *passim.*

22. These letters are in A.M.G., Al-2151, July; and especially 2152, August.

23. The series of letters between Villars and the king from the middle of August to the battle of Malplaquet is one of the most exciting documentary sequences that an historian will ever find. Reading them is a breathtaking experience (A.M.G., Al-2152).

24. These letters are to be found in A.M.G., Al-2152. Villars' wound did not heal, his fever threatened his life, but he had posted soldiers to shoot anyone who tried to amputate his leg. Louis sent his own physician, Sieur Marchand, to care for him. Red hot irons and Villars' good constitution finally cleaned out the wound and saved the soldier's life.

25. When the Duke of Orléans was in command of Philippe's armies the preceding year, he and several of his "creatures" caused a scandal by talking and plotting for the replacement of Philippe by the Duke of Orléans on the throne. The duke returned to France, but Philippe arrested his companions, and would not give them up at his grandfather's request. The whole affair evaporated after Vendôme's victories of 1710.

26. Louis to Philippe, November 11, 1709, A.M.G., Al-2179.

27. Louis to Philippe, January 4, 1710, A.M.G., Al-2265.

28. Torcy's *Journal (Journal inédit de Jean-Baptiste Colbert Marquis de Torcy . . . pendant les années 1709, 1710 et 1711* [Paris, 1884], p. 322) is most instructive for this period.

29. Torcy, *op. cit.,* p. 177.

30. A.M.G., Al-2215, fols. 111, 114, 128.

31. A.A.E., Holland, 228 (1710–11 sup.), fols. 71–75.

32. A.A.E., Poland, 123 (April–August), 251ff.

33. A.M.G., Al-2256, August 24, 1710.
34. Louis to Villars, July 22, 1710, A.M.G., Al-2216, fol. 83.
35. A.M.G., Al-2216, fol. 83, 2217, fol. 19.
36. A.M.G., Al-2217, fol. 197.
37. A.M.G., Al-2256, December 1710.
38. Torcy, *Journal*, p. 322.
39. Torcy, *Mémoires*.

33. PEACE FOR EUROPE

1. Torcy, *Mémoires*.
2. It is interesting to note that Fénelon, exiled to Cambrai, did not share this point of view. On June 15, 1710, he wrote to the Duke de Chevreuse: ". . . a man who came here from Versailles said that it was reported that the Duke de Bourgogne said to someone, who repeated it to others, that France's present sufferings come from God in expiation for the sins we have committed in the past. If the prince did in fact say this, he was doing less than justice to the king's reputation. Such criticism is a poor way of showing his affection for his grandfather. . . ." (*Correspondance de Fénelon*, ed. by Gosselin and Caron) (Paris, 1820), vol. I, no. 122.
3. Louis to Noailles, January 11, 1711, A.M.G., Al-2330, fol. 21; Louis to Philippe, January 27, 1711, A.M.G., Al-2333, fol. 3.
4. A.M.G., Al-2333, and *passim*.
5. This opinion is based upon both my own studies in the Archives and the considered statement of Legrelle whose knowledge of the Archives of the Ministry of Foreign Affairs for this period has never been exceeded. Cf. Legrelle, vol. VI, p. 359*ff*.
6. A.M.G., Al-2333, no. 38.
7. The negotiations of 1711 between England and France can be found in A.A.E., England, vols. 237 and 238; the best account of the French side is in Legrelle, vol. VI, pp. 5–53.
8. A.M.G., Al-2303, *passim*.
9. A.M.G., Al-2306 (Flanders), 2318 (Alsace), 2325 (Savoy), 2333 (letters of Louis XIV and Philippe V of Spain).
10. Cf. bk. V, ch. 34, p. 110.
11. *Arch. d'Alcala*, I, 2400, quoted by Baudrillart, pp. 469–70. This book is indispensable for the study of Louis' relations with his grandson.
12. Louis to de Bonnac, April 18, 1712 (A.A.E., Spain, 213, fol. 102).
13. April 28, 1712, cited by Baudrillart, *op. cit.*, pp. 480–81.
14. Philippe to Louis, April 22, 1712, signed by his own hand (A.A.E., Spain, 213 fol. 165).
15. A.A.E., Spain, 213, *passim;* see also Legrelle, *op. cit.*, vol. VI; and Baudrillart.
16. Arch d'Alcala, I, 2460; cited in Baudrillart, *op. cit.*, pp. 490–91.
17. Philippe to Louis, May 29, 1712, A.A.E., Spain, 218 fol. 255.
18. Quoted by G. M. Trevelyan, *England Under Queen Anne*, vol. III (London, 1934), p. 216.
19. *Quelques lettres de Louis XIV, op. cit.*, pp. 67–68.
20. De Vogue, *op. cit.*, vol. III, pp. 138*ff*.
21. A.M.G., Al-2380, fol. 62.
22. *Ibid.*, fol. 63.
23. There is an excellent account of this action in Sturgill, *op. cit.*, pp. 112–26.
24. A.M.G., Al-2380, fol. 163.
25. *Ibid.*, fol. 186.
26. *Ibid.*, fol. 246.
27. See A.M.G., Al-2383, 2384, 2385, *passim*.
28. A.M.G., Al-2386, fol. 108.
29. Legrelle, VI, pp. 360–61.

30. Baudrillart, *op. cit.*, pp. 546–47.
31. Torcy, *op. cit.*

34. THE LAST ACT

1. The *Journal de la Santé du Roi* should be studied by someone who understands modern medicine. Most historians do not know what the king's doctors really meant. The present author has his tongue in cheek when he speaks of "humeurs" or "vapeurs" and the like—he really knows nothing about it.

2. A.N., O¹-44, fols. 95, 99–100.

3. A.N., O¹-56, fols. 61*ff.*; O¹, vols. 44–60, and B.N. ms. franç., 6557, *passim*.

4. Madame de Maintenon to the Duke of Noailles, June 9, 1709, Geoffroy, II, p. 209.

5. See *Lettres* (Langlois, ed.), vol. V, *passim*.

6. *Ibid.*, pp. 235, 277, *passim*.

7. Cordelier, *Madame de Maintenon une Femme au Grand Siècle*, Paris, 1955, chap. IX; Louis Hastier, *Louis XIV et Madame de Maintenon*, Paris, 1957, 219*ff.*

8. Langlois' discussion of the problem does not solve it. *Lettres* (Langlois, ed.), vol. V, pp. 447*ff.* For all of Hastier's careful scholarship, his attempt to place the marriage so late does not really come to anything.

9. Geffroy, *op. cit.*, vol. II, pp. 48*ff.*

10. *Ibid.*

11. *Lettres* (Langlois, ed.), vol. V, no. 1420. It is most amusing to see that Madame de Maintenon recognized that in case she should die, the Princess des Ursins might easily have taken her place as wife of the king. In the short time that the princess was at Versailles, she made a great impression on Louis.

12. The little volume *Lettres . . . à Madame de Maintenon* (1822) and the packet in the A.N., K-121A are interesting and instructive.

13. The Duke d'Antin's comment about the court during these years is to the point: "It is only necessary to be happy to have enemies. It is a capital crime to be happy; secrets are rarely guarded, everyone seeks his own advantage; honest men are rare . . . ," etc. *Mémoires du Duc d'Antin* (1821), pp. 75–77.

14. Geffroy, vol. II, p. 126.

15. *Ibid.*, p. 189.

16. Boislisle, *Portraits et Caractères* (Paris, 1897) L 37 b, 5185.

17. A.N., KK-388, May 29, 1702.

18. *Gazette* (1701), pp. 276*ff.* The memoirists all tell the story in more realistic terms.

19. Elizabeth Charlotte came to the conclusion that Madame de Maintenon had spoken to Louis in her favor. It must have cost her much to write to the lady whom she usually called "the old wasp" or worse, in these terms: "If I had not had the vapeurs and fever, Madame, from the sad occupation of opening Monsieur's chests, perfumed with violent scents, I would have written sooner. . . . I am touched by the grace that the King gave to my son yesterday and the manner with which he treated me. Since these things are the results of your good counsels, Madame, please accept my marks of appreciation." Elizabeth Charlotte's correspondence is published in many editions and probably is not all published even today, for she wrote endlessly. One of the interesting collections of these letters was edited by Hans F. Helmolt, *Briefe der Herzogin Elizabeth-Charlotte von Orléans,* 2 vols. (Leipzig, 1908).

20. Baudrillart, "Philippe V et la cour de France, 1700–1715," *Revue d'histoire diplomatique,* third year sup. 1889.

21. The letters between the king and Philippe are to be found scattered in many places. Some are published in the *Œuvres de Louis XIV,* V and VI; many are published or extensively quoted in A. Baudrillart. A great many of them are copied in manuscript and bound by years in the Al series at the Archives of the War Ministry. Some are to be found in the National Archives at both Madrid

and Paris. Cf. Henri Froidevaux, "Une correspondence inédité de Louis XIV avec le roi et la reine d'Espagne 1701–1713." *Bulletin Soc. Vendomois,* vol. 9.

22. Louis to Philippe, September 9, 1707, A.M.G., Al-2051.

23. Saint-Simon (Boislisle, ed.), vol. XV, p. 469.

24. A.M.G., Al-2256, February 15, 1710. This child became Louis XV.

25. A.N., K-121, the Duke of Maine to Madame de Maintenon, April 11, 1711. See also A.N., O¹-1043, April, *passim.*

26. A.M.G., Al-2333, April 1711.

27. A.N., K-122, fol. 13. See also the sermons in the B.N., 8°, L37b 4390–94 *f. Relation du Service Solennel fait dans l'Église royale et nationale de St. Louis à Rome pour M. le D.* (8° Lb37 4395), 1711. The Grand Dauphin might someday be the subject of a Ph.D. thesis: his career does throw light upon the social and political world in which he lived.

28. Geffroy, *op. cit.,* II, pp. 295–308.

29. A.N., O¹-56, fols. 212–17.

30. Villars, *Mémoires,* vol. III, 139.

31. *Mémoires du duc d'Antin, op. cit.,* pp. 88–89. D'Antin was the only son of Monsieur and Madame de Montespan. After his mother's death, the king gave him the office in charge of the *Bâtiments,* which gave him frequent meetings with the king. He earned a measure of fame by removing a grove of trees on his estate overnight when the king expressed distaste for them.

32. A.N., K-122, no. 14.

33. A.A.E., France, 310, fol. 129.

34. V. Cronin, *Louis XIV* (Boston, 1965). This well-written book unfortunately is very superficial. The author should have spent more time on his basic research.

35. A.N., K-556, fols. 3*ff.*

36. B.N., ms. franç., 7013, fols. 412*ff.* See also J. C. Barbier, *Le testament de Louis XIV* (Paris, 1875), 8°L 37b 4985; and 8° Lc 1864 (1875), *Testament du Roy au deuxième Aoust 1714 et la Régence de M. le Duc d'Orléans* (n.d.), 8° Lb37 4442.

37. Dr. A. Corlieu, *La mort des rois de France depuis François I, Études médicales et historiques* (Paris, 1892). Le Felore Fontenay, "Journal historique de tout ce qui s'est passé depuis les premiers jours de la maladie de Louis XIV jusqu'au jour de son service à Saint Denis et l'avènement de Louis XV à la couronne de France," *Mercure Gallant* (Paris, October 1715). See also Dangeau (P. de Councillon, Marquis de) *Mémoire sur la mort de Louis XIV* (Paris, 1858), 8° L37b 4897.

INDEX

INDEX

THE AUTHOR

JOHN B. WOLF was born in Ouray, Colorado, on the 16th of July, 1907. He took his A.B. and M.A. from the University of Colorado and received his Ph.D. from the University of Minnesota in 1933. He taught history at the University of Missouri (1934–43), at the University of Minnesota (1943–66), and is now Professor of History at the University of Illinois at Chicago Circle. He received a Fulbright research fellowship at the Sorbonne in 1951–52 and was twice a Guggenheim Fellow, in 1959–60 and 1967–68.

Professor Wolf has traveled extensively in Europe, particularly in France, where most of the research for *Louis XIV* took place — in the Archives of the French Ministry of Foreign Affairs and of War, in the National Archives, in the Bibliothèque Nationale, and on numerous motor trips to visit the battlefields and other places where Louis XIV and his soldiers acted out their places in history.

Professor Wolf and his wife, Theta, live on Lake Michigan in Chicago and spend their summers either in Europe or at their summer cottage on Bone Lake, Wisconsin, where "neither telephone nor university committees disturb the peace" or his writing. In addition to this book, Professor Wolf is the author of *The Diplomatic History of the Bagdad Railroad; France, 1815 to the Present; The Emergence of the Great Powers — 1685–1715; The Emergence of European Civilization;* and coauthor of *History of Civilization.*